Taylor's Master Guide to Landscaping

Rita Buchanan

Taylor's Master Guide to

Landscaping

A Frances Tenenbaum Book

HOUGHTON MIFFLIN COMPANY

BOSTON   NEW YORK   2000

For information about permission to
reproduce selections from this book, write to
Permissions, Houghton Mifflin Company
215 Park Avenue South
New York, New York 10003.

Library of Congress Cataloging-in-Publication Data

Buchanan, Rita
    Taylor's master guide to landscaping / Rita Buchanan.
        p.   cm.
    "A Frances Tenenbaum book."
    ISBN 0-618-05590-8
    1. Landscape gardening. I. Title.

    SB473 .B737 2000
    712'.6 — dc21   99-054110

Book design by Anne Chalmers
Typefaces: Minion, News Gothic, Type Embellishments

Printed in the United States of America

WCT 10 9 8 7 6 5 4 3 2 1

Contents

Taylor's Master Guide to Landscaping

A well-designed land-scape surrounds your home with beauty and makes your life more comfortable and pleasant.

1 ❧ The Basics of Home Landscaping

LANDSCAPING the property around your home is an opportunity to surround yourself with beauty and provide a setting for your favorite outdoor activities. It's a way to put down roots, get in touch with nature, contribute to your community, and improve the environment. A well-designed landscape will enhance your quality of life, and it can even increase your property's value.

People approach landscaping from many different backgrounds. If you enjoy building, decorating, or photography, for example, that will influence how you think about developing and using your property. My own interest in landscaping grew out of a passion for plants and gardening, so I bring that perspective to this book. Many people follow a similar path. You don't *have* to be an avid gardener before you begin landscaping, but gardening experience does give you a head start. By making and tending a garden, you discover that you have the potential to create your own little world. At the same time, gardening teaches you how to choose plants that will thrive in your climate and situation, how to arrange them in a pleasing way, and how to care for them and keep them healthy and attractive. Gradually, as you become more aware of plants and your surroundings through gardening, you gain the knowledge and confidence to transform more and more of your property from what it was to what it *could* be.

In England, people use the word "garden" to mean all the area around their house, and they think of gardening as developing and caring for that entire space. This usage is starting to catch on here, but it isn't common yet. To most Americans, a garden is a particular and finite area. We often name or label our separate gardens, such as "my rose garden," "my shade garden," or "my kitchen garden." But what do you call your property as a whole? Americans don't have a standard term for the overall area, the sum of the parts. In this book, I'll call it your landscape, or your yard.

A typical home landscape includes many features, dominated by the house itself. There may be an attached deck or patio, a driveway and walkways, a garage or outbuildings, lawn, trees, foundation plantings around the house, hedges or other plantings around the perimeter, one or more gardens, play areas, maybe a swimming pool, perhaps some adjacent fields or woodland, and so on. Landscaping includes creating and caring for all of these separate elements. Even more, landscaping involves looking at the big picture and making sure that all of the parts seem to belong together—that they relate to each other (and also to the surrounding community and geographic region) and form a pleasing, satisfying whole. And, of course, a successful home landscape will suit your particular needs and interests, invite you to spend more time outdoors, and require only as much maintenance as you're willing and able to provide.

❧ WORKING ON YOUR OWN LANDSCAPE

Part of the fun of landscaping is that the process is so varied and includes so many different kinds of jobs. Starting with the physical work, there are simple routine chores, such as mowing the lawn and raking leaves; manual tasks that require skill, judgment, and practice, such as building a fence or dividing perennials; and dirty but satisfying projects, such as clearing brush or digging a new bed.

Along with the physical work of landscaping, there's also plenty of mental work. Learning about plants—how to identify and name them, what conditions and care they need, how fast they grow, when

GARDENING VS. LANDSCAPING

In gardening, you focus on plants. A garden plan or planting diagram (BLOW-UP) is a close-up of a particular bed that shows the number of plants used and how they're arranged.

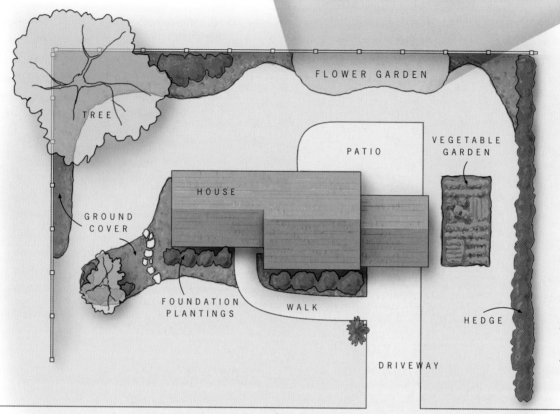

FLOWER GARDEN

TREE

PATIO

VEGETABLE GARDEN

GROUND COVER

HOUSE

FOUNDATION PLANTINGS

WALK

HEDGE

DRIVEWAY

Landscaping takes a broader perspective (OVERVIEW). It addresses everything that's growing or built around your house. A typical home landscape may include one or more gardens, a lawn, a patio or deck, trees and shrubs, a fence or hedge, foundation plantings, the driveway and walkways, and other elements. In landscaping, along with deciding how to plant a garden, you also think about where to put the garden, how big and what shape it should be, and how it relates to its surroundings.

they bloom, and so on — is like mastering a foreign language. If you love plants and are good at memorizing, this aspect of landscaping will be easy and fun; otherwise, you can always rely on the gardener's equivalent of tourist phrase books. The process called design or designing is a different kind of mental activity. It's not like being a student; it's like playing games or solving puzzles. Design involves observing and analyzing a situation, setting goals, making choices, developing plans, and evaluating results. It requires patience, persistence, and common sense; creativity helps, too.

People who do landscaping for a living usually specialize in one job or another. Look in the Yellow Pages and watch the crews working around your neighborhood, and you'll see that lawn services do grass, arborists do trees, horticulturists and nurseries grow plants. Masons work with stones and bricks, while carpenters use wood. Landscape architects and designers draw plans. Landscape contractors supervise installation as laborers do the grunt work.

It makes sense to specialize if you're trying to

earn a living, but if you're an amateur landscaping your own property, you can do everything yourself, or just do as much as you want and hire help with the jobs you don't have the strength, skills, tools, or time for. How you proceed will depend partly on how patient you are. If you're in a hurry to transform your property, hire lots of help (see page 28). Otherwise, you can learn as you go, making additions and improvements over the years, wearing many hats as you alternate from one task to another, and treating the whole project as a hobby, not a job. The alternation helps keep you from getting bogged down or overwhelmed — you can think until you're tired of thinking, then work until you're tired of working, going back and forth as you choose.

As you become interested in landscaping and want to learn more about it, you'll soon find that there's a mountain of reference material describing different kinds of plants, and there are volumes of detailed how-to information about manual jobs, such as laying bricks or pruning shrubs and trees. By contrast, it's hard to find guidelines for how to think

about your landscape and make choices and plans, such as deciding whether to build a fence or plant a hedge, choosing a ground cover for a particular site, defining the size and shape of a flower bed, or anticipating how fast a tree or shrub will grow and how big it will eventually get. Many people feel that *deciding* is just as hard as *doing* something, so I've addressed this concern repeatedly throughout this book. For a wide variety of common situations, I've given advice on how to identify the problem or opportunity, compare different options, and make up your mind.

Design demystified

Many people are confident in their ability to build things, grow plants, or care for a finished landscape but are intimidated by the idea of designing a landscape. This is partly because professional designers, like academics or politicians, speak a language of their own. Most "design talk" strikes me as vague, abstract, and lofty, so I avoid it. Good design is the basis for successful landscaping, and this book is all about design, but I've deliberately chosen to write in plain English and use down-to-earth examples. Design is so important that I don't want to risk boring or confusing you with the usual style of design talk.

Also, the success of big-name designers such as Ralph Lauren gives a misleading impression of what

design is all about. Most design work is not glamorous at all. Real-life design involves making decisions and plans that are, frankly, quite mundane. You make design decisions every time you get dressed. Does this shirt go with these pants? What color socks should I wear? Is it so cold that I need a coat, or will a sweater be enough? Home-landscape decisions involve similar questions. Would this gate go with our fence? What color clematis should we plant? Would mountain laurel grow well next to the house, or should we plant yews there instead? Designing a landscape is like filling your closet with a collection of flattering, comfortable clothes that go together, meet your needs, and suit your style and situation. This isn't mysterious. It's straightforward and satisfying work.

It's true that some people possess more creativity, ingenuity, and imagination than others, and their designs stand out accordingly. That's a welcome bonus that makes the world a more interesting place. But, fortunately, you don't need to be very creative yourself to design a fine landscape. You can take other people's good ideas and adapt them to your site. Borrowing is a time-honored design technique. Professionals do it routinely, and you can, too.

WHAT ABOUT SPONTANEITY? Some people reject design as an artificial, unnatural process.

Designing any landscape, even a simple one that looks casual and natural, involves planning, fine-tuning, and lots of decision-making. Here someone had to decide where to lay the path, how wide to make it, what surface to use, what plants to buy, and how to arrange them.

Look at nature, they say. Nobody designed the forests and meadows, yet what could be more beautiful? But what works in the wilderness doesn't work as well at home. You certainly can't take a spontaneous approach to building; there are too many practical constraints. It's okay to design something that *looks* irregular and random, but it has to *work* okay. For example, flagstones laid in a "crazy" pattern have to be flush and level, so you won't trip on the cracks. A rustic trellis built from crooked twigs has to be sturdy enough not to collapse under the weight of a vine. Spontaneity is better suited to planting than to building, but it's harder than you'd expect to create a planting that looks as if it grew there naturally. Most attempts at "random" combinations or patterns of plants or flower colors don't look natural at all; they simply look like mistakes.

Each landscape is unique

What kind of landscape you make depends partly on your vision, ambition, and interests. It also depends on the particulars of your site and surroundings. Designing a landscape that fits the site and makes the most of its potential is an intriguing challenge, with no single "right" answer. There are multiple solutions for any situation, each one unique. Moreover, every situation can be reevaluated from time to time, and the previous landscaping can be revised or replaced.

This book is full of ideas and advice about how to create new landscapes or remodel existing ones. It will help you think of things to build, plant, or do. You'll also find ideas in other books and in magazines and by visiting public and private gardens. But browsing for landscape ideas isn't like shopping from a catalog. You can't order a ready-made landscape; landscapes must always be custom-built. What you see in a picture suits *that* site and situation, but your place is different, so you can't copy an idea exactly. You almost always have to alter the size or scale of the design, use different materials, or choose different plants. That's good, because customizing an idea so it fits your property and meets your needs is much more satisfying than simple copying would be.

STUDYING THE GIVENS OF YOUR SITE AND SITUATION

Many factors affecting your landscape must be acknowledged, and can't be changed. These are the givens of where you are and what it's like there, immutable issues such as the size and shape of your lot, its topography and soil, the nature of your surroundings, and your climate. To work within these given limits, first you have to identify them. If you've been settled in one place for several years, you already know a lot about it, but even so, it helps to take a fresh look around. If you've just moved in—especially if you've come from another town or a different part of the country—you'll need time to

---

KEEPING TRACK

Here are simple, effective ways to keep track of information and ideas about your site and situation.

- **MAPS** or **PLAN VIEWS** are helpful for showing the size and shape of parts or all of your property and for indicating the location of existing buildings, trees, and other features. Sometimes you need a plan that's accurately measured and drawn to scale, but often a sketchy or cartoon-like map is enough to record what's where and serve as a reminder you can refer to later.

- **PHOTOS** are handy for showing you how any part of your property looks from another point of view (framing a scene as you would see it from an upstairs window, for example), reminding you how the same view changes with the seasons and over the years, and documenting how different plants look at the same time (which flowers bloom in late June, for instance). Also, you can carry photos with you to a garden center, club meeting, or lec-

ture, where you might find someone who could give you ideas or answer questions.

- Use a **CALENDAR** or journal to record weather events, such as first and last frosts, notable storms, dry spells, and cold snaps and heat waves; plant and nature events, such as the sighting of the first daffodil, the first ripe tomato, or the first robin; and your activities, such as the first and last times you mow the lawn, whenever you apply fertilizer or other products, or when you do any planting or transplanting.

- Keep **INVOICES** and **RECEIPTS** for plants and supplies that you've purchased. This helps if you want to buy more of the same or need to claim a refund.

- Make **LISTS** of plants you already have, plants you want to buy, and projects you want to do.

This yard is large but easy to maintain. There are broad sweeps of carefree shrubs and ground covers and an uncluttered, easy-to-mow lawn.

observe and learn about your situation before you lift a tool. Explore every corner of your land and every quirk of your climate. This will help you identify the challenges and opportunities that lie ahead.

How big is your lot?

When you buy a piece of real estate, the paperwork typically includes a plot plan or map indicating the property's location and boundaries, a deed with a surveyor's precise description of the property lines, and an estimate of the total area in square feet or acres. If you don't have this information, track it down through city hall, then go out and measure the site yourself to confirm the written record. Identifying your property lines and having accurate measurements is important if you are planning any construction; want to put up a boundary hedge or fence; need to calculate how much topsoil, mulch, or other material to apply to a given area; or want to figure how many plants a certain space would hold.

HOW MUCH CAN YOU MAINTAIN? Along with taking measurements, it's important to assess your property's size in general terms of what you can do with your landscape and how much time and care it requires. For example, you might have (or wish for) a place that's big enough for you to host large parties, plant an orchard, pasture a pony, or do whatever else would make you happy. But you don't want a lawn that's too big to mow, a flower bed too big to weed, or even a patio too big to sweep.

There are certain minimums for what counts as big enough. Even dwarf fruit trees must be planted 10 to 15 feet apart. That pony might need an acre or

more. Hosting a party requires plenty of parking space.

What counts as too big depends on your schedule. Here are some estimates for maintaining a lawn and closely tended plantings, such as mixed beds and borders, a vegetable or herb garden, or patio containers. If landscaping is your passion and your schedule lets you work outdoors full-time throughout the growing season, you might be able to keep up with an area the size of a football field (that's about 1 acre, or 44,000 square feet). If you're busy with work, family, and other commitments, you probably won't

This tiny yard is a labor of love. Keeping it so lush and immaculate requires hours of care every week.

have the time and energy to maintain an area much larger than a basketball or tennis court (between 2,500 and 5,000 square feet). If you're really busy, try managing an area the size of a large living room (about 250 to 500 square feet). It's great to *own* more land than that, but you'll want to choose low-maintenance uses for the outlying areas, such as mass plantings of ground covers and shrubs, natural or reforested woodland, or meadow or pasture that's mowed just once or twice a year.

THE SIGNIFICANCE OF SHAPE. The shape of an area can affect how it looks and feels.

A view of the Colorado Rockies gives a wide-open feeling to this small patio.

Usually, though, it's not the overall shape of a property that matters but the shape of its component parts. For example, a backyard that's 30 feet wide by 80 feet long invites you to stroll toward the back, like following an aisle or a hallway to see where it leads. By contrast, a backyard that's 80 feet wide by 30 feet long makes you feel as though you're facing a stage or panorama where all the scenery is spread out sideways—great for viewing from a porch or deck but less likely to pull you out for a walk. Shapes that are broad or nearly square are easy to use. Long, skinny shapes, such as a strip between the sidewalk and the street or between the house or driveway and the property line, are more awkward, so these narrow strips are often weedy and neglected. Designing ways to make narrow shapes useful and/or beautiful is a common challenge in urban and suburban landscapes.

What surrounds you?

No matter what size lot you have, there's a big difference between city and country, historic district and new subdivision, forest and ranchland, riverfront and desert. The character of your landscape is affected by its setting. How much sky can you see? At night, do you see the moon and stars, or artificial light? What's on your horizon? How far away are the neighbors? Do you hear traffic, dogs, children, church bells, factories, farm equipment, birds, surf?

For better or worse, all the sights and sounds around you are as much a part of your landscape as the features on your own property are. If you're lucky, you relish your surroundings. You might have a great view of natural scenery, or live in a pleasant community filled with attractive, comfortable homes and interesting, well-tended plantings. But most people don't have a perfect setting. Real-life situations usually involve some compromise. Maybe you chose your house because of its size or price, or because it's close to work or in a good school district, despite the fact that there's an eyesore next door, a utility pole out front, or a noisy freeway a few blocks away. Landscaping can't work miracles—there are some things you just have to accept—but a well-designed landscape can help screen out unpleasantness, and it can give you something nearby to focus on and enjoy.

Remember that landscaping is reciprocal. Anything you do that's visible from your neighbor's home or from the street affects their view, just as anything they do affects yours. You can't make your neighbors prune their hedge or mow their lawn or paint their shed or put their youngsters' toys away, but you can ask them to and remind them why you care, and you can set an example by doing the same things yourself. Many neighborhoods have been transformed because one household took the initiative to work on their landscape. Your efforts might inspire others to follow.

(ABOVE) *Although it's surrounded by neighboring houses, this fenced yard feels quiet, calm, and private.*
(RIGHT) *An enclosed garden is an oasis from the noise and hurry of the world outside. You'd never guess that this lot is in a busy city.*

CREATING ILLUSIONS. A recurrent theme in landscaping is the idea of denying or defying what's around you by creating an illusion. Projects such as this can be successful or futile. Illusions are like theater: they require the "willing suspension of disbelief." An illusion doesn't actually change your surroundings, but if you're willing to pretend and cooperate, you may forget where you are and what it's like there, at least for a while.

For example, one successful kind of landscape illusion is designed to give the impression of privacy in a busy, built-up town or city. It tries to isolate you from crowds, traffic, and commotion and create a feeling of calm. These landscapes are often small and may be totally enclosed by a fence, wall, or hedge. The illusion really works if the landscape screens out the background, captures your attention as soon as you enter, and engages all your senses, so you're immediately and fully distracted.

Another kind of illusion attempts to re-create the past, to restore an example of the original, natural landscape in a region that's been altered by development, farming, logging, grazing, and so forth. The

A smooth, level site is easy to develop, maintain, and use.

A gentle slope makes a good setting for graceful curved plantings, and you can easily mow a lawn on a site like this.

success of this illusion is typically limited by scale—there's a big difference between a backyard "prairie" and the primeval sea of grasses and wildflowers that spreads from horizon to horizon. Still, this kind of project is a fascinating adventure that changes how you view your surroundings, stimulates your interest in ecology and history, and gives you something to care deeply about. And in practical terms, restored landscapes can be very beautiful and are relatively carefree.

By contrast, another commonly attempted illusion is more trouble and less satisfying. This happens when people with fond memories of another part of

the country or world, perhaps a place where they once lived or vacationed, strive to duplicate the look and feeling of that distant landscape where they live now, even though the growing conditions and climate are totally different. Such displaced landscapes are like fish out of water; the plants don't thrive, and the imported materials and objects look too conspicuous to be comfortable. You can't simulate Colorado in Texas by planting some spruce and aspen trees, or recapture the feeling of New Mexico by building an adobe wall in Ohio, and why try? Wherever you live, a landscape that suits the surroundings makes more sense than a souvenir of someplace else.

(ABOVE): *Bold rock outcrops look dramatic but feel inhospitable. The level lawn is a perfect counterpoint that provides a sense of welcome and respite.*

(LEFT): *A steep site, especially one exposed to coastal storms, calls for retaining walls, safe walks and steps, guardrails, and sturdy, deep-rooted plants to stabilize the soil and resist erosion.*

Topography and drainage

Can you walk all over your property in regular street shoes, or are there places where you need hiking boots or rubber boots? Are there areas where you proceed confidently but visitors hesitate or turn back? Having to change shoes or to take a guest by the hand is a sign that you should scrutinize your property's topography and drainage.

LEVEL SITES VS. SLOPES. The topography of a piece of land—its contours and slopes—is hard to draw on a site plan or map, but it certainly influences what you can do with your property. Although it may be boring to look at, flat land is blessedly easy to live on and use. Slopes make a property more interesting to look at but less comfortable to explore, develop, and maintain. On flat sites, you can mow a lawn, play a ball game, tend a perennial border, lay a brick path, or build a fence and arbor without having to think about uphill or downhill. On sloping sites, you're always climbing or descending, watching where you step, adjusting your posi-

tion, trying to keep a grip on your tools. To build any hardscape (the nonplant features of a landscape) on a slope, you need informed and thoughtful design and well-engineered foundations, framework, and finishing. The results can be wonderful, but working on a slope adds time and expense to any project.

Of course, the degree of challenge and difficulty depends on the area of the site and how steep it is. You can almost ignore gentle, broadly rolling slopes that reach across an entire lot or throughout a neighborhood; they add character without posing much of an obstacle to gardening, recreation, construction, or other activities. At the other extreme, you'll definitely need professional help if your house is perched on a mountainside, canyon, or shoreline, in order to develop a satisfactory landscape that capitalizes on the dramatic setting while guarding against erosion and danger.

Some of the most common topographic problems are steep banks created during the construction of a house or drive. A bank such as this may be just a small part of your property, but it's often an eyesore and it's wasted space that's hard to use or enjoy. Throughout this book I'll offer advice for dealing with these challenging situations. For example, you might cover the bank with a carefree, long-lived, strong-rooted ground cover (see page 245, 321); build a deck over it (page 114); or reshape it into one or more level areas or terraces that are buttressed by retaining walls (page 215).

Runoff from a heavy rain can carve a gully, undercut pavement, dump a load of debris on your yard, or carry things away. Flood-water can do a lot of damage in a short period of time if you aren't prepared.

WATCH WHERE WATER GOES. Water moves both under and over the ground. You probably won't think about underground water unless you have a well or spring, but any property owner can and should study the surface flow. Walk around during or after a rain to see where water is moving and which way it goes. See how the water lifts, carries, and deposits loose soil, mulch, leaves, and debris as it flows along? Make note of this; places that wash after a normal rain are vulnerable to serious erosion in a

heavy downpour or flash flood and may need to be stabilized or altered. Observe how water flows between your land and your neighbors'; are there problems you should face together? Check to make sure that surface water and roof runoff flow away from your house. If that's not the case, and you have water flowing into the basement or crawlspace, you need professional help to correct the situation.

Low spots where water collects for just a few hours or days don't need special consideration, but watch for places that stay wet for days or weeks. These areas look different from drier ground — the vegetation might be lusher, or it might be stunted. There will surely be different kinds of weeds, and the soil itself will look and smell different from dry soil. A permanent wet spot provides the opportunity to grow special, water-loving plants (see page 253), but most garden plants won't grow well there. If you want to run a walkway or path through a wet area, you can put a crossing there (page 181).

It's fairly easy to alter drainage patterns and divert or capture runoff by filling low spots, burying drain tiles, digging trenches or swales, or building dams and retaining walls. You don't even need heavy equipment; you can make a big difference with a shovel and a wheelbarrow. But first call local officials to see what regulations might apply. You may get an unconditional go-ahead for small changes. Major changes, especially anything affecting a brook, river, lake, or designated wetland, are usually governed by guidelines and may require a permit.

Exposure

Surroundings and topography affect whether a site is exposed to the sun and wind or sheltered from one or both. There's a big difference between being down in a valley or up on a ridge, in level or hilly terrain, neighbored by other buildings or out in the open, surrounded by woods or by grassland and fields, or close to water. Exposure patterns affect plant growth and human comfort, and they influence how you perceive and use a landscape.

SUNLIGHT AND SHADE. The quality of light is part of the landscape; it colors how things look and how you feel. Light gives a sense of place as you travel. Think of the blinding white glare of sun reflected off snow in Colorado or sand in Arizona, the soft shady depths of an evergreen forest in Washington, the pastel glow of a fog-swept island in Maine, the stained-glass effect of sunbeams filtered through fall leaves in Vermont. At home, it's a joy to see your own landscape under different lighting — rosy sunrise, golden sunset, pale moonlight, dark storm clouds, a rainbow.

Seasonal lighting changes are as dramatic as a single day's passage from dawn to noon to twilight. Standing outdoors on a bright summer day, you just can't imagine how your yard would look in winter,

and vice versa. The shadows cast by buildings or trees vary more than you'd ever predict. Plants differ greatly in their need or tolerance for sun or shade, and you have to take this into account when deciding what to plant where. Many plants need full sun in summer but not in winter; some demand shade in summer but not in winter; others require different combinations. To arrange things right, you'll need to know exactly what parts of your property are sunny or shady at different times of year. Keep watch throughout the seasons, observe what parts of your land receive full sun and what portions are more or less shaded, and make notes or take photos to keep track of that information.

Also consider the exposure or orientation of sloping sites or areas next to buildings or walls. North-facing slopes and areas next to north-facing walls don't get any direct sun from fall until spring, and the soil in these places stays cool and moist in summer. South-facing slopes and sites are always much warmer and drier. In spring, there can be daffodils in full bloom against the south side of the house, while a patch of ice lingers along the north wall. East-facing slopes or sites enjoy the warmth of the sun in the morning but are shaded from afternoon heat. West-facing slopes or sites can get quite

hot in the afternoon, especially in summer. Standing next to the west wall of a brick or masonry house on a summer night, you can feel all the heat it has absorbed. As with sun and shade, you have to take orientation into account when positioning plants. Even more important, orientation affects how you'll feel about outdoor living spaces. The extra warmth of a sunny, south-facing patio might feel wonderful in winter and spring but oppressive in summer. A north-facing porch might feel cool and refreshing on a summer evening but damp and clammy the rest of the year.

Finally, consider daylength. Are there times of day or year when you want or need to be outdoors, but it's dark then? Decide where outdoor lighting would be helpful or desirable, and have it installed right away. It's a bargain, and you'll immediately be grateful for the safety, convenience, and pleasure it provides.

WIND. A gentle breeze is welcome on a summer day, but gusty or unrelenting winds are stressful to both people and plants. Steady winds can wilt leaves, dry out the soil, and stir up dust. Stormy winds can break trees, knock down perennials, or topple a trellis. If there's a prevailing wind in your area, go out on

This brick patio is cool and shady in summer but warmed by the sun from fall to spring when the trees are leafless.

ing precipitation, there are comparable *numbers* of plants for dry and rainy climates, but they're different *kinds* of plants—you can't grow fuzzy gray herbs in humid Louisiana or lush green ferns in arid Nevada. Choosing plants adapted to your climate is a key to successful landscaping. Well-adapted plants (which may or may not be native to your region, as long as they grow well there) are easy to care for, and because they're healthy and not under stress, they look better than misfits.

Beyond plant selection, weather affects how *you* relate to your landscape—whether you experience it directly or view it through glass. You know that glorious feeling when the air feels perfect and being outdoors is so delicious that you have to put everything else aside and go savor it. At times like that, the landscape is a place to explore and use. But when it's too hot or cold, too rainy or humid, or it's hayfever season or insects are biting, the landscape is like a series of murals outside your window frames—something you see but don't touch or smell.

Take climate and weather into account as you plan your landscape. With respect to hardscape, for instance, you might use a deck daily in California, but in Minnesota you'd be happier with an addition that could double as a cozy sunroom in winter and a bug-proof screened porch in summer. When planting, it's natural to focus on the season you like best and emphasize flowers that peak then, but don't overlook the rest of the year. Anticipate the time you'll spend indoors looking out, and give yourself a treat by composing a scene for that season.

Soil

If you've already been gardening awhile at your current home, you know about your soil. If you've just moved in, don't be surprised if the soil is different from any you've experienced before, and probably worse than what you're used to. Shallow, compacted, infertile dirt, not rich deep topsoil, is what's typical around both old and new homes. Don't worry too much about that. You can't *change* the basic character of your soil (you can't turn sand into clay, for example), but any soil can be *improved* enough that well-chosen plants will thrive.

If you do have any soil condition that could cause serious problems for construction or gardening, it is likely to exist not just on your property but throughout your neighborhood, so your neighbors and local authorities should be able to point it out and advise what, if anything, you should do about it. Potentially troublesome conditions include soil that's underlain with bedrock, hardpan, or caliche; places where the water table is close to the surface; clay soil that swells and shrinks dramatically when it absorbs water or dries out; soil that turns into a muddy slough in spring, when the surface thaws before the subsoil does; and unstable slopes or shorelines that are liable to erode.

In a frost-free climate like California's, you can enjoy bougainvillea and other flowering plants year-round.

a blustery day and look for places where the air is still, in the lee of a building or hedge. It's a relief to get out of the wind, isn't it? A sheltered nook is an enticing setting for relaxing outdoors or for growing delicate plants. If you don't have any shelter now, you may want to create some by planting a windbreak or building a fence or wall.

Climate and weather

Like sun and wind, everything else about climate and weather affects landscaping. Temperature and precipitation, in particular, influence which plants you can grow and what care they'll need. Extremely cold winters or hot summers limit the selection. Where temperatures are moderate year-round, you can choose from a much wider variety of plants. Regard-

The factors I've listed so far—the size and shape of your lot; its topography, drainage, exposure, and soil; and your surroundings and climate—are givens. You can tweak at them, but mostly you have to live within their limits. What's *on* your lot, though, is negotiable. You've seen instances where someone bought a lot in a desirable part of town, bulldozed a quaint little cottage tucked among old-fashioned shrubs, and put up a modern mansion ringed by a narrow, moatlike lawn instead. That's an extreme case, and I mention it only as a reminder of what's possible, to give you courage to undertake your own improvements.

The bulldoze-and-rebuild, down-with-the-old, up-with-the-new approach doesn't apply to many situations. Hopefully, your lot includes many features you want to preserve and just a minority of things you'd like to get rid of or change. What often happens, though, in the rush of everyday life, is that you simply accept things the way they are, whether you like them or not. You get blind spots, and you learn to ignore plants and structures you dislike. That can go on for years until someday you'll wake up bored and annoyed and decide it's time to *do* something.

Get started now by assessing what you've got and how you feel about it. Encourage everyone in your household to share their impressions. Ask friends and visitors to walk around the yard with you, and listen to their feedback. Take a fresh look at everything on your property and consider how you might improve it.

Assessing your structures and hardscape

Start by reviewing whatever has been built on your property—buildings, paved areas, fences and gates,

(**TOP**): *A blank slate. Although this house is several years old, it has virtually no landscaping. The new owners who just moved in will have to start from scratch.*

(**MIDDLE**): *A yard in "move-in" condition. Well-built hardscape and well-designed, carefully tended plantings are a winning combination. You'd be lucky to buy a house with a yard like this.*

(**BOTTOM**): *There's a house in there, but the yard's a jungle. Renovating this landscape will involve a lot of cutting and clearing.*

retaining walls, arbors and trellises, outdoor seating, raised beds, and so on. If you were trying to sell your house, what would a potential buyer think of these things? What do *you* think? Do an inventory, evaluating each structure on the following points.

- Was it built well in the first place, with good-quality materials and careful workmanship?
- Is it useful, convenient, well positioned, the right size?
- Is it in good condition, or does it need fixing, straightening, remodeling, cleaning, or refinishing?

After thinking it over, you'll probably decide to go on living with most things just as they are, partly because you'll dismiss some potentially desirable changes as unfeasible or too expensive. But you'll also identify some priorities and recognize changes that *are* possible and affordable. Sometimes the needed improvement is obvious and easily accomplished, such as when you need to repaint a weathered picket fence, remove an outgrown playset, straighten a sagging gate, or widen a narrow walkway. Doing a major remodeling, replacement, or addition takes more planning and may require special tools and skills, so you may want to get professional help; more about that later.

Assessing your plants

What's your immediate, emotional reaction to the plants around you? Ideally, you'd feel they look just right, suit the setting, and give you comfort and delight. More likely, though, you think there are not enough plants, or too many. You might wish some of them were bigger and more impressive, or smaller and not so overpowering. There are probably some plants you love and others that bore or annoy you. You might fret over how the plants are arranged and wonder if you should move or regroup them.

Designing with plants is the most fascinating part of landscaping, but it's also the hardest part, because there are so many kinds of plants to work with, each unique, and because plants keep changing all the time—they don't stay the same size and color from week to week or year to year. (By comparison, doing hardscape is a breeze—there are only a limited number of materials and styles, and once you build something, it stays put.) Refining your plantings isn't a one-time job, it's an ongoing process. Time and again, you'll look at what you've got and wonder how to improve it. This involves two kinds of thinking: looking at the big picture, and reacting to individual plants.

STUDY THE OVERALL EFFECT. To design an appealing landscape, you need to step back and see the forest, not the trees. It's hard to achieve this kind of detachment if you're a gardener who cherishes what's special about each individual plant. As a lifelong plant lover myself, I used to resist this big-picture talk as high-flown and pretentious; eventually, I realized that it's not. It's like the difference between a box of fabric scraps and a thoughtfully patterned quilt.

It might help if you take photos from an upstairs window or from across the street and look at the pictures instead of standing face to face with your plants. Critique the groupings, to see how the shapes and colors and textures fit together. Are there gaps, anomalies, or pile-ups? What seems missing or out of place, and why? Review the plantings again in every season, to see how the patterns change.

EXAMINE INDIVIDUAL PLANTS. Shaping the big picture takes time. I'll return to that topic throughout this book, and you'll dwell on it repeatedly as you develop your landscape. Meanwhile, consider your plants separately, too. Regarding each tree, shrub, ground cover, and so forth, ask questions such as these:

- Do you like it? Are you glad to have it growing on your property?
- What kind is it? Did it grow wild, or did someone plant it?
- How big is it now? How tall will it get, and how wide will it spread? How fast does it grow?
- Is it positioned right? If not, could it be moved?
- What's special about it—flowers, leaves, fruits, fragrance, form—and when do those features appear?
- Is it healthy and trouble-free? Does it cause any problems or need special care?

You can answer many questions about a plant even if you can't name it, but you'll learn more if you can get it identified. Ask knowledgeable friends for help, compare your plants to pictures in books, take photos of your mystery plants and see if anyone at a local nursery or garden center can identify them, or hire a horticulturist or landscaper to do an evaluation for you. From the start, keep a notebook in which to write down all your plants' names and the bits of information and ideas you have about them. Also, mark their positions on a map or plan, so you can keep track of what's where.

When you move into a new home, especially if you don't recognize the plants there, spend a year or more getting to know them before making any major changes. First impressions can be misleading. A shrub that's nondescript in winter might be the highlight of the garden in spring. A seemingly charming herb may sow a thousand weedy seedlings. A humble ground cover may earn your appreciation because it's so steadfast and undemanding. Take your time. Watch and wait. When you're ready, you can decide which plants to honor and which ones to move or replace.

❋ DETERMINING YOUR LANDSCAPE GOALS AND STYLE

Most home-landscaping projects are initiated in response to a complaint or a wish; you want either to solve a problem or to add an amenity. Often you can design a solution that does both jobs at once. At this point, you may have some vague ideas about what you want to do, but you probably need to focus and refine them and to set some priorities. Making lists is a good way to start. If you have a to-do list and a wish list, you can find entries that make a match; for example, you could match "fill that barren strip along the south wall" with "plant an herb garden."

Think about your schedule and interests as you're making plans. Part of deciding what you want to have is acknowledging what you're willing and able to take care of. For instance, you might have a sunny area that you'd like to fill with flowers. If you started a few clumps and patches of prairie wildflowers there, you'd have plenty of color all summer, and it would require only a few hours of maintenance in spring and fall. You could achieve a more sophisticated look by planting a border of classic garden perennials, but maintaining this might take a few hours a week. Which would you prefer?

Also, keep reminding yourself to think of the big picture. Step back from a project you're considering to anticipate how it will look from a distance.

Does it seem to belong there? Does it complement what you already have? The eternal challenge in designing a landscape is tying the parts together. To create an overall effect that's coherent, not chaotic, you'll have to reject some ideas because they simply don't fit.

It's much easier to make design decisions if you give yourself some guidelines and define your own style by specifying which colors, materials, and effects you want to use or avoid. Developing a landscape in your chosen style means surrounding yourself with what you like to see, and that's good. It's also a form of communication. How will other people respond to your landscape? What are you showing them about yourself? Finally, there's the matter of cost. Whatever your budget, you want the money you spend on your landscape to buy beauty, comfort, and happiness. These are things to think about as you make choices and plans.

Solving problems

Listen to yourself and the other people in your household, and you'll soon have a list of your landscape problems, expressed in statements such as these:

"Those bushes are so tall that I can't see out the window."
"Deer keep eating all our flowers."

The owners of this new house face a long list of landscape concerns. The lawn is too big, and the property looks bare. The backyard is too steep and soil is eroding. There's no level place to sit outdoors, and no screening or privacy. There are no paved walkways. In such a situation, what would you want to do first?

"We can't afford to water such a big lawn."
"I'm tired of looking at that weather-beaten shed."
"Don't go out back; there's too much poison ivy."
"I can't mow around the maple tree because its roots stick up."
"Watch your step; that path is slippery."
"Why are we growing so many vegetables? We don't eat them all."
"I can't relax on the patio because the neighbors sit there watching."

Listing your problems is the first step toward doing something about them, and the more specific you can be about describing just exactly what's wrong, the more likely you are to identify a good solution. Sometimes the job is obvious, and you just need to take time and do it: Whack down the bushes, paint the shed, spray the poison ivy. Or you may need to do some research: Instead of grass, what else could you plant under that maple tree? What could you grow that deer won't eat?

Often you can choose from alternative solutions: To shade the patio from the late-afternoon sun, you could plant a tree or build an overhead trellis and cover it with vines. What kind of tree? What kind of trellis and vine? Pick candidates from your wish list. Maybe you always wanted a redbud or a flowering cherry tree, or a clematis or wisteria vine. There are several alternatives to a too-big lawn. You could replace part of it with an unthirsty ground cover or shrubs, spread a gravel mulch, install paving, or build a wooden deck. Which solution would you prefer? Which could provide something else (in addition to less lawn) that you've been hoping for?

Adding amenities

Talk this over with your household. What would make your landscape more beautiful, more inviting, more useful, more fun? What plants, structures, or facilities do you long for? Some typical "wish-list" entries might be:

"I want an arbor covered with fragrant roses."
"I want to grow tomatoes and chili peppers and make my own salsas."
"I want a brick patio with a barbecue grill and an outdoor dining area."

What do you long for? (TOP): *An herb garden outside the kitchen door?* (CENTER): *A gazebo?* (BOTTOM): *A lily pond? Why wait any longer? Treat yourself to the landscape of your dreams!*

"I want a shady retreat where I can read and relax."

"I want a place to make compost."

"I want a fountain that makes a splashy noise."

"I want window boxes and hanging baskets dripping with colorful flowers that attract hummingbirds and butterflies."

Many of the things you wish for in a landscape are so simple and affordable that you can have them right away. Treat yourself. That's one of the reasons for buying a house, isn't it — so you can do what you want outdoors? Other amenities are more expensive, take more space, or require more planning to accomplish, but like any good thing in life, they're worth working for. People often squelch their longings and postpone making landscape improvements until they've finished decorating the house, sent the kids to college, or retired. Then they finally go ahead and immediately afterward proclaim, "Oh, this is so wonderful. I wish we'd done it years ago!" Why wait? The sooner you get what you want, the longer you'll enjoy it.

What's your schedule?

The one big drawback to expanding and enriching your landscape is that everything you add demands some of your time and attention. Plants have to be watered, weeded, and trimmed; structures have to be cleaned, refinished, and repaired; tools have to be sharpened, oiled, and put away. How much time do you have at home, and how do you want to spend it? Are you frequently home during the day, or mostly after dark? Does travel keep you away for days or weeks at a time? Your schedule affects how big a lawn you'll want to mow, whether you can hand-water or need an automatic irrigation system, what kinds of perennials and shrubs you should grow, and many other landscape decisions.

CUSTOMIZED LOW MAINTENANCE. Your preferences and attitudes play a major role, too, in determining what tasks you might want to reduce or avoid. Books and articles about low-maintenance gardening often imply that everybody dislikes the same jobs, but of course that's not so. Some people *love* mowing their lawn. Others love shearing bushes, pulling weeds, raking leaves, tinkering with tools. Low maintenance isn't a one-size-fits-all proposition. It's only important to minimize the time spent on tasks that you personally dislike. If you enjoy what you're doing, it's not a chore, it's a labor of love.

What's your style?

Each time you add something to your landscape, you make decisions that express your taste or sense of style. For example, imagine a rose-covered arbor. You could choose a rustic bentwood arbor made from

(TOP AND ABOVE): *Formal landscapes feature paved walks and edged beds arranged in geometric shapes and aligned with the house, and symmetrical groupings of just a few kinds of plants, which are often sheared. The formal style requires a level site or a series of level terraces supported by retaining walls.*

(RIGHT): *Informal yards may include rounded and irregular stones, rough or unpainted timber, asymmetric groupings of many different natural-shaped plants, and walks and steps that curve or zigzag toward the house.* (BELOW): *The informal style can be used on level or sloping sites of any size or shape.*

twigs and trunks with the bark left on; a wrought-iron arbor with squiggles and curlicues; a round- or flat-topped arbor built from milled lumber, painted or stained in any color or left to weather naturally; or a carefree white PVC arbor. The rose could be a relatively unassertive type that you can tie neatly to one side of the arbor, or one of those rambunctious monsters that wrap entire structures in a swirl of waving canes.

CHOOSING CONSISTENTLY. Choices, choices. You inevitably express yourself each time

you decide "I like this, I don't like that." The challenge is choosing deliberately and consistently. If you *don't* think about style and just build and plant at random, your efforts will probably look disjointed and hodgepodge. You know what I mean — there's a place in every neighborhood where the owners have one example of each thing they like, but nothing goes together. A little variety goes a long way. Too much variety, and it looks as though you can't make up your mind. It's fun to read magazines and know about the latest fads and fashions in landscaping, but you don't have to go along with every trend. Some ideas will "fit" you just right, while others won't suit you at all.

To avoid that hodgepodge look, you need to define some limits, so you can look at a picture, product, or plant and say, "That's fine for somebody else, but it would look out of place in *our* yard." Choosing things that complement what you already have—your house itself, other major structures, and big healthy plants that you're committed to—is a first step. Comparing opposites also helps you identify and articulate your style. For instance, with reference to landscape structures and objects, do you like antiques or modern pieces? Matched or assorted items? Rough or smooth-textured materials? Classical images or folk art? What about the plants in a bed or border? Do you feel they should be firmly staked and neatly trimmed, or is it okay if they flop and sprawl, perhaps tipping onto the path or lawn? Do you prefer brilliant or pastel flowers? Your style might be serious or whimsical, practical or romantic. Maybe you value stability and control, or relish spontaneity and change. Whatever you prefer, asserting a clear sense of style will give your landscape coherence and distinction.

What will your friends and neighbors think?

Do you want to blend in with or stand out from the style of the community or neighborhood you live in? This is an important, yet controversial, question of style. If your landscape is conspicuous and unique, your neighbors and visitors might react with admiration, emulation, amusement, bewilderment, envy, annoyance, or other mixed emotions. Do you care what other people think? If so, what reaction are you hoping for? Whom are you trying to impress, and why?

LAWNS AND ALTERNATIVES. Front yards are the focus of many debates. A uniform, velvety, weed-free lawn is the traditional, idealized front yard in most American communities, but you might decide to challenge that ideal. On a tree-shaded site, moss, ferns, and shade-tolerant ground covers and perennials grow much better than turfgrass. In arid climates, pavement and unthirsty plantings make more sense than a lawn. On sloping, tiny, or odd-shaped lots, mowing is inconvenient, and ground covers are easier to care for. Perhaps you just don't value a lawn and would rather fill your front yard with flower beds. A decade ago, anyone who replaced a conventional lawn with alternative plantings was cast as a black sheep. Nowadays, so many pioneers have led the way that people aren't as surprised anymore to see a front yard that isn't a lawn, but your neighbors may still be disappointed or disturbed. Talk it over with them. Explain what you're doing and why you think it's such a good idea. Maybe

they'll still be grumpy, or they might come around and follow your example.

PUBLIC AND PRIVATE SPACES. Along with whether and how you keep your lawn, onlookers will react to your other front-yard decisions. If you *don't* prune your shrubs, rake your leaves, pick up litter, or shovel the snow off your sidewalk, or if you *do* set out some pink flamingos, leave the sprinkler running all day, paint your picket fence purple, or pretend a giant weed is a wildflower—whatever you do, you may be hearing about it. Reconciling your landscaping plans and attitudes with community values often requires some compromise. New subdivisions can be very homogeneous, often deliberately so. There's more flexibility in older, mixed neighborhoods where the houses were built one at a time and have different architecture, hardscape, and

(**BELOW TOP**): *Replacing your front lawn with flowers on a street where everyone else grows grass will provoke mixed reactions. Some neighbors will be delighted, but don't be surprised if others act jealous or cranky about it.*

(**BELOW BOTTOM**): *Filling the backyard with flowers is your prerogative. A planting like this will generate only praise, especially since the rest of the yard is perfectly groomed.*

When it's time to sell your house, a landscape like this appeals to most buyers. The hardscape is well built along classic lines. The plantings are healthy, complete, permanent, and uncluttered.

plantings, but there, too, your neighbors have the right to comment on what they see in your yard. Try thinking of your property in terms of public and private spaces. In public spaces—areas that are on view to passersby—apply the Golden Rule, and don't flaunt neighborhood values without good justification. In private places that are screened by trees, shrubs, fences, or the house itself, or on lots that are set back away from the street or road, you can grow and do whatever you want.

What's your budget?

Landscaping doesn't have to be expensive, but it certainly can be. As a rough estimate, professional landscapers recommend that you spend 10 to 20 percent of the price of a new house on establishing a land-

scape. That expenditure might cover lots of construction, some grading and soil improvement, planting trees and shrubs, making a lawn, and preparing, planting, and mulching some beds. Remodeling or upgrading an existing landscape is usually less expensive. In any case, how much you actually spend and what you spend it on will depend on your budget, your priorities and goals, and many other factors, such as the size of your lot, what's already there, whether or not your work schedule and climate allow you to spend much time outdoors, how much of the construction and planting you're able to do yourself, or how patient you are.

LANDSCAPING AS AN INVESTMENT. Perhaps the first issue to resolve is whether to regard landscaping as a real-estate investment or as a way to enrich your life. How long do you plan to live in this house? The longer you plan to stay, the more sense it makes to please yourself by building and planting whatever you want. But if you're planning to sell the property within a few years, get a local realtor's advice about what will appeal to potential buyers. This will depend on your neighborhood and climate and on the current housing market. Landscaping is an uncertain investment. Typically, well-designed and well-built hardscape features such as decks and patios, driveways and walkways, fences, or irrigation

systems pay for themselves by raising the property value. Removing overgrown, brushy, or weedy plantings and adding fresh, healthy, colorful new flowers and shrubs may or may not add much to the selling price, but these actions are likely to speed up the sale, so your house won't stay on the market so long. On the other hand, amateurish, eccentric, or unfinished hardscape; labor-intensive gardens such as a big vegetable plot or perennial border; and special-interest features such as a rock garden or greenhouse may slow the sale of a house and even reduce its value.

LANDSCAPING FOR FUN. Whether or not it increases your property value, landscaping certainly increases your quality of life. Thinking of landscaping as entertainment or enrichment makes budgeting easier, too. Just compare your landscaping options with other treats you might desire. Would you rather have season tickets for a local sports team or put up a greenhouse? Take the family to Disneyland or build a deck? Eat out once a week or collect old-fashioned roses? Drink a bottle of fine wine or get a pretty terra-cotta pot and some herbs to plant in it? Buy a pair of stylish shoes or a truckload of mulch? Invest in your landscape to the extent that it brings you joy. You'll get comfort and beauty as immediate rewards, and any expense that you recoup when you sell the house can be a bonus.

For your own enjoyment, grow all the flowers you want. Be aware, though, that potential homebuyers might take one look at this yard and say, "It's too much trouble."

DON'T SKIMP ON CONSTRUCTION. The same rules apply to landscape construction and remodeling as to homebuilding: Invest in good-quality materials and skilled workmanship. You'll never regret a job done right, but you'll be disappointed immediately and forever after by cheap materials, such as untreated wood that's prone to decay, soft bricks that spall (crumble and chip) in freezing weather, or steel nails that drip rusty stains, or by compromised construction, such as shallow foundations, weak joints, or lines and surfaces that aren't square, level, or plumb.

YOU CAN SAVE ON PLANTS. Plants are another story. If you can muster up some patience, you can save a lot of money by forgoing specimen-size trees and shrubs. Smaller plants cost much less, and they typically grow faster, recover more quickly from transplanting, and look better in the long run. You can also see significant savings by starting a lawn from seed rather than sod and by propagating your own annuals, perennials, and ground covers from seeds, divisions, or cuttings.

Impatient homeowners, anxious to establish an "instant garden," often buy too many plants and set them too close together. This multiplies the initial price, and worse yet, it causes problems and waste a few years later when those plants crowd together and need major pruning and thinning. Buying plants that are inexpensive because they grow fast is a related problem; the initial price may seem low, but add the subsequent cost of controlling or replacing them, and the bargain is lost.

There are some occasions and situations when it makes sense to buy large plants, lots of plants, or fast-growing plants, but usually these strategies cost more than they're worth. By contrast, it's both thrifty and rewarding to watch a sapling grow into a tree, to fill a bed with ground covers that you've propagated yourself, and to collect well-mannered plants that don't grow out of scale or take over.

❧ MOVING AHEAD WITH YOUR PLANS

One of the great things about landscaping is that the rewards are so tangible. Spend a few hours working outdoors, and you can really see the progress you've made. Few aspects of modern life offer such immediate, yet lasting, gratification. Keep this in mind as you anticipate working on your landscape. You can probably do much more than you expect, faster than you expect. Remember to keep looking back at what

---

GETTING STARTED

What are some initial steps to take when you move into a house? You'll want to do more than just sit around making lists and plans; you'll want to begin doing something tangible. Here are some activities to start with.

- Haul away trash, construction debris, and unwanted structures. Get this stuff out of the way before you grow blind to its presence.
- Prune and groom dead, weedy, or overgrown brush, vines, shrubs, and trees. Pull weeds. Make the existing plantings look as good as possible while you're considering whether to keep, alter, or replace them.
- Proceed with any earthmoving, grading, or other projects that require heavy equipment. Big machines leave a wake of disturbance, so get this work done before doing any planting that might get damaged.
- Stabilize bare, disturbed soil that's liable to turn into mud or dust by sowing grass or a cover crop such as clover or by topping it with mulch; you can replace any of these later with permanent plantings or pavement, when you decide what you want to use where.
- Proceed with plans to build a deck, patio, pool, or other outdoor living area as soon as you can decide what you want. Get any work done on the house, including remodeling, additions, or simply painting or refinishing the exterior, before you start working on the adjacent plantings.

- If there aren't any flowers yet, prepare a bed and fill it with annuals. Besides the pleasure you'll derive from their immediate beauty and color, growing these inexpensive, disposable plants is a great way to learn about your soil and climate.
- Plant some daffodils and other bulbs the first fall after you move in. When they bloom the next spring, you'll feel as though you've already made a mark on the landscape. Bulbs are gratifying because a modest effort brings big results.
- Start a little nursery area for growing plants that you moved from your previous home, that are given to you, and that you buy. You can keep these plants in pots or plant them in the ground until you've decided where to use them in your landscape.
- Don't plant any trees yet. Most properties have only enough room for a few added trees, and when you first move in, it's too soon to decide which kinds you want and where to put them.
- Don't pave any surfaces with concrete, gravel, or crushed rock until you're *sure* about the location, size, and shape of such areas. These materials are easy to pour down but hard to remove if you change your mind.

you've already accomplished, and don't be daunted by what lies ahead. Take lots of photos to record your progress. (A related tip: Take "baby" pictures of trees, shrubs, and other plants when you first set them out; years later you'll be amazed at how much they've grown.)

To be fair, I should remind you again that landscaping is a job that's never "done." You may reach the point where everything looks perfect and meets your needs exactly, but that situation won't last indefinitely. Structures weather and age, plants get bigger or die back, and your interests and tastes change. It's reasonable to expect that every year you'll have to make some minor adjustments (in addition to routine maintenance), and that every five years or so you'll probably undertake a major project such as having an overgrown tree removed, renovating a garden, or building a new hardscape feature. This ongoing involvement is part of the fun.

Do you need a master plan?

In reference to landscaping, the term "master plan" can have two meanings. It can refer to a set of goals and a course of action, or to a scale drawing. You're sure to benefit from developing a master plan in the first sense, and I'll talk about that later. The importance of developing the other kind of master plan—a scale drawing of the intended landscape, like a blueprint for a building—is debatable. Drawing plans of individual garden areas or of parts of your property can be very helpful. It's a lot easier to compare different ideas on paper than to keep rearranging actual plants. Planning an entire landscape, though, is more than most people want to tackle, because it requires so many decisions at once.

Professional designers are adamant about plans. They think making a drawing is the only way to ensure that everything will fit its place and that all the parts will flow together. Landscape architects and designers are trained to think continually about the big picture, and they're experienced at translating back and forth from a flat plan to three-dimensional space, so designing on paper and planning everything at once feels comfortable and habitual to them. If you like maps and graphics, and if you are anticipating major construction, have a large piece of land, or expect to spend a lot of money on your landscape, hiring a qualified professional to draft a master plan might be a good investment. You wouldn't have to *do* everything right away—you could spread out the building and planting to suit your budget—but by planning ahead, you would have a clear view of where you're going and what you'll have when you get there, and you could avoid pitfalls and missteps along the way.

Could you draft a master plan yourself? Probably not. Because professionals work this way, most do-it-yourself books imply that amateur landscapers should do likewise, but I think that's unrealistic and inappropriate. It's very rare for an untrained homeowner to complete this task. You need to accurately map your existing landscape, juggle dozens of factors, and spend many hours sketching and tracing on overlays as you draw and revise each change and addition. Using a computer design program eliminates the need for tracing paper, but it doesn't alter the basic process, and it doesn't save much time, since it's the *thinking,* not the drawing, that goes slowly. Sooner or later, you'll probably get exasperated and give up.

Maybe that's for the best, because the ultimate test of a design isn't how it was planned, it's how it turns out. Sometimes a plan that looks good on paper wouldn't be attractive or functional when actually installed. I've seen countless plans published in books and magazines that simply wouldn't work in real life. You have to scrutinize a plan closely and ask: What would this design look like from various points of view, at different seasons, and over the years? Is there enough space to move around? Could you walk on the paths, climb the steps, mow the lawn? Would these plants all adapt to the same conditions? How soon would they fill the space—is there room for them to grow? Paper plans *can* be accurate and helpful, but they aren't necessarily so. It takes close evaluation and multiple revisions to develop a workable plan. Even professionals sometimes go astray and have to revise their plans once construction and planting are under way.

The incremental approach

Many homeowners don't need or want a master plan for their landscape; they just want some good ideas for solving particular problems or making wanted improvements. That's okay. If drafting a master plan sounds like something that's not going to happen at your house, you're in good company. Throughout history, people have made beautiful countrysides and villages without any plans or blueprints. Think of places you've seen pictured on calendars and postcards—scenes of rural and small-town life in Europe, England, Mexico, around the world. Those traditional landscapes are appealing because of their integrity, simplicity, and practicality. They rely on plants that are adapted to the climate and that thrive without special care, a narrow range of locally produced building materials, and an architectural style suited to the climate and materials. Anything that didn't survive, fit in, or work out has been eliminated.

Designers fault the incremental, piecemeal approach because so many amateur landscapes look disunited, but that's as likely to result from inconsistency, compromise, and haste as from lack of a master plan. You can proceed one step at a time toward a coherent and satisfying landscape if you observe the traditional guidelines. Use proven, well-adapted plants that won't surprise or disappoint you by

Using an incremental approach, the owners first added a second-story studio to this detached garage, which sits behind their house. The entrance to the studio is at the far end, upstairs (ABOVE LEFT). *Then they built a deck behind the house* (ABOVE RIGHT). *Later they upgraded from wood-chip to flagstone paths and replaced the shabby lawn with permanent plantings* (OPPOSITE). *The effort and expense were spread over a few years.*

growing too slow or too fast, taking over, or dying unexpectedly. Choose a style and stick with it. Limit how many kinds of plants, materials, and colors you use, so it doesn't look as if you kept running out or changing your mind. Scale the sizes and shapes of trees, lawn, planting beds, and various structures so they're all in proportion to each other, to your house, and to the overall lot, so nothing looks too small, silly, or insignificant, or too large, intimidating, or ostentatious. Keep reviewing what you've done, and if something didn't turn out right, adjust or remove it.

Think things through

How much planning should you do before you jump into a job? That depends on what kind of project you're thinking about. The price for acting impulsively is that replanting or redoing things later, if you change your mind, may be inconvenient, expensive, or impossible. Replanting a window box is trivial, but rearranging a foundation planting is heavy work. Moving a birdbath is no problem, but moving a swimming pool would be out of the question.

Indulge your spontaneity in designing temporary or seasonal plantings such as annual flower beds, patio containers, and holiday displays. The bigger and more expensive the undertaking, and the longer you want it to last, the more planning you should do. This sounds obvious, but remember how often you see something in a landscape that makes you ask, "What were they thinking of when they put *that* there?"

For most projects, an appropriate master plan would include lists, sketches, and a sequence or schedule. For example, you might form a plan like this: "This year, I want to cut down that tattered hedge and dig out the roots, build a wooden fence there, and remove the sod and improve the soil from an area in front of the fence, so that next spring I can plant a perennial border there." Along with the stated goal, you could collect ideas for an interesting fence, make lists of perennials you'd like to grow, and sketch planting diagrams for how you might arrange those plants in a border. Meanwhile, you could be contemplating master plans for developing other parts of your property. Of course, you need to coor-

WORKING STEP BY STEP

The advantage of planning ahead is that, ideally, you can organize the work in an efficient sequence, so you don't get in your own way and make things harder than they should be. Also, subdividing a job and finishing one step at a time gives you a sense of progress, like passing milestones as you travel. For example, to install an entire landscape at a new house, a contractor might follow a sequence such as this:

1. Erect temporary barriers around trees and large shrubs to be saved. Fell trees that are flagged for removal, haul away the wood, and grind the stumps. Clear brush and unwanted overgrown plantings. Demolish unwanted structures and hardscape. Clear away trash and debris. Identify any serious infestations of perennial weeds and destroy them.

2. Do any major grading and earthmoving (with respect for trees and caution for buried utility, water, and septic lines). Assess and adjust the drainage as needed. Stabilize slopes and build retaining walls if needed.

3. Install buried drain lines, irrigation systems, and wiring for outdoor lights and receptacles. Prepare foundations and lay paved walkways and patios.

4. Build or install other hardscape features—decks, fences, trellises, arbors, sheds, work and storage areas, permanent edgings or mowing strips for garden beds and borders.

5. Add topsoil, organic material, lime, fertilizer, and other amendments to the soil as needed, and prepare the soil for planting by tilling and raking.

6. Plant lawn, trees, shrubs, ground covers, and perennials as specified in the design, working carefully around any existing trees and shrubs. Mulch the planted areas and begin watering as needed.

7. Do a final cleanup.

dinate the different projects—don't plant a tree where you intend to build a deck later, or fence off an area where truck access would be handy. Plan ahead, think things through, and use your common sense.

Who will do the work?

There's a full spectrum of possibilities here. You can try to do everything yourself (with help from the rest of your household and from whatever family, friends, and neighbors you can recruit), or you could hire help with parts or all of the job. Consider your abilities and interests and do what makes sense.

LANDSCAPING BY YOURSELF. Satisfaction, self-expression, and involvement are the main benefits of doing something yourself. You'll earn the sense of achievement. You can do things *your* way. You'll stay busy, and you'll undoubtedly learn a lot. Investing yourself in this way will deepen your attachment to your property.

But there are drawbacks to doing your own landscaping. The process will almost certainly take longer than if you hired help. You might hurt yourself. You'll face moments of uncertainty as you make plans and decisions. You'll get tired and leave things unfinished. You'll get interrupted, make mistakes, and change your mind. Sometimes you'll end up redoing or undoing jobs you'd done before, things that "seemed like a good idea at the time." Your designs and workmanship may look amateurish.

DIVIDING THE WORK. Like many homeowners, you may decide that it doesn't make sense to do everything yourself. Think of landscaping as a set of

many different tasks, and consider how they match up with your interests, skills, energy, and schedule. Work at the jobs you really enjoy, using skills and knowledge you have already mastered or want to develop. If you anticipate that a task would be too much for you to tackle, find someone else to do it. Putter away at projects where you aren't impatient for results; hire help for jobs you want done as soon as possible.

Don't do a job yourself simply to save money; that's often false economy. When you factor in the costs of buying tools and correcting mistakes, and consider the speed of completion and the quality of the results, hiring help may seem like a bargain. If your spare time is limited, it's especially important to focus on the tasks you really care about doing and think you can do well.

HIRING HELP. You can hire help for any kind of landscaping job, from design and planning to construction, plant selection, site preparation, planting, and maintenance. Of course, hiring help doesn't take all the work out of your hands; it simply changes your role. Now instead of doing the job yourself, you have to become a manager, and that requires its own set of skills. If you want good results with a minimum of surprises and setbacks, you'll have to put some time into supervision. Follow these steps:

▪ Decide what you want done. For example, if you need to do something about a dying tree, do you want someone simply to fell it? To cut it into firewood and stack that for you? To chip or haul away the brush? To grind the stump and

fill in the hole? To clean up afterward? Think it through and list everything you'd include as part of the job.

- Hire cautiously. How do you know if the people you're considering can and will do what you want? Interview them. Ask about their training and experience. Confirm that they are bonded, insured, and licensed according to your state's laws. Call their references, go visit their previous job sites, or review their portfolio.

- Discuss the job. Describe what you have in mind, and ask if they've done similar work before. If you don't know exactly what the job would involve or how it should be done, ask them to explain the "right way" to do it. Be frank about your budget. If you can't afford the very best, ask how they could cut costs without cutting corners. Be sure they're aware of and plan to comply with any relevant codes or regulations. See if your personalities are compatible. Do they listen to what you're saying? Do you like the ideas that they propose?

- Agree on a written contract. This may be brief or lengthy, depending on the job. The bigger and more expensive the project, the more terms you should clarify in the contract. Most professionals have a basic contract form that makes a good starting point. Read that carefully, discuss any questions, and add any provisions that are missing. The final contract for a big job should (1) describe the work to be done, (2) state estimated costs for materials and labor, (3) specify the terms of payment (usually a deposit on signing, with balance on completion for small jobs; add a few intermediate payments for large jobs), (4) estimate the starting date and completion date, and (5) state any guarantee that applies (both construction and plants are often guaranteed for one year). Also, before the work starts, discuss how you'll handle any contingencies or unforeseen problems, or extra tasks that you might want to add on to the original job description.

- Monitor progress, and review the finished work. Keep an eye on how the job is coming along, express your interest, offer praise and appreciation, and ask questions about anything that concerns you. Be sure the project is completed to your satisfaction before making the final payment.

Hire qualified tradespeople for jobs you can't do yourself, such as resurfacing this old patio with mortared brickwork. Word of mouth is the best way to find good help. Otherwise, interview carefully, check references, and go see examples of their completed work.

Trying to find and hire the kind of help you need can be confusing because several job titles include the same word, "landscape," although the people in these jobs have very different backgrounds, skills, and outlooks.

- **LANDSCAPE ARCHITECTS** are trained to address the major issues of property development, such as the siting of buildings and driveways, grading, drainage, soil and slope stabilization, and hardscape design. They also have some training in plant selection and placement, although this is usually not their strongest interest or skill.

    In nearly every state, only people who have completed a university training course and passed a national examination and some kind of state licensing program can use the title "landscape architect." Most registered landscape architects are members of the American Society of Landscape Architects and use the initials "ASLA" after their name to indicate this. The profession is small; ASLA has only about 13,000 members.

    Most landscape architects are based in metropolitan areas and work only on large-scale commercial or municipal proj-

ects. Some gladly undertake residential jobs, especially if they're called in early and the site offers particularly interesting opportunities and challenges, but you usually don't need a landscape architect to develop a typical home landscape. You might hire one to consult on an hourly basis if you have a specific problem, such as an eroding slope that needs a retaining wall.

- **LANDSCAPE DESIGNERS** are not licensed and may or may not have any formal training, so their qualifications vary. Some designers are amateurs with limited background, while others are extremely knowledgeable and skilled. They also vary in creativity. Some have a narrow repertoire of ideas that they use repeatedly, while others are prepared to observe your particular situation, listen to your concerns, and pose an innovative solution.

    A good landscape designer can address all the issues of a typical home landscape, including both hardscape and planting, and can develop plans for landscaping an empty, undeveloped site or for renovating an older, existing landscape. Some

Landscape architects tackle projects like this that involve major site work and construction. This job included grade changes, retaining walls, walkway design, an irrigation system, outdoor lighting, and planting.

designers want to work only on larger projects, but others gladly undertake small jobs, such as developing a plan for converting a front yard from lawn to xeriscape or designing plantings to surround a swimming pool.

Some landscape designers work independently, and you can hire them on an hourly or project basis to help you develop a plan or design a planting. Then you can do the follow-up work yourself or hire contractors to do it. Other designers have a full- or part-time affiliation with a nursery or a landscape contractor who also provides installation, construction, and planting services. In that case, different employees of the same company could do your entire job from design to finished work.

- **LANDSCAPE CONTRACTORS, OR LANDSCAPERS,** do the physical work of landscaping. This is the largest group of landscape workers, and it includes a wide range of individuals, skilled and unskilled, conscientious and careless. Word-of-mouth recommendation is the best way to find a landscaper whose work will satisfy you.

Landscapers may do installation work, such as grading, construction, and planting, or maintenance work, such as mowing, pruning, leaf-raking, or both. Hiring maintenance help is easier, because once you find an individual, team, or crew you like, you can arrange to have them come back on a routine basis. Generally one person or team can do all different aspects of maintenance work.

Getting a new landscape installed is more trouble, because it requires specialized workers with different equipment and skills — one crew to build a wooden privacy fence, another group to install an irrigation system, others to lay a masonry patio, someone else to plant trees and shrubs, and so on. You may be able to find a general landscape contractor who can organize the entire project for you, scheduling and supervising all the separate subcontractors and work crews, but often (especially if you don't want or can't afford to have everything done at the same time) you end up in the general-contractor role yourself and have to find, coordinate, and supervise all the different tradespeople.

- **GARDEN DESIGNERS,** like landscape designers, are a mixed lot. Some have training in horticulture and design, but many are self-taught amateurs. There's considerable overlap between what garden designers and landscape designers do, but in general, those who choose to call themselves garden designers are more interested in plants than hardscape. Garden designers often have a specialty, such as perennial borders, herb gardens, water gardens, or plantings that attract birds and wildlife. They usually aren't very interested in ordinary situations, designs, and plants, such as a simple front yard with a lawn and evergreen foundation planting.

- **GARDENERS, OR PROFESSIONAL GARDENERS,** are hands-on workers skilled at maintaining existing plantings, regaining control of an overgrown or neglected yard, and creating and caring for new plantings. A good gardener is smart, observant, and hard-working. She recognizes all the common plants in your area and most uncommon plants, too, and knows how to help plants look their best. Gardeners prune, groom, weed, mulch, water, and do other routine and specialized plant care, but generally don't do lawn care.

- **HORTICULTURISTS** usually have a degree from a two- or four-year college program, and are skilled at identifying plants, growing them, and diagnosing plant problems. Most horticulturists work in the nursery business or at public gardens, while a few teach or write about gardening. Horticulturists don't necessarily have much hands-on experience in tending home landscapes and may not have any design training or skills. You might hire one as a consultant to name the trees, shrubs, and perennials on your property and give you some information about caring for them, but not to help with the actual work of creating or tending a landscape.

Garden designers are masters at choosing, combining, and arranging plants to create colorful displays like this perennial border.

Arranging plants to make satisfying patterns of color, form, and texture is the artistic part of landscaping.

2 ❧ Designing with Plants

THERE ARE MANY WAYS to interact with and think about your landscape—as home base for your daily routines, space to use for work or play, something to care for, or a project to pursue. This chapter treats the landscape as scenery to look at and move through. It addresses the visual effects you can create with plants, and the feelings that different landscapes invoke.

Designing with plants is the most artistic part of landscaping and is often compared to painting. This is where you can express yourself as bold or subtle, contemporary or traditional, predictable or surprising. There's more to success, though, than just indulging your opinions and preferences. It always comes back to this: A landscape artist can depict whatever situation she or he wants, but a landscape gardener has to work with an actual site and integrate a new planting with existing plants, the house, the background or neighborhood, and the terrain.

Landscape design is also compared to interior decorating, but that's inappropriate because you can't treat plants like furnishings. You can set a chair wherever you choose, but a plant will only grow on a suitable site. A chair stays the same size and color forever, while plants continually grow larger (although they may die back in winter) and change color from season to season. Arranging plants requires knowledge and imagination. You need to know how fast each one grows, how big it will get, and what it does at different times of year, then you have to imagine how it would fit a particular situation and coordinate with what's around it.

Landscapes are dynamic, and a successful design takes that into account. It's relatively simple to create a planting that looks good at one point in time, like the mini gardens they set up at flower and garden shows, or like the photos you see in garden magazines and books (which are often "staged" or enhanced with lots of extra flowering plants that are added just for the purpose of taking the photo). It's more difficult, but also more important, to design a planting that looks good month after month and year after year, so I'll elaborate on those challenges later in this chapter.

Finally, a designer needs to think of both the forest and the trees, the big picture and the details. You need to think of whole planted areas, or *plantings* (other names for plantings are "beds," "borders," and "gardens"), and consider their overall shape, size, and placement with respect to the size of your lot and your house. Within the plantings you can position some key plants as single specimens, but mostly you'll arrange *groups* (two or more of the same kind of plant grown side by side) and *combinations* (two or more different plants grown side by side). In a successful design the plants and plantings are all coordinated—they don't stand alone—and although each plant is individually beautiful, the sum is greater than the parts.

If all this sounds like too much to think about, you can always hire a landscape designer to draft the basic layout, to advise you on plant selection, or to plan the entire project. A professional can save you time and money, solve problems you'd struggle over, and offer ideas you'd never dream of.

On the other hand, I don't think it's unreasonable to hope that you can design a landscape yourself. Just keep in mind that it isn't easy, and it can't be done fast. Be patient, take your time, and don't hesitate to change your mind or to make revisions. And remember that you don't have to tackle the whole yard at once; you can do one section at a time, learning as you go.

This landscape includes open space where you can walk around and planted areas, or plant-ings. Within the plant-ings there are groups, *or multiples of the same kind of plant, and* com-binations *of different plants.*

🌱ASSESS WHAT YOU HAVE NOW

Most of this chapter is organized and written in terms of how to do things "right" — how to design a new or remodeled planting that looks pleasing and seems to belong on the site. There are sections on looking at the big picture, making plant combina-tions, working with color, planning for year-round interest, planning for future growth, and deciding how many plants to use and how to space and arrange them. I've tried to articulate guidelines that are versatile enough to apply to a wide range of situ-ations and styles.

But if you find it hard to relate general design guidelines to your specific needs, start by identifying some of the things that might be "wrong" with your current landscape. Focusing on a particular design problem can help you decide what you need to learn and do.

Make a habit of scrutinizing what you see. What are your impressions when you look at your front yard from across the street, from the front door, from an upstairs window? How about the backyard and side yard? Other areas that are not visible from the

street or the house? Looking at different parts of your land from different points of view is the starting point for developing or refining a design. Do this kind of evaluation repeatedly, as your impressions will change with the seasons. Hopefully you're happy with what you see and only want to tweak a few details here and there, but you might be feeling either dissatisfied or ambitious enough to be plan-ning a major new planting or renovation project.

Record your problems and progress with pho-tos. A photo album is probably the most helpful tool you can refer to when designing your yard. It's so enlightening to see pictures of the same area or same plants taken from different points of view and over a period of time. If you haven't yet, start taking pic-tures now, and mark the dates on them so you can keep them in order. "Before" and "after" pictures show you how much progress you've made and inspire you to tackle new projects. Looking at photos is an indisputable reminder of how fast plants grow; that's encouraging and useful whenever you plant a new little shrub or tree. And taking photos is the most convenient way to record which plants bloom at the same time, along with showing their size and placement. Even photos of your "failures" — plants that died, combinations that didn't look as good as you hoped, plantings that were overcrowded—show lessons that you've learned the hard way and can guide your future efforts.

Common situations and solutions

If you're disappointed or frustrated by what you see around your yard, you may have one of the following problems. Naming the problem is the first step toward solving it. Possible solutions are given here as brief summaries; use the rest of this chapter to learn more about following through with your redesign.

YARD IS EMPTY. Most new houses and a surprising number of existing homes have virtually no landscaping, perhaps just a few trees and a lawn. In this case, start by outlining areas that you want to fill with plants, as opposed to places where you may want to make a patio or build a deck, lay walkways, install a pool, or put up a storage shed. Don't be in a rush. Making all these decisions about how to divide the space takes time and can't happen until you've lived in the house for a while. Meanwhile, as soon as you think you've decided on the size and location of a planting bed, go ahead and prepare the soil and plant annuals there. You'll have flowers to enjoy right away, and you'll get a second chance to define the shape of the bed at the end of the growing season. By

then you'll be more ready to design a permanent planting.

A tight budget is no reason not to plant your yard. Mail-order nurseries sell all kinds of shrubs and trees in small sizes at bargain prices. Learn how to divide perennials, and you can start with a single plant and have a whole patch a few years later. Befriend an older gardener whose land is already crowded with plants, offer to help with big jobs or special projects, and you'll always come home with valuable knowledge and starts of proven, recommended plants.

YARD IS PLANTED BUT LOOKS BORING. Perhaps there's too much green and not enough color. Expand the planted area or replace some of the existing plants with others that bloom over a longer season or at a different time of year. Consider adding plants with colored or variegated foliage. If, along with color, your plants are similar in leaf size and texture, insert contrast by adding plants of a different habit and character, such as waving ornamental grasses or large-leaved perennials.

NEW PLANTING LOOKS DISAPPOINTING. If you're concerned only because the plants are small, be patient; they'll soon grow. If you sense that the design isn't right—perhaps the bed is too small or the shape is too fussy, or there are too many

Well-proportioned and neatly tended plantings surround this house, but the effect is boring because almost everything is stiff and green. There's only a tiny strip of flowering pink impatiens for contrast. A summer-blooming shrub, large-leaved hosta, or fluffy clump of grass would add welcome variety here.

Combining so many kinds of plants and materials gives a hodgepodge effect. To refine this planting, you might take out the yellow marigold and use only red, pink, and white flowers. Remove the Japanese stone lantern, which is out of context here. Add more stone blocks across the front to make a continuous edging, and pull out those functionless 4x4 posts.

kinds of plants and not enough of each kind—try to identify the problem now and revise the planting as soon as possible, before the plants get established.

When you've got the basic size, shape, proportion, and placement of a bed just right, it will look as if it belongs there as soon as you've laid it out. If the plants are grouped appropriately, they'll look right, too, even when they're small. Trust your impressions, and keep moving things around until you're satisfied.

BACKGROUND IS UNATTRACTIVE. Screening out the background with a fence or hedge is the best solution; for ideas, see page 193. But in situations where screening is unfeasible, just strive to make the planting so appealing that it holds your interest and distracts your attention from what lies behind. This actually works well. Think of the times when you've stopped to admire a beautiful garden in an unlikely setting, such as in a commercial district or a rundown neighborhood. Focusing on the garden, you forget where you are.

YARD IS ROOMY BUT TOO SIMPLE, FEATURING JUST A FEW BIG OLD SHRUBS OR TREES. Count your blessings—this is an ideal starting point! Create beds big enough

to frame and flatter those prize specimens and choose an assortment of low and medium-size plants that will complement, coordinate, or contrast with them.

THERE'S A VOID WHERE AN ESTABLISHED PLANT DIED OR GOT DAMAGED. First clear away the remains and trim any damaged shoots off adjacent plants. Simply replacing the plant you lost with another of its kind is one option, but a single new plant will be conspicuous for years before it fills in and catches up with established neighbors. Another approach is to expand the hole and revise the surrounding area, adding several new plants. Ironically, rather than exaggerating the effect of the loss, this may mitigate it.

PLANTS ARE MISMATCHED, LOOK HODGEPODGE. This is a very common problem, especially among gardeners who love plants. It usually means you have too many different kinds of plants and not enough of each kind, and that you accumulated them for their individual merits without thinking of how they'd go together. Deciding on a color scheme is one good way to sort things out. It can help you determine what plants to keep, how to rearrange them, and what plants to give away, dis-

card, or consign to the back forty. Your resulting beds may still be fussy and complex, but at least if the colors are coordinated, there will be some logic to the design.

COLORS LOOK GAUDY. Are you objecting to the leaves or flowers of a particular plant? If so, take it away. But if the problem seems more general, it's probably that adjacent plants contrast too much and clash with each other. Rearranging them might help, adding some intermediate colors might bring harmony, or perhaps you should keep a few favorite plants and choose color-coordinated replacements for others that you remove.

YARD LOOKS STIFF AND TIGHTLACED. Are there too many shrubs that have been sheared repeatedly? Are the plants arranged in straight rows or geometric-shaped beds? If you want to transform this situation into something more casual and natural-looking, you'll likely have to rip out the existing plants and start over, although you might be able to transplant or work around a few of them.

YARD LOOKS MESSY, UNKEMPT. This probably means you have too many herbaceous and deciduous plants and aren't keeping up with the maintenance (grooming, staking, pruning, cleanup, and so forth) they require. Identify the floppiest plants and replace them. In general, evergreens of all kinds look neater than deciduous plants, and of course woody plants have better posture than herbaceous ones do.

LOOK AT THE BASIC LAYOUT

Focusing on perceived problems is one way to begin thinking about design. A more comprehensive approach is to step back and look at the big picture. This addresses the basic issues of how you want to use your property and how you want it to look and feel. It takes some detachment and imagination. You have to see beyond how things are now and envision how they *could* be.

Imagine walking through an unfurnished, undecorated house. Even when it's empty, the house as a whole and the rooms within it can communicate welcome feelings such as grace and comfort or distressing feelings such as confinement or inconvenience. There's plenty to respond to as you judge the

This planting looks disheveled and unstructured in midsummer. There are too many plants with vertical stems and fine-textured foliage. Substituting some broadly mounded plants with wider, larger leaves would help the design. Also, that narrow strip between the edge of the blacktop driveway and the stone edging for the bed looks fussy and is full of weeds. Why not remove the edging and extend the planting right out to the pavement?

(TOP): *The line between open space and planted bed curves along the contour line here. The lawn is nice and level, while the sloping bed makes an ideal stage for displaying this collection of dwarf conifers and other special shrubs.*

(MIDDLE): *In this courtyard, carefree brick flooring provides practical open space, and the planting beds are filled with evergreen shrubs and ground covers.*

(BOTTOM): *A fenced rose-and-herb garden is the centerpiece of this Santa Fe landscape. The plantings are lovely, but because of the spacious gravel paths they don't overwhelm you.*

size, shape, and arrangement of the rooms and their relation to each other.

Likewise, the division of a landscape into planted and unplanted areas and the sizes, shapes, and relations of those areas create impressions that you see, feel, and respond to, and you can think and talk about these aspects of a landscape without reference to particular plants just as meaningfully as you can talk about an unfurnished house. In fact, it's helpful at this point not to focus on the plants; just think of them as green blobs.

Distinguish between planted and unplanted areas

The unplanted parts of your yard—the driveway, sidewalks or walkways, patio, deck, lawn (even though grass is a plant), or any areas that are surfaced with gravel, rock, or mulch in lieu of a lawn—are places where you can walk without watching your step, the kids can play games, the dog can run, and you can set up a table and chairs and have a party or a yard sale. Unplanted areas are useful space.

By contrast, anywhere you dig a bed or hole, improve the soil, and add plants becomes off-limits. You may be able to walk through it on designed pathways or steppingstones, but you can't wander at random or you'll crush the plants.

Sorting out how you're going to use different parts of your property deserves your attention because it has both practical and visual consequences. How much open, unplanted space you need depends on how many people use your yard and what they do outdoors. Beyond those needs, extra open space is optional. You might like the sense of spaciousness and freedom, or you might think unplanted areas are missed opportunities. Suit yourself.

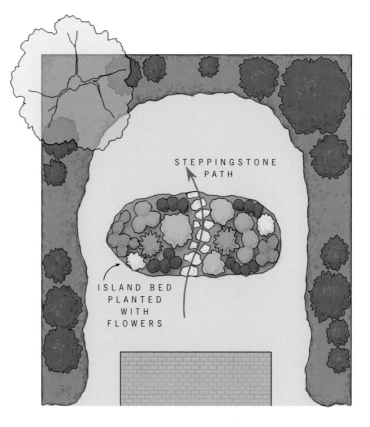

PLANTS AND OPEN SPACE

Arranging plants around the perimeter of your yard leaves open space in the center where you can walk around, play, or gather with family and friends.

Adding an island bed gives you something to look at and a place to grow more plants, but it reduces the open space. To avoid a sense of crowding and obstruction, include a path so you can walk through the island and don't have to go around it.

Context is another consideration. If your view includes plenty of open space — treeless cropland or rangeland, a big park, distant mountains, a body of water — you may want to bring that spacious feeling right up to your house by keeping your landscape open and simple, with short plants, or you may react by ringing yourself with trees, shrubs, and densely planted beds. If surrounded by a real forest or a "forest" of buildings, you may yield to the pressure and let plantings crowd right up to the house, or sweep them away to maintain a precious patch of open space. Again, it's up to you.

KEEP PLANTINGS OUT OF THE WAY.

No matter how beautiful it is, any plant or planting that blocks your path or limits your activity is an annoying obstacle, and chances are that sooner or later someone will knock it down or at least curse it. So before thinking about how you want a planting to look, make sure you're locating it in a place where it will be welcome, not resented.

One conventional solution is to put plantings around the perimeter of a property and right around the house, leaving expanses of open space between. This usually works well. It looks formal and stereotyped if the plantings are narrow bands of uniform width, such as sheared evergreen hedges and foundation plantings, but the design can be varied, natural, and interesting if you combine many kinds of plants and give the beds an undulating profile.

Another common approach is setting plants or beds like islands in a sea of lawn or pavement. Making islands is tricky and a little risky because an island is a potential obstacle. Realizing this, many people timidly create small islands, but that looks silly and doesn't solve the problem. A better solution is to make a big, assertive island that demands and earns its space and to include openings or pathways so you can move through the island instead of having to go around it. Or fill the entire area with plantings if you aren't using the open space.

PLANT ANY UNUSED SPOTS.

You can hardly go wrong by filling any unused or uninviting areas with plants. Watch how you use your property, where you do and don't spend time, where company

(LEFT): *Fill unused areas with masses of carefree wildflowers or other cheerful plantings. This dry side yard was no place for a lawn, so the owners wisely transformed it.*

(RIGHT): *This bed is wide enough to balance the walkway and is generously filled with plants. Because you see the bed up close, you can appreciate the detailed variety of flowers and leaves, but the overall effect is unified by a color scheme that coordinates with that of the house.*

gathers or never goes. Any place where you're unlikely to walk or linger might be better planted than empty. This includes spaces that are too exposed, noisy, or narrow, or where the ground is sloping, rough, or too wet for you to walk, play, or rest there in comfort. It also includes stretches of lawn where you never walk except to push the mower or fertilizer spreader; instead of grass, you could plant something else there. Design plantings to make these areas look interesting and attractive, and provide pathways as needed for access or crossing.

Match the scale of a planting to its surroundings

The idea of "one size fits all" doesn't work any better in landscaping than it does in clothing. A grove of tall trees looks majestic on a country estate but would overwhelm a city yard. A precious collection of dwarf succulents would sparkle in the roomlike setting of a small enclosed yard but would dwindle to

insignificance on a wide-open lot. Try to relate the scale and complexity of a planting to the overall size of your yard, the size and style of your house, and the size of any established trees.

WHAT SIZE FITS YOUR HOUSE AND YARD? Basically, small houses and yards call for small plants and plantings, and large houses and yards call for large plants and plantings. This concept is simple and should be obvious, but drive down any street and you can find a landscape where the scale of the plantings is all wrong. A hugely overgrown shrub looks as awkward and intimidating in a small yard as a whale in a swimming pool, while a single row of flowers along the edge of a two-car driveway looks as ridiculous and pathetic as a rubber ducky adrift in the sea.

Judging scale is easy once you realize it's an issue and if you're willing to be honest about what you see. If you have trouble assessing your own yard, eaves-

INCORPORATING SPECIAL COLLECTIONS AND GARDENS

If you have a passion for a particular group of plants, the idea of keeping them out of the way will sound absurd. If you love irises or daylilies or rhododendrons, for example, of course you'll want to give them a prominent place in your yard, where you can admire them, compare and study them, and show them off. Likewise, if you're eager to have a lily pond, a rock garden, an herb garden, a vegetable patch, a mini orchard, or any other special garden, you'll want to feature it, not shove it to the sidelines. That's fine. Here are some tips for integrating collections and specialties into a landscape.

- **PICK THE MOST FAVORABLE CONDITIONS.** Give your chosen plants every advantage by locating the collection or garden where growing conditions are most suitable. Consider sun and shade, shelter from wind, soil quality and drainage, fencing from deer or other herbivores, convenient watering, and so on. Sometimes the ideal place for growing your favorite plants is right beside your house; for advice on that, see page 101.

- **BECOME AN EXPERT GROWER.** Whatever plants you've chosen, dedicate yourself to learning how to grow them well. It's not enough to simply acquire a collection of plants; anyone can shop. Masterly care is what makes a collection so stunning that it can stand as the centerpiece of a landscape. What you're showing off is not just plants but also the evidence of your knowledge and skill.

- **MAKE THE AREA BIG ENOUGH.** If you decide to devote part of your yard to a plant collection or specialty garden, don't skimp. Make the area big enough to look significant, not trivial, in the context of the yard as a whole (see page 38). Make it big enough to accommodate the additional plants that you'll inevitably acquire. And make it big enough that you can take pride in it, become knowledgeable about the plants, and derive authority from your commitment. After all, part of the reason for collecting plants is the sense of identity it gives you, but you can't claim to be a specialist in daylilies, for instance, if you have only a dozen cultivars.

- **ADJUST THE SHAPE TO THE SITE.** Collectors sometimes get stuck in an agricultural mindset and arrange their plants in straight rows or rectangular blocks. Break out of that box and try curved shapes instead, especially if you're working on a sloping site. Rows can curve, meander, or radiate. Beds can tuck into a corner, wrap around a patio, climb a hill, or sit like islands in a lawn.

- **DIVERSIFY AND INCLUDE COMPANION PLANTS.** Diversity is the difference between a collection (which often resembles a mere crop) and a garden. Reach beyond the focus of your collection and think about combinations (see page 50). Choose plants to complement, coordinate, or contrast with your favorites. For example, if you collect tree peonies, which bloom briefly in spring, complement them with shrubs and perennials that bloom throughout the summer and fall. Use an underplanting of dianthus, catmint, or hardy geraniums to unify a collection of different roses. Add evergreen herbs or dwarf fruit trees for winter interest in a vegetable garden. Don't begrudge the space that other plants take away from your collection; appreciate how they enhance the overall effect.

- **INVEST IN HARDSCAPE.** Manifest your commitment by treating your collection as a permanent feature in the landscape, not just a temporary encampment. Lay a nice paved walk that leads out to, through, and around the area. Put a fence or wall around it, mark the entrance with a gate or arbor, or make a masonry mowing strip to separate it from the lawn. Include a bench or table and chairs, so you can sit and enjoy your plants.

- **DOWNSIZE THE LABELS.** Identifying the plants in a collection is important, but try to do it in a subtle way. You've probably seen gardens where the plant labels are visible from 1,000 feet. That's distracting, especially if they're white plastic or shiny aluminum. There's no need for oversize labels; you can always walk closer if you need to read the name of a plant. Small wooden, plastic, or metal markers tucked in the ground at the base of a plant or tied to its limbs are usually sufficient. Make yourself a map of the planting, too, as a backup in case labels get lost, faded, or misplaced.

---

drop on what other people say about it, and take their reactions to heart.

Generally it's shrubs and trees that seem too large for an area, although vines and ground covers can get overwhelming, too. In any case, if you have plants that have outgrown their space, cut them back or take them out.

There are various explanations for why something may seem too small, and these invoke different reactions. If you've just planted a new tree, it will look short and skinny compared with your house or any mature trees in sight. But that's understandable because it's obviously young. Everyone knows it will grow, and most people respond to baby trees with encouragement, not disdain. Likewise, perennials sprouting up in spring are a happy sight even as mere tufts, because you know they'll soon make an impressive show. By contrast, a bed or border that's too small, too narrow, or sparsely planted usually looks silly or amateurish at best, and it may appear downright stingy.

HOW FAR ARE YOU LOOKING? Many things that are visible up close can't be seen from a distance. Complex combinations of many small plants with fascinating details are effective only at short range. Use them near your house, right outside a window, along a walkway, or in a tiny yard. When you get more than a few steps away from a planting like this, you just can't see what's going on. It's like trying to read a newspaper from across the room. To make a planting that looks clear, distinct, and impressive from across the yard or across the street, you need to think big, like an artist painting a billboard. The farther away the planting is, the bigger the area it takes to make an appreciable effect. This applies both to the overall size of a bed or border and to the areas filled by each group of plants.

DON'T SKIMP; MAKE PLANTINGS BIG ENOUGH. A handy guideline for working around trees and shrubs is to make the bed or planted area at least as wide as the plant's mature spread. Follow the drip line of a tree, for example. This serves the practical purpose of keeping plants out of the way, so you won't have to keep trimming shrubs that reach or flop out onto a pathway or lawn or swerve or duck as you walk under or around taller shrubs and trees.

Most people are more likely to make a bed too narrow than too wide, so when in doubt err on the generous side. Shrubs and trees in too-small beds

recall cartoons of elephants on tiptoe in ballet slippers; they're top-heavy and unstable, their feet are pinched, and they look disrespected and silly. Widening the bed at the base of a plant like this gives it dignity and ease and makes it seem more relaxed, graceful, and comfortable. If you don't make it big enough at first, you can enlarge a bed years later when you see how the plants grow. For a bed that contains an assortment of shrubs, trees, and other plants, the edge can wind in and out to accommodate their varying widths.

Another way to determine an appropriate size for a planting under or around big shrubs or trees or next to a house is to look at the shadows cast when the sun is fairly low in the sky (early morning, late afternoon, or at midday in winter). Make the planting as big as the shadow. Shadows move around, so the bed won't necessarily line up with the shadow, but using the shadow for inspiration will ensure that you make the planting large enough. Don't be surprised if this approach suggests that you should plant an entire section of your yard that's currently open space or lawn. Be confident; it really would

Bold plantings with broad sweeps of color are clear and satisfying, especially in wide-open spaces.

look better if you developed that space by adding plants. Even a bed of ground cover would assert a use of space that's proportioned to the trees and/or house.

RELATING BED WIDTH AND PLANT HEIGHT. A conventional guideline recommends making the average width of a bed or border about two-thirds the mature height of the tallest plants you expect to grow there, or conversely, if you outline the area first, choosing some plants that will grow about one and a half times as tall as the bed's width.

Don't think twice about breaking this rule; it's too restrictive for most situations. When you're thinking about the height of plants in your yard, it's not enough to focus on how things look, you have to consider how they *feel*. It makes a great deal of difference whether plants are short enough that you can see over them or tall enough to block your view. For example, if you want to put an island in your yard yet retain a feeling of openness, use mostly short plants, regardless of the bed's width. To deliberately provide a feeling of enclosure or separation, include some taller plants even if the bed is narrow. A hedge or row of plants intended specifically to provide screening may be two to three times taller than it is wide.

SET AN IMAGINARY CEILING. If you were designing an estate with vast grounds and broad vistas, you'd want to pay attention to the height and placement of specimen trees, the shape of their crowns, and how these sizes and shapes relate to the areas of other plantings and lawns. From a distance, all of that is visible and meaningful.

Up close, though, in a typical home landscape, it's as if there were an imaginary ceiling. People may glance at the sky from time to time, but they don't spend much time looking up. Mostly they look around and down.

This helps resolve two situations that would otherwise be design challenges. One situation is a house surrounded by tall trees. On an average lot, there isn't room to design plantings in proportion to the full height of those trees, so ignore their tops; don't look up. Prune off the lower limbs as high as you can reach, thin the crowns to let some light through, and then work around the trunks to create a shade-tolerant understory landscape of smaller plants that are scaled to each other, the lot, and the house.

Another challenging landscape situation is common in expensive new developments, where builders erect castle-sized houses on tiny lots, with as little as 6 feet between the house walls and the prop-

Mature trees dominate this yard. Their size, and the shadows they cast, suggest that the entire area should be filled with plantings, as it is. This continuous under-planting is very wide, but all the plants are short enough that even a child can see over them. As a result, it feels open, not crowded.

erty lines. It would take an acre or more to create plantings in proportion with a house that size. On a tiny lot, you have to think differently. There's nothing you can plant in a space 6 feet wide that's in proportion to a house 30 feet tall. Again, an imaginary ceiling is the solution. Don't look up. Develop the space at ground level into a rich and interesting outdoor room with plants and plantings scaled to that kind of space.

Use formal elements sparingly and deliberately

Plants in straight rows or neat patterns, mirror-image or symmetrical plantings, shrubs sheared into geometric shapes—these formal elements are the hallmarks of a man-made landscape. You never see things like this in nature. That doesn't mean you shouldn't use them in your landscape. They can be stunning. But since they obviously don't occur by chance, their placement should be as deliberate as their appearance.

So, align straight hedges or edgings with the sides of the house or the property lines, making them parallel or perpendicular to some prominent or meaningful existing feature. Use a single sheared shrub as a focal point. A matched pair of plants can mark the beginning or end of a path or the sides of an opening or passageway.

Novices often make symmetrical designs because they're uncertain about how else to arrange plants or simply because they like the looks of symmetry. While it's true that a symmetrical planting can mirror the repose and dignity of a house with a symmetrical facade, the effect is flawed if the two sides of a planting differ, as they typically do because of slight differences in growing conditions or circumstances. It takes frequent pruning, fussing, and luck to achieve true symmetry or to create a homogeneous effect in any geometric pattern of evenly spaced plants. If even one plant grows slowly, gets knocked over, or succumbs to a pest or disease problem, it leaves a hole that's hard to refill.

DON'T BE AFRAID OF STRAIGHT LINES. Although you should think twice before filling a straight row with one kind of plant, don't be afraid of straightness in general. If you're making a bed in front of your house, beside the patio, or along the driveway, there's no reason why its edges should not be straight. The simplest shape for such a bed is a rectangle parallel to the adjacent structure. After all, a straight line is the shortest distance from point to point. It's the most convenient route to walk along and the easiest shape to mow along or to edge.

Don't call attention to an edge by outlining it with a row of short "edging" plants unless you delib-

eratery want the bed to look prim. If you simply fill the bed with a variety of interesting plants that come right out to the edge, no one will think twice about the fact that it's straight. You can let some or all of the plants cross over and obscure the edge if the planting adjoins pavement, decking, or gravel. Where a planting adjoins lawn, though, it's impractical to let plants flop over the edge, because they get in the way of mowing and can even smother the turf.

Make pleasing curves

Disdain for straight lines leads many people to design curved edges for their beds and borders or for patches of ground covers or the shape of the lawn. Sometimes this doesn't work right and the curves just look like meaningless squiggles. There are a few tricks to making curved edges that look natural and inevitable.

RELATE CURVES TO THE TOPOGRAPHY. On a sloping site, it looks good if curves follow the contour lines. You may have seen this done on a large scale in farmland. It works just as well in a small yard. One way to envision where the lines or

Parallel to the house wall, a straight walk is the shortest, most direct path to the door. Straight doesn't necessarily mean rigid. That's the beauty of combining plants with hardscape; the plants soften the edges.

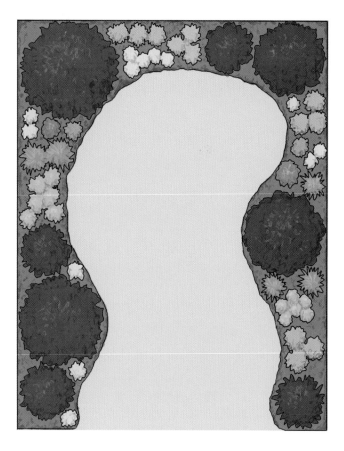

RELATE CURVES TO THE PLANTS

When you design a bed with a curved outline, make each convex curve swing out around a single specimen of a broad, substantial plant, such as an evergreen shrub or a big clump of ornamental grass. Fill the areas inside the concave curves with groups of smaller, shorter plants.

Follow the drip line to make a bed that curves gracefully around the base of a tree. This flowering crab apple is underplanted with pachysandra, an evergreen ground cover.

edges would go is to imagine that your yard is flooded with water. Estimate how a shoreline would curve in and out, then follow the curves of that imaginary shoreline to outline a planting area. You might carry this a step further. Use taller plants—whatever you choose—above the "shoreline," and put lawn, a fine-textured low-growing ground cover, gravel or mulch, or pavement on the lowest, most level part of the yard to symbolize a pool of water there. It's an artifice, but one that's quite convincing and satisfying.

RELATE CURVES TO THE PLANTINGS. Another basis for shaping curves is to make them bulge *around* a substantial plant. This works on either flat or sloping ground. If you're creating a bed around one or more existing trees or mature shrubs, think of an imaginary shoreline again, and pretend that the trees or shrubs are bluffs or headlands. The shore would curve out around them and recede back into bays beside or between them. If you're starting from scratch, you can first outline the shape of a curved bed and then use plants to give the curves meaning. Where the bed curves outward, put a broad, rounded evergreen shrub or an ornamental grass that forms a big clump, and position it so that when the shrub or grass is mature it will fill out and down to the edge of the bed. Walking around that plant will give meaning to the curve. Or put a multi-

trunked tree with interesting bark there, and plant some dark evergreens behind it to make a background so the tree stands out as if it were in a display case. Fill the bays of a bed with smaller plants that look "softer," as if they could be pushed back or washed away.

LOOK AT THE NEGATIVE SPACE. Any edge or outline defines two shapes, one on either side of the line. Perhaps your backyard is just lawn now and you want to put a border around the edge. When you're outlining a border, you tend to focus on what will go inside it. Try looking instead at the area that will remain as lawn. Is it a pleasing shape? Do the curves look graceful and natural? The area between prominent features is sometimes called "negative space," but it isn't really negative or empty. In a landscape, that empty space is usually where you'll walk, sit, and spend the most time. Try to see it and appreciate it for its own sake, and try to refine its shape. Fine-tuning the curves of a negative space simultaneously improves the shape of whatever it's next to.

KEEP REFINING CURVES UNTIL THEY LOOK RIGHT. Be patient when you're designing a planting with a curved or undulating edge. Making natural-looking curves takes some tweaking and adjusting. Mark a tentative outline, consider it from all angles, and then pull it out here, push it back

there, until you think it's just right. As an additional test for any planting that's adjacent to a lawn, try running the lawn mower along the curved outline. If you can't negotiate the curves in a single pass and need to keep backing up and starting again, the curves are too small and sharp. Make them bigger, wider, more gently rounded. The edge will be easier to mow and will look better, too.

COMBINING AND ARRANGING PLANTS

Once you've outlined an empty new bed or decided to renovate or expand an existing one, it's time to think about which plants to grow there. Even if you want or have room for only a few kinds, there are many possibilities to consider. You can borrow ideas you've seen in another garden or in a photograph or develop your own.

Either way, you'll be concerned with expressing a purposeful style; making combinations; observing color, form, and texture; and using repetition. These topics, or principles of design, may seem hard to comprehend at first, but once you grasp an idea you'll start noticing examples of it everywhere and

Look at the beds, then look at the lawn. The shape of the lawn is the negative space. When you're designing an area like this, observing the outline of the negative space helps you refine the curves.

(Text continued on page 48)

Any slope that's steep enough to catch your attention is likely to be unused space. If you aren't spending time there, you may as well cover it with plants.

First build a path and steps (see page 159) if you need a way to climb or cross the slope, and consider the possibility of making terraces and retaining walls (page 214). Give priority to the hardscape, and if you plan any construction, finish building before you start planting.

Although you can impose straight lines on a slope by building a level retaining wall that runs sideways or a fence that climbs uphill, do this sparingly. In general, a sloping site calls for an informal design with curved, not straight, lines. Don't try to fit a formal rectangular or square plot onto even a moderate slope; it will look crooked and tippy. Formal designs look best on level sites. On a slope, take advantage of the topography and strive for a graceful, natural-style design that follow its contours.

Any slope, natural or terraced, is a dramatic setting for displaying plants, especially if you consider the point of view. It makes a big difference whether you're at the bottom of a slope looking up or at the top looking down. If the slope is in your front yard and your house is either uphill or downhill from the street, you'll probably want to consider both perspectives, the view from and toward the house. But in other situations—for example, if your backyard slopes up to the property line—you'll spend more time looking one way than the other, so you can design the planting accordingly.

In any case, whatever else you grow, underplant it all with a dense, preferably evergreen ground cover to stabilize the soil, protect against erosion, and deter weeds. For more on ground covers, see page 319.

■ **LOOKING UPHILL**. If a slope rises in front of you, you naturally tend to look uphill. Rather than exaggerate the vertical emphasis in this case, try to balance it with horizontal interest. Avoid straight-trunked trees, conifers that point up, narrowly erect shrubs, and spiky flowers. Use perennials and grasses that have a mounded or floppy profile, such as *Artemisia* 'Powis Castle', calico aster (*Aster lateriflorus* var. *horizontalis*), red valerian (*Centranthus ruber*), bleeding hearts (*Dicentra*), hardy geraniums, golden hakone grass (*Hakonechloa macra* 'Aureola'), catmints (*Nepeta*), fountain grass (*Pennisetum*), and floppy species of penstemons and salvias. There are also many fine trailing perennials that will spill over the edge of a wall or tumble down a slope. Many of these put on a remarkable show of bloom at one season or another. For recommendations, see page 150.

Mounded, arching, and trailing shrubs are especially good for sloping sites. It's impressive to look up and see them cascading toward you like a waterfall. A few big shrubs can cover a slope more easily and effectively than dozens of smaller shrubs or perennials. Most of the following shrubs will spread at least 5 to 6 feet wide, and some reach 10 feet or wider. Many form roots wherever the stems touch the ground; in this sense, they serve like a large-scale ground cover. Some outstanding broad-leaved candidates for this looking-uphill situation are most kinds of abelia, bearberry (*Arctostaphylos uva-ursi*), beautyberry (*Callicarpa*), most cotoneasters, deutzia, most forms of winter creeper (*Euonymus fortunei*), forsythias, hypericums, winter jasmine (*Jasminum nudiflorum*), leucothoes, Cape plumbago (*Plumbago capensis*), fragrant sumac (*Rhus aromatica*), 'White Meidiland' and other trailing "landscape" roses, and *Stephanandra incisa* 'Crispa'. Most trailing cultivars of various conifers—such as creeping junipers; pros-

(LEFT): *Use waterfalls as an inspiration when choosing plants for a site that will be viewed from below. Plants with trailing, tumbling, and arching stems are good for this situation.*

(BELOW): *Geraniums and roses lean toward you as you face this retaining wall and bank.*

trate forms of many pines, firs, and spruces; and weeping hemlock—are also ideal for slopes.

Weeping trees, and trees with dangling flowers, are great plants for uphill sites, as it's entrancing to look up into their boughs. If you have room for a small tree on a slope, you could try a weeping Japanese maple *(Acer)*, 'Lustgarten Weeping' Kousa dogwood *(Cornus kousa)*, Oyama magnolia *(Magnolia sieboldii)*, 'Red Jade' crab apple *(Malus)*, weeping parrotia *(Parrotia persica* 'Pendula'), weeping Higan cherry *(Prunus subhirtella* 'Pendula'), or weeping Japanese snowbell *(Styrax japonicum* 'Carillon'). Your local nursery may not stock any of these trees normally, but they can order one for you.

Don't bother putting vines on a slope that you'll be looking up at, as you'll only see the bottoms of their leaves. Vines don't trail down; they climb up, and their leaves always face toward the light.

■ **LOOKING DOWNHILL.** When a slope drops off below you, or when you're designing a planting that will be viewed primarily from a deck, second-story window, or other raised vantage point, you get an overview that shows off the basic layout of an area—the shape of the planting beds and how you've subdivided them. It's very satisfying if these shapes are bold, simple, and harmonious.

When you're looking down onto plants, anything that's pointy or skinny or predominantly vertical doesn't amount to much, so don't bother with stiffly upright grasses, perennials, or shrubs. In general, arrange low, small plants in wedge-shaped patches that fit together into a tapestry (or use a single ground cover throughout the entire area).

For larger specimens that can rise above and stand out against the low background, consider some of the following. All look especially good from above. Most of these look best if spaced far enough apart that they can develop fully rounded shapes, and one plant of a kind is often enough, except for the smaller perennials.

Try perennials with large leaves, such as bergenias, brunneras, heucheras, hostas, lungworts *(Pulmonaria)*, and 'Helene von Stein' lamb's ears *(Stachys byzantina)*. Colored or variegated forms of these perennials are particularly intriguing. For a real conversation piece, try cardoon *(Cynara cardunculus)*, Scotch thistle *(Onopordum acanthium)*, silver sage *(Salvia argentea)* or clary sage *(S. sclarea)*, or mulleins *(Verbascum bombyciferum, V. olympicum)*. All are biennials that form giant (up to 3 feet wide) rosettes of silver-gray leaves during the first season of growth. You'll peer into these rosettes with amazement; they're very engaging.

Most clump-forming grasses and ferns look neat from above, as do the bold, architectural rosettes of agaves, yuccas, small fan palms, and New Zealand flax *(Phormium tenax)*. Likewise, you'll enjoy the top view of deciduous shrubs that form dome-shaped mounds of equal-length stems (when thoughtfully pruned), such as various hydrangeas, 'Hidcote' and other hypericums, 'Anthony Waterer' and related summer-blooming spireas, and cultivars of *Weigela florida* (prune weigela hard immediately after it blooms).

Another group of plants that look outstanding from above are perennials that bear big, up-facing clusters of colorful flowers, such as yarrows *(Achillea)*, butterfly weed *(Asclepias tuberosa)*, asters, chrysanthemums and daisies, coreopsis, gaillardia, sundrops and evening primroses *(Oenothera)*, most kinds of phlox, black-eyed Susans or coneflowers *(Rudbeckia)*, pincushion flower *(Scabiosa)*, and 'Autumn Joy' and other sedums. You can't help but smile as you look down on these flowers and watch the butterflies that are drawn to them.

(BELOW): *When viewed from a second-story deck, the plants appear to be holding their leaves out as if they were waving and smiling up to you. Actually, they're facing toward the brightest part of the sky.*

(RIGHT): *Overlooking the Pacific, this path takes you past splendid succulent rosettes and masses of flowering geraniums and sea lavender.*

Shopping is easier if you know what you're looking for, and a good way to define what you want is by answering key questions. With landscape plants, you first have to match the plant to the site. For that, review the questions on page 232. Then decide how you want the plant to look and what role it should fill in your design by asking the following questions.

- How tall do you want it to get?

- How wide an area do you need to fill? Will one plant grow that wide, or should you use a group of them?

- What shape are you looking for? Some common plant shapes, or habits, are columnar, spiky, vase-shaped, spheri-cal, mounded or cushionlike, flat, weeping, vining, or irregular or asymmetric.

- What texture are you looking for in the leaves and twigs? Think of terms such as "huge," "bold," "coarse," "stout," "massive," "bulky," "bland," "pliable," "tiny," "fine," "dainty," "delicate," "wispy," "see-through."

- Does it matter if the foliage is evergreen or deciduous, or if the stems die down in winter?

- Do you want a certain color to stand out, or is plain green okay? If you're looking for a color, what month(s) or season(s) do you want it to show?

(Text continued from page 45)

suddenly it will be meaningful and clear. And although the examples and applications are countless, the principles themselves are very simple. I think of them not as rules or recipes but as pointers that remind you what to look at and that help you analyze and interpret what you see.

Substitute plants to adapt an idea

Much of what we react to when looking at a planting or landscape is quite basic and general. This is good news, because it means that you can copy design ideas without worrying about identifying, obtaining, or trying to grow the kinds of plants used originally. You can usually re-create an effect that you've admired in some other setting by substituting plants that will thrive in your own climate and growing conditions (see page 233).

The idea for a design rarely depends on particular plants. Few plants are so distinctive that they can't be replaced with something else that has a similar size, shape, color, and texture. That's why it's helpful to talk about design ideas in basic terms rather than focusing too closely on the specific plants used.

The magnificent colors, textures, and forms of those conifers and other shrubs are what's special about this garden. Added details — that dot of red flowers, the sundial, lamp, and bird-bath — seem undersize and anomalous in this context. Removing them would simplify and strengthen the design.

Instead of naming the plants you see, try to summarize the dominant impression or overall effect you feel.

Your description of what you're looking *at* also specifies what to look *for*. So, for instance, if you admire a planting you see in a magazine that shows how white brightens a shady corner, you can proceed to brighten your own shady corner with any number of shrubs or perennials with white flowers or white-variegated leaves. Define the idea first. Then you can come up with a list of possible plants, either by doing your own research or by getting help from friends or professionals.

Show a sense of purpose and style

Professional garden designers, like interior decorators and wardrobe or image consultants, usually make a big deal about choosing a style and sticking with it. As with anything else, you can go overboard with this and end up hidebound. Most amateur landscapers, though, demonstrate the opposite shortcoming; their yards seem too random or eclectic, without any clear structure, pattern, or theme. There's a happy medium between these extremes. Make the basic layout of your yard simple and satisfying, then have fun with the small stuff and details.

RESOLVE ANOMALIES. Anything that's unexpected catches your attention. It can be an empty gap in an otherwise full planting, one plant that sticks up taller than everything around it, a clashing color, a tropical with oversize leaves, a geometric shrub in a casual setting, or an asymmetric plant in a formal garden. Although unexpected features can be masterful additions to a landscape when they're sized and placed just right, more often they are distractions that make you ask, Why is *that* there?

Using contrast and surprise is tricky, so devote extra time to studying what works and doesn't work. Look for plants that stand out and ask, Does that look deliberate or accidental? If it's too weird, maybe you should get rid of the plant. Or dig it up and put it in a pot — people expect to see weird plants in pots. Sometimes moving the plant to a different position or changing its neighbors will make it look right. Often the problem is that the anomalous plant is too small; this makes it look timid and tentative. Maybe it will seem to belong when it grows larger, or maybe you should surround it with more of its kind to make the effect look more purposeful.

KEEP FOCAL POINTS TO A MINIMUM. A focal point is a special plant or object that's positioned to catch and hold your attention. It's something to focus on and it invites you to pause a moment. Obviously, you can't focus on more than one thing at once, so if there are multiple focal points in your field of view you get confused and don't know which way to look. Instead of this, try to arrange things so you see only one focal point at a time and have to turn around or walk a ways before

This yard has a single, unambiguous focal point: the blue gate at the end of the walk. The plants cheer your passage but don't distract you from that goal.

(LEFT): *Daffodils and daylilies complement each other. The daffodils bloom when the daylilies are mere tufts of foliage; later in the season, the full-grown daylilies hide the withering daffodil leaves.*

(RIGHT): *The lavender, santolina, and lamb's ears combined in these layered crescents are equable companions. They share silver-gray color, fuzzy-leaved texture, mounded habit, and a preference for dry, sunny sites.*

you see the next one. You can easily judge whether or not your focal points are clear and effective by watching how visitors respond to them. Do they see what you intended? Do they get the point?

A focal point gets its importance from *what* it is and from *where* it is. In terms of placement, the obvious positions for a focal point are at the beginning or end of a path, at a corner or turning point, or in the center of a bed. These are places where people will look anyway, expecting to find something. What you put there should be special. If it's a plant, choose one that looks good throughout the growing season or, better yet, year-round; that gets big enough to fill a prominent role; and that has excellent foliage, a pleasing shape, long-lasting flowers, or other virtues. For an object, choose something such as a bench, arbor, rock, fountain, or sculpture.

Saying that you shouldn't have too many focal points doesn't mean your garden can't be full of interesting treasures. It's a matter of perception. A garden can be complex and richly textured if everything works together as a whole. The problem comes when you have too many features that rival each other and clamor for your attention. These aren't focal points; they're clutter.

Think in terms of combinations

Few plants are interesting enough to stand alone. One of the most common mistakes amateur landsca-

pers make is setting a single perennial, shrub, or tree by itself someplace out in the yard. These isolated plants rarely have enough stature or beauty to perform solo. Don't expect too much of single specimens. Plan combinations instead.

To make successful combinations, think about how two or more different kinds of plants can complement, coordinate, or contrast with each other. It's helpful to focus on these interactions one at a time, although they easily overlap. Imagine a patch of bearded irises flanked by clumps of ornamental fountain grass. The plants coordinate in overall size and habit, but the broad iris leaves contrast with the slender grass leaves, and the iris blooms in spring, complementing the grass, which flowers in late summer and fall.

Talk to yourself as you think about putting plants together. Choose a starting point—a plant that's already growing in your yard or something you know you definitely want to buy. Identify what's special or distinctive about it, then describe what would complement, coordinate, or contrast with it. Putting a problem into words usually makes it much easier to grasp and solve. Instead of waiting and hoping for inspiration to strike, you can just go ahead and decide what you want and need.

COMPLEMENTS. Plants can complement each other by making up for each other's shortcomings. The most important way this happens is in timing. A shrub that blooms in spring and turns plain green afterward needs some companions that bloom in summer and fall. Early-flowering bulbs make good complements for perennials and shrubs that don't start growing until late spring. Evergreens complement deciduous or herbaceous plants that are leafless or die down to the ground in winter. Choosing something that will add interest in a different season is an easy yet worthwhile place to start when you're making plant combinations.

Complements can also serve by screening visual flaws. For example, using daffodils or other spring bulbs to add early color requires a reciprocal relationship. The grasses, perennials, or whatever else grows among the bulbs should quickly grow tall and full enough to hide the bulb foliage as it yellows and withers in early summer. Likewise, you'll probably want to complement a "leggy" shrub or perennial (an upright plant that drops its lower leaves, so the stems are bare below) by planting something shorter, bushy, and dense in front of or around it.

Fragrance is another basis for combining plants. Camellias, for instance, have flowers that are lovely and large but virtually scentless, while sweet olive flowers have a lovely aroma but are too small to notice. Camellia and sweet olive shrubs grow in similar conditions, so they make excellent complements.

COORDINATES. Plants can coordinate in many ways. Let's start with color. If neighboring plants flower at the same time, it always looks nice if their colors are coordinated. You can hardly go wrong by combining shades of pink, purple, and blue or by mixing yellows and golds. And color coordination certainly isn't limited to flowers. Foliage colors are often more useful because leaves last longer than flowers do. It's fun to make combinations where one plant's flowers coordinate with another plant's leaves, or with its berries, pods, or bark. Try pairing a pink-flowered rose with a purple-leaved plum, or combine red-stemmed shrub dogwoods with red-berried hollies for winter color.

Along with color, plants can be coordinated in terms of their size, form, habit, and/or texture. For example, it's easy to assemble a collection of shrubs that are compact, rounded, neat, and dense, with lots of small leaves. They may be deciduous or evergreen and their leaves and flowers can vary in color, but they'll all go together. Or you could cover a patch of ground with assorted mat-forming plants that crowd together in irregular shapes like puzzle pieces.

Take note of how plants look and act, and group those that have similar styles. Plants with stiff stems, erect posture, well-groomed foliage, and symmetrical profiles send a different message than do those with floppy stems, leaves that turn brown or drop off early in the season, and loose or irregular shapes. It's not that one style is better than the other, but they don't combine well.

Even though they vary in color, habit, and other visual aspects, plants that are native to the same habitat seem to go together. Maybe it's just that we're accustomed to seeing certain combinations in the wild, so when we see the same or similar plants arranged in a garden it looks familiar and "right." Certainly plants adapted to the same growing conditions are likely to thrive together, so they're coordinated in terms of health and vigor.

In general, coordination is a great approach to choosing plants and designing plantings. It can lead to a comforting harmony and unity. But a planting in which everything is too well coordinated can look bland and boring. You can take it all in at a glance; the parts get lost in the whole. Worse yet, it may seem prissy or contrived. If so, it's easy to liven things up by adding some contrast.

CONTRASTS. Contrast makes any planting seem more interesting and spontaneous, and it also calls attention to the features of each plant by comparison

This fascinating planting makes maximum use of contrast. Each plant is different from its neighbors in terms of size, shape, texture, and color.

to something different. There are countless possibilities for using contrast, starting with color combinations such as violet and yellow or dark green and white. Try contrasting plants with tiny or large leaves or fuzzy or glossy leaves, or with different habits, such as upright, vase-shaped, arching, mounded, trailing, or vining. Dull/bright, leathery/lacy, coarse/delicate, stiff/pliable—any basis for contrast can be illustrated with plants.

Working with contrast almost always requires some fine-tuning. Just because two plants are different doesn't mean they'll set each other off. Before you dig holes and plant them in the ground, simply set plants side by side in their pots and contemplate them for a few days to be sure you like the effect. Or pick sprigs of each plant and put them in a vase together to study how the colors, forms, and textures interact.

The problem is that it's a short step from contrast to clashing or even to chaos. Occasionally you'll see photos of a garden where someone has arranged a collection of disparate plants in a way that looks eclectic, open-minded, and exciting, but that requires a certain knack or flair that most of us lack. Usually a combination of plants that contrast too sharply or in too many ways looks random, absurd, or unsettled.

There are two good strategies for taking advantage of contrast without overdoing it. One is to create transitions that bridge the gap between contrasting colors, sizes, or styles. Instead of putting strongly contrasting plants side by side, separate them and include intermediate plants between and around them. For example, pink and yellow flowers often clash, but adding peach-colored blossoms may unify them. Bridge the vertical span between trees and ground covers with storied layers of knee-, waist-, and head-high shrubs or perennials.

Another way to avoid jarring contrasts is to change only one or two factors at a time and have the plants be coordinated in other ways. Imagine a combination of compact evergreen shrubs and dwarf conifers—all slow-growing plants in the same size range, but with leaves and needles of varying shapes and textures and in different shades of green and gold. The similarities in size and habit will unify the group while variation in texture and color provide variety.

(TOP): *These hostas and euonymus differ greatly in leaf size and texture, but their colors coordinate, so that reduces the contrast.*
(LEFT): *Color isn't everything. With enough variety in form and texture, a planting catches your interest even in black and white. Looking at black-and-white photos of your yard gives you a fresh perspective and points out strengths and weaknesses you might otherwise overlook.*

Look closely at color

Color captures and holds your attention more than any other feature of the landscape, and observing, enjoying, and working with color can easily become a passion. If you're fascinated with color and want to learn more about using it in a garden, you can find excellent books on this topic. Studying landscape paintings and photographs and taking art classes will also heighten your awareness of color, help you develop and refine color ideas and combinations, and increase your confidence.

On the other hand, I think the role of color is often overrated. Focusing too much attention on color can distract you from looking at size, shape, form, texture, and other aspects of landscape design that are at least as important. A well-designed landscape looks good even in a black-and-white photo; color is a bonus. For that reason, and because you can easily find more information about color in other books if you choose, I'll just outline some basic guidelines here.

TAKE NOTE OF THE BACKGROUND AND SURROUNDINGS. Anything you plant

White, pink, and wine red flowers coordinate quietly with this house. Silver, gray, and blue would also work well here, and you might try a pale yellow.

Contrasting colors are exciting. These orange roses really zing beside that blue gate.

will blend in with or stand out against the surrounding vegetation and scenery. Evergreens offer a welcome contrast to tan lawns and gray tree trunks in winter but get overlooked in the verdure of summer. Flowers of any color stand out against green leaves, but pale and pastel flowers may seem inconspicuous against gray, silver, or dusty green foliage. Take note of what's already around you, then you can decide whether to use contrasting or coordinating colors.

What colors are your house and hardscape? Almost any color flower looks good with white, cream, gray, and other pale or pastel paints and stains and with natural stone, wood that's weathered to a silver-gray color, and adobe. It's harder choosing plants to go with anything painted barn red or other vivid colors, buildings and walkways made of brick, and golden or reddish brown wood. Pink and purple, in particular, usually clash with these backgrounds. Before you buy plants and set them in the ground, test different possibilities by setting bouquets of cut flowers or foliage next to whatever structure you're working around, then step back to see how the colors look together.

Relate your use of color to the style of your house and neighborhood and to your own taste and personality. Stick with pastel shades of just a few coordinated colors for a formal, conservative, traditional look. Use more contrast and brighter colors for an informal, casual, contemporary look.

USE COLORED FOLIAGE THOUGHTFULLY. Choosing flower colors is mostly a matter of developing your own style and taste, but there's a different issue to consider with colored foliage. Plants with gold, blue, purple, or silver-gray leaves are uncommon in nature, and they really stand out if the surroundings are otherwise plain green or tan. Vividly colored plants may look fake or pretentious in a rural or informal setting. If you have a natural-style landscape but want to collect some colored plants, grow them in containers near the house, not planted out in the ground. Putting something in a

Colored foliage isn't "natural." The yellow shrubs here stand out as something special, even in autumn. Position colored plants carefully and be sure they're healthy and well groomed, as they attract extra attention.

pot signifies that it's exceptional and excuses its oddness.

If your landscape looks deliberately designed, however, and has a personal, artistic style, use colored foliage generously and emphasize it by repetition. A single plant of a different color stands out from its surroundings. It can be a wonderful focal point, but often it just looks like an oddball. Before you timidly take it away, consider adding different plants in the same color group to repeat the idea and create a theme. If, for example, you put three or more gold plants in the same area, your purpose will be clear.

A big advantage of colored foliage is that it's effective throughout the entire growing season or even year-round. It lasts much longer than flowers do. When there are flowers, colored foliage can enhance them by means of coordination or contrast. For a subtle, harmonious effect, coordinate silver-gray or purple foliage with pastel pink, lavender, and blue flowers, or deep gold foliage with pale yellow, creamy, and white flowers. For more excitement, contrast yellow foliage and bright blue-violet flowers, or pale gray foliage with vivid scarlet flowers, or deep purple foliage with tropical oranges and magenta.

One caution: Because they're so prominent, colored plants must always be in excellent condition. The foliage should stay healthy all season (replace plants that get chewed or diseased or that die down early), and keep the plants well pruned and groomed.

KEEP VARIEGATED PLANTS NEARBY.
Variegated plants—plants with leaves that are striped, rimmed, spotted, or blotched with white, yellow, or other colors besides green—are freaks of nature that have been discovered and propagated by gardeners. They appeal mostly to collectors: you either love them or hate them.

If you love them, there are plenty of variegated plants to choose from, including some trees, many evergreen and deciduous shrubs, some vines, and scores of grasses, hostas, irises, and other perennials. You can't go wrong growing variegated plants as novelties in containers. The challenge is placing them in a garden in a way that features their beauty and seems inevitable, not artificial.

Consider these guidelines. First, keep variegated plants where you will see them up close and can distinguish and appreciate the patterns in their leaves. Seen from too far away, the colors blur together, and the plant may look pale or diseased. Second, coordinate adjacent foliage. Surrounding a variegated plant with solid-color neighbors that repeat the same tone of green, gold, gray, or any other color that appears in its foliage "frames" the plant and makes it look special, yet integrates it at the same time. Don't be afraid to use two or more variegated plants in the

same bed or even to put them side by side, *if* they share the same colors but have different leaf sizes, shapes, and patterning, or if they have leaves of the same size and shape but with different patterns and colors. Just don't vary everything at once; keep most factors the same for continuity's sake.

OBSERVE HOW COLORS CHANGE. The
appearance and even the visibility of different colors varies with distance, lighting, the time of day, and the weather.

All colors show up best when you're looking away from or at an angle to the sun. When you're looking toward the sun, you mostly see dark silhouettes rimmed with bright sparkles—an effect that can certainly be delightful, but it isn't colorful.

If you like the looks of colored foliage, use it generously. Repeat the same colors in different plants with different forms and textures to create a rich, varied display.

PLANTS WITH COLORED LEAVES

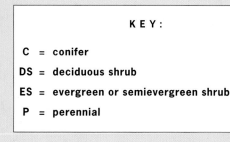

> **KEY:**
>
> **C** = conifer
> **DS** = deciduous shrub
> **ES** = evergreen or semievergreen shrub
> **P** = perennial

Here are some outstanding, widely adapted shrubs, conifers, perennials, and grasses that have richly colored leaves. These plants are fairly small, ranging from under 1 foot to a maximum of 6 to 8 feet tall. Try something in this size range to get started. If you decide you like the effect of colored foliage, you can escalate to using larger shrubs or trees with colorful leaves.

Except where noted, all plants named here prefer sites with well-drained soil and full or part sun.

SILVER, GRAY

- **'Powis Castle' artemisia** (*Artemisia* cv.). **ES**. Pungent, scalloped foliage. **ZONE 6**. **'Lambrook Silver' wormwood** (*A. absinthium*). **ES** or **P**. Even lacier and more silvery. **ZONE 5**. Many other artemisias are silver or gray.

- **'Lochinch' butterfly bush** (*Buddleia* cv.). **DS**. Lavender-blue flowers in summer. **ZONE 6**.

- **Bush morning glory** (*Convolvulus cneorum*). **ES**. Big white or pink flowers in summer. **ZONE 8**. **Ground morning glory** (*C. mauritanicus*). **ES**. Small blue flowers all summer. **ZONE 7**.

- **Silverberry** (*Elaeagnus commutata*). **DS**. Very sweet-scented flowers in spring. **ZONE 3**.

- **Dead nettle** (*Lamium maculatum* cvs.). **P**. Good ground cover for part shade, with pink or white flowers in early summer. Try 'Beacon Silver', 'Pink Pewter', or 'White Nancy'. **ZONE 4**.

- **Texas ranger** (*Leucophyllum frutescens*). **ES**. Blue-violet flowers follow rains in spring and summer. **ZONE 8**.

- **Russian sage** (*Perovskia atriplicifolia*). **P**. Blue-violet flowers in summer. Upright, fine-textured. **ZONE 5**.

- **Rosemary willow** (*Salix elaeagnos*). **DS**. Very slender leaves. Prune hard every spring. **ZONE 5**. **Coyote willow** (*S. exigua*). **DS**. Very silvery leaves. **ZONE 5**.

- **Common sage** (*Salvia officinalis*). **ES** or **P**. Beautiful blue-violet flowers in early summer. Pungent gray-green leaves. **ZONE 5**. Many other salvias also have gray or silvery foliage.

- **Lavender cotton, or gray santolina** (*Santolina chamaecyparissus*). **ES**. Bushy and dense, with rough, curly, pungent-scented foliage. Yellow flowers in summer. **ZONE 6**.

- **Lamb's ears** (*Stachys byzantina*). **P**. Lows mats of large, fuzzy, gray leaves. Violet flowers in summer. **ZONE 5**.

BLUE, BLUE-GREEN, BLUE-GRAY

- **'Boulevard' Sawara cypress** (*Chamaecyparis pisifera*). **ES**. Upright and cone-shaped, with fluffy-looking foliage. **ZONE 5**.

- **Maiden pink** (*Dianthus deltoides*) **and cottage pink** (*D. plumarius*). **P**. Broad low mats of grassy blue-green foliage topped with fragrant rose, pink, or white flowers in early summer. **ZONE 4**.

- **Blue fescue grass** (*Festuca glauca*, a.k.a. *F. ovina*, cvs.). **P**. Neat, pincushion-like clumps of wiry blue leaves. **ZONE 4**.

- **Blue oat grass** (*Helictotrichon sempervirens*). **P**. Like blue fescue grass, but forms larger clumps with wider leaves. **ZONE 4**.

- **Hostas** (*Hosta*). **P**. Some of the best blue-leaved hostas are 'Blue Angel', 'Fragrant Blue', 'Hadspen Blue', 'Halcyon', and 'Love Pat'. Part shade. **ZONE 4**.

- **Junipers. ES**. Blue rug juniper (*Juniperus horizontalis* 'Wiltonii') is a prostrate ground cover. 'Blue Star' juniper (*J. squamata*) makes a low, irregular mound. 'Grey Owl' juniper (*J. virginiana*) is a midsize shrub with arching shoots. Many other junipers also have blue or blue-gray foliage and are hardy at least to **ZONE 4**.

- **'Heavy Metal' switch grass** (*Panicum virgatum*). **P**. Dense, upright clumps of blue-gray foliage, topped with airy seed heads. **ZONE 5**.

- **'Jackman's Blue' rue** (*Ruta graveolens*). **P**. Scalloped foliage is almost iridescent, with a hint of turquoise. **ZONE 5**.

- **Colorado, or blue, spruce** (*Picea pungens*). **ES**. Dwarf cultivars such as 'Fat Albert', 'Globosa', and 'R. H. Montgomery' stay small for decades and have very blue needles. **ZONE 3**.

PURPLE, BRONZE, RED

- **'Crimson Queen' Japanese maple** (*Acer palmatum*). **DS**. Shrubby, not tree-sized. Fine-cut leaves stay dark red or bronzy all summer. Needs part shade in hot climates. **ZONE 5**.

- **Bugleweed, or ajuga** (*Ajuga reptans* cvs.). **P**. Good ground cover for part or full shade. 'Bronze Beauty', 'Burgundy Glow', and 'Catlin's Giant' have gorgeous leaves. Blue flowers in early summer. **ZONE 3**.

- **'Prince' calico aster** (*Aster lateriflorus*). **P**. Dense and twiggy, with small dark leaves and stems. White flowers in midfall. **ZONE 4**.

- **'Bagatelle' and 'Crimson Pygmy' Japanese barberries** (*Berberis thunbergii*). **DS**. Dwarf, rounded shrubs with garnet-burgundy foliage. **ZONE 4**.

- **'Royal Purple' smoke tree** (*Cotinus coggygria*). **DS**. Rounded leaves are uncommonly dark wine-purple. Fluffy pink flower heads in summer. **ZONE 5**.

Lighting conditions influence the color of leaves and also affect what we see. (LEFT): *Purple-leaved plants, such as 'Palace Purple' heuchera, require plenty of sun to develop rich colors and look best when lit from the front.* (RIGHT): *Most blue-leaved plants, such as these 'Halcyon' hostas and 'Sissinghurst White' lungworts, prefer part shade. Their colors look most intense when seen in a shady site on a sunny day, enhanced by blue light from the sky.*

- **Purple hop bush** (*Dodonaea viscosa* cvs.). **ES.** 'Saratoga' and 'Purpurea' are good cultivars with glossy dark leaves. Showy pink pods in fall. Tolerates desert conditions. ZONE 8.

- **'Chocolate' white snakeroot** (*Eupatorium rugosum*). **P.** Purple-brown leaves, white flowers in fall. ZONE 4.

- **'Palace Purple' heuchera** (*Heuchera micrantha*). **P.** Glossy purple-brown leaves. Best in part shade. ZONE 4.

- **'Red Baron' Japanese blood grass** (*Imperata cylindrica*). **P.** Upright, narrow leaves are truly red. ZONE 5.

- **Red fountain grass** (*Pennisetum setaceum* 'Rubrum'). **P.** Arching leaves are purple-bronze. ZONE 9.

- **Dwarf purpleleaf plum** (*Prunus* × *cistena*). **DS.** Leaves stay dark red-purple all summer. Pink flowers in spring. ZONE 3.

GOLD, YELLOW, CHARTREUSE

- **'Aurea' and 'Bonanza Gold' Japanese barberries** (*Berberis thunbergii*). **DS.** Compact habits, yellow-gold foliage. Part shade. ZONE 5.

- **'Gold Mop' Sawara cypress** (*Chamaecyparis pisifera*). **ES.** Stays small for years, but eventually exceeds 8 feet. Stringy foliage. Part shade. ZONE 5.

- **'Buttercup' English ivy** (*Hedera helix*). **ES.** Slow-growing and unaggressive. New shoots are butter yellow. Part shade. ZONE 6.

- **Golden hakone grass** (*Hakonechloa macra* 'Aureola'). **P.** Soft, arching blades are golden yellow. Part shade. ZONE 5.

- **Hostas** (*Hosta*). **P.** 'August Moon', 'Gold Drop', 'Piedmont Gold', 'Sum and Substance', and 'Zounds' have all-gold leaves. Part, not full, shade. ZONE 4.

- **Junipers. ES.** *Juniperus chinensis* 'Gold Coast', 'Old Gold', and 'Saybrook Gold' and *J. horizontalis* 'Mother Lode' are all low shrubs that spread much wider than tall. Foliage is yellow-gold in summer, copper or bronze in winter. ZONE 3.

- **Gold moneywort** (*Lysimachia nummularia* 'Aurea'). **P.** Prostrate ground cover, butter yellow in summer, coppery in winter. ZONE 4.

- **Golden privet** (*Ligustrum* × *vicaryi*). **DS.** Small leaves are bright yellow in full sun. White flowers in early summer. ZONE 5.

- **'Dart's Gold' ninebark** (*Physocarpus opulifolius*). **DS.** Lobed leaves are clear yellow-gold. White flowers in late spring. ZONE 2.

- **Spireas** (*Spiraea* × *bumalda* cvs.). **DS.** 'Gold Flame', 'Gold Mound', and 'Magic Carpet' all have changeable foliage that ranges from pink to coral, gold, chartreuse, or copper. Pink flowers in early summer. ZONE 3.

- **Gold feverfew** (*Tanacetum parthenium* 'Aureum'). **P.** Scalloped leaves are clear yellow-gold. White flowers like tiny daisies from late spring until frost. ZONE 5.

- **'Rheingold' American arborvitae** (*Thuja occidentalis*). **ES.** A dense, slow-growing shrub with fluffy foliage, gold in summer, copper-bronze in winter. ZONE 3.

(TOP LEFT): *Try coordinating flower and foliage colors. The gold spirea and blue spruce blend well with the yellow and pink flowers in this border.*

(TOP RIGHT): *Variegated leaves are most interesting when seen up close. From a distance, a tree or shrub like this variegated dogwood usually looks ghostly or albino, a showy but surreal effect. You have to stand beside it to see that the leaves have green blotches.*

(RIGHT): *Your reaction to colors depends on lighting. Plants with white flowers, white variegation, or silver foliage look best on cloudy days or at dusk. On sunny days, the glare from white and silver makes you squint.*

White and pale colors disappear into the general sparkle of reflections on a sunny day but gleam entrancingly from shady corners or at dusk. Yellow is conspicuous and prominent under almost all conditions and clearly visible even at a distance, while blue, lilac, and lavender look best when you're standing nearby on a cloudy day; in bright light they get "washed out" and at a distance they fade into the haze. Bright red, magenta, and orange hold their own in blazing midday sun and also look striking in the gold, slanting light of sunset or short winter days; some people think these colors look too bold, even gaudy, under subtler light conditions.

On many plants, the colors of the flowers and leaves are affected by temperature and may change from month to month, or vary from place to place if the same kind of plant is grown in different climates. Typically, hot weather bleaches or fades flowers and makes them paler, while cool weather produces richer, more saturated flower colors. Many plants have leaves that are green in warm summer weather but turn gold, purple, or bronze in the cool short days from fall to spring. Other plants that are "supposed" to have gold or purple foliage may turn plain green in hot weather.

For all these reasons, the colors you see in photos are sometimes misleading. When you're seeking particular colors to use in combinations, there's no substitute for looking at a living plant. You may buy or order something that you think will work but decide it's wrong when you set it in place. Then you'll have to try again. Fine-tuning color combinations often requires some trial and error.

LOOK AT UNDERTONES. It's rare to find a "pure" color in plants. Plant colors are almost always a mixture, and it usually takes a compound name such as "yellow-green" or "reddish purple" to describe what you see. Learning to watch for and identify undertones is very important when you're trying to match or coordinate colors. For example, pink with a gold undertone looks quite different from pink with a hint of blue in it.

WITH FLOWERS, TIMING IS CRITICAL. Combinations involving flowers depend on timing and serendipity. It doesn't matter whether two or more flowers have coordinated or contrasting colors unless they happen to bloom at the same time. But as any town that hosts an annual dogwood, lilac, or rose festival can attest, plants don't read calendars. Early or late, they bloom when they're ready, and this varies from plant to plant, so flowers that coincide one year may get out of step the next. Your chances of achieving an overlap are best if you use plants that keep blooming for weeks or months, not just days (these long bloomers also do more to earn their space in your yard). If you're serious about designing

Combinations based on flower color, such as the rhododendron, magnolia, and peony growing here, work only if the plants bloom at the same time. The undertones must coordinate, too. These three flowers are all pink-purple, with a blue undertone. An orange-pink would clash here.

successful flower combinations, you need to keep your own records or photos of plants in your garden or neighborhood. You can't necessarily copy a combination you see in a book or magazine, as plants that are synchronized in another climate may not flower together in your yard.

Since flowers come and go, you can arrange to have a sequence of different color schemes and combinations as the year progresses. For example, you could decide to feature yellows and blues in spring, pinks and purples in summer, and reds and whites in fall, and choose flowers for each season accordingly. Or you can observe how the native vegetation in your area changes colors with the seasons and use those colors and that schedule as a basis for planning a seasonal cycle in your landscape.

Combinations based on texture and form give your eyes a lot to explore and capture your interest in every season.

Combine varied textures and forms

"Texture" refers to the size of a plant's parts—its leaves, twigs, stems, flowers, or fruits. Form is the outline or shape you see when you look toward a plant. Texture and form are as important as color, and as with color you can use these aspects of a plant's appearance as a basis for making combinations that coordinate or contrast.

Any plant with tiny, thin, pliable, or delicate parts looks fine-textured. Plants with big, thick, stiff, or coarse parts are coarse-textured. Some plants are hard to categorize because they combine textures. A perennial may have broad leaves and wispy flowers, while a tree or shrub may have a stout trunk, limbs, and twigs but dainty little leaves. That's okay; just react to what you notice first or feel is most important. The terms "fine" and "coarse" are sometimes used to imply value judgments, but that isn't appropriate here. A landscape with only fine-textured plants would be boring. Coarser textures are essential for contrast and variety. Push the limits and include coarse, fine, and everything in between to make an interesting landscape.

A plant's form is determined by how the stems grow and branch—whether they point up, out, sideways, or down, and whether they angle stiffly or bend

softly—and also by pruning, which can enhance, alter, disguise, or ruin a plant's natural, inherent form. Woody plants develop a form as they mature and it stays pretty much the same year-round, independent of leaves. Herbaceous perennials usually have changing forms; they look one way when in bloom but may be quite different earlier or later in the season.

COMFORTABLE, EASY-TO-USE FORMS. The most common and popular plant forms are rounded or mounded, matlike or trailing, vase-shaped (narrow at the bottom and wider on top), fountainlike (with arching stems), drumlike (flat on top), pincushion-like (lots of stems pointing in all directions), and conical (like Christmas trees). It usually looks good if most of your shrubs and perennials have one or another of these forms, and you can combine these forms freely; they all go together.

VERTICAL SHAPES. Also common but more challenging to a designer are tall, skinny plants with straight, erect stems. These stand out like an exclamation point or like a fence post or flagpole. Sometimes this effect is good for contrast, but a little goes a long way. Be cautious about using extremely narrow conifers, rigid clumps of grass or bamboo, or tall perennials such as lilies or delphiniums as single specimens. Such plants usually look better in groups where the width is proportioned to the height. Particularly jarring, like pictures hanging crooked on a wall, are skinny plants that should be vertical but are slightly tilted instead. These are candidates for staking, straightening, or removal.

Trees are a special case. You expect a tree trunk to be straight as a pole; how prominent it looks depends on how many trees surround you. A single tree or a few trees really stand out, but in a grove of trees or a woods there are so many trunks that your perception is altered and you start taking vertical lines for granted and don't notice them as you do on an open site, where most lines are horizontal or rounded. (This reminds me of a story about how designers sometimes get blinded by their own dogma. Once I visited Falling Waters, the famous Frank Lloyd Wright house in Pennsylvania. Everything about that house is short and wide, and the tour guide went on and on about Wright's devotion to nature and his contention that horizontal lines are more "natural" than vertical lines. He felt that way because he grew up on the prairie. The irony is that Falling Waters is surrounded by dense woods, with a myriad of tree trunks outside every window and no horizon in sight.)

WEIRD FORMS. This includes trees and shrubs with windswept, weeping, contorted, or spiraling limbs; all kinds of topiary; trees pruned in Japanese styles; and giant succulents and cacti. Some people disdain such plants and avoid them altogether, while others love them and collect all they can find. As a compromise, I'd say one weirdo can make a good focal point, or at least a conversation piece, but I think one is enough for most yards.

To make the most of a weird plant, don't try to integrate it with more familiar forms. Give it a special place and treat it as a specimen. Put it at the front of a bed, at a corner or end, or in its own island. Leave plenty of open space around it—don't crowd it with other plants of similar height; just spread short or creeping plants at its base.

Use repetition for unity

Repetition is a versatile technique for unifying a large planting or visually connecting different areas. You can use it in many ways, subtle or obvious. Using repetition as a tool in designing a landscape gives you a satisfying sense of purpose, and recognizing

Repetition unifies a planting. Broad low mounds of evergreen junipers and pines are the backbone of this long bed, flanked by a variety of smaller plants in bloom.

Let's say you have a big red oak tree in the corner of your lot and you want to fill the area underneath it with three kinds of plants: 'Pleasant White' azaleas, 'Royal Standard' hostas, and Christmas ferns. You'll need several of each kind. How many, and how will you arrange them?

One way to answer these questions is by doing a mockup. Use three different kinds of boxes, pots, stakes, or whatever to symbolize the three kinds of plants and the space each plant will eventually fill. Keep adding and taking away and arranging and rearranging these objects, stepping back often to judge the effect from different distances and points of view, until you like what you see. Then count how many of each plant you need to buy, and leave the mockup in place to guide the planting process.

In addition to making a mockup, try planning the layout on paper to crosscheck your ideas and estimates. Also, observe these general principles:

- **PLANT SELECTION.** When you're buying plants to use as a group, be sure to select ones that match, as any difference in flower or leaf color, texture, or habit stands out.
- **ODD NUMBERS.** For some reason, groups of three, five, seven, etc., plants usually look better than even-numbered groups. This applies only where the plants are separate, not merged into a patch, and for groups of fewer than a dozen or so plants.
- **PATTERNS AND SHAPES.** It's common to arrange three plants in some kind of triangle and to make five into a "W," star, or pentagon. For larger groups, try wedges or diamonds with sides of different lengths and slightly curved, not straight. Irregular, crooked, or rounded shapes fit together well, and you can design them to follow variations in the terrain or to wrap around specimen plants and hardscape. By contrast, plants arranged into squares and other neat geometric shapes almost always look out of place except in formal gardens on level ground.
- **LINES.** Straight or curved, a single-file line of plants doesn't look natural. It can look deliberate, and that makes sense if the plants serve as an edging or hedge. But a single row of plants that slashes across or meanders among other shapes looks accidental. If you've inadvertently drawn a line with plants, revise it by digging up the ones at both ends and replanting them along the sides to make a fatter shape.
- **SPACING.** When you're using a group of plants to fill an irregular area, arrange them at approximately equal spacing, so each plant is separated from its neighbors by 1, 2, or however many feet, but make crooked or curved rows that are slightly offset from each other so the pattern is a little irregular.
- **DEGREE OF SEPARATION.** Gardeners tend to split into two camps on this topic. On one hand are those who think neighboring groups of plants should be kept distinct. The groups may be shaped so they fit together like a jigsaw puzzle, but they don't overlap. Each kind of plant has its own place. This effect looks neat and controlled.

On the other side are gardeners who mix plants freely and welcome blurred edges; their idea of a group includes satellite plants that are scattered at varying distances from the nucleus, and their groups are interconnected and overlapping, not separate. This gives a more natural and spontaneous look.

Aside from the difference in looks, there's a practical consideration here. It's easier to maintain separated groups of plants. Where two or more kinds of plants overlap, it takes longer to sort your way through them when you're doing any pruning, cutting back, deadheading, division, or other maintenance.

- **HEIGHT VARIATION.** If you are desperately eager to crowd as many plants as possible into a garden and can't bear the thought of keeping them separate horizontally, separate them vertically. Combinations of shorter and taller plants can be set closer together than pairs of equal-height plants can. Mixed-height combinations look good and are generally easy to keep track of and to maintain.

repetition brings a special delight to most viewers. It's a form of communication; when someone discovers your pattern, they see your thoughts.

REPEAT A LAYOUT. Making a symmetrical or mirror-image design is one form of repetition, but this is usually too obvious to be interesting, and the effect is easily flawed by even minor differences in how the plants grow. Reserve this for formal gardens; it's not a good approach for most landscape situations.

A less rigid way of repeating a layout is to choose a combination of plants, say, A, B, C, and D, and treat them as a repeating module that can be rearranged in many ways: ABCD, DCBA, ACBD, DACB, and so forth. This is an easy and effective way to fill a border with plants that bloom in different seasons. Because each kind of plant reappears throughout the area, when it comes into bloom it will spread a broad swath of color.

REPEAT FAVORITE PLANTS. One of the pleasures of walking through a woods, meadow, or other wild landscape is seeing certain plants repeatedly as you move along; you quickly learn to recognize and appreciate them. Most natural ecosystems are dominated by (and named for) a key group of plants that are relatively abundant, then enriched by a great diversity of plants that appear much less often. This is a good pattern to copy.

Admittedly, there's a risk in repetition: the plants may all succumb to some horrid disease or insect. That happens sometimes, but it certainly isn't inevitable. Look around any region or neighborhood and you'll see lots of dominant plants that are abundant and indisputably healthy. So if you have a

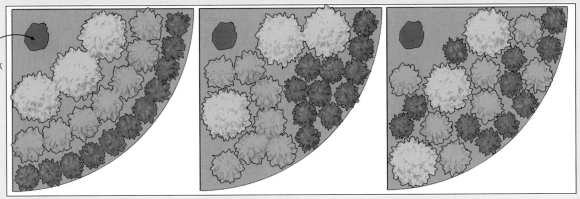

TREE
TRUNK

*If you have space in the
corner under a tree for 3
shrubs, 7 large perenni-
als, and 11 smaller
perennials, you could
arrange them in con-
centric rings* (**LEFT**), *in
free-form groups* (**MID-
DLE**), *or intermixed*
(**RIGHT**).

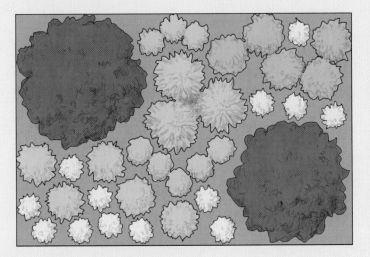

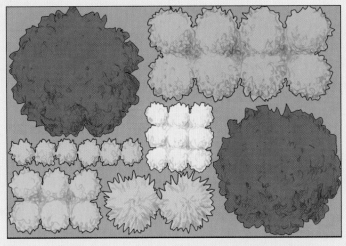

ACHIEVING A NATURAL LOOK

*Imagine that you want to fill the area around two shrubs with some
perennials. Different ways of arranging those plants produce different
effects. Using odd numbers of plants arranged in angled rows and
irregular or overlapping groups creates a more relaxed, natural look*
(**ABOVE**).

*Using even numbers of plants positioned in pairs, straight lines, or
blocks usually creates a stilted, artificial look that can be unsatisfying*
(**ABOVE**).

favorite plant that grows well for you, don't be reluctant to include it in different parts of your yard.
Propagate what you have or buy some more and
spread them around.

USE A SINGLE GROUND COVER. If you
have several beds and borders around and throughout the yard that feature an assortment of trees,
shrubs, and large perennials, choosing one ground
cover to use everywhere gives a single color and texture to them all. An evergreen ground cover is best
for this job, because it fills the shape of the bed year-
round. This mitigates the patchiness typical of mixed
plantings in winter, when leafless or dormant plants
leave "holes" in a bed.

**REPEAT A COLOR, FORM, OR TEX-
TURE.** This is subtler than repeating a kind of

plant. Select a certain feature, such as blue flowers in
June, chartreuse foliage, neat hemispheric form, or
heart-shaped leaves. Find three or more kinds of
plants that display this feature (this will take some
research and becomes a fun treasure hunt). Plant
them around the yard—not side by side, but spaced
apart from each other. In an overview, you may see
them all at once, but when walking around, you'll
come upon them recurrently.

You can use the same idea to connect your landscape with something in the background. If your
neighbor has a beautiful big purple beech tree, for
example, you might repeat that purple color by
planting a purple smoke bush and 'Palace Purple'
heuchera in your yard.

Repeating colors throughout a landscape is
almost always a good idea. Any single plant of contrasting color stands out from its surroundings and

Consider more than flowers when choosing plants. For example, many azaleas have pink flowers, but 'Weston's Pink Diamond', shown here in late April (LEFT) and mid-October (RIGHT) also has vivid fall foliage.

grabs your attention, even if its placement and stature don't deserve such special recognition. Repetition makes the difference between a single oddball plant and a color theme. Your gaze moves back and forth among like-colored plants, appreciating the pattern, and you don't fixate on any one of them.

Repeated forms and textures are less obvious to most viewers, but in a quiet way they too can create themes in your garden, and as with color, you can use repetition to turn a would-be prima donna into a member of the chorus.

Anticipate seasonal changes

This is a big challenge for people who approach landscaping from a background in gardening. Most gardeners start out with a passion for flowers and think almost solely in terms of their color, size, shape, and fragrance. Catalogs, magazines, and books encourage this way of thinking by overwhelmingly emphasizing flowers in their photos and write-ups.

But depending on flowers when you design a landscape can lead to disappointment. That's because most plants bloom for a limited period, then quit. Wax begonias, impatiens, and other tender bedding plants that bloom nonstop are exceptional, as are tropical shrubs such as bougainvillea and hibiscus. It's a big deal if a hardy perennial, shrub, vine, or tree flowers for longer than a month or so or blooms more than once a year. If you focus primarily on flowers, you're likely to end up with a garden or yard that looks glorious for a single peak season but disappointing the rest of the time. It's one thing to have certain beds or plants that look bare or bad for months at a time, but how much space are you willing to devote to plants that have definite off-seasons?

Your desire to design plantings that always look good will depend a lot on the size of your property. If there's plenty of space, it's easy to justify using some of it for ephemeral beauty. In smaller yards, it's more important for each plant to earn its position by performing nonstop or offering different features in different seasons, such as flowers in spring, great foliage all summer, and berries in fall.

Your climate and schedule are factors, too. In a place such as New Hampshire, where winters are cold, the ground stays covered with snow, and days are so short that you leave for work before it gets light and return home after dark, it doesn't matter so much if there are big blank spots in your yard where all the perennials are dormant and the shrubs are deciduous. Or if you have a summer home that you

DESIGNING SUSTAINED, YEAR-ROUND DISPLAYS

A four-season landscape never serves up a feast of color, just a series of nibbles. At any point in the growing season, there might be just one or a few kinds of plants in bloom. Actually, there's a plus to that. It helps you focus on each plant during its moment of glory. Individual specimens don't have to clamor for attention. They each have a turn. But the challenge is that each plant needs a certain amount of space even if it's not in bloom, and most of the time it won't be. That's why it's so important to consider foliage and form along with flowers when you're choosing plants.

- **WORK BACKWARD.** The best way to plan for ongoing interest is to start with winter and work backward. The basic attributes that make a garden attractive in winter—a clear design with well-proportioned areas, some hardscape features, some plants with evergreen foliage, and a few key trees and shrubs that are placed and treated as specimens—will serve you well year-round. When they're in place, the whole picture will come together and everything else you add will be enhanced by the context.

- **FOCUS ON FOLIAGE.** Healthy leaves in a range of colors, shapes, and sizes can make a garden that always looks good, whether or not anything is in bloom. Pay attention to foliage and think backward from fall to spring as you're choosing deciduous and herbaceous plants, especially perennials, for this reason: Most of these plants make fresh new leaves that look lovely in spring, but over the course of the summer leaves get weathered, tattered, chewed on, or dotted by disease, or they turn tan and fall off. A plant whose leaves are still attractive at the end of the season is preferable to one that turns ugly or goes bare early. Leaf retention isn't strictly related to flowering time. Plants that retain healthy, attractive foliage may bloom in spring, summer, or fall. So you can have an ongoing sequence of flowers, if you choose, without making compromises over foliage.

- **EXPECT MORE FROM EACH PLANT.** It's not asking too much to expect each plant to have at least two noteworthy features—extra-early or late bloom time, uncommonly profuse or long-lasting flowers, fall foliage color, evergreen foliage, foliage that's colored or variegated in summer, showy fruits, distinct shape or habit, and so forth. Research this when you're selecting plants, and if you're initially drawn to a plant by one feature, ask what else is special about it. It sounds obvious, but a plant that delights you repeatedly is a better choice than one that performs briefly and then recedes into the background.

- **KEEP TWEAKING THE DETAILS.** Achieving the best appearance over the longest season takes some experimentation, revision, and fine-tuning. As you watch your landscape month after month, there will be times when you're satisfied that all is well and times when you're bored because there's not enough color or variety. Watch for dull times and blank spaces, identify what you need, and go shopping. You might say, I want more flowers in late winter and early spring, or some yellow foliage for that bed that's so plain and dark all summer, or colorful berries to linger in late fall after everything else has quit. Keep filling gaps and extending the season at both ends by adding more plants or replacing ones that don't do their share.

This long border, anchored by pine and spruce trees, also includes a dozen deciduous shrubs that bloom and fruit at different times and repeated groupings of several perennials that flower in sequence. Daffodils begin the show in spring. **(TOP):** *Yellow daylilies, gold coneflowers, and white mountain mint dominate the display in midsummer.* **(MIDDLE):** *White boltonia blooms during fall foliage season.* **(BOTTOM):** *By winter, the perennials are cut down, but bright red holly berries, rose hips, and red-twig dogwood look cheerful until the next spring.*

Plantings fill in fast. Here are two views of the same landscape, taken when the beds were first laid out (BELOW) and again four years later (BOTTOM). About half of the plants are shrubs; the rest are perennials. Over time, as the shrubs continue to grow, most of the perennials will be removed and given away or discarded.

rarely visit in winter, a one-season landscape is fine. But if you live in southern California and spend time outdoors year-round—or wherever you live, if you're home during the daytime and constantly viewing your yard—you'll want plants that give and give.

DESIGNING COORDINATED, PEAK-SEASON DISPLAYS. If you crave the dramatic impact of a synchronized show of bloom when everything seems to be happening at once, or if that kind of gardening suits your climate or schedule, here are some tips on how to make it happen.

Mark a calendar. There's no better way to determine what flowers when in your garden or neighborhood. Make notes of everything that blooms during whatever season you want to feature. After a few years you'll clearly identify which flowers are

ephemeral and which stay bright and fresh-looking for weeks, and you'll know which blooms coincide.

Pick proven performers. Don't waste space or risk gaps by using plants that bloom sparsely or sporadically or sometimes skip a year. Go for steadfast, dependable plants that flower abundantly and reliably.

Fill the frame. For maximum impact in a small enclosed space, be sure there's something in bloom at all levels from underfoot to overhead, so you're totally surrounded with flowers. In large open areas, extend the planting as far as possible, like a sea reaches to the horizon.

If you want to compensate for the off-season dullness that's such a common consequence of focusing on a single season's flowers, one solution is to shift the focus around your property so that different areas peak at different times. For instance, you could dedicate the front yard to spring, the side yard to midsummer, and the back to late summer and fall. This works quite well if the areas are detached or screened so that each space feels like a separate space or room. One after the other, each area can surround you with its magic and then subside into the background again. At any point in time, your property will seem smaller than it is because you'll take some areas for granted and won't bother to explore them, but over the course of the year you'll fall in love again and again as each area's planting reaches its prime.

On a larger scale, consider how your garden relates to its surroundings. Enjoy what's already out there, and design new plantings to fill seasonal voids. For example, if the neighbor's yard looks great in June, focus on another month at your place. If wildflowers color the countryside in spring, follow them with garden plants that bloom in summer or fall. Where fall color is overwhelmingly brilliant, enjoy the free show and work at growing flowers that peak earlier in the season.

❦ PLANNING FOR FUTURE GROWTH

Perhaps the biggest challenge in landscaping is anticipating how plants—especially long-lived perennials, ground covers, vines, shrubs, and trees—will develop over the years. If you want to end up with full, vigorous specimens and an overall effect that's neither puny nor pinched, you need to plan ahead and space and arrange plants according to their potential. This requires researching how wide and tall each plant is likely to get, how fast it will grow, and how long it will live.

Admittedly, your best-laid plans may go astray. Some plants will grow bigger and faster than you expected, while others will inexplicably lag behind or die. Even experienced garden designers admit that choosing and spacing plants so that they'll fill an area

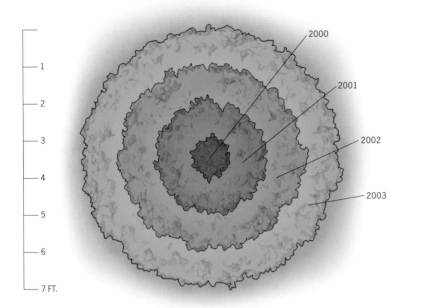

1

2

3

4

5

6

7 FT.

2000

2001

2002

2003

HOW FAST PLANTS SPREAD

Plants grow faster than you expect and expand in all directions unless confined or pruned.

If you choose a perennial or shrub whose runners or branches grow 1 foot per year and start with a plant that's 1 foot wide, by the fourth year it will be 7 feet wide.

within a reasonable amount of time yet not become crowded too soon requires both knowledge and luck. But the chances of success are certainly greater if you start with some kind of plan than if you just proceed willy-nilly.

Different approaches to spacing plants

The main problem, along with needing to know your plants, is that if you allow enough space for future growth, a bed will look sparse at first. People take different approaches to resolving this conflict, as you can see from driving around any town or neighborhood.

WIDE SPACING. At one extreme are those who space very generously. Some people, perhaps because their budget is limited or because they aren't avid plant collectors, buy a minimum number of trees and shrubs and set them far apart. Their yards, although simplistic, can eventually display some remarkable specimens because the plants were unlimited by competition.

OVERPLANTING. At the other extreme are those impatient or naive homeowners who want an "instant" landscape, so they overplant, or buy more plants than are needed and set them too close together. This is an expensive, wasteful, and ultimately frustrating approach. If you put plants too close together, or too close to a building or pathway, they'll be squeezing each other or getting in your way within a few years. Along with misshapen growth, crowded plants are hard to care for, they don't bloom as well as well-spaced plants, they're more susceptible to disease and pest problems, they require extra watering, and they're liable to flop over during storms because their stems are thin and weak.

Avid gardeners who eagerly collect all kinds of plants also tend to space them much too close

together. If you do this, your plants can't reach their full potential, and you'll soon have to thin, revise, and rearrange the plantings. This can be fun if you love gardening, but it's also a lot of hard work and some plants will get lost in the shuffle.

SHEARING FOR SIZE CONTROL. Most landscape contractors who design and install "conventional" suburban and commercial plantings use tough, adaptable shrubs, ground covers, and trees; space them fairly close together for immediate impact; then rely on annual (or more frequent) shearing to control their size. Shearing works, but it is time-consuming, disguises a plant's individual character, and tends to homogenize a landscape.

STRATEGIC COMBINATIONS. This is the approach that I recommend. It involves identifying the most valuable and desirable plants (mostly trees and shrubs, but also long-lived perennials and boldly architectural plants such as palms and succulents), which you hope will mature into well-shaped, perfectly placed specimens, and giving them priority as you plan and plant. Then you can fill in around and between them with shorter plants. Some of these will be designated as temporary fillers that get removed after one or more seasons; others may persist as long-term ground covers or low companions to the taller specimens.

Making strategic combinations is a way to compromise between short-term and long-term goals. It's intended to promote optimal development of permanent plants, while offering a dense, colorful look in the meantime. The following sections will explain how to implement this strategy.

Research how big plants will get and how fast they grow

Most plants have an innate tendency to develop a typical shape and to reach a certain size. Ideally, you

This 8-foot 'Boulevard' false cypress is now 10 years old. It was started from a rooted cutting the size of the new baby plant in the pot at lower right. Over the years it has been transplanted four times (to larger pots, a nursery bed, and this final site) and pruned repeatedly. This is considered a dwarf conifer. Standard conifers grow even more quickly from seedlings or cuttings to full-size trees.

To determine how fast a particular shrub grows, start at the tip of a stem and follow it down, looking for a point where the bark changes color and texture. That marks the junction between new and previous growth. This juniper, for example, has put out about 6 inches of new growth so far this year. You can use this technique to assess plants at a nursery or in a garden.

match the shape, size, and growth rate of the plant to the open area on the site, hoping that the plant will grow to fit the space in a reasonable period of time without getting too much bigger afterward.

When you're thinking about how much space a plant needs, don't be influenced by what size it is when you buy it. At most nurseries, the difference between smaller and larger sizes of the same kind of plant represents just one or two years' growth. That's insignificant compared with how many years the plant will live in your landscape and how big it will get in the long run. Space plants according to what size they will reach someday, not what size they are now.

Whenever you buy a plant, look it up in your reference books to find out how big it's likely to grow. Better yet, find a specimen that's already established in your neighborhood. Visit local public and private gardens whenever you get a chance, study what you see there, and use these observations to plan your own plantings. The following guidelines will help you interpret what you read, hear, and see when you're researching a particular plant.

TREES. A tree described as small typically grows no more than 15 to 25 feet tall, or about the height of a two-story house. A medium tree can reach 25 to 50 feet tall, or the height of a three- to five-story building. A large tree will grow to 50 feet or more in height. Most trees are slim when young. Their crown usually doesn't expand much sideways until they've reached more than half their mature height; this may take one to several decades.

When mature, many trees have a spread approximately equal to their height. Trees described as narrow, columnar, or fastigiate remain upright and skinny. Trees with spreading, umbrella-like, or weeping crowns start widening and developing their characteristic shape when they are still relatively young, and they grow wider than they are tall.

When young, a fast-growing tree under favorable growing conditions can add 2 to 4 feet or more of new growth at the end of every limb in a single year. Such a tree will quickly transform a bright sunny site into a cool shady one. An average young tree puts out 1 to 2 feet a year; even at that rate, a sapling will reach the top of a two-story house in less time than it takes a child to go from kindergarten to college. A young slow-growing tree adds less than 6 inches a year. All trees gain height more slowly as they age.

SHRUBS. A prostrate or creeping shrub may cling to the ground or reach up to about 1 foot tall. A dwarf shrub typically grows 1 to 3 feet tall; a small shrub, 3 to 5 feet; a medium-size shrub, 5 to 10 feet; and a large shrub, over 10 feet. A compact cultivar of any shrub will be smaller than normal, but if the shrub is normally large, "compact" may simply imply medium-size, not small. Of course, these are the potential heights of unpruned plants.

With shrubs, there's no single rule of thumb relating height and spread. Many shrubs are taller than wide; these are described as erect, narrow, upright, or (if they tend to be bare at the base and leafy on top) leggy. Broad, spreading, or mounded shrubs grow wider than they are tall. A rounded shrub usually grows about as wide as it is tall. A dome-shaped shrub is hemispheric. A shrub described as vase-shaped, fountainlike, or arching commonly has a spread equal to or wider than its height. A suckering shrub sends up new shoots around the edge and spreads to form a patch or colony, usually of erect stems that are taller in the center and shorter around the sides. Suckering and creeping shrubs can eventually grow quite wide; in nature, individual plants sometimes cover an acre or more.

Other than slow-growing shrubs, which put out just a few inches of new growth each year and for that reason are rarely pruned, it's hard to generalize about the growth rate of a shrub because that depends on when and how the shrub is pruned, as well as on growing conditions and variety. If unpruned, many shrubs grow at least 1 foot taller annually for a few to several years, then slow to a rate of just inches a year. The same shrubs, if pruned hard every year or every few years in winter or spring, might send up new shoots 2 to 6 feet tall, or even taller, in a single season. Shrubs that spread sideways may extend a few inches or a foot or more in all directions every year, continuing until they encounter an obstacle or a change in growing conditions.

PERENNIALS. Perennial plants of all kinds—including perennial bulbs, ferns, grasses, and ground covers as well as flowering perennials, such as daylilies and daisies—are so popular, widely grown, and well described that you can generally find fairly specific numbers for the typical heights of these plants. The range is very wide; perennial stems, stalks, or leaves can hug the ground or reach 8 to 10 feet in height. Most perennials display their full height in the second or third growing season after you plant them.

The recommended spacings typically given for perennials are less reliable, because they are intended to create a "filled-in" effect within a year or two and don't indicate what will happen afterward. When reading descriptions of perennials, look for the key term "forms a clump" or "spreads." Virtually all perennials send up more stems every year. In clump-forming perennials, the stems are spaced close together. Clumps do gradually widen (established clumps of some perennials can eventually fill a circle 6 feet in diameter or even wider), but mostly they just become denser every year. Clump formers may

do well at recommended spacings for many years.

Spreading perennials fill in well at the normally recommended spacings; that's good if you're using them as a ground cover or to fill large areas. However, some perennials can spread as much as 12 inches in all directions every year, and that causes trouble if they interfere with adjacent plants, sprout up where you don't want them, or spread into the lawn. Books and catalogs should warn you about this but often don't, so pay attention. If you spot that a perennial is growing faster than you expected, take immediate action and dig it up before it turns into a problem.

Make strategic combinations

When gardeners talk about plant combinations, they're usually thinking about color. Combining

PLANNING FOR FUTURE GROWTH

When you're planting shrubs, do your best to estimate how wide they'll spread at maturity. Draw circles of that diameter, center each shrub in its circle, and outline the shape of the bed that they will fill someday. Prepare the soil and plant the shrubs. At planting time, they'll look small and there will be empty space between them.

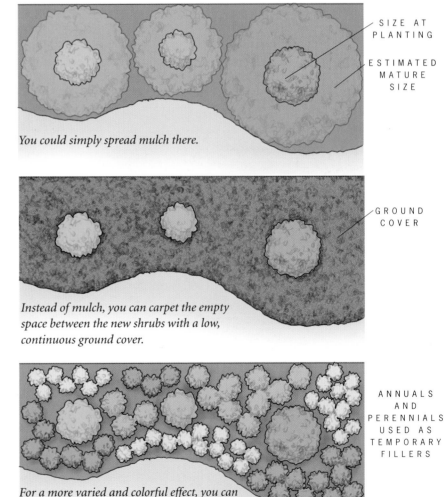

You could simply spread mulch there.

SIZE AT PLANTING

ESTIMATED MATURE SIZE

Instead of mulch, you can carpet the empty space between the new shrubs with a low, continuous ground cover.

GROUND COVER

For a more varied and colorful effect, you can plant annuals and clump-forming perennials between the shrubs, removing them later as needed so they never impinge on the shrubs.

ANNUALS AND PERENNIALS USED AS TEMPORARY FILLERS

plants so that their flowers and foliage will harmonize or contrast is an important principle of design (see page 50), as is making compositions based on plant form and texture (page 60). Consider those visual effects whenever you're putting plants together.

But the topic here is a practical aspect of making combinations. Along with appearance, you need to think about competition and long-term consequences when you combine plants. Of course you want a planting to look good as soon as possible, but you don't want the plants to stunt, overwhelm, or disfigure each other. For example, it's a shame to let an aggressive perennial smother a valuable baby shrub, and this can happen in a single season.

Making strategic combinations is about planning ahead, envisioning how you want your yard to look in five or ten years, and using that goal as a basis for short-term decisions. You need to be optimistic, patient, and ruthless. The first step is choosing your long-term plants, the ones that will become key specimens in your yard, and siting them so that they can remain in place for the foreseeable future. Then follow this rule: Either everything that's planted near, between, or around a key plant must remain shorter than it is, or you must be ready and willing to remove the temporary filler plant before it threatens the shape and vigor of the permanent plant.

CENTER PLANTS IN CIRCLES. If it's not crowded or shaded by other plants or nearby buildings, almost any perennial, shrub, tree, or other plant will assume a rounded shape. This pattern is very conspicuous when you look out from a tall building or an airplane window and survey the landscape below.

A fully rounded specimen is a handsome sight. This is especially true of slow-growing and long-lived shrubs but can also be said of anything you plant, even annuals. Research the plant you've chosen and make a generous, optimistic estimate of how wide it's likely to spread. Then outline a circle that size, and set the plant in the center. To arrange a group of plants, center each in a circle of its own, and let adjacent circles barely touch. Be sure to position any plant at least one-half its mature width away from any boundary, walkway, or building.

Using circles to symbolize the mature size and shape of plants whenever you're drawing a plan on graph paper or working directly on the ground to stake out a planting helps you center the plant in the right spot to begin with and also serves as an important reminder that the full area of the circle "belongs" to that plant. Don't plant anything else inside that circle that would inhibit the development of the intended specimen. Leave the area open (just cover the soil with mulch), fill it with ground-cover

DISTINGUISH THE PERMANENT PLANTS

Not all plants are equally valuable in terms of cost, prestige, and permanence. When you're designing a planting, give priority to the slow-growing specimens, which can and should remain in the same place for decades, becoming ever more impressive and beautiful. Make sure they're sited right and have enough room to develop fully.

What plants are potential specimens? To some extent you can judge by price. Often (not always) plants that cost more are worth more, because they're especially desirable and/or slow-growing. But you should also research a plant's eventual size, its typical life span, and its performance under your local conditions.

- **TREES.** Most broad-leaved trees are potential specimens, except for short-lived, trouble-prone species of birch, cherry, mountain ash, poplar, and willow. Conifers vary. Many grow fairly quickly and become much too large for a typical lot, but slow-growing species, such as California incense cedar (*Calocedrus decurrens*), lacebark pine (*Pinus bungeana*), and Japanese umbrella pine (*Sciadopitys verticillata*), and dwarf or compact cultivars of most other species are excellent long-term choices.

- **SHRUBS.** Many evergreen shrubs make outstanding specimens that live for decades, gradually widening into broad

upright or mounded shapes. Consider species and cultivars of aucuba, barberry (*Berberis*), boxwood (*Buxus*), camellia, daphne, euonymus, holly (*Ilex*), Indian hawthorn (*Rhaphiolepis*), mahonia, mountain laurel (*Kalmia*), leucothoe, oleander, osmanthus, photinia, pieris, pittosporum, rhododendron, and viburnum in this group. Among deciduous shrubs, the most attractive and shapely (both in and out of leaf) and long-lasting specimens are kinds of buckeye (*Aesculus*), barberry, sweet shrub (*Calycanthus*), Harry Lauder's walking stick (*Corylus avellana* 'Contorta'), cotoneaster, daphne, witch hazel (*Hamamelis*), hydrangea, various shrub roses, and lilac (*Syringa*).

- **PERENNIALS.** Perennials that form such impressive, long-lived clumps that they deserve specimen status (even though they may die down to the ground in winter) include bear's breeches (*Acanthus mollis*), lily-of-the-Nile (*Agapanthus orientalis*), blue stars (*Amsonia*), false indigos (*Baptisia*), gas plant (*Dictamnus albus*), queen-of-the-prairie (*Filipendula rubra* 'Venusta'), perennial sunflowers (*Helianthus*), large-stature daylilies (*Hemerocallis*), mallows (*Hibiscus*), large hostas, and peonies (*Paeonia*). Also, most clump-forming grasses, bamboos, palms, cacti, yuccas, agaves, and tropical perennials should be treated as specimens and given plenty of space and a prime location.

Now you see the daylilies in this curving bed. Look closely and you'll see yews in there also. Someday those yews will form a continuous evergreen hedge. Before then, the clumps of daylilies can be removed, divided, and planted elsewhere.

plants that will always stay shorter than the centerpiece, or use temporary plantings there and remove them as the specimen grows.

USING GROUND COVERS. Most plants grow best if they have no competition and the soil around them is simply covered with mulch, but some ground covers have such weak or shallow roots that they pose a minimal threat and can serve as a living mulch. These bantamweight ground covers can be used in almost any planting to add a low carpet of color and texture. There aren't many candidates in this group—most good ground covers are aggressive enough to be competitive—but some annuals and perennials can be recommended.

China pinks *(Dianthus chinensis)*, edging lobelia *(Lobelia erinus)*, sweet alyssum *(Lobularia maritima)*, forget-me-not *(Myosotis sylvatica)*, portulaca or moss rose *(Portulaca grandiflora)*, annual phlox *(Phlox drummondii)*, garden verbena *(Verbena × hybrida)*, and creeping zinnia *(Zinnia angustifolia)* are nonthreatening, low-growing annuals that you can safely intersperse among any new planting. Many of these annuals self-seed, or you can replant them for a few seasons until the permanent plants have filled in.

Some shallow-rooted, fast-growing perennial ground covers that can be planted right around potential specimens without inhibiting the more valuable plants' growth are ajuga or bugleweed *(Ajuga reptans)*, purple poppy mallow *(Callirhoe involucrata)*, hardy ice plants *(Delosperma)*, most pinks *(Dianthus)*, bloody cranesbill *(Geranium san-*

guineum cvs.), spotted dead nettle *(Lamium maculatum* cvs.), moneywort *(Lysimachia nummularia)*, mazus *(Mazus reptans)*, Corsican mint *(Mentha requienii)*, rock soapwort *(Saponaria ocymoides)*, strawberry geranium *(Saxifraga stolonifera)*, creeping sedums, creeping thymes, creeping veronicas, and sweet violet *(Viola odorata)*. These perennials fill in so fast that they'll make a good show in the first or second growing season, but they may get shaded out a few years later as the permanent plants grow taller. That's okay. These will have done their job as temporary fillers. In the long run, you may not need or want a ground cover among the permanent plants.

Most long-lived perennial ground covers, such as pachysandra and vinca, are too powerful to put right next to a baby shrub or tree (remember that most tree and shrub roots grow quite close to the surface of the soil). A vigorous ground cover can steal a lot of nutrients and water from the ground, leaving a less aggressive plant at a great disadvantage. So in general, plant perennial (and also shrubby or vining) ground covers out around the perimeter of a permanent plant's circle and let them grow toward each other over the years. That way the shrub or tree will have had time to get established before it has to compete with the ground cover.

USING TEMPORARY FILLERS. If you're anxious to create a "full" effect right away, deliberately select plants that grow quickly but are easily removed, replaced, or transplanted. Over the years, you'll keep removing these temporary plantings to prevent overcrowding; never let them inhibit or overwhelm the permanent plants. Don't invest too much money or emotion in short-term plants, as you have to be willing to get rid of them, or at least move them elsewhere, when they get in the way.

When choosing plants to use as temporary fillers, follow these two principles: First, anything you plant as a filler must stay shorter than the adjacent permanent plants, to avoid shading the latter from the side or, worse yet, flopping over onto them and smothering them. Second, use plants you can remove or destroy with minimum disturbance to the permanent plants' roots.

Many clump-forming perennials can be used as temporary fillers and remain in place for about three to five years. Since you know you'll be removing them, choose plants that tolerate or require periodic division or renewal, such as asters, coreopsis, daisies, daylilies, garden mums, hardy geraniums, heucheras, and sedums. Avoid perennials that spread by runners, as it's harder to remove them.

Annuals are my first choice for filling empty space around young shrubs or perennials. They come in all colors and provide immediate gratification, yet they're cheap and expendable, so you won't hesitate to discard them immediately if they begin to impinge on the permanent specimen. And you don't have to dig them up; simply cut off the stems at ground level.

❦ LAYOUT AND DESIGN TECHNIQUES

When it comes down to the final, nitty-gritty business of deciding exactly which plants to include in a bed, how many of them to use, and where to dig the holes, most gardeners balk and squirm. These are hard decisions.

The various techniques described below can help you experiment with and finalize a planting design. I don't think any one method is good for all occasions. They are different ways of working and show different dimensions. It's good to alternate between two or more approaches as you're planning a bed to be sure that you're considering all the important variables. Design a planting one way, then another, and crosscheck the results.

Remember that you don't have to resolve everything at once. It's okay to leave gaps in a planting, places you can fill later. If you can't make up your mind or if you have been to all the local nurseries and can't find a plant you want, just leave an open space or put some annuals there for now.

No matter how you develop a design, after you're done and the plants are in the ground, draw yourself a map or diagram — even a rough one will do — showing what plants you used and where you put them. Keep this handy so you can refer to it when you forget a plant's name.

Measure how much space there is to fill

To measure the length and width of small beds, use a yardstick or tape measure. For larger areas, measure distances in paces, determine the length of your average stride, and multiply to figure the distance in feet. My average stride is about 30 inches, or 2½ feet, so if I figure a bed is roughly 10 paces long, that equals about 25 feet.

When planting next to a building, think about plant heights with reference to the architecture. If you want a shrub that will grow up to a windowsill, or one that would reach the eaves, measure the building to determine the ideal plant height.

Out in the open, a fast way to estimate how tall a plant you want must be is by comparison to your body. If you're looking for a ground cover that does not get more than knee-high or a hedge that grows above your head but not taller than you can reach, decide what height you want, then convert to feet and inches later by measuring yourself. (For handy reference, it helps to know a few of your own dimensions, such as the height of your knees, waist, or chest.)

Mockups

This is the fastest and most accurate way to estimate whether a planting will feel welcome or "in the way," to outline an area that looks just right (not too big or small), to symbolize the height of plants up to 6 to 8 feet tall, and to pinpoint the position of major plants and focal points.

Improvise with whatever markers you've got handy. Hoses, ropes, or stakes and string are good for outlining edges, while stones, empty plastic pots, empty cardboard boxes, or stakes can mark individual planting spots. A shovel or digging fork stuck in the ground can symbolize a medium-height shrub, and a bamboo stake or a tripod of beanpoles can stand for a tree. Better yet, to site the initial planting hole and also visualize the eventual impact of a full, round specimen, use both a tall stake at the hole to indicate the approximate mature height and a circle of shorter markers to mark the plant's potential circumference.

GROWING ANNUALS AS A MOCKUP. If you're not in a hurry, using annuals as prototypes is a smart idea. There's no better way to assess how it will feel to look at and walk around a planting, and a showy bed of annuals will make you feel good and impress your neighbors while you're learning about potential long-term plants and making up your mind.

Consider height first, and choose annuals that will grow approximately as tall as the permanent plants you're considering. Space the annuals about 1 foot apart, using as many as it takes to fill an area.

SKETCHING OVER A PHOTO

This is an easy way to start planning a design. Take a photo of your house or of the area you want to develop (RIGHT). *Have a big enlargement made. Lay tracing paper or plastic film over the photo and use colored pencils or erasable markers to draw your ideas, as shown here. Design several alternatives and compare them. At this point, it isn't necessary or desirable to be thinking about specific kinds of plants. What's important is thinking about the basic layout of planted and unplanted areas, desired heights and spreads, and how many different kinds of plants you might use.*

Sunflower, castor bean *(Ricinus communis),* and cleome can grow 4 to 8 feet wide in a season and make good surrogates for medium or large shrubs. Dozens of annuals grow 1 to 4 feet tall and can simulate smaller shrubs, and dwarf or creeping annuals such as wax begonias, sweet alyssum, and portulaca can stand in as ground covers.

Using annuals is also an excellent way to observe how different flower colors look against the color of your house and hardscape or in the context of your surroundings. Any flower color that exists in perennials or shrubs can also be found in annuals. To compare and choose from a variety of colors, plant a mixture of annuals.

Photo tracings

This is a good way to decide how tall plants should be in relation to adjacent buildings, established trees or shrubs, or other backgrounds. It's also a good way to set approximate boundaries for the overall size of a planting and to determine a minimum grid unit (see below).

Take photos of the area you intend to develop from different points of view and have them blown up into 5x7 or larger prints. Get some transparent plastic sheets (like the kind used for overhead projectors) or a tablet of tracing paper at an office supply store. Then lay the plastic or paper over the photo and try sketching different plantings. Your drawings don't have to be artistic; simple cloudlike blobs are enough to suggest plants of different sizes, shapes, and positions.

An important lesson that comes clear with this technique is that big, simple shapes almost always look better outdoors than fussy designs with too many small details.

Using an imaginary grid

This is a way to make sure you use plants or groups that are big enough to show up from whatever distance you'll usually view the planting. Once you have outlined a bed and are ready to think about filling it with plants, imagine that it's divided into a grid—like a patchwork quilt—where each piece or block holds one plant or one kind of plant.

Decide on the smallest area that would be visible and look good. That's the minimum grid size. For nearby viewing, you might set the minimum area at about 1 to 2 feet wide. For farther away, minimum grid sizes could be 3 to 4 feet wide or 6 to 8 feet wide. Consider the average mature spread or width of a plant to figure how many you need to fill a unit on the grid.

Like a patchwork quilt, these broad beds are made from blocks of different-colored plants. The average block, or grid unit, is an area about 3 feet wide, and the gardener used as many of each plant as needed to fill that area.

Of course, not all plants or groups have to be the same size and shape. The basic unit is a minimum area, but some of the plants or groups should be larger than that. As for shape, single plants will be round, but groups can be whatever shape fits and looks good. Successful plantings usually resemble crazy quilts, where the pieces are of assorted sizes and materials, rather than matching blocks.

Drawing plans

Since it shows only the width or spread of plants, not their height, most people find it hard to visualize a planting from a plan, but drawing plans is a good counterpart to other planning techniques. It can help you focus on how much space individual plants need, how many of them you can fit in an area, and how to arrange them there.

Get a tablet of graph paper ruled at four squares per inch. Let one square equal 1 square foot, and start by drawing the outline of the bed or planting area you have to fill; tape sheets together if the area is too large to fit on one page. Trace a few copies of this outline so you can pick one up when you want a fresh start.

DESIGNING WITH PLANTS

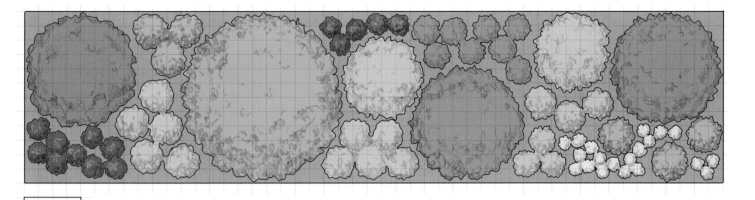

MINIMUM
GRID
SIZE

PLANNING A DESIGN ON GRAPH PAPER

As a convenient scale, let one square of the paper equal 1 square foot of the planting. Draw circles to indicate individual plants, making the diameter of each circle equal the expected mature spread of the plant. Draw a square or circle in the margin to remind yourself of the minimum grid size for your planting. As you fill in the design, do visual comparisons to make sure that the area of each group of plants is approximately equal to or greater than the minimum grid size.

Here the dimensions of the planting are 12 by 40 feet, and the minimum grid size is 4 by 4 feet. Large plants easily exceed the minimum size; that's good. With small plants, use three, five, seven, or as many as needed to fill the minimum area, and arrange them in natural-looking clusters and drifts.

If you have already decided about some of the permanent plants you want to include or are working around established specimens, go ahead and draw appropriate-size circles to indicate them directly on the plan. In addition, draw a square in the margin to indicate the minimum grid size. Refer to the square as a reminder that any section of the planting has to be at least that large.

Basically, there are two ways to proceed with a plan. You can look at the available space and say something like "There's room here for three plants that each grow about 4 feet wide," then come up with some appropriate candidates and choose among them based on all the many factors of site suitability, height, appearance, and how they relate to other plants you've already decided on. Or you can already have narrowed your choices to certain plants and use the paper plan to determine if they'll fit the space and to decide how to arrange them. Keep a plant encyclopedia handy, because you can't make a plan without stopping to check plant spreads and look for alternative candidates as you explore different ideas.

Drawing even a simple plan for a small area usually involves lots of drafts and revisions. Eventually you should zero in on a design that shows the major, permanent plants as large circles. Groups of smaller or temporary plants can fill other shapes that are always at least as large as the minimum grid size.

Don't be afraid that starting with circles and grids will make a homogeneous, artificially uniform garden. It never turns out that way. These are just planning tools. In actual gardens, plants vary so much in height, habit, texture, and color that the result is never boring, no matter how simple the plan looks.

COMPUTER DESIGN AIDS. Drafting plans with a computer instead of on graph paper sounds like a great idea, and various landscaping programs are available on CD, but their drawbacks become evident as soon as you try them. It's hard to draw with a mouse. The size of your monitor limits the scale at which you can work; for large plantings, it's easier to work on taped-together sheets of paper than to scroll around the screen or constantly zoom in and out. Eventually you'll need to print out a plan that you can carry outdoors, and what size will that be? The programs are interesting if you like playing with your computer, but in practice they aren't nearly as useful as conventional design techniques.

In this brand-new development, everyone has begun their landscaping by planting around their house. Almost every yard has a curved bed that wraps along both sides of the main walk from the driveway to the front door, then extends to the far corner of the house and projects out as a rounded peninsula. A small tree is planted in the peninsula. An assortment of rounded shrubs are spaced along the walk and across the front of the house.

3 ❧ Landscaping Around Your House

THE AREA immediately around your house is special and deserves high priority as you develop your landscape. This is true regardless of the overall size of your property. On large lots, there's a distinction between what's nearby and what's farther away. On small lots, all you've got is land close to the house. Either way, the house is where you spend the most time, so nearby space gets the most scrutiny, appreciation, and use.

A house dominates its surroundings in many ways. Visually, it's the center of attention on most lots, especially if it faces and is visible from the street. It gives you something to build against and provides shelter and security for a deck or patio. It affects growing conditions and creates microclimates different from those of sites out in the open.

Certain issues take on extra importance when you're landscaping around your house. One is community standards, which may pose implicit or even explicit guidelines for how you should develop and maintain any parts of your land—especially the front yard—that are in public view.

Another concern is hardscape. Most projects near or next to a house involve some building or remodeling. The closer it is to your home, the more important it is for the hardscape to be well designed, safe, in full compliance with local codes, and carefully built from good-quality materials. Invest in the best; you'll never regret it. If your landscaping plans call for hardscaping, finish the construction first and add plants afterward.

As for plants, the general guidelines for selecting and designing with plants apply here as elsewhere. Although there are a few cautions regarding plants close to a house, there are special opportunities, too, and it's important to use a lot of plants around a house. Their rounded shapes, soft and varied textures, motion, seasonal changes, and natural growth are indispensable for balancing the rigid structure, flat surfaces, straight lines, and permanence of architecture and hardscape.

❧ GETTING IN AND OUT

A good starting point in landscaping around your house is to focus on how you come and go. How well does the driveway function, and how does it look? Do you have enough parking space? Can you and your visitors walk from a car to the house without watching your step or getting your shoes wet? Do you have a place to stand and linger over greetings and farewells? Is it easy to pack the kids and their gear into the car? What about unloading groceries, carrying out the trash, or getting the mail—not just on a sunny spring morning when life is a joy, but how about doing these basic tasks after dark or in the rain or snow? Ideally, landscaping should facilitate your routine activities (at the very least it shouldn't interfere with them), and hopefully it can provide beauty and pleasure as well.

Driveway and parking

Considering how much we depend on cars, it's amazing how heedlessly many driveways are built. If yours is too steep, narrow, or slippery, or if it leads blindly into a busy street, you owe it to yourself to get estimates on what would be involved in fixing it. Likewise, if your driveway or parking area is too dark, look into outdoor lighting. The price of driveway improvements may be daunting, but it's definitely a worthwhile investment.

You'll need to hire a contractor if you want to widen, lengthen, or alter a driveway, add a turnaround, or expand a parking area, and it's worth talking to at least a few different businesses to com-

Do your gardening right next to the house if you want to preserve a natural setting like this pine forest in the Colorado Rockies.

If you want to relocate a driveway or remove a former driveway or parking area that's no longer needed, it's possible to reclaim the land for gardening or other uses. You may need to work with two different contractors on a project like this—one to dig up and cart off the old pavement, and another to loosen the compacted subsoil, haul in enough fresh topsoil to bring the area up to grade, and prepare it for planting—but both parts of the job will go quickly and be fairly inexpensive. You *could* do some or all of this work yourself, but it's uncommonly strenuous, as the soil under an old driveway is packed dense as rock.

PAVEMENT. Aside from layout, pavement itself is the big issue with driveways. A simple gravel or grass driveway may be okay in a rural setting, if it doesn't get much wear and the drainage works right so the surface doesn't turn to mud. In town, most driveways are topped with blacktop (also called asphalt or macadam) or concrete. Both have drawbacks. Blacktop costs less at first but needs more upkeep and gets hot in the sun. Concrete costs more and lasts longer but stains badly and glares in the sun. In both cases, repairing cracks or other damage involves patches that are hard to disguise.

In terms of design, both blacktop and concrete are so bland that a conventional driveway is a big blank spot in the landscape. There's no texture, no pattern, nothing to break it into smaller units or to catch and hold your interest. Featureless driveways are so familiar that you might think they're inevitable, but of course there's an alternative. Look at the kinds of pavement used in public places, at

pare their opinions and estimates. Although the basic formulas and codes for laying out driveways are fairly standard, one contractor might point out a problem or solution that another had overlooked. If your site has steep slopes, the driveway is long, or there are large trees nearby, you should also consult a landscape architect, who can help you avoid problems with runoff, erosion, and tree damage.

Imagine how different your yard would look if the driveway was paved like this!

pedestrian malls or parks, and all over Europe—grids and swirls made of bricks, authentic cobblestones or cut-stone blocks, or, most commonly nowadays, interlocking concrete pavers (see page 124). Pavement can be an art form! I don't know why it's such a low priority in our residential landscapes.

If your driveway is a prominent feature in your front yard and you seriously want to upgrade its appearance, classy pavement is the way to go. Finding what you want will take some research. Check the Yellow Pages and call local contractors. Watch for ads and articles in lifestyle and home-improvement magazines and see if the paving manufacturers have a representative in your area. Go to home and garden shows. Keep your eyes open as you drive around town, and when you see interesting and uncommon pavement, try to find out who installed it. Once you've settled on what you want, expect to pay at least twice as much for special pavement as for a

(BELOW LEFT): Subdividing an expanse of pavement makes it less imposing. Here stripes of inlaid cobblestones divide the concrete into rectangles that are in scale with the wall, gate, planters, and shrubs. Changing from concrete to gravel at the gate adds variety and marks the transition from one area to another.

common blacktop or concrete driveway; even so, resurfacing a driveway costs no more than many smaller landscaping or home-improvement projects, and it makes a great visual impact.

DESIGNING AROUND A DRIVEWAY. If resurfacing your driveway is out of the question, or if the front of your house is dominated by that other common design dilemma—a broad garage door—you face a challenge. How can you compensate for or counteract such large blank surfaces? The area of a driveway or a garage door is so large that you can't overlook it, but when you do look at it, there's nothing there. It's visually empty.

This isn't an easy problem to solve, but one approach is to balance the scale and bareness of the driveway and door with simple plantings of comparable area. That might be an expanse of ground cover alone or, better yet, ground cover surrounding a group of large shrubs, a grove of small trees, or a single specimen tree with a broad graceful crown. The point is to fill large areas with just a few kinds of plants or a few big plants; as a result, the driveway and door won't seem so large anymore.

Note that an expanse of lawn doesn't provide the visual weight you need to balance a driveway or

(ABOVE LEFT): Framing a driveway with bold, large-scale plantings that come right up to the edge of the pavement helps integrate it into the landscape. The idea is to balance the big expanse of pavement with plantings (not just lawn) of comparable area. Evergreen shrubs adjoin this Oregon driveway.

(ABOVE RIGHT): Broad patches of perennials and grasses serve the same role in a Missouri yard.

(BELOW RIGHT): You can't keep plants out of a gravel driveway. If you're lucky, flowers will grow there. (Usually you just get weeds.)

garage door; lawn is too bland and just adds to the problem. If your front yard is mostly driveway and lawn, the best thing you can do to improve its appearance is to outline a big bed, dig up the turf there, and replace it with other plants.

From the perspective of the street, it's rarely feasible and not necessarily desirable to try to hide a driveway, parking area, or garage door with plants. When you're driving toward a house, you want to be able to see where to go.

But from a point of view inside the house, you might want to screen a driveway or parking area, so you don't have to sit and look out at your cars or squint at the glare reflecting from your driveway. Plants used for this purpose don't have to make an opaque screen; a lacy, fine-textured, see-through screen works just as well and looks subtler. You could use a few clumps of ornamental grasses with slender waving seed heads, or a few upright-growing or vase-shaped shrubs thinned by pruning to eliminate all the weak inner twigs. Use the viewpoint from inside the window to decide where to plant such a screen and how tall and wide to make it, then mock up the planting with stakes, and consider it from all sides. Adjust the placement and height of the stakes until you like what you see, then choose plants that will suit the site and reach the size you want.

Entries

When visitors approach your house, is it obvious which way they should come and what door they should use? Which door(s) do you use? Are the various entries to your house all clear, convenient, and safe?

Start with the main or front door, if you have one. Even if you use it only for special occasions, it's important to make it look generous, warm, and welcoming. A main entry that's undersized, neglected, or obscured by overgrown shrubs sends an unfriendly message. If you do use it daily yourself, then it's all the more worthwhile to design a main entry that's cheerful and pleasant. The walk that leads to the door should be as unmistakable and gracious as a red carpet. Make it broad, direct, and smooth. Use paving that's appealing to look at and comfortable to walk on.

Treat yourself by upgrading any side, rear, or service entries in addition to the main or front door. Most of the same considerations and guidelines apply to all entries, but the details will vary depending on how you use the different doors and how you view them, too.

SHOW THEM THE DOOR. The sight of the door itself is the primary clue about where an entry is, so don't let shrubs or trees block it out of view. If the door is small or modest, you may want to call attention to it with bright paint, colorful plants, or a wreath or other decorations.

A door that's hidden in an alcove, behind a projecting wall or screen, or around a corner is an uncertain destination. First-time visitors may feel hesitant to approach if they aren't sure where to go; they may be afraid of violating your privacy and knocking at the "wrong" door. In such a case, the

(BELOW): *What a pleasure to arrive at a home like this, with a broad, smooth, well-lit walkway that leads directly from the parking area to the front door. You and your guests could come and go quickly and safely, day or night, in any weather.*

(BELOW): *The swirling pattern in the brick pavement leads you through the alcove and directs you to the door. An extension of the same pavement could serve as a terrace or driveway. Note the repeated use of bricks here, in the paving, the wall, and the house itself.*

walkway must be especially broad and clear, as a narrow or overgrown path would increase the sense of doubt.

PROVIDE A LANDING. A landing, porch, or reception area outside a door is both symbolic and practical. It should be big enough to accommodate at least a few people plus their shopping bags, toys, parcels, or gear. Builders often skimp on this and pour concrete slabs that are both too small for comfort and visually undersize in proportion to the house.

If your landing looks like a token afterthought, enlarging it (or more likely, replacing it with something larger, which might be a grade-level patio or a raised porch or deck) will bring your house up to date and give you some surprisingly useful outdoor space. If the landing is big enough, you'll linger there with friends and visitors. You may even want to add a bench or chair and sit there yourself sometimes, and a front landing is a great place to grow special plants in containers. For help in designing a new front landing, see the guidelines on designing an outdoor room on page 107.

LAY A CONSIDERATE WALKWAY. Your main or front walk is the most immediate and direct link to the world outside your home. Negotiating it should be a safe, comfortable, and pleasant experi-

ence, both for you and for your guests. Yet walkways are often poorly designed or built, and as a result they may be annoying, awkward, or even dangerous.

Trying to repair or remodel an existing walk is unlikely to be satisfactory. If your walk has problems or simply looks bad, you'd probably better get it removed and replaced, and I'd recommend that you hire a landscape contractor if the walk is more than 20 to 30 feet long or requires climbing more than a few steps. You can tackle a secondary walk or a garden path yourself, but the main walk is a pretty significant feature on your property and you want to be sure it looks professional (and to be sure that it gets done, if you're the kind of person who tends to leave half-finished projects lying around). At any rate, whether you hire help or do it yourself, here are important points to think about in designing a main walkway.

Acknowledging that most people arrive by car nowadays, a main walk should originate at the most-used parking place or wherever people get out of their cars to approach your house. There's no point in having a front walk that leads out to the street or public sidewalk if you and your visitors routinely pull up into the driveway. If parking is on the street, a walk should lead all the way to the curb, if possible, so you can stay on pavement and not have to take a few steps across grass or dirt. Check local rules regarding the strip of land adjacent to a street or road; usually you can lay a walkway or grow plants there if you get permission in advance, but some towns forbid or regulate such improvements.

From the place of arrival, a main walk should lead directly to the main entry. It doesn't have to be straight as an arrow—gentle curves are okay, but don't impose unnecessary delays or difficulties by

(LEFT): A walk that leads around to the side or back of a house can be narrower than the main front walk, but it should be direct, safe, and easy to use.

(BELOW): A wooden deck with wide, angled steps leads to a matching wood house. The geranium, potted plants, and vine soften the sharp lines of the architecture.

laying out a "scenic route" with pointless meanders, detours, or obstacles, and don't expect that people using the walk will want to stop and smell the flowers. That's romantic nonsense. The place for a casual stroll is in a pleasure garden out back. Design your main or front walk for the sake of people who are in a hurry, people carrying briefcases or boxes or babies, and people who tire easily or walk with difficulty. Remember, too, that you'll be using the main walk not just on beautiful days but also in bad weather and at night, when all you want to do is get from the car to the door as fast as possible.

A main walkway should be at least 5 to 6 feet wide to allow two people to walk side by side, and that's if adjacent vegetation is short. Make it wider if the walk goes beside or between plants taller than waist-high; impinging plants impose a crowded feeling under any condition, and especially so when their foliage is wet.

The walk should be graded so water drains off quickly. The surface should be easy to walk on in any kind of shoes and should provide good traction in all weather. It should be level and uniform, with no irregularities to trip you. Concrete, brick, stone, and wood surfaces all have pros and cons in terms of initial cost, appearance, upkeep, and safety (see page 159).

Any steps should be wide and not too steep, and a long climb should be broken up with one or more landings. Wherever there are steps, a handrail may be welcome, too. An experienced contractor will know the guidelines for constructing safe outdoor steps; to learn more about steps yourself, see page 183.

PLANTING BY ENTRIES AND WALKS.

One or more special plants near your main entry can highlight it as a destination and center of attention. A plant used for this can stand out in various ways. Many people choose a Christmas-tree-shaped conifer or some kind of evergreen that's sheared into a neat geometric shape, but you could go the other way and opt for something distinctively irregular—a small tree with multiple trunks, a weeping crown, or strongly textured bark, or, if your climate allows, a clump of bamboo, a shrubby palm, or a bold-leaved tropical.

Containers are good for marking an entry. Growing something in a big pot lifts it up, sets it apart, and makes it look more special. One way to use containers is to fill them with a sequence of seasonal plantings—spring bulbs, heat-loving annuals and tropicals for summer, and cool-season annuals for fall and winter. Another approach is to put permanent plants—usually shrubs or evergreen perennials, but you can try small trees, herbaceous perennials, grasses, or other plants, too—in planters large enough that the plants can grow there for years.

A matched pair of plants symbolizes and marks an entry. The convention is to use two formal evergreens here, but you could have unsheared, natural-looking evergreens, an informal pair of deciduous shrubs or small trees, or anything you want in two big containers.

Or if you like the idea of repetition, instead of pairing plants at the door try putting the same kind of plant at both ends of the walk, to signify departure and arrival, or at intervals along the walk, like mile-

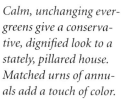

Calm, unchanging evergreens give a conservative, dignified look to a stately, pillared house. Matched urns of annuals add a touch of color.

Symmetry, neatness, a tasteful color scheme, and conspicuously contented plants make a great first impression when you arrive at this home.

stones marking the way. You wouldn't necessarily want or need to use large plants in this way—small rounded shrubs make subtle but effective markers, especially if they have colored leaves. Consider various kinds of wormwood *(Artemisia),* lavender, sage, or other shrubby herbs with silver or gray foliage, for example; all are semievergreen or evergreen, can be sheared or left natural, and release fragrant or pungent aromas when you brush against them. Clumps of ornamental grasses are good walkway markers, too, offering soft textures and rustling movement.

There are a few other points to keep in mind when planting near a walkway or doorway. First, keep plants out of the way, by planting them far enough back in the first place and pruning—or even removing—them when they grow too far out. Don't put scratchy or thorny plants where anyone might bump into them. And be careful where you put any expensive, rare, or delicate plants, especially short ones; don't position them where they might accidentally get trampled.

Outdoor lighting

You can think of outdoor lighting in terms of convenience, safety, and security or in terms of the atmosphere or ambiance it can create. Both roles are important, but they're quite different. Spotlighting or task lighting helps you see where you're going or what you're doing outdoors at night. It can be bold or subtle, and the fixtures can be plain or decorative. Artistic or atmospheric lighting is used mostly to create effects that are pleasing to look at, and the source of the light should usually be inconspicuous or hidden. I'll emphasize practical lighting here.

HOUSE-CURRENT LIGHTING. Fixtures that are attached to a building, mounted up in a tree, or on a pole and used to light large areas run on standard house current. Visit a lighting store or big home-improvement center to see examples of different fixtures. They range from utilitarian to quite elegant. With regard to the bulbs they use, ask how bright they are, what color the light is, and (for fixtures mounted where replacing bulbs would be inconvenient) how long the bulbs can be expected to last.

As you're thinking about what areas you want to have lighted and how many light fixtures you'll need, think about switches, too. First, do you want different lights on separate switches or connected? Then decide how the switches should be controlled. Along with standard wall switches, think about light-sensitive switches that turn on at dusk and off at dawn, motion detectors that turn a light on when you enter the area and turn it off later, and timers. If you choose an automatic sensor or switch, you'll want a wall switch also so you can override the system sometimes.

Once you've decided what you want, an electrician can quickly install outdoor fixtures and switches for you. Any house-current wiring must conform to local codes. Don't tackle this job yourself unless you're *absolutely* sure you know what you're doing.

LOW-VOLTAGE LIGHTING. Low-voltage systems start with a transformer that converts standard house current into 12-volt DC current. These systems are designed for homeowners to install and are safe, convenient, and versatile. Years ago, the appeal

Masses of flowers catch your eye here, but take another look and admire that paving. Think how different the effect would be if that were plain concrete, without the pebble surface and stone insets. Textured paving adds extra interest to any landscape.

of low-voltage systems was limited because the only fixtures available looked cheap and tacky, but that's changed a lot. Now there are many attractive styles of low-voltage fixtures, suitable for use as pathside, wall-mounted, or overhead lighting. These lights aren't as bright as house-current lighting can be, but they're adequate for safely finding your way around. Visit home-improvement stores to see what's in stock there or obtainable by special order.

You can buy transformers and fixtures separately or together. Either way, read all the fine print about where and how to install them. The transformer has to be plugged or wired into an outlet supplying house current. If you already have a waterproof outdoor outlet with GFCI (ground fault circuit interruption—that means the power shuts off instantly if water gets in) and buy a plug-in transformer, you can proceed on your own. If you need to have an outdoor outlet installed, or if you choose a wired-in transformer, or if you have any doubts or questions, call an electrician. *Don't* plug the transformer into an extension cord.

Usually a switch or timer is located on or built into the transformer, although you could arrange to have an indoor wall switch also or instead. Talk to the electrician about that if you want it.

The wire(s) that runs out from the transformer generally extends about 50 to 100 feet and can accommodate a certain number of fixtures. Follow the guidelines that come with your setup, and don't overload the system or the lights will go dim and the transformer may burn out. Do a tentative layout first and decide where you want the fixtures to go before you attach them to the wire (they connect easily with built-in fittings or screw-on wire nuts).

Low-voltage wiring doesn't have to be buried—you can just tuck it behind some plants or cover it with mulch. But if there's any risk of tripping on it, or if you suspect that local squirrels or chipmunks might gnaw through it, you'd better bury the wire a few inches deep in the soil.

SOLAR LIGHTS. Solar-powered outdoor lights seem like a great idea, but they don't quite fulfill their potential yet. Only a few models are available. Most are pathside lamps with a collector panel on top, which has to face the sun. When fully charged, these lamps cast a light that's comparable to that of a small flashlight, enough to mark the edge of a path or to indicate a corner or landing, but their storage capacity is limited. If they turn on automatically at dusk, they may run down before dawn, and they're dim or useless during prolonged cloudy spells.

ATMOSPHERIC LIGHTING. Creating artistic effects such as spotlighting your house, uplighting into a tree, or backlighting some shrubs is surprisingly tricky. When done well, the results can really enhance the appearance of your property at night from indoors and out, but this isn't a do-it-yourself project. It takes judgment and fine-tuning to choose suitable fixtures and get their placement and direction right; otherwise there can be spooky shadows, disorienting bright spots, and unwelcome contrasts. If you want to invest in atmospheric lighting, hire an experienced outdoor-lighting designer (when interviewing potential designers, be sure to visit some of their finished jobs at night to see the style of their work) and have a licensed electrician do the actual installation.

Utilities

Any of the various lines, cables, and pipes that connect your house to the world may occasionally need monitoring, repair, or replacement, so you don't want to inadvertently pave or build over them. Even more, avoid accidentally digging into or cutting a line when you do any construction or soil preparation. Most utilities have a phone number you can call for help with locating buried lines. Take advantage of that service, and proceed cautiously in any case when you're working around the house.

Don't let plants impede access to whatever hookups, vents, meters, hatchways, electrical outlets, water taps, or light fixtures are mounted on the outside walls of your house. It's okay to flank these fixtures with pliable, soft-leaved shrubs that are easily pushed aside, but neither you nor your servicemen want to plunge through prickly hollies or junipers. Prune lower tree limbs out of the way. Lay stepping-stones through a bed of ground covers. You may not need to get at any of these connections or fixtures very often, but when you do, it shouldn't be a nuisance.

❦ DESIGNING YOUR FRONT YARD

Any discussion of planting in front of your house has to start with the questions, Does your house have an obvious "front" side, and if so, does that side face visitors when they arrive? Some houses, especially contemporaries, don't have a definite front, and houses of any age are sometimes sited sideways or at an angle, so they don't directly face the street or driveway. These situations encourage original, creative landscape designs because they aren't associated with timeworn conventions and expectations. The main concern is to make it obvious to anyone who's coming to see you how they should approach the house and where the entry is.

Most houses do have a front side that faces the street. This presents some wonderful possibilities for showing the world how special you are, but the convention in most neighborhoods, especially suburban subdivisions, is to fill front yards with stereotyped plantings of lawn or ground cover, shade trees, some flowering shrubs, and sheared evergreens.

Other neighborhoods, both old and new but especially where the topography and architecture offer a variety of settings, demonstrate an open-mindedness toward innovative landscaping. In this context you can feel free to put up a fence or plant a hedge, replace your lawn with native plants, make a cottage garden, plant an extravagant perennial border, put up an arbor and cover it with billowing roses, or arrange some chairs or a bench where you can sit and watch the world go by.

What's your neighborhood like, and do you want your property to blend in or stand out? For that matter, do you have a choice, or are your options restricted by municipal zoning regulations or homeowners' association codes? These are your basic concerns in developing a yard that's exposed to public view. Anticipate local reactions before you do anything out of the ordinary, since it might be welcomed as a benefit to the neighborhood or rebuked as an eyesore.

I'll assume that you have some flexibility, that you want to create a front yard that's regarded as something special, that you want it to look neat and well cared for without actually requiring extra care, and that you want the plantings to frame and flatter your house. And although you certainly want to enjoy the view from the house toward the street, the main focus here will be on designing plantings that face out and look good from the public point of view. (Note that if you're already happy with your front-yard plants and you just want to learn more about caring for them, you should refer to pages 261–352. The discussion here is about designing new plantings and revising or remodeling older yards that aren't attractive anymore.)

What style suits you, your yard, and your house?

What kinds of plants you choose and how you arrange them determines the style of your landscape. There are many options. If your house already has a certain architectural style, that's an obvious starting point, but many houses are neutral enough to coordinate with various landscaping styles. Sometimes the topography of the site, its natural features, or existing plants suggest one style or preclude another. Mostly, though, it's up to you to decide what you like and express it through the choices you make.

CONTEMPORARY STYLES. Driving around in different parts of the country, you see a variety of front-yard landscape styles. Sometimes they're related to the house; more often they say something about the owner and the neighborhood. These styles don't actually have names, but it's easy to label them. Along with creating different impressions, these styles involve quite different budgets and time commitments. Here are a few examples; you can probably think of others.

"Calm and controlled" is a very widespread style. This is the landscape equivalent of a business suit, and its appearance varies little from season to season, year to year, and place to place. Characterized by its simplicity and grooming, it features a low-cut and weed-free lawn, sheared evergreen shrubs, and deciduous trees with the lower limbs removed. There may be a small, crisp-edged flower bed; like choosing a tie, this is where you can show some color and express a bit of individuality. You can also distinguish a yard like this by selecting top-quality plants; that's like having a custom-tailored suit made from exquisite fabric.

In the "take it easy" style, the goal is to achieve a casual but neat yard that requires little routine care. It should look good year-round and have some seasonal highlights, too. The keys to reducing maintenance, as emphasized throughout this book, are matching plants to the site and climate, replacing at least some of the lawn with ground covers and pave-ment, choosing plants that don't grow too big for their spot, keeping the design simple, and restricting how many kinds of plants you grow.

"Look what we bought" landscapes are seen in remodeled yards as well as in new developments. They feature classy hardscape, sculpted beds, trees so big they have to be carried in and planted with specially equipped trucks, fancy-shaped specimens, and lots of shrubs and smaller plants crowded for immediate impact. Although impressive at first, these

SOME HISTORIC AND REGIONAL LANDSCAPE STYLES

A landscape style encompasses the materials and architecture of the house and hardscape, the choice and arrangement of plants, and ornaments. Here are brief discussions of a few popular styles, including comments on their advantages and drawbacks.

- **COLONIAL** landscapes are suited to authentic or reproduction Early American houses. Typically the front yard is a squared-off area enclosed by a board or picket fence and/or clipped evergreen hedges (usually boxwood). The yard is subdivided into a geometric arrangement of raised beds filled with assorted flowering shrubs, berries, small flowering and fruit trees, old-fashioned perennial flowers, and herbs. There is no lawn. Paths are surfaced with bricks or gravel. The beds are edged with boards plus a low clipped edging of some dense, fine-textured herb or shrub. Ornaments could include a sundial, bee skep, or bench. Side yards and backyards might be shaded by native deciduous trees and floored with an evergreen ground cover such as English ivy or periwinkle. Because of the hardscape and evergreens, colonial landscapes look good year-round, with added color in summer, and they're relatively easy to maintain.

- **MEDITERRANEAN**- or Spanish colonial-style landscaping was introduced by the Catholic missionaries who settled in New Mexico and California. Variations on this style are popular throughout the Southwest today, because it's so well suited to both traditional and contemporary architecture in sunny, arid sites. The hardscape includes thick stucco walls around the perimeter, no lawn, packed dirt or tile floors, natural weathered or brightly painted wood, and built-in seating. Special features are colorful tiles, small fountains or pools, and specimen plants in large terra-cotta pots. Characteristic plants include citrus, bay, and other small evergreen trees; roses; and lavenders, rosemary, and other shrubby herbs. Fragrant plants are preferred. Mediterranean landscapes are easy to care for, partly because the enclosed area is usually relatively small, and they look good year-round and age gracefully.

- **VICTORIAN** landscaping prevailed throughout much of the 19th century and is suitable for houses of that era or style today, if you have the space and time for it. Authentic Victorian landscapes require generous grounds, a large number of plants, and skilled maintenance. The practice of surrounding a house with sheared evergreen "foundation plantings" dates to the Victorian era. Other typical features are grottoes, arbors, benches, and sculptures in a variety of quasi-classic and rustic materials and styles; uncommon trees and shrubs set as specimens on a smooth green lawn; well-groomed "carpet" beds of colorful annuals; and a conservatory filled with potted ferns and tropicals, many of which get carried outdoors for the summer.

- **COTTAGE**-style landscaping, or cottage gardening, is associated with small English villages. Despite its romantic appeal, it isn't suitable for most American front yards, because it requires continual grooming and attention during the growing season and typically looks messy or bare during cold winter months. In addition, it's surprisingly hard to arrange plants in a way that looks casual and spontaneous. If you're entranced by the cottage style, try it on a small scale in a side yard or backyard first before converting your front yard to it. A cottage garden features natural or painted wooden fences around the perimeter, no lawn, extensive crowded beds accessed by narrow grass or dirt paths or steppingstones, and plants trained vertically against the house and on arbors and trellises. It uses a wide variety of plants closely intermingled, including fruit trees, berries, flowering shrubs, shrub and climbing roses, clematis and other flowering vines, herbs, old-fashioned perennials, self-seeding biennials and annuals, and sometimes even vegetables.

- **ORIENTAL**- or Japanese-style landscapes look out of context with most American homes and are intended for private settings such as a secluded side yard or backyard, rather than public front yards. If you are intrigued by this style and want to try it anyway, think about how you can adapt it to your site. Maybe you should omit the most overt symbols, such as stone lanterns and highly sculpted trees. Also, avoid culture clash by rigidly excluding features that are *not* Oriental, such as petunias, geraniums, and other common bedding plants, or alien hardscape such as white picket fences. Stick with characteristic plants such as large and small conifers, maples, flowering cherries, azaleas, bamboo and grasses, peonies, and chrysanthemums. For building materials, use stone (both boulders and gravel), wood, and bamboo. You may want to include a quiet pool or pond.

landscapes are sometimes impractical and difficult to maintain in the long run.

"Put on a show" landscapes aren't very common, but if there's one around, you can't miss it. These are designed to stop traffic with joyful displays of colorful flowers—a bank of daffodils, a bed of daylilies, a hedge of lilacs—continuing in sequence throughout the season. Although it's not necessarily costly or demanding, this style does require informed plant selection and a bit of luck. A major drawback of these landscapes is that they usually have down seasons when the plants are past bloom or dormant. Also, if the plants are struck by frost, disease, or some other catastrophe, your disappointment is magnified by the scale of the planting.

"We're having fun" landscapes might follow any style or no style at all, but they make you smile and wave. The owners are always out there building and planting, enjoying what they've already done and planning new projects. It may seem as though they'll never finish, and they probably won't; what would they do then? Folks like this are an asset to any neighborhood, as their enthusiasm is contagious and they're usually quick to share plants, ideas, and information.

TRADITIONAL STYLES. Some landscape styles have a historic or geographic origin or started as a school of thought among landscape architects and garden designers. These traditional styles are generally associated with particular settings and usually don't adapt well to different contexts. In that sense, whether or not to consider one has already been decided for you. If your house and lot call for a colonial landscape, for instance, go ahead with it. Otherwise, look elsewhere for ideas.

Pursuing authenticity is fun, but it isn't fast. It takes a while to track down the information you need. There's at least one book about most established styles (although these books go out of print, so you may have to get them through a library or used-book store). A book will show outstanding examples of the style, discuss its guiding ideas, illustrate typical hardscape features, and list appropriate plants. In addition, seek out and visit relevant historic sites and restorations. Many of these institutions have put a lot of research and thought into establishing or restoring gardens appropriate for their period, and some host conferences or publish newsletters.

NATURAL LANDSCAPES. A different approach to the topic of landscape style is to focus on plants and nature, not architecture and human concerns. In this approach, what matters is not the appearance and arrangement of your house but the ecosystem in which you live. What kinds of plants, or plant community, would grow there naturally? It might be an evergreen forest, a deciduous woodland, a scrubby dryland, or a grassy prairie. Would you like

to preserve, encourage, or re-create that natural landscape?

Horticulturally, it makes good sense to copy or preserve native-plant communities. It's the obvious model for designing long-term, low-maintenance landscapes. Enough people have tried this approach in recent decades that you can find advice and plants appropriate for your site and climate. There may be a local group of native-plant enthusiasts that you can join, and perhaps a book written for your area.

Even so, advocates of natural landscaping are a small minority. You'll have peer support if you move into a neighborhood where the developer carefully preserved the existing vegetation, but if you try to reestablish a natural landscape in a conventional neighborhood, your neighbors may scoff or protest. When you listen to their concerns, you'll probably find that the problem isn't that you're growing native or wild plants, it's the perception or fear that you're going to let plants grow wild and get out of control. It's not the particular kinds of plants; it's the hands-off style that people react to.

To make sure your actions won't be interpreted as laziness or carelessness, be vigilant about pruning, thinning, and cleanup. Get rid of anything that looks dead. Spend time out front and make it clear that you care about what plants are growing on your land and aren't using "natural" as an excuse. Keep the house itself, the driveway, and the mailbox and streetside uncommonly neat. If it's obvious that you're conscientious and responsible, the neighbors may still think you're odd, but they won't have any genuine cause for complaint.

What do you have to work with?

As with any landscaping project, designing your front yard involves making the most of your site and situation. Start by taking a fresh look at what's there now, reconsidering how you currently use the space, and imagining what you might do there instead and how you would like it to look.

FIX UP THE HARDSCAPE. If you need or want to do any construction in the front yard—repaving the driveway, moving or widening the front walk, adding or rebuilding a gracious landing at the entry, building or repairing steps or a retaining wall—get all that work done before you get serious about planting. Except for trees and big old shrubs or woody vines, most plants are relatively short-lived and portable compared with hardscape, so it takes priority. Furthermore, the size, scale, style, and function of the house and hardscape are the basis for designing plantings in your front yard. So build first, then plant around what you've built.

EVALUATE AND ACT ON THE EXISTING PLANTS. Plants that are already established in your front yard may be an asset or an obstacle. Stand and look toward the front of the house as you evaluate each plant in terms of size—does it look inappropriately large or small, compared with the house; placement—does it rub against the house, block your view, crowd a walkway or entry, or stand alone or too far off in any direction; and color—do its flowers or foliage clash with the house?

Looking at the big picture, the yard as a whole, which plants grab your attention? Do you notice them for a good reason, because they're gorgeous or radiant or unique, or because there's something wrong about them? You'll want to feature any fine plants, but don't hesitate to get rid of the clunkers.

Which, if any, plants have the potential for anchoring a redesign and serving as starting points for making combinations? Anything that's well sited, shapely, and healthy deserves consideration, even if it's not an exciting plant. It's there, it's bigger than what you could buy to replace it, and you can use it as a background and expand around it.

Working around existing plants is a two-step process. It's hard to imagine the future while you're looking at the past. First make a clean sweep, then try to start over. Do an assessment and determine what you want to do with each plant—save, protect, prune, transplant, or remove it—then follow through on those decisions. Once everything is spruced up and only the chosen survivors are still in view, you'll be better able to appreciate what you have and to visualize a plan that will work around it.

HOW BIG IS THE AREA? The less distance there is between your house and the street, the less sense it makes to subdivide the area into "next to the house" and "farther away." If space is limited, use it all. Develop the whole front yard, not just a strip next to the house.

The goal of using all available space applies to large yards, too, and it's always good to think and plan in terms of the big picture. For larger yards it will take longer to carry out your plans, because there's more work involved, but don't let that inhibit you. If you envision a front yard that includes several hardscape and planting projects, you can complete them one at a time over a period of months or years.

Here's one way to think about areas. Look at your house from across the street, or look at a photo taken from that point of view. How big is the face of the house, including its roof? Use that area to set the scale, and imagine filling a comparable area on the ground with plantings. If the house is large and the lot is small, this affirms that you should go ahead and develop the whole yard, to achieve a sense of balance.

If your front yard is dominated by a driveway, the best design solution is to counteract the "nothingness" of the driveway with big plants or large plantings that are unified by a color theme and by

These Phoenix home-owners replaced the front part of their lawn with spring-blooming wildflowers. To reassure the neighbors, the remaining lawn is impeccably groomed and there's plenty of hard edging and pavement to confine the "wild" plants.

repeated use of a few kinds of plants or of certain plant habits or textures. See page 61.

When designing a front yard and laying out plantings, you're more likely to err on the side of being too timid than too bold. Think big. You might protest the "think big" advice because you've seen yards where everything looks too crowded and the plants seem to overwhelm the house. Over decades, that can happen, yes. Plants do keep growing and growing. But even in that case, the problem may not be that the areas originally outlined for planting were too big or even that individual plants are too big now. More often it's that there are too many plants too close together. If you thin some of them out, the remaining ones might look just right.

HOW MUCH LAWN OR OPEN SPACE DO YOU NEED OR WANT? In most American neighborhoods, it's uncommon to actually use the front yard as a place to relax, play, or entertain. If you're not going to spend time there, why preserve any of the area as lawn? If the only time you walk on your front lawn is to mow, fertilize, or care for it, perhaps you don't need grass there.

It's true that a lawn can serve a useful design role as negative space, and its fine texture contrasts with adjacent plantings. But a fine-textured ground

cover could serve a similar purpose and requires less care. Which ground cover to use in a case such as this is an important decision. Does it have to sustain occasional foot traffic? Should it be evergreen? Would you like it to stay as short as a lawn, or can it grow up around your ankles or even taller? Some ground covers can be mowed from time to time, to keep them uniformly low and neat. See page 321 for more on replacing lawn with ground cover.

If you have more lawn than you need or enjoy but don't want to get rid of it altogether, convert some of it into planting beds where you can grow flowering shrubs, perennials, or whatever you want, and retain wide strips of lawn as pathways. If you enjoy gardening and want to get out there to admire and care for your plants, you'll need the convenient access and durable surface that grass paths provide; no ground cover is as traffic-proof as turf. The trick here is to use your lawn mower to lay out the shapes of the paths and beds, to make sure any curves are easy to negotiate.

On level sites, you can replace an area of lawn with pavement or gravel, but don't do this until you've thought it through carefully. A paved or graveled surface glares and gets hot in the sun, and it's *not* carefree. You have to rake or sweep away leaves, twigs, and other plant debris that lands there, and

Perfect for busy people, this simple planting requires just a few hours of annual care, looks good year-round, and will satisfy for years before it looks crowded or dated. The dark green conifers and purple-leaved barberry foliage coordinate with the house. Including a few pink dahlias and mums, while optional, adds welcome highlights.

(RIGHT): *Summer is short in this Colorado ski town, so you have to make the most of it. Like an alpine meadow, this yard is packed with flowers. The colors are especially vivid at high altitude and suit the brightly painted house. A rail fence lets passersby enjoy the blooms but keeps these out of reach.*

(BELOW): *Building a wall or fence in front of your house enhances your privacy but may be interpreted as antisocial or unneighborly. To contradict that impression, fill the area between the wall and the street with generous masses of flowers as a goodwill gesture.*

you may have to pull weeds. Removing pavement or gravel is a tiresome job if you change your mind about it later. It makes sense to use gravel or decomposed rock as a mulch for natural-style plantings in arid climates, but in conventional plantings or rainy climates, you'd probably be happier replacing lawn with a ground cover instead.

WHAT HAPPENS ALONG THE STREET?
Streetside planting is limited in some situations. If there's a strip of ground between the street and the sidewalk, inquire about local restrictions before you even think about doing anything there. You might be welcome to proceed as you wish; more likely, you'll need to keep plants under a certain height, choose from a limited list of recommended plants, or follow other guidelines.

Even if there's no sidewalk and your yard runs uninterrupted to the edge of the street or road, you may have to work around other challenges, such as a roadside drainage ditch or swale that occasionally floods, a highway supervisor who insists on mowing or spraying the roadsides every summer, snowplows and possibly road salt in winter, or careless motorists who drive off the pavement and park on your yard. What it adds up to is this: Don't plant delicate or valuable plants where they're liable to get hurt. Use plants that are tough and resilient, quick to rebound from untoward treatment, to make a streetside buffer zone. Plants that spread underground and grow back from the roots if they're accidentally cut down or knocked over are good candidates; this group includes some shrubs and some vines as well as many perennials, wildflowers, and grasses.

How about putting some kind of marker, barrier, or screen between yourself and the road? It doesn't have to be (but could be) an opaque fence or dense hedge that's tall enough to totally enclose you from public view. A picket, rail, or iron fence will do, or any planting that's high and/or wide enough that you can't step over it. Even marking just the corners helps define an edge and gives you something to work back from. Again, you'll need to check about possible restrictions on maximum height and minimum setback for anything you want to put by a street or road, but if you get the go-ahead, give this some serious consideration. For more on fences, hedges, and screening, see page 193.

Dressing a house with plants

In evaluating existing plants or thinking about where you'd put new ones, it helps to have a drawing that's just a silhouette or profile of the house itself. You can make this by taking a photo and then tracing just the lines of the house, ground, and hardscape onto a blank sheet of paper. Omit all the existing plants when you first make the tracing, then draw in, one at a time, the ones you want to preserve and work around. Looking at a simple drawing that shows how your house would look *without* any unwanted plants will help reassure and motivate you to proceed with taking them away, and it's the starting point for planning what you might grow there instead. Likewise, if you have no or few plants around the house now, a photo or tracing is very helpful as a tool for designing new plantings.

Although you need to follow up with other planning strategies—a scale drawing on paper, a mockup on the ground, or both—to get the final positions and spacing right, tracing on photos is a great way to begin the design process, since the goal here is to present the public with an attractive portrait or picture of your house "dressed" with flattering plants. You might run through half a tablet of tracing paper before you settle on the ideal design, but it's a fast, fun, and easy way to try different alternatives.

TREES AND HOUSES. When you see trees and a house in the same picture, you react to their relative sizes and the distance between them, and also to the placement and shape of the trees compared with the house's roofline.

In terms of height, it looks normal and balanced if the trees in your yard are somewhat taller than the longer dimension—height or width—of the front of the house. Of course, it may take years or decades for trees to grow that tall and they'll look small in the meantime, but you'll cheer them on. On the other hand, when the surrounding trees are much taller

than a house, they dwarf it and become the center of attention. That's okay if the surrounding trees are part of a majestic forest or grand estate, but in typical suburban neighborhoods a too-tall tree seems hulking or intimidating, as if daring you to challenge its dominance. Go ahead; if you have a too-tall tree and don't like it, have it removed.

Along with too-tall trees, too-close trees are troublesome. They crowd uncomfortably against a house and can even damage it, and they get in the way, make it too dark inside, and limit what else you can grow. It looks better and *is* better if a tree is far enough away that there's some open space between its crown and the siding or roof of the house; they definitely shouldn't rub together.

If you're thinking about planting one or more trees around your house, use the trace-on-a-picture method to determine their ideal height and place-

A tree too close to a house eventually leads to trouble. This big old beech is sound and healthy, but it's rubbing against the eaves.

your house. It looks welcoming and gracious if you extend plantings out along those lines, as if your house were standing with outstretched arms. Whatever you plant there will seem to reach out toward the street and lead your eye from the house down to the ground. Using this angled position looks more casual and natural than setting plants square in front of the house. Starting at the corners is also important because corners are such strategic positions. They anchor and frame what you see from any side of the house, and they mark the transition from one side to another, which often corresponds to a transition from public to more private space.

A corner or diagonal planting bed will be shaped like a peninsula. How far out should it extend, and what shape should it be? Relate the length of the bed to the height of the house and stake that out first, then adjust the width and outline. For a one-story house, a bed might reach out 10 feet or so, far enough to encompass a small tree or tall shrub and some shorter plants. For a two-story house, the bed could reach out 20 to 30 feet and include a larger tree and masses of shrubs, perennials, and ground covers. Include a pathway as a shortcut through any corner bed that sticks out so far that you don't want to walk around it.

DON'T HIDE A PRETTY HOUSE. If your house is well designed and carefully built, it could stand alone, simply rising up from the ground. Some houses look best this way. I especially like to see beautiful masonry in full view, unhidden by plants. Outstanding wood construction is worth showing off, too. With a fine specimen of a house, the thing to do is reveal it and frame it, not hide it or block it. Or if there's a special feature or detail on your house — a carved door, a broad porch, a leaded window, a stone chimney, a tile roof, whatever it might be — display it, don't hide it. Keep plants off to the side, down below, or far enough in front that you can see around and behind them.

Instead of screening a pretty house, frame it with trees that will grow taller than its roofline, set behind it and off to the sides. Or plant masses of shrubs far out in the yard, back in the corners of your lot, or as screening around the perimeter to help balance the visual weight of the house.

In front of the house, keep things simple. Lawn, pavement, or a low ground cover can carpet the full front yard. Use low shrubs along the main walkway or beside the front door. If you want something taller, choose a small tree with an interesting silhouette — a multitrunked specimen with a narrow crown would be good — and position it at least half its height in front of the house, so that you can see the house behind it. Surround the tree with a bed of ground cover, or combine it with one or more low, spreading shrubs and a big rock. Keep the planting simple, though, and secondary to the house.

This pink dogwood looks okay now because it's young and slim, but it will outgrow that space within a few years. It would have been better to plant it on the other side of the walk so it could spread naturally and develop its characteristic horizontal branch pattern without impinging on the house.

ment. In addition, sketch trees with different shape crowns — fastigiate (erect and skinny), conical (like a spruce), vase-shaped (like an elm), round, oval, spreading, weeping, or irregular — and see which shape looks best in conjunction with your house's roofline and shape. It often looks better if the tree's profile contrasts with that of the house, rather than repeating it. For example, consider rounded or oval trees for boxy houses, and upright trees for sprawling, ranch-type houses.

If your goal is to shade the house with one or more trees, see page 102.

WORK OUT FROM THE CORNERS. This is a simple but helpful tip for getting started with planting around a house on an empty lot. Imagine diagonal lines running out from the front corners of

Two views of the same yard show wise placement of plants. (LEFT): *The birch tree is set far enough out from the house to avoid conflict and provide screening.* (BELOW): *A bed of low cotoneasters runs along the main walk, joining the birch to the bed of low and narrow evergreens that decorate the front of the house without overwhelming it.*

FOUNDATION PLANTINGS. The idea of planting shrubs to hide a house's foundation originated in Victorian architecture and sentiment, when houses were huge and their owners had an exaggerated notion of modesty. Later it became design dogma that you need a row of shrubs to "tie down" a house and "connect" it to the ground. Now sheared shrubbery is as ubiquitous as mowed lawns in American landscapes.

Some house foundations truly are ugly or incongruous and *should* be hidden. Using plants is an obvious way to do it, although you might work wonders with paint, stucco, siding, or lattice instead. But on most 20th-century houses the foundations are quite low and inconspicuous. If there's nothing to hide, why plant shrubs there? It's purposeless. Of course, you *can* copy this stereotyped style, but you don't *have to*. Again it's a question of community attitudes. If all the other houses in your neighborhood are ringed with a "green caterpillar" of sheared evergreens, you may hesitate to uproot yours (you could modify it, though, by widening the bed and putting other plants in front of the existing evergreens; see below). But if you don't feel duty-bound to uphold the conventional standard, you can pursue other options with your front yard.

If you want or feel you need a foundation planting, conforming to neighborhood standards is pretty straightforward. Look at the plantings around other houses on your side of the street (not across the street, as those plantings have a different exposure), find out what the plants are, and notice where and how they're used—at the corners, along the front, under windows, and so forth. Then copy what you see, putting the same plants in the same places in your yard.

To design a custom planting, see the box on page 94.

WIDENING A FOUNDATION BED. Two common problems with existing foundation plantings, typically sheared evergreen shrubs, are that they are too narrow and don't extend far enough out in front of the house, and that they're too static. You can solve both problems at once by expanding the bed. Bring it several feet farther out into the yard and extend it diagonally out from the corners of the house. Then add more plants.

A ready-made evergreen background is really quite an asset, and your boring old foundation planting might be the beginning of a great new garden. It's much easier to design a planting to be seen primarily from one point of view—the street side in this case—against an established background than to create a freestanding island.

Don't start digging the new bed immediately in front of the shrubs, because their roots surely reach out farther than the sheared tops do. Leave a buffer

DESIGNING A FOUNDATION PLANTING

If you want to design a new foundation planting that's customized to your house, not copied from the neighborhood, use the trace-on-a-photo method and keep these tips in mind.

- How high is the foundation? The shortest plants should be about that tall.

- Set tall plants at the corners (on a diagonal out from the house) and at the main entry, and connect them with shorter plants in between.

- If the facade of the house isn't symmetrical, there's no reason for the planting to be.

- Unless you deliberately want to block the view in or out, choose shrubs that won't grow higher than the sill for planting in front of windows. Shrubs can be centered under the windows or not. Sketch your design both ways and see which looks better.

- The taller the house, the deeper the planting should be. A shallow row of shrubs around the bottom of a big tall house looks as inadequate as a bikini. Widen the planting bed. Make it reach farther out into the lawn, perhaps wrapping around a tree that's out there, and fill the newly expanded area with a low ground cover.

- Use repetition—multiples of the same plant, or plants with similar size, shape, habit, texture, and/or color—to unify and harmonize the planting. Keep contrast to a minimum here, remembering that the point of a foundation planting is not to call attention to itself but to frame and flatter the house. Also, keep focal points to a minimum. In terms of plants, include just one that counts as a focal point or, better yet, none at all. In this setting, the front door of the house should be the focal point.

- If you want a group of matching shrubs to merge together into a continuous block of green, plant them closer than usual to start with and shear their fronts and tops, but don't cut between them.

- If adjacent shrubs or plants are of different kinds, space and prune them so they don't push each other out of shape.

- Individual plants or groupings of like plants must be big enough to show up from a distance. Try this guideline: Make sure each plant or group is as big as the average window on the front side of your house. When viewed from the street, windows are big enough to show up clearly. Foundation plants should be that big, too.

- Although evergreens of all kinds (including conifers, broadleaved evergreens, evergreen vines, ground covers, and perennials) aren't the only choice for foundation plantings, they do set the standard. Deciduous trees and shrubs are welcome if they present a neat silhouette in winter; to do this, they need good natural growth habits and thoughtful thinning and pruning (not shearing, as sheared deciduous shrubs usually look unhealthy and abused in winter). Herbaceous plants leave a hole for months at a time when they go dormant; that's fine in other settings but questionable in a foundation planting, where it could too easily be interpreted that something's died or gone wrong. If you want to include some herbaceous perennials or annuals, choose kinds whose foliage stays healthy throughout the growing season, and position them carefully *after* you've laid out a basic framework of evergreens.

Traditional foundation plantings wrap around the base of a house. In this example there are about a dozen different kinds of evergreen and deciduous shrubs, some sheared and some natural, to provide a variety of textures and some seasonal color from flowers and leaves.

An established foundation planting, such as these clipped yews, makes a good background for a colorful border of flowering shrubs and perennials. You can't see it in the photo, but there's a narrow walk between the evergreens and flowers.

strip about 2 feet wide, and smother any turf there by covering it with overlapping sheets of newspaper topped with a layer of bark chips or other long-term mulch. This way you'll avoid damaging the shrubs' roots, and the mulched path will provide access so you can continue shearing the shrubs. Begin the new bed in front of the path. When viewed from the street side, you won't see the path; you'll see the new plants in front of it. The path probably will show when you're looking out from inside the house, but it won't be obtrusive, and it's a small price to pay for preserving healthy shrubs.

Focus on height, color, and texture when you're

choosing plants for the new bed. As for height, the new plants should mostly be shorter than the existing evergreens. If the evergreens are only knee-high, that might mean filling the bed with ground covers, creeping shrubs, or mat-forming perennials, but that's no problem—there are scores of colorful plants that happen to be short. And you could interrupt a bed of short plants with one or more specimens that stick up taller, especially if they're wispy or wandlike on top, like grasses and some flowering perennials, or if they're trees or shrubs pruned to reveal interesting bare trunks.

As for color and texture, choose plants that con-

This contemporary foundation planting was designed to combine the year-round presence of evergreen hollies and conifers with the freshness of pink impatiens and geraniums in summer.

Creeping fig fits against this old brick house like custom upholstery, but creating that look requires frequent clipping. If untended, this vine would obliterate the stairs and door and reach to the roof. Meanwhile, the railing makes a sturdy support for a yellow climbing rose.

A few horizontal wires provide adequate but almost invisible support for the tendrils of this flowering clematis vine.

trast with the static evergreens but coordinate with each other. You might start with a color theme that complements your house and look for flowers and foliage in those colors. Since sheared evergreens are basically fine-textured, stiff, and geometric, include some plants with large leaves, pliable or arching stems, or irregular profiles in the new expanded bed.

The front edge of the bed can be straight or curved; either way, it should be crisp and neat. If it abuts lawn, consider installing some kind of permanent edging or mowing strip. If the expanded foundation bed leads out to the main walkway or another paved area, prune as needed to keep adjacent plants from flopping or creeping too far onto the pavement.

VERTICAL PLANTINGS. Vines, climbing roses, and espaliered shrubs and trees are typically high-maintenance plants that need frequent training, tying up, pruning, and grooming. It's a tradeoff. Vertical plantings can be very beautiful, but caring for them is a labor of love, and they can become a nuisance. In particular, read the discussion of vines on page 311 before you make a commitment.

In terms of design, the advantage of vertical plantings lies in their shape: they're tall and flat. You can frame a doorway, screen a porch, or fill a blank space on the wall of the house, spreading the color and texture of leaves and blooms across an area many feet tall and wide with plants that stick out only a foot or so. Because their stems are relatively supple and trace arches and curves, not straight lines, vines are indispensable for "softening" the hard edges and flat surfaces of buildings, like swag draperies.

But be cautious. Keep any vines that climb by means of adhesive rootlets (such as English ivy, creeping fig, or climbing hydrangea) away from wooden walls and trim. It's okay to let clinging vines run up a brick or masonry wall or chimney, but stand ready to cut them back if they head toward a wooden surface or the roof.

Any other plants that you grow against a wall of your house—vines that climb by twining, tendrils, or scrambling, and espaliered shrubs and trees—will need some kind of support. This might be a trellis, a sheet of lattice, or heavy-gauge wire or polypropylene rope stretched vertically or horizontally between screw-eyes or masonry clips mounted on the wall. Always leave at least a few inches of space between the support and the wall, so air can circulate back there and so you can reach behind the support, if needed, to do painting or other maintenance.

Plan, build or buy, and install the support first. Then you can guide the plant into the desired shape as it grows. Lay some steppingstones so you can get to and stand at the base of a vertical plant whenever you need to work on it. Convenient access is important, as climbing roses need weekly attention during the growing season, and most vines and espaliers

Espaliers are trees, shrubs, or woody vines deliberately trained to grow flat against a wall. Their limbs have to be bent and tied into place when still young and tender, and they then harden in that position as they mature. Traditionally, espaliered limbs were spaced and set at definite angles. Now it's common to train them more informally and casually.

At first, espaliers are usually trained to horizontal wires or a wooden trellis or grid. After a few years they may grow stout enough to stand on their own against a wall without any support.

Espaliers need annual pruning and occasional trimming, grooming, and tying, repeated year after year. They're high-maintenance plants, but that's fun if you like to putter with them.

The following plants are good candidates for espaliering against a house wall, and they can be kept under 10 to 12 feet tall, so you can maintain them from a stepladder. Because growing conditions vary so much from one wall to another, monitor your intended site over a period of time and do some book research or get local advice before finalizing your plant selection.

- **Fruits.** Apple, crab apple, cherry, fig, peach, pear, and citrus trees are often grown as espaliers, partly because they fruit well if treated this way. Ask a nursery to help you choose a dwarf cultivar or a grafted plant grown on a dwarfing root-stock. **HARDINESS VARIES.**

- **Camellias** (*Camellia japonica, C. sasanqua,* and hybrids). Evergreen foliage; lush rose, pink, or white flowers in winter or spring. **ZONE 8 OR 7.**

- **Flowering quince** (*Chaenomeles* cvs.). 'Enchantress' (pink), 'Nivalis' (white), and 'Toyo Nishiki' (rose, pink, and white) are cultivars with upright growth habits suitable for espaliers. Deciduous, but the crooked stems look interesting in winter. **ZONE 4.**

- **Dogwoods** (*Cornus florida, C. kousa,* and others). White flowers in spring, red berries in fall, and garnet fall foliage. Deciduous. **ZONE 5.**

- **Rose-of-Sharon** (*Hibiscus syriacus).* Rose, pink, white, or blue-purple flowers in summer. Deciduous. **ZONE 5.**

- **Oakleaf hydrangea** (*Hydrangea quercifolia).* Terminal clusters of papery flowers open white in early summer and darken to a pinkish tan. Large lobed leaves turn garnet in fall. Stout twigs have russet bark that peels and curls. Deciduous. **ZONE 5.**

- **Winter jasmine** (*Jasminum nudiflorum).* Yellow flowers in late winter. Tiny leaves, but twigs have green bark. Deciduous. **ZONE 6.**

- **Magnolias** (*Magnolia* spp. and cvs.). Many kinds of magnolias stay under 10 to 15 feet tall and can be espaliered. Most deciduous kinds have white, pink, rosy purple, or creamy yellow flowers in spring. Evergreen magnolias have white flowers in summer. **HARDINESS VARIES.**

- **Pyracantha, or firethorn** (*Pyracantha* cvs.). Tough, thorny stems. Small evergreen leaves. Bright orange, red, or yellow berries last for months, from fall until new white flowers appear the next spring. 'Apache', 'Mohave', and 'Teton' grow upright and are suited for espalier. **ZONE 6.**

- **Yew pine** (*Podocarpus macrophyllus).* Evergreen conifer with relatively long, flat, dark green needles. **ZONE 8.**

- **Weeping conifers.** Weeping (often named 'Pendula') cultivars of various firs, cedars, spruces, and pines can be espaliered. Check the estimated growth rate and mature size and choose a slow-growing plant that won't overwhelm you.

A red-berried pyracantha looks dramatic against a white masonry wall. Training an espalier like this makes a good hobby. It doesn't take a lot of skill or time, just desire, patience, and persistence.

need care at least once a month in summer and perhaps a major once-over in winter or spring also.

The microclimates next to a house or other building offer a varied set of growing opportunities. Each side is unique, particularly in terms of light, temperature, and moisture. (See page 246.) There are big differences between north- and south-facing walls or between a dry strip that's sheltered by overhanging eaves and rarely gets rained on and another bed that gets soaked by runoff from the roof. On all sides, the soil near a house is usually compacted and infertile and needs thorough preparation before you plant anything.

Another point to remember is that ill-chosen or ill-placed plants can actually harm the roof, siding, and foundation of your house or other buildings. These problems are often insidious and develop slowly over several years before you notice something's wrong. Then the repair may be expensive. Going through or hearing about an experience like this makes people cautious about having plants near the house, yet most damage can be avoided by foresight, awareness, and routine inspection.

An underused advantage of planting next to the house is convenience. There's no better place for plants that you want to tend or enjoy often, on short notice. Put your "pet" plants right outside the door, so you can visit them in your slippers, and take advantage of the shelter and varied growing conditions near the house to grow small, tender, or fragile plants that wouldn't stand up farther out in the open.

Drainage and runoff

Any house should be sited and built with provisions for weathering an occasional deluge, and the same setup should cope easily with normal rain. If you have a problem with water pooling around your house or leaking into the basement, postpone landscaping and deal with the drainage problem first. Consult with local contractors and/or landscape architects to identify where the water is coming from and how to redirect it. The solution may require installing a system of gutters and drainpipes and/or buried drain lines, regrading the soil around the house to speed runoff, building channels and berms uphill from the house to avert water that's flowing toward it, or (messiest of all) digging to expose the exterior of the basement wall so it can be repaired and sealed. It's hard to imagine getting any of this work done without damaging any nearby plants.

SOIL MOISTURE. Hopefully you don't have any drainage problems and can think about growing conditions instead. What to look for is extremes.

(LEFT): *Snow slides off the steep roof of this house and attached sunroom and piles several feet deep in winter. This would crush a conventional evergreen foundation planting, so the area, which faces south, is filled with hardy perennials instead. Since the perennials are dormant in winter, the snow doesn't bother them, and they bloom happily in summer* (BELOW).

Building a new house invariably upsets the surrounding soil, and you have to compensate before you can plant anything there. Around older houses, too, the soil is usually quite compacted, infertile, and dotted with old junk and buried debris.

Even in a rainy climate, any soil that's sheltered by the house eaves, by a projecting roofline, or under the overhang of a second-story balcony or deck can be surprisingly dry. In addition, if rains typically come from one direction, the leeward side of the house will be drier than average. Dig a few test holes at different places near the house and out in the open to compare levels of soil moisture. Choose suitable plants for sites where the ground tends to stay dry; this is fairly easy for sites that get at least part sun, but there are few candidates for sites that are both dry and darkly shaded. (In that case, you may need to leave the immediate space empty and set plants farther away from the house where there's both more light and more moisture.) Plan to water as needed. A soaker hose is handy for routine watering of a narrow strip beside the house, but from time to time you'll want to water by hand or with a sprinkler to wash dust off the foliage.

While soil under an overhang gets quite dry, soil under the drip line of a roof that's not equipped with gutters gets extra wet during a rain. Where rain runs off a roof during a summer shower, it knocks down soft-stemmed plants, so choose stiff or resilient plants to grow under the drip line, or plant anything you choose but set it a little farther away from the house. Roof runoff will wash away most organic mulches and also splashes soil up against the house. Mulch the strip from the drip line to the house with gravel or rocks, or see if you can establish a low, dense, evergreen ground cover there. Test single plants of different ground covers to see how they perform for a year or so, then choose the winner and buy or propagate enough of that kind to fill the area.

SNOW PILE-UP. In snow country, identify where snow piles up as it slides off a steep roof or gets shoveled off a porch or sidewalk. Some shrubs and evergreens can eventually survive the burden of snow as they mature and their stems get strong, but as young plants they're liable to get crushed or broken. If you want to get shrubs established in a snow-prone site, you need to protect them for the first several winters after planting. Use an A-frame shelter made from two pieces of plywood hinged together at the top. Better yet, fill these sites with annuals or herbaceous perennials that die down to the ground in winter, ornamental grasses that you can cut down in fall or spring, deciduous shrubs that can be pruned severely every spring, and/or prostrate ground covers.

Soil beside a building

Unless you've already improved it, the ground next to your house is probably dense, compacted, and infertile. Maybe the "soil" is just fill dirt that was added to adjust the grade when the house was built, or sand and gravel added to speed drainage. It might look smooth on top but be loaded with construction debris or buried junk below. Because lime leaches out of fresh concrete, the soil around a new house tends to be alkaline, even if your native soil is typically acid; this extra alkalinity persists for several years.

Don't expect plants to grow there until you've done some groundwork. Follow the general guidelines for soil preparation (see page 277). Start with a spade or fork and dig cautiously, watching closely for buried utilities. Don't use a rototiller near a house until you're sure the site is hazard-free. Seek local advice on what amendments to add and how much of each to use, depending on what soil you're starting with and what plants you want to grow. After you're done loosening and amending the soil, carefully rake the bed to restore its previous grade, and be sure it pitches down away from the house.

SOIL CONTAMINATION. Under certain specific circumstances, the soil beside a house may be contaminated. The soil around an old wood house may have a high lead content owing to chips of paint that have flaked or been scraped off and settled into the ground. Where termites are common, there may be insecticide residues around an old wood house that's been sprayed heavily and repeatedly. Acid rain can leach arsenic from a pressure-treated wood deck (see page 114).

If you're in one of these situations and you fear there might be soil contamination around your house, check the Yellow Pages and call an environmental lab for directions on how to collect a soil sample and have it tested. They can interpret the test results and give you advice. In general, such contamination poses little risk if the soil remains undisturbed, but there might be problems if pets or children were tempted to play in a newly worked bed.

And although there's virtually no chance that plants would absorb anything from the soil, play it safe anyway and plant only ornamentals, not edible plants, in a contaminated area.

RAISED BEDS AND CONTAINERS. Where the existing soil is extremely poor, you can create much better conditions by building a raised bed and filling it with purchased soil. This would involve making a retaining wall (see page 214) around the front and sides of the bed and using the house foundation as the back side. Check with a local building inspector before you pursue such a project. Raising the soil level against the outside of a house is unwise if there are termite problems in your area.

Growing plants in containers (see page 124) is another way to get around the problem of poor soil next to a house. Shrubs or even small trees can live for many years in large planters or tubs, yet these freestanding containers don't involve the cost, commitment, or risk of raised foundation beds. Pots or containers that are small enough to be portable are especially good for seasonal plantings that you want to rearrange continually. It's quite easy to install a drip irrigation system (see page 267) if you can't keep up with the frequent watering that containers need.

Large, built-in planters are the best solution if extremely poor soil, pavement, or steep terrain make it difficult to plant next to a house.

Use window boxes, pots, and planters to grow herbs and other plants where pavement covers the soil next to a house.

Convenience

No place is better than right next to the house for plants that you want to monitor closely and visit often. These could be herbs or salad vegetables that you harvest, roses and other flowers to admire and pick, any plants you collect, or seedlings or other baby plants that you've propagated. If you love bird watching, put a feeder and birdbath right outside your favorite window and plant shrubs where the birds can perch and rest.

Although you can expand them to fill the space available, any of these special plantings can fit into a corner or run lengthwise along the side, back, or front of a house—wherever there's space and the exposure is suitable. In any case, you'll enjoy them most if you lay a path or steppingstones for access so you can walk there without having to cross wet grass or change your shoes.

HERBS AND TREATS. Beside the kitchen door is the traditional place to grow culinary herbs. That's for good reason: You'll use them much more than if you had to walk across the yard to get them. If the plants are nearby, you can even run out in your robe and slippers in the morning to get some parsley and chives for a breakfast omelet. Plant herbs along any unshaded east, south, or west wall. Most herb plants are fairly small and you need only one or a few of each kind, so you can tuck them in among other, larger plants.

If you love to cook, or simply to snack on fresh produce, consider a tiny kitchen garden along a sunny wall. Boost the soil with lots of compost for maximum productivity. (Remember that the soil on most sites is perfectly safe for growing food; if you unfortunately have contaminated soil, cover it with gravel or some kind of paving and grow edible plants in containers.) Cherry tomatoes, chili peppers, salad greens, and everbearing strawberries and raspberries are desirable choices. They produce bountifully—a single cherry tomato plant may yield more than you can eat, and a 4-foot-square patch of salad greens is enough to feed any family. You can harvest from these plants repeatedly over a long season, and they're good-looking, easy, and fun to grow.

ROSES. Roses are excellent shrubs for sunny east, south, and west walls, and a few roses can tolerate part shade and will even grow against a north wall. You'll get daily pleasure from their flowers and fragrance, and it will be easy to keep up with deadheading, pruning, watering, and pest and disease control. Most roses are fast-growing and there are scores of cultivars, both new and old-fashioned, that are remarkably trouble-free and rewarding.

Choosing is the hard part, as there are so many wonderful roses. Look for a long season of bloom (some roses flower almost continually from late spring until hard frost), disease-resistant foliage, hardiness (although the microclimate next to your house is more protected than open areas of the yard and you may succeed here with roses that would otherwise freeze), height and spread (allow plenty of space, as most roses reach full size in just a few grow-

Roses wind through the porch rail and climb the corner post in this impeccably groomed garden.

ing seasons; because they're thorny, you don't want them to spread too far and get in your way, nor do you want to have to keep cutting them back), and flower color (coordinate it with your house walls).

A COLLECTION OF SMALL PLANTS. If you're obsessed with any group such as dwarf conifers, succulents and cacti, or alpines or with a genus such as daylilies, hostas, or irises, you'll want to check your "babies" first thing in the morning, as soon as you get home from work, and whenever you get a chance. If there's a promising site beside the house, plant your favorites right there. You'll get immeasurable pleasure, and the collection will be an excellent conversation piece to share with visitors.

If your plants are too small, too many, and too varied to look good from across the yard, as usually happens with a collection, do this: Immediately next to the house, plant a dense row of upright-growing evergreens to make a solid background, or let evergreen vines climb up onto a masonry foundation or brick wall to make a curtain of green. This simple evergreen backdrop will look fine from a distance. Widen the bed in front of it to accommodate your collection, and enjoy your special plants from up close.

A NURSERY BED. Any extra-small plants that you buy, along with seedlings, rooted cuttings, and

other plants you propagate yourself, need more frequent watering and attention than larger, older plants do. They also need extra shelter from hot sun, dry wind, and stormy weather. A cold frame or raised bed set against the house is a safe and handy place for a little nursery. This of course might look out of place against the front of a house, but if you've got space against a less conspicuous side or rear wall, why not use it for something you'd enjoy? And like any other collection, a bed of little plants you've grown yourself is a fun feature to show to your friends.

Trees for summer shade

If your house has several large windows on the south and west sides that cause heat buildup on sunny summer days, well-sited deciduous trees can provide welcome shade and natural air conditioning. But it's one thing to appreciate the advantages of natural shade if your house is already protected by well-sited trees; it's something else to plant trees to shade a new house.

It takes years for even a fast-growing tree to get tall enough to provide much shade. Normally, deferred gratification is no reason not to plant a tree, but if you're going to need curtains, blinds, or the like to shade a window while a tree is growing, why not rely on these indefinitely? Or instead of using a tree, you could shade a window more directly with a large nearby shrub or a vine-covered trellis or overhead structure.

Don't rush out and plant a tree solely for the purpose of shading a house. Trees get too big and have too much impact on the landscape. You need to consider other factors than shade when choosing and siting a tree.

SITING A SHADE TREE. To think it through, first decide where you'd need a tree by standing by a window at the hottest time of day. Face toward the sun, look down at the ground, and imagine a line that runs between you and the sun. Follow that line out at least 10 to 15 feet from the house for a small shade tree and at least 25 feet for most trees, then go drive a stake in the ground to mark the tentative planting spot. Repeat this process from other windows or other parts of the house, or at different times of day, if you want more shade.

Now respond to each stake and consider what it

ATTRACTING BIRDS

Birds will come right up to your house to seek food, water, and shelter, and it's wonderful to get a close look at them. Start by putting up a feeder, but don't mount it permanently at first, as you may have to move it a few times before you find the ideal location. You'd like to watch birds outside the window where you spend the most time, but since you need to refill a busy feeder every day or so and to take it down to clean it from time to time, it should also be easy to get at—not on the far side of the house, in a bed of prickly junipers, or where snow drifts up in winter. Bird preference is an inscrutable factor, but undeniable. Sometimes birds will ignore a feeder in one position, but if you move it 20 feet away they'll flock to it. So if the first place you put it isn't optimal, keep moving the feeder until you find the right place.

You don't have to arrange a smorgasbord. Hulled sunflower seeds attract all kinds of seed-eating birds, and there's very little waste or litter to accumulate on the ground. If you provide sunflower seeds through the summer as well as winter, you'll get to see a whole different assortment of birds when the migrants are present and to watch parents and their chicks. In cold weather, put out some suet to attract woodpeckers and other insect-eating birds, but take the suet feeder down in spring because when the greasy suet gets soft it can damage their feathers. Add a hummingbird feeder from spring to fall.

Along with seeds, birds really appreciate a shallow basin of fresh water for drinking and bathing. In cold climates, using a heater to keep the water open in winter draws many extra bird visitors.

Birds need a place to perch while they're waiting their turn at a feeder or birdbath; a nearby tree or tall shrub is preferred, although they'll land atop a fence or even on the roof sometimes. For shelter at night and on stormy days, they seek out evergreens, especially dense, prickly conifers.

If you have a cat that catches songbirds, don't keep a feeder; it isn't fair. If birds that are attracted to a feeder keep flying against one of your windows, try moving the feeder closer to the house; that usually reduces the number of crashes. And if squirrels, crows, or jays are driving you crazy, try one of the new feeder models designed to repel these unwanted seed eaters.

Attract chickadees and other birds to your window by providing a basin of clean water, a feeder stocked with seeds, and brushy shrubs for shelter.

implies. Is that a suitable place to plant a tree? Do you want a tree there? Would it block a good view or hide the house from the street? A tree that shades the house will also shade the yard—do you want shade in that area? If everything works out and you think a tree sited to provide shade would also serve other roles and wouldn't get in the way, then go ahead.

CHOOSING A SHADE TREE. A shade tree should be deciduous, so it doesn't block welcome winter sun (although it's surprising how much shade even deciduous trees cast in winter; look at the long shadows they cast). It needs to grow about 25 feet tall to shade the windows and roof of a one-story house and 40 feet or taller for a two-story house. In the world of trees, those are considered small or medium size. You don't need a huge, towering tree just to shade a house, and trees that reach forest proportions are usually much too large for an average yard.

There's little to be gained from buying a large specimen tree. Even the largest tree that can be moved is too small to provide much shade. Getting shade from a tree takes patience. You'll have to wait at least five to ten years, and over that interval a tree planted from a 5-gallon can will catch up with and usually surpass an expensive, boxed specimen.

Be skeptical of cheap, fast-growing species touted as instant shade trees, such as silver maples; most willows, cottonwoods, and poplars; fruitless mulberries; and Siberian elms. These trees do grow fast, but they're generally undesirable. Their wood is typically weak, brittle, and vulnerable to storms. They're also subject to various insects and disease problems. It's better to invest in a quality tree that's strong and healthy, and some of these desirable trees (see the box on page 105) grow almost as quickly as the trashy ones do.

Study the guidelines on page 285 for more information and directions on planting and caring for a tree. See the list on page 119 for smaller, slow-growing trees suitable for shading a patio.

Site an oak or other large shade tree at least 25 feet away from the house, on the south or southwest side, in order to shade the windows from the heat of the afternoon summer sun.

RECOMMENDED DECIDUOUS SHADE TREES

If you want to plant shade trees to cool your home and shade part of the yard, here are some good candidates to consider. All are readily available in the areas where they grow well, and they're healthy, trouble-free, and shapely. These trees grow fairly quickly but don't have the weak wood and breakage problems usually associated with fast-growing species. All grow to about 40 feet or taller. They cast adequate shade in summer but don't drop burdensome amounts of leaves in fall. Check with local nurseries to determine which of these trees are best suited to your site.

- **Red maple** (*Acer rubrum*). Showy red flowers in very early spring; red leaves in fall. 'October Glory' is an outstanding cultivar. Prefers moist soil. **ZONE 4**.

- **River birch** (*Betula nigra*). Yellow fall color. Curly peeling bark is eye-catching in winter. 'Heritage' is a very popular cultivar. Tolerates wet sites. **ZONE 5**.

- **European hornbeam** (*Carpinus betulus*). Yellow fall foliage. Tolerates dry sites. **ZONE 5**.

- **Yellowwood** (*Cladrastis lutea*). Sweet white flowers in early summer; yellow fall color. Prefers good soil. **ZONE 3**.

- **Green ash** (*Fraxinus pennsylvanica*). Yellow fall color. Buy only seedless cultivars, such as 'Marshall's Seedless' or 'Summit'. Tolerates poor soil. **ZONE 3**.

- **Thornless honey locust** (*Gleditsia triacanthos* var. *inermis*). Fine-textured foliage casts a light shade. Yellow fall color. 'Moraine' and 'Shademaster' are good cultivars. **ZONE 4**.

- **Kentucky coffee tree** (*Gymnocladus dioica*). Picturesque in winter, with thick twigs and ridged bark. Fragrant greenish flowers in early summer; gold fall foliage. Female plants make interesting pods. **ZONE 4**.

- **Silver-bells** (*Halesia carolina*, a.k.a. *H. tetraptera*, and *H. monticola*). Dangling white (rarely pink) flowers in spring; nice bark and silhouette in winter. **ZONE 4**.

- **Chinese pistache** (*Pistacia chinensis*). Good for fall color, even in warm climates. Tolerates poor, dry soil. **ZONE 7**.

- **Sargent cherry** (*Prunus sargentii*). A beautiful cherry, the best for most yards. Pink flowers in spring; vivid fall foliage; rich brown bark. **ZONE 5**.

- **Oaks** (*Quercus* spp.). Many oaks make fine shade trees. Get local advice about which oak would do best in your climate and soil.

- **Scholartree** (*Sophora japonica*). Fragrant white flowers in early summer; bright green, compound leaves; green twigs in winter. **ZONE 5**.

- **Littleleaf linden** (*Tilia cordata*). Small, very fragrant flowers in early summer. 'Greenspire' is a good cultivar. **ZONE 3**.

- **Lacebark, or Chinese, elm** (*Ulmus parvifolia*). Flaking, multicolored bark is distinctive. Small, dark green leaves hang on until late fall. Disease-resistant. **ZONE 5**.

A private, airy room like this invites you to spend more time outdoors. Here the extensive brick flooring continues farther away from the house, and the size and shape of the room are defined by the rectangular trellis overhead.

4 ❧ Outdoor Rooms

An OUTDOOR ROOM is a place to rest, eat, entertain, play, or work outdoors. It can be a simple concrete patio furnished with a few chairs and a barbecue grill, a warm brick terrace surrounded by trellised vines and climbing roses, an elaborate split-level deck built under a splendid old tree, or a shady glade with a soft wood-chip floor and a rustic twig bench. Whatever it is, an outdoor room is likely to be the most-used part of your yard. It's wonderful how much time you spend outdoors—and how much you enjoy it!—when you have a convenient, comfortable place to go.

An outdoor room can also enhance the view from indoors. Looking out through a window or doorway, you'll appreciate the overall architecture, thoughtful details in the construction, special ornaments you've collected, and favorite plants you've gathered nearby.

If you don't have an outdoor room yet, this chapter covers what to think about when designing and planning a new one and getting it built. The focus is on simple rooms that are open to the air. In these rooms, the main element is the floor. To wall or outline the area and provide screening for privacy and shelter, you might build a fence, put up a lattice or trellis, plant a hedge, or grow plants in pots and planters. For shade, you could locate the room under an existing tree, plant a shade tree, or build a wooden overhead structure or arbor to support vines.

Part of the pleasure of using an outdoor room depends on how you've furnished and equipped it. There are lots of possibilities regarding seating, tables, storage, fireplaces and grills, kitchen or bar setups, lighting, and so on. I'm not sure these furnishings count as landscaping, so I'll leave choosing them up to you. However, I will include swimming pools, reflecting pools, fountains, or water gardens here and talk about landscaping around them.

❧ DESIGNING AN OUTDOOR ROOM

Deciding on the placement, size, shape, and style of an outdoor room can be quite straightforward, especially if you're thinking of something simple, but sometimes you have to work around challenges posed by the house or the site. At any rate, it's worth thinking through some alternative plans before you make a final decision.

If they're adjacent, coordinate the outdoor room with the house itself in terms of design, style, and materials, as you would if you were building an addition. There's more freedom in designing rooms that are set apart; make the playhouse of your dreams out there. In either case, check every aspect of construction, material selection, and finishing to make sure the room will hold up to your climate and won't require extensive maintenance, since you want to spend time enjoying the space, not caring for it.

Whether you plan to build it yourself or hire a contractor, contact the local building inspector before you go very far with your planning. Find out if you need to apply for a building permit and, if so, what kind of plan you need to submit. Ask about zoning laws and building codes, and don't hesitate to pick the inspector's brain for advice about foundations, materials, and finishes. Likewise, as you talk to potential contractors and shop at lumberyards and home-improvement centers, solicit opinions on how different designs and techniques function in your climate and get feedback on what would look and work best with your house. These professionals will point out possibilities and pitfalls you wouldn't have thought of, particularly if you are new to the region and have moved in from another part of the country.

As you're planning, think about where you'd like to have outdoor lights, the switches that control

Nestled against a dramatic rock outcrop and flower garden, this free-form flagstone terrace is the perfect getaway for summer evenings, furnished with comfortable chairs, lanterns, and a freestanding fireplace.

them, electrical outlets, and water taps or irrigation lines, so these utilities can be installed and buried as construction proceeds and won't have to be added later.

Although it's definitely worth taking the extra care to work around existing trees or noteworthy old shrubs, it's generally best to ignore existing plants when you're designing an outdoor room and to clear them out of the way when doing the construction. Once the hardscape is finished, you can turn to soil preparation and replanting. But think continually about the potential for incorporating plants as you design an outdoor room. Leave space for borders around the edge. Consider built-in planters that are large enough for small trees, shrubs, and other permanent plantings, and plan on plenty of portable containers for smaller plants and seasonal displays.

Choosing the site

Location is everything in real estate, and it certainly affects how much you'll use and enjoy an outdoor room. Which side of your house offers the best exposure, where you would go to enjoy good weather? Is there a door now on that side of the house? If not, could a carpenter make a doorway there? Perhaps you could design a room that wraps around two sides of the house, including the side where the door

is. Or you could make a walkway to connect the ideal site and the closest door.

It would be wonderful if your outdoor room offered a great view of some scenic vista and if the setting was peaceful and private. If you have those assets, site the room to take advantage of them. Unfortunately, many lots offer neither vista nor privacy. That's okay. You can create both your own backdrop and a sense of seclusion by surrounding the room, at least partially, with a fence, hedge, trellis, or some other outdoor "wall."

CHECK ABOUT SETBACKS. Setback codes may restrict your options. Most apply to decks, not necessarily to ground-level patios. Ask locally about minimum setbacks between any construction and the property line. If any side of the house is already close to a lot line, there may not be enough space to add an outdoor room there.

CONNECTED OR DETACHED? An outdoor room can adjoin the house or be set apart. The closer the better, in terms of convenience. You're much more likely to step out into an adjacent room than to walk even 20 feet farther away, and more likely to carry food or supplies with you. If an outdoor room is too far away, you won't take advantage of it.

But despite the inconvenience, there are a few

situations where you might consider building a free-standing patio or deck. One is to preserve the dignity of an older house or to avoid clashing with any house that has a distinctive architectural style. Another is to keep from damaging or having to remove valuable plants that are established around the house. If the ground right around the house is sloping, you might prefer a level site farther away. Or you might deliberately seek the seclusion and privacy of a remote, hidden site, and it would give you a destination to go to.

ROOMS AS PASSAGES. An outdoor room can be a cul-de-sac, a place where you go, turn around, and come back. Often, though, it functions like a landing or a wide spot in the road. If there's a place where you now step out the door onto a simple walkway, imagine what it would be like to have a room there instead. You could still walk back and forth and get where you need to go, but the area would seem bigger and more inviting as you passed through it. For example, you could walk across a patio and out into your backyard, or go out from the kitchen onto a deck and then step down to the driveway, or come up the main walk to an entry terrace and then into the front door. This kind of transition is so pleasant that you may end up with outdoor rooms outside every door!

TOPOGRAPHY AND LEVELS. The nature of the site determines what kind of floor you can build and may affect where you decide to put an outdoor room. On sloping ground, you can't pour a concrete slab for a patio or lay any kind of masonry without doing some grading first. This may not be a big job —you might even do it yourself—but it may be unaffordable or undoable if the area is too large, the slope is too steep, the soil is unstable, or the site is hard to get at and the soil would have to be brought in or hauled away by wheelbarrow rather than by truck.

If the ground near your house slopes but there's a level site farther away, you might opt for a detached terrace or patio and make a walkway that leads to it. Otherwise, build a deck or porch. Working with wood is the easy way to create a level floor on a sloping site; that's one of the many reasons why decks are so popular. Of course, the steeper the site, the trickier it will be to build there, but you can find a deck contractor who will enjoy this kind of challenge.

How many steps are there from the door down to the ground where you are thinking about putting a room, and at what level would you want the outdoor floor to be? It could be approximately level with the floor inside the house (usually a step down of about 1 inch is recommended), level with the ground, or in between. Although it complicates construction, any situation that requires a few or more steps is a welcome design opportunity, because the geometry of steps is so pleasing, especially if they're built on a generous scale. You could have a split-level deck, a deck with inset steps and landings, a big flat deck with steps that angle off the edge, or a broad, gracious bank of steps that leads from the house down to a terrace or from a terrace down to a lawn or garden.

Determining size, shape, and style

It's easy to check the size and shape of a potential outdoor floor that will be at or close to ground level. Simply outline the area with stakes and strings and live with the layout for a while to see what you think. Look at the outlined area from all points of view— from the doorway, an upstairs window, across the yard. Do the size and shape look right, compared with the house and the rest of the yard?

Set some furniture out there. Invite some friends over. Would the area be large enough to serve your needs? You're more likely to err on the small

(BELOW LEFT): *Before this deck was built, a short flight of steps led from the house down to a sloping lawn. Now the split-level octagonal deck provides outdoor living space, a broad landing, and a multidirectional passageway between the house, a separate garage in the foreground, and the lawn and garden beyond.*

(BELOW): *Building a raised deck is the easiest way to create a level outdoor floor on a sloping site. Note the attractive railing here. It's safe and sturdy, in compliance with codes. Rails are an important feature of raised decks and deserve close consideration.*

stakes-and-string mockup for a raised deck and instead need to rely on drawings, computer-assisted design tools, and/or scale models. Since you can't test a drawing or model by walking on it, take extra time to think through the design, whether you draft it yourself or hire a deck designer. Get a builder's input, too, to make sure the design is feasible and complies with codes.

SIMPLE SHAPES WORK BEST. You can't go wrong with a rectangle that's aligned with the house, especially if the house itself is a basic box shape. At worst, a rectangle is boring, but that's only when it's empty; the area will become interesting as soon as you add outdoor furniture, planters, and other fittings.

Remember, too, that the pattern of the decking or pavement is as conspicuous as the overall shape of the floor or room. For example, even if their basic shape is rectangular, decks with boards set on the diagonal or patios made from random flagstones create a very dynamic impression.

Some situations do call for uncommon shapes. It's fun to make a detached patio or terrace round or octagonal, particularly if it's located where you can get an overview from a second-story window or deck. A ramada backed into a corner of your lot might be a triangle, vee, or quarter-round. A room adjacent to the house might start as a rectangle but have a curve along the outside edge or have a jog that parallels the wall of the house. Outlining an irregular

(ABOVE): This room is well fitted to the site. A free-form floor of dry-laid bricks mirrors the sinuous tree trunks. Although the outline of the floor is curved, the surface is level, like a pool of still water.

side, so don't be timid about moving the stakes to expand the outlined area.

Consider traffic patterns. Where would you cross the proposed room as you move from one place to another in the yard or back and forth to the house? Adjust the outline to accommodate preferred pathways; either make crossing the room a convenient part of the route, or keep the room out of the way and let walkers bypass it.

The same principles regarding size and shape apply to raised decks or porches as to ground-level outdoor floors, but you usually can't do a simple

(RIGHT): An attached room should coordinate with the house in terms of material, style, and color and must be well built. Planters substitute for some of the railings here. Check with your local building department to see if that's permitted in your area.

shape might help you fit the room onto a sloping site, work around a big tree or rock, connect two buildings, or incorporate or avoid a walkway. The key to designing irregular rooms is to keep the lines simple. Choose one or two basic shapes—such as a 120° angle or a curve drawn on a set radius—to use repeatedly. Don't mix shapes at random or vary the outline too much; that looks fussy and is trouble to build.

MATERIALS AND STYLE. An outdoor room that's attached to a house should coordinate and look like an integral part of it, not a wayward afterthought. The sense of belonging starts with making sure that the placement, size, and shape of the outdoor room are in scale with the house (not too big or small) and balanced (not lopsided or eccentric).

Beyond that, the choice of materials and finishes determines style. For instance, a Victorian house shouldn't have an unfinished pressure-treated deck with blunt square railings; it needs a painted porch with turned spokes and shaped moldings. A colonial shouldn't have a bare concrete slab for a patio or terrace; flagstone or gravel would be more appropriate, or perhaps bricks. Consult reference books on period architecture and home-remodeling magazines for more information if you're trying to preserve the integrity of an older house.

If your house is generic 20th-century suburban and there's no particular style to heed, choose just a few materials to build with, pay attention to their colors, and stick within a limited color scheme. For example, you might use rust red bricks, tan gravel, and either weathered gray or white painted wood. Using the same materials and colors repeatedly gives a deliberate look that's very pleasing.

One of the fun things about building a room apart from the house is that you have more freedom to do what you want. Some codes may still apply, but they're almost always more liberal than for attached construction. And if the room is out of sight, you don't have to worry about style and other people's opinions. You—or your kids—can make a council circle, a vine-covered grotto, a treehouse, or a thatched beach hut. Getting to enjoy yourself like this is one of the rewards of owning land.

DESIGN AND COST. Building or laying the floor is the initial and often the major expense in building an outdoor room, so price that first. Would you rather have a larger patio made with inexpensive concrete pavers, or a smaller one surfaced with dressed stone? An irregular shape made of poured concrete, or a simple rectangle of bricks? Does your deck layout take advantage of standard lumber dimensions and minimize cut-off ends? Get some preliminary cost and feasibility estimates before you set your heart on any particular combination of design and materials, as you may want to reconsider and choose a smaller size, simpler shape, or less expensive flooring. Similar tradeoffs apply when

Indulge your fantasies in a detached playhouse. As long as the construction is safe and sturdy, the design can be as whimsical as you want.

you're planning to build a fence, wall, or overhead or other structure.

Outdoor floors can be made of a variety of materials, all of which have pros and cons in terms of cost, appearance, ease of installation, durability, care requirements, and how they feel underfoot. Whatever it's made of, an outdoor floor should be continuous and uniform, with no cracks or bumps that you might trip on, so you can walk on it safely after dark or when you're carrying something or involved in a conversation and can't look down. You shouldn't have to watch your step.

A floor should also provide good traction and not be slippery. Achieving this depends on the material and your climate. In rainy climates, and especially on shady sites where algae grow on outdoor floors, wood, tile, bricks, and some kinds of flagstone can all feel slick. Safe footing is important, so use your own experiences with local pavements as a basis for making decisions, and talk to local contractors, too.

When comparing cost, remember that the price of the material itself is only part of the total cost of a floor. Delivery charges, site preparation, and labor factor in, too, and these may differ greatly from one material to another. Compare bids or estimates that are based on the total project, not just the surface material. Also consider how long the floor is likely to last and what kind of maintenance it will need; a material that's more expensive at first may be a bargain in the long run.

What if your house already has a concrete slab, flagstone patio, or other outdoor floor, but it is too small, is badly worn, or looks dated? You may be able to resurface or add on to it, or it might be better to remove and replace it. Perhaps you can recycle the used materials for paths, walls, or other construction projects around your yard.

Mortared tiles make a neat, clean floor. Tile works best in sunny climates, as it tends to be slippery when wet.

Grade-level floor toppings

Several kinds and grades of materials can be laid flush with the ground. Almost always, you'll need to prepare the site first by grading it so that it is basically level but slopes slightly away from the house. Then, depending on what kind of surface you're using, your soil, and your climate, you'll need to prepare some kind of base or foundation. This usually involves removing a few or more inches of soil and replacing it with crushed rock.

The materials and techniques used to pave grade-level outdoor floors are basically the same as for walks and paths, so I have grouped most of this information in the next chapter and will only review some key points here.

LOOSE MATERIALS. Various kinds of gravel, crushed rock, and wood or bark chips are the easiest floors to install yourself. They require minimum site preparation, and they're good for sites with trees because they minimize root damage. But the appearance is very casual and informal, and loose materials can be a nuisance. They get in your shoes or catch in the tread on the soles. The surface shifts around and you have to rake and relevel it. Loose materials seem to collect leaves, debris, and litter, and tree or weed seeds that blow in are likely to sprout there. For these reasons, most loose materials are best suited for rustic homes, natural landscapes, or outdoor rooms that are set apart from the house.

One advantage of wood chips is that it's easy to remove and recycle them if you change your mind about where you want to have an outdoor room and how big you want it to be, or if you haven't decided yet what you want to use for permanent flooring. Wood chips are the only topping to consider for temporary use.

Gravel, by contrast, is one of the most difficult materials to remove, so don't ever spread it anywhere unless you're sure you want it there. For more about using gravel, crushed rock, or aggregate as paving, see page 151.

POURED-CONCRETE SLABS. Poured concrete goes down fast, is long-lasting and easy to care for, costs less than other masonry, and is especially well suited for designs with curved edges. It tends to look and feel cold in the winter and glaring hot in the summer sun, and it may crack, shift, settle, or heave on an unstable or poorly drained site, but all of those problems can occur with other kinds of masonry, also.

There are a few drawbacks unique to concrete.

The first is that a poured-concrete slab typically looks utilitarian and bland. There's no need for this, as many variations are possible. Stain can be added to dye concrete in many colors. The concrete can be stamped when wet to create surface patterns that simulate old-fashioned brick or stone pavements. It can be topped with different types of gravel or aggregate, which give a textured surface. You'll have to call around, but you can probably track down a contractor who's interested and equipped to do something out of the ordinary with concrete.

Another problem is that it's hard to clean or repair stained or damaged concrete slabs. Homemade patches don't work very well, and they show. There are some refinishing techniques that contractors can use, but these aren't widely available. Finally, demolishing and removing an old concrete slab is an exhausting job, so don't have concrete installed unless you want it for the long term. For more about poured-concrete paving, see page 137.

MASONRY PAVEMENTS. This category encompasses a wide and wonderful range of materials in many colors and styles, including cast concrete pavers, bricks, tiles, flagstones, and cobblestones. When properly installed, these make particularly attractive and long-lasting outdoor floors. They're much classier than poured concrete and more formal than most wooden decks. You can choose one or another kind of masonry to coordinate with any

style of house and any kind of landscape. These materials are endlessly versatile, and their patterned surfaces are always pleasing to look at.

Masonry pavements are more popular where winters are mild than in snowy climates. You'll hear skeptics say, why invest in pretty paving if it's going to be buried under snow for months at a time? But that's true only on the north side of a house, where the sun doesn't shine, or if you don't shovel. Where the sun can reach, if you clear most of the snow off a paved area, the rest will soon melt and the resulting

(ABOVE): *Giant squares of cut flagstone make a traditional-looking patio, edged with brick to match the house and the wall. This is a good floor for a dining area. You can slide those chairs around and the legs won't catch in any cracks.*

(LEFT): *Over the years, a dry-laid brick floor settles into place and develops a mossy patina that symbolizes tradition and permanence.*

dry spot will be an inviting place to walk or sit on mild winter days.

People sometimes complain that masonry floors are slippery when wet, but concrete and wood can be slippery, too. A little texture makes any outdoor floor feel safer underfoot. The ideal surface is just rough enough to not feel slick when wet but still smooth enough that you can walk on it barefoot.

The main drawbacks of masonry are its high cost and the effort and skill required for installation. Good masonry pavement is expensive, but it's a worthwhile investment that retains its value and ages gracefully. For more about masonry paving, see page 140.

Wooden decking

Decks have many advantages as outdoor floors. They're resilient and comfortable to stand and walk on. Compared with concrete or masonry, a wooden surface is warmer in winter and cooler in summer. The grain of the lumber is attractive, the patterns of the decking and railings are intriguing, and the out-

line or shape of a deck can be straight, angled, or curved. You can build low or raised decks on sloping, rocky, wooded, or poorly drained sites where ground-level construction would be complex and expensive, and a deck can easily incorporate steps and have two or more levels.

Although a deck is the most popular addition you can make to many home landscapes, I won't elaborate on deck design and construction in this book. It's too big a topic, and there are plenty of good how-to and idea books devoted solely to decks. I'll just touch on a few aspects of decks as outdoor floors.

USE DURABLE LUMBER. Almost all kinds of wood decay quickly when exposed to the weather, especially if they're set into the ground as posts or laid horizontally as floorboards. Termites and other wood-eating insects wreak havoc, too. Don't waste time building a deck from untreated pine, oak, or other susceptible lumber. It won't last. You can use other woods for fencing, trellises, or other vertical or decorative construction, particularly if you're going

---

USING PRESSURE-TREATED LUMBER SAFELY

Gardeners sometimes question the safety of pressure-treated lumber, but according to tests conducted by the Environmental Protection Agency, the U.S. Consumer Product Safety Commission, and other public agencies, this wood is acceptable for use around the home and garden. There are some cautions, but they're very specific. To be safe, follow these guidelines.

- When carrying, stacking, or building with pressure-treated wood, wear gloves and/or wash your hands thoroughly afterward. Also, change your clothes when you finish work for the day. The amount of preservative that gets absorbed through the skin is negligible, and thorough washing further reduces that risk.

- Wear a dust mask when you're sawing or sanding to avoid inhaling fine particles. Work outdoors over a tarp, and put all cut-off ends, shavings, and sawdust in the trash.

- Finish all pressure-treated wood projects by applying an oil-based stain or similar wood sealer, and reapply it every two years. This helps seal the preservative inside the wood and greatly reduces the risk that residue will come to the surface or get leached out. Finishing the wood also improves its appearance and reduces weathering, cracking, warping, and splintering.

- Don't let toddlers play with or on unfinished pressure-treated wood. They're more at risk than older children or adults because they keep putting their hands in their mouths and can actually ingest some of the preservative. This doesn't cause any immediate problems, but if they play on CCA-

treated wood for hours a day, over a period of time arsenic can accumulate in their bodies.

- Repeated tests have shown that there is negligible leaching of the CCA preservative from fences, posts, retaining walls, or other situations where pressure-treated wood is installed vertically, but leaching can occur under unfinished deck floors, because they're horizontal and water can pool there rather than immediately running off. In particular, if acid rain pools on unfinished deck boards, or if you use deck cleaners that contain oxalic acid or citric acid, the acid can leach arsenic out of the wood. Soil tests have found high levels of arsenic in some cases under decks. This isn't necessarily a problem if you never go under the deck or do anything there, but you can easily prevent leaching by finishing the wood with a sealer or stain.

- Never burn pressure-treated wood under any circumstances —not in a fireplace, woodstove, or open fire. Burning concentrates the copper, chromium, and arsenic used in the CCA treatment to a dangerous level in the ashes. Instead of burning, you should put scraps, sawdust, and shavings of pressure-treated lumber in the trash or take them to a landfill.

- Disposal is an issue if you have an old pressure-treated deck and want to tear it down. Perhaps you could recycle the wood, which will probably hold up for many years to come, by making raised beds, compost bins, or other garden projects. Maybe you could give it to someone else who would like to recycle it. Otherwise, send it to the landfill.

---

to paint or finish it or don't mind replacing it from time to time. But durability is a special concern for decks, because they're close to the soil and because the most vulnerable surfaces—the buried posts and the bottom of the floor—are out of sight and out of reach, so you can't monitor or maintain them.

There are only a few native North American trees whose wood resists decay and termites. These include chestnut (now extinct, but occasionally and expensively available when old buildings are taken apart and recycled), black locust and Osage orange (both sometimes available as posts but rarely as boards), bald cypress (often simply called cypress, and sold mostly in the South), several kinds of cedar, and redwood. Of these timbers, only cedar and redwood are readily available. The better grades (boards with close, uniform grain and no knots) of cedar and redwood make beautiful, durable decks, but they're fairly expensive.

Currently the most widely used wood for deck building and other garden construction is called pressure-treated lumber. This is yellow pine, Douglas fir, or other softwood lumber that's been treated with a preservative called chromated copper arsenate (CCA). Pressure-treated lumber lasts for decades. The CCA process was developed in the 1930s and boards from the original tests are still in good condition. It is sold in a few quality grades and two levels of treatment: Ground Contact, which is required for posts or any other pieces that touch soil, and Above Ground, which is suitable for decking, rails, fencing, and the like.

You can find pressure-treated wood at any lumberyard at affordable prices, but there are a couple of drawbacks to this type of lumber. The wood is not particularly attractive or easy to work. It's wide-grained and it can be splintery. The copper in the CCA treatment gives the wood a greenish cast, although that's easily disguised by staining (see below). Finally, although it's generally safe, there are a few safety measures to observe with CCA pressure-treated lumber (see the box on page 114).

Although it's by far the most commonly used, CCA isn't the only preservative used to pressure-treat wood. There are alternatives. The ACQ process and the Kodiak formula both include copper but avoid the hazardous arsenic or chromium. ACQ- and Kodiak-treated timbers are as long-lasting as CCA-treated lumber and cost only a little more, but you'll have to call around to find a lumberyard that stocks them. Kodiak-treated wood has a pretty brown color, not the usual greenish tinge.

"Lumber" made from virgin or recycled plastic is another option for outdoor construction. It's not common and it is fairly expensive compared with CCA-treated wood, but it's strong, durable, weather-resistant, surprisingly attractive, splinter-free, and easy to work. Different manufacturers produce different products; polyvinyl and high-density

polyethylene are the most common. Plastic lumber comes in the full range of standard lumber dimensions and in white, tan, brown, and sometimes other colors. Big lumberyards and home-improvement stores may have samples you can examine and more information.

FINISHES. Although you can leave decks built from cedar, redwood, or pressure-treated wood exposed to the weather, bare wood is liable to warp, crack, splinter, and mildew. Furthermore, it looks raw, neglected, and simply unfinished.

Decks so often go unfinished that people sometimes ask if you *can* finish them. Of course you can, and you should. Don't use paint or varnish; those materials don't stand up to wear and they flake badly. Choose a sealer or stain that's designed to soak into the wood, and apply it as recommended on the label. Sealers are usually clear and let the color and grain of the wood show through. Semitransparent stains show the wood grain but are tinted, usually in shades of brown. The tinted colors look warm and natural and hide the greenish color of pressure-treated wood. You'll need to reapply any of these finishes every other year or so, as they gradually dry out and also wear off underfoot.

Treat new decks as soon as the wood has dried out enough for the finish to soak in. This may be immediately after construction or within a month or so. Ideally you'd seal the bottoms of the boards as well as the tops. For most decks, that means you have

Grade-level brick paving leads to a raised wooden deck with built-in seating around the edge. Painting the deck dark brown helps blend it into the surroundings.

Nobody wants to see what's lurking beneath your deck. Enclose its underpinnings with vine-covered lattice (RIGHT), a flowering hedge and garland of hanging baskets (BELOW), or a rock wall with planted crevices (BOTTOM).

to finish the boards before nailing them down. Most builders don't bother and simply finish the top surface.

If you have an old deck that's never been finished, you probably should scrub it first with a solution of household bleach, trisodium phosphate, citric acid, or some other deck cleaner (but see page 114). Follow the directions for surface preparation on the label of whatever finish you've chosen. After cleaning, rinse well, then let the wood dry for a day or so before you apply the finish. Buy some extra gallons of finish, as you'll be surprised how quickly it soaks into the old dry wood. You'll be really pleased at how much better the deck looks afterward.

ENCLOSE THE UNDERPINNINGS. In terms of landscaping, the major concern with raised decks is how to treat the area underneath them. It's almost always too dark and dry to grow any plants down there, the gridwork of beams and joists is usually an eyesore, and although 4x4 posts are functionally adequate for supporting a deck, they sure look skimpy.

It's easy to screen low decks, ones that are no more than a few feet off the ground, with plants. Dig a bed around the edge and fill it with plants. Choose kinds that will grow at least as tall as the deck floor, so that when you're looking from the yard toward the deck, they'll fill that otherwise empty space. See the box on page 124 for suggestions of bushy perennials and shrubs that grow about 2 to 3 feet tall. Include some taller plants too, so you'll get to see them peeking up around the edge as you sit on the deck. For example, try some fragrant, long-blooming shrub roses, such as 'Carefree Beauty' (pink), 'Easy Going' (yellow), or 'Iceberg' (white); or flowers that attract butterflies and hummingbirds, such as butterfly bush, hibiscus, salvias, and agastaches.

For decks that are raised several feet off the ground, perhaps the best solution is to sheathe the area with siding to match the house, or to enclose it with lattice or trellises and let vines grow all over these vertical structures. Leave openings where needed if there's a door or window under the deck, or if you use the space there for storage. Of course, you could screen the deck with shrubs, but it would take years for them to grow tall enough to be effective. Moreover, shrubs tall enough to hide the underpinnings of a second-story deck are typically so wide that they reach far out into the yard; that wastes a lot of space that you could put to better use.

SHADE OR CEILINGS FOR OUTDOOR ROOMS

Looking up to the sky is one of the joys of being outdoors and not anything to sacrifice lightly. But there are situations in which some kind of ceiling enhances an outdoor room. The extreme would be a rainy climate, where you'd want an actual roof of some kind. A porch, gazebo, or garden house is a great place to relax on a rainy evening or sit out a thunderstorm. But getting a roof built may be a more complicated or expensive project than you're ready to consider.

Providing shade is a simpler matter than staying dry. Basically, you can get shade from a tree or by building some kind of overhead structure or arbor, which may or may not be covered with vines. One consideration is the time of day when you want shade. Shade is usually not required in the cool of morning. If you want to spend time in the outdoor room between midmorning and midafternoon, you need shade directly overhead. Unless you build an outdoor room under an existing shade tree, building an overhead structure is the fastest way to get midday shade. Planting a new shade tree that will eventually shade the room and perhaps the house itself or a big part of the yard might be a good solution, but it will take years to grow big enough to shade a picnic table at lunchtime. By late afternoon and early evening, the sun is lower in the sky, so a small tree or even a large shrub planted on the west side of an outdoor room will provide enough shade for late-day use.

Putting a floor under a tree

The space underneath a big tree can be an ideal site for an outdoor room, but it depends on the tree. If the tree is neat and doesn't drop much litter, go ahead. It will be cool and shady there, and you'll enjoy the spreading limbs, the rustling leaves, and the birds. But think twice before putting a floor under a messy tree whose flowers, fruits, pods, or needles would stain the floor, attract wasps, crunch underfoot, or stick to your shoes or feet.

If you have a suitable tree or trees, prune it first (or have it pruned) to remove any low-hanging, dead, weak, or damaged limbs and to open up the crown and reveal its branch patterns. Then decide on the size, shape, level, and type of floor you want. The two best options are a floor made of loose materials or a wooden deck. Neither of these will do major damage to the tree's roots either during installation or construction or in the future, nor will the tree roots damage them. But putting concrete or masonry flooring under a tree is asking for trouble; one way or the other, something will have to give. Either the tree will suffer, or it will eventually crack the pavement.

SPREADING LOOSE MATERIALS UNDER A TREE. Wood or bark chips or compactable gravel are good floorings under a tree. You can fill an area of any shape and the look is casual and natural. The floor won't necessarily be level; it will follow the contours of the ground. Maintenance

(ABOVE): *The shingled roof keeps this gazebo dry, so you could enjoy a meal there during or after a rain.*

(RIGHT): *Wood chips work fine as the flooring for this shady hideaway. They decompose slowly, but you can easily add a fresh topping every few years.*

can be a nuisance if you have to keep raking litter off the loose surface, and seedlings of the tree itself or of weeds may sprout up there, but these aren't inevitable problems. Note the general discussion of loose materials (see page 112) and the following additional points.

What, if anything, is growing under the tree now? If you want to preserve any healthy existing shrubs or perennials, you can spread the chips or gravel around them. The floor doesn't have to be like wall-to-wall carpeting; it can be a broad, meandering path with one or more areas that are big enough for a bench, table and chairs, or whatever you want to put there.

If there's any weak or weedy grass or ground cover under the tree, kill or remove it first (see page 274), and cover the area with a lightproof barrier—overlapped sections of newspaper or a sheet of landscape fabric—to suppress any lingering shoots that might sprout up later, before spreading the chips or gravel.

What's growing outside the area under the tree? If there's lawn there, you'll want to install some kind of permanent edging or mowing strip to keep the lawn from spreading into the chips or gravel and simplify mowing and maintenance. Or dig up a band of lawn around the edge of the area under the tree and surround the floor with plantings of shrubs, perennials, and ferns. The inner edge, between the floor and the plantings, can be a casual, irregular line broken here and there by plants that straddle it. Maintain the outer edge of the bed, between the plantings and the lawn, as you choose (see page 154). It will be less prominent and easy to care for than an edge between loose material and lawn, and adding the plantings will make the area a lot more interesting. Likewise, an edging or adjacent bed is needed if you want to keep a vigorous ground cover from moving into a loose floor.

BUILDING A DECK UNDER A TREE.
Building a deck is the best solution if the ground around the tree slopes or the tree's roots are exposed, and it's the only way to create a smooth, level floor under a tree. A deck can be as low as one step off the ground, as much higher than that as you want, or split-level. The outline can be a familiar shape or an irregular one. It doesn't have to be centered around the tree; in fact, a deck seems bigger and you have more space for a table and chairs if the tree is off toward one end, not in the middle.

The opening(s) in the deck around the tree's trunk(s) should be big enough to allow for future growth. A tree's trunk may widen a few inches or more in a decade.

A deck needs to sit on concrete footings, and digging the holes for these will inevitably cut through some tree roots. There isn't much design flexibility in locating footings; they have to go where they're needed, but if you see major tree roots on the surface, try to design the deck around them if possible. The farther away from the trunk the footings can go, the less likely you'll hit big roots. Once the footings are poured, the rest of the construction takes place aboveground, so further root damage is minimal.

Rain that falls on a deck will run down through the cracks and soak into the ground below, so in rainy climates a tree will still get the water it needs after a deck is built. In arid climates, however, or during dry spells in any region, the tree may need watering. Running a soaker hose around the edge of the deck, set at a slow drip for hours at a time or long enough for the water to fully saturate the surrounding soil, should give the tree what it needs.

Planting a patio shade tree

If you're patient and you plan to stay in your house for a decade or more, you can plant a tree to shade an outdoor room. One of the medium-size shade trees recommended in the box on page 105 can eventually shade a large patio or deck throughout most of the day.

But even a much smaller tree planted by the south, southwest, or west side of an outdoor room will provide enough shade to shelter a table and

A custom-rounded deck and wood-chip mulch turn this redbud tree into the centerpiece of an outdoor room, while protecting its roots. This particular tree casts such dense shade that it would be hard to grow anything beneath it.

KEY:

D = deciduous

E = evergreen

S = full sun

PS = tolerates or prefers part shade

These small trees are especially suitable for planting next to a patio, terrace, or deck. Any one of them would delight you through the seasons and over the years. They'll grow big enough to cast some shade and provide a sense of shelter overhead. Some grow rather quickly, while others are slower. The flowering kinds start blooming when they are still small, perhaps the first year after you plant them.

- **Maples** (*Acer* spp. and cvs.). **D, S** or **PS.** Trident maple (*A. buergerianum*). Vivid fall color, handsome peeling bark. Tolerates poor, dry soil. **ZONE 4.** Amur maple (*A. ginnala*). Fragrant white flowers in spring, red fruits in summer, red fall foliage. Adaptable, tolerates poor soil. **ZONE 3.** Paperbark maple (*A. griseum*). Slow but desirable. Appreciated for its glossy, curling brown bark. **ZONE 5.** Japanese maples (*A. palmatum* cvs.). There are dozens of kinds, with more or less finely cut leaves in shades of green, red, bronze, and purplish. Most grow slowly and prefer part shade and moist soil. **ZONE 6 OR 5.**

- **Serviceberry, or shadbush** (*Amelanchier* spp. and cvs.). **D, PS.** White flowers in early spring, tasty blue-purple berries in summer, great fall foliage, handsome bark. Often multi-trunked. **ZONE 4.**

- **Musclewood, or American hornbeam** (*Carpinus caroliniana*). **D, PS.** Smooth gray trunks have a lean, sinuous, muscular look. Yellow fall foliage. Interesting papery fruits. Slow-growing but trouble-free. **ZONE 3.**

- **Palo verdes** (*Cercidium* spp.). **D, S.** Often leafless, but the twigs, branches, and trunk all have green bark. Bright yellow flowers appear in spring and sometimes in summer, after a rain. Fast-growing. For desert climates. **ZONE 9 OR 8.**

- **Chitalpa** (x *Chitalpa tashkentensis*). **D, PS.** Fast-growing and vigorous, with large, trumpet-shaped pink, white, or lavender flowers over a long season but no messy pods. **ZONE 6.**

- **Japanese clethra** (*Clethra barbinervis*). **D, PS.** Very fragrant white flowers in mid- to late summer. Yellow fall foliage. Beautiful trunk bark. Naturally shrubby, but easily trained into tree shape. **ZONE 5.**

- **Dogwoods** (*Cornus* spp. and cvs.). **D, PS.** There are many excellent cultivars and hybrids of flowering dogwood (*C. florida*) and Kousa dogwood (*C. kousa*). Cornelian cherry dogwood (*C. mas*) and the similar *C. officinalis* bear yellow flowers in very early spring and big red berries in summer. Most dogwoods have wonderful red fall foliage. **HARDINESS VARIES; MOST ARE ZONE 5.**

- **Magnolias** (*Magnolia* spp. and cvs.). **D or E, S or PS.** Cultivars of *M.* × *loebneri* are fast-growing and widely adapted, with fragrant white or pink flowers in early spring and deciduous leaves. Sweet bay magnolia, also a fast grower, has slender semievergreen leaves and sweet white flowers in summer. There are scores of other fine magnolias that form neat small trees. **HARDINESS VARIES; MANY ARE ZONE 5.**

- **Crab apples** (*Malus* spp. and cvs.). **D, S.** Beautiful (and sometimes fragrant) white, pink, or rose flowers in spring. Red (sometimes purple, orange, or gold) fruits in fall and winter. Get local advice on which crab apples grow best and resist diseases in your climate. Habits range from shrubby to upright, rounded, or weeping. **MOST ARE ZONE 4.**

- **Flowering cherries** (*Prunus* spp. and cvs.). **D, S.** 'Hally Jolivette' (double, pale pink), 'Kwanzan' (puffy, double, rose-pink), and 'Snow Goose' (single, pure white) are a few of the many outstanding cherries. Most bloom in early spring. Some have yellow fall foliage and glossy cinnamon-colored bark. When choosing a cherry, ask about its resistance to local diseases and pests. **HARDINESS VARIES.**

- **'Majestic Beauty' Indian hawthorn** (*Rhaphiolepis*). **E, S.** Can be trained into a small tree, with leathery leaves and long-lasting displays of fragrant, pale pink flowers. **ZONE 8.**

- **Japanese snowbell** (*Styrax japonica*). **D, S** or **PS.** Dangling clusters of fragrant pink or white flowers in late spring. Variable fall color. Needs good, moist soil. **ZONE 5.**

- **Stewartia** (*Stewartia pseudocamellia*). **D, PS.** An ideal tree. Lovely foliage with varied fall colors, round white flowers in summer, and patchy, multicolored bark. Needs good, moist soil. **ZONE 5.**

- **'Ivory Silk' tree lilac** (*Syringa reticulata*). **D, S.** Fluffy, creamy white flowers in early summer. Neat upright habit, tight glossy bark. **ZONE 3.**

- **Blackhaw viburnum** (*Viburnum prunifolium*). **D, S** or **PS.** White flowers in late spring, dark fruits in fall, glorious red-purple fall foliage.

'Ivory Silk' lilac is an ideal patio tree: neat, shapely, multi-featured, tall enough to shade a table and chairs but small enough that it doesn't dominate or overwhelm the site.

chairs or a bench, and if you don't need a big tree, why plant one? A small tree, one that reaches 15 to 25 feet tall, is typically all you need for shading a patio.

Even if you don't need the shade, a small tree can be a welcome feature because it does give you something to look up at. Choose one with lovely flowers, colorful fall foliage, interesting bark or twigs, or other features and details that you'll enjoy watching up close. Make sure that it is neat and doesn't drop messy litter and that it has deep roots that won't heave or buckle a paved floor.

Building an overhead structure

An overhead structure designed to provide shade can be built onto a house or other building, projecting out over an adjacent outdoor room, or it can be a freestanding structure. Either way, you may need to get a building permit and comply with local codes, so check into that first.

Sound construction starts with sturdy, well-set posts or columns. These are typically 4x4 timbers, but 6x6 posts often look better, not so skimpy. Posts don't have to be square. Round white columns are

more formal. Round poles made from trees are more casual. And they don't have to be wood; they could be metal or masonry, or some combination of solid core and decorative veneer. Posts normally need to be set on poured-concrete footings that extend below the frost line, but in some cases you can build up from existing footings that support a deck or from a poured foundation wall that runs under the perimeter of a concrete slab or mortared masonry terrace. Your local building inspector will have definite advice about what's acceptable practice. Follow codes and standard construction guidelines regarding the size, number, and spacing of beams and rafters that complete the framing.

You can top the rafters with 1x4s, laths, poles made from saplings, or purchased wooden lattice. Use sealer or finish on all the wooden parts of an overhead structure to enhance their beauty and to protect them from sun and rain.

VINES TO PROVIDE SHADE. Decide before you build it whether or not you want to grow vines that climb up a post and sprawl across the top of an overhead structure. A big vine is surprisingly heavy

A vine-covered arbor shades a poolside terrace. This simple post-and-beam structure is topped with a sheet of shade cloth (a screenlike mesh woven from black plastic). That provided shade immediately after construction, before the vine reached the top. Now it catches leaves or litter that drop off the vine and keeps them from blowing into the pool.

and can sag or topple an inadequate structure. To support a vine you may need to use larger beams and rafters or set them closer together, or both. When in doubt, overbuild. You'll never regret a structure that's stronger than it needs to be, and besides, sturdy structures look more impressive than lightweight ones.

Some of the best vines for covering an overhead structure are too vigorous for most other landscape situations, so if you like these plants this is a chance to indulge. Suitable candidates include kiwis (*Actinidia;* these have separate male and female plants, and you need both if you want fruit), akebia, trumpet creepers *(Campsis),* anemone clematis *(Clematis montana)* or evergreen clematis *(C. armandii),* vigorous climbing or rambling roses such as 'American Pillar' (pink) or Lady Banks (small yellow or white flowers), and all kinds of wisterias.

All of these vines tolerate full sun, grow fast, and soon provide plenty of shade. One plant can quickly spread to cover an area of 50 square feet or more. You'll probably need to tie it to the post or give it a rope to twine around as it initially climbs to the top, but once it reaches the rafters you can let it spread on its own. If a growing tip drops down between the rafters, tuck it up again or trim it off and new growth will sprout up on top. Every year or two in late winter, you'll need to spend some time on a stepladder, reaching up and pruning out tangles of old growth.

Also, check from time to time to make sure the vine isn't heading for your roof or the siding of the house; if so, prune it hard. Vines have a lot of leaf surface exposed to the sun and wind and therefore transpire a lot of water, so don't forget to give periodic deep soakings during dry weather.

PLANTING OUTDOOR "WALLS"

An outdoor room feels cozier, more intimate, and more protected if it's sheltered on one or more sides by some kind of wall, fence, hedge, or other vertical border. This can, but doesn't have to, be a continuous, high, opaque, or weatherproof structure, such as the wall of a house or other adjacent buildings. Unless you need a windscreen, a visual barrier, or a security fence, an outdoor wall can be primarily symbolic and decorative. A low hedge or rail, an openwork trellis, or a few posts supporting an overhead arbor makes a fine wall for an outdoor room. It doesn't take much to define the space and create a distinction between "in here" and "out there."

Chapter 7 is all about locating, designing, and building or planting fences, walls, hedges, and screens, especially those suitable for property boundaries. This section includes ideas for outlining smaller areas with plants and for adding vertical interest to outdoor rooms.

Because you see and enjoy them from up close, the plantings around an outdoor room can be more complex and varied than plantings viewed from a distance. In addition, the nearby location means that this is a good place for valuable or delicate plants that you wouldn't risk putting out by the street. Finally, pay attention to fragrance. Some plants bear flowers that smell odd or even unpleasant or that have a fragrance that's pleasing from a distance but too powerful or overwhelming from up close. You'll soon get rid of any plants whose aroma bothers you. But other plants smell positively delicious, and relaxing in an outdoor room surrounded with your favorite fragrant plants is a marvelously refreshing experience. I've included some of my favorites in the plant lists in this section.

Planting against house walls and fences

If your outdoor room is adjacent to the house, you can soften and decorate the vertical surface of the house wall by training an espaliered tree or shrub against it. See page 97 for recommended plants that are amenable to this kind of training. Growing an espalier is a good hobby. It's an unfinished work of art. The initial training—getting the main trunk as tall as you want and directing the side shoots as you choose—takes minimal effort but a fair amount of vision and patience over the first few years. After that, plan to spend a few hours every spring pruning the espalier and a few minutes a month throughout the growing season on pruning, pinching, and tying the new shoots.

Espaliers can be formal or informal. Either way, if you keep up with the grooming, they tend to look quite neat. Vines usually look wilder, more spontaneous, and more exuberant, but that makes a welcome contrast to the rigidity of most architecture. The challenge is achieving a casual, spirited look without letting the vine take over. Be careful about what vines you grow and where you plant them. For more on choosing and maintaining vines, see pages 206 and 311.

Small-scale hedges

A few upright plants or a narrow or short hedge can define the edge of a room, while adding color, texture, and seasonal change. Plants are "soft" compared with hardscape, and using plants for walls and edgings offers a welcome contrast to the hard surfaces of nearby buildings and pavement.

Plants need time to grow, so you need a little patience to grow a hedge. A hedge doesn't provide the instant privacy you can get by putting up a fence. But hedge plants mark a border or outline as soon as you plant them, and they serve a psychological role

long before they grow tall enough to actually block your view. And in many cases you don't ever need much height. Often short plants are enough to surround an outdoor room.

Most of the plants used for boundary hedges grow too tall and wide and are too vigorous and "common" to use around an outdoor room. For small, special situations you need plants that are more restrained and refined, such as the narrow shrubs recommended in the box on page 123. If you don't need or want the continuity of a solid screen, you could use fewer of these narrow shrubs and space them a little ways apart, to appear like columns or posts. This defines the outer edge of a room but doesn't block the view or stop a breeze. Buy three, five, seven, or more plants and space them 4 to 8 feet apart. As soon as they're in the ground, the room will feel more secure, as if you'd framed it in somehow, although all you've done is set out a few skinny shrubs. As they grow taller, the sense of enclosure they provide will become more and more convincing and satisfying. Group lower, rounded shrubs and perennials on one or both sides of a narrow hedge or around and between more widely spaced shrubs to fill in the planting.

SHORTER EDGINGS. Plants don't have to be tall to provide a sense of enclosure. Surrounding or edging an outdoor room with plants that are only knee- or waist-high will do the job, especially if their growth form is basically upright. Vertical stems, like a row of pickets, define a border or edge.

There are so many fine plants in this size range and growth form that you could easily shop at a nursery and come home with a mixture—one of these, one of those. Because you'll be seeing and enjoying the planting from nearby, this is one landscape situation where it's fine to indulge a passion for plant collecting. To make it look like more than just a collection, though, decide on some theme or idea that will unify it. You might pick a certain color scheme for the flowers, coordinate flowers with colored foliage, or focus on evergreen foliage and vary the leaf sizes and shapes.

Using a variety of plants calls attention to the details of a planting but diminishes its overall effect as a border or edge. To emphasize the sense of outlining and enclosure and "tie a room together," use one kind of plant to make a continuous low hedge. Again, because there are so many candidates to choose from, decide how to narrow your search. How tall an edging do you want? Do you want to clip or shear it, or let it grow naturally? Do you care if it's evergreen? Do you want it to flower? And, of course, as for any situation where you're planting multiples of one kind of plant, be sure it's a plant that is well matched to the site and will thrive in those growing conditions.

SHRUBS FOR A NARROW HEDGE

Surprisingly few shrubs are narrow in relation to their height. Here are some of the best ones to try, both evergreen and deciduous, with and without showy flowers. To make a continuous hedge with any of these shrubs, plant them in a single row (straight or curved), spaced about 2 feet apart.

These shrubs grow naturally to about 4 to 8 feet tall and about half that wide, or they can be maintained in this size range by pruning.

- **'Graham Blandy' English boxwood** (*Buxus sempervirens*). **E.** Dense, almost columnar habit. Small glossy leaves. **ZONE 5.**

- **Japanese camellia** (*Camellia japonica*). **E.** Blooms late winter to spring. Use 'Debutante' (light pink), 'Glen 40' (deep red), 'Kumasaka' (rose-pink), or 'Purity' (white). **ZONE 8.**

- **Enkianthus** (*Enkianthus campanulatus*). **D.** Small flowers in spring. Vivid fall color. **ZONE 5.**

- **Rose-of-Sharon** (*Hibiscus syriacus*). **D.** Hollyhock-like flowers all summer. Try 'Aphrodite' (pink with red center), 'Bluebird' (violet-blue), or 'Diana' (white). **ZONE 5.**

- **Hollies** (*Ilex* spp. and cvs.). **E.** Use *I. crenata* 'Jersey Pinnacle' (**ZONE 6**), *I. attenuata* 'Foster #2', or *I. vomitoria* (**BOTH ZONE 7**). All have narrow, upright habits and small stiff leaves.

- **Florida anise** (*Illicium floridanum*). **E.** Smooth, spicy-scented leaves. Unusual flowers and fruits. **ZONE 8.**

- **Junipers** (*Juniperus* spp. and cvs.). **E.** *J. scopulorum* 'Moonglow' and 'Skyrocket' are very skinny and tight, with blue-gray foliage. *J. chinensis* 'Robusta Green' and 'Torulosa' are narrow and irregular, with deep green foliage. **ZONE 4.**

- **'Boeticus' myrtle** (*Myrtus communis*). **E.** Thick, larger-than-average leaves and dense, upright habit. **ZONE 8.**

- **Heavenly bamboo, or nandina** (*Nandina domestica*). **E.** Fine-textured foliage with vivid winter color. White flowers, red berries. **ZONE 7.**

- **Holly-leaf osmanthus** (*Osmanthus heterophyllus*). **E.** Spiny, hollylike leaves. Tiny but very sweet-scented flowers in late fall. 'Gulftide' is a very good, compact cultivar. There are also variegated and purple-tinted forms. **ZONE 7.**

- **Yew pine** (*Podocarpus macrophyllus*). **E.** Slender, dark green needles. **ZONE 8.**

- **Azaleas** (*Rhododendron*). Look for cultivars described as upright or even as "leggy." Among evergreen azaleas, try Southern India hybrids such as 'Fielder's White' or 'George Lindley Taber'. Among deciduous azaleas, many of the Exbury, Mollis, and *viscosum* hybrids are upright growers, especially for their first decade or so. **HARDINESS VARIES.**

- **Roses** (*Rosa*). **D.** Most hybrid tea roses, such as 'Mr. Lincoln' (red), 'Tiffany' (pink), 'Tropicana' (orange), and 'Pascali' (white), are upright growers. 'Louise Odier' (pink), 'Reine Victoria' (dark pink), and some other shrub roses are also erect, but most roses spread wider than tall. **ZONE 6 OR 5.**

- **'Tuscan Blue' rosemary** (*Rosmarinus officinalis*). **E.** Fragrant leaves, narrow upright growth, dark blue flowers. **ZONE 8.** 'Arp', another upright cultivar, stays shorter but is hardy to **ZONE 7.**

- **'Miss Kim' lilac** (*Syringa patula*). **D.** Fragrant lilac blossoms in late spring, disease-resistant foliage. **ZONE 4.**

- **'Hicksii' yew** (*Taxus × media*). **E.** Has multiple leaders, all quite stiff and erect, and bright green needles and red fruits. **ZONE 5.**

- **'Emerald' American arborvitae** (*Thuja occidentalis*). **E.** Forms a very slim cone. Lustrous, aromatic foliage stays green all winter. **ZONE 3.**

'Emerald' arborvitae is slender and upright, good for hedging in tight quarters, since it doesn't spread sideways as most shrubs do.

COLORFUL PLANTS FOR LOW EDGINGS

These shrubs and perennials are compact and bushy and grow about 2 to 3 feet tall and wide. They're ideal for creating low hedges around an outdoor room. When massed, the effect of any of these plants is bold and exciting, yet orderly. Most need a good spring pruning but are otherwise carefree. Except where noted, all prefer full or part sun.

- **Blue star** (*Amsonia tabernaemontana, A. hubrechtii*). **P, D.** Willowy stems topped with pale blue flowers in spring. Slender leaves turn a lovely yellow in fall. **ZONE 3**.

- **Blue spireas** (*Caryopteris* cvs.). **S, D.** Mounded green, gray-green, or gold foliage is covered by rich blue or blue-purple flowers in late summer. **ZONE 6 OR 5**.

- **'Nana Gracilis' Hinoki cypress** (*Chamaecyparis obtusa*). **S, E.** Upright but irregular, with twisted sprays of shiny emerald green foliage. **ZONE 5**.

- **'Heatherbun' Atlantic white cedar** (*Chamaecyparis thyoides*). **S, E.** Forms a cone or mound. Fluffy-textured foliage is gray-green in summer, maroon-purple in winter. **ZONE 4**.

- **Rock rose** (*Cistus* spp. and cvs.). **S, E.** Rounded shrubs with very showy, large, white or pink flowers. **ZONE 8**.

- **Hostas** (*Hosta* spp. and cvs.). **P, D.** An excellent seasonal edging for shady sites. Thousands of cultivars offer solid or variegated leaves in shades of green, blue, gold, or white, along with violet, lilac, or white flowers in mid- to late summer. **ZONE 3**.

- **Hydrangea** (*Hydrangea macrophylla*). **S, D.** 'All Summer Beauty', 'Forever Pink', 'Pia', and 'Pink Beauty' are compact cultivars with neat foliage and showy flowers all summer. **ZONE 6**.

- **Tutsan** (*Hypericum androsaemum*). **S, SE.** There are green, variegated, and purple-leaved cultivars; all turn purple or bronze in cold weather and have small yellow flowers and red-black fruits. Tolerates shade. **ZONE 6**.

- **'Victor' crape myrtle** (*Lagerstroemia* cv.). **S, D.** A very compact form of this popular shrub. Dark red flowers continue all summer. Disease-resistant foliage turns yellow in fall. **ZONE 6**.

- **Lavandin** (*Lavandula × intermedia*). **S, SE.** Bushy plants, larger and more vigorous than common English lavender. There are lavender-, purple-, and white-flowered cultivars, all very fragrant. Gray-green foliage. **ZONE 5**.

- **Heavenly bamboo, or nandina** (*Nandina domestica*). **S, SE.** 'Harbour Dwarf', 'Wood's Dwarf', and 'Moonbay' are dwarf cultivars that form compact spheres. Fine-textured foliage turns vivid red-purple in winter. **ZONE 7**.

- **Peonies** (*Paeonia* cvs.). **P, D.** A showy seasonal hedge with large, fragrant rose, pink, or white flowers in late spring and colorful foliage in fall. **ZONE 4**.

- **'Prelude' Japanese andromeda** (*Pieris japonica*). **S, E.** A compact cultivar of this popular shrub, with white flowers in spring. New shoots are tinted pink. Prefers shade. **ZONE 5**.

- **Indian hawthorn** (*Rhaphiolepis indica*). **S, E.** Clusters of pink, rose, or white flowers hide the dark leathery foliage for weeks in spring. 'Ballerina', 'Enchantress', and 'Indian Princess' are compact cultivars. **ZONE 8 OR 7**.

- **Roses** (*Rosa*). **S, D.** There are scores of long-blooming and carefree roses in this size range, ideal for low hedges. Some tolerate part shade. Try 'Angel Face' (lavender), 'Easy Going' (yellow), 'Eutin' (dark red), 'Gruss an Aachen' (light pink), 'Iceberg' (white), or 'Nearly Wild' (pink). **ZONE 5 OR 4**.

- **Spireas** (*Spiraea japonica, S. bumalda* cvs.). **S, D.** Bushy, mounded shrubs with fine-textured foliage and rose, pink, or white flowers in early summer. There are many cultivars, including several with very colorful foliage. **ZONE 3**.

Planters

Growing plants in big pots, tubs, or planters around the edge of an outdoor room combines the solid impression of knee-high hardscape—the planters themselves can function like a low wall—with the variety, color, and softness of plants. It's the perfect solution for many situations.

You could grow as many plants as you want in separate pots, using containers 6 to 12 inches in diameter or larger. This has the advantage that you can move plants farther apart as they grow and can add or remove plants at different seasons or when they start or finish blooming. But tending a collection of potted plants is time-consuming, especially in the heat of summer, when you need to water them all at least once a day and fertilize every week or so. In addition, plants in small pots tip over on windy days, and that gets to be a nuisance.

Using bigger pots or planters simplifies care, and as the lower part of an outdoor wall, they look more substantial, too. You can buy plastic, fiberglass, and wooden planters, usually round or square, in

sizes up to about 2 feet tall and/or wide. These are big enough for growing individual perennials or shrubs that get up to 4 to 5 feet tall and wide, or you could combine a few smaller plants in one big pot.

BUILDING PLANTERS. Best of all for edging an outdoor room are permanent planters built of wood or masonry. These are usually made about 2 feet high, 2 to 4 feet wide, and as long as you want. It's uncommon to find such planters ready-made, but you can build them yourself or hire a handyman to do it.

Make outdoor planter boxes from a rot-resistant wood such as pressure-treated lumber, cedar, or redwood, and apply a generous coat of wood sealer

or oil-based stain to the inside and outside of any wooden planter before filling it with soil. If you're going to set a wooden planter box onto a terrace or deck, be sure to drill several ½-inch holes in the bottom and use blocks to support the box an inch or so off the floor, so water can drain out and away. If you want to make a wooden planter that sits on the ground, it doesn't need a bottom—you can just build the four sides, like a raised bed, and let plants root down through it into the soil below.

Masonry planters are usually four-sided structures that set on the ground. The sides, or walls, can be made of mortared bricks or stones or concrete blocks. Since planters don't have to meet the sort of structural standards applied to higher walls, this

(ABOVE LEFT): *Matching planter boxes surround this wooden deck and steps. Marking the edge is important for reassurance and safety wherever there's a drop-off.*

(ABOVE RIGHT): *A planter built into the knee wall around this raised deck holds a specimen pine tree. A dwarf or slow-growing tree can live for years in a planter like this. (Think of bonsai; those trees live for centuries!)*

(LEFT): *Potted plants and built-in planters mark the edges and level changes on this attached deck. Note that sandbox at lower left. When the children outgrow it, it can be converted into another planter.*

might be a good first project if you want to try your hand at working with mortar, or you could hire a mason to build a mortared planter for you. An easy way to build a masonry planter yourself is by using cast-concrete "wall stones" that stack in interlocking layers. These are dry-laid; no mortar is required. You'll find different sizes, styles, and colors of these concrete "stones" at any home-improvement or building-supply store. Begin by digging a trench, laying a gravel base, and leveling it. After that, stacking the concrete units is simple, and there are special, easy-to-use corners and capstones.

GROWING PLANTS IN PERMANENT PLANTERS. Unlike for smaller pots, where it's almost always best to use a soilless potting mix to promote rapid drainage, the soil for larger planters should include some real earth. Real soil holds up better in the long run than soilless mixes, which decompose and settle over a period of months or years. You can make a good blend yourself by mixing two parts (measured by volume, not by weight) good garden soil with one part coarse, gritty sand and one part peat moss. Add about 1 cup of ground limestone and 2 cups of composted steer manure per bushel of soil mix.

Watering is the main chore in maintaining a planter. In the heat of summer, you may need to water once a day. Installing an automatic drip system on a timer is an easy way to simplify that task. Fertilizing is essential, too. Use a balanced, water-soluble fertilizer mixed at half the recommended strength and apply it every two to three weeks from when new growth starts in spring until late summer.

Many kinds of small trees, shrubs, and perennials can be grown for years in large, permanent planters. Eventually most plants outgrow a planter and need to be removed and set into the ground. Then you can replace them with something different for a change. You can also use planters for short-term or seasonal plantings of annuals, tropicals, herbs, vegetables, or whatever you want to grow.

❦ WATER FEATURES

Water captures and holds your interest like nothing else, and a water feature adds sparkle and serenity to an outdoor room. There are many possibilities, depending on your space, budget, climate, and interests. If you want to get into the water, consider full-size swimming pools in standard or free-form shapes, lap pools for exercise, shallow wading pools for young children, and heated spas for relaxation. If you'd rather stay dry, sit back, and enjoy the sight and sound of water, you might like a fountain, a little pool with a built-in waterfall, a reflecting pond, or a water garden with water lilies, other aquatic plants, and fish.

Any of these features can be the centerpiece of an outdoor room. You can add small features to an existing room, or install a swimming pool, in-ground spa, or lily pond and build a room around it. At minimum you'll want a patio, deck, or some other type of floor around or beside the water. You'll probably want some kind of outdoor walls for privacy, but it's better not to have a ceiling. Water belongs under an open sky, so you can see it mirror the sun by day and the stars at night.

Practical considerations

When you're planning any water feature, think about safety, utilities, weatherproofing, site selection, and design. Safety is an issue if there are children around. Municipal zoning codes aptly describe most water features as "attractive nuisances" and require some sort of fencing or barrier around them, so inquire locally about this. The utility requirements for most water features are fairly simple and straightforward, but unless you already have convenient and adequate water and electrical hookups, you may need to hire a plumber and electrician, so that's something to factor into your budget and schedule.

Weatherproofing is mostly winterizing. In freezing climates, you'll probably need to do some preparation in fall as you shut down the pump, drain the lines, cover the water, and so forth, and then start up again in spring. Meanwhile, a winterized pool or pond is a forlorn sight, but maybe you can overlook it as you daydream about the happy days of summer. Other weather concerns have to do with maintaining the water level. In arid climates, water evaporates so fast from the surface of a pool that you'll probably want a valve that refills it automatically. In any climate, a prolonged downpour can flood a small water feature, so any basin or pool should have an overflow channel, even if it's just a simple notch in the rim.

Accounting for convenience, utility hookups, safety, and privacy will limit your options for where to site a water feature. Other things to consider are topography and trees. Level sites are best for all but the smallest features. It's much more challenging to install a pool or pond on a slope. In addition, choose a site without nearby trees, if possible, to cut down on the amount of leaves and litter that you'll need to filter out of the water.

Design considerations

For design ideas, it helps to think in terms of styles and color themes. For example, to preserve a natural-style landscape, install a free-form in-ground pool with a dark gray or green (not bright turquoise) finish, or build an artificial pond with a small waterfall at one end. Use boulders and evergreens (to minimize leaf drop) around the edge. In a Mediterranean-style outdoor room (see page 86), consider a rectangular reflecting pool lined with gleaming tiles or a small spouting fountain set into a masonry wall. In an American-style suburban setting, contrast the cool color of a traditional turquoise pool with a decking of warm reddish brown bricks or stained wood, and surround it with lots of annuals and perennials that bloom all summer in shades of blue, violet, pale yellow, and white, or go tropical and surround it with palms and colorful vines and shrubs.

For a shady yard surrounded by trees, consider a babbling fountain rimmed with moss and ivy.

The main challenge, in terms of design, is making the water feature seem to fit in. Think about coordination, repetition, and harmony, not contrast. Because water is so inviting, it always becomes the center of attention and tends to stand out too much and overwhelm its surroundings. That tendency gets exaggerated if a pool or fountain is strikingly differ-

LANDSCAPING AROUND A POOL

The challenge is incorporating a pool into your yard at an affordable price. If cost is no limit, you can have a spectacular free-form in-ground pool with colorful tiles, an adjacent spa, a smooth terrace or deck for lounging, a shady retreat, a bathhouse, stylish fencing, and lush plantings all around.

- **UPGRADE THE "FLOORING."** On a tight budget, or if you already have a pool and want to upgrade it, focus on the lounging area, the fence, and the plantings. Start with the lounging area. It's nice if this is as large as the pool itself. Lawn isn't good, because grass clippings get into the water. A smooth outdoor floor is much better. For an in-ground pool, consider wooden decking or dry-laid pavers instead of the conventional poured concrete. Whatever surrounds the pool should slope away from it, so that surface water doesn't run into the pool. For an aboveground pool, you could pair a smaller deck or landing that's raised to water level with a larger floor at ground level. This doesn't have to surround the pool; it can be set off to one side.

- **TURN THE FENCE GREEN.** Chain link, the most common kind of pool fencing, is stark on its own, but if there's space along the base of a chain-link fence, you can disguise it — in fact, you can transform it into something desirable! — by letting English ivy, creeping fig, euonymus, or other evergreen vines climb up through it.

- **PLANT BOLDLY.** For poolside plantings, think big and bold. Because the pool itself is big, nearby plants and plantings should be big. More is better. Don't be timid here. Fill beds around the outer edge of the pool deck with fountainlike ornamental grasses, landscape roses and other summer-blooming shrubs, and robust perennials that form broad, bushy, long-flowering clumps, such as Japanese anemones, purple coneflower, daylilies, rose mallow or hardy hibiscus, coneflower or rudbeckia, Russian sage, Jerusalem sage, and various salvias. Use cannas, gingers, calla lilies, elephant's ears, and other large-leaved tropical bulbs in the ground or in large containers. Stuff big pots and planters with colorful annuals.

Avoid plants that continually drop petals or litter that could blow into the water. Those listed above are neat.

Don't worry about the effect of chlorine from the pool water. How often does pool water splash as far away as the plants are growing? Chlorine isn't likely to be a problem unless you put plants right next to the edge of the pool.

A traditional swimming pool is the centerpiece of a calm, formal landscape with cut-stone paving, clipped hedges, and a muted color scheme.

A contemporary pool and spa are lapis, not turquoise, with free-form shape, random stone edging, and mixed plantings with varied colors and textures.

(RIGHT): *Natural-looking but totally man-made, this stone fountain and pool is plumbed with a recirculating pump and includes a flexible waterproof liner and an overflow drain (a desirable but often overlooked feature).*

(BELOW): *Small and simple, a Japanese-style fountain brings the entrancing tinkle of running water into any garden.*

ent in size, materials, style, and color from its surroundings. So ask yourself, in considering and siting a new water feature or working around an existing one, what would fit here? How can I make this blend in? What would tie it all together? Answering questions such as these helps you integrate a design.

Swimming pools and spas

A swimming pool is a great place to relax—or exercise—in warm weather. Kids love pools, and most grownups do, too. Fresh, clear water is so refreshing.

But pools have several drawbacks. They take a lot of room and require continual monitoring and maintenance. Although there's been some progress in designing biological filters and natural care systems, most pool owners still depend on an arsenal of chemicals to maintain water quality. Pool pumps are noisy. Most communities mandate that any pool be surrounded by a childproof fence; sometimes double fencing (one fence around the property, another around the pool itself) is required. During cold weather, when a pool is covered or closed, it's just a big blank spot in your yard. All told, an in-ground pool is a big commitment of space, a major investment, and an ongoing responsibility. It won't necessarily increase your property's value and may even decrease it. Aboveground pools share some of these drawbacks but are smaller, cost less, and are more easily removed when they're not wanted anymore.

Spas and hot tubs are so much smaller than swimming pools that by comparison, it's easy to fit them into a landscape. You'll probably want a site that's close to the house, for convenience, and screened by walls, fences, or plants for privacy, with an electrical hookup to run the pump, filter, heater, and lights. Check local authorities to see what, if any, kind of fencing, gates, or other security measures are required.

Fountains and waterfalls

Everyone loves the sound and sight of running water; it's both refreshing and soothing. You can buy small fountains in a wide range of traditional and contemporary styles from catalogs and garden centers. Some kinds can be mounted on a wall. Others rest on the ground or can be set inside a pool. All models have three basic elements. There's a spout of some kind where the water comes out, a basin or reservoir below where the water collects, and a hidden electric pump that recirculates the water. Most ready-made fountains include all three components in sizes designed to work well together.

Small pools with splashing waterfalls are normally custom-built and include more elements. Along with the pool itself (which has a framework or foundation and a flexible plastic or rubber liner), the decorative edging (usually rocks), and the waterfall (typically a simple spillway over a protruding rock lip), there are hidden underpinnings, one or more filters, a pump, perhaps a float valve, and maybe some underwater lights. You can get enough information from the manufacturers and suppliers and from water-gardening books to put everything together yourself, or you can have a water-garden contractor design and build something wonderful for you.

Running water is especially welcome in dry climates. A fountain like this is a perfect feature for a walled, Mediterranean-style landscape.

WIRING AND SWITCHES. Installing a fountain or pool usually doesn't require a plumbing connection, as you can simply fill it with water from a hose as needed. But you do need an electrical hookup to run the pump. For safety's sake, and to comply with standard codes, you should only plug a fountain pump or any other appliance used under water into an outlet or circuit equipped with a ground-fault circuit interrupter (GFCI), which immediately trips off the current if anything happens to bring water in contact with the wiring. Outdoor outlets at new houses are normally GFCI-equipped, but if you have any doubts about your outdoor wiring, call an electrician.

If you need to use an extension cord to connect the fountain's pump to an outlet, be sure to use a waterproof cord that's designed for outdoor use, not an indoor extension cord.

Flipping an on-off switch is more convenient and safer than repeatedly plugging and unplugging a cord to turn the pump off and on. If your setup doesn't come equipped with a switch, you can have an electrician install one. Follow the manufacturer's instructions for maintaining the pump and protecting it from winter damage.

Reflecting pools and water gardens

Still water serves as a mirror, reflecting the ever changing sky, the sun and clouds and moon, nearby plants—even your own gazing face—until a breeze stirs the surface, raising ripples and bubbles that break the spell. It's very easy to add a still-water feature to an outdoor room or garden area. These features rarely require any special plumbing or wiring and usually aren't covered by any local regulations or codes.

A reflecting pool doesn't have to be more than a few inches deep. The only problem with making it too shallow is that the water will evaporate quickly and you'll need to refill it often, but that's no issue if you're watering plants in the area anyway. If you keep the water less than about 1 inch deep, birds will come to bathe there. For a small reflecting pool or birdbath, you can simply set a broad, shallow stone, ceramic, metal, or other kind of basin on a pedestal, or lay it on the ground and use blocks around the edge to hold it level and steady. Make a larger reflecting pool by digging a hole or building a frame and installing a flexible pond liner, as for garden pools. You can cover the liner with smooth rocks, if you choose. Add a few drops of household chlorine bleach to the water occasionally to keep algae from growing on the rocks.

Pools or ponds for raising water lilies, other plants, and fish need more water than reflecting pools but can still be quite shallow. A maximum depth of 2 feet is plenty, and many plants do fine in as little as 6 to 12 inches of water. Although pools

designed for plants and fish sometimes have pumps and filtration systems, they generally don't include fountains or waterfalls, so the surface of the water is still, like that of a reflecting pool. However, if you're growing water lilies or floating plants, their leaves will spread to cover some or all of the pond surface by mid- to late summer.

MINIATURE WATER GARDENS. A half-barrel planter lined with a sheet of plastic holds enough water to grow a miniature water lily and a few vertical water plants along with half a dozen goldfish. For a larger pool or a different look, buy a sturdy preformed plastic or fiberglass tub from a water-garden supplier. These tubs are usually round but also come in oval, rectangular, or irregular shapes. They range from 2 to 5 feet wide and 1 to 2 feet deep, holding up to 200 gallons of water. You can set them on a patio floor and build a stone or wood frame around them. If there isn't a water-garden supplier in your area, visit a farm store. Plastic or galvanized-steel livestock water tanks or feeding troughs cost less but work as well as the preformed pools sold by water-garden specialists, and their agricultural look goes unnoticed once you've planted in and around them.

LARGER WATER GARDENS, MADE WITH LINERS. The easiest and best way to make a pool that's more than a few feet wide or long is by using a flexible pond liner purchased from a water-garden supplier. A pond liner is a big sheet of rubber or polymer that can be fit into any shape and makes a seamless waterproof lining. Good-quality liners

(ABOVE): Still water reflects the sky and invites you to linger and watch. It doesn't take much water to lend a mesmerizing effect. A reflecting pool can be quite small and very shallow.

(RIGHT): This shallow lined pool greets visitors in an outdoor room that serves as an expanded entryway. Its curving shape mirrors that of the dwarf pine on the left side of the gravel path.

cost at least $1 per square foot, but they are 40 mils thick, are resistant to ultraviolet light and freezing, and have about a 20-year guarantee. They're much more satisfactory than cheap sheets of polyethylene, which soon turn brittle, crack, and leak.

Like swimming pools, a water-garden pool can be set into the ground or raised above it. Most directions recommend digging a hole and recessing the pool into the ground. One advantage of this is that you can make the pool in any shape you can dig. Moreover, you can try to simulate a natural look if you choose. However, *don't* install an in-ground pool in a place where water would collect naturally or where surface runoff will carry debris into the pool and cause flooding. Choose a level or raised site for an in-ground pool.

Although you don't read as much about them, raised pools have several advantages. You don't have to peer down so far to see the plants or fish or bend over so far to tend them. The water stays cleaner because less debris blows in. Raised pools are easier and faster to build—you make a wood or masonry frame instead of digging a hole—and easy to move or remove if you change your mind someday and don't want a pool anymore. Also, if you already have an outdoor room, you can add a raised pool without disturbing the existing floor. Two possible drawbacks: Raised pools are usually built in simple rectangular shapes and in smaller sizes than in-ground pools.

The companies that sell pond liners provide guidelines for building pools. For more information, consult a water-gardening book. One tip that most directions fail to mention is that for any pool, inground or raised, it's a good idea to install an overflow drain (flexible 1-inch plastic pipe is good for this) at some point around the rim. Run the pipe out onto the lawn or into a planting bed. That way, if there's a heavy downpour, the extra water will be carried away from the pool instead of flooding over the edge.

WATER PLANTS AND FISH. You can order plants and fish from mail-order specialists or find them at local nurseries and pet or fish stores. Along with water lilies and lotuses in sizes ranging from dwarf (small enough to grow in a half-barrel) to large (spreading 8 to 10 feet or wider), there are scores of other aquatic plants, both hardy and tender, to choose from. Most water plants should be planted in pots of heavy garden soil, then set down into the pool so that water covers the soil to a certain depth; plant suppliers will provide detailed information on this. They'll also give you guidelines on achieving the right balance of plants, goldfish, and water snails. (The snails, along with underwater plants called oxygenating plants, help control the algae that turns pond water green.)

With a pool for a centerpiece, you can expand a patio water garden by growing plants in pots. Almost any water-loving plant that's described as a *marginal* or *emergent* plant (water-garden catalogs list lots of these plants, including many with gorgeous foliage and flowers) will grow quite well in a container of ordinary potting soil sitting in a saucer, crock, or cachepot with an inch or two of water at the bottom. These plants need constant moisture, but their roots don't have to be fully immersed. Grouping several potted specimens around your pool will make a lush, exotic display.

(LEFT): *Boulders, grasses, and evergreens offer a fascinating range of shapes and textures that contrasts with the clear, still water in this manmade pool.*

(BELOW): *A wide rim of mortared flagstone frames this formal pool, which is raised slightly aboveground. The water lilies are planted in plastic tubs that sit on the pool bottom. Goldfish are carefree, tame, and entertaining, and they help control algae in a pond.*

Pavement deserves more appreciation. Imagine walking on this smooth, clean, level walk, and then think about what it would be like if there were just a dirt trail there instead.

5 ❧ Pavings and Edgings

NOWADAYS MOST people take smooth, easy-to-clean, quick-drying pavement for granted. Surrounded as we are by public sidewalks, streets, freeways, and parking lots, it seems as if there's pavement everywhere.

But if there isn't enough pavement in your own yard, you really miss having it. When you move into a new house that doesn't have paved walkways and landings yet, the mud, dust, ruined shoes, and tracked-in dirt soon get on your nerves. Or if you live in an older house where the pavement is so scanty or irregular that you have to watch your step, that's frustrating, too. In arid climates and for small yards, pavement is a practical alternative to lawns. In any case, adding or replacing pavement is a landscape improvement you'll really appreciate.

This chapter covers the practical aspects of choosing, installing, and maintaining pavement made from poured concrete, brick, flagstone, and other masonry and from compacted gravel or rock aggregates. The same information applies to pavement used for patios, terraces, and other outdoor floors (for more on those topics, see page 112), for walks or paths (page 159), and for driveways (page 77).

If you're contemplating a project, you'll need to choose what kind of pavement you want and decide where you want it. Whether or not to install it yourself depends on your time, energy, ambition, and skill. In most cases, an experienced contractor could do the job faster and probably better than you would. But here I'll explain basic techniques and procedures so you can see what's involved and determine whether you want to give paving a try (if so, start with a small project) or hire help.

Paving is a long-term investment. You'll get decades of pleasure, convenience, and satisfaction from a well-laid masonry walk or a well-designed concrete patio. So it's definitely worth spending extra time and money to carefully prepare the site, get the kind of surface you want, cover a big enough area, be sure it's installed right, and include sturdy edgings.

❧ BASIC SITE PREPARATION

Many problems with existing pavement are the consequences of hasty or inadequate site preparation. Regrettably, these are hard to solve after the fact. About the only way you can deal with an underlying problem is to lift up the pavement and start over again. Obviously, it's better to plan ahead, be cautious, and prevent such disruption and expense.

First, check on buried utilities. If you suspect that there might be water, sewer, gas, electric, phone, or other lines buried under the area you intend to pave, call the customer service department of the relevant utility to arrange for help in locating where the lines go and in finding out how deep they are and if there's any reason to think twice before paving over them. Make sure these concerns are addressed before any pavement goes down, so you won't have to think about them again.

Evaluate nearby trees. This is a two-way concern. Looking one way, installing pavement can do serious damage to the roots of nearby trees. If you're worried about that and you have a valuable tree — especially one with shallow roots that are visible near or at the surface — consider relocating the paved area, using gravel or wood chips instead of concrete or masonry, or building a raised deck or boardwalk instead of installing grade-level pavement. (See pages 112 and 114.) If you can't help severing and removing a tree's roots, the root damage may

(ABOVE): *Dry-laid paving made of irregularly shaped flagstones is the easiest kind of pavement for a homeowner to install, looks casual and natural, and coordinates well with plants.*

kill it, although trees sometimes take years to die.

But looking the other way, some trees have strong, shallow roots that will reach underneath nearby pavement, grow thicker, and gradually crack and heave the surface. This doesn't happen all at once. Usually you've got a few years' notice. Watch the area between a tree's trunk and the pavement, and if you see that the ground is getting lifted, you know the pavement's next in line, and you can decide whether to sacrifice it or the tree.

Either way, what I'm saying here is that trees and pavement are uncertain partners. Sometimes things work out fine, but there's always a chance that you'll end up losing one or the other. In any particular case,

it depends on the kind of tree, how deep and extensive its roots are, how much of its root system the paving covers, and fate. Consult with a local arborist for more specific guidance and decide what risks you're willing to take.

Clearing and rough grading

After you've determined a design and marked the outline of the area to be paved, dig up and transplant all desirable garden plants that aren't too large to move. Strip any sod and lay it elsewhere or compost it. Kill any perennial weeds (see page 273). Get down to bare ground, then go further and make sure you've removed any buried roots, rhizomes, or bulbs. I've seen daffodils, lily-of-the-valley, and other indomitable perennials sprout up through 2 inches of blacktop. The same plants have an uncanny ability to locate and emerge through cracks in concrete or masonry. It's actually rather charming and amazing to see old favorite garden plants pop up through pavement, but not when cursed weeds come back to taunt you.

With plants out of the way, study the grade. If the area you want to pave is sloping or irregular now, it can and should be more or less leveled or smoothed out. Although driveways often run uphill or down, most other paved areas on residential lots should be level or nearly so. You can easily drive a car on a slope that's too steep for safe, comfortable walking. For pedestrians, the combination of level walkways and steps is almost always preferable to a ramp. If you do decide to lay a walkway that climbs or traverses a slope, at least make it level from side to side. And, of course, patios, terraces, landings, work areas, and any other paved surfaces should be completely level, with only enough pitch to provide for runoff.

For small projects or on gentle slopes, you can do the required grading by hand. For larger projects, steep slopes, or any situation where you're uncertain or daunted, call for help. A landscape contractor

(BELOW): *The roots of this big old maple tree had cracked and heaved the old sidewalk. When the city replaced the paving, they shaped a well around the base of the tree.*

(BELOW RIGHT): *Here's another way to pave around trees. The mason left a space around the tree trunk at upper right, poured separate concrete slabs, and then laid cobblestones in the cracks between the slabs and the gap between the slabs and the tree. The cobblestones let water drain through and will "give" as the tree roots thicken over the years.*

can handle most situations, but for really steep slopes you may need a landscape architect or a soil engineer.

WORKING ON GENTLY CONTOURED GROUND. Height differences of just a few inches from here to there can be addressed in the normal course of excavating soil, preparing a base, and laying pavement. Determine where you want the finished height of the pavement to be. Use a level as you go around the edge and mark that height with stakes and string. Then work down from there, removing more soil from the high spots and less from the low spots as needed to make a flat-bottomed hole. Go ahead and build up the base, pavement, and edgings.

Once the pavement is completed, use a hoe or rake to smooth out the contours of the surrounding soil. Even out any abrupt cuts or drop-offs and make the soil ease right up to the edge of the pavement. You may need to dig up some plants and set them aside while you fine-tune the grading around or along the edge of the pavement, then replant them afterward. That's inconvenient, but smoothing out the surroundings makes any paved area look more natural, as though it belongs there.

WORKING ON STEEPER SITES. Certainly one problem with major grading jobs is the amount of soil to be moved, but that's not the primary issue.

More important is an understanding of soil and topography, an awareness of the difference between cutting and filling, and an ability to judge stable vs. unstable situations. This takes skill and experience. Don't risk disappointment or liability. Get professional help with any paving job that involves grade changes of more than several inches.

In general, cutting into a slope and laying a base and pavement over undisturbed soil works okay, because undisturbed soil is usually (not always) fairly stable. You will have to deal with the raw bank where the soil was cut away on the uphill side of the leveled area. This may require a retaining wall, or perhaps you can establish a dense ground cover there.

Importing fill dirt and laying pavement on top of a filled area is riskier. Anytime this is done, the contractor should make every effort to compact the fill as densely as possible. Even so, it's likely to settle over time, and as it does, the pavement will sink with it. If you're having fill work done, tell the contractor that you're worried about subsidence and ask what he's doing to minimize or prevent it.

The success of a fill job also depends on the site. Filling a small bowl-shaped depression usually works okay if the fill is well compacted. But trying to fill a dip where a driveway or walkway crosses a swale or drainage area is asking for trouble. Unless you provide a culvert (see page 182) for the water to run

Building a ramp, instead of a step, into this mortared tile pavement lets you roll a wheelchair or baby stroller in and out of the house.

You can't lay a floor on a sloping site; you must alter the grade first. Here cutting into a hillside made a level area for the mortared flagstone floor. The retaining wall braces the slope on the uphill side of the floor.

through, it will make its own way, almost certainly to your dismay.

A common but challenging situation is trying to build a paved terrace or patio on a sloping site by bringing in fill dirt to raise the downhill side and make a level area. In this case, along with compacting the added soil, you definitely need to have a sturdy retaining wall along the downhill edge (see page 214). If the edge simply tapers off, the fill dirt is likely to erode and slump. In addition, the edge of a pile of fill looks ugly, it's hard to get plants established there, and it's a headache trying to care for plants in such a spot.

Assess the drainage

Only on sites where the soil dries promptly after a rain can you lay pavement directly on the ground. That's uncommon. Almost always, you need to remove some of the existing soil and replace it with a base of free-draining crushed rock. What kind of rock aggregate to use and how much of it is required depends on your soil and climate, so get local advice. Site preparation also depends on what kind of pavement you're installing, as discussed in the sections on concrete, masonry, and aggregate pavements later in this chapter.

It's hard to judge drainage on short notice or if you've just recently moved into a house, since drainage problems are normally latent and show up

only on a seasonal or occasional basis. Wait a few months or longer to see what happens during a heavy storm. Or if you're impatient, run a hose out to the low spot(s) in a potential path, let it flow awhile, and see if the water soaks in or puddles. Anyplace where puddles linger or the ground stays muddy for more than a day or so after a rain has poor drainage and is sure to need attention.

FROST HEAVING. Frost heaving is a seasonal problem that's related to poor drainage. Water expands when it freezes, so soil that's saturated with water heaves up in cold weather. Any pavement or path surface likewise gets lifted. Although the heaving subsides again when the ground thaws, the pieces don't fit back exactly as they were before, and repeated cycles of freezing and thawing gradually disrupt the surface of a path and make it bumpy. In regions where the ground freezes in winter, it's especially important to make sure that water drains out from underneath a path. Again, this almost always requires building a crushed-rock base.

MUD SEASON. Another related problem is spring mud season in cold, wet climates. Mud season happens when the surface starts to thaw while the subsoil remains frozen. Water can't drain down into frozen ground. During mud season, which lasts for days or weeks, walks and paths that have adequate drainage throughout the rest of the year may be temporarily impassable. If possible, the best way to deal with mud season is to stay away from the soupy spots until the ground warms and dries out.

(OPTIONAL) INSTALL A BURIED DRAINPIPE. A good crushed-rock base is sufficient for most situations, but where drainage is uncommonly poor, an extra precaution is to install a drainpipe to carry water away from under the pavement. I'll describe how to do this for a path or walkway. If you need to drain a larger area before making a patio or terrace, get local advice on how many drain lines are needed and how to position them.

For a single drainpipe under a walk, excavate the soil as usual, then dig a trench about 8 inches deep and wide under the center of the walkway. Spread 1 to 2 inches of coarse crushed rock in the bottom of the trench, then lay in a 4-inch PVC perforated drainpipe. Use a hose to run some water into the pipe and make sure it flows downhill, pointing away from the house or any buildings. Cap the top end of the pipe, to keep soil from washing in. At the outlet end, you can direct the runoff onto a lawn or a bed of plants that appreciate extra water, or run it into a drain or ditch. Fill in around and over the drainpipe with more crushed rock. Cover the crushed rock with a layer of porous landscape fabric to prevent soil particles from filtering down and silting up the pipe. Then proceed to lay the normal aggregate base.

❦ POURED-CONCRETE PAVING

Poured concrete is the most widely used pavement because it's so versatile, affordable, and durable and because it costs less than brick, stone, or other masonry paving. It's suitable for all climates and sites, and it can be integrated with both formal and informal landscapes and with both traditional and contemporary homes. Concrete readily fits into both curved and rectangular designs, and it's easy to incorporate steps or levels into a design.

But concrete has various drawbacks. If the surface is too smooth, it's slippery when wet. Slabs are liable to crack. Oil, paint, and rust leave indelible stains. Unwanted concrete is hard to remove.

Concrete's appearance is typically banal, but there are several ways to make it look more attractive and interesting. You can order it in various colors or arrange to have a pebbled, etched, or grooved surface. Concrete combines quite gracefully with other materials, and making combinations gives you the advantages of concrete—low cost and easy maintenance—along with the visual interest of the other material. For example, one way to mitigate the blankness and expanse of a concrete slab is by leaving the timber framing in place and including wooden dividers that subdivide the overall area into smaller shapes. Bricks, stones, or metal can be used in a similar way to surround or subdivide a slab.

Because it is fluid and conforms to any shape, concrete can be poured right up to the base of a vertical edging or wall, such as the wall of a building or a retaining wall or garden wall, made from wood, stones, or brick. Where steps are required, you can use concrete for the risers and lay something else on top for the tread, or vice versa. Talk to a landscape contractor, not just a paving specialist, for projects like this.

While newly poured concrete is still soft, you can press bricks, tiles, or stones down into it, setting them flush with the surface (this is easier said than done). You can place individual elements in key locations, scatter them at random across the surface, make lines or geometric shapes, or create a mosaic. In any case, work this out in advance with your concrete contractor. There's only a limited time period when you can set things into the concrete, so plan the pattern ahead of time by laying things out on the foundation, then make a drawing that shows what you want to put where. Plan to be present on the day of the pour so you can answer any last-minute questions and watch as the design gets set in place.

Installation

In general, pouring concrete is not a do-it-yourself job. It's better to hire a contractor. He'll make it look easy, but it's not. In fact, if you've ever tried it yourself, you'll be all the more impressed when you watch workers who really know what they're doing. Wet concrete is heavy, sloppy stuff, yet you need a surprisingly light touch when finishing its surface. You also need to be totally prepared in advance and to work quickly once the pour begins. There's almost no leeway for correcting mistakes.

If you do want to try it yourself, start with a short walk or other small project. First, check with the local building department to see what, if any, codes apply to your planned project. Then line up one or more experienced helpers who have done some concrete work and know what's involved, and spend some time visiting construction sites to watch how the pros do it.

You can't learn how to install concrete by reading about it; you have to actually see and touch it. But I'll explain the basic process here so you will know what's involved, can talk to a contractor about what you want, and will understand what he's doing as the job proceeds.

SITE PREPARATION AND FORM BUILDING. A contractor will check the grading and drainage, excavate as needed, and install a gravel base suitable for your climate and site (usually 2 to 6 inches deep).

Poured concrete is the most versatile paving material, excellent for floors, walks, and steps. It can be molded into curved or straight shapes, and it combines well with stones (RIGHT), bricks (BELOW), wood, and other materials. You can choose from several colors and surface textures when having new concrete installed.

Then he'll build sturdy forms around the perimeter, setting the tops of the boards at the desired level for the surface of the slab (usually allowing for 4 inches of concrete), and lay reinforcement mesh inside. To provide for rapid runoff and surface drainage, the forms will be built with a pitch of about ⅛ to ¼ inch per foot. Attached slabs must slope away from the house. Detached slabs or walks can slope whatever way you choose.

Wooden forms can be made temporary or permanent; ask your contractor about this. Permanent forms made of substantial, rot-resistant timbers can attractively frame the area and provide welcome contrast in texture and color, but to not look skimpy, these should be much thicker than the boards typically used as temporary forms.

Except for very small projects, your contractor will probably recommend subdividing the area with more boards that run crosswise or form a grid; these are meant to be left in place and become a permanent part of the design. They're called expansion joints, because they relieve the stress and tension that occur when slabs expand and contract owing to temperature changes. Again, it looks better and costs only a fraction more if these boards are thicker than average.

Pay special attention to form building if you undertake a concrete project yourself. Make sure that the forms are very sturdy. Check and double-check them to ensure that the surface of the slab will be level and properly pitched.

MIXING AND POURING CONCRETE. Concrete is made by mixing cement (a dusty powder prepared from limestone and clay) with sand, crushed rock or gravel, and water. Although fluid at first, it soon starts to harden. Once the ingredients are mixed, you need to spread and finish it within a couple of hours.

Except for small projects or on inaccessible sites, it's uncommon to mix concrete on site. Normally a contractor will have ready-mix concrete delivered by truck. Ready-mix is sold by the cubic yard. One cubic yard of concrete will pave an area of about 80 square feet to a thickness of about 4 inches. If you want to have the concrete colored or to have an exposed-aggregate finish, sort this out before placing the order.

Things happen fast when the truck arrives. The contractor will start at one end or corner and pour concrete into the forms, using a hoe to spread it around and to make sure it's settled down into the corners and along the edges. He'll fill sections of the form one at a time.

To level the surface, two people (one on each end) will pull a 2x4 *screed* along the top of the form, jiggling it back and forth with a sawing motion. They'll shovel more concrete into any low spots as needed and screed it again. They'll use a trowel or edging tool to round off the edges and a *float* to further level and smooth the surface.

For outdoor purposes, concrete shouldn't be too smooth or it will glare in the sun and be slick in the rain. While it's still soft, the contractor can make a rough, grainy, or grooved surface by lightly brushing the concrete with a stiff broom. An even nicer surface, called exposed aggregate, is made by washing the surface of the soft concrete to reveal attractive gravel that was included in the mix.

CURING. Although you can walk on new concrete after a day or so, it continues to harden, or *cure,* for weeks afterward and turns out best if you keep it from drying too quickly during this time. The contractor may cover it with plastic and recommend that you keep it covered for a few weeks, or ask you to spray it daily with water. Temporary forms can be removed after the concrete has hardened, usually within a few days.

Maintenance, renovation, and replacement

Other than sweeping or hosing it clean, concrete needs virtually no maintenance. If weeds sprout up through any cracks, kill them with a contact herbicide, by flaming, or by pouring scalding water on them. Turfgrass and trailing ground covers growing around the edge of a slab can spread several feet across it in a single growing season if you let them, but when you get fed up and want to peel them off it's as easy as rolling up a rug. Or you can maintain a neat edge next to concrete by trimming plants there with a sharp edging tool or string trimmer.

A well-installed concrete slab should look good for decades, but things can go wrong. The surface may get stained. It may flake or erode. The slab may crack or heave if the ground underneath settles or tree roots intrude. Even if it's still in good shape, you may want to remodel the area somehow. Here are some options.

WORKING OVER OLD CONCRETE. If the slab is in basically good condition, a contractor can refresh its surface by staining, coating, or recovering it. These are specialized services, not universally available, so you'll have to call around to find someone who can help you.

If the slab is still level and hasn't heaved or shifted, you can spread sand on top and lay pavers, flagstones, or bricks there. If the existing slab isn't as big as you want the new floor to be, you'll need to excavate around the perimeter and lay a gravel foundation there before spreading the sand. Even if you compact the gravel as thoroughly as possible, the juncture between it and the concrete may show up later as a slight ridge in the finished surface, but it should be fairly subtle.

If the slab is badly cracked, don't try laying pavers on it. Whatever caused the slab to crack would heave the pavers sooner or later. Have the slab removed and start again from scratch, or get a deck built over the cracked slab. A builder will probably have to remove some of the old concrete to install the deck's foundation, but most of it can remain; it won't show and won't do any harm down under a deck.

REMOVING OLD CONCRETE. Removing a concrete slab is hard work. You might be able to break it apart yourself with a sledge hammer or a rented air hammer, if it's fairly thin and it wasn't reinforced, but you'll be sore afterward. Most concrete that's been poured in recent decades does have metal reinforcement inside, so it takes heavy equipment to break it apart.

Concrete rubble can be recycled to make rustic steppingstones or retaining walls, although it always looks like what it is and doesn't compare with real stones. You might use rubble this way if you think it will soon get hidden by moss or trailing plants. Or you might have a place to use some rubble as fill that will get buried. Otherwise, have it hauled away.

Unlike poured concrete, whose surface is continuous or has just a few joints or seams, masonry pavement is a fascinating mosaic of separate elements set close together. It has an overall pattern determined by the shape of the pieces and how they are arranged. This patchwork effect makes masonry a perfect element for landscapes, because it evokes the natural patterns of leaves and flowers and works on a similar scale. Bricks, for example, are about the same size as many plants' leaves, so brick pavement coordinates beautifully with plants. Along with bricks, masonry pavement can consist of tiles, cast-concrete pavers, flagstones, or cobblestones, and all of these materials can be used separately or in combination.

Masonry pavement is endlessly varied and versatile because there are so many materials to choose from, in different sizes, textures, and colors, and so many ways to arrange them. It combines well with all kinds of architecture and all styles of landscaping. It can be used for large or small areas, for rectangular or curved shapes, for wide floors and narrow walks. Steps can be incorporated, if needed (although building steps is much more complicated than simply paving a level surface; see page 183).

Get it done right

If done well, masonry work lasts for decades, even centuries, and never looks out of fashion. It's expensive, but it retains its value and doesn't depreciate. But it's critical that you prepare a stable, free-draining base; invest in good bricks, stones, or pavers; and install them carefully. Cheap, hasty, or poorly done masonry soon becomes an annoying eyesore, and its surface can get so irregular that it's hard to walk on, even dangerous.

Installing masonry pavement is a good do-it-yourself project if you're a patient, thorough, detail-oriented worker. There's a lot of digging and hauling in preparing the base, but as a reward, the final step of actually laying pavers in place is particularly satisfying. If you want to give masonry a try, use the dry-laid technique and start with a small project such as a landing, the area under an arbor, or a garden terrace big enough to hold a bench and some potted plants. Then, if you like the work and think you have the knack for it, you might tackle a larger project such as a walk or patio. Solicit plenty of local advice, study construction manuals, think through the job before you begin, and don't rush—take the time to do it right, and you'll have something to be proud of.

It is, however, better not to tackle a masonry project yourself unless you're totally committed to doing it, as you're likely to get bogged down or be disappointed by your results. Get recommendations and references from friends, neighbors, local nurseries, or landscape contractors and hire a mason or paving contractor to do the work for you. In particular, hire help if you want mortared pavement, if your project covers a large area, or if there are any problems posed by the site, such as a steep slope, unstable soil, or poor drainage.

Dry-laid vs. mortared construction

There are two common ways to lay bricks, flagstones, or pavers. One is to set them on a bed of sand or finely crushed rock, carefully positioning and leveling them, and then use more sand to fill any cracks. This approach is called dry-laid or dry-set pavement. The advantages are that it doesn't take too much skill to install, requires less of a base, and is easier to adjust or relevel if it shifts or heaves. Furthermore, you can lift and replace individual pavers if they ever get stained or damaged. If you use good materials and install them carefully, dry-laid pavement lasts for decades, even centuries. But it can easily be removed and recycled if you change your mind. The main drawback with this kind of pavement is that weeds grow in the cracks.

Although you'll probably want to hire a contractor for big jobs such as patios, main walks, or driveways, you can install small expanses of dry-laid pavement yourself. It's a fun and satisfying project.

The other approach to masonry pavement is to set the bricks, stones, or pavers in a base of wet mortar and use more mortar to grout the cracks. Mortared pavement has a more finished and formal look that's uniform, neat, and weed-resistant. When done right, it's strong, beautiful, and permanent. But it takes judgment to mix mortar of the right consistency and skill to apply it without making a mess, and you need to work quickly and accurately. Unless you happen to have experience with this kind of work, I'd encourage you to omit the mortar and lay masonry pavers in a bed of sand, as described above. If you want a mortared walk, hire a mason to make it for you.

Mortared pavement needs a more substantial foundation than dry-laid pavement. Typically, it's laid on a concrete slab. Around the edge there should be a reinforced-concrete footing that reaches down below the frost line. This adds to the cost of installation. (Although if you already have an old concrete slab in fairly good condition, laying mortared pavement on top of it is an affordable upgrade.)

A long-term drawback of mortared masonry walks is that the mortar is almost certain to crack over time. It may remain in place, but the cracks will show and can be invaded by weeds. Also, mortared pavement is hard to repair when stained or damaged. You can't simply lift out individual elements and replace them, as you can with pavement set in sand; you have to redo whole areas, and places where you've patched or replaced the mortar are nearly impossible to conceal or disguise. Finally, if you change your mind someday, removing mortared pavement is a big job and you can't reuse the bricks or stones without chipping off the old mortar, a tiresome task.

Choosing and buying pavers

If you're having a mason lay your pavement, he'll show you photos and samples of different materials and get what you want. But for background information, or if you want to tackle a project yourself, shop for paving materials at home-improvement centers, building-supply stores, and stoneyards throughout your area. You'll find several appealing options, which will differ greatly in appearance and price but be fairly similar in terms of installation and upkeep. As for price, don't decide on the basis of the pavers alone, since that's only a fraction of the total job cost. Figure or get estimates for the entire project, from site preparation to final cleanup.

Calculate the area of your intended floor in square feet, then ask the supplier to help you figure how many pavers you'll need. With manufactured materials such as bricks, there's not much waste unless you need to cut pieces to make them fit. However, you may need to buy more than would be required if they're sold only by the pallet load, not by the count. Flagstones don't fit together as neatly, so buy some extras in order to have plenty to choose from as you work.

CONCRETE PAVERS. These are very popular because they come in so many colors and shapes, including several that simulate bricks or stones. Their surface can be rough or smooth; look for ones that are gritty, not slick, if you live in a rainy climate and are concerned about traction. Big square or rectangular pavers are usually about 2 inches thick. Smaller sizes and interlocking blocks may be thicker. If you can't find a wide variety of pavers at your local home-improvement center or building-supply store, check with paving contractors and stoneyards, or attend a local or regional home and garden show. At those shows you see a lot of these products on display.

Pavers are affordable and easy to install. They're very durable and they hold up to any climate. They have been used extensively in commercial landscapes over the last few decades in Europe, Canada, and the United States and are increasingly popular for home-landscape projects. If there's a drawback, it's that they may look too uniform, manufactured, or commercial, but that effect diminishes as they age. There are special cleaners, stain removers, and sealers designed to be used with concrete pavers. The sealers add a sheen, intensify the color, and help the pavers resist wear, stains, and water.

BRICKS. Bricks are designed for different situations and purposes—walls or floors, interior or exterior, and so forth. If you're hiring a mason to lay

Brick paving goes with any style of landscaping and is always popular. Traditional patterns, or bonds, shown here in mortared pavement, include basketweave (RIGHT) and herringbone (BELOW). Running bond, shown here in dry-laid pavement (BOTTOM), has the bricks set end to end in parallel rows that can be straight or curved. This particular example was tricky to make because it required cutting so many bricks where the straight and curved sections come together.

a mortared floor, take his advice on what bricks to use. For dry-laid paving that you're going to install yourself, choose special paving bricks, which measure a full 8x4 inches. They fit together snugly and it's easy to keep them aligned and to make neat patterns. By contrast, standard building bricks measure 8x3¾ inches, leaving a ¼-inch gap for mortar. You don't want gaps when you're setting bricks in sand; the surface will be more even and stabler if the bricks butt together.

You may find paving bricks, or brick pavers, in other shapes and sizes along with the standard 8x4. Try laying some out to see how they fit together before you decide which ones to get. Thickness varies, too, from about 1½ to 2 inches. As long as all your bricks are the same thickness, it doesn't matter what the measurement is.

Weather resistance is a concern with bricks. They're rated according to their durability. Use only SW (severe weather) bricks for paving in cold climates. Where the ground never freezes, you can get by with MW (moderate weather) bricks. Old bricks that are salvaged from demolished buildings are rarely suitable for paving; they crack, crumble, or flake apart after just a few seasons on the ground.

TILES. Quarry tiles and other ceramic tiles are made of fired clay, like bricks. Although gorgeous, they're often too pricey and also too slippery for outdoor flooring, but you may find a bargain or locate some tiles with a surface that's rough enough to be safe. Again, ask locally about their weather resistance. Tiles are usually installed on a concrete slab, using mortared construction, but they can sometimes be set in sand, depending on the site.

FLAGSTONES. Flagstones are split or cut from several kinds of rocks, so they come in a range of colors, textures, and hardnesses. Natural flagstones come in irregular shapes and varying thickness and typically have slightly rough surfaces. Dressed flagstones have been sawn or cut to a uniform thickness and standard width or shape; these look more formal but are sometimes slippery. Visit stoneyards and quarries in your area to see what's available.

Flagstones for paving are usually about 2 inches thick; thinner slabs are liable to crack. As for size, the bigger the better. Although you'll need some small or narrow pieces as fillers, it's best if most of the stones are at least 12 inches wide. When you work with stones, you soon learn to translate size into weight and to recognize one-person stones that you can move alone, versus two-person stones that you need help lifting and no-way stones that are too big to handle. Take your helper to the stoneyard to test-lift a few samples before you buy a pallet of big stones.

You can plan to dry-lay stones in sand yourself. It's easier for amateurs to work with irregularly shaped stones that fit together like puzzle pieces than with dressed or cut stones. If you've got some extras to pick from, you can almost always find a random stone that fits the spot, or that's good enough. With cut stones the expectations are higher; they should fit together as snugly and neatly as bricks. Another problem with cut stones is that you may end up having to trim a whole row of stones along one side of the floor to make them fit the space. This is a tricky and nerve-racking job, whether you do it the old-fashioned way with a chisel and hammer or use an electric masonry saw.

Flagstones are flat slabs about 2 inches thick. They come naturally in random shapes that fit together like puzzle pieces (BELOW) or are sawed into square or rectangular shapes that form geometric grids (BELOW RIGHT).

STONE BLOCKS. Cobblestones, river rocks, Belgian blocks, and other small paving stones should be about as thick as they are wide. They can be set in sand, packed as close together as you can fit them, or cast in mortar. Paving made from small rocks looks intriguing but isn't easy to live with. It works better for driveways or parking areas, or for decorative edgings around the edge of a smooth pavement made from another material, than for patios or other outdoor floors. The surface is a little too irregular for comfort, because the grooved seams tend to catch a shoe or the leg of a chair.

MOLDED-CONCRETE PAVEMENTS. You may have seen advertisements for or examples of plastic molds that are supposed to make concrete walks or patios that resemble brick or flagstone paving. The molds come in different patterns. Each is about 2 feet square overall and is subdivided into smaller rectangular or random shapes. The mold is roughly 2 inches thick, big enough to hold the contents of one 80-pound bag of ready-mix concrete. You lay the mold in place, mix the concrete with water, pour it into the mold, trowel the surface smooth, wait a few minutes for the concrete to set, and then lift off the mold, move it to the next location, and repeat. You end up with an array of little concrete slabs with wide cracks between them, which you need to fill with sand or soil.

What's wrong with this system? First, the cracks are too wide. Wide cracks encourage weeds and allow the separate paving pieces too much leeway; they shift around, rather than holding each other in place as tightly fitted pieces do. Second, unless you prepared a base underneath the pavement—a critical step that most directions omit—the individual elements will heave and settle and the surface will become quite irregular after a year or two. Third, unless you install an edging—another step that's omitted from the directions—the sides of the pavement will tip.

It's hard to think of a situation where this kind of molded concrete would give lasting satisfaction. If you can't afford the kind of masonry you want, choose something else in the meantime while you save up some money. Consider alternatives such as wood chips (ideal for temporary paving because they're so easy to remove and you can recycle them as mulch) or steppingstones rather than wasting your time and money and getting disappointed.

Preparing a base for dry-laid paving

Rarely is it satisfactory to lay pavers right on the soil surface. This only works on a level area where the ground slopes away around the edges, the soil is sandy or gravelly, and the climate is warm and dry. In

This unusual combination resulted when an old driveway was filled in. It includes random flagstones, square-cut stone blocks, and rounded cobblestones. You can see the difference in texture. Cobblestone pavement has an irregular surface that looks interesting but is difficult to walk on.

most situations, if you just lay pavers on the soil, the floor won't stay flat for long. Parts of it will sink down into the mud during a rainy spell. If your soil is clay, you know how it shrinks and swells; that makes pavers tilt and dip. Anyplace where waterlogged soil freezes in winter, pavers get heaved awry. Watching these problems as they occur, you might hope that everything will revert back to normal afterward, but it usually doesn't work that way. Once masonry pavement gets out of line, it either stays bad or gets worse; it doesn't fix itself.

Even more so than with other pavements, the long-term success of a masonry job depends on site preparation, which involves excavating the existing soil, burying a drain line if the site is poorly drained, and building up a base of compacted aggregate. Don't skimp; more is better. The benefits of a deep base more than repay the effort and expense of making it.

What kind of aggregate to use and how deep it should be depends on your climate, your soil, and the site's drainage. Because there are so many variables, get local advice. Talk to the building inspector (while asking if you need a permit for your project), to local masons and paving contractors, and to landscape contractors.

Although it involves a lot of shoveling, hauling, and raking, you can prepare a base for dry-laid pavement yourself. But if you're going to hire a mason to lay the pavement, he'll want to do the whole job. His reputation is at stake, and the success of a masonry surface depends on doing the preparation right.

ESTABLISH THE FINAL LEVEL. Unless you're going to build raised edgings along its sides or

around its edges, plan to set the surface of a masonry pavement a little higher than the adjacent ground. Raising it ½ to 1 inch is enough. That way, if the pavement adjoins lawn, you can run the lawn-mower wheel on it to mow right up to the edge. If it's next to a planting bed, make the pavement just high enough that soil and mulch don't keep spilling down onto it, but not so high that the bed appears sunken.

Once you've decided where you want the finished surface of the pavement to be, use stakes and strings to mark that height. You'll measure down from there when excavating and making the base.

Water will soak down through the cracks and base of dry-laid pavement, but if you live in a rainy climate it's good to speed runoff by pitching or crowning the surface. A masonry floor that's adjacent to the house should slant away from it, so that water all runs off to the far side. A freestanding floor can slant to one side or from the center outward to all edges; either way is okay. A path can slope from end to end or have a slight crown—that is, be higher along the centerline and lower on both sides. In any case, a slope of ¼ inch to the foot is standard. An easy way to check this is to take a 4-foot board and nail a 1-inch block under one end. Set the board on the surface you're checking and put a spirit level on top of the board; when the bubble is centered, the pitch is correct.

Be thinking about level and pitch as you work on the base. You'll need to give it a final check after spreading the sand, before you start to lay the pavers.

EXCAVATE THE SOIL. Generally, to prepare for dry-setting pavers, you'll need to excavate and remove the existing soil to a depth of 6 to 12 inches.

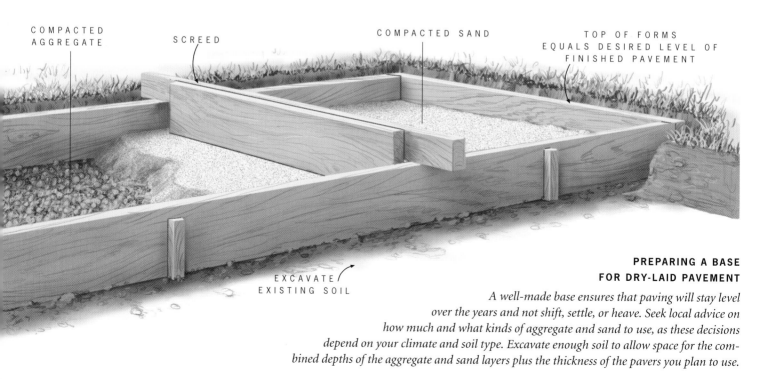

COMPACTED AGGREGATE

SCREED

COMPACTED SAND

TOP OF FORMS EQUALS DESIRED LEVEL OF FINISHED PAVEMENT

EXCAVATE EXISTING SOIL

PREPARING A BASE FOR DRY-LAID PAVEMENT

A well-made base ensures that paving will stay level over the years and not shift, settle, or heave. Seek local advice on how much and what kinds of aggregate and sand to use, as these decisions depend on your climate and soil type. Excavate enough soil to allow space for the combined depths of the aggregate and sand layers plus the thickness of the pavers you plan to use.

Starting from the finished surface level, subtract the thickness of the bricks, stones, or pavers you plan to use, then the recommended amount of sand, then the amount of coarse aggregate, and dig down to that depth.

This initial digging and hauling is the hardest part of laying masonry, as the soil is likely to be very compacted and you have to move it all out of the way. Figure out what you're going to do with that soil or dirt. Try to think of some way you could use it on your property, so you can shovel it into a wheelbarrow as you dig and move it one load at a time. Depending on the volume and quality, perhaps you could use it to fill low spots, make raised beds, level a hillside terrace, or shape a berm.

If you've hired a mason or contractor, he'll probably bring in a little front-end loader to scoop up the soil, dump it into a truck, and haul it away.

SPREAD, LEVEL, AND COMPACT THE AGGREGATE. Get local advice about what kind of gravel, crushed rock, or other aggregate to use as a base and how deep to lay it. A typical recommendation would call for from 2 to 8 inches of ¾-inch or coarser gravel or crushed rock, topped with 1 to 2 inches of rock dust, fines, or sand, into which you'll set the pavers.

Figure the area of your path in square feet, and the sales clerks at the gravel yard or building-supply store can advise you on how many tons of aggregate and sand to buy. Decide where you want the delivery truck to dump the piles. Put them as close to the work site as possible.

Spreading aggregate goes faster than excavating the original soil. Dump wheelbarrow loads here and there and spread the aggregate out with a rake, then set a spirit level on a 2x4 to check if the material is approximately level in all directions. Despite its weight, rock aggregate doesn't spontaneously settle into a dense layer. You have to deliberately compact it. For large areas, rent a power tool called a plate compactor (this looks kind of like a floor polisher—you walk along behind it as it vibrates against the ground). You can compact small areas with your feet by stomping all over the surface. After you've compacted an area, check it again to see if it's level. Add and compact more aggregate as needed to bring up any low spots.

Some contractors recommend putting a sheet of porous synthetic landscape fabric on top of the coarse aggregate before you add the sand. This makes a barrier that water can trickle through but keeps sand from silting down and clogging the pore spaces in the gravel base. It isn't mandated, but this step certainly doesn't do any harm. (The same layer of fabric is often described as a weed-prevention barrier, but that's wishful thinking, as most weed problems in pavement originate from seeds that land on the surface; they don't sprout up from below the fabric.)

ADD THE SAND. Spreading sand is even easier than spreading the coarse aggregate, and you need only a relatively thin layer of it. Dump piles of sand here and there, rake it out, and then smooth the surface by *screeding*, or dragging a board evenly across it. You don't have to compact the sand, but double-check that (1) its surface is level, (2) there's a pitch or slope of about ¼ inch per foot, and (3) the top of the sand is one paver thickness below the desired finished height. If it doesn't line up right, make adjustments and rescreed the sand.

Edgings for masonry pavement

An edging is an important part of masonry pavement. Like a cinch, a sturdy edging squeezes the pavers together. It also keeps the outside units from tipping or sliding out of place when stepped on.

In traditional construction, you install the edging after you've outlined the area and removed the soil, and you position it so the top of the edging will be flush with the finished pavement. Building the edging establishes what that level will be, and you use the edging as a reference as you proceed to add the aggregate and lay the pavers. These edgings are meant to be permanent, and they show, so they have to be neatly made from pressure-treated or rot-resistant lumber, poured concrete, or masonry. See page 154 for more on edgings.

The new approach to edging masonry pavement is to determine the level with a temporary grid of stakes and strings, add the aggregate and pavers, then install a PVC edging afterward. The PVC edging comes in rigid or flexible strips. It has an L-shaped profile, like an angle iron, and fits against the side of the pavement but doesn't show from above. You use special 10-inch spikes to fasten it down, nailing them through the base of the L, then rake soil or mulch over it.

Both approaches have pros and cons. Building the edging first gives you a frame to work in and helps you keep track of the level, but you need to measure accurately to make sure the edging holds a round number of pavers—otherwise, you'll have to do a lot of cutting or fudge the fit by leaving extra-wide gaps. A well-built edging looks good and adds to the final design. But the new PVC edging is easy to install and minimizes the annoyance of cutting and fitting (although you may still need to cut some pavers, depending on the pattern you've chosen).

Maintenance, renovation, and replacement

Masonry pavement should be relatively carefree. The worst problem is weeds that sprout from any cracks. If you ignore them, they'll go to seed and the problem will get worse. Try hand pulling, if you can get a grip on the weeds; cut or scrape them out with a pointed weeding tool; use a propane-fueled weed

SETTING DRY-LAID PAVEMENT

Putting the pavers in place is a piece of cake after you've done the hard work of preparing the base and building the edging. Whatever kind of paver you're laying—concrete pavers, bricks, tiles, flagstones, or cobblestones—the basic principles are the same.

1. First, recheck that the sand base is smooth, properly leveled, and correctly pitched. From now on, don't step directly on the sand. Lay scraps of plywood on the sand, and step or kneel on them.

2. Start in one corner or along one edge and work backward until you end up at the far side. Fit the pavers as close together as possible. Any gap or crack is a potential trip-up and a place for weeds to grow. If a ridge of sand gets pushed up between two pavers, lift one and sweep the sand away. Use a rubber mallet or a length of 2x4 to tap recalcitrant pavers into line. If you're setting bricks or rectangular pavers, use a chalk line to make sure each row is straight. Gaps are inevitable with irregularly shaped flagstones, but try to keep them to 1 inch or less. Sometimes there will be triangular spaces several inches wide where three or four stones come together. Break a few flagstones into fragments that you can pick from for filling these spaces.

3. Meanwhile, use a board and level to continually monitor that all the pavers are flush with the edging. If any are too low or too high, lift them and adjust the sand underneath as needed, then reset them and check again.

4. Stop often, get up, walk a few steps away, and admire what you've done. Scrutinize the alignment and the evenness of the surface. If any problems are becoming apparent, undo and revise that area immediately. There's no shame in having to do the job twice to get it right, but you'll kick yourself for years afterward if you leave an obvious problem unresolved.

5. Finally, sprinkle the surface with more of the sand you used underneath the pavers, and sweep it down into the cracks with a stiff-bristled broom. Spray the area with a hose or wait for a hard rain. Some of the cracks will reappear, so add more sand and repeat until they are filled.

Various kinds of flagstones, bricks, and other masonry pavings are typically sold by the ton or by the pallet load. You pay extra for delivery. Have the driver bring the pallets as close to your work site as possible.

flamer; or spray actively growing weeds with a contact herbicide. You'll need to reweed the paved area a few times each growing season.

Any kind of creeping turfgrass is particularly weedy in pavement and can spread from the cracks to completely hide the pavers over just a few growing seasons. Mowing doesn't control this; you have to kill the grass or say good-bye to your floor.

Ants often nest in the sand under dry-laid pavement. They're rarely more than a minor nuisance, but if you want to get rid of them, use boric-acid bait stations.

To protect and enrich the surface of a masonry walk, you can spray or paint on a clear liquid sealer. This isn't obligatory, but it has cosmetic value. A few different brands and products are available. Look for them at hardware and home-improvement stores if you're interested.

MINOR REPAIRS. One of the advantages of dry-laid pavement is that you can lift and reset or replace individual pavers or areas that have shifted or cracked or gotten stained. If the bricks or pavers were laid as close together as possible, it's hard to pry one out, but once you get the first one you can easily lift the ones around it and take up as much of the pavement as needed. Add or remove sand if you need to relevel a surface that's gone awry, then fit the pieces back in place and refill the cracks. You can hardly do this kind of piecemeal repair with mortared pavement, as it's much harder to remove a damaged piece or area and any patch you make will be very conspicuous.

SERIOUS PROBLEMS. Shifting, heaving, cracking, and settling are major headaches because fixing them involves lifting the pavement and correcting the underlying problem, which might be poor drainage, too shallow a base, unsettled soil, or intrusive tree roots. These issues shouldn't arise with new pavement, but they do show up after decades. If the walk or patio doesn't get much use and you don't mind its irregular appearance, the obvious thing to do is postpone fixing it. But if it's too rough to walk on or it looks like an earthquake zone, you'll have to remove it, solve the problem, and start over.

REPLACEMENT. Demolishing mortared masonry is like removing a concrete slab: you have to break it apart. The individual bricks or stones can be recycled, although the remaining mortar disfigures them, and chipping it off is a tedious job. Removing dry-laid masonry is much easier, since you can simply lift the pieces and set them aside. Usually most of them will still be good and can be reused for another project. If you don't have any use for the old pavement yourself or know anyone who wants it, you can always have it hauled away and dumped as fill.

If you plan to install new pavement in the same area, you probably should excavate and replace the old base, especially if there were problems with shifting or settling. Likewise, if you want to replace the pavement with lawn or plantings, you need to get rid of the old base and replace it with fresh soil. Don't try to dig up a previously paved area yourself unless you're a masochist. Hire somebody with machines to do the work.

Plants and masonry

Incorporating plants with masonry paving softens the surface, blurs the edges, and gives a more natural feeling and casual style. One way to include plants is to let them grow up through the floor at scattered intervals here and there. But some people don't look where they're walking and will stomp on a creeping plant, while others go out of their way to step around anything green, even a weed. You know your family, friends, and visitors, so choose accordingly. Few plants other than turfgrass and weeds can sustain continuous foot traffic, but there are several low-growing plants that can spring back from an occa-

It looks as though this pavement doesn't function as a driveway anymore, so why work around it? You could leave the strip next to the house as a walkway but remove the other strip and haul it away. Judging from how they've settled, these slabs are thin and demolition would be a fast, easy, and gratifying job.

sional flattening. See the box on page 180 for a list of creeping plants that combine well with stepping-stones. The same plants can be integrated with pavement.

Any plant taller than just a few inches stands far enough above the pavement to be perceived as an ornament or an obstacle, depending on your attitude. Encouraging tufted plants to sprout up here and there changes an outdoor floor from a functional space to a garden area. Rock gardeners are masters at this and create mosaics of gemlike plants in a meandering matrix of pavement. A planted floor is perfect for leisurely viewing, but it certainly doesn't double as a play area for children or a place to host a cocktail party.

PUT PLANTS AROUND THE EDGE. A more practical way to combine plants with an outdoor floor or walkway is to grow sprawling plants around the edge, while keeping an uninterrupted opening in the center. Suitable plants can tolerate an occasional misstep, but they can't be walked on regularly. Several perennials and a few shrubs will spread from an adjacent bed onto pavement that's at the same level, so you can grow these around grade-level patios or walks. These same plants can also trail down, so they could spill over a raised edging and down onto the pavement.

(RIGHT): *The grid of green thyme growing between these square-cut stones is artistic but impractical. You don't want to walk across something like that. And you have to keep trimming it or the thyme will flop and spread to fill the entire area. One season's uncut growth would totally cover the stones.*

(**ABOVE**): *Push the idea of "pavement interspersed with plants" to the limit and it turns into "garden mulched with flagstones." This Denver garden is a stunning example, with myriad details to discover and enjoy.*

(**LEFT**): *Creeping junipers are a popular edging for walks, although they tend to spread fast. If a juniper reaches out too far, don't just trim it back. Instead, lift it up, reach underneath as far as you can, and prune off the lower limbs.*

When choosing sprawling plants to grow beside pavement, pay special attention to exposure. Pavement that bakes in the sun gets extra warm, and smooth surfaces reflect sunlight back onto nearby plants; these factors exaggerate the difference between sunny and shady sites. Some plants bask in the added light and warmth, but shade-requiring plants would quickly wither there.

Also, find out how far a plant is likely to spread. Avoid vines and vigorous shrubs that reach too far out. Perennials that spread a few feet each season and get cut back hard once a year are good, along with compact, slow-growing shrubs. Here's a tip for pruning sprawling plants: Think of their stems as overlapping like layers of petticoats. Lift them up and reach underneath to remove the bottom layers or innermost petticoats first. Then let what's left drop down again and shear any shabby parts off the top.

PLANTS TO TRAIL OVER THE EDGE OF A FLOOR

These perennials, grasses, and shrubs grow 6 to 12 inches tall and spread 1 to 4 feet wide. If planted around the perimeter of a paved area or in a slightly raised bed adjacent to it, they will spread to form a casual, rounded patch that overflows the edge. Stepping on them now and then may bruise some leaves or break a stem but won't do fatal damage.

TRAILING PLANTS FOR SUNNY SITES

- **Aubretia** (*Aubretia deltoidea*). **P, SE.** Soft gray foliage. Rose, pink, or purple flowers in spring and summer. **ZONE 5**.
- **Basket-of-gold** (*Aurinia saxatilis*). **P, SE.** Gray leaves. Bright yellow flowers in spring. **ZONE 3**.
- **Heathers and heaths** (*Calluna vulgaris* cvs. and *Erica* spp. and cvs.). **S, E.** Twiggy and fine-textured. Different kinds bloom in sequence, almost year-round, usually with white, pink, lilac, or purplish flowers. Some have colorful foliage, especially in cold weather. **ZONE 5**.
- **Dalmatian bellflower** (*Campanula portenschlagiana*). **P, D.** Glossy green foliage. Blue-violet flowers all summer. **ZONE 4**.
- **Snow-in-summer** (*Cerastium tomentosum*). **P, SE.** Silvery leaves. White flowers in early summer. **ZONE 4**.
- **'Tom Thumb' cranberry cotoneaster** (*Cotoneaster apiculatus*). **S, D.** Tiny leaves, great fall color and berries. Very dense and compact. **ZONE 5**.
- **'Nikko' deutzia** (*Deutzia gracilis*). **S, D.** Low, slow, and neat, with white flowers in spring and purple fall foliage. **ZONE 4**.
- **Pinks** (*Dianthus* cvs.). **P, SE.** Mats of grassy blue-green foliage topped with very fragrant rose, pink, or white flowers, usually in late spring or early summer. **ZONE 4**.
- **'Vancouver Gold' broom** (*Genista pilosa*). **S, SE.** Dense and twiggy. Masses of yellow flowers in late spring. **ZONE 5**.
- **Sun rose** (*Helianthemum nummularium*). **P, SE.** Forms loose mounds. Abundant flowers come in almost all colors and open from spring through summer. **ZONE 5**.
- **Perennial candytuft** (*Iberis sempervirens*). **P, E.** Glossy emerald green foliage. Masses of white flowers in spring. **ZONE 3**.
- **Junipers** (*Juniperus*). **S, E.** This is a warning, not a recommendation. Few junipers are suitable for edgings. Most spread too far, too fast.
- **Missouri primrose** (*Oenothera missouriensis*). **P, D.** Big yellow flowers week after week in summer. **ZONE 5**.
- **Rock soapwort** (*Saponaria ocymoides*). **P, SE.** Masses of tiny flowers are usually bright pink, but there's a white form, too. Blooms from spring into summer. **ZONE 4**.
- **Sedums** (*Sedum*). **P, D.** There are many creeping forms, but some go too far, too fast. Try 'Ruby Glow' (a.k.a. 'Rosy Glow'), 'Vera Jameson', or *S. sieboldii*, all of which bear pink flowers in late summer or fall. **ZONE 3**.
- **Lamb's ears** (*Stachys byzantina*). **P, SE.** 'Big Ears' is the best cultivar for edging, offering big, fuzzy gray leaves. Rarely blooms. **ZONE 4**.

TRAILING PLANTS FOR PART SHADE

These plants prefer partial or afternoon shade and can't take full sun, especially in hot climates, but most would get straggly in too much shade. Those marked * are your best bets for fully shaded sites.

- ***Bugleweed, or ajuga** (*Ajuga reptans*). **P, SE.** 'Catlin's Giant', which has uncommonly large glossy leaves and blue flowers, is best for edging. **ZONE 3**.
- **Lady's mantle** (*Alchemilla mollis*). **P, D.** Masses of tiny yellow-green flowers on arching stems in early summer. **ZONE 3**.
- **Variegated Japanese sedge** (*Carex morrowii* 'Aureo-variegata'). **P, E.** Slim leaves are smooth as plastic and arch in all directions like a fountain. Pale creamy yellow. **ZONE 6**.
- **Golden hakone grass** (*Hakonechloa macra* 'Aureola'). **P, D.** Forms a soft, arching mound of slender green-and-gold-striped leaves that lean toward the light. **ZONE 5**.
- **Irises** (*Iris*). **P, D.** Try dwarf crested iris, *I. cristata*, which forms mats of short leaves, or Japanese roof iris, *I. tectorum*, which has taller, especially lovely leaves. Both bloom in spring, with white or purple flowers. **ZONE 3**.
- **Siberian cypress** (*Microbiota decussata*). **S, E.** A shade-tolerant conifer with graceful arching stems and feathery foliage. Green in summer, turns purple-bronze in winter. **ZONE 3**.
- **Creeping phlox** (*Phlox stolonifera*). **P, SE.** Dense mats of smooth green leaves. Bright white, pink, or purplish flowers in spring. **ZONE 3**.
- ***Creeping raspberry** (*Rubus calycinoides*). **S, E.** Forms a neat mat of glossy leaves. Bears few if any berries. 'Emerald Carpet' is a fine cultivar. **ZONE 6**.
- ***Saxifrages** (*Saxifraga*). **P, E.** Try strawberry geranium, *S. stolonifera*, with round leaves and runners, or London pride, *S. umbrosa*, which forms mats of smooth leaves. **ZONE 7**.
- ***Sedum** (*Sedum*). **P, E.** *S. ternatum* grows in shade, making small rosettes of flat round leaves. White flowers in early summer. **ZONE 5**.
- ***Foamflower** (*Tiarella cordifolia*). **P, SE.** Forms dense low mats of soft foliage. New cultivars have leaves with fancy markings or shapes. All bear white flowers in spring. **ZONE 3**.
- ***Sweet box** (*Sarcococca hookeriana* var. *humilis*). **S, E.** Spreading shrub with glossy, pointed leaves. Tiny but fragrant flowers in early spring. **ZONE 6**.

ROCK-AGGREGATE PAVING

Gravel, crushed rock, volcanic rock, brick dust, and other kinds of rock particles, or aggregates, make a surface that's sometimes called semi-pavement. It's firmer, neater, and drier than dirt, but nowhere near as stable, clean, and carefree as concrete or masonry. Aggregate costs less than other paving materials, is easy to install, and makes a practical flooring for outdoor work or storage areas such as the space under a raised deck, around a compost bin, or next to a firewood rack. You can apply aggregate under and around trees without damaging their roots, and although aggressive tree roots may project up through an aggregate surface, at least it won't get cracked or heaved as concrete or masonry would.

Unfortunately, aggregate semi-pavement has many practical drawbacks. It demands constant maintenance. It shifts around and doesn't stay put. You have to rake it often. It settles and becomes uneven. It invites weeds and accumulates litter and debris. Anyplace where you disturb or try to patch the surface remains conspicuous. Finally, it's hard to remove unwanted aggregate. For these reasons, think long and hard before bringing rock products onto your property. Consider the alternatives and use aggregate only where you're convinced that it's going to be an acceptable long-term solution.

Depending on the color and particle size, aggregate pavement can appear quite natural or alarmingly fake. Small, irregular, multicolored gray or brown particles blend into most landscapes, while particles sized 1½ inches or larger shout for attention (this can be good or bad) and white rocks always look alien. The appearance of aggregate depends on climate, too. It seems more appropriate in arid climates, where it's not uncommon to see bare ground. In moist climates, there's no natural equivalent for semi-pavement, as any wild or untended place that isn't solid rock is covered by plants.

Choosing and buying an aggregate

Various kinds of aggregates aren't equal or interchangeable, and choosing an appropriate material is the key to a satisfactory paving. The bagged products sold at garden centers are rarely suitable. Not only are they overpriced, but their colors are usually too vivid and their particles are too big. A better use for these colored stone chips is as a conspicuous decorative mulch.

To choose aggregate for pavement, visit building centers, stoneyards, and/or quarries; solicit advice from the staff (and from local paving and landscape contractors); and plan to buy in bulk and have a pile of material delivered.

WHAT TO AVOID. Anyone who has lived with it will tell you that a uniform, round aggregate, such as pea gravel, is totally unsuitable for pavement because the particles continually roll, slip, and shift underfoot. This is annoying and tiring to walk on, even dangerous. Pea gravel is also hard to confine; it leaps across any edging.

Most forms of washed, graded, crushed rock are inappropriate for home paving. Although the fragments are angular and don't roll like peas, they still shift underfoot and don't settle down. Coarse grades, with particles sized 1½ inches or larger, are especially rough to walk on.

(BELOW LEFT): Aggregate paths need some kind of slightly raised edging, such as the stone blocks used here, to keep stray particles from spreading sideways. Note the fine particles and neutral color of this aggregate. That's the best kind to buy for paving.

(BELOW RIGHT): Fine aggregate covers the largest area here, but there are at least five other forms of mineral matter: small river rocks, boulders, cast concrete, cut flagstones, and square concrete pavers. What makes this work is that they're all the same neutral gray color.

WHAT TO SEEK. What you need for pavement is a gritty mix of angular particles in assorted sizes (usually ¾ inch and smaller, or even ½ inch and smaller) that will pack down into a relatively firm and stable layer. Such a surface is easy to walk on and the particles tend to stay in the intended area (although they can get knocked out of place by skidding wheels, snow shoveling, or rough play).

Depending on where you live, aggregates of this kind are called fines, processed rock, road bond, crusher run, or decomposed granite. A product such as this will be loose and easy to spread when first delivered, but it packs down fast after it's gotten rained on or walked on, or you can rent a roller or power compacting tool to smooth and firm the surface right after you've spread the material around. Packed aggregate makes a much more durable and satisfactory outdoor floor than loose gravel does.

HOW MUCH TO BUY. Some quarries don't want to bother with small orders from novices, while others welcome you. Call around until you find the material and service you need. Gravel and rock may be sold by the ton or by the cubic yard. Figure the area you want to cover in square feet, decide how deep you want to spread the material, and ask the supplier to estimate how much you should buy. Get more than you need and pile the extra in an out-of-the-way place to use for filling depressions or for repairs.

If you want to estimate the amount yourself, here are some ballpark guidelines. When you spread it about 2 inches thick, 1 ton of aggregate will cover about 100 square feet, or 1 cubic yard will cover roughly 160 square feet. So, for example, to cover 800 square feet to a depth of 2 inches, you'd need approximately 8 tons (800 divided by 100) or about 5 cubic yards (800 divided by 160).

Installing aggregate

First kill or remove any unwanted plants that are growing in the area (see page 274). Build edgings (page 154) that project at least 1 to 2 inches higher than the finished pavement surface to help confine the aggregate, or build grade-level mowing strips about 6 inches wide to separate an aggregate path from a lawn (the mowing strips will also help keep the turfgrass from invading the aggregate).

DO YOU NEED A BASE? If the site is very well drained and the ground stays firm even after a heavy rain, or if the area is detached from the house and you'll never go out there during wet or messy weather, you can spread the topping directly on clear, weed-free ground. Otherwise, prepare a base by excavating the existing soil and spreading a layer of coarse crushed rock for drainage. Usually the base should be 2 to 4 inches thick, and the topping about 2 inches thick.

WHAT ABOUT PLASTIC OR FABRIC? Everyone else will tell you to lay down sheets or rolls of black plastic or of synthetic landscape fabric before spreading aggregate, to suppress weeds and to separate the topping from the soil below. I'm telling you not to, because any plastic or fabric that you spread will someday work loose and flap up around the edges. When that happens, and it always does, the

This all-too-typical example shows what can go wrong with gravel in the landscape: alien pale color, oversize particles, weeds, torn flaps of the landscape fabric that was supposed to prevent weeds, and wretched strip edging that is writhing out of the ground.

only cure is to remove it. By that time, you'll also have learned that there's no such thing as a weed barrier.

If you want to keep aggregate separate from the soil because you have the idea that someday you might want to remove it, a sheet of plastic or fabric isn't the answer. Choose a different solution. Removing unwanted aggregate is such an obnoxious job that you should never spread this material in a temporary context.

SPREAD, LEVEL, AND COMPACT THE AGGREGATE. Minimize hauling by having the material delivered as close as possible to the site, and spread a tarp before the pile gets dumped to simplify cleanup afterward. Use a wheelbarrow or cart to distribute the aggregate across the area, dumping small piles at regular intervals, then spread it around and level the surface with a metal rake.

Check the level by eye or with a spirit level set on a 2x4. For floorlike areas, make the surface approximately level, with a slight pitch away from the house or other nearby buildings.

As you're shaping the surface of an aggregate path, build in a slight *crown;* that is, make the surface about ½ inch higher in the center than at the sides. This helps the surface dry faster after a rain. It also anticipates wear patterns. You walk more in the center of a path than along the edges, so the center gets more compacted over time. If you build it high to start with, the path may end up level from side to side, but if you build it level it will eventually get a depressed channel down the center, and that invites puddles and ice to form in the path.

Aggregate needs to be packed down or compacted. You can rent a power tool called a plate compactor to work over large areas, or use a lawn roller filled with water. Go back and forth several times in different directions. After you've compacted an area, check it again to see if it's level. Add and compact more aggregate as needed to bring up any low spots.

Maintenance, renovation, and replacement

Weeding, vacuuming up or blowing away plant litter and debris, and raking to restore the surface are ongoing chores with aggregate pavement. Loose gravel shifts around so much that it needs almost daily raking. Even compacted aggregate needs occasional raking and redistribution, as the places where you walk get packed down and loose particles shift around and accumulate in untrod areas.

TRY TO CATCH SPILLS AND LITTER. If you have gravel paths between raised beds in a garden, keep a tarp handy. Spread it over the path whenever you're digging in the beds to do any planting or transplanting or when you're trimming or pruning plants. Catching any soil or litter on the tarp greatly simplifies cleanup. It's almost impossible to remove the evidence if you spill soil onto gravel; it settles into the crevices and shows like a stain.

TOPPING A WORN SURFACE. To renovate or top up an older aggregate pavement, get similar material if possible. It's unlikely that you can make a precise color match, but try to get a similar kind (in size and shape) of particles. Scoop up a sample of the

This close-up shows an inevitable problem with gravel pavement: weed seedlings. There are dozens of seedlings per square foot, and this is a 10-by-120-foot driveway. Imagine hand pulling that many weeds, only to watch more sprout after the next rain.

old gravel and take it with you as a reference. Try to level the existing surface and put on a generous layer of new stones. If the old surface is too uneven or if you don't add a thick enough topping, the new stones will shift into any low spots and the old high spots will stick up like bald heads, making a patchy, bicolored effect.

REPLACEMENT. If you have an outdoor area surfaced with any kind of rock product and decide to replace it, one solution would be to build a low wooden deck over it. Alternatively, you could build a raised masonry floor by working up from the existing pavement. You'd need to build edgings, level the existing aggregate (perhaps adding more), add sand, and then lay the pavers, flagstones, or bricks.

But to build a new floor at ground level or to reclaim a graveled area for planting, you have to scoop up and get rid of the gravel and the compacted soil beneath it. That's not a bad job if you can get machinery into the area, but it's very slow, heavy work to do manually.

❦ EDGINGS

Edgings outline and separate different parts of a landscape, such as paved areas, lawn, and plantings. They aren't always necessary. One of the advantages of poured concrete, for example, is that it hardens into a monolith and doesn't need to be protected or contained by an edging. Likewise, steppingstones and wooden decks and boardwalks all have integral edges. Sometimes you can maintain the edge between a lawn and a bed of ground cover simply by mowing there. In many cases, the best way to maintain the edge of a bed or border is by cutting a shallow trench in the soil and renewing it periodically to uproot any trespassing plants.

But edgings are usually required to stabilize a masonry or aggregate walkway or outdoor floor, and to restrain the soil, mulch, and plants in raised beds and borders and keep them from spilling onto adjacent pavement or lawn. Edgings can guide feet and wheels and prevent you from accidentally running off a walk and damaging nearby plants. Conspicuous edgings mark and emphasize the boundary between where it's okay to walk and where you shouldn't step.

If you need an edging, it should be stable and sturdy enough to support your weight if you step or lean on it. Nothing less will do the job. Focus on function first, then consider style and appearance. Edgings that are constructed on the site, as you'd lay pavement or build a wall or fence, are the most satisfactory in the long run. They stay put, do the job, and look honest and substantial.

Garden centers and catalogs offer various lightweight plastic, wood, wire, and cast-concrete, plaster, or terra-cotta edgings. Most of these are overpriced knickknacks. None are suitable for edging pavement and few can even support a low raised bed. They tip over, give way if you lean on them, and need frequent resetting. I'd recommend that you shop around and see what it would cost to build a stable, functional edging before you buy one that's merely decorative. You might be surprised at what a bargain it is to invest in quality.

Commercial strip edgings

Those strips of steel, aluminum, or plastic edgings that you see so often in commercial landscapes, outlining beds and occasionally along aggregate paths, don't perform as well as you'd hope. That's why you see them—it's because they heave, pull loose, and stick out. Or sometimes they were set too high in the first place and the ground settled around them, or someone tried to fit the edging onto a slope or curve and it popped straight out again.

Anyway, these edgings are often disappointing in a home landscape. They don't extend deep enough to confine plants that run underground; likewise, any creeping plants dash right over the top. Really, these edgings work best as a visual aid to mark where the edge of a bed is supposed to be, so you know where to cut when you're trimming there with a string trimmer, edging tool, clippers, or spade. An inset mowing strip that's wide enough to support a mower wheel is much more effective and convenient for separating a lawn from adjacent beds and doesn't cost that much more than strip edging to install.

The various kinds of lightweight aluminum or plastic strip edging that are marketed to homeowners are usually a waste of money. They just aren't substantial enough to hold up to kneeling gardeners, children at play, lawn mowers, cart wheels, and the like.

Masonry edgings

Concrete, bricks, and stones can be used to edge masonry or aggregate paths, to contain raised beds, or as an inlaid mowing strip around the edge of a lawn. A masonry edging can be straight or curved, and it can run along level ground or go up or down hill. The style can be rustic or formal, traditional or contemporary.

An inset or buried masonry edging should be stable enough not to tip or sink when you stand or step on it or run a mower or cart wheel over it. A raised edging should not only contain the soil pressing against it and resist the force of gravity, it should also be sturdy enough to withstand accidental kicks or bumps, and to support your weight when you lean against it. In other words, a practical edging should hold up to everyday wear; you shouldn't have to be careful of it. Decorative edgings often fail to pass this test, and you have to mince around them.

Like masonry pavement, masonry edgings are most satisfactory if you prepare a base first by exca-

vating some soil and replacing it with free-draining crushed rock and/or sand. This is especially important in cold-winter climates, where edgings laid on unprepared ground are likely to frost-heave.

Dry-laid masonry edgings can easily be repaired or reset if individual elements heave or get knocked out of line. Mortared masonry edgings are theoretically stronger and neater than dry-laid ones, but even if they're properly installed over a poured-concrete footing, cracks are likely to occur and are nearly impossible to repair.

You can install dry-laid edgings or mowing strips yourself, and because it's a relatively simple project, making an edging is a good place to experiment if you want to try learning how to do mortared masonry. Hiring a mason to lay edging may be difficult because it's a small job. Be patient and you may find someone who can help you out between other jobs or during a slow season.

CONCRETE EDGINGS. Poured concrete makes a sturdy permanent edging, good for driveways and main walkways or as a substantial mowing strip. It needs to extend at least several inches underground, and preferably down to the frost line. The top can be at grade level or raised as high as you want. The main problem with making a concrete edging is building all the forms. If you're going to do that much woodworking, in most situations you might as well make wooden edgings. But if you want the look and permanence of concrete, it's a good investment.

INSET MASONRY EDGINGS. A traditional edging for dry-laid brick paths is a "soldier" row of bricks set on end along each side of the path and buried so that the tops of the bricks are flush with the rest of the path or project slightly above it. You can use cobblestones or stone blocks that are at least 8

inches thick in a similar way. After preparing the aggregate base, line up the bricks or stones along the edges of the path, then add the sand base and install the pavement. It's the buried part of a soldier row that does the job of providing stability and keeping the edges of the path from tipping or spreading sideways.

For mowing strips, bricks can be laid on edge and set side by side lengthwise, to make a strip or edging about 8 inches wide and 4 inches deep. Dig a trench about 6 inches deep, spread 2 inches of coarse

(**ABOVE LEFT**): *Poured concrete makes sturdy, carefree, permanent mowing strips and raised edgings. Because it needs a foundation that reaches down to the frost line, it's most practical for mild climates where the soil doesn't freeze.*

(**ABOVE RIGHT**): *This uncommonly smooth pavement with matching edging looks like bricks at first glance, but it's actually tiles mortared onto a concrete base. Note the neat seams and mitered corners.*

(**LEFT**): *A brick mowing strip is a great convenience and looks good, too. Buy enough bricks to make it nice and wide, as shown here, and you'll never regret it.*

A brick mowing strip can be curved instead of straight. Look how it sweeps in and out around these trees. What a graceful line it draws.

Random shapes and rough textures give this masonry a casual look. The mortared edging is made of flat stones stacked a few courses high, like a low retaining wall.

A row of white stones makes a symbolic edging here that reminds you not to step into the planted area.

sand or rock dust in the bottom, and then lay the bricks on that. As you proceed, keep checking that the top of the edging is level and smooth, and raise or lower any individual bricks that are too high or too low. Also check that their ends are neatly aligned. Fit the bricks as close together as possible, then fill any cracks with sand and pack it in firmly. When you're making a curved edging, the cracks between bricks will be wider at the outside edge, so take special care to pack plenty of sand there.

RAISED MASONRY EDGINGS. Raised brick or stone edgings are built like short retaining walls. These combine well with masonry, aggregate, wood-chip, or turf path surfaces, do double-duty by supporting beds along the sides of a path, and usually look great.

For dry-laid masonry, dig a trench where the edging is to go and lay a base of 2 to 4 inches of crushed rock. For mortared masonry, dig a trench and pour a concrete footing twice as wide as the edging and at least as deep as it is tall. The bottom of any masonry edging should be buried partway below grade level—about 2 inches is deep enough for an edging 4 to 8 inches tall.

For a simple, rustic edging, use a single row of fieldstones or other rocks gathered from your property. If they aren't all the same size or thickness (they probably won't be), bury the thicker rocks far enough that the top of the edging comes out level. For a more refined edging, use squared-off stone blocks or bricks laid in neat, level courses. Try to make the front face of an edging as smooth as possible; it looks better that way and is easier to trim or rake up to.

Timber edgings

Wood makes attractive and versatile low edgings for any kind of pavement and for raised beds, and it can be incorporated into many landscape styles. It certainly goes well with contemporary homes and natural or casual landscapes, but wood edgings were already popular in colonial days, so they're appropriate with historic homes and traditional landscapes, too.

Because wood rots in contact with the ground, most wood edgings nowadays are built from pressure-treated lumber. Used railroad ties are long-lasting and used to be popular for strong, stout edgings, but they aren't readily available or affordable anymore. If you have a place to harvest your own logs or poles, you can use them for rustic edgings. Log edgings look good in casual gardens, but realize that they'll probably decay, crumble, and need replacement within a decade or so, unless you happen to have access to cedar, cypress, black locust, Osage orange, or other naturally rot-resistant timbers.

Note: The techniques described here are for low edgings *only.* Don't extrapolate them to higher retaining walls. Making a timber retaining wall more than about 2 feet tall requires engineering and construction techniques beyond the scope of most homeowners.

HORIZONTAL TIMBER EDGINGS. Timbers sized at least 4x4, boards 2x8 or wider, used ties, or logs laid on edge are good for edging straight-sided or rectangular areas. You can dig a trench and set them into the ground so the top edge is flush with or slightly above the surface of an adjacent path, or mount them aboveground for raised edgings.

A horizontal edging looks best if the timbers are level, so check for that by eye or with a spirit level as you work. If the site itself is nearly level, you'll have to make only minor adjustments (adding or removing soil as needed) to set all the timbers level with each other. This style of edging doesn't adapt easily to sloping sites, but if you want to try running a horizontal edging up a slope, use short lengths of timber and "stairstep" them. Start at the bottom. Set the first timber and make sure it's level; then set the next higher one, overlapping the ends by at least 2 feet, and continue up the hill.

It's not enough to just lay timbers on the ground. The force and weight of soil, pavement, or people pushing against them will make the timbers splay or fall over. You have to stake or pin them in place. Drive sharpened 2-foot stakes cut from pressure-treated wood or 2-foot lengths of iron rebar along the outside edge of the timber. Space the stakes about 6 inches from every end, joint, or corner and every 2 to 3 feet along the sides. These stakes will show, but it's better to see stakes than to have an edging get knocked out of line. A way to hide the staking is to use 4x4 or larger timbers or logs, drill ½-inch holes through them, and drive the rebar through the holes.

Corners need careful cutting and fitting. There are special corner connectors designed for making raised beds from 2x6 or wider boards, which are made from sheet metal or plastic and are preset at 60°, 90°, or 120° angles. If you can't find anything like this at a local building-supply center, you can order them by mail from garden-supply catalogs. If you're working with 4x4 timbers, overlap them at the corners, like stacking a log cabin, and then drill a hole that goes down through all of them and drive a rebar through.

VERTICAL TIMBER EDGINGS. A stockade-style edging with timbers or logs set vertically side by side looks attractive and can be fitted along curved paths or on sloping sites, but it uses a lot of wood, most of which is out of sight. Decide how far you want the edging to project aboveground and cut landscape timbers or poles of naturally rot-resistant wood into sections at least three times that long, planning to bury the bottom two-thirds. For exam-

ple, to make an edging that stands 6 inches high, cut pieces 18 inches long and bury them 12 inches deep. Dig a trench as deep as you need, set the pieces in place, recruit a helper to hold them plumb and steady, and then fill the trench with aggregate and pack it down as firmly as possible.

You need to connect the timbers somehow to keep them aligned. Otherwise, one or more may tip out if the edging gets knocked or bumped. Nail a 2x4 to the back sides as a stringer for straight edgings. Use fencing staples to tack heavy-gauge wire or cable along both the front and back sides of a curved stockade edging, pulling the wire as tight as possible as you go along.

(TOP): *Landscape timbers work best for straight, low edgings on level sites. Installation gets more complicated when you have to go around corners or fit the edging onto a slope.*

(BOTTOM): *A vertical timber edging made of treated posts makes an interesting low edging, but the construction is more trouble than you'd expect and it requires a lot of wood, most of which is hidden underground.*

A walk like this is easy to live with. It's wide and smooth. The steps aren't too steep, they're separated by landings, and the slightly curved route is interesting but not inconvenient.

6 🌿 Walks, Paths, Bridges, and Steps

SOME PROPERTIES have only a few main walks, the practical ones used for everyday coming and going. They don't need any other paths, because they're set up like pedestrian malls, with plenty of open space in the middle and attractions lined around the edge. For example, imagine a yard that's mostly lawn, with perhaps one or two shade trees, a patio and some plantings next to the house, and a mixed border of perennials and shrubs around the perimeter. In a situation such as this you can go anywhere you want simply by crisscrossing the lawn. Open, mall-like yards are easy to maintain and provide room for entertaining, for children and dogs to romp, and for lawn games.

But as you transform an open lawn into a garden, or if your land is already crowded with plantings or covered by woods or native vegetation, you need to map out some routes. A network of walks and paths shows you and your guests where and where not to walk, leads you to special attractions, subdivides the space, organizes and outlines plantings and garden beds, and provides access through overgrown areas that would otherwise go unvisited. Making—and maintaining—walks is the key to enjoying any piece of property that's filled with plants.

🌿 DESIGNING WALKWAYS

Most walks have a primary purpose, and if you identify that role and focus on it as you design and develop any route, the result will gratify both your eyes and your feet. The function or purpose of a walkway will influence your decisions on where it should go, whether it should take a direct or an indirect route, how wide it should be, and what kind of surface it needs. The range of possibilities is very wide. On a single property, you might have a smooth, cut-stone walk that climbs a few steps from the curb and then leads straight to the front door, a narrower concrete walk from the back door to a detached garage or toolshed, a ribbon of lawn that winds among shrubs and flower beds in the backyard, chip-covered paths between and around raised beds in a vegetable garden, and a steppingstone trail that serves as a shortcut through a bed of ground covers between your house and the neighbor's.

In any case, certain basic questions guide design decision-making. How often will the walk be used? Will you go there at night or in bad weather, or only on pleasant days? Does the site slope enough that you should build some steps into the path? How many people will be walking together? What kind of shoes will they be wearing? What if anything will they be carrying or pushing? Addressing practical concerns helps you make paths that are safe and convenient.

Other important aspects of path design have to do with appearance and style. Most people look down while they're walking, and the character of your walkways goes a long way toward defining the style of your landscape. Style depends partly on a walk's shape and width and also on the texture and neatness of its surface, the nature of its edges, and what grows beside it. Picture a ruler-straight mortared brick walk with clipped boxwood edgings. A raked gravel path with herbs tumbling from raised beds along both sides. An old flagstone path with mossy cracks, like a network of green veins. A mowed grass path that leads off into a meadow. Think of the impressions different walks have made on you as you decide what effect you want to create.

Finally, there's the matter of how walks subdivide a yard into smaller areas. Laying out walks is like drawing lines on a map. We tend to focus on the line of the walk itself, especially for practical walks, but you also need to look at the size and shape of the areas on either side of it, make sure they're graceful and useful, and think of how you'll develop them after the walk is built.

Resolving common walk problems

The existing walks and paths around an older house or established garden often have shortcomings. Among the most common problems are poor siting, inadequacy, and disrepair. Remodeling your walks — which usually consists of widening and resurfacing them but may include regrading a walk or rebuilding steps — is a very satisfying upgrade that will improve the look of your property and brighten your attitude as you come and go.

WALK IS TOO NARROW. Walkways often are, or seem to be, too narrow for comfortable passage. Widening them is a worthwhile upgrade.

For example, in suburban developments built since World War II, the main walk leading toward the house is typically made of poured concrete and may be only 3 feet wide. Making narrow walks was a way to economize when these houses were built, but the long-term price is inconvenience and a stingy look. If the surface is still in good condition, you can widen such a walk by adding contrasting bands of pavers or bricks on both sides. But if the existing walk is badly cracked or heaved, you'd best remove it and start anew.

Sometimes the walk itself is of adequate width, but it's gotten overgrown or crowded by plants. You know what to do about that. Prune, shear, whack, peel up, pull back, uproot — do whatever is needed to regain control. Plants that overtook a walkway once are likely to do it again, so unless you don't mind doing periodic sieges, you might want to replace those aggressive old plants with new ones that are more restrained.

WALK IS TOO WIDE. This is uncommon; walks are much more frequently too narrow than too wide. It's most likely to occur on the walkway you have the least control of: a city sidewalk that crosses the front of your property. And even there, your per-

(BELOW LEFT): *These plants look lovely but they're crowding the steps. If they were set farther away from the sides of the walk, you could enjoy looking at them without having to brush them out of the way.*

(BELOW RIGHT): *The actual pavement is wide enough here, but it's a squeeze passing between these overgrown box-woods. When shrubs close you out, it's time to prune or replace them.*

ception that the walk is too wide is probably a matter of looks, not function. Wide walks are just right for groups of children walking to and from school, although they may seem blank and empty the rest of the time.

See what's allowed under local codes. You're almost certainly forbidden to let plants block a public walkway, but replacing an area of lawn just inside a sidewalk with a low hedge (see page 224) or a flower bed will add color, height, and texture and call your attention away from the walk.

WALK IS INDIRECT OR ROUTE IS INCONVENIENT. Shortcuts worn into the dirt are a sure sign that an existing walkway doesn't go where it needs to. It's futile to keep reminding people to stay on a misplaced path. Take a hint and pave the shortcut or lay steppingstones there.

Sometimes there isn't a shortcut, but you wish there were. If it's your own yard, you might dutifully detour around an obstacle or barrier of some kind, needlessly adding steps to a much used route that should be as convenient as possible. Look for a more direct way. That might mean cutting an opening through a hedge or fence, laying a path through a planting bed, or building a new set of steps to climb a slope or get up onto a deck. Making a shortcut is generally a fairly simple, inexpensive, and fast project, and you'll really appreciate the results.

WALK SURFACE IS TROUBLESOME. It's no fun, and it may be downright dangerous, to walk on a path that's muddy, icy, or slippery when wet; on material that shifts underfoot (as do soft sand and loose gravel); or on masonry that's bumpy, tilted, cracked, or uplifted by tree roots. Usually a bad surface is a symptom of deeper problems and can't simply be patched. You may need to remove the existing walk and build a new one. Future problems can be prevented by careful construction, which includes preparing the site, allowing for drainage, laying a proper base, avoiding tree roots, and choosing a skid-proof pavement or topping.

WEEDS GROW IN THE PATH. Crabgrass, dandelions, oxalis, and all the other weeds that typically grow in lawns are equally troublesome in paths surfaced with turf, gravel, or wood chips and in the cracks of masonry paths. Perhaps you can keep up by hand pulling, or you can use a propane-fueled weed torch around masonry, but I think this is one situation where herbicides are a justifiable convenience. A preemergent herbicide applied in spring will prevent many annual weed seeds from germinating. Spraying with a contact herbicide in summer helps control deep-rooted perennial weeds. Weed control is more or less a chronic problem in most paths and, whichever method of eradication you use, requires routine, ongoing attention.

Burying a sheet of weed-barrier fabric when you build a new path, although commonly recommended, is only minimally effective because most weeds sprout from seeds that land on top of the path, rather than poking up from beneath it.

WALK EDGES ARE CRACKED, TILTED, OR IRREGULAR. The edges of a walk are like the collars, cuffs, and hems of your clothes. They're conspicuous and they need extra attention if you want the walk to look well groomed, not worn and shabby. Even more than neat, the edges of a path should appear sound. If the pavement or topping is crumbling or falling away, you question the stability of the rest of the path.

Securing the edges of a masonry or aggregate walk normally requires some kind of permanent edging, and that should be installed at the time a path is built. (See page 154.) It may be possible to add or replace edgings along an older walk while preserving the rest of its surface, but it's generally easier and better to go ahead and rebuild the entire walk.

This walk is due for renovation. The bricks have heaved and settled over the years so much that the surface is tippy and uneven, especially between those steps. It's time to lift out the bricks and set them aside, upgrade the base to provide better drainage, and then re-lay the bricks.

PATH IS TOO STEEP, OR STEPS ARE SCARY. It's hard to climb and harder yet to descend a sloping or ramped path that's too steeply inclined. Even in dry weather, you're likely to slip. When the surface is wet, icy, or muddy, forget it. Where ramps are needed to provide access for wheelchairs or wheeled tools, the incline should be no more than 1 in 12. Garden paths and nature trails that are used simply for pleasure can make steeper climbs, but in general, walks and paths on hilly sites should include steps.

Unfortunately, outdoor steps are often poorly designed and carelessly built. Typically the risers are too high and make the climb too steep. Treads are often too narrow, so you can't set your feet down straight and flat. Sometimes the risers aren't uniform and some steps are unexpectedly higher or lower than others. Perhaps the treads aren't level. These are hazards. Bad steps are awkward, tiring, and even dangerous to use. Replace them, the sooner the better. Having safe, comfortable, attractive steps is a priority on any sloping site.

PATH IS POINTLESS, UNUSED. Sometimes, especially in older neighborhoods, you see walkways or steps that have obviously been abandoned. Perhaps they lead to a street that's gotten so busy that cars never stop or park there anymore; now everyone pulls into the driveway. Or they might lead to the site of an outbuilding long since taken down. It's easy to postpone removing an unused path and dismiss it as a trivial annoyance, but it's also easy to hire someone to come demolish it and take it away. Getting rid of it will give you a fresh start and encourage you to reconsider how you use that part of your yard.

Designing practical walkways

The main walks you use for everyday coming and going should be direct, clear, smooth, and roomy. Naturally, they should also be attractive, but function has priority here. A good main path shows you where you want to go and how to get there with no ambiguity. The layout should avoid sharp curves, detours, and meanders and head directly from point A to point B. Make any walk that gets used day and night in all weather as undeviating as possible.

The surface should be smooth enough not to stub your toe, catch your heel, or throw your ankle. The ideal width varies, depending on who uses the path and what they're carrying or pushing. Lighting (see page 83) is essential for main walks used by visitors and is welcome for any other path you might use at night.

FRONT WALKS AND OTHER MAIN ENTRIES. Any house that's lived in already has one or more walks leading from the doors out into

(ABOVE): *Although picturesque, these steps are a hazard because they're too irregular. The danger of tripping or slipping is increased when the stones are wet and covered with slippery leaves.*

(LEFT): *These steps are ornamental, not functional. They're too narrow, tippy, and irregular for safe passage.*

and through the yard, so you rarely start from scratch to design these main walks. However, existing main walks often call for a redesign. You may want to reroute them, to make them more direct and convenient, or to widen or resurface them.

Start at the ends. Right outside the door, is there room for an expanded landing of some kind, a place where a few people could gather for hellos and good-byes, where kids could dump their gear, where you could work on a project such as refinishing a piece of furniture, or where you could set out a bench or chair and some potted plants? This could be a wooden deck, concrete patio, or masonry terrace. At the far end of the walk, typically a parking area, is there enough room on both sides of the car for everyone to get in and out without stepping on plants or soil? Sometimes you need to make or expand a landing strip or loading zone beside a street or driveway, especially if you have children or other passengers riding in the back seat.

Conventional guidelines recommend a minimum width of 4 feet 6 inches to accommodate two people walking abreast, but that's barely sufficient even for sedate adults who aren't carrying anything. For lively children or anyone toting bags or gear, a minimum of 5 to 6 feet is more realistic. And no matter how wide the walk is, people and dogs will occasionally go over the edge, so flank walkways with tough, resilient plants that can spring back from accidental missteps.

The best surfaces for main walks that get everyday use are poured concrete, concrete pavers, and dry-laid or mortared flagstones or bricks. Wooden decking and boardwalks are good, too, and compacted aggregate is okay for casual landscapes in arid climates.

SERVICE PATHS. You may have a few important but secondary routes in addition to the main walks that lead in and out of your house. These would be the paths that lead, for example, to the compost bin, garbage cans, or woodshed or barn. Although they may be narrow—3 feet wide is usually sufficient for one person toting a load—these should be so direct and smooth that your feet can follow the route automatically regardless of what you're carrying or what's on your mind. Mundane paths such as these are sometimes surprisingly inconvenient. Upgrading them is an easy way to improve your quality of life. Smooth out the surface by filling low or muddy spots and removing potential trip-ups. Steppingstones set flush in a bed of aggregate make good service paths for many situations, or you could simply use compacted aggregate. Straighten out the route as much as possible, avoiding needless jogs. Make sure steps are predictably spaced, level, and skid-proof. Design gates so you can operate the latch with one hand.

(LEFT): *Main walks should be wide, smooth, level, and direct, with a skid-proof surface that dries quickly.*

(BELOW): *The service paths that connect your house with outbuildings or storage areas get frequent use, so make them pleasant and convenient. This one uses dry-laid stone blocks.*

Work paths in a garden provide access to the beds and open space where you can park a cart or lay down your tools.

To decide how wide a work path should be, get some sticks or stakes about 3 to 4 feet long, drive them in the ground to simulate plants on either side of a path, and try pushing your garden cart or other tools between them. Keep moving the stakes farther apart until the passage seems comfortable, and make the path that width. Then, even if the path is wide enough, consider building some kind of sturdy edging on both sides to serve as bumpers or curbs. Edgings are especially helpful if you garden in the evenings until you can barely see. It's a great relief to feel the wheel of a loaded cart rebound from an edging rather than plunging off into an adjacent bed.

Wheeled tools can't negotiate steps, particularly if the wheels are small, as they frequently are. So work paths need ramps at every grade change. You may be able to carve ramps out of the existing soil, but often it helps to bring in a few wheelbarrow loads of extra soil or aggregate to build up a longer, wider ramp. Occasionally you might want to use 2x12 pressure-treated boards as ramps for the wheels to run on, if the soil is so soft or damp that the wheels would make ruts in it. At doorways where you have to roll a tool up into a storage shed or garage, make wooden wheel ramps or use packed aggregate to build up the path into a gradual ramp as wide as the door.

Designing garden walks and trails

Designing the paths that define a garden's layout or lead you on a stroll is less straightforward but more fascinating than making practical walks. If a new path doesn't *have* to go anyplace, the challenge is deciding where you *want* it to go. Sometimes you'll be guided by the topography of the site or the placement of existing plants. An open site, though, is like a blank canvas. You can go anywhere on it, via paths that are straight or curved, wide or narrow.

MAPPING OUT WALKS AND BEDS ON AN OPEN SITE. Imagine moving into a house with an empty lawn. An avid gardener would regard that open space as untapped opportunity and quickly set about digging up the turf, preparing beds, and filling them with all kinds of rare and wonderful plants. By default, the strips of remaining lawn would become paths. A landscape architect would probably take the opposite approach and lay out a network or grid of paths first, then start planting afterward.

The advantage of the avid gardener's approach is its flexibility. If you change your mind about the size, shape, or placement of a bed, you can move its plants, dig up more lawn, and reseed or resod an area that you'd dug before. Nudge the outlines back and forth until you're pleased with the results. Although it's a little tiresome to maintain neat edges, fine-textured green grass paths combine beautifully with

WORK PATHS AND RAMPS. Work paths are where you can push garden carts, wheelbarrows, chipper/shredders, and other tools; set down buckets and hand tools; and pile trimmings as you tend flower beds and borders, vegetable gardens, and other plantings. You may not need work paths if your plantings are small and surrounded by lawn, but large gardens do need to be intersected by paths. Work paths do double duty. They provide access, a way for you to get into or move between planted areas, and they also serve as workstations. In gardens that need a lot of maintenance, you may spend hours a week standing or kneeling on the work paths. For economy and comfort, work paths are usually surfaced with grass or low-growing plants or with wood chips or aggregate, perhaps with flagstones for decoration or added durability at key locations.

An overview shows you the layout of paths and beds in this hosta lover's garden.

lush, varied, colorful plantings, so don't be in a hurry to replace the grass with other path surfaces. You can always convert from grass to chips, aggregate, or pavement later, when you're sure you know exactly where you want a path to go and how wide you want it to be.

On the other hand, designing the paths first is efficient and decisive. Use stakes and string to mock up different layouts. Assess them from different points of view, and remember to keep looking at the big picture, including both the paths and the beds, and to consider how they relate to each other and to the size and shape of the overall area.

Try walking along the would-be paths with a companion, and try pushing a lawn mower or cart around. Be sure to make the paths wide enough. Usually garden paths feel too narrow. What happens is this: You lay out a path on open ground and it seems fine. But later, as plants grow up on both sides, they reach out like fans clamoring for autographs and you can't walk through without brushing them aside. Anticipate such crowding, make the paths extra wide to begin with, and set plants away from the edges to preserve a clear passage.

When you're designing a new garden on an open site, planning for wide enough paths may seem like a waste of space, but that impression is deceptive. Later, when the beds are filled with plants, the total space that the plants fill will seem much greater than the area devoted to paths, because plants get tall but paths stay flat. A bed of plants is three-dimensional, while a path is two-dimensional. Although it doesn't show up when you're drafting plans on paper, that makes a huge difference in how you perceive the results.

PATHS AND YOUR SENSE OF SPACE.
How you lay out paths and divide a yard into different areas affects your perception of the yard's size. Of course, this also depends on the height of the plants growing in beds between the paths. The effect is most pronounced if the plants are taller than you are (see page 41), but even if they're only knee-high or waist-high, your sense of space will be affected by the layout.

If you make straight paths that run the full length of the yard or run diagonally across it, you can sight down the longest possible span. But ironically, that makes the yard seem smaller, since you can take it in at a glance or see it all at once. By contrast, if you

Winding through a narrow path surrounded by tall plants is an emotional experience. Some people love it, while others wouldn't even step in there.

divide the yard into a maze of meandering paths, you can't (or don't) look very far ahead and you don't have an overview. Wandering around slowly in a situation such as this, you're likely to be fooled into thinking the area is much larger than it really is.

A simple design with plants around the perimeter or in geometric beds may actually fill a large area, but it's easy to grasp and you never feel lost in it. A convoluted design with islands, peninsulas, and bays keeps you going in circles, so you lose your sense of direction and space. You can take advantage of this to make a small yard seem rich and complex, but not without risk. If there are too many blind curves, especially if you can't see over the plants, the effect can be pretty intense. Some people would find that exhilarating and stimulating, but others would say it's cluttered and claustrophobic. Personally, I wouldn't complicate a small yard that's already surrounded by trees and buildings; I'd keep the design simple, the paths straight, and the plants low. The result may look undeniably small, but at least it feels like open space that way.

STRAIGHT PATHS NEED DESTINATIONS. A straight path needs to point to something. Otherwise, it's literally pointless, and you look down it with confusion and disappointment. A straight path can lead onward, through a gate or door or over a bridge, implying that you'll keep walking. It can lead to a windowlike opening in a fence or hedge that reveals a vista or an overview. Or it can

(ABOVE): *This walled garden is small but it doesn't feel crowded, because you can see across the plants as you walk along the path.*

(RIGHT): *The gazebo at the far end is a perfect focal point and destination for a straight path like this. Note how the path and gazebo are exactly the same width. The beds are scaled to match, and look at those immaculate edges!*

come to a stop at a bench, fountain, sculpture, or stunning plant. Whatever you use as a focal point at the end of a path needs to be hefty—a bit oversize and impressive—to earn its position. If it's too small or trivial, again the path seems pointless.

CURVED PATHS SHOULD BE INTRIGU-ING. On a curving path, the destination is hidden, so you're drawn onward by the lure of the unknown. What's around the next bend? you ask. Maybe the path leads to a quiet retreat, a bench hidden in a shady corner, or to a sunny glade in the woods, an unexpected shoreline, or a marvelous old tree. Who knows. It might even turn out that there was no destination; you simply end up back where you started from, but that's okay, too.

When you head down a curving, meandering path, you expect the journey itself to be rewarding, not just a means to an end. So in designing such a path, include lots of incentives along the way. Line the path with a variety of special plants, particularly ones with inviting textures (fuzzy buds, curly bark,

glossy leaves, velvety flowers, and so on) that make you want to stop and touch them. Use stones, sculptures, found objects, and plaques or signs to delight, provoke, and amuse visitors. Make the path itself interesting by putting some surprises in its surface. Insert some special tiles or stones into a brick trail, or set steppingstones in a river of moss, or let creeping plants seed into a gravel or chip path. Changes in the path surface make you look down and slow down, prolonging and enhancing your walk.

SHAPE CURVES THOUGHTFULLY. Curves seem gratuitous unless they relate to the topography and the plantings, and curves should almost always be broader and more gradual than your initial attempt to outline them. See page 43 for guidelines on designing curved planting beds; the same principles apply to curved paths.

A meandering network of paths invites you to slow down and explore the details of a complex, varied planting.

It's tiresome to walk on paths that slope like this unless you have one leg longer than the other.

Here's how to make a path that traverses a sloping site. Level the surface from side to side. Build a retaining wall on the uphill side and a reassuring edging on the downhill side. This path is slightly ramped, but the climb is gradual enough that the path doesn't need steps.

Walkways on sloping sites

Slopes complicate walkway design, partly because it's hard to compare different potential routes. Until the walk is built, a sloping site may be quite difficult to negotiate—awkward to climb or descend and hard to traverse. Any given route might be easy to follow afterward, once steps are installed and the surface is graded, but it's hard to predict that. Looking at or trying to walk on a rugged or steep hillside can be so discouraging and confusing that you bypass that terrain or walk around it and postpone the project of developing it. Even a gentle slope is off-putting. And yet without a path, the area is wasted, off limits, out of reach.

Building steps is treated later in this chapter. For now, I'll just note two key points about relating paths to slopes.

STRAIGHT WALKS SHOULD RUN ON THE LEVEL. In a home landscape, walks that are straight should be level, or nearly so, from one end to the other and also from side to side. A straight path that's inclined like a ramp tends to look institutional. Unless you need a ramp to accommodate someone who relies on a wheelchair or to roll bicycles, strollers, carts, or tools up and down, use a combination of steps and level runs to fit a straight walk onto a sloping site.

Straight paths are a major element in formal gardens (gardens that are laid out on a geometric grid, typically aligned with the house). For this type of landscape design, the entire area should be graded before you begin construction and planting, so that all the walks and beds are flat and level, not sloping or contoured.

CURVED PATHS CAN FOLLOW THE GRADE. Once you've got curves in two dimensions, you may as well have curves in three dimensions. That means paths that curve from side to side can also climb up and down. Curving paths easily hug a hillside or roll across undulating ground. The result looks natural, informal, and inviting.

To traverse the side of a hill, you can lay a path along a contour line or let it climb at a gentle slope. In either case, carve out a terrace so the surface of the path is level from side to side, not banked. Make the terrace at least 3 feet wide for walking single file, 5 feet wide for two people to walk side by side.

To make a walk that curves as it climbs a hill, arrange the steps in a radial pattern like a section of spiral staircase. Depending on how you angle them and how many steps you use, a curved set of steps can simply insert a slight bend in the path or it can provide a full 180° switchback. Of course, you can arrange the steps to turn either left or right as you climb.

If you want to make casual-looking curved steps for a garden path or nature trail, you can carve the shape into the hillside, use landscape timbers for the risers, and fill in behind them with aggregate. (See page 151.) Making more formal-looking curved steps of masonry, poured concrete, or wood is another story. Building curved shapes with these materials is complicated enough that you'll need to hire an experienced contractor.

This concrete-and-aggregate path is beautifully fitted to the site, with gradual steps that climb around a curve and level stretches that follow along a contour.

MAKING A TRAIL THROUGH A WOODS

If you own a patch of woodland, you'll enjoy it more if you make a trail that invites you to hike in, around, and back out again. With a trail to follow, you won't get disoriented, you'll be sure to pass your favorite spots, and you'll minimize the impact of your foot traffic on low-growing plants, tree roots, and the forest soil.

- **CHOOSING A ROUTE**. Leave your saws and pruners on the shelf at first, and get a roll of bright-colored plastic flagging tape. Spend time exploring your woods and use the tape to mark special finds, such as the biggest trees, uncommon kinds of trees, patches of wildflowers, springs or waterways, interesting rocks, and mossy fallen logs. (You might use different colors of tape to mark different categories.)

Depending on the layout of your land and how much of it is wooded, you might choose some point at the edge of the woods to serve as an entry and exit and make a trail that goes around in a loop, or you could enter the woods in one place and come out another. Your entry point can be as subtle or secretive as a creature's bolthole, or you can call attention to it with a path that leads there, stone pillars, an arch, or some other symbolic structure.

Start from the entry and begin figuring how to lay a route that leads from one flagged feature to the next, like connecting a series of dots. Add more flags, spaced every 5 to 10 yards, to mark the route as you plan it. The route will almost certainly be roundabout; that's part of the fun and it makes your piece of woods seem like a vast forest. You may want to interrupt the convolutions with a straightaway here and there for a change of pace, but that's optional.

- **MAKING THE TRAIL**. The final construction of a woodland trail involves clearing an opening aboveground as well as smoothing out the surface you walk on. Do the pruning and cutting first. Cut brushy growth at ground level and trim low tree limbs back to the main trunks. You'll encounter many small (or larger) trees that are in the way of the path. Sometimes it will make sense to route the path around a tree, and other times you'll decide to cut the tree down. If you do fell a tree to lay a path, cut the stump as close to the ground as possible. Where an already downed tree lies across your route, saw through the log to make way for the path.

The ground in a woods is often irregular, with roots and rocks that stick up in your way and low wet spots to negotiate. A supply of gravel really helps here. Although it's a pain to cart gravel into a woods, there's nothing better for filling low spots in a trail or raising the grade of a path so you can walk over a tangle of projecting roots or rocks without stumbling on them.

Wood chips make such a good surface for forest trails that you may agree it's worth the effort of hauling them in. Or if you have a chipper, you can chip brush and tree limbs as you go along and spread the chips on the trail. Otherwise, the combination of packed dirt, gravel fill as needed, and a natural topping of autumn leaves or conifer needles works just fine.

To make a trail through a woods, first you have to explore the area and choose a route, deciding which trees to go around and where to go in and come out.

What's involved in building a walk depends on the site and soil, how much grading or foundation work is required to level it out and improve the drainage, and the kind of surface you've chosen. Consider how much use the walk will get as you undertake site preparation and material selection. Walks that get everyday use require careful construction, durable toppings, and sturdy edgings. Lesser paths and trails can be more simply and sparingly made.

In any case, spending time on site preparation prevents problems that would mar the appearance of a path, make it unpleasant or inconvenient to walk on, or shorten its life. First, lay out the design. Decide on the placement and width of the path, and mark where the edges will be. Locate where any steps will go. Pause at this stage for at least a few days to assess the layout from all angles and make any improvements.

Next, clear the ground. Remove weeds, strip off sod, transplant desirable plants, and get rid of roots, stumps, rocks, debris, or other obstacles. Grade the area, cutting high spots and filling low spots to make the path level from side to side and level or gently sloping from end to end.

Where steps are needed, make or install them before you finish the rest of the path. Focus on getting the proportions and dimensions of the steps right. Afterward, you can easily adjust the grade of the path so it lines up with the top and bottom of the steps. This is easier than finishing a path first and having to fit steps into a fixed gap.

If you're going to surface the path with gravel or masonry, you'll probably need to prepare a base first to provide for good drainage. (See page 144.) Paths topped with turf, creeping plants, moss, or wood chips usually don't need a base, nor do steppingstone paths.

Edgings

How you treat the edges of a walk is as important as what you choose for its surface. Edge treatments have a big impact on the appearance and durability of any walk or path. See page 154 for advice on how to build edgings.

There are only a few instances in which you can ignore edgings. One is a trail cut through a woods. There it's more important to keep up with pruning brush or limbs that grow across the path and hit you in the face than to maintain the edges at ground level. Boardwalks and poured-concrete walks usually don't have or need distinct edge treatments, since they're integral from side to side. Steppingstone trails don't need edgings, since the perimeter of each stone is an edge in itself.

You need some kind of demarcation or edging along turfgrass, wood-chip, and stone-aggregate paths to separate the path surface and adjacent areas, to keep plants from crossing into the walkway, and to confine the turf or path topping. A shallow trench cut between grass paths and adjacent planting beds works fine but needs frequent renewal. An inlaid masonry mowing strip makes a much more permanent and convenient edging for a grass path. Raised edgings are good along wood-chip or aggregate paths, to keep loose particles from spilling sideways.

Brick, concrete-paver, and flagstone walks benefit from an edging that extends a few inches underground and keeps the elements along the edge from spreading or tilting sideways. This should be installed when the path is built. Depending on what you use for an edging, its top may be hidden underground, flush with the surface of the path, or raised above it. Buried or flush edgings are inconspicuous and are good for walks that cross a lawn, as you can run the lawn mower on the walk to mow right up to the edge.

Along any walkway, raised edgings add an extra feature to your landscape. They can do double duty by supporting raised beds adjacent to a walk, and they are needed along the uphill edge of any walk that traverses a slope to keep soil and plants from spilling down onto the walk surface. You may also want a raised edging along the downhill side of a walk that crosses a slope, for psychological benefit. A short edging is too low to actually serve as a guardrail, but it looks reassuring to see it there.

A sturdy raised masonry edging helps keep plants, soil, and mulch off the surface of a path.

Plants growing beside a walk don't substitute for built edgings in terms of structural benefit, but they remind visitors to stay on the path, highlight the lines and shapes of a garden's design, and generally look nice. Plants beside a path get extra appreciation because they're right there to be seen, and they're easy to reach and care for. Here are some recommended short edging plants.

For suggestions of colorful, compact perennials and shrubs that grow 2 to 3 feet tall and wide and make wonderful low hedges along walks or paths, see the box on page 124. For sprawling plants to blur the edge of a path, see the box on page 150.

The following plants are all short, compact, and upright or rounded. Most grow to about 1 foot tall and wide or can be kept that size by shearing or pruning. Plant them 6 inches away from the sides of a walk for a low edging that won't get in your way.

These plants all look good at least throughout the growing season, and in some cases year-round. Although they're all desirable and worthwhile, they're also common, readily available, and fairly inexpensive. (They're also easy to propagate at home from seed, cuttings, or divisions.) Low plants along a frequently used main walk are damage-prone, so use expendable or replaceable plants there and put your choice treasures in more protected locations.

- **ANNUALS.** Look for compact or "edging" strains of flossflower (a.k.a. ageratum), wax begonia, English daisy, Madagascar periwinkle (a.k.a. vinca), lobelia, China pinks, dusty miller, French marigold, and pansy. Most of these annuals bloom nonstop for months; when they wear out or freeze, replace or remove them. Most annuals do best on sunny sites.

- **ANNUAL HERBS.** Parsley, 'Spicy Globe' basil, Mexican mint marigold (*Tagetes lucida*), and sweet marjoram are usually grown as annuals. All are fragrant and tasty. They do best on sunny sites.

- **HARDY PERENNIAL HERBS.** Hyssop (*Hyssopus officinalis*), 'Munstead' English lavender (*Lavandula angustifolia*), winter

savory (*Satureja montana*), germander (*Teucrium chamaedrys*), and 'English' common thyme (*Thymus vulgaris*) respond well to clipping and can be used for neat, low, hedge-like edgings on sunny sites. All are rather shrubby, have semievergreen foliage, and are hardy to Zone 5.

- **HARDY PERENNIALS.** Here are some affordable, reliable perennials. Most are hardy to Zone 5 and can be divided to increase your stock if you want to make a continuous edging without buying lots of plants.

For **PART SHADE**, try the dwarf astilbes *Astilbe chinensis* 'Pumila' and *A. simplicifolia* 'Sprite', which bear pink flowers in late summer; heartleaf bergenia (*Bergenia cordifolia*), with rosy pink flowers in spring; coralbells and heucheras (*Heuchera* cvs.), which offer profuse flowers or gorgeous foliage, but not both; small hostas (*Hosta* cvs.) such as 'Ginko Craig', 'Gold Drop', and 'Hadspen Blue'; or clumping foamflower (*Tiarella wherryi*), which has neat foliage and white or pale pink flowers in spring.

For **SUNNY SITES**, try calamints (*Calamintha nepeta, C. grandiflora*), which have a neat, bushy appearance and fragrant leaves; 'Blue Clips' and 'White Clips' Carpathian bellflowers (*Campanula carpatica*), which flower from June to frost; 'Clara Curtis' chrysanthemum (*Chrysanthemum rubellum*), for its pink daisies in late summer and fall; 'Goldfink' coreopsis (*Coreopsis lanceolata*), which bears gold flowers all summer; alpine strawberry (*Fragaria vesca*), with neat foliage and tasty berries; bigroot geranium (*Geranium macrorrhizum*), which offers rosy purple flowers in early summer and big scented leaves; 'Stella de Oro' daylily (*Hemerocallis*), which produces its gold flowers all summer; or 'Butterfly Blue' pincushion flower (*Scabiosa columbaria*), for its summer-long show of blue flowers.

- **GRASSES AND GRASSLIKE PLANTS.** These all form tufts or clumps of slender, grassy leaves and are hardy at least to Zone 6.

Choosing and installing popular path surfaces

Price, appearance, adaptability to straight or curved designs, walking comfort and safety, installation requirements, ease of and need for maintenance, and durability should all be considered when you're comparing different toppings for a walk or path. As you'd expect, there are tradeoffs. Grass, wood-chip, and gravel paths cost much less and are easier to install than brick, paver-block, stone, poured-concrete, or board walkways, but the inexpensive toppings are also less weatherproof, more trouble to care for, and less permanent.

You'll almost certainly want to use different top-

pings for walks and paths that serve different roles and lead through different parts of your property. Typically you move from more formal, "harder" walks near the house to more casual, "softer" surfaces farther away. Places where one path intersects with or leads into another can feature a simple butting of one surface against another, or you could introduce a third material to mark the transition. For example, you might lay a single flagstone at the fork where a grassy garden path diverges from a main brick walk, or insert a landscape-timber step at the point where a wide gravel path funnels down into a narrow mossy trail.

Coordinate the toppings of your walks and

For edging paths, choose compact plants that are dense, short, and upright, such as lilyturf (**LEFT**) *or bergenia and sword fern* (**BELOW**). *These perennials all have evergreen foliage.*

Clumps can be divided every two or three years, in spring, to increase your stock.

For **PART SHADE**, try variegated Japanese sedges (*Carex morrowii* cvs.), which have glossy, semievergreen leaves striped with gold or yellow; lilyturf (*Liriope muscari* cvs.), which produces semievergreen dark or variegated leaves and lilac or white flowers in summer; or blue-eyed grass (*Sisyrinchium angustifolium*), which offers

smooth, neat leaves and bright blue flowers in late spring.

For **SUN**, try blue curly chives (*Allium senescens* 'Glaucum'), for its twisted blue-gray leaves and lilac flowers in summer; blue fescue grass (*Festuca glauca*), with wiry blue-green leaves and wispy tan flowers in summer; or 'Little Bunny' fountain grass (*Pennisetum alopecuroides*), a dwarf grass with fuzzy plumes in late summer.

paths with your house and other hardscape and the general style of your landscape. A stately old colonial or Victorian house calls for fairly formal main walks surfaced with brick or cut stone; away from such a house you could use grass or gravel for garden paths. Poured concrete, concrete pavers, and bricks go well with many contemporary homes. Random flagstone walks, chip paths, and boardwalks are appropriate for casual homes with natural-style landscapes, especially on wooded, mountain, or shoreline sites.

POURED CONCRETE. Concrete is very widely used for main walkways leading to the front and side doors of a house, for walks between a house and a

garage or other outbuildings, and as extensions of a concrete patio or terrace. Poured concrete is familiar, affordable, durable, nearly weed-proof, and easy to maintain. An advantage for walkways is that concrete works equally well for straight and curved shapes, and you can build steps right into a walk. Drawbacks are that concrete is liable to get cracked or stained; if it does, it's difficult to repair or clean. Also, it's hard to remove an unwanted concrete walk.

Although poured-concrete walks typically look plain and pale, they don't need to. Color can be added with concrete dyes, the surface can be textured, and the overall effect can be enriched by combining poured concrete with brick or wood edgings

(LEFT): *Boardwalk works well for a main walk that gets frequent use. Steppingstones, less convenient and comfortable to walk on, are okay for a secondary side trail.*

(BELOW LEFT): *Masonry is the most popular and versatile pavement for walks. These cut stones are dry-laid on a sand base.*

(BELOW RIGHT): *Mortared masonry such as this brick walk requires skillful installation but is stable, permanent, and weedproof.*

or by laying stones or tiles into the concrete. However, these design improvements must generally be done at the time the concrete is poured. Some contractors have methods of retopping and modernizing a plain old concrete walk, but these techniques aren't widely practiced and don't always give satisfactory results. For more about poured concrete, see page 137.

MASONRY. A well-made masonry walk is a prized addition to any landscape. You'll never tire of studying its patterned surface, you'll appreciate how it coordinates with all kinds of plants, and you'll admire how gracefully it ages. Building one does require a significant commitment in time and materials, but the result is an heirloom. It's one of the most satisfying and long-lasting hardscape features you can add to your yard.

See page 140 for guidelines on site preparation, material selection, installation, and maintenance. The same principles and pros and cons apply to brick, concrete-paver, flagstone, or cobblestone toppings whether they're applied to paths, patios, or driveways.

A gravel path that's tight and tidy like this is an inspiring sight, but it's a rare achievement. Usually gravel is a messy nuisance.

AGGREGATE OR GRAVEL PATHS. Crushed rock, gravel, or other rock aggregates make a path topping that is fairly inexpensive and easy to install. Gravel looks casual and blends well into natural-style landscapes, and it coordinates with both traditional and contemporary homes. English gardening books praise the crunchy sound of walking on gravel; although somewhat esoteric, I suppose that's a possible advantage, too.

But maintaining gravel is a chronic headache. Even compacted aggregate tends to shift underfoot and needs frequent raking to relevel it. Edging is definitely needed to confine any aggregate and keep it from spilling into adjacent areas, but stray pieces will leap across even the best edging. Fine particles stick to your shoes and track indoors. Aggregate is an ideal seedbed for many pernicious weeds, and uprooting these weeds disrupts the surface of the path. It's hard to clean up any messes where you've accidentally spilled soil, plant debris, or other litter on the path. If you ever need to add more aggregate to fill low spots, raise the surface, or extend a path, it's almost impossible to match the color of the original product, so patches are conspicuous. As a final insult, if you decide to remove a gravel path, digging it up is a pain.

I don't recommend gravel paths, but many people love them. If you're interested, see page 151 for guidelines on site preparation, material selection, installation, and maintenance. The same principles apply to gravel, crushed rock, and other aggregates whether they're applied to paths, patios, or driveways.

WOOD PRODUCTS. Chipped or shredded bark or wood from any kind of tree can be used for casual, natural-looking, soft-to-walk-on paths. These materials are especially suitable for shady sites under and around trees and large shrubs, in woodlands, and for work paths that provide access to flower beds or vegetable gardens. They're good temporary toppings for paths that you're uncertain about, that you might want to relocate or remove at some future date. Or if you haven't made up your mind yet about what kind of hard, permanent topping you might want to use on a path or can't afford to buy it yet, you can use wood chips in the meantime. When you want to remove them, you can just rake them up and use them for mulch or mix them into the compost pile.

Wood products have some drawbacks. They can be slippery when wet, and crumbs tend to stick to your shoes and get tracked indoors. They sometimes host fungus or mushrooms. Chips inevitably scatter off the sides of a path. That's a nuisance if they land in a lawn, but not if they land on a mulched planting bed. Weeds or garden plants that spread by seeds or runners all grow eagerly in wood-chip paths and you'll have to uproot them regularly. Also, you'll need to rake the chips occasionally from the edges back toward the center of the path.

If you live in a forested region, you can find a

variety of wood products at local sawmills and woodyards. Although you should seek already composted materials when you're using wood products as mulch, that isn't necessary for path toppings. Raw, uncomposted bark or chips are okay. For paths on sloping sites, use coarsely shredded bark, not chips of wood or bark. Chips wash or slide downhill, whereas shreds tend to cling together, mat down, and stay in place. Regardless of the color when you buy them, wood or bark chips usually bleach and age to a light silvery gray on sunny sites; they stay darker on shady sites.

On well-drained sites, you can spread wood products directly on the ground, but chips will float and wash away anywhere water collects or sink into the mud if you spread them on wet spots and walk there. To prevent problems, fill individual low spots

This grassy path is dotted with tiny English daisies. You can tell where people walk, because the daisies aren't quite as tough as turf is.

or depressions with gravel before spreading chips, or prepare a base for the entire path.

All wood products decompose in a few years' time (or faster), so you need to renew the surface periodically with a fresh topping. Fortunately, wood products are inexpensive and fairly lightweight and easy to transport and spread. They're usually sold by the cubic yard. One cubic yard of chips will cover 150 square feet to a depth of about 2 inches when compacted.

Turf paths

The dense, fine texture of healthy grass makes a beautiful contrast with the colorful flowers and lush foliage of adjacent plantings, and grass paths look lovely in a sunny garden. But grass paths need mowing, fertilizing, weeding, aerating, and all the other routine care you'd give a lawn, plus some extra TLC to compensate for the extra wear and compaction caused by localized foot traffic. They don't hold up to heavy everyday use and are liable to get worn down to the dirt on sites where the grass is weak because of shade, competition from tree roots, or poor, dry soil. Grass stays wet after a rain or dew, and fresh or damp clippings stick to your shoes and get tracked indoors. Most grasses turn brown when dormant (in summer or winter, or both, depending on the kind of grass and your climate).

Many gardeners end up with grass paths by default, because that's what they have left after carving beds out of a lawn. If you were starting from scratch, you could create new grass paths on an open site by seeding or sodding. Grass paths can be straight or curved, level or sloping. Test the placement, width, and shape of a potential grass path by pushing a lawn mower along it, and make any adjustments so it will be easy to mow.

ALTERNATIVES TO GRASS. Roman chamomile, white clover, creeping thyme, and a few other low-growing perennials can be used instead of or along with grass in paths, for variety. They sustain foot traffic almost as well as turf does and can be mowed, fertilized, and otherwise treated like grass, but they usually don't look quite as neat and uniform as turf does.

MOSS. On shady sites with acid soil where moss thrives, encourage it. It makes lush soft paths that are surprisingly durable and carefree. It holds up well to moderate foot traffic but isn't deep-rooted, so accidental missteps can kick up divots. (If that happens, set the disturbed clump back in place, water well, and it will reestablish.)

Moss turns brown during dry spells, but it recovers and greens up as soon as there's rain again. Weeds can be a problem in moss. Try cutting them down with a lawn mower or weed trimmer; that may

Although often used in public settings, boardwalks are an overlooked option for home landscapes. They're a good solution for situations where the ground is rocky, full of tree roots, sandy or unstable, or boggy. In terms of cost and durability, they're comparable to brick or flagstone, and wooden walks are pleasant to walk on and easy to maintain.

Most boardwalks are built like low decks, with concrete piers and pressure-treated beams and decking. A typical boardwalk would be about 6 feet wide and would need two beams spaced 4 feet apart. Depending on the dimension of the lumber used for the beams, you'd need to set piers every 6 to 12 feet. Digging the holes for some piers is much less work than excavating an entire area to lay an aggregate base for a walk, and it does much less damage to tree roots. In addition, you've got some leeway in digging the holes for the piers. If you hit a root or rock in one location, you can move back and forth a foot or so and try again.

Pressure-treated wood is the usual choice for decking a boardwalk, although you could use redwood, cedar, or cypress. Any wood should be sealed with a waterproof finish. It's a good idea to apply finish to all surfaces of the boards before you build the walk. Renew the finish by painting a fresh coat on the tops and ends of the boards every year or two as needed. For more on pressure-treated and other wood, see page 114.

A boardwalk costs no more than a masonry path on a square-foot basis and is a much easier way to traverse a rough or sloping site. This pressure-treated lumber was finished with a dark stain that improves its appearance.

be enough to weaken or subdue them. Otherwise, try hand pulling or spot-treat the weeds with a contact herbicide. Use a soft-tined rake or leaf blower to clear tree leaves off moss paths in fall, as a thick buildup of leaves can smother moss.

Steppingstones

Steppingstones are ideal for shortcuts. Use them where you need to cross through a wide planting bed or a patch of ground cover. They're good for access, too, if positioned where you have to step into a bed to tend the plants there. Providing one or more steppingstones in these situations minimizes the risk of treading on fragile plants, reduces soil compaction and root damage, and keeps your shoes dry.

These stones also make good markers. Use a big broad steppingstone to signal the end of a trail, to call attention to a fork in a path, to underscore the transition between different parts of the yard, or as a welcome mat where a patio leads off into a lawn. As a subtle but unmistakable marker, you can set a steppingstone in almost any situation, as these stones coordinate well with almost all path surfaces and landscape styles.

Steppingstones can serve as the treads for casual, infrequently used steps (see page 187), but this is a little tricky. You need to use broad, heavy stones and set them very securely, lest they tip if you step too close to the edge. Likewise, when using steppingstones to bridge wet spots or small streams (see page 181), it's important to use big stones set as steady and stable as possible.

FEW OR MANY? When used sparingly, steppingstones catch your attention and you tend to step onto them carefully and deliberately. Walkers wel-

Imbedding steppingstones flush or nearly so with the surface of an aggregate or wood-chip path works very well, as does insetting them in a mulched bed.

Setting steppingstones in turf is often recommended, but in truth this is a high-maintenance combination. There are two options, both troublesome. If you set a steppingstone flush with the soil so you can roll the lawn-mower wheels over it, most kinds of turf will creep out across it and you'll have to trim the grass back to the edge at least once or twice a year. You can do that by slicing around the edge with a sharp garden knife. Another issue is that a stone set flush with the ground is indented below the surface of the lawn; depending on how long you let your grass grow, it may look forlorn down there.

Alternatively, if you set the stone high enough that its surface is level with the top of the mowed grass, the stone will look more impressive but you can't mow over or around it. Instead, you have to trim all the way around it every time you mow the lawn, using a string trimmer or hand shears. That gets tiresome by the end of mowing season.

Like turf, many ground covers and creeping perennials will grow out over steppingstones, but since these other plants don't need to be mowed like grass does, you can set the stones high. Depending on the kind of plants, you'll need to trim around the stones at least once or twice a year. The combination of steppingstones and creeping plants looks so attractive that you may be glad to keep up with the trimming, at least for short paths composed of just a few stones.

MATERIALS AND SIZES. A steppingstone should be a single slab or paver with a minimum diameter of 12 inches. The shape can be round, square, or irregular, as long as the stone is big enough to support your entire foot. For places where you will stop and stand on the stone with both feet, 12 by 18 inches would be a minimum size. Bigger is always better. Although large steppingstones are heavy to transport to the site and set in place, they're much easier to walk or stand on. For stones used as markers, a slab 2 by 3 feet is none too big. Steppingstones should almost always be at least 2 inches thick, as thinner pieces of most materials are likely to crack.

Cast concrete and flagstone are the best materials for steppingstones. It's tempting to use rounds cut from logs, but they tend to be very slippery in wet climates and decay fast unless you have access to a kind of rot-resistant wood.

For concrete steppingstones, you can buy precast slabs or cast your own. The precast ones you find at garden centers work fine. They're usually either round or square, 2 to 3 feet in diameter, with a textured or pebbly surface. To cast your own, you need to buy or make a mold. Buy bags of ready-mix con-

Spacing is the problem with a steppingstone path. You have to adjust your stride to the placement of the stones, and it's frustrating if that distance feels uncomfortably short or long.

come occasional, thoughtfully placed steppingstones.

But steppingstones aren't particularly well suited for paths more than 15 to 20 feet long, especially if a path gets used by different people. That's because the point of these stones is that you're supposed to step directly on them, but people have different strides. In theory you could adjust your stride to match the spacing of the stones, but sometimes you just don't want to bother, or you think whoever laid the stones didn't know what they were doing and put them too close together or too far apart. So you disregard the stones and let your feet land as they may.

If you're making a long steppingstone path, you'd better acknowledge that people won't necessarily follow your lead. Do your best to position the stones at a comfortable, natural spacing. But set them flush in a bed of aggregate or chips so that walkers can step anywhere, on or off the stones. Think of the stones as pattern elements, but make the path as smooth overall as a parquet floor or an Oriental carpet.

crete (the mix includes both cement and aggregate), add water and stir as directed on the bag, and scoop it into the mold. Adding some dye when you mix the concrete makes prettier stones. You can also sprinkle or set colored pebbles, shells, or beach glass in the top of the steppingstone. Set these decorative additions in place while the concrete is still soft and gently push them down flush with the surface.

For flagstone steppingstones, you can use natural stones in irregular shapes or quarried stones that have been sawed square. Again, aim for a minimum diameter of 12 inches and a minimum thickness of 2 inches. A steppingstone doesn't have to be a slab of uniform thickness, but it does need at least one good flat side. You can use a stone with a rounded or slanted bottom if you set it in place so the top is level. Perhaps you have suitable stones on your property or permission to gather stones from someone else's land. Otherwise, visit local quarries or stoneyards to buy steppingstones.

SETTING STEPPINGSTONES. Placement, height, and stability are the things to think about as you're setting stones. Each stone should be placed so it's easy to land your foot on it. Depending on the number of stones and the context, it can be flush with the ground or raised. The surface should be level, and the stone should be so steady that it doesn't rock or tip even if your foot lands off center.

Establish placement first. To set a single steppingstone, first lay it on the ground, right side up, approximately where you want it. Step back and forth a few times to test the placement. Move it forward or back or from side to side as needed. Stand a little ways away to look at its orientation. Rotate it if you think that would look better.

If you're setting more than one stone, lay them all out to check their placement and spacing, or simulate the arrangement with scraps of plywood or cardboard. Walk back and forth repeatedly, and move the stones or scraps farther apart, closer together, or side to side as needed until walking on them feels comfortable, natural, and automatic. If other people will be using the path, ask them to check the spacing also. The result will probably involve some compromise. Whatever spacing you settle on, be consistent, so each step spans the same distance.

As for height, steppingstones can be set fully into the ground so their surface is flush with the soil or the surrounding path surface. This minimizes the risk of tripping and is good for any path that has more than a few steppingstones, any path that gets used frequently by visitors who may not be wary or sure-footed, and any path that gets used after dark. But raising a steppingstone above the surrounding soil or path surface makes it more visible, keeps it cleaner (soil and mulch sometimes spill onto flush-set stones), and slows the progress of some kinds of creeping plants. A raised stone can also keep your feet dry as you cross water or mud. You can raise a stone just a little or leave its full thickness aboveground.

Once you've decided on placement and height, set the stones one at a time. First use a shovel or trowel to make a few cuts around the edge of the stone, marking its place, then set it directly aside, without flipping or rotating it. Clear away any plants or debris, and dig a hole a little wider than the stone and deep enough to hold however much of the stone you want to bury plus an inch or so of sand. Spread a layer of coarse sand across the bottom of the hole.

Setting a stone so that its surface is level and it doesn't tip or rock takes some tinkering. Position the stone in the hole, check it by placing a spirit level on its surface, and then test it by standing on it with both feet and trying to rock it. Note which way it leans or tips. Then lift the stone, adjust the sand beneath it, reset the stone, and check it again. Repeat until the stone is level and steady, then pack sand around it firmly to refill the rest of the hole.

Follow the same process for setting consecutive stones. In addition, check to see that they're level with each other (if the site is level) or that they climb at the same slow, steady pace (if the site is sloping). Either way, use a straight piece of 2x4 to check for continuity. Span three stones with it and make sure the stone in the middle is aligned with its neighbors. Repeat along the length of the path.

SETTING STEPPINGSTONES

The height of a steppingstone in relation to its surroundings influences appearance and maintenance. **(TOP):** *If set at grade level in turf, mowing is easy but the stones look recessed.* **(MIDDLE):** *If set at mowing height in turf, the stones are flush with the lawn and look good, but you have to trim around each stone every time you mow.* **(BOTTOM):** *An ideal solution is to set steppingstones slightly above grade in a bed of ground cover. This looks fine and requires only occasional trimming.*

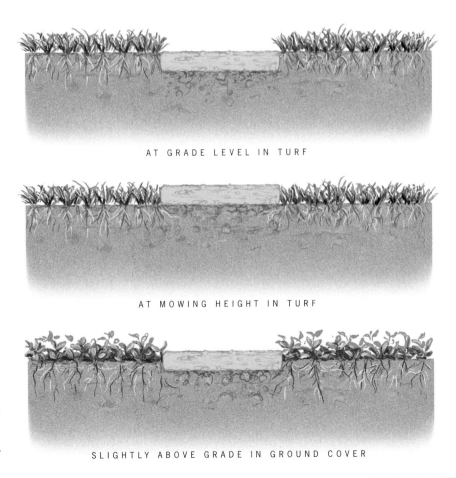

AT GRADE LEVEL IN TURF

AT MOWING HEIGHT IN TURF

SLIGHTLY ABOVE GRADE IN GROUND COVER

These perennials grow 1 to 4 inches tall and form low mats that spread to about 1 foot or wider. They can withstand being stepped on occasionally, but daily crushing would discourage them. They will gradually reach over the edge of a steppingstone and need to be trimmed back when they spread too far. You can trim them at any season, with a sharp garden knife, grass clippers, or pruning shears. The following are all evergreen or semievergreen. Except where noted, they require full or part sun and well-drained soil.

- **Mt. Atlas daisy** (*Anacyclus depressus*). Rosettes of ferny gray-green leaves. White daisies on short stalks in summer. **ZONE 5.**

- **Pussytoes** (*Antennaria dioica*). Very fuzzy, rounded leaves. Tufts of white or pink flowers in early summer. **ZONE 5.**

- **Sandwort** (*Arenaria montana*). Slender gray-green leaves. White flowers in early summer. **ZONE 4.**

- **Roman chamomile** (*Chamaemelum nobile*). Bright green, fine-textured, fragrant foliage. Seedlings have daisylike flowers; 'Treneague' is nonflowering and forms a neater, denser mat. **ZONE 5.**

- **Cheddar pinks** (*Dianthus gratianopolitanus* cvs.). Dense mats of short, grassy, blue-green or green-gray foliage. 'Tiny Rubies' is especially compact, with carmine flowers. **ZONE 4.**

- **Blue star creeper** (*Laurentia fluviatilis*). Shiny little green leaves; pale blue flowers in late spring. Prefers moist soil. **ZONE 8.**

- **Mazus** (*Mazus* spp.). Shiny mats topped with purple or white flowers that dangle on short stalks in summer. Prefers moist soil. **ZONE 5.**

- **Corsican mint** (*Mentha requienii*). Forms shiny, mosslike mats of tiny leaves that smell like crème de menthe. Prefers moist soil. **ZONE 6.**

- **Moss** (many kinds). Where moss grows naturally, encourage it. A few nurseries are starting to sell moss. It's a fine ground cover for shady sites with acid soil. Turns brown if it dries out, but greens up again with the first rain. **HARDINESS VARIES.**

- **Partridgeberry** (*Mitchella repens*). Vining stems lined with small oval leaves. Plump red berries ripen in late summer and last until birds eat them. Takes full or partial shade. **ZONE 4.**

- **Moss phlox** (*Phlox subulata*). Many fine cultivars; 'Emerald Blue' and 'Emerald Pink' are especially good. They bear masses of flowers in early spring. Shear them hard after they bloom. Foliage is fine-textured but wiry, like stiff moss. **ZONE 4.**

- **Scotch moss, Irish moss, or pearlwort** (*Sagina subulata*). Very compact and mossy, with bright green leaves and tiny white flowers. *Arenaria verna* is a similar plant that goes by the same common names. There are gold-leaved forms of both species. **ZONE 5.**

- **Sedums** (*Sedum* spp.). Gold moss sedum (*S. acre*) and many other species form low, tight, evergreen mats of tiny succulent leaves. Most have vivid gold, pink, or white flowers in late spring or summer. **ZONE 4.**

- **Thymes** (*Thymus* spp.). There are many excellent creeping thymes that form low, dense mats of wiry stems with tiny leaves and flowers. Foliage can be fuzzy gray or shiny green in summer; some kinds turn maroon in winter. Most bear masses of pink, purple, or white flowers in summer. **ZONE 4.**

- **Veronicas** (*Veronica* spp.). There are many creeping veronicas that form mats of fuzzy gray-green, shiny green, or bronze foliage. Most bear gorgeous blue-violet flowers in spring. **ZONE 4.**

These steppingstones are level and flush, and they are "mortared" with woolly thyme, a creeping ground cover. That makes the path easier to walk on, because it seems like a continuous surface, not just a row of dots.

When a walk or path comes to a boggy spot, ditch, brook, or gully, you need to design some way to get across without getting wet. The possibilities include steppingstones, bridges, and culverts. Which solution is best for your situation? It depends. Study the site and identify your needs. How long a span is it? How wide a path do you need? Is the area always wet, or just sometimes? What's the high-water mark? Would you need to cross at high-water times, or could you wait until the water recedes? Along with crossing on foot, would you ever want to roll a cart or power tool across? Steppingstones are only good for casual or occasional pedestrian crossings. For most purposes, you need a culvert or bridge.

Think about style, too, and whether you want your crossing to be a conspicuous feature in the landscape or simply a welcome solution to a messy problem. Bridges stand out more than steppingstones or culverts do, and they can be designed to look rustic, traditional, contemporary, or foreign. Choose whatever style coordinates with your house and the rest of your landscape. A bridge draws plenty of attention anyway and you don't need to exaggerate its visual impact by picking an anomalous style.

Observe the water level over time

Installing any kind of crossing is something you think about for a while before doing it, and that's good. As you monitor a stream, ditch, or boggy spot for a year or two, you can observe how high and how quickly the water rises after a heavy downpour or during spring snowmelt or runoff season. Also note how long it stays up and how fast it subsides to normal flow. Ask old-timers in the neighborhood to tell you about the worst flooding they've seen, and remember that what happened once can happen again. High water is powerful, and you have to plan for it. I emphasize this because small streams can surprise you. What looks like a babbling brook one day can be a roaring torrent the next.

Use the difference between normal and flood stage as a basis for deciding whether you can handle a crossing project yourself. Tackle only relatively stable waterways. For any case where the water volume fluctuates notably, get advice from a hydrologist, an engineer, a landscape architect, or local or state agencies. Construction in this situation is likely to be governed by regulations and codes, you may need a permit, and you probably should hire a qualified contractor to do the work.

Steppingstone crossings

These aren't practical for everyday use, but they're suitable for garden paths or nature trails. They can

be placed in rock-bottomed brooks or streams, artificial (man-made) waterways with stable bottoms, or low spots where water pools after a rain because the soil there is so compacted that water doesn't drain down through it. If you can walk across the site without sinking in, you can put steppingstones there.

However, steppingstones are futile in situations where wet ground is soft or mushy. If your boots sink in, a stone would sink in, too. In fact, it's surprising how quickly and completely even a big stone can disappear into the mud, and it's an astonishingly messy job trying to retrieve a sunken stone should you want to try again or put it someplace else.

INSTALLING STEPPINGSTONES. Use a rake or hoe to smooth the area where you want to set a stone, removing pebbles, debris, roots, or tussocks. Choose a big slab of uniform thickness, flat on both the top and bottom, and thick enough to project above the normal water level. You'll need help handling a stone this size and setting it in place. Ease it

This wooden bridge, built like a deck, has a sturdy rail to lean against. It seems high above the water now, but at flood stage the brook rises almost to the beams.

into position, then trying stepping on it. It probably won't be level or steady at first. Tip it sideways and put one or more shims underneath it, then lower it back into place and try again. Keep adjusting the shims until the stone sits just right.

If you need two or more steppingstones for a crossing, set them one at a time. Space them close enough to provide for short steps, not long hops.

Culverts

Culverts are used to confine flowing water to a restricted channel as it moves under a walkway or driveway. This is a great solution for situations where a path has to cross a small ditch or brook and presently dips down and up again. Putting a culvert there would let you level out the path and walk or roll right across the water.

USE A BIG ENOUGH PIPE. Get local advice on how big a culvert you need. Almost certainly, the answer will be bigger than you'd expect, because culverts should be designed with reference to the maximum flow, not the normal flow. Culvert pipes are sized by diameter, in inches or feet. Small (4-inch) drainpipes made of plastic suffice only for minor jobs. Often you need larger concrete drain tiles or corrugated steel pipes. Depending on the situation, you might use one big pipe or two or more smaller ones side by side. The pipe(s) should be at least a foot longer than the path is wide.

INSTALLING A CULVERT. You can install a culvert pipe yourself or with a helper. Along with the pipe, you'll need an assortment of medium to large rocks to stack walls at both ends of the pipe, along with a supply of crushed rock to fill in around the culvert and to level out the path. (Pouring concrete around the culvert is a worthy alternative to filling in with crushed rock.)

Work on a warm summer day when the water level is down. Dig any rocks or weeds out of the way, make a trench through the center of the channel, and spread a shallow bed of crushed rock there. The pipe should slope very slightly downstream and its bottom should be just a little below the natural bed of the stream or ditch (if you set it too low, silting will soon reduce its capacity). Roll the pipe into place, watch the water flow through it, adjust its height or position if needed, and then lay a few big rocks along both sides to hold it steady.

Arrange big rocks around the inlet end of the culvert to withstand the rush of high water and to funnel the flow into the pipe. Stack the rocks up to and over the top of the pipe. Use more rocks to build up a sturdy wall around the outlet end of the pipe. Then fill the entire area along both sides of the pipe with crushed rock, packing it in as firmly as possible. Extend this crushed-rock base as far as needed to

level out the path on both sides of the culvert, then lay the final path surface on top.

Bridges

You need to know the flood-stage water level in order to design and build a bridge. For small ditches and streams that drain a limited watershed, flood stage may be just a foot or so higher than the normal water level. You can handle a situation like that. Also, you can bridge a man-made waterway such as an artificial brook or garden cascade that's powered by a recirculating pump. And you can likewise bridge still water, such as shallow ponds or boggy areas. What you shouldn't tackle without a lot of research, experience, planning, and a permit is bridging any natural stream that's part of a large watershed and hence subject to dramatic flooding.

PIERS, BEAMS, AND DECKING. The understructure of a bridge includes poured-concrete piers or masonry abutments built on opposite sides of the brook, and beams substantial enough to cross the span between them and carry the expected load. Follow local codes and the charts in deck-building books to figure what size piers and beams you need. Codes and common sense usually dictate that the piers or abutments should be set well out on the banks, beyond the high-water line, so they don't snag debris and/or get washed away during floods. At any rate, the piers must be high enough to support the beams above the high-water line or the whole bridge is likely to get washed away.

Narrow pedestrian bridges may simply have piers at both ends spanned with beams laid side by side. Bridges like this are sometimes made as narrow as 2 feet wide, but a minimum of 3 feet is more comfortable. For a wider bridge, top the required number of beams with crosswise decking. Make a bridge 4 to 5 feet wide for two people walking side by side or if you want to roll carts or tools across. Again, you can apply deck-building guidelines to the framing and construction of wooden bridges.

A bridge with a flat deck is easiest to design, build, and use. Bridges with bowed decks look charming, but they're more trouble to make and much harder to walk across. If you want a little bowed bridge, try out the ready-made models available at garden centers. The ones that are quite curved are slippery underfoot even when dry and impassable when wet. That doesn't matter if you want the bridge mostly as an ornament, but for a bridge that functions as part of a path, a flat deck is much safer.

RAILINGS OR BUMPERS. Building codes typically require a sturdy handrail for any deck that's more than 30 inches aboveground. That's very lenient. For safety's sake, lower decks need railings too, and bridges certainly do. Whether or not it's required by code, build a railing on any bridge whose

deck is more than a foot or so above the normal water level. Make it at least 36 inches high (better yet, 42 inches high), and anticipate that people will lean heavily on it as they gaze down into the water, so make it very sturdy.

For bridges that are within 1 foot of the water, use 2x4s to make low bumpers along both sides or add wide fascia boards that stick up about 2 inches above the decking. It's surprising how much psychological and practical benefit bumpers provide. They make you feel safer as you walk or stand on the bridge, and they're indispensable for keeping wheels from rolling off the edge when you push a tool or cart across.

❦ DESIGNING AND BUILDING OUTDOOR STEPS

Outdoor steps are obviously useful, but they can be much more than that. Well-designed, solidly built steps are a sort of outdoor sculpture. They're satisfying to look at and pleasant to climb. They're good to sit on, too. Whether or not you build them yourself (in many cases you'll want to hire a contractor), it's fun planning the layout of steps, choosing materials, and thinking about how they will fit in with the adjacent path and the surrounding landscape.

Steps are a conspicuous feature in any setting. You can maximize this and make them on a grand scale, broad and stately, or call extra attention to them by using material whose form, color, or texture stands out from the surroundings. Or you could minimize their presence by making them seem to blend in; well-placed stone steps can look so inevitable and ancient that visitors will wonder if they are natural outcroppings. Or just make casual, friendly steps that look comfortable and reassuring. Whatever style you choose, steps are a great addition to a landscape and they transform a sloping site from a problem into an asset.

Dimensions

Steps have three dimensions: the width from side to side, the depth from front to back, and the height from bottom to top. Of these, width is the most inde-

(RIGHT): *Both grand and charming, this combination of steps, retaining walls, and narrow planting beds fills a half-moon shape and leads from a raised terrace down to the lawn. These steps are well designed, with uniform spacing, low rise, and deep tread. They look gracious and feel comfortable underfoot.*

(BELOW): *For curved steps like this made of cast concrete, hire a contractor. Figuring the layout, building the forms, and making everything uniform and level takes experience and skill. Investing in well-built steps will give you years of pleasure and satisfaction.*

essarily *determined* by the site. You normally have at least a few, and sometimes many, suitable options to consider.

WIDTH. In general, outdoor steps should be as wide as the rest of the walk or path they're a part of. Usually that means a minimum of 3 to 4 feet wide. It's often desirable to make steps much wider than that. If they're 6, 8, or 10 feet wide, they look more gracious. Wide steps become a gathering place for people to sit, or they can serve as staging for a display of potted plants. Next to a house, wide steps expand the landing. In a garden, wide steps can ease seamlessly into a terraced hillside.

Occasionally, you might try the tactic of making very narrow steps on a garden path or trail. Squeezing through a bottleneck slows people down and implies that something significant is happening or lies ahead, some big change in style or scenery, like climbing up a cliff and getting a wonderful overview, or stepping down into a cavelike secret room. But it's pointless to do this if there isn't any reward at either end of the passage. Unless the context supports their significance, narrow steps just seem tight.

HEIGHT, OR RISE. The overall climb from the bottom to the top of the steps is called the *total rise,* and the vertical distance from one step to the next—how high you lift your foot—is called the *rise,* or *unit rise,* or *rise per step.* Most outdoor steps have something, such as a piece of timber or a row of cut

pendent variable. You can make steps as narrow or wide as suits the site, without regard to their depth or height. Depth and height are much more constrained. These must fit within a limited range of measurements and proportions or the steps will feel awkward to use.

Although steps should ultimately appear to *fit* the site, their dimensions and placement aren't nec-

stone, that establishes the rise and serves as a *riser,* but some steps are constructed without risers.

The unit rise for outdoor steps is typically between 4 and 7 to 8 inches. You could have a rise as short as 2 inches—the thickness of a typical paver or brick—but that's generally not a good idea. If a single step has too low a rise, you may overlook it and trip on it. If steps in a series have a too-low rise, you'll get impatient and climb them two at a time. Generally, 4 inches is the lowest desirable rise for a few steps. Go to at least 5 inches for a series of many steps.

Indoor steps sometimes have a very steep rise of 9 to 10 inches, or even more in old colonial houses, but that's uncomfortable, and it's unnecessary and inappropriate outdoors. Outdoor steps should have a maximum rise of 7 inches except in rare circumstances where space is so limited or the climb is so steep that you have to go to a maximum rise of 8 inches.

The total rise is determined by the site. Next to a building, deck, or other structure, it's the distance from floor level down to the place on the ground where the steps end up. On a hillside or bank, it's the distance between level areas at the top and bottom. Using a water level (see the drawing at right) is an easy and accurate way to measure the total rise.

You can usually round the total rise up or down by an inch or two, because you can make up that kind of difference by adjusting the grade of the adjacent walkways. Rounding helps make the numbers come out even as you divide the total rise into fewer or more steps. For example, if you have a bank with a total rise of about 35 or 36 inches, you could divide it into nine 4-inch steps, eight 4½-inch steps, seven 5-inch steps, six 6-inch steps, or five 7-inch steps.

Which is better: fewer, steeper steps or more, shallower steps? That's for you to decide, but first you have to consider the depth of the steps, or the run. And you're constrained by the ideal ratio between rise and run.

DEPTH, OR RUN. A single step set out in the middle of a path doesn't have depth to speak of, it's just a vertical blip. But when you have two or more steps in a row, the horizontal distance from one to the next is called the *run,* or *unit run,* or *run per step.* Also called the *tread,* it's where you set your foot down, and it should be deep enough that you can set your foot flat and not have to perch on your toes.

Although building codes sometimes allow a minimum unit run or tread depth of only 9 inches, that's terribly small for outdoor steps. A run of 11 to 12 inches feels much more comfortable and safer to walk on. A run of 14 to 16 inches is even better. In fact, for walks that climb long, gentle slopes, you can design outdoor steps with treads so deep that you take two or three paces on each one.

Multiply the unit run times the number of steps to figure the *total run,* or overall depth of the set of steps. Unlike total rise, the total run is determined only partly by the layout of the site. As you fit steps into a slope or bank or extend them out from a building, you usually have enough leeway to accommodate different total runs. It comes down to a judgment call based on how you want the steps to look and feel.

BE CONSISTENT. Even more important than the actual dimensions you set is making all the steps the same. Your feet will feel the difference and register it as an uncertainty or a hazard if the unit rise varies by even ½ inch from one step to the next, or if the unit run varies by as little as 1 inch. Consistency is critical for steps close to a building or for steps that have been built from wood or masonry. Farther out in a garden and where steps were obviously carved out of a slope, you can be a little less precise, but it's still desirable to do the best you can at maintaining an even, measured pace.

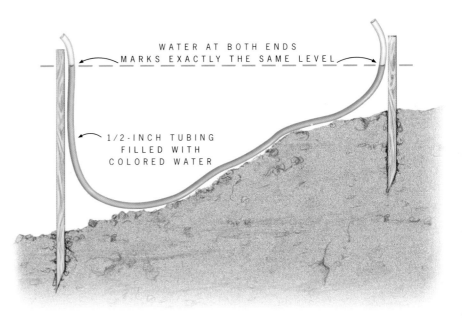

WATER AT BOTH ENDS MARKS EXACTLY THE SAME LEVEL

1/2-INCH TUBING FILLED WITH COLORED WATER

USING A WATER LEVEL

This simple, inexpensive, easy-to-use tool is very accurate. Buy a length of clear plastic ½-inch tubing; it's sold by the foot at any hardware store. Add a few drops of food coloring to some water and pour it into the tubing. Get a helper to hold the other end, and observe how water moves back and forth in the tubing until it reaches the same level at both ends.

To measure the height of a bank, drive stakes at the top and bottom of the slope. With your helper, hold the tubing between the stakes and draw marks at the water level. Measure from the ground up to the line on both stakes, then subtract. The difference equals the height of the bank.

To level the tops of a row of fence posts, draw a reference line on the first post at the desired height. Then run the tubing from the first post to the second. Line up the water level with the reference line, and draw a line at that level on the second post. Continue along, marking the desired level on one post after another.

RATIOS OR PROPORTIONS FOR STEPS

There's a standard formula for designing outdoor steps. Make twice the unit rise plus the unit run equal 26 inches. Easy examples that meet this formula are 4-inch rise and 18-inch run, 5-inch rise and 16-inch run, 6-inch rise and 14-inch run, and 7-inch rise and 12-inch run. You get the idea—as the rise gets higher, the run gets smaller. This way, the combination of rise and run stays within the range of a comfortable stride, so you can climb the steps as you would walk.

Let's work an example with this formula to see how the unit rise and number of steps affects the total run. Consider a bank with a total rise of about 35 or 36 inches. If you make nine 4-inch steps, the total run would be 9 times 18 inches, or 162 inches (13½ feet). But if you make five 7-inch steps, the total run would be 5 times 12 inches, or only 60 inches (5 feet). What a difference: total runs of 13½ feet versus 5 feet to climb the same distance! (Of course, there are countless intermediate options for this or any example or site.)

If you follow the formula, the unit rise also determines the total run or overall "footprint" of the steps, how much space they fill in your garden, and how dominant they look. Sorting out this issue is the big challenge in designing most steps. It's a tradeoff between more and fewer steps, low or high rises, shallow or deep treads, and compact versus expanded total run.

ALTERNATIVE RATIOS. Actual steps vary widely from the formula and sometimes work well anyway. If you're thinking about building some steps, do a serious comparison of existing models. Take a measuring tape as you go around town and check the measurements of different outdoor steps in parks and public places, in shopping malls and commercial developments. You'll find a lot of variation, including some steps that feel very inviting and others that are downright annoying. Measure the ones you like best and copy those dimensions at home, if you can make them fit the site.

**RECOMMENDED
DIMENSIONS FOR OUTDOOR STEPS**

These drawings, done to scale, represent three combinations of rise and run that stay within the range of a comfortable stride: 4-inch rise and 18-inch run (LEFT), 5-inch rise and 16-inch run (CENTER), and 6-inch rise and 14-inch run (RIGHT).

HOW RISE/RUN RATIOS AFFECT OVERALL DIMENSIONS

A flight of steps can be condensed or spread out, depending on how much space is available and what effect you want to create—a long gradual climb (LEFT) or a short steep climb (RIGHT). These two sets of steps both conform to standard proportions. They have about the same total rise but very different total runs.

Combining steps with landings

When a walk climbs a long, steep slope that requires many steps, breaking it up with one or more landings that run on the level gives people a chance to pause and catch their breath, adjust their grip on anything they're carrying, and look around to see how far they've come. As a rule of thumb, don't make a continuous set of more than 10 or 12 steps in an outdoor walk or garden path. If you need that many steps, divide them into two or three shorter climbs with landings in between.

A landing can be continued straight in line with the path, or the steps and landings can be set at different angles. For example, you can use landings to help a path zigzag up a long hill, where you'd take several steps up, turn onto a level landing that traverses the hill for a short distance, turn again and climb some more steps, and so on.

On a long, gentle slope where the total rise calls for just a few steps, you could cluster them at one end or the other and level the entire area in between, but that would involve a fair amount of earthmoving. There's less grading to do if you space single steps here and there along the length of the path and level each landing separately. When you incorporate occasional single steps into a path, make sure each step has the same rise, but don't worry about standardizing the distance between steps if they're more than a few paces apart.

Building garden steps

Steps that lead directly into your house count as part of the house, so I won't elaborate on them here except to suggest that they should coordinate with it in style, choice of materials, and quality of workmanship, and to emphasize that the three most important concerns in designing and building steps are safety, safety, and safety. You've probably encountered all the typical problems: steps that are tippy and unstable, slippery, too steep, irregular, unlit—it's a rogues' gallery. Enough can go wrong in designing and building house steps that most homeowners should forgo any idea of doing the job themselves. Hire an experienced contractor instead.

Likewise, any steps that are part of the main walk leading into your house are critical because they're used by all kinds of visitors and often exposed to public view. You might try making these yourself, but it's a job to take seriously. Some of the precast concrete paver and wallstone systems (see page 221) include modules for simple, easy-to-make steps that turn out well. If you're a careful carpenter, you could make wooden steps. Otherwise, hire a contractor, especially if you want a concrete or masonry main walk with built-in matching steps.

Farther out on your property, any steps that form part of garden paths or trails should also be safe, convenient, and pleasant to use, but the standards aren't quite as strict. If visitors don't want to climb some steps you've built way out in the garden, they can just turn around and go back to your house. You yourself may use the steps only on nice days, not in foul weather or after dark.

You can design and build fair-weather or garden steps yourself. One method is to simply set steppingstone treads in place, one for each step. This works okay if you need to make only a few steps on a narrow path, if the slope isn't too steep, and if you stabilize and cover the soil around the steppingstones with dense plantings of creeping plants to protect against erosion.

Another approach is to install risers, then fill in the treads behind them with packed aggregate, perhaps topped with pavers, bricks, or flagstones set in a bed of sand. Installing risers is better than setting steppingstones for any path that is 3 feet or wider, for slopes where you need a series of several steps, or in situations where erosion is likely due to loose soil or high rainfall.

PLAN THE LAYOUT FIRST. Whether you intend to lay treads or to install risers, do the same basic planning before you start to build steps. Use stakes and string or spray paint to outline the route you want the path to take as it climbs the slope. It really is worthwhile to measure the total rise, spend time figuring, designing, and comparing your options, and then decide on the total number of steps, the unit rise, the unit run, and the total run. If you can't bear the idea of doing all that figuring and planning, you can go ahead and proceed by trial and error, continually testing the steps as you build them, but you'll have to do a lot of extra tweaking and revising if you work that way.

WORK YOUR WAY UP. Start at the bottom of the slope and work up when building steps, installing one step at a time. Remember that consistency is the key to safe, comfortable steps. Use a yardstick to make sure that all the steps in a series have the same rise and run. When you get to the top, you may have to raise or lower the grade of the path or trail to make it line up with the top step. For that reason, finish the steps first, then complete the path afterward.

Setting steppingstones as treads

Both natural stone and cast-concrete steppingstones are suitable for step treads. Choose a closely matched set of stones if you're making more than one step. Steppingstone treads should be approximately rectangular and have a fairly straight edge that can serve as the front of the step. They should be at least 2 inches thick, 14 to 16 inches deep, and 24 to 30 inches wide. (If you can get them and have someone to help

You can install steps like this yourself, using cast-concrete steppingstones, if you're patient enough to make sure each stone is absolutely level and stable.

you set them in place, you could use much thicker and wider stones, up to 6 to 7 inches thick and 36 inches wide, but it's hard to find matched stones in that size range and they're very heavy.)

PLACE EACH STONE CAREFULLY. Starting at the bottom, level out the end of the path. Then cut into the soil where you want to set the first step. Use a sharp spade to make a neat vertical cut for the riser, and remove enough soil to make a level area about the size and shape of the stone.

Lay the stone in place, aligning its front edge with the vertical cut you made in the soil. Check the rise by putting a piece of 2x4 on the stone and measuring from the bottom of the 2x4 down to the surface of the path. Set a spirit level on top of the 2x4 to see if the stone tread is level in all directions. Step on the stone and try rocking it to see if it's stable or tippy.

You'll almost certainly have to make adjust-

ments, so lift the stone aside, remove or add soil beneath it, and then put it back in place. Recheck its rise, levelness, and stability. Repeat until the stone is set just right, then pack dirt or crushed rock firmly along the sides and back of the stone.

Set each successive stone the same way, working up the slope. Carve a terrace into the soil; carefully position the stone, checking particularly to make sure that each step has the same rise and run; and pack fill around the stone to keep it from shifting. Keep testing the steps as you proceed by walking up and down the ones you've already laid. Remember that consistency, levelness, and stability are essential. If you detect any variation, awkwardness, or unsteadiness, go back and fix those problems before you continue upward.

PROTECT THE SOIL WITH PLANTS. Erosion is the main problem with steppingstone steps. If the soil under a stone gets washed away, the step will tilt. Try to minimize this risk by disturbing the soil as little as possible when you set a step. Make the terraced area you cut into the hillside approximately the size of the stone, or just a little wider and deeper. Leave the existing vegetation in place, or replace it promptly with creeping plants that quickly establish a good mass of roots and a dense cover of top growth. The perennials recommended in the box on page 180 are good candidates for stepside stabilization.

Stacked-stone steps

Although I need to mention this, I don't recommend it: Another way to build steps is to assemble masses of stones, rather than setting stones singly onto a dirt base. When built right (which usually means building on a massive scale), stacked-stone steps last virtually forever, as evidenced by ancient monuments such as the Great Wall of China or Machu Picchu.

But for today's amateur homeowners, there are two serious problems with stacked-stone steps. First, you probably can't find or handle individual stones that are big enough to make steps, so you'll end up stacking stones to achieve the desired rise and piecing stones to make a big enough tread. All this stacking and piecing means there are lots of seams in the work, and to someone walking on the steps those seams are red flags that warn of an uneven and perhaps tippy surface. Second, unless you do a lot of chiseling and shaping, stones rarely fit neatly and snugly enough to make square, level steps, so you end up using a lot of shims to adjust the heights and to fill gaps. That aggravates the already shaky appearance. Only skilled stone masons can make dry-laid stone steps that look — and are — safe and stable to walk on.

Using mortar would solve the problems, hold the stones together, fill cracks, and give the steps a smoother overall look, but making mortared stone steps is a challenging job even for experienced masons, so don't even think of trying it yourself.

Installing risers, then filling in the treads

This is a good method of building steps. First you install risers (usually made from landscape timbers), mounting them securely on the slope, then you fill in behind them with firmly compacted gravel. You can leave it at that and let the tops of the risers and gravel backfill serve as treads, or you can surface the treads with pavers or flagstones set in sand or with creeping plants rooted in pockets of soil. Because the risers serve as a series of mini retaining walls, steps built this way help stabilize a slope and resist erosion. You can make a straight or curved path with steps of any width, and you can easily standardize the measurements for the rise and run.

PROBLEMS TO PREVENT. Steps of this kind are very common in contemporary home landscapes, but more often than not they show certain problems. These problems can be avoided by careful construction. For example, sometimes the risers are tilted from one end to the other. Prevent that by using a level as you install them. Sometimes the risers start tipping or leaning downhill. Prevent that by fastening them more securely when you install them. Often the treads are sunken or dished out behind the risers. Prevent that by thoroughly compacting the

Building steps this way isn't recommended. It's too hard to level the treads and to maintain the same unit rise. Also, seeing the irregularly shaped crevices between the stacked stones makes you hesitate to climb.

Landscape timbers make good risers for outdoor steps. To install them, start at the bottom of the slope and work up. Make sure each timber is level, then stake it securely. Pack soil or aggregate behind each riser and compact it firmly to make the tread level with the top of the timber.

backfill when you build the steps and topping it up afterward if it continues to settle.

WHAT TO USE FOR RISERS.

Pressure-treated 6x6 landscape timbers make good risers. Old railroad ties work well, if you can get them. If you have a place to cut your own black locust, cedar, or other rot-resistant wood, you can use round logs or poles about 8 inches in diameter instead of squared timbers. Cut the timbers or logs as long as the path is wide so you can use a single length for each riser. You could use stones for risers, but suitable stones are hard to come by and heavy to handle. They should be fairly square in cross section, about 6 to 8 inches high and deep, and as long as the path is wide. (Putting shorter stones side by side doesn't work nearly as well as using one long stone, because it's too hard to level and align a series of stones.) Unless you're well supplied with stones and experienced at setting them, make wooden risers.

INSTALLATION GUIDELINES.

As always, start at the bottom and work uphill when installing risers, and check repeatedly with a yardstick to make sure that each step has the same rise and run. Be as consistent as possible. Work slowly and carefully. Doing your best to position, level, and stake each riser is the key to making an attractive, comfortable, and durable set of steps.

Wooden risers must be secured in two ways. First, dig a shallow trench so you can bury about 1 inch of a square timber or 2 to 3 inches of a round pole. Use a spirit level to make sure the riser is perfectly level from side to side, and if it's a square timber, make sure its top is level from front to back. Add or remove soil from the trench as needed until the riser is correctly positioned.

Then stake the riser to keep it from tipping or rolling downhill. Either drive ½-inch holes through the riser about 6 inches from each end and every 2 to 3 feet in between and drive 2-foot lengths of rebar through the holes and into the ground, or drive similar lengths of rebar or wooden stakes at similar spacing along the downhill edge of the timber.

If you have big, long stones to use as risers, basically you can set them like timbers, using stakes along the front edge. If you have really large stones, thick enough that you can bury them halfway, you can omit staking them. If you need two or more smaller stones to make a wide enough riser, butt them as close together as possible and make sure they're flush across the front and top edges of the riser.

BACKFILLING.

Use a hoe or shovel to pull soil downhill and fill in the space behind each riser after you've positioned and staked it, leveling out the area that will be the tread and also the place where you will install the next riser. Pack down the soil as firmly as possible by stomping on it with your feet and whamming it with the end of a 2x4. Be especially thorough about firming along the back edge of the riser.

Depending on the slope you're working on and the proportions of your steps, you probably won't have enough soil to bring the treads up level with the tops of the risers. In that case, use a compactable crushed-rock aggregate to fill in, and pack it firmly. Even if you do happen to have enough native soil to complete the steps, you may want to remove some of it and use aggregate instead for a neater and more attractive topping.

SETTING PAVERS ON THE TREADS.

There are two ways to combine timber or stone risers with paver treads. You can partially fill the area behind the risers and set the bricks, flagstones, or concrete pavers so their surface is flush with the top of the riser. Or you can bring the backfill up level with the riser, then lay pavers on top of the entire area, extending them out over the riser. (This adds the thickness of the paver to the height of the riser, so if you're going with this option, bury the risers deep enough that the total rise won't be too great.)

Either way, dry-set the pavers on the treads as you would for a path, fitting them as close together as possible. Make sure the entire surface of the tread is smooth and level. Pack sand into the cracks, and plan to add more sand from year to year as it settles or washes away.

GROWING PLANTS ON THE TREADS.

The combination of hard timber or stone risers and treads carpeted with soft green creeping plants looks nice but is tricky to achieve. That's because compacted soil and foot traffic make life hard for plants grown on steps like this. To give them a better chance, inset steppingstones into the treads so you can step there, rather than crushing the plants. Dig planting holes along the sides of the steps and replace the dirt you dig out, which is probably just subsoil, with good garden soil when you insert your plants.

Choose creeping perennials from the list on page 180. Once they get established, creeping plants will reach out across the treads and fill in around the steppingstones. Eventually you'll need to trim them back on a regular basis.

A see-through gate in this bougainvillea-covered arch welcomes visitors, while defining the transition between public and private space.

7 ❧ Fences, Walls, and Hedges

VARIOUS KINDS of "outdoor walls" or vertical features serve many roles in landscaping. They can create privacy, block an unwanted view, reduce noise, filter the wind, limit the passage of people and animals, mark the boundaries of your property, enclose a smaller area and make it feel snug, and act as a background for plantings. Often a single feature fills two or more roles simultaneously.

Along with serving many functions, vertical features come in many styles, plain and fancy. There are all kinds of wood and metal fences, freestanding masonry walls, masonry or timber retaining walls, and hedges short and tall. Choose what suits your needs, your taste, and your situation.

Well-placed and carefully built or planted vertical features are long-term, even permanent, parts of a landscape. If your property already has a good fence, wall, hedge, or any combination of these, you realize what assets these landscape elements are. Moreover, you appreciate how little care they require. Hedges call for pruning or shearing plus the routine watering, weeding, mulching, and so on that you give all plants, but fences and walls need only minimal attention from year to year. High benefits and low maintenance are a winning combination; that's why these features are so popular and desirable.

There's not much to learn or do if you're happy with what you have, but there is a lot to think about if you are starting from scratch and want to add vertical features to a new property or if you are remodeling an older landscape and want to replace what's there. So this chapter discusses what to consider when you're planning to build a new fence or wall or plant a hedge, and it will address both the practical and decorative issues.

❧ DECIDING WHAT YOU NEED AND WANT

Planning any vertical feature begins with questions. Where will it go? Do you want to surround your entire yard or just part of it? What role(s) do you want a fence, wall, or hedge to serve? Do you want to be able to see over it, or see through it? What styles, materials, and colors would look good with your house and landscape? Does your site pose any particular challenges—sloping ground, rocky soil, wet spots, trees—that you'll have to work through or around? Are your options limited by local codes, deed restrictions, or homeowners' association rules?

The two main issues here—what you want the new feature to *do* and how you want it to *look*—go hand in hand, so you'll have to alternate back and forth in your thinking as you consider your options and focus on a final plan. Take your time, and be flexible. Putting up any kind of vertical feature, especially one intended to be permanent, involves several choices and decisions and may require some compromise and creative problem-solving, especially if you are constrained by codes or are trying to seek agreement with your neighbors on a property-line structure or planting.

Designing a vertical feature for your site

Almost any fence, wall, or hedge serves at least two roles. A security fence around your swimming pool can double as a trellis for morning glories. A dense hedge that keeps the neighbors from watching what you do in your backyard keeps their dogs out, too. A masonry wall that muffles traffic noise also blocks dust and fumes. But sometimes one purpose conflicts with another. For example, an evergreen screen

that serves as a windbreak will also block your view. So try to anticipate possible drawbacks, as well as advantages, as you plan.

VISUAL SCREENING. Screening works both ways. It keeps others from looking into your yard, creating privacy, and it blocks the view as you look out, walling out anything you don't want to see and producing a sense of enclosure.

As for privacy, it's both practical and pleasant if at least part of the area around your house is closed off from public view. You can use the private place for an outdoor room, as an outdoor workshop or puttering place, or for storage without worrying about who's watching and how it looks. You can relax, get away from the world, and find peace and quiet there.

In some neighborhoods the desire for privacy is well understood. Screening is routine, and most homes have a fence, wall, or hedge around the backyard, or around the entire property. In other communities, one lawn leads into another in a continuous sea of grass. In neighborhoods like that, where screening off a major part of your yard is likely to be regarded as antisocial, don't position a screen on the property line. Put it closer to the house; keep it just high and wide enough to effectively screen your deck, patio, or outdoor living area; and make it ornamental. For example, plant a colorful hedge of flowering shrubs, or build a latticelike fence and cover it with vines. Using conspicuous, showy plants downplays the fact that your primary motive is privacy, so the result is less jarring to the neighbors.

A screen 6 feet high is tall enough that people in the yard or house next door can't see you unless they're looking out an upstairs window or they live uphill and can see down into your yard. For privacy in that particular situation, you would need shade trees or a tall hedge instead of or in addition to a standard 6-foot screen, but these carry a price. The taller the screen, the more shade it produces. It's especially undesirable to have a tall screen on the south side of your house in winter, when the sun is low in the sky, as even a relatively short screen casts a long shadow then. If you feel it's essential to have a tall screen to the south of your house, plant deciduous trees or shrubs. It's worth sacrificing some privacy in winter to let the sun shine through.

How tall a screen it takes to block the view looking out from your yard depends on how far away from the screen you're standing. If you're sitting or standing close to a 6-foot screen, you can't see much over and beyond it, but as you move farther away more is revealed. From 50 feet or more, a 6-foot screen is just a token strip across your field of view. The practical implication of this phenomenon is that if you want to close off the view of your surroundings for any reason, you need either a normal-height screen nearby or a much taller screen farther away. Match the height of the screen to the area you're trying to enclose — a tall hedge or row of trees around a large yard; a much shorter hedge, fence, or wall around a small yard.

To estimate the screening effect of any feature you're considering, make a mockup. Drive temporary stakes at the ends and corners of the potential fence, wall, or hedge. Buy a roll of plastic flagging tape (its high visibility makes it better than string for this situation) at a hardware store or garden center and run it between the stakes at the estimated final

(**LEFT**): *Freestanding drystone walls are the traditional boundary markers in New England. Although they're low enough that you can easily see or even climb over them, their intent is unmistakable.*

(**ABOVE**): *The abbreviated version of a drystone wall, useful where space or stones are limited, is a balanced rock corner marker.*

height. Step back, walk around, and observe it from all sides to see how the screen would affect your view.

Keep any screen as low as possible, because it's a short step from enclosure to claustrophobia. Being walled in by too high a screen makes you feel as if you're down in a canyon. Too much screening blocks off the sky and sun as well as the surroundings. This often happens when a hedge grows too tall and overwhelms a small yard; usually the solution in that case is to cut the hedge down.

Another way to mitigate the potentially claustrophobic effect of screening is to leave (or create) windowlike gaps, places where you can look through and see out. You could prune an opening through a hedge or cut one section of it lower than the rest. Install an openwork panel in an otherwise solid fence. Put a gate through a wall. A peek at what lies beyond satisfies your curiosity and actually enhances the feeling of enclosure. Such partial screening can be even more effective than trying to totally block out the surroundings.

BOUNDARY MARKER. It doesn't take much of a marker to stake your claim. In fact, an excellent way to indicate the extent of a property is simply to mark the corners and any jogs in the outline with iron stakes, concrete piers, or stone cairns. These may already be in place and recorded on your property deed.

But marking the corners normally isn't enough. It's often desirable or necessary to erect a practical or symbolic barrier along the property lines. Unfortunately, this is tricky. It makes sense to position a fence, wall, or hedge exactly on the property line if both neighbors agree. In practice, though, it's so common for neighbors to disagree on the height, style, and upkeep of a boundary marker that these delineators are often placed off to one side or the other, not centered along the property line. This gets confusing because you lose track of the actual legal boundary as the years go by or when either property changes hands. New neighbors are likely to assume that their property runs all the way to an existing fence, wall, or hedge, even if it doesn't. So what should you do?

When you move into a situation where some kind of marker is already present, don't assume that it's on the property line. Use the information in your deed or survey to determine the actual boundary.

Before installing a new boundary marker, establish the exact location of the property line and make every effort to solicit your neighbor's cooperation. If you can come to an agreement, center the marker on the line; in the long run, that works best for both parties. If you can't agree, then do as you choose on your side of the line.

Frontage along a public street or road is a special situation. You'll need to inquire locally to determine how wide the right-of-way is (be sure to check whether it's measured from the center or from the shoulder of the pavement) and if there are regulations regarding minimum setback and maximum height for roadside screens.

In any case, a vertical feature along the front, side, or back of your property doesn't necessarily have to be a continuous or opaque screen, nor does it have to be high enough that you can't see over it. Unless you need a substantial barrier for other reasons, a symbolic marker, such as a rail fence or a knee-high hedge or wall, is usually sufficient to outline a property. For extra impact, mark the corners with something bigger and taller, such as a bed of ground cover and a grove of trees, a grouping of shrubs, or a few clumps of a big ornamental grass.

ENHANCE LANDSCAPE DESIGN. Vertical features give structure to a landscape by organizing it into distinct areas that you can identify and name: the backyard, the rose garden, the sheep pasture, and so on. By dividing it into smaller, separate areas, you increase the complexity of your property and make it more diverse and interesting, and you can accommodate a wider range of activities. This kind of subdivi-

A wooden fence on the property line is common in crowded suburban neighborhoods. Note how this fence is stepped up the slope and how its height is extended with latticework on top. Along with privacy, a fence like this provides a perfect background for a colorful flower border.

sion makes a property seem larger, because you have to walk around and explore it, rather than seeing the whole area at a glance.

Locating any kind of planting in front of a fence, wall, or hedge simplifies the design process, because it typically means you have to think only about how the planting will look from one side, when viewed against the background. This is much easier than designing a planting that looks good from all directions. Having some kind of continuous vertical background helps unify a diverse collection of plants, and considering the dimensions of the background helps you determine the ideal height and width of the planting or of particular plants. Finally, any planting seems more significant when it's framed by a background rather than floating in open space.

NOISE FILTER. A high, dense barrier can take the edge off some kinds of noise, but don't expect too much here. It's hard to screen out the sound of barking dogs, screaming children, or loud music.

Mostly, what a barrier can mitigate is your awareness of passing traffic, both by reducing the noise you hear and by blocking your view of the vehicles and the turbulence they cause. To screen an area next to a busy street, erect the highest fence or wall allowable under local codes, then plant a thick evergreen hedge inside it, as the combination of hardscape and foliage reduces sound more effectively than either does alone. If space or budget constraints mean you can't have both a structure and a hedge, build a sturdy structure and cover it on both sides with vigorous leafy vines.

WINDBREAK. You can't stop a steady wind, but you may be able to deflect or dissipate it and reduce the associated noise, dust, and dryness (and salt spray in coastal areas) in order to create a more comfortable outdoor living area or a more sheltered microclimate for plants.

Windbreaks are usually a form of hedge, made from tough, adaptable, fast-growing trees and/or shrubs. Face into a prevailing wind to determine where a windbreak should be planted, and use stakes to mark out a tentative position and arrangement. In open country, the distance between the windbreak and the area you want to shelter should be 10 to 20 times the height of the tallest trees. In built-up areas, to save space, windbreaks can be planted much closer to the area you want to screen, at a distance of 2 to 4 times their height. The windbreak should be longer than the area you want to shelter. If you have space, plan to use at least two rows of plants, taller ones in back and shorter ones in front. The rows don't have to be straight and parallel. They can be staggered or curved. Each row can be a single species, or you can combine different kinds of plants for a more varied and natural look. Within each row, space the plants

farther apart than is normal for a hedge. Remember, you're trying to filter, not block, the wind.

Of course, you're out of luck if the appropriate planting site is unavailable (for instance, off your property or where the driveway is) or if a windbreak would constitute an unacceptable barrier or obstacle. On the other hand, a windbreak in the right place can serve double duty as a visual screen, a space divider, or a background for a shorter planting and might be a welcome design feature.

Using fences as windbreaks is more complicated, as an inappropriate fence can cause annoying turbulence and make the wind seem even worse than usual. Since it's tricky figuring where a wind fence should go, how tall it should be, whether it should be solid or slatted, if the top should be angled, and so forth, get advice from different professionals—an architect, a landscape architect, and an engineer—before making any final decisions.

SECURITY, SAFETY. An uncrossable barrier (commonly a fence or wall, perhaps flanked with a thorny hedge) offers protection and peace of mind if you want to keep small children from wandering away, if you need to limit access to a swimming pool or other attraction, or to safeguard your home and possessions from intruders.

Lightweight temporary fencing is enough to confine babies and toddlers, but it takes more to keep older children or the public away from a pool or out of your yard. In most areas, any pool more than 18 inches deep must be enclosed by non-climbable fencing 54 to 60 inches high with self-closing gates. Check to see if further requirements are specified by your local codes.

Also check with local law-enforcement personnel before making plans or decisions regarding security fences or walls. The interaction between screening and crime is complex. On the one hand, increased privacy means your property and possessions are hidden from public view. On the other hand, it means any burglars or stalkers who do penetrate beyond the screen can escape notice. If you're vulnerable to crime, you'll probably want to accompany screening with an electronic security system.

ANIMAL CONTROL. What kind of enclosure it takes to keep an animal in or out of your yard depends on the kind of animal and how determined it is. In general it's easier to keep your own animals home than it is to keep out stray dogs, wandering livestock, or wild animals.

Those buried "invisible" fences and accompanying collars are a very effective way to confine your own dog(s). To keep other dogs out you need a continuous, solid fence or wall at least 3 to 4 feet tall. A hedge usually doesn't work, as many dogs would squirm through if tempted.

Various types of electric, woven-wire, and

This split-rail fence is lined with woven wire to help keep the sheep inside the pasture and keep coyotes and other predators out.

board fences can keep most horses, ponies, burros, sheep, llamas, and cattle where they belong. Goats are more of a challenge; they will discover and take advantage of any gap in a fence. Also, more than other livestock, goats are excellent climbers and jumpers. If you have a goat, you'll spend a lot of time trying to outwit it, and you'll often lose.

But even goats are cooperative compared with varmints such as woodchucks, raccoons, coyotes, and deer (for more on dealing with deer, see page 256). Don't kid yourself; there's no easy way to fence out these critters. You usually need to bury or stake

down the bottom of a fence so they can't cross beneath it. You may have to add an electrified strand along the outside or on top so they can't go over it. And, of course, you'll need to be vigilant about maintaining the fence and keeping gates closed. Otherwise hungry animals will climb, jump, or dig their way into your yard if you're growing anything they want to eat.

STABILIZE A SLOPE, CREATE LEVEL TERRACES. Building a retaining wall transforms a sloping site into level terraces, which makes the area easier to use and more enjoyable. Such a wall also reduces erosion and slows runoff. Designing and building a retaining wall is treated later in this chapter (see page 215), but I mention it here in order to point out that a retaining wall, like any other vertical feature, can do double duty. If you're on the downhill side looking toward it, a retaining wall can serve as a screen, boundary marker, background, or barrier.

On the other hand, if you're on the uphill side, you can't see the wall; it's a drop-off. In some situations this could be disconcerting or dangerous, and you need to build a fence or plant a hedge on top of the retaining wall to create a visual and physical barrier, like putting a guardrail along a cliff.

The drystone retaining wall separates the sloping lawn below from a level terrace above, where there is a swimming pool surrounded by lush flower beds. The low picket fence reiterates the boundary line and doubles as a safety feature.

Other factors to consider

Along with its suitability for accomplishing any of the functions and roles described above, there are some other practical issues to consider when you're planning a vertical feature. Any of these may lead you to choose a fence versus a hedge, for instance, or vice versa. Remember to weigh all your options: all kinds of fences and hedges, freestanding walls and retaining walls, even berms. Your first idea may not be the best solution.

It often makes sense to combine different treatments—hedges along both sides of the yard and a fence across the front, for example—but if you do that, give some thought as to how they will intersect at the corners. Furthermore, if you're planning to run two treatments in parallel, such as a chain-link security fence combined with an ornamental flowering hedge, decide which should go on the inside (closer to your house) and why.

CODES. Check with your local building department before you begin any construction, to find out about restrictions pertaining to setbacks, heights, foundations, and other elements that may be imposed.

Many areas have codes that restrict the height of a fence or wall, typically to 42 inches in the front yard and 72 inches in the backyard. If you want to build higher than that, you'll need to obtain a variance. Sometimes you can finagle a way around the codes by putting a fence on top of a wall to gain extra height. Almost always, you can train a bushy vine along the top of a fence or wall for extra screening.

You'll probably need a building permit for any masonry wall over 3 feet tall, and you will also need an engineer's approval for any kind of retaining wall that's over 3 feet tall. These are for your own good, but they may require you to build a much more substantial (and expensive) foundation and wall than you would do voluntarily.

Normally there aren't any codes that apply to hedging, but homeowners' association rules may specify which plants you can or can't use and how tall you can let them grow. Also, if you plant a hedge along a street or road, you'll probably be required to keep it trimmed so it doesn't impede traffic or visibility.

SITE CONSTRAINTS. Some sites pose special challenges that complicate construction or planting. Rocky ground, for example, makes it hard to dig postholes for a fence, planting holes for a hedge, or a foundation trench for a wall. You may have to redesign the layout to work around unmovable stones or rock outcrops.

Where trees are growing, digging and construction will inevitably sever some roots and cause soil compaction. Keep damage to a minimum by digging as few holes or as small a trench as possible, piling

construction materials off to the side, keeping heavy equipment out of the area, and watering the tree(s) during any dry spells for at least a year afterward to compensate for the loss of roots.

Slopes complicate construction. It's more trouble to design and build a fence or wall for a hillside than to do a similar project on level ground. This is true whether you're going up and down or across the slope. The main challenge is deciding whether to angle the top edge so it runs parallel to the ground, or to shape it into a series of level sections, like stairsteps. With a hedge you don't have to worry about that; a uniform-height hedge looks great as it rolls up and down across sloping terrain. But the work of planting and tending a hedge is more tiresome on sloping than on level ground.

If you want to follow an established curve—along the edge of a driveway, for instance, or along the shore of a creek or lake—it's almost always easi-

Masonry walls hug the earth and can be fitted to any site. This adobe-block wall in Arizona surrounds a big development and extends for miles, running up, down, and around.

Echoing the curved pavement, low clipped boxwood hedges lead through a side yard to a rose-covered arbor.

er to build a wall or plant a hedge than to erect a fence. With a wall or hedge you can easily make continuous, graceful curves. Fences can angle at each post, like connecting a series of dots, but doing that is more trouble than building a straight fence and the result is a jagged line, not a smooth curve.

If growing conditions are totally unpromising, don't bother trying to plant a hedge. It's futile expecting hedge plants to grow in shallow, compacted, bone-dry, or poorly drained soil, or in dense shade. Build a fence or wall in those conditions.

Likewise, choose a fence or wall instead of a hedge if the available space is narrow—along the side yard between the house or garage and the property line, for example. Hedges require a minimum depth of at least 2 feet plus clearance on both sides.

CAN YOU INSTALL IT YOURSELF? Any gardener can plant a hedge. If you have the aptitude, tools, and ambition, you can build a wood fence. Metal fences, though, are too specialized to tackle. In most situations, you can build a low freestanding or

retaining wall of dry-laid stones or concrete wall blocks yourself. Hire a mason or contractor for any wall higher than 3 feet, for most timber retaining walls, and for any mortared masonry wall.

COST AND VALUE. The pricing for almost any kind of new vertical feature that you might add to your yard is done on a per-linear-foot basis. Per-foot figures can range from as low as a few dollars or less for planting a hedge to $50 or more for hiring a mason to lay a drystone wall or a carpenter to build a custom-designed wood fence. If you're soliciting bids from contractors, ask them to break down the bid into separate estimates for materials, labor, and design. This can help you decide which materials to use. If labor costs are high anyway, you might as well spend *more,* not less, on materials, to get the most value out of your investment. Likewise, if you're doing the job yourself and your labor is free, invest in time-tested, top-quality materials, using whatever would be best suited to the project, so that you'll be satisfied with the results for decades.

Fences and walls are expensive enough that you'll wonder how much they increase your property's value, especially if you're planning to sell your house in the foreseeable future. Ask a local realtor for advice. Basically, anything that enhances privacy, security, and comfort makes your property more usable and should add to its value, but whether this will actually affect the selling price or speed of sale depends mostly on the local real-estate market. And as with any home improvement, the perceived value of a fence, wall, or hedge depends only partly on the initial cost and choice of materials. The design, style, quality of workmanship, ease of maintenance, current condition, and life expectancy figure in, too.

MAINTENANCE AND LIFE SPAN. Well-built masonry walls require very little or no routine care and can endure for centuries. Wood fences usually need a fresh coat of paint or stain every few years; if this is done, they may last for decades. Untreated wood, though, may rot out in 20 years or less. Virtually all hedges need to be pruned at least once a year, and closely clipped hedges may require shearing three or more times during the growing season. Most hedges also need watering, fertilizing, weeding, and mulching. A hedge made from appropriate plants should last at least 20 years. Some hedges survive much longer than that, sometimes for a century or more.

Openings

Almost any vertical feature needs at least one opening that you can walk or drive through. These should line up with existing walks and drives and be at least as wide as the pavement. Along with the obvious, frequently used openings, try to anticipate where you might want access for occasional or special purposes, such as having a truckload of mulch or firewood delivered into the backyard.

You might also want windowlike openings. These don't have to go all the way to the ground. They're for visibility, not access. A well-placed opening could frame a view of your land or your surroundings. It could reveal a natural vista, overlook a city or harbor, show sunrise or sunset, whatever. To plan where you might want to leave an opening, drive stakes on either side and tie a length of flagging tape between them. Then step back and look through the opening you've framed to check its placement and size. Move the stakes and tape until you're satisfied.

GAPS AND GATES. You can simply leave an open gap in a fence, wall, or hedge. Gaps are convenient to pass through because you never have to bother with opening or closing them.

But gaps provide no security. If you want to close off the view or to keep people or animals in or out, you need gates. Gates in a fence are usually made of the same material and in the same style as the adjacent siding. For a wall or hedge, consider wrought-iron or wooden gates. If you can't decide whether you want a gate, can't choose a style or find what you want, or can't afford one now, you could leave a gap for the time being and plan to add a gate later. The only problem with that approach is that the size of the opening must match the gate, and if a ready-made gate doesn't fit into your gap, you'll need to get one custom-built.

In general, gates for walkways should be 4 feet wide. Wider openings are handy if you need to go through with riding lawn mowers, garden carts, or other cumbersome tools. Driveway gates need to be at least 12 feet wide. For openings of that breadth, it's better to have paired gates, like a swing-through door, instead of a single wide gate, as wide gates are clumsy and often drag on the ground.

To prevent sagging, wooden gates should have a

This wrought-iron driveway gate was a wise investment. It suits the house, adds dignity and security, lasts indefinitely, and needs minimum care.

(ABOVE): *This wooden gate looks light and airy (notice the circular cutout) but is very well built, with a diagonal brace, heavy-duty hinges and latch, and sturdy side posts.*

(BELOW): *Limblike lines of a rustic gate contrast with the thick solid wall. Gates like this are relatively simple to make but are tricky to install. It's hard to get them to fit right, hang square, and swing freely.*

diagonal brace that runs from the bottom of the hinge side to the top of the latch side. Any gate must be securely mounted to a sturdy post that's sunk at least 3 feet into the ground and preferably set in concrete. Use heavy-duty hinges attached with long screws.

ARBORS AND ARCHES. To make any gap or gated opening more impressive, build an arch or arbor that reaches over your head. Arches and arbors are especially satisfying at entryways, such as the main entry from a public sidewalk into your front yard, or at the entry into a secluded, enclosed garden area. Passing under an arch or arbor feels more symbolic—it marks more of a transition—than going through a topless opening.

Arches and arbors are typically made of wood. (Masonry arches made of brick or stone are even more impressive than wooden ones, but they're much more expensive to build.) If you choose wood, you can buy a ready-made model or kit to install or have one custom-built. The only problem with ready-made or kit arbors is that they're usually too small and lightweight; they look insubstantial and insignificant. They're suitable for outdoor rooms or other small areas but not for main walks or entries. To look right and to provide comfortable passage, the opening inside an entry arch or arbor should be at least 4 feet wide, 7½ to 8 feet high, and 3 feet deep.

This wooden arch and fence, designed and stained to match both buildings, connect a house and garage and separate utility and pleasure areas. The wide, ungated arch allows easy passage for carrying or carting groceries, firewood, garbage, or garden tools back and forth.

Bigger is better. Also, the corner posts should be 4x4 or larger timbers, not just 2x4s.

A key step when installing or building any overhead arch or arbor is to make sure the corner posts are plumb and the top is level. This is another problem with ready-made arbors. They're often just set on ground that's not level, so they tilt. This makes them look as if they're likely to fall over. To set the arbor straight, make footings by digging holes about 1 foot wide and deep at each corner, filling the holes with well-packed gravel, setting concrete pavers on top, and using a level to make sure all the pavers are level. Then set the arbor on the pavers and check to make sure its posts are plumb. If the arbor is tilted, set it aside, add or remove gravel under the pavers as needed, and try again.

An even better solution for installing a ready-made arbor is to set posts (see page 212) on either side of it and bolt or strap it to them. This not only holds it level and plumb, it will also prevent the arbor from blowing over in a windstorm.

PILLARS. Another way to make any gap or gated opening more impressive is to flank it with masonry pillars. These can stand alone or double as gateposts or the end posts of a fence or wall. Plan ahead, and if you want to install outdoor lighting fixtures on top, have the wiring built into the pillars.

Entry pillars are typically between 2 and 4 feet square and 4 and 8 feet tall. They're often built of concrete block and veneered with brick or stone, to save construction time and money. They need a good concrete foundation, about twice as wide as the pillar and as deep as the frost line. Choose a mason whose work you admire to build your entry pillars, because of their prominent location. Don't try to build them yourself. It's much harder than it looks to get all four corners plumb and square and to make two pillars that match.

Planting next to a vertical feature

A fence, wall, or hedge makes a great background for planting. Vines and climbing roses are an obvious choice for this situation, but if you make a wider bed you can grow perennials, ferns, ornamental grasses, flowering shrubs, or whatever else you'd like there. Even common, ordinary plants gain esteem when sited against a background, and prize specimens of bold or distinctive plants look outstanding there.

There are just a few practical concerns when planting in front of or along a vertical feature. One is preserving access. If you need to routinely paint a fence or shear a hedge, leave some open space; don't plant right against it. If you're planting between a fence or wall and a walkway, choose plants that won't spread too wide and block the walk, or keep them

Clipped evergreen hedges are the traditional background for perennial borders in English gardens. The effect is lovely, as seen here, but difficult to create and maintain.

tied or pruned out of the way. The other concerns relate to growing conditions.

TEMPERATURE. Any vertical feature creates some of the same microclimates as the walls of a house or other building do (see page 246), albeit on a smaller scale. In particular, plants are sensitive to the differences between the cool shade on the north side of a fence or wall and the buildup of reflected light and heat on the south and west sides. Air and soil temperatures can vary by 20 degrees or more from one side to the other. That constitutes distinctly different climate zones, so you must choose plants accordingly. When you're planting right against any structure, temperature extremes are the most important factor to take into account, even more than exposure to sun or shade.

WIND. Plants may be affected by airflow near any vertical feature, but before you can take this into account, you have to watch closely on a windy day to see how the currents work. The air may be fairly still close to *both* sides, or there may be turbulence or gusts on one side or the other. Normally most plants appreciate still air, since a steady wind has a drying effect and pulls moisture from a plant's leaves and the soil. But in muggy climates air circulation is beneficial and plants that are sequestered in a still spot are prone to mildew and other fungal infestations. So what to plant in different locations will depend on your climate as well as on the kind of plant you want to grow. You may have to sort this out by trial and error. If a plant gets mildewed or infected, move it to a breezier spot. If it wilts and dries out too fast, move it to a more sheltered spot.

Brick pillars support lattice panels to make a fence that is substantial but doesn't block the breeze or light. Roses and fountain grass flourish in a bed of well-prepared soil.

SOIL QUALITY. The soil next to any existing feature is likely to be compacted and infertile, but you can address that by improving the soil as you normally would for planting (see page 277). Usually you can till the soil—and add plants—right up to and against a fence or wall.

Be more careful about digging and planting near a hedge. Depending on what type of plant(s) is used in the hedge, the plants' roots may totally fill and dominate the topsoil throughout a strip at least as wide as the hedge is tall. For example, a hedge 8 feet tall probably has a root zone at least 8 feet wide. If you want to plant next to an established hedge, leave an undisturbed strip, commonly about 2 feet wide, between the drip line of the hedge foliage and the edge of any bed you dig. Just spread mulch there; leave it alone otherwise. Digging too close to a hedge may harm it, and any new plants you try to insert too close won't have much of a chance, as the hedge-plant roots will reenter the disturbed soil sooner than a new plant's roots would get established there. Finally, you'll need a place to stand and walk every time you have to prune or shear the hedge, and that 2-foot strip makes a barely adequate workspace.

SOIL MOISTURE. A 6-foot wall or fence may create a rain shadow, a dry strip up to 1 to 2 feet wide at the base of the leeward side. Watch for this, and give extra water to plants growing there if they need it.

A dense hedge may also create a rain shadow, but more important, a hedge's roots compete with nearby plants for water. That's why the soil at the base of a hedge is often bare except for tough weeds, weedy grasses, or ground covers that were planted about the same time as the hedge itself. If you're trying to establish or maintain other plants in front of or along a hedge, be prepared to water them generously during dry spells, and be sure to leave the 2-foot separation strip so the hedge and other plants aren't rooting into the same patch of soil.

Retaining walls are a special situation because of how water moves through the soil on a slope. Ordinarily the soil right behind the top of a wall dries out quickly, while the soil right in front of the base of a wall holds extra moisture. Take this into account and plant moisture-loving plants at the base of a retaining wall and ones that need good drainage at the top.

VINE SUPPORTS. Although I urge anyone to be cautious about planting vines against a house or at the base of a tree or shrub, you can be more carefree about letting them take over a fence or wall. Read the discussion of how vines climb (see the box on page 314) and do research on any vine you're considering to determine what kind of support it needs. Only vines with adhesive tendrils or rootlets can climb a smooth-surfaced fence or wall. Vines that climb by twining or curly tendrils need something to wrap around, such as hairy twine or rope, netting, or wire mesh. Install the support when you plant the vine, and guide the young shoots toward it. Once they get a grip, they'll take off and continue climbing on their own. If you don't direct them back to the support, vines are liable to tumble forward and clamber among any other plants growing in the area.

Where does that ivy come from? Is it climbing up the wall or trailing over the top? Look closely and you'll see that it's emerging from tiny planting wells at the base of the wall. Its roots extend under the brick pavement and absorb water that seeps through the cracks.

RECOMMENDED VINES AND CLIMBING ROSES

The following plants make good decoration for a standard 6-foot fence or wall. All need to be guided to a support of some kind, such as strings, ropes, a piece of netting, or a trellis, as they can't get a grip on a bare, smooth surface. Except where noted, they prefer sunny sites. Ask local nursery staff for advice as to whether any particular plant can take the heat of a south- or west-facing exposure in your climate; plants that can't would do better facing north or east.

PERENNIAL AND WOODY VINES

These are relatively small-statured vines that are easily controlled by pruning. Although most can reach 15 feet or taller if unpruned, they're much more manageable than truly vigorous vines that often reach 30 feet or more.

- **Climbing aster** (*Aster carolinianus*). Small, daisylike, lavender-pink flowers in fall. Deciduous. **ZONE 7**.

- **Cross vine** (*Bignonia capreolata*). 'Tangerine Beauty', the best cultivar, bears masses of orange flowers in late spring. Evergreen. **ZONE 7**.

- **Bougainvillea** (*Bougainvillea*). Vivid papery bracts in all colors but blue. Cultivars differ in vigor, habit, and hardiness, so read the fine print. Evergreen. **ZONE 10**.

- **Clematis** (*Clematis*). All clematis are lovely, but some get huge. For small spaces, choose any of the large-flowered hybrids, with blooms in shades of white, pink, rose, purple, red, or blue; or golden clematis (*C. tangutica*). Deciduous. **ZONE 4**.

- **Wood vamp** (*Decumaria barbara*). Lacy white flowers in early summer; large, glossy leaves. Deciduous. Prefers part shade. **ZONE 7**.

- **Climbing bleeding heart** (*Dicentra scandens*). Dangling clusters of yellow flowers in summer. Lacy foliage is deciduous. Prefers part shade. **ZONE 6**.

- **Carolina jasmine** (*Gelsemium sempervirens*). Sweet-scented gold flowers cover the foliage in spring. Evergreen. **ZONE 7**.

- **Honeysuckles** (*Lonicera*). Goldflame honeysuckle (*L. × heckrottii*) has lightly scented yellow-pink flowers. **ZONE 6 OR 5**. Trumpet honeysuckle cultivars (*L. sempervirens*) have scentless scarlet, orange, or yellow flowers. **ZONE 5**. 'Dropmore Scarlet', a hybrid, has scentless coral-red flowers. **ZONE 4**. All are semievergreen.

- **Mandevillas** (*Mandevilla*). The hybrid 'Alice du Pont' mandevilla bears rose-pink flowers almost nonstop. Evergreen. **ZONE 10**. Chilean jasmine (*M. laxa*) has very fragrant, large, white flowers in summer. Deciduous. **ZONE 8**.

- **Silver fleece vine** (*Polygonum aubertii*). Frothy clusters of white flowers in summer. Very adaptable and fast-growing, but dies down to the ground in winter. **ZONE 4**.

- **Magnolia vine** (*Schisandra chinensis*). Small but fragrant white flowers on separate male and female plants. Females, if pollinated, bear showy clusters of red berries in fall. Deciduous. **ZONE 5**.

- **Star, or confederate, jasmine** (*Trachelospermum jasminoides*). Sweet-scented starry white flowers in late spring and early summer. Evergreen. **USUALLY ZONE 8, BUT 'MADISON' IS HARDY TO ZONE 7**.

Trumpet honeysuckle blossoms are scentless, but hummingbirds love them and they appear over a long season.

ANNUAL VINES

Try some of these if you are intrigued by the look of vines but don't want to wait for results. These grow fast, reach at least 6 feet tall but don't grow out of bounds, and bear colorful flowers or pods from early or midsummer until the end of the growing season.

Sow the seeds where you want them to grow, or start them in pots indoors in early spring and transplant them after the last frost. In most areas you'll have to replant them every year, but some of these vines self-sow or come back from the roots in mild-winter climates.

- **Love-in-a-puff** (*Cardiospermum halicacabum*). Interesting balloonlike pods, 1 inch wide, that ripen from green to red-brown.

- **Cup-and-saucer vine** (*Cobaea scandens*). Cup-shaped, blue-purple or white flowers sit on leafy "saucers."

- **Hyacinth bean, or lablab** (*Dolichos lablab*). Uncommon purple-green foliage, spikes of pink or white flowers, and fuzzy magenta pods.

- **Glory vine** (*Eccremocarpus scaber*). Lipstick-shaped flowers in shades of red, orange, or yellow.

- **Morning glories** (*Ipomoea*). Big round flowers can be blue, white, red, or bicolor.

- **Moon vine** (*Ipomoea alba*, a.k.a. *Calonyction aculeatum*). Very fragrant, pure white flowers, 6 inches wide, open at dusk.

- **Cypress vine** (*Ipomoea quamoclit*). Lacy foliage and star-shaped scarlet flowers.

- **Sweet pea** (*Lathyrus odoratus*). Sweet-scented rose, pink, lavender, or white flowers. Prefers cool weather.

- **Firecracker vine, or exotic love vine** (*Mina lobata*). Arching spikes of papery orange, yellow, or cream flowers.

- **Scarlet runner bean** (*Phaseolus coccineus*). Showy red (also available in coral-pink and white) flowers, lush foliage, and edible beans.

- **Black-eyed Susan vine** (*Thunbergia alata*). Gold (sometimes available in orange or white) flowers with recessed brown "eyes."

- **Canary-bird flower** (*Tropaeolum peregrinum*). Bright yellow flowers have feathery, fringed petals.

CLIMBING ROSES

Roses don't climb on their own; they must be tied to a support. Use twist-ties or twine to fasten the new shoots in place. You'll have to do this repeatedly throughout the growing season. The following cultivars perform well in most parts of the country, are generally hardy and disease-resistant, and bloom abundantly over a long season. 'Altissimo' (red), 'America' (coral), 'Autumn Sunset' (peachy yellow), 'Climbing Joseph's Coat' (red-orange-yellow), 'Golden Showers' (yellow), 'New Dawn' (light pink), 'White Dawn' (white), 'William Baffin' (rosy pink), 'Zépherine Drouhin' (cerise).

Sweet pea quickly covers a fence but must be replanted each year, as it's an annual vine.

Many neighborhoods restrict fence height to 6 feet, but sometimes you can exceed that by building a wall first and setting the fence on top of it, as done here. This fence is a "good neighbor" design; its front and back sides look the same.

Fences have several advantages over walls or hedges. They go up faster, providing almost instant results, and they come in a great variety of materials, styles, and prices. They're skinny, requiring almost no space at ground level, and they can be fitted to almost any site regardless of climate. A fence can serve as an effective barrier or marker without seeming ponderous or dense or totally blocking your view. Finally, fences are relatively easy to repair or to remove. For all these reasons fences are the most popular and widely used vertical features.

Most fences have an average life span of 20 years or more, and the materials and styles most popular nowadays need relatively little maintenance, so if you choose well and have it carefully built or installed, you won't have to think about a fence again for quite a while. As with other hardscape features such as paving or decks, it pays to invest in durable materials, timeless design, and sound craftsmanship. A good fence will give you immediate satisfaction and adds to your property's value, in case you're planning to sell.

Installing fencing is not a do-it-yourself task for most homeowners. The initial hurdle is digging holes and setting all the posts; that's a big job, and it must be done right (see page 212). Then there's all the measuring, cutting, fitting, leveling, and assembly. You know yourself: Would you do a careful job? Would you finish? If you think you can build a good fence and you have some experience in construction or carpentry, go ahead. But if you're uncertain or ambivalent, hire a contractor who has the tools and skills to do the job quickly and well.

Fence design

Whether or not you build the fence yourself, you'll need to decide what you want it to accomplish, where you want it to go, what you want it to look like, and what materials will be used. In regard to function and practical roles, review this chapter's introductory section on planning vertical features. This section adds to that by highlighting concerns that are unique to fencing.

PLACEMENT, HEIGHT, AND THE TOP EDGE. Finalize your decisions on fence placement and height by making a mockup with temporary stakes at the ends, corners, and gates. Use colored flagging tape to mark the bottom and top edges of the fence, and check from all sides to make sure you're satisfied with how a fence of that height would affect your privacy and view. Remember that fence height is regulated by codes in many areas, and don't exceed the prescribed limits.

Slopes pose a special design challenge. You have to decide whether the top of the fence should be divided into a series of level sections, like stairsteps, or run at an angle or contour parallel to the ground. Normally both options are available, but it usually seems easier to build one way or the other, depending on what material you choose and who's doing the work. As for appearance, both stepped and angled or contoured fence tops can look good; it depends on the particular situation. You can use the stakes-and-tape setup to mock up both types of fence tops and see which you prefer. See page 213 for how to use a spirit level to monitor the top line of a fence.

SOLID OR OPEN? The *feeling* created by a fence depends on whether it's solid or open. This is

very important but hard to anticipate. A solid, 6-foot fence gives a dramatic sense of enclosure. You simply can't imagine what that's going to be like until the fence is built. Ideally it's comforting, but it may seem overwhelming, like being stuck in a windowless cubicle.

A shorter or see-through fence has a much "lighter," friendlier, and less imposing effect. It's surprising how little material is really needed to make a symbolic fence that defines an area. A simple grid is enough.

When in doubt, go for an open fence design, as you can always "fill" a fence later by covering it with vines, but you can't do much to mitigate the stuffiness and trapped feeling caused by opaque fencing around a too-small yard.

WHAT ABOUT THE OTHER SIDE? Some fences look about the same on both sides, but others have a front and back. If you're sharing a property-line fence with a neighbor, keep this in mind and choose a style that rewards you equally. If no one's looking at it and the back side doesn't matter, it may cost less or be simpler to build a one-faced fence.

COORDINATING WITH WHAT YOU HAVE. What color and style of fence would suit the architecture of your house, the tone of the neighborhood, or the nature of your landscape? If your house is painted, you could repeat the color of the house or its trim on the fence. For a brick, stone, or natural-finished wood house, consider a natural wood fence. Rail fences go well with ranch-style homes, picket fences suit cottages, and wrought-iron ones complement Mediterranean architecture. Likewise, unfinished wood or rustic wood fences are a match for casual, natural-style landscapes, while neatly made, smooth-surfaced fences suit well-groomed lawns and formal gardens.

Fence materials and styles

Choosing a kind of fence is more complicated, but also better, than it used to be, because there are new products to consider. As you shop around to see what's available, assess durability and ease of maintenance along with appearance and initial cost. Local fence contractors in most areas will be able to tell you about and supply most kinds of conventional wood fencing and chain-link fencing, but some of the new plastic and metal fences are made by only a few manufacturers, so if you're interested in them, you'll need to do some Internet or telephone research to track down a local distributor, see samples, and make arrangements for installation.

Fences use a basic set of parts. The primary element is the vertical *posts.* There may be special corner posts and gateposts that are longer and larger than average. Sometimes masonry *pilasters* are used instead of posts, especially for wrought-iron fences

or for gates. Posts can be connected with horizontal *rails* or *stringers,* then some kind of *siding* can be installed. This might be vertical pickets, side-by-side boards, panels, lattice, or lengths of wire or plastic mesh or netting.

As you're seeking information and getting estimates for different kinds of fencing, you'll need some basic facts and figures. Stake out the proposed fence line, determine where the corners and gates will go, use a tape measure, and make a sketch or map of the project. Start at one corner and measure the *run,* or distance (measure in feet and inches, rounding off to the nearest inch) to the next corner or gate. Write that on your map. Then turn the corner and start again, or measure the gap you've allowed for a gate and start again on the other side. Continue all the way around. You need to know how many corner posts, how many gates, and the total run to estimate the cost of a fence. Depending on the kind of fence, whoever makes the estimate for you will figure how many regular posts are required.

METAL FENCING. Metal fencing comes in a wide range of styles and costs. In its least expensive form it's indispensable as farm fencing. Inexpensive strands of barbed or smooth wire (which can be electrified or not) and rolls of wire mesh fencing are effective for confining farm animals or for keeping critters out of a vegetable patch. These are among the easiest fences to install. You can drive lightweight wooden or metal posts or stakes by hammering them into the ground. Then stretch the wire or mesh taut along the length of a run (this is the hardest part of the job and requires a helper or some kind of tensioning system), and staple or clip it in place. One tip: Install the fencing on the side of the post that the animals will be leaning against, so they press it toward the posts. If you put it on the far side, their weight may pry it off.

Chain-link fencing is too often dismissed as merely inexpensive and utilitarian. Actually, those are virtues. If you need an affordable, carefree, long-lasting security fence, chain link is probably your best choice. Don't try to install it yourself; have a contractor do it. A problem with chain-link fencing is that the galvanized version is such a conspicuous color. If that bothers you, get the black-coated kind instead; it's almost invisible. If you have an old chain-link fence that's gotten rusty, it's too much trouble trying to clean, prime, and paint it. Let it rust. It will take years or decades before the rust weakens the metal so much that the fence becomes useless. In the meantime, cover it with English ivy, honeysuckle, or other vines, or plant a hedge in front of it.

The bottom edge of a wire mesh or chain-link fence can touch or even be buried in the soil. This is the best way to keep animals from burrowing under a fence. However, plain steel mesh or fencing will

Such combinations save money, and the contrast between the metal fence and its surroundings actually calls attention to it and highlights its presence.

Another look-alike that's not widely available but worth considering is a coated steel fencing that mimics wood. It comes in rail, picket, and privacy styles and in white and other colors. It's priced to compete with wood, and its advantages are low maintenance (it doesn't have to be painted) and durability (it doesn't rot).

PLASTIC FENCING. This is a rapidly developing group of products. There are several manufacturers producing "lumber" from new or recycled plastic. This material comes in standard timber dimensions for do-it-yourself projects and in prefab posts, panels, and other pieces for fencing. Prefab plastic fencing comes in white and other colors and in picket, rail, board, and lattice styles.

Why plastic, you might ask, but it actually has some advantages over wood. The initial costs are

(BELOW): Vinyl fencing has a factory-made perfection that looks fake, but it doesn't rot or warp and never needs painting. Those are significant advantages for an installation around an area like this 2-acre horse pasture.

(ABOVE): Chain-link fencing is easily hidden by vines, such as this clematis with fluffy seed heads.

rust sooner or later, so use galvanized or coated metal in applications where the fencing will touch the ground.

Wrought iron is the most expensive fence material, mostly because it involves so much skilled workmanship to make and install it, but it offers an ideal combination of strength, durability, and delicate, see-through appearance. Occasionally you can find antique wrought-iron panels or gates at a salvage yard and put them to use. Before investing in new wrought iron, consider some of its look-alikes, such as cast steel and cast aluminum, with painted or powdered-metal finishes. These are less expensive, lighter, and rustproof, and you'd be hard-pressed to tell the difference simply by looking at them. Both wrought iron and its imitators combine well with wood fencing, masonry walls, and sheared hedges.

comparable, but plastic lumber doesn't warp, shrink, splinter, or rot. However, it may mildew, fade, discolor, crack, or get a chalky surface, depending on the kind and quality of the plastic and your climate. Be cautious, talk to different vendors, and ask them to show you their earliest installations in your area so you can see how the products have held up over time.

For information about plastic-mesh deer fencing, a totally different kind of plastic fencing, see page 257.

WOOD FENCING. Wood is by far the most widely used material for fencing, despite its ever-rising cost and some inherent drawbacks, such as its susceptibility to insects and fungus and the recurrent chore of painting or staining its surface. It's natural and familiar, available everywhere, and easily worked with common tools.

Cost is an initial concern when you're considering wood fencing. One way to keep the price down is to use less wood in the siding. If full privacy isn't required, choose a lattice, picket, or spaced-board type of siding, rather than solid panels or close-set boards. Use standard-dimensioned timbers or pre-cut or prefab parts, rather than custom-milled or fancy-shaped pieces. If the back won't show, make the fence with just one good side; that usually uses less material and is easier and faster to build.

Durability is another big concern when you're buying and building with wood. You should definite-ly invest in pressure-treated lumber or naturally rot-resistant woods such as cedar, cypress, redwood, or black locust for posts. These woods are also best for rails and siding because they far outlast normal woods, especially in humid climates, on shady sites, or where the fence will be surrounded by leafy plants. A fence made of pressure-treated or naturally rot-resistant lumber should last 20 years or more, even if unfinished. It will look better, though, and be less likely to warp, crack, and splinter if you apply a water-repellent finish. (See page 114 for more on woods and finishes for outdoor projects.)

People often economize and use pine or other softwood boards, locally milled hardwoods, or various kinds of stakes, poles, or rustic timbers for fence siding. (But not for posts; posts should always be made of treated or rot-resistant woods.) Depending on your climate (wood decays faster in humid regions) and the kind of wood, you can expect 5 to 15 years of service from ordinary woods if they're left bare. They last longer if coated with paint, stain, oil, or another water-resistant finish.

When installing any kind of wood fencing siding, mount it up off the ground. Leave about 2 to 3 inches of space between the soil or mulch and the bottom edge of panels or of vertical pickets or boards. This is to keep the wood dry and help it resist decay.

If you plan to let a fence weather naturally or to use a clear finish or transparent stain, be sure to invest in galvanized or stainless steel nails or screws,

Finishing a wood fence with an opaque stain, instead of paint, means it will be easy to maintain. Stains must be reapplied occasionally, but they don't flake like paint does.

Rustic fencing made from natural poles has intriguing texture and color. Use naturally rot-resistant wood, such as cedar, to postpone decay.

to avoid those skinny rust stains that streak like tears from plain steel nail heads.

Aside from the wood used, the durability of a fence depends on how it's assembled—how the joints fit and how the pieces are fastened together. Novices often make mistakes through inexperience. If you're thinking about building a fence, spend time studying construction books and recruit a friend with some carpentry experience to give you advice or help with the project.

One of the fun things about wood fencing is that there are so many styles and variations. You can find ideas in books and magazines, or if you're hiring a contractor, ask him to show you his portfolio of finished projects and choose from those examples. Although many intriguing and attractive styles of wood fencing are relatively easy to build, some kinds of detailed work are more trouble and hence more expensive. So if you're considering different styles, get estimates for each of them, as costs may vary significantly.

BAMBOO, REED, AND SAPLINGS OR TWIGS. For small fences and trellises around outdoor rooms, it's fun to work with rustic or lightweight materials such as bamboo, purchased rolls of reed matting, poles made from saplings (with the bark intact or peeled off), pliable twigs, and the like. Small rustic projects are charming and easy to make.

The drawback with these materials, and the main reason for using them only on a small scale, is their vulnerability to decay. In humid climates or when surrounded by vegetation, rustic twigs and poles decay and weaken in a matter of years. They last longer in arid climates, but they eventually become weak and brittle. To prolong their life span, keep these materials up away from the soil. Use them only as siding, not as posts. Choose pressure-treated or rot-resistant wood for the posts. In addition, protect the surface of rustic materials with a clear, water-repellent finish, such as a deck sealer, on the wood; that hardly affects the appearance but does increase the life span.

Setting posts

Setting posts is the critical part of building or installing any fence, gate, arbor, trellis, or railing. Only lightweight wire or mesh fences can be hung from wood or metal posts that you drive or hammer into the ground. For anything more substantial, you need to dig a deep narrow hole, set the post into it, and hold the post plumb as you pack dirt, gravel, or concrete around it. This can be hard work, and it's also fussy work, but there's no shortcut. A weak, wobbly, or tilted post looks bad, doesn't hold up the structure it's supposed to be supporting, and can even be dangerous, if you lean against it and it falls over.

CHOOSE A SUITABLE POST. Posts are usually made of pressure-treated or naturally rot-resistant 4x4 timbers. Sizes smaller than 4x4 are suitable only for very light duty. Corners, long or heavy gates, and tall fences or arbors may call for 6x6 timbers. It's common to combine 6x6s for end posts and gates with 4x4s for intermediate posts.

Posts can be round instead of square. Cedar, cypress, and black locust poles, for example, are often simply tree trunks with the bark and sapwood removed.

Plastic lumber, 2-inch galvanized steel pipe, and cast-concrete or cut-stone posts are used in some situations.

To determine how long a post to buy, decide how far you want it to project aboveground, then add half that measurement to determine the minimum length. For instance, if you want posts to project 6 feet aboveground, add 6 plus 3 and buy posts at least 9 feet long. Actually, in that case you'd probably have to buy posts 10 feet long, but that's okay. You can cut off the extra.

DIG A DEEP ENOUGH HOLE. As a rule of thumb, plan to set the bottom end of a post at least 2 feet into the ground or one-half the distance that will project aboveground, whichever is greater. This means digging holes much deeper than a lazy person would dig, but you'll never regret setting a fence post too deep. Setting posts deep enough is especially important in soft, wet, sandy, or unstable soil; on sloping sites; on windy sites (the force of a strong wind blowing against a fence can be enough to push it over); if the fence or gate is made of uncommonly heavy materials; or for any fence, gate, or railing that will get leaned on by people or animals.

Although holes should be deep, they don't need to be wide. In fact, a relatively narrow hole—about two and a half to three times the width of the post—works fine. It's better not to dig a bigger hole, as undisturbed soil is stabler than soil that's been removed and replaced.

A shovel isn't a handy tool for digging a posthole. A clamshell-type digger works much better. If you need more than a few holes, hire someone with a tractor-mounted auger to dig them for you, or rent a two-person, gas-powered posthole auger. Using a power auger is still hard work, but it's much easier and faster than digging holes with a clamshell digger.

Buried rocks complicate hole digging. If you run into a rock before you reach the required depth of the hole, you either have to change your design plan and dig a hole in a different location, or get out the shovels and crowbars, enlarge the hole, and remove the rock.

If you run into tree roots, reach down into the hole with loppers or a pruning saw and cut them off neatly at the edge of the hole. This does less harm to the tree than tearing or hacking at the roots.

Use a tape measure to check the depth of the hole. Dig it a few inches deeper than needed, then put some coarse crushed rock or gravel in the bottom of the hole for drainage.

MAKE SURE THE POST IS PLUMB. This is a two-person job. Set a post down into its hole, resting on the gravel. While one person holds the post, the other uses a spirit level to check that it is plumb in both directions. The helper must try to hold the post steady as you fill the hole. As an alternative, you can nail temporary braces to two adjacent sides of the post to hold it plumb.

FILLING THE HOLE. For a low, lightweight, or openwork fence, it's okay to backfill the postholes with soil. Backfilling with soil is also okay if you expect to move or remove the posts or fence some-day, and for mounting a single post to support a mailbox, bird feeder, or other object. Add a few shovels of soil, pack that much firmly into place on all sides of the post by tamping it with a length of 2x4, then add some more, pack it in place, and continue until the hole is full. Keep the spirit level handy and check the post a few times as you fill the hole to make sure that it remains plumb.

Soil is inadequate for supporting posts that are intended to be permanent and that will support a tall or solid fence, an overhead arch or arbor, or any fence or structure that you intend to cover with vines (full-grown vines are very heavy and also catch the wind like a sail). For posts in these situations, fill the holes with concrete. Plan to use one 80-pound bag of ready-mix concrete for every one or two postholes, depending on how deep and wide they are.

Set the post on the gravel in the bottom of the hole, make sure it's plumb and install the temporary braces, and then mix up some concrete in a wheelbarrow according to the directions on the sack. Shovel concrete into the hole on all four sides of the post, tamping it down with a 2x4 to make sure there aren't any voids. Continue until the hole is full, then add some extra concrete and shape it into a low mound so rainwater will flow away from the post and soak into the ground. Use the spirit level and check again to make sure the post is still plumb. Adjust it right away if needed. You have only about 15 minutes before the concrete starts to set; after that, it's too late to straighten up a post that has tipped. Wait two days for the concrete to cure, then remove the braces and continue with fence construction.

SPACING. Setting a single post, such as for a mailbox, is easy. Just put it where you want it. Installing two or more posts gets more complicated, as you need to decide how far apart to put them and to make sure they line up.

Spacing depends on the project. If you're installing a ready-made panel, trellis, railing, or gate, measure its width and decide whether it should be mounted between two posts or in front of them. As you work, check repeatedly to make sure the posts are the right distance apart, measuring to the nearest ¼ inch.

If you're building almost any kind of wood fence with 2x4 stringers, the posts can be up to 8 feet apart, but they're often set closer than that. For lightweight wire mesh or other fencing that comes on a continuous roll, posts may be 10 feet or farther apart. For these situations, the distance between any two adjacent posts is up to you and depends on the project and the site. Just be consistent. For each run, measure the total distance between two ends or an end and a corner, and divide it into equal segments. Do a trial calculation first, and if the numbers come out awkward, perhaps you can simplify things by set-

ting the ends a little farther apart or closer together. For example, if your first calculation suggests spacing posts 7 feet 1¼ inches apart, maybe you could bring the ends closer together to round the spacing off to an even 7 feet. If that doesn't seem feasible, just keep your tape measure handy and keep checking as you go along.

To set two or more posts, use stakes to mark the locations and dig all the holes first. Then start at one end, set the first post, make sure it's plumb, and pack soil or concrete around it. Now set the other post (if you need just two) or the post at the far end of the run (if you're setting a whole row of posts) tentatively in its hole. Measure again and make sure it's positioned at the right distance from the first post. If the posts are square, rotate the second post as needed so its front edge is in the same plane with the first post. Finally, make sure the second post is plumb, then pack soil or concrete around it.

ALIGNMENT. To align a row of posts, run a string from one end to the other, resting along their front edges, and then as you proceed to set the intermediate posts, make sure each one touches lightly against the string. Double-check yourself by standing at one end and sighting down the line. Remember that you have about 15 minutes to adjust a post's position before the concrete hardens permanently.

To align the tops of the posts as you go along, run a second string over the tops of the two end posts, then add or remove gravel from underneath each intermediate post to make its top meet the line. Sometimes it's easier not to worry about the tops as you set the posts. Just pay attention to getting each post plumb and in line. Then come back afterward and saw the tops off any posts that stick up too high.

WALLS

Walls are in a different league from fences. They're weightier, literally and figuratively. Walls have a dignity and permanence that fences can't match. They're substantial, impressive, and durable.

In terms of mass and form, walls are more like hedges than fences. Unlike fences, both walls and hedges have noticeable thickness, and they can be rounded instead of straight. But unlike hedges, walls are virtually maintenance-free, and a well-built wall will outlast most hedges.

Walls can blend into the landscape, following contours and tracing curves as if they were part of the natural geology of a place, or they can stand out as geometric, obviously man-made structures. They can be short or tall, rough- or smooth-surfaced, rustic or refined, natural-colored or painted, left bare or draped with vines.

Basically, there are two categories of walls: free-

(LEFT): *This inviting structure begins as a knee-high retaining wall, then rises into a freestanding wall as it climbs beside the steps. Developing such an organic design is one of the pleasures of wall building.*

(BELOW): *Needed to support a 6-foot grade change, this concrete retaining wall bears fossil-like impressions of the boards used to mold it. A narrow planting bed between the wall and the driveway affords space for the espaliered pyracanthas and a few patches of pansies.*

standing and retaining. Freestanding walls are exposed on both sides. Like a fence or hedge, they can serve as a privacy screen, boundary marker, or background. Retaining walls back up to a bank, slope, or terrace, and their primary function is to hold the ground in place. These different roles involve different design and construction.

Situations that call for retaining walls

A retaining wall can be a requirement or an amenity, depending on your site. In places where it's a requirement, the need is usually obvious at the time the house is built, so the wall should be installed then also. But sometimes developers or owners underestimate the seriousness of the situation, or problems arise or intensify years after the house was built. At any time, if it becomes clear that you *need* a retaining wall to stop soil erosion, contact local experts and start gathering advice and estimates. You may be in for a major building project and will have to observe local codes. Before hiring a contractor, check references, go to see similar retaining walls that they've finished in your area, and discuss their track record and guarantee.

If you don't need a retaining wall but simply *want* one as an amenity, engineering is less of a concern and you may decide to build the wall yourself or to work with a general landscape contractor, not an engineer or a wall specialist. The final structure must be sound and suitable for the site, but you have some leeway in determining the placement, shape, and height of the wall and what materials can be used to build it.

UNSTABLE SLOPES. This is a regional occurrence. Some parts of the country, primarily the mountainous West, are notorious for landslides. When heavy rains saturate particular kinds of clay, whole hillsides are liable to drop away. If you live in an area that experiences this kind of soil slippage, seek expert local advice before you buy or build a house. The best strategy is to avoid developing particularly vulnerable sites. Trying to retain unstable soil on a large scale is expensive and may be a futile exercise. Where it seems feasible, it requires site-spe-

(RIGHT): *The lake is calm now, but its shoreline is vulnerable at other times to erosion and undercutting from wave action and ice. Waterfront properties typically need substantial retaining walls.*

(BELOW): *Low drystone walls are enough to protect the banks of this small brook (lower right) from high water, ice, and burrowing rodents. A level terrace provides a pathway for walking beside the water, and another retaining wall along the uphill side supports a terrace planted with wildflowers.*

cific engineering and substantial walls, usually made of reinforced concrete and/or massive timbers.

SHORELINES. Ocean, lake, and riverside properties are vulnerable to erosion from waves and high water. Steep banks get undercut and then collapse. Again, this is a regional issue. If you're losing ground, your neighbors are, too, and everyone will have opinions on the performance of various kinds of breakwaters, storm walls, and retaining walls. These are sometimes installed on a community basis and sometimes done piecemeal by individual landowners. Either way, building a major waterfront retaining wall is an expensive project that must be designed by an engineer and built by a professional.

It's a different story if you have just a little brook, an earth-bottomed pond, or lake frontage; the shoreline is fairly shallow; and the water level is fairly constant. There it's fun and easy to reinforce and stabilize the shoreline by standing in the water on a warm summer day and building a low dry-laid stone retaining wall against the bank, or simply covering the bank with a close-fitted layer of riprap. You may be able to gather enough stones from right around the area. If you have to import stones, consider using broken concrete rubble; it's ideal for this situation because the pieces are angular and fit together well.

CUTS, MAN-MADE BANKS. Building houses, driveways, and streets on sloping terrain or in hilly neighborhoods usually involves making some cuts with a bulldozer or backhoe. Cutting into a bank leaves an area that's steeper than it was before and also strips away any topsoil that was there. For some reason, developers and builders are blind to the problems that cut banks so obviously pose: they're too steep to walk or work on, and the combination of accelerated runoff and poor soil makes it quite difficult to establish or maintain any plantings there.

The typical builder's solution is to hydromulch the area, seeding some kind of cheap, fast-growing turfgrass. That leads to a weedy patch of lawn that's hard to water and mow. Such banks persist for decades as nuisance areas in a landscape. Ordinarily they aren't big enough to count as serious problems, or the developer wouldn't have been able to walk away from them. But they're annoying to live with, unsightly, and a waste of space.

Replacing the bank by building one or more retaining walls and making level or slightly sloping terraces at the top and bottom makes it much easier to grow plants there or to use the land for recreation, outdoor living, or other purposes. Whether or not you can build the wall(s) yourself depends on scale and your ambition. Generally, if a bank is currently covered with grass and you're able to mow it, that's a situation you could handle yourself if you choose to. If the bank is so steep or unstable that plants won't grow there or that loose soil and rocks fall off, get help. Likewise, if you need or want a wall more than 3 feet tall, get help.

(Note that another solution to an awkward bank that is difficult to maintain as lawn is to cover it with a vigorous, dense, weed-resistant ground cover; see the box on page 321. To regain space wasted by an awkward bank close to the house, build a deck that extends out over it; see page 114.)

STABLE, MODERATELY SLOPING SITES.

A gently sloping or rolling lot is scenic, and it's easy enough to design and tend a lawn or other permanent plantings there, but there are a few reasons why you might want to alter such a site by adding one or more retaining walls to support level terraces.

You could build a wall for its own sake, just

Formerly lawn, this slope was transformed into a series of level terraces by cutting and filling. The stones used for the walls came right out of the ground (this site is in New England). You could use purchased stones, concrete wall-stones, or timbers instead.

HOW TO CUT AND FILL

To terrace a slope, start at the bottom and work up.

Build the first retaining wall. Pull soil downhill to backfill behind the wall, and compact it firmly. Now you have a level terrace to stand on as you proceed.

Build the second wall, and pull soil downhill to backfill behind it. Continue uphill until you reach the top of the slope.

Make short walls and wide terraces on gentle slopes. Steep slopes require taller walls and narrower terraces. Use the guidelines for designing steps (see page 186) to figure the ideal wall height (the unit rise) and terrace width (the unit run).

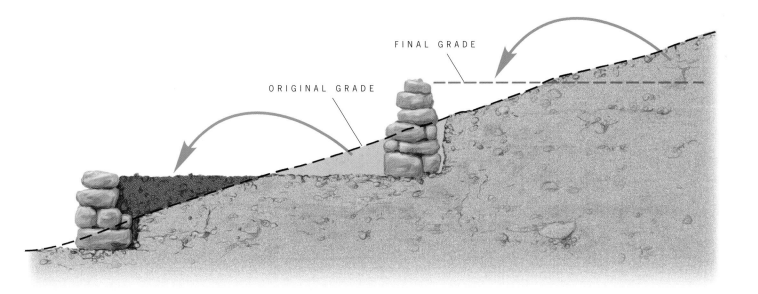

FINAL GRADE

ORIGINAL GRADE

because you like the look of stones. A wall gives structure to a garden, serves as a focal point, and makes a great background for any plants that reach up in front of it or trail down over the edge. Adding a wall is especially desirable if you have a window or outdoor living area that faces uphill, so that you're looking directly at the wall. It's less rewarding to look downhill over a wall.

Or you might want to build a wall and terrace because slopes, even gentle ones, are inconvenient as outdoor floors. It's better to have a level place where you can set a table and chairs, host a barbecue, fill a wading pool for the kids, or display a collection of container plants. Slopes are also inconvenient for growing vegetables, herbs, and flowers that need frequent attention or harvest and ongoing care. It's more fun to grow these plants on level terraces.

There are three ways to transform a slope into a level area or terrace. (1) You can cut into the slope, take soil away, and build a retaining wall at the uphill edge. This is good if you plan to lay pavement, as the undisturbed subsoil makes a relatively stable base. It's not good for garden beds, though, as it takes a lot of work to make subsoil suitable for planting. (2) You can build a retaining wall at the downhill edge of the terrace and bring soil in to fill the area behind it. This is good for gardening, as you can add soil that's customized for whatever plants you want to grow. But if you plan to build a floor on a filled area, you must go out of your way to deliberately compact the fill. (3) You can build short retaining walls at both the top and bottom edges and rearrange the existing soil, cutting into the uphill side of the terrace and using that soil to fill the downhill side. This is called cutting and filling. It has the advantage of not requiring any import or export of soil. The problem with cutting and filling is that you tend to end up with nice loose topsoil on the downhill side of the terrace and raw hard subsoil on the uphill side, and you have to take those varying conditions into account as you proceed to develop the terrace into a floor or garden.

RAISED BEDS AND PLANTERS. If you want to add vertical interest and variety to a level or gently sloping site, outline a shape or an area, build a low retaining wall around the edge, and fill it with soil to create a raised bed or planter. For more about raised beds, see page 278.

Engineering and design concerns related to retaining walls

These are the questions to ask when you're talking to potential contractors or thinking about building a retaining wall yourself. The answers will vary depending on the steepness of the site, height of the wall, soil type, and wall material. Often there are several solutions or answers to any questions. Compare the advice you get from different sources. Also check to see if local building codes specify certain requirements for retaining walls. In many areas you need an engineer's approval and a building permit to build a wall more than 3 feet tall.

STABILITY. What will hold up the wall and keep it from tumbling forward? Dry-stacked walls rely on gravity and friction, and they also lean slightly backward into the slope. Mortared, timber, and poured-concrete walls must be anchored somehow, typically via long rocks set sideways as tie-ins, buttresses on the front side, stakes or reinforcing bars that reach down into the ground, or screw anchors that connect back into undisturbed soil behind the wall. All of these are installed as a wall is built.

What kind of a foundation does the wall need? This depends on material, soil, and climate. Generally, dry-stacked and timber walls are laid on a bed of packed gravel and installed with the first course, or

Developing a steep, unstable slope calls for experienced engineers and contractors. Here massive timbers make a series of walls and narrow planting beds. The plants will gradually trail over the edges and soften the appearance.

Blocky chunks of sandstone fit snugly in this dry-stacked wall. Note the staggered joints, level courses, and slight batter. Natural stones are a very versatile building material. It's easy to make a curved shape with split-level beds for plants like this orange-flowered penstemon and pink Jupiter's beard.

row, of stones or timbers partway below grade level. Mortared and poured-concrete walls need a much more extensive foundation—thicker than the wall itself and deeper than the frost line—or they're liable to crack someday when the ground shifts owing to frost action or changes in soil moisture content.

HEIGHT. You can reshape many sites by building either one tall retaining wall or two or more shorter ones with terraces between them. Building more walls sounds like more work, but it isn't necessarily. In fact, it may actually simplify the engineering and construction process, as short walls are easier to design and build.

Moreover, a steplike series of short walls often looks better, and it's safer. A single retaining wall more than 5 to 6 feet tall is a pretty imposing structure in a home landscape, and that kind of drop-off is scary, too. If you have a high wall, you'll probably need or want a protective railing, fence, or hedge along its top edge. By contrast, walls only 2 to 3 feet tall have a friendly feel; you want to sit on them.

DRAINAGE. How will water get through, under, past, or around the wall? As rain or irrigation water soaks down through the soil above the wall, it has to get out somehow. Drainage normally isn't a problem with a dry-stacked wall, because water can seep out between the stones or blocks. Watertight walls must be provided with outlets or weep holes (usually plastic pipes or clay drain tiles) that run through the wall from back to front, near the base, or a buried drain line that runs lengthwise behind the base of the wall,

carrying runoff to either end. Water pressure can build up behind a tight wall if drain lines are absent, inadequate, or blocked, causing the wall to crack or give way.

PLACEMENT, SHAPE, AND CONTOUR. The best way to design a retaining wall is to work directly on the site; don't bother trying to draw it on paper. Go lay out a tentative arrangement with stakes and string, using the string (or flagging tape, which is more visible) to mark the top edge of the wall. Stand back, look from all sides, and then try again, moving the stakes and string until you're satisfied.

Pay special attention to the top edge. As a rule, the top of a retaining wall should be level or stepped. (If you can't tell whether it's level by eyeballing it, use a water level as described on page 185.) Sometimes it looks okay if the top of a wall is angled or contoured to make it approximately parallel to the ground. Each site is unique, and you'll just have to keep moving those stakes and string until you make up your mind.

A wall can be straight, angled, or curved. If you want it to be straight, think about making it parallel to any nearby structure such as your house or the street. An angled or curved wall can be concave and cut into the slope, or convex and bow out with the slope, or it can go back and forth. What would look right? Try different shapes and see what you like.

The trickiest part is deciding what to do at the end of a wall. It can gradually taper off, angle into the slope and disappear, or lead right up to another structure, such as the corner of your house, a flight of steps, or a stone pillar. Keep an eye out for retaining walls around your neighborhood and community to observe different end treatments.

Retaining-wall construction

Contractors can build big, sturdy retaining walls from materials that an average homeowner is rarely equipped to handle: poured concrete, steel beams, stout timbers, big blocks of cut stone or concrete, or mortared masonry. If you need to have a wall built, get local experts to advise you on the performance, durability, appearance, drawbacks, and costs of these different materials as installed in your soil and climate.

Poured-concrete walls, if properly designed and reinforced, are good and strong, but a plain concrete surface looks stark. A good mason can start with a concrete core and add a mortared masonry veneer that makes it look as if the wall is solid stone. Or you can plant clinging vines (such as English ivy, Virginia creeper, euonymus, or climbing hydrangea) at the base and let them cover the concrete with greenery.

Timber construction appeals to some do-it-yourself homeowners, but even for low edgings (see page 156) there are often problems with timbers warping, heaving, or getting knocked out of line. Building a timber retaining wall more than 2 feet tall requires careful joinery, strong fasteners, and a

Trailing evergreens soften the profile of this mortared stone retaining wall, which is old enough to be covered with mosses and lichens. Well-built walls last for decades at least, and sometimes for centuries.

proven anchor system. Furthermore, timbers big enough for tall walls are hard to find, expensive, heavy to handle, and tough to cut.

MASONRY WALLS. A dry-stacked, or dry-laid, wall made from natural stones or a concrete-wall-stone system is a good choice for most home-landscape situations. These walls are attractive and trouble-free. There are several reasons to choose a dry-stacked rather than mortared wall. Because it "gives," a dry-laid wall is unlikely to crack when the soil freezes or shifts. And water can seep through a dry-laid wall, so you don't have to worry about providing for drainage. A dry-laid wall costs less to install, because it doesn't require the substantial foundation that a mortared wall needs. It takes less skill; you can build the wall yourself. If you get partway into a project and find you've wavered off-level or off-line, you can undo that part of the wall and rebuild it. If you change your mind later and want to make the wall higher or wider, you can add to it. Working with mortar is another story; you have to get everything right the first time, as you don't get a second chance.

The major reason for using mortar is that it strengthens a wall and makes it solid and rigid. Mortar holds all the pieces in place so they won't be dislodged by accidents or animals. When it's done right, a mortared wall looks dignified, classy, and professional. But a sloppy mortared wall is undeniably an eyesore. A mortared wall that has cracked or chipped for some reason is ugly, too, and irreparable.

BUILDING WITH NATURAL STONES. The best stones for wall building are brick-shaped or blocky, with two flat parallel sides. Building with round fieldstones or river rocks is possible but harder, as they don't stack well. Unless you happen to have a ready supply of suitable stones on your property or access to a place where you can collect them, you'll have to buy stones. Visit local stoneyards and quarries to see what's available. Stones for wall building are usually sold by the ton. For a wall roughly 2 feet thick, multiply the length of the wall times its height and divide by 10. You'll need at least that many tons of rock, and it's good to buy about 25 percent extra so you'll have plenty to choose from.

Set aside the best, biggest, flattest stones to use on top of the wall as *capstones.* Save crooked, ugly, and small pieces to use as fill behind the wall. You can take the stones as they come or learn to shape them with a chisel and mallet. Shaping stones takes practice but lets you achieve a much closer fit.

Lay stones flat, with the broadest side parallel to the ground, not on end or on edge. Choose whichever face looks best for the front side of the wall, and try to align all the faces so the front of the wall is a smooth plane. Use bigger stones along the front of the wall, and fill in behind them with smaller stones.

Several basic guidelines apply whether you're building with natural stone or concrete wallstones. Some variations and tips related to one or the other material are noted below. For your first project, plan to build a retaining wall of uniform height that's level on both the top and bottom edge and that backs against a cut bank. It can be straight or curved. Later you can try building walls that are taller on one end than on the other, or that run uphill and have a stepped profile, or that are built as freestanding walls and backfilled afterward (as for raised beds).

1. If you're building a steplike series of two or more walls, start at the bottom of the hill and work your way up.

2. Dig a trench about 2 feet wide and deep enough to hold about 4 inches of packed gravel plus part or all of the first course of stones. The surface of the packed gravel should be level from side to side and from front to back.

3. Starting at one end or at a corner, lay the first, or base, course of stones in place on the gravel, fitting them snugly side by side. Check often to make sure that each stone is level, that they're all at the same height, and that the front of the wall follows the intended line. Do this by eye or, for a straight wall, stretch a string from end to end and align the stones with that. For a curved wall, you can outline the desired shape with a hose or rope or by spray-painting it on the ground.

4. Fill in behind the first course with small or scrap stones, if you have any, plus crushed rock or dirt. Use a piece of 2x4 to ram or pack the dirt firmly into place. This is important. Try not to leave any gaps or air spaces behind the stones.

5. Add the second course of stones, overlapping them with the first so that the joints are staggered. This course should be set slightly back from the first. A setback, or batter, of about 1 inch for every 1 foot of height helps keep a dry-stacked masonry retaining wall in place. Keep checking as you work from one end of the wall to the other to make sure that the top of the course is level.

6. Add fill behind the second course and pack it down firmly.

7. Continue until the wall is as high as you want it. Use capstones for the final course. Fill in behind them with topsoil.

As you lay each course, try to keep its top surface level and make sure it's steady and it doesn't rock. Often this will require propping up a stone with wedges or shims. That's okay. Shimming is an essential part of wall building. Here and there set a long stone sideways into the wall to serve as a *tie stone;* this adds stability. Don't forget to give the wall a slight setback, or batter; make it lean into the slope.

Fitting natural stones is like working a three-dimensional puzzle. You'll spend a lot of time staring at shapes, trying to figure out which stone to use next in order to create a tight fit, maintain level courses, continually stagger the joints, and create an attractive pattern. If you have a knack for it, it's a lot of fun and immensely satisfying.

BUILDING WITH CONCRETE WALL-STONES. Several manufacturers around the country are producing concrete wallstones and paving stones now in a variety of styles, textures, and colors. If there's an annual home and garden show anywhere in your area, that's a good place to meet and talk with local distributors, see examples of the products and sample installations, and pick up some literature. Home-improvement centers and building-supply stores usually carry at least one or two brands of these stones, so you can see a limited selection there if you can't make it to a home show.

The price of building a wall with concrete stones is comparable to or sometimes lower than the cost of using real stones, and the concrete stones are definitely easier to install because of their uniform size and shape. Although the systems from different manufacturers vary in minor ways, most are quite cleverly designed. They stack firmly and automatically create a staggered arrangement and a uniform setback. You can make straight walls or concave or convex curves. There are special units for turning corners or building steps into a wall. The main drawback with these walls is that they tend to look rather "raw" and bland, but that impression is soon forgotten as you fill beds above and below the wall with a variety of plants.

Any concrete-wallstone system comes with detailed installation instructions. For systems that produce particularly tight-fitting walls, the instructions will recommend that you bury a 4-inch perforated drainpipe in a bed of gravel behind the wall and backfill with crushed rock, not packed dirt, to facilitate drainage. Otherwise, the directions are similar to the basic dry-stacked wall guidelines.

Freestanding walls

Freestanding walls are typically placed where you'd otherwise put a fence—along a boundary line or around the edge of an outdoor room—and a wall is sort of a heavy-duty upgrade from fencing. Walls provide security and privacy, they help block sound, they create microclimates, and they carry prestige. For all these reasons, exclusive gated communities are surrounded with walls, not mere fences. On a smaller scale, a wall adds structure, class, and visual interest to any property.

Freestanding walls are almost always built of stones, concrete blocks, bricks, or other masonry materials, using either mortared or dry-laid construction. A mortared brick or block wall can be quite shallow—as thin as 8 to 12 inches, the depth of a single brick or block—and up to 6 feet or taller. Dry-laid stone walls, by contrast, are usually at least 2 feet thick and often as thick as they are tall. Dry-stacked walls are rarely built more than 3 feet tall, partly because a taller wall must be so thick that it requires masses of stones and fills up too much space.

Walls are notably carefree and durable except for a few common problems. If tree roots grow under a wall, they will break it apart. Frost action and the dynamic nature of clay soil can heave and crack a mortared wall if the foundation was inadequate. And streetside walls are regrettably vulnerable to colli-

sions from cars and trucks, a problem that's compounded by the difficulty of repairing mortared work. But if it can avoid these problems, a wall will endure for a lifetime, perhaps for centuries.

FREESTANDING-WALL DESIGN. The materials and styles used for freestanding walls and the very presence of these walls vary a lot from region to region around the country. Old drystone walls are ubiquitous in New England and these walls are still being built or rebuilt there, because suitable rock is so abundant and the dry-stacked technique is so well adapted to cold climates where the soil freezes deep. In general, though, you see a lot more walls in mild-winter regions than in cold climates, because less of a foundation is required there. Throughout the South and Southwest and along the West Coast, residential neighborhoods feature all kinds of wonderful walls made from stone, brick, poured concrete, stuccoed blocks, and adobe, with appealing surface textures and patterns and interesting contours and silhouettes.

A wall is a big investment and a long-term commitment; it becomes part of your property. For those reasons, it makes sense to take a fairly conservative

This stuccoed adobe wall incorporates an arch topped with an antique timber. Walls like this are patted into shape, and the resulting curves are so appealing that you want to rub your hands along them.

approach to wall design and choose a material and a construction technique that match or coordinate with your house and neighborhood. There's also a practical reason to choose an established wall style. Local contractors have had more experience building familiar walls and are better prepared to anticipate and prevent any problems. When you experiment with an unfamiliar or untested wall-construction technique, you're taking a chance. The wall might crack.

The way to diverge from the norm and set your wall apart as something special is in the details and cosmetic touches. Make round rather than square corners. Let the top edge be stepped, scalloped, or pinked. Frame a gateway with an overhead arch. Choose a wrought-iron grill or wooden grate to fill a windowlike opening in the wall. Build openwork blocks into the wall to let the breeze through, or use glass bricks to let in light. Use rough-textured boards to add texture to a poured-concrete wall. Add brick or stone veneer to a concrete-block wall. Hire an artist to insert tiles, design a mosaic, or paint a mural on a smooth concrete wall. Install a wall fountain. Details such as this don't add much to the overall cost of a wall and don't compromise its structure, but they make it unique.

To resolve the basic issues of where to locate a freestanding wall, what shape to make it, and how tall it should be, follow the general design guidelines at the beginning of this chapter.

BUILDING A FREESTANDING DRY-STACKED WALL. Building a dry-stacked stone wall 2 to 3 feet tall and wide is a job you might tackle yourself. Follow the same guidelines and process that apply to dry-stacked retaining walls (see page 218). Basically, a freestanding wall is two retaining walls that lean together, back to back, and that are tied occasionally with stones that run all the way from one side to the other. The sides should be slightly battered, making the wall somewhat narrower on top

than at the bottom. An amateur can do a fine job building one of these walls if you pay attention to how the stones fit together. Always stagger the joints; set one stone over two, or two over one. Remember that gravity and friction are what hold the wall together, and make sure each stone rests securely on the ones beneath it and touches as many other stones as possible. Use shims and wedges to fill gaps and prevent rocking or shifting.

BUILDING A FREESTANDING MORTARED WALL. This is a job for pros. You may find an individual mason who can undertake all parts of the project, but more likely you'll work with a contractor who manages a crew of specialists.

If you plan to have a masonry wall built on your property, consider incorporating a custom feature, such as an alcove sized for a special bench (TOP) or a spouting wall fountain (BOTTOM).

The first challenge is knowing what kind of foundation is required by your soil, climate, and local codes and making sure that it gets properly built. The success of a wall depends on its footing, so it's important to hire someone who understands what's needed, who has years of experience in your area, and whose work and reputation are unquestioned.

Building the visible, aboveground part of a mortared wall is a skilled craft, and you'll enjoy watching how it's done. Getting everything level and plumb, stacking one course after another, inserting reinforcement rods, fitting the joints, shaping the top, finishing the surface, making both sides of the wall look good, putting in the details you've chosen —there's a lot going on. The project will extend over a period of days or weeks, perhaps even months, until finally the wall stands complete. Both functional and sculptural, a freestanding wall is one of the most attractive and valuable features you can add to your landscape.

Broadly mounded azaleas illustrate the general rule that most shrubs grow wider than tall. Hedges require more space than a fence or wall, but they create inimitable results.

❧ HEDGES

Compared with other vertical features, hedges have two main advantages. They're relatively inexpensive to create, especially if you start with small plants, and they're alive and dynamic, not inert. Hedges change with the seasons, send out tender new growth, blow in the wind. They can bear flowers and fruits. Some hedge plants smell good. Hedging offers many possibilities because plants themselves are so varied. Don't limit your thinking to the stereotyped prisms of greenery that you see in every neighborhood. Hedges also come in many other shapes, colors, and sizes.

But hedges have some major drawbacks, too. First, it takes a minimum of a few years to establish a hedge that forms a dense, continuous screen. Afterward, a hedge continues to require pruning and other care throughout its lifetime. Hedge plants are vulnerable to bad weather, insects, and diseases, as well as the kinds of accidents that could damage a fence or wall. Hedges also fill more space than walls or fences do. Even the thinnest hedge is at least 2 feet thick. Normally hedges are at least 4 to 6 feet

thick, plus you need to allow some additional open space on both sides so you can approach the hedge to tend it.

The main reason for making a hedge is because you want the textures and colors of live plants and are intrigued by the design opportunity. Other good reasons are that hedges make affordable and attractive screens or boundary markers for large properties and that they're useful as windbreaks on exposed sites.

Designing a new hedge

Basically, a hedge is a group of plants arranged in a row and spaced close enough together that you perceive the overall effect, not the separate parts. Use just one kind of plant for a solid hedge, or different kinds for a mixed hedge. The principal issues are what kinds of plants to use and how to arrange them to achieve the results and style you want.

As a reminder of how important it is to choose appropriate plants for a hedge, look at existing hedges around your neighborhood. You'll see that hedges often spread too wide and get in the way, or grow too tall and cast unwanted shade. They may be vigorous on top yet bare at the base, or be straggly, uneven from one end to the other, or infested with weeds. Many hedges are made with boring, ugly, or ill-suited plants.

These problems are frequently blamed on the plants, although it's really not their fault—it's the responsibility of whoever selected them. Choosing suitable plants is the major challenge in making a hedge. Of course, upkeep is an issue, too. Hedges go bad if you don't take care of them. Sometimes a neglected but originally well-conceived hedge can be restored over a few years' time by diligent pruning, grooming, weeding, and fertilizing. But if a hedge's problems are due to poor plant selection, the only solution is to uproot it and start again.

MEASURE THE AVAILABLE SPACE. Hedges can be as short as your boots, taller than your house, or any height in between, but the range between 3 and 7 feet tall is the most practical, as such hedges are the most useful and the easiest to maintain. Letting a hedge grow taller than you can reach adds drama to a large garden, but it offers only an incremental gain in privacy, while casting considerably more shade, especially in winter.

There are many situations—around the edge of a patio, for example—where a hedge is welcome but you want to be able to see over it. Use stakes and string to mock up an ideal prototype hedge, measure how tall it is, and choose plants whose average mature height matches your needs. Don't get trapped in a rat race of nonstop pruning to keep down a too-tall hedge.

Most shrubs spread at least as wide as they are tall. Only a limited number of plants remain slender as they mature. In many situations, you'll have to prune or shear the sides to keep a hedge as narrow as you want it. Usually the thinnest you can make a hedge is about one-half its height. For instance, you might keep a 6-foot-tall hedge to about 3 feet thick if you select upright-growing shrubs and keep trimming them as they grow. For spaces too narrow to accommodate a hedge, build a fence instead and cover it with vines.

SHEARED OR NATURAL? Shearing or clipping evens out the surface of a hedge, calls attention to its overall form, diminishes your awareness of the individual plants themselves, and emphasizes that the gardener is in control. A sheared hedge typically contains just one kind of evergreen shrub and has a formal, well-groomed, geometric look.

In an unsheared, or natural, hedge, the shrubs are hand-pruned to enhance their health and vigor without disguising their natural shape. The plants have a neat but somewhat irregular profile, not a flush, smoothly shorn surface. The effect is usually more colorful and dynamic than that of a formal, sheared hedge, and the hedge may feature flowers or fruits as well as foliage. And you aren't restricted to one kind of plant. A natural hedge can include a variety of shrubs side by side.

As for size, both sheared and unsheared hedges can come in heights from short to tall. You can keep a sheared hedge narrower than an unsheared hedge. But decide which style you want before you begin a hedge, as it's hard to change from one to the other afterward.

Formal hedges look pretentious or out of place in rural areas and in natural-style gardens. But they're perfect for small urban and suburban lots because they combine so well with buildings and pavement. Plant them along lines that reach out from the corners of your house, run parallel to a walk or boundary, or surround a patio, and the hedges will seem like living extensions of the architecture and hardscape. You'll need patience, though, as it can take several years before a formal hedge starts to look mature.

If your landscape style is casual or you have a large property, you'd probably be happier with a natural hedge. Natural hedges aren't totally carefree, but the upkeep is less than for a sheared hedge. In addition, natural hedges normally develop faster. Depending on what shrubs you choose, a natural hedge may start looking full just a few years after you plant it.

PERMANENT OR SEASONAL? Hedges are often designed to be permanent and unchanging, like green architecture. That's why most hedges are made with evergreen shrubs. But it's a short step from static to boring. If you don't need the year-round structure, shelter, and screening that evergreens provide, consider using deciduous or herbaceous plants. These make more exciting hedges because they change with the seasons.

UNIFORM OR MIXED? Where uniformity is the goal, a hedge must include just one kind of plant. Otherwise it's more interesting (and more fun, if you're an avid plant collector) to include a variety of shrubs. Mixed hedges are almost always maintained in a natural style, not sheared.

It's hard to make a uniform hedge if soil moisture and quality or sun/shade exposure varies from one end to the other. Any single kind of plant would reflect the gradient, growing better in some places than in others. So design a mixed hedge for a varied site, choosing plants adapted to the different growing conditions, rather than striving for a homogeneous look.

Minimizing contrast is the key to designing a mixed planting that seems like a hedge. Select plants that are basically similar in height, width, and rate of growth but that differ in habit, texture, season of bloom, flower color, or leaf color. If you want to combine evergreen and deciduous shrubs, position the evergreens first to be sure they'll seem spaced right in winter, then fit the deciduous shrubs in between them.

Recommended plants for different kinds of hedges

Take your time and do plenty of homework before you buy plants and make a hedge, as success and satisfaction depend so much on choosing the right kind of plant(s). Any hedge plant should be trouble-free and well adapted to your climate and growing conditions and have a natural mature size and shape that approximate the hedge you have in mind.

Most hedges are made with shrubs, but certain trees, grasses, perennials, and even annuals can also be used for hedging, and cacti, large succulents, and tropicals such as bananas can be used for a bold effect in suitable climates.

The following recommendations can serve as a starting point if you're planning a hedge. Copy out or photocopy the list for whatever situation you're considering, then continue to narrow the selection by checking the descriptions and photos of individual species and cultivars in a good plant encyclopedia and asking advice from local experts. Also follow the guidelines on pages 48 and 231 for assessing any particular plant. All this research really is worthwhile because you'll probably be buying, caring for, and living with several plants—perhaps dozens—of whatever kind you choose, and you don't want a large-scale disappointment.

SHRUBS FOR SHEARED HEDGES. Looking around at contemporary landscapes, especially at commercial properties maintained by hired crews, you have to conclude that almost any kind of tree or shrub can be sheared. But the ideal is a slow-growing plant with dense, twiggy growth and small leaves or short needles (preferably but not necessarily evergreen).

The presence or color of flowers isn't much of an issue here, since shearing often prevents blooming, but foliage color is something to consider. Pure deep green is the classic favorite. Blue-green and silver-gray are almost as versatile and timeless. Think twice before making a hedge with gold-, bronze-, or purple-leaved plants. At best, it would be dramatic and memorable, but it might be just an eyesore that serves as a local landmark.

There's little to be gained by choosing a rare or little-known plant for a sheared hedge, as the plant's individual character is subservient to the overall effect. Talk to local experts and choose a well-tested,

Slow-growing, fine-textured boxwood is a favorite choice for clipped hedges. Its tiny evergreen leaves glow in the summer sun.

reliable cultivar that's recommended for your area. Don't be too proud to settle for a familiar plant if it's a good one. Some of the best candidates are various kinds of barberries *(Berberis)*, boxwood *(Buxus)*, cotoneaster, elaeagnus, euonymus, holly *(Ilex)*, junipers *(Juniperus)*, sweet bay *(Laurus nobilis)*, leptospermum, ligustrums or privets, true myrtle *(Myrtus communis)*, sweet olive *(Osmanthus)*, evergreen cherries *(Prunus)*, evergreen azaleas *(Rhododendron)*, alpine currant *(Ribes alpinum)*, yews *(Taxus)*, arborvitae *(Thuja)*, and hemlocks *(Tsuga)*.

SHRUBS FOR BROAD UNSHEARED HEDGES.

An unsheared hedge displays the inherent, natural shape of its constituents. In most cases, that means it will have a softly rounded profile and spread wider than it is tall. For example, a forsythia hedge that's 6 feet tall may spread 12 feet wide. Such a broad, billowing hedge overwhelms a small garden but looks very gracious on wide-open properties of a half acre or more.

If you have the space, there are scores of wide-spreading shrubs to choose from. Try chokeberries *(Aronia)*, sweet shrubs *(Calycanthus)*, flowering quince *(Chaenomeles)*, shrub dogwoods *(Cornus)*, cotoneasters, brooms *(Cytisus)*, hydrangeas, *Kerria japonica*, bayberry and wax myrtles *(Myrica)*, oleander *(Nerium oleander)*, mock orange *(Philadelphus)*, ninebark *(Physocarpus)*, pittosporums, many kinds of shrub roses, spring-blooming spireas, and many viburnums. All of these have wonderful flowers, fruits, and/or fall foliage in addition to a pleasing mounded profile.

SHRUBS FOR SMALLER PROPERTIES.

Three main groups of shrubs — narrow, compact, and slow-growing — are suitable for situations where space is limited. For names of narrow, upright-growing shrubs that reach or can be kept at 4 to 8 feet tall and about half that wide, see the box on page 123.

There are smaller-than-average forms of almost any shrub, often indicated by common names that include the word "dwarf" or "petite" or by the cultivar names 'Compactum' or 'Nana' — for instance, dwarf cranberry bush viburnum *(Viburnum opulus 'Compactum')*. Plants in this size group usually grow about 2 to 3 feet tall and wide. Note that compact plants aren't necessarily slow growers. They may reach their mature height in just a few years. Then they continue to broaden as they age and typically end up wider than tall. For names of colorful flowering plants that make hedges about 2 to 3 feet tall and wide, see the box on page 124. For low plants to use as edgings along walks or paved areas, see the box on page 172.

Slow-growing plants such as boxwoods, camellias, dwarf conifers, evergreen daphnes, some hollies, and most rhododendrons and azaleas may eventually become quite large, but not for many years or even decades, as they grow only a few inches per year. Because they're slow, these plants cost more to buy and mature specimens are truly prized. These are great plants to invest in if you plan to live in the same home for many years. By the time (if ever) that the hedge gets big enough to make you feel crowded, you'll be so devoted to it that you won't begrudge its girth.

ORNAMENTAL GRASSES.

A row of clump-forming grasses makes an inexpensive, trouble-free hedge that reaches full height by the third growing season and then persists indefinitely, getting thicker and denser over time. A grass hedge looks very dramatic when it blows in the wind, and although it changes with the seasons, it actually makes a good substitute for a formal hedge of clipped evergreens. A good grass hedge should stand up to ordinary weather through the summer, fall, and winter. Cut off the old growth, leaving short stubs, anytime between late fall and when new growth starts in spring. Grasses are ideal for good property-line hedges because your neighbor doesn't have to help with the maintenance.

Choose grass species or cultivars that form stiff, erect clumps and aren't too tippy or floppy. Some good grasses for hedging are big bluestem *(Andropogon gerardii)*, feather reed grass cultivars *(Calamagrostis × acutiflora* 'Karl Foerster' or 'Stricta')*, ravenna grass *(Erianthus ravennae)*, Japanese silver grass cultivars *(Miscanthus sinensis* 'Graziella', 'Malepartus', and 'Strictus' are the most erect)*, switch grass cultivars *(Panicum virgatum* 'Heavy Metal' or 'Prairie Sky')*, and 'Sioux Blue' Indian grass *(Sorghastrum nutans)*. All reach 5 feet or taller. Space plants at least 3 feet apart for a dense hedge and 6 to 8 feet apart for a more open look.

HARDY PERENNIALS.

Although it dies down in winter, a row of perennials looks stunning when the plants are in bloom and has a hedgelike presence throughout the growing season. Perennial hedges are good for marking the transition between a carefully tended garden and a natural landscape beyond; for foundation plantings around detached garages or other outbuildings; and as edgings along walks, driveways, or roads in climates where snow buildup would damage woody plants.

Perennials suitable for hedging form clumps that gradually widen but can persist for decades without needing division, and they have foliage that stays neat and healthy throughout the growing season. Some of the best candidates are cultivars of species of blue stars *(Amsonia)*, false indigos *(Baptisia)*, gas plant *(Dictamnus albus)*, daylilies *(Hemerocallis)*, rose mallows *(Hibiscus)*, hostas, and peonies *(Paeonia)*. Any of these should be spaced 2 to 3 feet apart for hedging purposes.

ANNUAL HEDGES. You can make a hedge in a hurry with some of these plants, and it will surely be the talk of the neighborhood. Planting an annual hedge creates privacy fast on an empty lot, helps you visualize what a hedge would do for your garden, and buys time while you're deciding what shrubs to use for a permanent planting.

Choose annuals that get tall and bushy but are sturdy enough not to flop over, such as spider flower (*Cleome hassleriana;* airy clusters of rose, pink, or white flowers), standing cypress (*Ipomopsis rubra;* fine foliage and scarlet flowers), sunflower (*Helianthus annuus;* pinch young plants to make them branch out), burning bush (*Kochia scoparia;* the dense, fine-textured foliage is bright green in summer, turning crimson after frost), castor bean (*Ricinus communis;* bold foliage in shades of green, red, or bronze), candle plant (*Senna alata;* loves hot weather, bears yellow flower spikes), or Mexican sunflower (*Tithonia rotundifolia;* bushy, with bright orange flowers). You can direct-seed these plants or start them indoors about a month before last frost. Space them 1 to 2 feet apart for a hedge.

TREES FOR TALL HEDGES. If you want a hedge, windbreak, or screen that grows higher than you can reach, the natural style works best, as shearing a tall hedge from a ladder or scaffolding is an awkward job. Many conifers are suitable for tall hedges because they grow fairly quickly, soon reach 20 feet or taller, are less than one-half as wide as they are tall, and retain their lower foliage as they mature. Get local advice on which of the following would be best suited to your climate and growing conditions: incense cedar (*Calocedrus decurrens*), Japanese cedar (*Cryptomeria japonica*), Leyland cypress (x *Cupressocyparis leylandii*), true cypresses (*Cupressus*), spruces (*Picea*), arborvitae (*Thuja*), or hemlocks (*Tsuga*).

There are a few kinds of broad-leaved trees with narrowly upright growth. Usually designated by the cultivar name 'Columnaris' or 'Fastigiata', these are interesting but not readily available. Because they tend to drop their lower limbs as they mature and become bare at the base, they aren't as good for screening as conifers are, but they're fine as boundary markers.

SALT-TOLERANT PLANTS FOR COASTAL HEDGES. Plants along the ocean shore must tolerate salt spray, wind, and usually poor soil. It's a challenging combination, but some shrubs and trees do fine there. Get local advice on which particular species and cultivars are best suited to your climate. In general, salt tolerance is higher than average in the following groups of shrubs: elaeagnus, hollies (*Ilex*), hydrangeas, junipers (*Juniperus*), privets (*Ligustrum*), honeysuckles (*Lonicera*), bayberry and wax myrtles (*Myrica*), oleanders (*Nerium oleander*), sweet olive (*Osmanthus*), Indian hawthorn (*Raphiolepis*), rosemary (*Rosmarinus officinalis*), rugosa rose (*Rosa rugosa*), lilacs (*Syringa*), tamarisks (*Tamarix*), and viburnums.

Starting a hedge

The general guidelines on planting and tending young shrubs or other plants presented on pages 276 and 310 apply to hedges as well as to other situations, so refer to those pages along with the special considerations given here.

With shrubs, you'll probably be starting with plants grown in 1- or 5-gallon containers, although some evergreens are commonly sold B&B and some deciduous shrubs are sold bare-root. Grasses, perennials, and trees used for hedging are often sold in containers but may be bare-root or B&B. In any case, if you want to make a solid hedge from one kind of plant, buy all you need from one supplier. Explain that you want the plants for a hedge and need a matched set propagated from a single stock and similar in size and age. Buy a few extras and plant them nearby in case you need to replace a plant that gets damaged, doesn't grow right, or dies.

SPACING AND ALIGNMENT. Depending on the kind of plant and how tall and wide you want the hedge to grow, shrubs for a sheared, formal hedge are normally spaced just 1 to 3 feet apart. This uncommonly close spacing is needed to create a dense, full hedge.

For an unsheared, natural hedge, it isn't necessary or desirable to crowd plants too close together. Research the average mature spread for your chosen plant(s) and plant them about one-half to two-thirds (depending on how fast they grow) that far apart. For example, if you're planting shrubs that reach roughly 6 feet wide, plant them 3 to 4 feet apart. At this spacing, the hedge won't fill in as fast as a crowd-

Eastern red cedar and other fast-growing, upright conifers are suitable for tall hedges or windbreaks. Removing their lower limbs destroys part of their grace but improves visibility. This effect is sometimes called a "hedge on stilts."

Burning bush euonymus has vivid fall color. These plants are spaced about 6 feet apart. In a few more years, they'll fill in to make a broad, spreading hedge with lovely layered limbs.

ed hedge would, but it will have a more graceful, generous look in the long run. You can allow even more space, setting plants their full width apart, for a hedge that looks like a string of beads.

In any case, it's almost always best to arrange the plants single-file in one line. Disregard anyone who tells you to set hedge plants in a zigzag pattern or in staggered rows. Excessive width is already a problem with most hedges, and anything other than a single row takes extra space. Widening a hedge doesn't improve its appearance, and it makes pruning or shearing more difficult. The only reasons to plant in two or more rows are to create a windbreak with plants of varying heights, to create an architectural or sculptural effect with plants sheared at different heights, or to deliberately transform a wide-open space into a brushy thicket in order to attract birds or wildlife.

PLANTING. If the plants will be set closer than about 3 feet apart, dig a trench approximately 18 inches deep and 24 to 30 inches wide where you want the hedge to go. If the plants will be spaced farther apart than that, you may prefer to dig separate holes of comparable dimensions. Pile the excavated soil off to the side and incorporate organic matter, mineral amendments, and fertilizer into the bottom of the trench or holes with a digging fork. Add more amendments to the soil as you backfill. Doing this kind of soil preparation is time-consuming and tiring work, but it gives the hedge a good start. Prepare the entire trench or all the holes before you begin to plant.

Starting at one end, set all the plants into the trench or holes and refill with just enough soil to hold them upright. Then step back to double-check the spacing, and sight from one end to the other to check the alignment. Adjust or rotate any plants that don't look right. Check again, then finish refilling the trench, watering generously as you go along to settle the soil in place.

Surround each shrub with a circular patch of mulch at least 2 to 3 feet in diameter (or mulch a continuous strip the length of the hedge) and keep weeds, grass, and other plants away from the young shrubs, as they'll grow faster when there's no competition. Over the coming months and years, continue to weed, water, mulch, and fertilize the shrubs in a hedge as you would care for an individual plant of that kind.

SHAPING A YOUNG HEDGE. Shaping must begin while the plants are still young. Some shrubs are fairly bushy when you buy them, with several main stems that branch near the base, but more often young shrubs are skinny or leggy. If so, prune them hard—leaving stubs just 6 to 12 inches tall—the first winter after planting. Do this for any young hedge, whether or not you plan to shear it.

For sheared hedges, begin shearing at least once a year, and usually two, three, or more times, cutting back each flush of new growth by one-third to one-half. Shear right after the shoots have elongated and before the wood hardens. This is usually in spring or early summer, but some hedges, especially in mild climates, send out additional growth later in the season. By the third year or so, you can begin to establish the hedge's profile. Whatever shape you choose for the top—rounded, flat, or pointed—make the hedge wider below, so light can reach the lower leaves. This keeps the plants from going bare at the base. For more on shearing shrubs, see the box on page 303.

For unsheared hedges, hand-prune each shrub in late winter or spring. Look inside and remove any dead, weak, or senile shoots by cutting them back to a main stem or to the ground. Then, one at a time, shorten shoots that stick too far up or out by trimming them back to a healthy bud. Don't shear—just prune—but don't neglect pruning, as it stimulates new growth and keeps a hedge healthy. For more on pruning shrubs, see page 301.

Healthy, vigorous plants make a successful landscape. This vast sweep of daylilies is a glorious example.

8 ❧ Choosing Plants That Will Grow for You

MOST PEOPLE don't have much practice at choosing landscape plants and don't know how to go about it. They focus on flowers instead of considering the plant as a whole. But landscaping is not like filling a little flower bed or window box with annuals that you'll discard a few months later. Trees, shrubs, ground covers, and other major plantings are meant to last for decades, and they grow quite large. Both problems and successes are magnified by time and scale, so when you do get the chance to create or expand a landscaping planting, savor the opportunity and take a thoughtful approach.

The key to success is picking plants that suit the site. A plant that's adapted to the climate and growing conditions and scaled to the available space appears comfortable and "right" and requires only routine care. An inappropriate plant—one that's stressed in any way—demands extra attention yet never looks as good. Understanding the relation between plants and growing conditions helps you make wise choices when you invest in new plants. It also helps you interpret the performance of plants that are already growing in your yard. A plant that's thriving obviously has the conditions it needs, but a plant that always seems weak or sick may be poorly sited; if so, you might as well move or replace it.

Throughout this book I discuss other issues to consider when you're choosing landscape plants, such as how tall and wide they grow, their typical shape or *habit,* and the appearance of their leaves and flowers. Those attributes are indisputably important. But first you have to ask, what plants would grow well on this particular site, in these particular conditions? Then you can pick and choose according to how different plants look. So this chapter covers the basics that determine survival versus failure. Everything else has to follow, because it doesn't matter how lovely a plant *could* be in ideal conditions if it dies or sulks when planted in *your* yard.

The term "growing conditions" encompasses temperature, light, moisture, soil quality, and other factors. I'll discuss these separately later in the chapter and also talk about how they interact. Understanding these factors is essential if you want to become an advanced gardener. But there are also some shortcut approaches to choosing plants, and I'll begin the chapter with these guidelines.

❦ STRATEGIES FOR CHOOSING PLANTS

How you choose plants depends mostly on your personality. It happens that I like to take a rational approach to decision-making and work through a checklist of considerations. I've included many examples of the checklist strategy in this book for those of you who work that way.

My deliberate approach drives some people crazy. They say it's too hard, there's too much to think about, it's too slow, and it inhibits spontaneity and passion. Or it just seems upside down to them. I'm suggesting that you study the site and pick a plant that would grow well there. Perhaps you feel impelled to choose a plant and then look for (or create) a place where you hope it will grow. Do that if you like. Sometimes it won't work because try as you may, some plants aren't meant to grow in your yard. Admittedly, my strategy doesn't always work either, because even plants that seemingly *should* match the site don't always come through.

Here's another personality issue. Do you want your landscape to blend in with the neighborhood or to stand out as something different? Do you want to grow the same or similar kinds of plants as your neighbors have, or are you always looking for

Choosing plants that will grow well in your yard takes patient observation and research. Explore local nurseries and gardens, make notes on what you see, and study reference books and plant encyclopedias.

uncommon or unusual plants? If you pursue the uncommon, you have an extra challenge, because you'll have to learn by trial and error whether or not each plant you covet will actually thrive in your yard. There's no prestige in having a rare plant if it looks miserable.

Some of us are obsessed with plants and eagerly spend hours studying the descriptions and photos in books, magazines, and catalogs, as well as visiting gardens and nurseries to see living specimens. You may not have the time or aptitude for all that. No problem. You can hire someone to choose plants for you. Scout for a trustworthy consultant and take his or her advice.

Be fair, but thorough, when considering a plant

Descriptions in books, magazines, and catalogs usually emphasize how beautiful a plant looks, but beauty is only part of the story. Adaptability, vigor, need for care, and "attitude" matter, too. As you spend time over the years living with and caring for a plant, you come to realize that how it acts is as important as how it looks. Consider a plant's drawbacks and weaknesses along with its charms and virtues.

People sometimes react to a disappointing or problematic plant by complaining that no one warned them about it. Often the truth is that information about that plant or problem was available, but they didn't seek it out. Learning about landscape plants before you buy them is like interviewing candidates for a job: you have to ask probing questions and read between the lines. It's easy to discover

CHECKLIST FOR CHOOSING PLANTS

Ask these questions when you're considering a tree, shrub, ground cover, perennial, or any other plant for your landscape. A knowledgeable staff person at a local nursery should be able to give you the answers, or you can look up the plant in a reference book or plant encyclopedia.

- Is it adapted to the climate—hardy enough to survive the winter, tolerant of summer heat, not vulnerable to late-spring or early-fall frosts, strong enough to hold up to wind and storms?

- Is it adapted to the site's soil conditions? Is it sensitive to soil pH? Does it require routine or special fertilization?

- Does it prefer moist or dry sites? Once established, can it survive on normal rainfall?

- How much sun or shade does it need or tolerate?

- Is it susceptible to any pests or diseases that are common in this area?

- How tall will it reach? How wide will it spread?

- How fast does it grow? How long does it live?

- Does it spread out of bounds? Does it produce unwanted seedlings? If you decide you don't want it anymore, is it hard to get rid of?

- Does it need pruning, trimming, grooming, staking, division, or other routine care? How often, and how big a job would that be?

what's good about a plant. The challenge is finding out about any shortcomings or attributes that might cause trouble or disappointment in your yard.

Yet don't automatically reject a plant just because you've heard someone badmouth it. Very few plants are totally worthless. Usually the truth is that the plant was put in the wrong site or situation, where its needs or tendencies were unsuitable or unwelcome. In a different context, the same plant might have been a perfect choice.

Crosschecking is a good strategy. If you're considering a particular plant, try to find a specimen growing in your area. Observe it yourself and see what you think. Look in at least two different books and compare what they say about the plant. Compare what you read with the impressions you get from talking to local experts or the staff at your favorite garden center.

Take hints from your surroundings

A straightforward way to assess what *could* grow in your landscape is to study what *does* grow throughout your neighborhood and region. Make a habit of observing plants as you drive and walk around. Notice what grows in untended areas—on vacant lots, along roadsides, or in undisturbed natural areas. Look at your neighbors' yards. Scrutinize commercial landscaping jobs. Go on garden tours. Visit any botanic garden or public display garden within driving distance. Looking at and learning about the plants around you is especially important when you move to a new location, but even after you've lived someplace a long time, it's still a helpful way to find ideas, inspiration, and answers. Here are some clues to gather and how to interpret them.

PLANTS FOR SPECIFIC SITUATIONS. If you're looking for plants to fill a particular role— a short evergreen plant to grow along the north side of your house, for example, or broad spreading bushes to spill down an embankment, or a flowering vine to train along a fence—watch for comparable situations as you drive or walk around town and see what's growing there. You'll get lots of ideas this way and notice candidates that might be just right for filling that spot in your yard. Choosing a plant because you've seen it thriving in a similar spot right in your

Every plant has various attributes that may count as virtues or shortcomings, depending on your situation. Lantana, for example, is a carefree, colorful ground cover for hot, dry sites in mild climates, where it self-seeds so readily that some people call it a weed. But on cold, wet, or shady sites, it doesn't grow at all.

own community, and based on your own observation of how it looks and grows, is a particularly reliable and satisfying way to make landscape decisions.

No matter where you live, there are avid gardeners experimenting with a wide variety of plants, especially now that gardening has become so popular. Learn from their efforts, and copy their successes. When you spot a plant you like, you may not know what it is. See if anyone can name it for you. Don't be shy about asking the homeowner or gardener. Most people would be pleased that you admired one of their plants and would gladly tell you all they know about it. Or if there's no one around to ask, make notes to yourself or take a snapshot that you can compare with pictures in books or show to a friend or acquaintance who knows about plants.

Chances are you haven't watched for landscape situations and plants before, but you weren't motivated. When you start working on your own yard, you've got a reason to notice these things. Looking for plants and learning about them can become a habit or an obsession just like spotting sports cars, dogs, antiques shops, or anything else you're interested in.

Eastern redbud, popular throughout the eastern United States, is a small deciduous tree that flowers in early spring. It normally has pink flowers (LEFT), *but if you want something special, you can buy a white-flowered redbud* (RIGHT).

Observe particular plants

True plant lovers develop the knack of watching for and recognizing particular kinds of plants. One reason for doing this is to determine whether a plant is likely to grow in your area. For example, let's say you saw a lovely photo of a redbud tree and think you'd like to have one. The question is, would a redbud grow in your yard? Redbuds bloom in spring, so you're mostly likely to notice one then. Keep an eye out as you travel around, and see if you spot any. Ask friends if they know of any local specimens and can tell you where to observe one. Be patient and persistent when tracking down a plant. It may take awhile to determine whether or not it's growing in your region. When you're ready, here's how to interpret your findings.

THE PLANT IS COMMONLY GROWN AND SEEMS TO THRIVE. This means you can plant it with confidence. If you see plenty of healthy redbuds around town, you can probably have one, too.

The only trouble with picking a popular, proven plant is that it might seem too common, not unique

or distinctive. Most people don't see this as a problem, but if you do, here's a good solution. There are common and uncommon varieties of almost any plant. Nearly all redbuds, for instance, have bright pink-purple flowers and plain green leaves. But if you want something special and are willing to take the trouble to order it, you can get a redbud with pure white flowers, or with purple leaves, or with variegated green-and-white leaves.

Going with an uncommon cultivar of a locally common plant has two big advantages over trying a rare, untested plant. First, odds are good that the uncommon form will grow as well as a common plant would, while an untested plant might die. Second, your friends, neighbors, and visitors (and, eventually, would-be buyers of your home) will appreciate it more. If a plant is too unfamiliar, people may think it's weird. But if residents of your area already know and love common redbuds, they'd be delighted and impressed to learn that you have a special, uncommon redbud.

THE PLANT SEEMS TO THRIVE BUT IS UNCOMMONLY GROWN. This could mean that it costs more than comparable plants, that it grows more slowly, or that it's more difficult for nurseries to produce. Or perhaps it's never been promoted or popularized and it isn't readily available. None of these issues should concern you; if you think the plant has merit and can find one to buy, go ahead.

THE PLANT IS COMMON BUT DOESN'T SEEM TO THRIVE. Forget it. Grow something else.

THE PLANT OCCURS, BUT IT'S UNCOMMON AND IT DOESN'T SEEM TO THRIVE. This calls for more investigation. There's probably a mismatch between the plant's requirements and the local climate and growing conditions. The plant might be stressed by winter cold or summer heat, sensitive to acid or alkaline soil, intolerant of wet or dry soil, vulnerable to certain insect pests or diseases, susceptible to acid rain or air pollution. Local landscapers, horticulturists, nursery staff, or other plant experts can probably identify and explain the problem to you.

Realizing the risk and challenge, you might decide to grow the plant anyway, if you can provide it with an unusually favorable site and/or give it extra care. Better yet, look for a similar or related plant with different requirements or tolerances. Research often reveals a suitable substitute. For example, eastern redbud, native throughout much of the eastern United States, wilts if the soil gets too dry in summer, while western redbud, a similar but shrubbier species native to California and Arizona, is well suited to arid climates or dry sites.

PLANT ISN'T SEEN AROUND THE AREA. If a plant seems to be absent from your area, you might well conclude that it's not adapted to the climate and growing conditions. On the other hand, perhaps no one has tried it. Which explanation is more likely? It depends partly on where you live. Around cities such as Philadelphia, Seattle, and San Francisco, where there's a long tradition of adventurous gardening, if a plant *can* be grown, it's pretty likely that someone has tried it. In rural areas or regions where gardening is less popular, many potentially successful plants have gone untested. By taking a chance, you could be the first to have an uncommon, special plant in your yard.

Distribution also depends on how long a plant has been in cultivation and readily available from nurseries. Many plants that are common now have been popular for centuries. Almost any place that these old favorites can be grown, they are being grown. But when new plants are discovered or developed, it takes awhile for nurseries to produce and promote them. Because they can be mass-propagated and grow fairly quickly, newly introduced perennials can go from rare to common status in just a few years. Slower-growing shrubs and trees may linger in the available-but-uncommon category for decades.

Notice plant combinations

Along with observing particular plants, watch for

As you observe plants around your neighborhood and region, watch for combinations— plants that grow in the same conditions and look good together, perhaps flowering at the same time like this white crab apple tree with white candytuft (an evergreen ground cover) growing beneath it.

pairs or groups of plants that grow in similar conditions and look good together. For example, if you're interested in redbud trees and happen to spot one, take note of what's growing underneath it and around it. What does well as a ground cover under redbuds in your area? Look for nearby shrubs and perennials that you could combine with a redbud to complement or contrast with its flowers and foliage. Revisit the tree when it's not in bloom to get ideas for companion plants that add interest later in the season.

Don't hesitate to ask for help

If you're daunted by the thought of choosing plants yourself, get help. There are several ways to proceed.

You could hire a landscape designer (see the box on page 28) to draft a plan for your yard (or any part of it) and specify appropriate plants. Then all you'd need to do afterward is learn the names of the plants and follow directions on how to care for them. To find a landscape designer, check listings in the Yellow Pages, ask at local nurseries, and watch crews at work around town and find out who's in charge of projects you admire. Before hiring anyone, ask to see a portfolio of their work and/or visit some landscapes they've designed.

You could observe the site where you want a plant to grow, noting the growing conditions; decide how big you'd want the plant to get and any special features you'd like it have (such as evergreen foliage, bright flowers in spring, and so on); and then ask a local plant expert to recommend something suitable. Finding a local expert is the key here. Have faith; there's someone out there. Every vicinity has its plant lovers. Ask at nurseries, watch the garden features in the local newspaper, attend talks and lectures, and go on garden tours. Some experts give advice freely, others consult for a small fee. Someone who can advise you what plant would grow well in a particular situation can't necessarily draw up a landscape design for you; knowing plants is one specialty, while design is something else. But if you only want to fill a certain gap or niche, you don't need a designer, you just need a suggestion of what plant to shop for.

Throughout this book I've included lists of plants recommended for various situations. This will help you by reducing the field of candidates, but you'll have to do some more research in order to make the final cut. You can find more information about and photos of these plants in the plant encyclopedia of *Taylor's Master Guide to Gardening*, in *Taylor's Guide to Growing North America's Favorite Plants*, or in other reference books. Or, since the plants I've recommended are all readily available and well known in areas where they grow well, if you photocopy a list and show it to local experts, they can help you select from it and they can probably name additional plants that would serve a similar role.

Experiment with untested plants

If you want to create a landscape that features uncommon plants, or if you're developing a site with challenging growing conditions, such as extensive areas of dry shade or poorly drained soil, you'll end up learning from experience and by trial and error. Although this is a time-consuming and often humbling process, the results can be magnificent. To approach landscaping this way, you have to love plants, be willing to change your mind and revise your plans over time, and welcome unexpected successes and not fret over the inevitable failures.

It's easy to get started. Study reference books and catalogs, make shopping lists of plants that sound wonderful and are likely candidates for your growing conditions, and buy one of each, collecting as many plants as you can find and afford. (For landscape use, you often need more than one plant of a kind, but you can buy or propagate extras later after you've determined that a plant will grow for you. For experimenting, one is usually enough.)

MAKE A TRIAL BED. You may as well admit that untested plants are a gamble. Don't even bother setting them in what you hope will be a permanent place in your landscape. That's generally too optimistic. They may not even survive, let alone thrive. If you're going to end up replacing or moving them later, why not face up to that now and put them in a special bed until you see how they perform.

Prepare at least one bed (or multiple beds if you have different growing conditions to deal with), plant your new plants there, and watch how they grow. This bed isn't for show; it's a trial ground. Don't worry too much about "designing" it, as you'll end up discarding, replacing, moving, or propagating all the plants over time. If you're worried about appearances and you think such a bed would look too utilitarian for your yard, fence it off, or just edge or screen it with some colorful annuals (in the ground or in pots) and no one will notice that it's there.

Record-keeping is important. Keep a list of which plants you buy, when and where you bought them, and where you put them in the ground. Be sure to label each plant, and sketch maps or planting diagrams, too, so you can be sure to keep track of what's where.

Observe herbaceous plants for at least a year or two, and watch woody plants for a few years. Some plants will die. Others will survive, but you'll be unimpressed with them. Some will thrive and delight you. As you discover which ones succeed and see how they grow, you'll get ideas for where and how to use the plants in your landscape, and you can start moving them to their permanent homes.

This is the cardinal rule for choosing landscape plants. Any place where you might dig a hole and plant a tree, shrub, or other plant has a set of circumstances that affect how that plant will grow. Winter cold, summer heat, wind, exposure to sun or shade, timing and amount of precipitation, depth and quality of the soil, the presence of other plants or buildings nearby, pests and diseases that are widespread problems in your area—these all influence a plant's survival and appearance.

Plants are more or less adaptable, but they each have certain limits. If the growing conditions are within those limits, the plant thrives. If they're not, it suffers or dies. Fortunately, there are plants for every situation. In nature, plants grow in rain forests and deserts, marshes and prairies. In landscaping too, there are plants for any setting. To make a good match, you start by observing the conditions, then do some research to determine what plants would grow well there and select from those candidates.

This attitude of accepting and working with your climate, soil, and site requires more thought and planning at first, but it involves much less work in the long run and gives much happier results than the opposite approach of buying plants regardless of their needs and then trying to alter or modify the growing conditions to suit them.

Temperature, light, water, and soil are the main factors affecting how well a plant grows in your yard, how vigorous and contented it looks, when it sprouts out and when it goes dormant, and when and how it blooms. These factors are all interrelated, but I'll talk about soil later and focus on climate and exposure first.

Length of the growing season

Plants grow year-round in places such as San Diego and Miami, but in most parts of the continental United States there's a more or less dramatic difference between winter, the dormant season when deciduous trees and shrubs are leafless and herbaceous plants have died down, and the time from spring to fall when flowers and fresh new foliage fill the scene. The growing season begins when plants sense that days are getting longer and that air and soil temperatures are warming, and it slows to an end when days get shorter again and the air and soil cool off. Temperature and daylength are the signals that tell plants when to grow and when to rest.

Many plants adapt readily to either short or long growing seasons, but when you're making choices it's worth asking, is our growing season long enough for this plant to develop, mature, and make a good show? And conversely, will this plant look good throughout the growing season, or will it poop out early? In northern or mountain regions where the growing season may be as short as four months, look for plants that start growing as early as possible, and realize that plants that don't start blooming until fall may flower briefly, if at all. In southern or coastal regions where the growing season may continue for eight to nine months or longer, look for plants that bloom continually or repeatedly, not just in a single burst, and for plants whose foliage looks good throughout the summer and fall. Where the season is long, it's a waste of space to grow perennials and shrubs that bloom briefly in spring or early summer and then look ratty or tattered for months afterward.

Frost

The growing season is typically several weeks longer than the frost-free season—the number of days between the last frost in spring and the first frost in fall. You need to be aware of the average frost dates for your region if you want to fill flower beds with tender annuals such as zinnias or petunias, to use tropical plants in outdoor containers or beds, or to grow heat-loving vegetables such as tomatoes and squash. Some annual plants keep flowering or producing month after month, but others go to seed and give up early. Where the frost-free season is longer than four to five months, you'll need to make two or more successive plantings of these short-lived annuals to renew or sustain the display.

FROST SENSITIVITY VARIES. Many perennial and woody landscape plants flower and sprout new leaves before the last spring frost, or continue blooming and retain their foliage through the first few frosts in fall. The flowers on spring-blooming daffodils and forsythia, for instance, and on fall-blooming asters and chrysanthemums aren't dam-

The lovely blossoms of 'Christmas Cheer' rhododendron, along with those of flowering cherries, magnolias, and many other shrubs and trees that flower in early spring, are vulnerable to frost. A cold snap turns the petals brown immediately.

Ivy geranium is treated as an annual or a house-plant in most parts of the country, but in a frost-free climate like southern California's, it grows as big as a shrub and blooms outdoors year-round.

aged unless temperatures drop into the mid-20s. Other plants are more vulnerable. If flowering cherries and magnolias are hit by even a light frost in spring, their petals get brown and mushy and drop off. If Japanese maples get frosted in fall, the leaves wither and turn dull tan instead of bright red.

FROST OCCURRENCE VARIES. Frost doesn't strike evenly across a large area. Its distribution is patchy but predictable. Go out and look around on frosty spring or fall mornings and you can see patterns in your yard. In some places the ground will be white; in others, not. Frost strikes first in open, sunny areas; this can happen even if the air temperature is higher than 32°F. Under a tree or close to a building, frost may not form until air temperatures drop to 30°F, 28°F, or colder. Driving around on a frosty morning, you'll notice that low-lying valleys may be covered with a heavy frost whereas surrounding hillsides are untouched—that's because cold air flows downhill, like water. Because pavement and buildings retain so much warmth, densely developed urban areas have a frost-free season several weeks longer than the neighboring suburbs and countryside do.

You probably didn't take frost patterns into account when you bought your house (some gardeners do!), but now that you've moved in, watch how

frost strikes your property. In cold regions, take advantage of sheltered pockets that escape early and late frosts by putting annuals and other sensitive plants there so you can enjoy a few extra weeks of color in spring and fall. Where winters are mild, use frost-free spots to grow tropicals outdoors year-round.

Summer temperatures

Any plant grows best at a certain temperature range, and if temperatures get too hot or too cold, it slows down, goes dormant, or dies. The optimum temperatures (and also the extremes that are tolerated) vary greatly from one plant to another. Grasses (including turf, ornamental, and weedy types) are a good example, as they fall into two main categories. Cool-season grasses, such as Kentucky bluegrass and feather reed grass, are lush and green in cool weather but go dormant and turn brown in hotter weather. Warm-season grasses, such as Bermuda grass and pampas grass, don't turn green until the weather gets good and warm, and they turn brown again as soon as it cools off in fall.

In plant descriptions in catalogs and gardening books, the expression "Thrives in hot weather" roughly translates into night temperatures of 70°F or higher and days in the 90s or even above 100°F. A plant that's said to prefer cool summers likes nights in the 40s or 50s and daytime highs in the 60s or 70s. Most plants grow best if there's at least a 10-degree difference in day and night temperatures.

TAKE ADVANTAGE OF MICROCLIMATES. To some extent, you can push the limits and grow plants not normally suited to your summer climate. To succeed with plants that need extra heat, put them in full sun on a south-facing slope; against the south or southwest side of a building, fence, or wall; or next to a stone or cement walk, patio, or drive. A location next to brickwork, stone, or masonry is especially good because these materials absorb heat in the day and radiate it at night. To protect plants from excess heat, put them in a place that's shaded from the midday and afternoon sun, water if needed to prevent wilting, and use enough mulch to help keep the soil from getting hot and dry.

HEAT AND FLOWERS. Where summers are cool, heat-loving plants may grow healthy leaves but fail to bloom or bear fruit. For instance, you can grow a tomato plant in Seattle, but you may not pick any ripe, red tomatoes; you can grow a crape myrtle, but it may not bloom. On the other hand, cool summers mean you can grow glorious lupines, delphiniums, and fuchsias.

In general, individual flowers last longer in cool weather than in hot. Consider roses, for example. Many kinds of roses (hybrid teas, floribundas, modern landscape roses, new English roses, and others) have an unusually wide temperature tolerance and bloom over a very long season through hot and cool weather. Their flowers remain colorful and fresh-looking for two to three weeks in cool weather, but the petals fade and drop after just a few days when it's hot.

Prickly pear cacti and citrus trees are undaunted by the glaring sun and 115°F temperatures of a summer day in Tucson.

PLANTS THAT FLOWER IN HOT WEATHER

Where summers are hot, many popular, old-fashioned garden plants don't do well—the flowers fade or drop off fast, or the foliage gets tattered and unsightly, or the plant dies young. Other plants, however, grow and flower best in hot weather. Every year nurseries introduce more new heat-loving plants—native species as well as discoveries from Mexico, Central America, South Africa, and Australia.

- **Anisacanthus** (*Anisacanthus wrightii*) is a small evergreen shrub with red-orange flowers.

- **Angel's trumpet** (*Brugmansia*, formerly *Datura*) is a bushy, upright shrub with huge trumpet-shaped flowers in shades of lavender, pink, orange, gold, or white.

- **Bird-of-paradise** (*Caesalpinia gilliesii*) is a fast-growing shrub with finely divided leaves and yellow flowers. **Red bird-of-paradise** (*C. pulcherrima*) has glorious clusters of red-orange flowers.

- **Cannas** (*Canna* cvs.) are perennials that form patches of upright, leafy stems and bloom all summer in shades of red, orange, pink, or yellow.

- **Tropical, or Chinese, hibiscus** (*Hibiscus rosa-sinensis*) are sturdy, erect shrubs, several feet tall, with showy single or double flowers, 2 to 10 inches wide, in shades of red, orange, pink, yellow, white, or bicolor. **Rose-of-Sharon** (*H. syriacus*) is similar but hardy and bears single or double flowers in shades of lilac, lavender, blue, or white.

- **Crape myrtles** (*Lagerstroemia indica*) are small trees, usually 10 to 25 feet tall, that bloom all summer with showy clusters of pink, rose, lavender, crimson, or white.

- **Mandevillas** are vines. *Mandevilla sanderi* 'Red Riding Hood' is compact and bears dark pink flowers. *M. × amoena* 'Alice du Pont' is larger, with big pale pink flowers. Chilean jasmine (*M. laxa*) has fragrant white flowers. Golden trumpet (*Allamanda cathartica*) is similar to mandevillas and bears large yellow flowers.

- **Blackfoot daisy** (*Melampodium leucanthum*) is a low, mounded, shrubby perennial with daisylike white-and-yellow blossoms.

- **Oleanders** (*Nerium oleander*) are typically large shrubs that bloom all summer with clusters of single or double flowers in shades of pink, red, salmon, cream, or pure white.

- **Passionflowers** (*Passiflora*) are vigorous vines with large, lobed leaves and complex flowers in shades of violet, blue, red, pink, or white.

- **Cape plumbago** (*Plumbago auriculata*) is a shrubby vine with ice blue or white flowers. It blooms nonstop for months.

- **Pomegranate** (*Punica granatum*) is a rounded shrub with bright orange or white flowers. The cultivars with double, carnation-like flowers bloom all summer but don't bear fruit.

- **Yellow bells** (*Tecoma stans*) is a fast-growing shrub with large, clear yellow flowers and bold compound leaves.

- **Verbenas** (*Verbena*) are perennials. 'Homestead Purple', 'Sissinghurst Pink', and other low-growing hybrid cultivars hug the ground and spread 3 feet or wider, blooming from spring to fall in shades of purple, pink, or red.

- **Chaste tree** (*Vitex agnus-castus*) has slender spikes of lilac flowers and spicy-scented compound leaves.

Bougainvillea, purple-top verbena, and Mexican daisy are some of the many perennials and shrubs that bloom best in hot weather.

HEAT AND FOLIAGE. For most kinds of leaves, it's meaningless to talk about the effect of heat alone, since there's so much difference between dry heat and moist heat and between a hot shady site and a hot sunny site.

For example, in Houston, where 100°F temperatures are often accompanied by 95 percent relative humidity, conditions are just right for plants such as elephant's ears, which have huge tender leaves. But in Phoenix, where 100°F temperatures may go along with 5 percent relative humidity, you see leafless cacti and shrubs and trees with tiny leaflets that drop off when it gets too hot and dry. Big tender leaves would dry to a crisp in Phoenix.

Colored and variegated leaves are affected not only by temperature but also by light intensity and daylength. The interactions can take many forms. Some perennials, shrubs, and trees have leaves that start out blue, purple, red, gold, or striped when they emerge as new growth in the cool of spring, then turn plain green in hot weather. Other plants start out green and then turn colored when the weather gets hot. Some evergreen plants are green in summer and turn bronze, coppery, purple, or other colors as temperatures cool off in fall, and, of course, many deciduous shrubs and trees have vivid fall color. At any temperature, usually full or part sun produces the richest, most intense colors. (For a list of recommended plants with colored foliage, see the box on page 56.)

HEAT ZONES. The American Horticultural Society has published a heat zone map that divides the United States into 12 zones based on the average number of days each year when the temperature climbs above 86°F. The idea is that someday a great number of garden plants will be rated according to their ability to tolerate fewer or more days of heat.

Personally, I think the heat zone concept is a great oversimplification. It's meaningless to focus on heat alone, since plant performance and survival are affected by the interaction between heat, soil moisture, humidity, and exposure. There were enough problems already with misunderstandings caused by the single-mindedness of the hardiness zone system (see below), and adding a second zone system just leads to more confusion. At any rate, the heat zone system is too new to be widely used yet, so I'll disregard it in this book.

Winter survival

A plant is considered *hardy* in your climate if it can survive an average winter in good condition without special protection. A *tender* plant is damaged or killed in an average winter. These are relative terms; a plant that's hardy in Dallas could be tender in Detroit. To be more precise, horticulturists use different systems of measuring and rating hardiness. One of the most familiar and most widely used systems is the USDA hardiness zone system (see the box on page 226). Checking its zone rating is a good way to estimate if a plant is hardy enough for your climate; it's not a guarantee, but it's a handy guideline.

Plant parts differ in hardiness. A cold snap can destroy flower buds without affecting the leaf buds, blacken leaves without hurting the stems, or kill a plant's top without damaging its underground parts. For several groups of woody plants, including bamboos, citrus, hollies, and rhododendrons, enthusiasts have compiled records stating at what degree Fahrenheit different parts have been harmed or remained unhurt. This information is sometimes given in catalogs and reference books along with or instead of USDA zone ratings.

Fall foliage colors vary from year to year, depending on the weather. A warm, rainy summer followed by a cool, dry fall produces the most vivid display.

USDA HARDINESS ZONES

The United States Department of Agriculture (USDA) has divided the United States and Canada into 11 hardiness zones that correspond to the average low temperatures in winter. For example, USDA Zone 5 has average winter lows of −10° to −20°F. A plant that is rated as hardy to Zone 5 should normally survive the winters in that zone, and also in warmer zones, but is liable to freeze and die in colder zones.

To find out what USDA zone you live in, refer to the standard USDA map, or better yet, ask the staff at a local nursery or an experienced local gardener. To find the USDA zone rating for any plant you might want to grow, check the write-ups in reference books and catalogs. Most landscape plants have been assigned a USDA zone number, but don't be surprised when you encounter discrepancies and disagreements. One source

may say that English lavender is hardy to Zone 5, while another book assigns it to Zone 6. That's because winter survival depends on many factors other than cold temperatures, such as wind chill, snow cover, and soil moisture, along with growing conditions the previous summer, the plant's age and general vigor, and pure fate.

Also keep in mind that the USDA zone system refers only to cold hardiness; it doesn't describe climate in general. For instance, Halifax, Nova Scotia; Columbus, Ohio; and Santa Fe, New Mexico, are all assigned to USDA Zone 5 because of their winter lows, but in other ways these cities have quite different climates. This points out that the hardiness zone system is a very specialized rating and not a broadly useful concept.

Gardeners routinely attribute winter damage to cold temperatures, but other factors are often involved. To increase winter survival, you need to be aware of these factors and know how to anticipate and mitigate their effects, as described below and on page 283.

WIND CHILL. Wind makes cold air feel even colder; this affects woody plants as it does people. Exposure to or shelter from wind can make a difference equivalent to one or two USDA hardiness zones. So, for example, if you have an enclosed, sheltered, windless site in Zone 6, you might succeed with Zone 7 plants. But if you have an exposed, windy site in Zone 6, it's a good precaution to rely on plants rated as hardy to Zone 5.

SNOW COVER. Snow is an excellent mulch. It's very effective at regulating soil temperature, preventing frost heaving, and protecting roots and any other plant parts that it covers. After a cold winter, you can often see the benefit of snow on spring-flowering shrubs, as branches that were under the snow are lined with bloom, while higher branches are barren because flower buds that were exposed to the air got frozen. A perennial, ground cover, or low shrub that would freeze in an exposed part of your yard where snow melts quickly might survive and thrive in a corner where snow accumulates and forms a continuous cover from late fall through spring. Reliable snow cover can make a difference equivalent to one USDA hardiness zone.

SOIL MOISTURE. In rainy climates or wet sites, many plants die in winter because their roots rot, not because of cold. Root rot is a common problem anyplace where the soil stays wet and muddy for weeks

at a time in winter or spring. By contrast, plants in arid climates or on well-drained sites sometimes survive temperatures much colder than predicted. Good drainage can make a difference equivalent to one or two USDA hardiness zones.

GENETIC VARIATION. In most species that occur naturally across a wide geographic region, plants found wild on northern or high-altitude sites can tolerate more cold than southern or lowland populations can. Nurseries have collected and propagated unusually hardy strains of several native trees and some native shrubs. It's worth seeking these out if you want to try growing plants that are not normally considered hardy in your zone.

SUMMER HEAT. Remember that there's absolutely no correlation between USDA hardiness zones and average summer temperatures. Dallas and Seattle both have Zone 8 winters but have very different summers.

Summer heat can affect winter survival for better or worse; it depends on the plant. Some have increased cold hardiness if they're growing where warm summers allow them to build up lots of carbohydrate reserves, while others are so weakened by summer heat that their hardiness is diminished after a hot season.

CHILLING REQUIREMENTS. We usually worry about too much cold in winter, but for some plants and some situations, the concern is getting enough exposure to cold. Peonies, poppies, tulips, lilacs, apples, birches, and some other kinds of herbaceous perennials or deciduous shrubs and trees require a winter dormancy or rest period—generally a certain number of days when the average tem-

Winter is particularly hard on broad-leaved evergreens, such as this Oregon grape. It's not just the cold that damages them. Heavy snow or ice breaks their stems, and the combination of cold air and bright sun will "burn" their leaves, or make them turn brown and drop off.

perature is below 40°F. Otherwise they may not bloom well, or they may gradually weaken and die. For some of these plants, horticulturists have selected or developed special varieties that require less cold. Look for these if you live in a region where winters are mild.

Sun and shade

All plants need light to grow and flower, but some require more light than others in order to perform well. To keep it simple, most books and catalogs name three lighting conditions—full sun, part sun (or part shade), and full shade—and describe plants as adapted to or tolerant of these different light levels.

"Full sun" generally means direct, unblocked exposure to the sun for at least six hours a day during the growing season. In northern or cloudy climates where the sun isn't too hot, many sun-loving plants do better with continuous sun from dawn to dusk. Across the southern United States where the summer sun is intense, many plants that are described as needing "full sun" actually appreciate some shade during the midday hours.

"Part sun" or "part shade" can refer to a site that gets direct sun for a few hours a day and is shaded the

Trees cast ever-moving shadows. The patterns of sun and shade vary from dawn to dusk and from season to season. In July, the sun shines on these pink astilbes for a few hours in the morning, then they're shaded for the rest of the day. This counts as part shade.

So many limbs have been removed from this big old oak tree that you look through it and see patches of sky. The kind of shade it casts is called high, light, or dappled. Rhododendrons, ferns, and many other plants grow well in a situation like this.

rest of the time by a nearby building, or to the dappled pattern of light and shade cast by trees with high, open branching and not-too-dense foliage. Part shade beside a building is a fine situation for many plants. Part shade under or near a tree is fine at first but is often a temporary condition. Over a few years' time a site that's partially shaded by trees frequently becomes fully shaded as the trees close in overhead. Plants below get less and less light unless you keep pruning off nearby trees' lower limbs and thinning their canopies. In this situation, if you won't be able to keep up with the pruning, don't choose plants designated for part shade; plan ahead and get ones that tolerate full shade.

"Full shade" means little or no direct exposure to the sun, because the site is shaded by trees, buildings, or other barriers. Usually we talk about plants that "tolerate" full shade, since only a minority of plants actually require or prefer it.

Most plants that prefer shade also prefer moist soil, but shady sites aren't necessarily moist. Dry shade is common under the eaves of a house and under trees with aggressive, shallow roots (not all trees are greedy, but many are). Watch plants in these situations and supply water as needed.

NOT ENOUGH SUN. If they aren't getting enough light, most plants develop weak, straggly stems and thin leaves that are spaced farther apart than usual, and they flower sparsely or not at all. Plants that are supposed to have purple or gold leaves may be plain green instead. These symptoms indicate that you should move or get rid of those plants and replace them with more shade-tolerant species, and/or do some pruning on nearby trees.

Plants that get light from one side but are shaded on the other side may grow and flower well, but they typically become asymmetric as their stems reach toward the light. Plants growing right next to a building, for instance, face out into the open, regardless of what compass direction that is. When you look out a window at nearby plants, you mostly see the backs of their leaves and flowers.

This bed of hostas and ferns runs along the edge of a shady woods. They're all leaning away from the dark trees and toward the open sky. At this time, the hostas are still getting enough light to bloom, but they will cease flowering in future years if the trees go unpruned.

PLANTS FOR SHADY SITES

These plants generally grow well on sites that are shaded for part of the day by nearby buildings or tall trees, and some tolerate full shade all day. Plants marked * require a certain amount of light to bloom well; if the site is too shady, they produce healthy foliage but no flowers.

SMALL TREES AND LARGE SHRUBS

Few large trees tolerate full shade, but these small (under 25 feet tall) trees and large shrubs adapt well to partial shade.

Japanese maple (*Acer palmatum*)
Serviceberries (*Amelanchier*)
Eastern redbud (*Cercis canadensis*)
Fringe trees (*Chionanthus*)
Flowering dogwoods and cornelian cherry
    (*Cornus*)
Silverbells (*Halesia*)
Witch hazels (*Hamamelis*)
Sweet bay magnolia
    (*Magnolia virginiana*)
Stewartias (*Stewartia*)

MEDIUM AND SMALL SHRUBS

Aucuba (*Aucuba japonica*)
Some bamboos
Boxwoods (*Buxus*)
Sweet shrubs (*Calycanthus*)
Camellias (*Camellia*)
False cypress (*Chamaecyparis*)
Summersweets (*Clethra*)
Enkianthus (*Enkianthus campanulatus*)
Hydrangeas (*Hydrangea*)
Most hollies (*Ilex*)
Mountain laurel (*Kalmia latifolia*)
Leucothoes (*Leucothoe*)
Spicebushes (*Lindera*)
Mahonias (*Mahonia*)
Siberian cypress (*Microbiota decussata*)

VINES AND CLIMBERS

Akebia (*Akebia quinata*)
Porcelain berry
    (*Ampelopsis brevipedunculata*)
Dutchman's pipe (*Aristolochia durior*)
Some clematis (*Clematis*)
Wintercreepers (*Euonymus fortunei* cvs.)
Carolina jasmine
    (*Gelsemium sempervirens*)
Ivies (*Hedera*)
Climbing hydrangea
    (*Hydrangea petiolaris*)
Some honeysuckles (*Lonicera*)
Virginia creeper and Boston ivy
    (*Parthenocissus*)
'Zépherine Drouhin' and some other roses
    (*Rosa*)
Hydrangea vine
    (*Schizophragma hydrangeoides*)
Star jasmine
    (*Trachelospermum jasminoides*)

Bayberry and wax myrtle (*Myrica*)
Heavenly bamboo (*Nandina domestica*)
Sweet olives (*Osmanthus*)
Andromedas (*Pieris*)
Pittosporums (*Pittosporum*)
Most rhododendrons and azaleas
    (*Rhododendron*)
Sweet boxes (*Sarcococca*)
Skimmia (*Skimmia japonica*)
Snowberries and coralberries
    (*Symphoricarpos*)
Yews (*Taxus*)
Cleyera (*Ternstroemia gymnanthera*)
Highbush blueberry
    (*Vaccinium corymbosum*)
Some viburnums (*Viburnum*)

GROUND COVERS AND PERENNIALS

Plants marked * survive but don't flower well in too-dense shade. Plants marked # can be used to form fairly dense, weed-proof, long-term ground covers on sites too shady for turfgrass.

Bear's breeches (*Acanthus*)
Bishop's weed (#*Aegopodium podagraria*)
Carpet bugle, bugleweed, or ajuga
    (*#*Ajuga*)
Lady's mantle (*#*Alchemilla mollis*)
Wild gingers (#*Asarum*)
Bergenias (*#*Bergenia*)
Green-and-gold, or golden star
    (*#*Chrysogonum virginianum*)
Bugbanes (*Cimicifuga*)
Lily-of-the-valley (*#*Convallaria majalis*)
Bleeding hearts (*Dicentra*)
Foxgloves (*Digitalis*)
Bishop's hats (#*Epimedium*)
#Ferns
Wintergreen, or checkerberry
    (*Gaultheria procumbens*)
Sweet woodruff (#*Galium odoratum*)
Hellebores (#*Helleborus*)
Coralbells (*#*Heuchera*)
Hostas (*#*Hosta*)
Dwarf crested iris (*#*Iris cristata*)
Dead nettles (*#*Lamium*)
Lilyturfs (#*Liriope*)
Moneywort (*Lysimachia nummularia*)
Mondo grasses (#*Ophiopogon*)
Moss
Pachysandra (#*Pachysandra*)
Creeping phlox
    (*#*Phlox divaricata, P. stolonifera*)
Jacob's ladders (*Polemonium*)
Solomon's seals (*Polygonatum*)
Primroses (*Primula*)
Lungworts (*#*Pulmonaria*)
Foamflowers (*#*Tiarella*)
Piggyback plant (#*Tolmiea menziesii*)
Toad lilies (*Tricyrtis*)
Myrtle or periwinkle (*#*Vinca*)
Violets (*#*Viola*)

White-variegated hostas and white-striped ribbon grass brighten the shady sitting area under this well-pruned cherry tree. The sheared hedge behind this border is made of yew, one of the few conifers that tolerate shade.

TOO MUCH SUN. Wilting is the most common result of too much sun, but it's caused not so much by the light itself as by the combination of too much sun and the resulting high temperatures and dryness. Many plants can tolerate extra sun if you water them enough to keep the soil from drying out. Bleached or faded leaves, leaves that are smaller than normal and perhaps curled or distorted, and leaves that turn crisp and brown around the edge are other symptoms that often indicate too much sun. If you have a plant that shows this kind of leaf damage, you suspect too much sun is the problem, and the plant is small enough that you can dig it up and move it, try transplanting it to a shadier location.

Note that whenever you move, plant, or transplant a plant in full leaf (not a dormant plant), it's particularly vulnerable to too much sun for the first week or so, even if it will be sun-tolerant later when established. Prevent drastic wilting and leaf damage by planting during a spell of cloudy or rainy weather, or use an inverted box or basket, a tepee of leafy twigs, or an old sheet or similar fabric to provide temporary shade for newly moved plants.

WINTER SUN. Plants don't need sun when they're dormant, and the combination of bright sun and cold air can be damaging, particularly to broad-leaved evergreens. Even on cold winter days when air temperatures are below 32°F, the sun can warm dark-colored foliage and stems up to 80°F or warmer. But as soon as the sun sets or goes behind a cloud, the leaves or stems cool off instantly. Such sudden and dramatic temperature changes can make the foliage on evergreen trees, shrubs, vines, and perennials turn brown, tan, or white. The discoloration usually shows on the south or southwest side of the plant, and it's intensified if snow cover reflects the sunlight back up onto the plant. Severe sunscald can weaken or kill these plants. To prevent this, plant evergreens where they will be partially or fully shaded by buildings or trees (even dormant deciduous trees cast sufficient shade for this purpose) during the winter months.

Conditions next to a building

To a plant, the difference between growing along the north or the south side of a house — normally a distance of 50 feet or less — can equal that between two sites 100 miles apart. It's a matter of temperature more than of light. The north side of a building is somewhat cooler, and the south side is much warmer, than nearby sites in the open. A fence or wall affects light and warmth in ways that are similar to the effect of a building, but less pronounced.

SOUTH-FACING WALLS. If the south wall is exposed to the full direct sun, both the air and soil beside it get hotter and drier than anyplace else on the property. A white or light-colored wall reflects glaring sunlight onto nearby plants, while a dark wood, brick, or masonry wall absorbs heat from the sun and stays warm for hours afterward. This extra warmth and dryness makes nearby plants start growing earlier than usual in spring and continue later in the fall. In summer, the extra warmth is a bonus in cool climates and coaxes more blooms from heat-loving shrubs and perennials such as roses, butterfly bush, lavender, salvias, and warm-season ornamental grasses that might languish out in the open. Where summers are hot, south-wall conditions quickly bake plants with soft green leaves, but there are plenty of shrubs and perennials with tough, leathery, or hairy foliage that can take the sun and heat, and succulents can, too.

NORTH-FACING WALLS. The soil beside a north-facing wall gets direct sun for only a few morning and evening hours in midsummer, if at all, so plants growing there are protected from extreme heat and dryness. During the growing season, conditions here are quite favorable for many plants, unless the area is heavily shaded by nearby trees or other buildings. The early and late sun plus bright skylight at midday provides enough light for sturdy growth, and temperatures are moderate. Year-round, air and

Shaded by tall trees and sheltered by a wood fence along the left side and the two-story brick house in the rear, the camellias and azaleas around this patio are protected from extremes of heat, cold, and wind. The microclimate here is milder than average regional conditions.

soil temperatures next to a north wall can be 20 to 30 degrees cooler than beside a south wall. Ironically, the area beside a north wall is less stressful for plants in winter, too, because conditions are consistently cold, with little variation from day to night or week to week. It's easier for most plants to survive continuous cold than alternate heating and cooling.

EAST- AND WEST-FACING WALLS. East- and west-wall conditions are intermediate between north and south. Both offer more sun than north walls but avoid the extreme heat and dryness of south walls. Typically, east walls, which get morning sun, are cooler, moister, and less stressful to plants than west walls, which bake in the hot afternoon sun. You can grow almost anything next to an east wall. Choose plants with tough leaves that don't wilt readily for next to a sunny west wall.

EXPOSURE AND EVERGREENS. Orientation has special impact on broad-leaved evergreens, such as hollies, rhododendrons, and English ivy, in climates where winter days can be sunny but with subfreezing temperatures. On cold clear days, the midday and afternoon sun can warm the surface of dark evergreen leaves up to 60°F or higher. But when the sun sets or goes behind a cloud, the leaves are suddenly chilled to air temperature. Those sudden and extreme temperature changes "burn" or discolor the leaves; such damaged leaves fall off in spring and have to be replaced. Winter burn is more likely and more severe if the evergreens are planted on the south or west side of a building, less so if they're on the north or east side.

Precipitation and soil moisture

In any climate, newly planted trees, shrubs, ground covers, grasses, and perennials may need watering for several weeks or months, until their roots get established. Afterward, a landscape plant that's matched to the climate and site should be able to survive on normal precipitation.

Regarding soil moisture, there are two issues: how much water falls onto the site, and how much is absorbed and retained. Even in a rainy climate, places where the soil is rocky or steeply sloped will dry out faster than normal, and in arid climates there are low, wet spots where runoff collects. Deep soil retains more moisture than shallow soil, clay holds more water than sand, and soil that's been amended with organic matter and topped with mulch stays moist much longer than bare, mineral soil. So it's not enough to match the plant to the climate in a general way. The plant has to match the particular hole where you're going to put it.

Another factor is the rate of water loss to the environment, or evapotranspiration. Water evaporates much faster from the surface of the soil and through plant leaves when weather conditions are hot, sunny, or windy than in cool, cloudy, or still weather. A plant that can easily survive a monthlong summer dry spell in foggy coastal Oregon might not make it through a week in California's ovenlike Central Valley. When you're choosing plants for a dry spot, think about both the soil and the demands of your climate.

WATERING. Watering allows you to grow countless plants that wouldn't survive otherwise, and it stimulates faster, lusher growth on any plants that are stressed by dryness. How much you want to rely on watering depends on your attitudes, priorities, and budget. Occasional watering can be a pleasant task that doesn't involve much trouble or expense. For plants that routinely need watering, consider an automatic irrigation system. (For more on watering, see page 261.)

In theory, it doesn't matter to a plant whether the soil gets moistened by rain or by irrigation, but in reality, plants respond almost instantly and with obvious gratitude to a warm, soaking rain, especially if it comes after a dry spell. Leaves that were dusty, grayish, and perhaps a little shriveled before the rain look clean, bright, and expanded afterward. Although you can grow beautiful plants in an irrigated landscape, you can't duplicate that rain-washed phenomenon; you just have to appreciate it when it happens.

CONSERVING WATER. There are several ways you can cut back on watering your landscape. Xeriscaping was designed to reduce water use in arid climates ("xeric" means "dry"), but its basic principles make good sense wherever you live:

- Group plants into zones, according to how much water they need. Put plants that need the most water close to the house. Farther away, use plants that need occasional deep soaking or no watering at all.
- If you want a lawn, keep it small and use a grass that's adapted to your climate. If you're not too attached to turfgrass, consider replacing the lawn with paved areas for outdoor living and beds of colorful, low-maintenance, unthirsty ground covers.
- Before planting, improve the soil by digging deep and adding plenty of organic matter.
- Cover the soil around and between plants with mulch to keep it cooler and to retain moisture.
- Irrigate efficiently, using a system designed to avoid waste. Monitor how much water is applied and how far it soaks into the soil.

Dominated by the massive trunk of a tall palm tree, the xeriscape in this Phoenix front yard includes sculptural, succulent aloes, agaves, and cacti, along with low, flowering clumps of penstemon and evening primrose.

PLANTS FOR DRY SITES OR DRY CLIMATES

After two to three years on a site, when these plants have established good root systems, they can survive for several weeks or even months (depending on the evapotranspiration rate) without rain or irrigation. Low-growing species or cultivars of plants marked # may be used as ground covers.

TREES

Many acacias (*Acacia*)
Strawberry tree (*Arbutus unedo*)
Most cedars (*Cedrus*)
Hackberries (*Celtis*)
Palo verdes (*Cercidium* and *Parkinsonia*)
Desert willow (*Chilopsis linearis*)
Russian olive (*Elaeagnus angustifolia*)
Most eucalyptus (*Eucalyptus*)
Kentucky coffee tree (*Gymnocladus dioicus*)
Goldenrain trees (*Koelreuteria*)
Crape myrtles (*Lagerstroemia*)
Sweet bay (*Laurus nobilis*)
Olive (*Olea europaea*)
Most pines (*Pinus*)
Chinese pistache (*Pistacia chinensis*)
Mesquites (*Prosopis*)
Locusts (*Robinia*)
Japanese pagoda tree (*Sophora japonica*)
Jujube (*Ziziphus jujuba*)

VINES

Queen's wreath (*Antigonon leptopus*)
Cross vine (*Bignonia capreolata*)
Carolina jasmine (*Gelsemium sempervirens*)
Silver fleece vine (*Polygonum aubertii*)
Wisteria (*Wisteria*)

PERENNIALS

Lily-of-the-Nile (*Agapanthus*)
Desert marigold (*Baileya multiradiata*)
Jupiter's beard (*Centranthus ruber*)
Most #euphorbias (*Euphorbia*)
#Blue fescue grass (*Festuca*)
Blanket flower (*Gaillardia*)
Gaura (*Gaura lindheimeri*)
Sun rose (*Helianthemum*)
Blue oat grass (*Helictotrichon sempervirens*)
Red yucca (*Hesperaloe parviflora*)
Bearded irises (*Iris*)
Red-hot poker (*Kniphofia uvaria*)
Blackfoot daisy (*Melampodium leucanthum*)
Many penstemons (*Penstemon*)
Russian sage (*Perovskia atriplicifolia*)
Matilija poppy (*Romneya coulteri*)
Many sages (*Salvia*)
#Stonecrops or sedums (*Sedum*)
Many #verbenas (*Verbena*)

SHRUBS

Century plant (*Agave*)
#Bearberry and manzanita (*Arctostaphylos*)
#Artemisias or wormwoods (*Artemisia*)
Groundsel bush (*Baccharis halimifolia*) and #dwarf coyote brush (*B. pilularis*)
Butterfly bush (*Buddleia davidii*)
Bird-of-paradise (*Caesalpinia*)
Lemon bottlebrush (*Callistemon citrinus*)
Siberian peashrub (*Caragana arborescens*)
Blue-mist shrub (*Caryopteris × clandonensis*)
Ceanothus, wild lilac, and #New Jersey tea (*Ceanothus*)
Mountain mahogany (*Cercocarpus*)
Rock rose (*Cistus*)
Smoke tree (*Cotinus*)
#Cotoneaster (*Cotoneaster*)
#Brooms (*Cytisus* and *Genista*)
Indigo bush (*Dalea*)
Hop bush (*Dodonaea viscosa*)
Wild buckwheat (*Eriogonum*)
Apache plume (*Fallugia paradoxa*)
Most #junipers (*Juniperus*)
#Lantanas (*Lantana*)
Lavenders (*Lavandula*)
Tea tree (*Leptospermum*)
Texas ranger (*Leucophyllum frutescens*)
#Oregon grape or mahonia (*Mahonia*)
Myrtle (*Myrtus communis*)
#Heavenly bamboo, or nandina (*Nandina domestica*)
Photinia (*Photinia*)
#Pittosporum (*Pittosporum*)
Cape plumbago (*Plumbago auriculata*)
Some cherries (*Prunus*)
Pomegranate (*Punica granatum*)
Firethorn or pyracantha (*Pyracantha*)
Indian hawthorn (*Rhaphiolepis*)
#Most sumacs (*Rhus*)
#Rosemary (*Rosmarinus officinalis*)
Lavender cotton (*Santolina*)
Texas mountain laurel (*Sophora secundiflora*)
Tamarisk (*Tamarix*)
Yellow bells (*Tecoma stans*)
Chaste tree (*Vitex*)
Bear grass or yucca (*Yucca*)

Gray-leaved plants, such as the lavender, lamb's ears, and curry plant used in this California xeriscape, look their best in arid climates. They can't tolerate much humidity; it rots their leaves. A site like this, with dry pavement and good air circulation, suits them fine.

HUMIDITY. Some plants respond well to high humidity. Moist air keeps their leaves and flower petals soft, supple, and fresh-looking. Too much humidity, though, favors the spread of molds, mildews, spots, rusts, blights, and other fungal and bacterial diseases that infect, disfigure, and weaken leaves, flowers, and stems. In humid climates where days are hazy and dew forms every night, plants with soft, fuzzy, or hairy leaves are particularly likely to rot or "melt down" in humid weather. Avoid growing these plants, or space them far enough apart that air can circulate around and between them to reduce disease problems.

FIRE RISK. In arid regions prone to summer brushfires, it's dangerous to let dry dead grass, stalks, and brush accumulate around your house. Mow it down and rake the litter away from a zone at least 30 to 50 feet wide, or keep the plants around the house moist and green by watering them regularly. Contact local authorities for more advice and information about doing what you can to reduce the risk of fire, and for lists of plants that can survive a brushfire.

Soil

You may think of soil, dirt, or ground as a surface to walk on, but to plants, soil provides food, drink, support, and shelter. And since plants are stationary—they can't move around like animals do—their growth is very dependent on the nature and quality of the soil immediately around their roots. Some plants tolerate shallow, hard, or infertile soil, but others need deep, loose, rich soil. If a plant is sited in inappropriate soil, it may not die, but it will probably be stunted and won't reach its full potential.

Experienced gardeners judge the quality and fertility of a plot of land by observing the plants growing there. Any plot that supports a healthy stand of cultivated, wild, or weedy plants obviously has good potential for landscaping. But if a plot is barren or hosts straggly or sparse vegetation, there's some kind of problem to solve—the soil may be infertile, poorly drained, extremely compacted, very shallow, or underlain with buried construction debris. These common problems are fairly easy to diagnose and to work around or correct if you tackle them before you do any planting. Once plants are established, howev-

The soil in your yard can and often must be altered to suit the plants you want to grow. It took commitment and effort to create a lawn and flower bed behind this home in the Colorado mountains.

er, there's little you can do to modify or improve the soil.

TOPSOIL. On an undisturbed site, the soil is stratified, with one or more underlying layers of mineral-based subsoil topped by one or more layers of topsoil. Subsoil is inert dirt, but topsoil is an ecosystem! Along with mineral particles, it includes roots; fresh and decomposing plant parts; humus, enzymes, acids, and dissolved nutrients; fungi and bacteria; ants, earthworms, and many other invertebrates; and burrowing rodents, moles, and shrews. If you're lucky, your land is covered with a thick layer of healthy topsoil that's easy to dig, fragrant, full of life, and fairly uniform from one place to another.

Most residential lots, though, are not like this. Usually there are places where the original native topsoil was scraped off or covered up when the site was graded and developed, and areas where the soil has gotten compacted by frequent foot traffic or play. There may also be garden sites where the soil has been cultivated and improved. Variation in the soil doesn't necessarily spell trouble, but it's something to be aware of—don't assume that the soil in your backyard is the same as the soil out front. Explore your soil by digging test holes in different locations. See how hard it is to dig, what color the soil is, how it feels in your hand, and how deep you have to go before you hit a color or texture change.

More than climate, soil can be altered to suit the needs of particular plants you want to grow. Organic vegetable growers are especially passionate about soil improvement and tell inspiring stories of transforming barren lots into abundant gardens by amending

the soil generously with organic matter and minerals (see page 277). If you take a similar approach to preparing the soil for planting a lawn, annual flower bed, or perennial or mixed border, you'll be very pleased with the results.

On the other hand, many trees and shrubs and several ground covers grow just as well or better if planted into native, unamended soil. You don't necessarily need to make major improvements to your soil before planting in it, and it probably isn't feasible or within your budget to improve the soil across your entire property. Focus your soil-improvement efforts on those areas where they will have the most effect.

SOIL PH. Acidity or alkalinity is measured on the pH scale, which ranges from pH 0 to 14, with pH 7 being neutral. Typically regions of high rainfall have acid soil (with pH numbers lower than 7), while arid regions tend to have alkaline soil (with pH higher than 7). Many plants aren't fussy about pH and adapt to any but extreme conditions. Some plants do require a certain pH level; this information is usually noted in reference books. Rhododendrons, azaleas, blueberries, gardenias, and camellias are good "indicator" plants. If any of these thrive in your neighborhood or region without requiring special soil preparation, you almost certainly have acid soil. If none of these grow locally, that probably means your soil is neutral or alkaline.

It isn't practical to change soil pH on a large-scale or long-term basis, but you can do it on a small scale in order to grow certain plants that wouldn't otherwise thrive in your yard. Mixing pulverized

This colossal rose-of-Sharon has never been pampered yet looks quite satisfied. Sometimes, instead of trying to improve your soil, it's easier to just choose an adaptable plant, dig a hole for its roots, backfill with the same soil, and hope for the best. This method sounds careless but works surprisingly well. If the plant survives at all, it's liable to thrive.

Moss and azaleas need acid soil, and they either get what they want and thrive, as seen here, or don't have it and die.

poor drainage are wet sometimes but not all the time —they can become totally dry during droughts.

Poor drainage is a problem for hardscape and can cause pavement to settle, heave, shift, or crack. It also harms plants in several ways. Soil particles are separated by countless tiny pores through which water and air can flow, but if the pores are saturated with water, no air gets in. Roots need air, and they are liable to rot and die without it. So plants can drown in poorly drained soil. Another problem is that plants growing in poorly drained sites develop very shallow roots, because moisture is so close to the surface. But shallow roots leave plants unprepared to cope during droughts, when any available moisture is deeper in the soil.

There are two common causes of poor drainage, and a few different solutions. One cause is simply lowness, a difference in elevation. Water flows downhill over the surface of the ground and collects in depressions. A second cause, which often accompanies the first, is a layer of compacted soil, impermeable clay, or rock that slows or stops water from percolating down and away.

DRAINS, DITCHES, AND SWALES. One solution to poor drainage is to provide a way for the water to drain away. A system of buried drain tiles (perforated pipes laid in a bed of gravel) works well but is expensive and intrusive to install. It's generally worth doing to ensure the success of hardscape projects, such as pavement or walls, but not necessarily so to improve growing conditions for gardening.

Open ditches are effective for carrying surface runoff out of an area, but ditches are ugly, inconvenient, and hard to maintain (they get clogged with weeds and fill up with sediment). The main advantages to ditches are that you can dig one quickly and that a ditch will disrupt only a narrow strip of soil.

It takes more time and patience to shape a broad, shallow swale, subtle enough that you scarcely notice it when you're walking or mowing, but a swale can direct the flow of water as well as a ditch and looks better—if you notice it at all. A swale in a lawn is inconspicuous under ordinary conditions. You notice it only when it's filled with water after a heavy downpour.

RAISING THE GRADE. Another solution to poor drainage is to raise the soil level. For example, if there's a little hole or low spot in your lawn, adding enough soil to level it out will keep water from pooling there. Depending on your budget and ambition —and how much it would disrupt the existing landscape—you can bring in enough soil to raise a larger area and grade the surface into a smooth, shallow slope. This is sometimes done to redirect water away from a house (a concern that should have been addressed before or when the house was built) or to fill a concave area in a lawn or next to a driveway or

limestone (calcium carbonate) into the soil helps reduce acidity and raise pH. Adding generous amounts of peat moss or composted pine bark helps lower the pH of alkaline soil. (Adding sulfur or sulfur compounds such as aluminum sulfate, magnesium sulfate, or iron sulfate is another way to lower soil pH, but these are short-term treatments that have to be repeated at least once a year.)

Poor drainage and compacted soil

A site is considered poorly drained if water remains on the surface for more than a day or two after a rain. Or if you dig a wastebasket-sized hole, fill it with water, and the water doesn't soak away within a day or so, that indicates poor drainage. Most sites with

These plants tolerate heavy, wet soil and survive on sites that are swampy or water-logged for part of the year, where many other plants would die. The best time to plant them is right after the wettest season. They're more likely to establish good roots as the soil dries out than when it's at its soggiest.

TREES

Swamp maple (*Acer rubrum*)
Silver maple (*A. saccharinum*)
River birch (*Betula nigra*)
Northern white cedar
    (*Chamaecyparis thyoides*)
American holly (*Ilex opaca*)
Sweet gum (*Liquidambar styraciflua*)
Southern magnolia (*Magnolia grandiflora*)
Sweet bay magnolia (*M. virginiana*)
Sour gum, or tupelo (*Nyssa sylvatica*)
Sycamores (*Platanus*)
Cottonwoods (*Populus*)
Swamp white oak (*Quercus bicolor*)
Pin oak (*Q. palustris*)
Willow oak (*Q. phellos*)
Live oak (*Q. virginiana*)
Tree willows (*Salix*)
Bald cypress (*Taxodium distichum*)
Arborvitae, or eastern white cedar
    (*Thuja occidentalis*)

SHRUBS

Chokeberries (*Aronia*)
Groundsel bush (*Baccharis halimifolia*)
Sweet shrubs (*Calycanthus*)
Buttonbush (*Cephalanthus occidentalis*)
Summersweet (*Clethra alnifolia*)
Red-osier dogwood (*Cornus sericea*)
Titi (*Cyrilla racemiflora*)
Possum haw (*Ilex decidua*)
Inkberry (*I. glabra*)
Winterberry (*I. verticillata*)
Sweetspire (*Itea virginica*)
Spicebush (*Lindera benzoin*)
Bayberry (*Myrica pensylvanica*)
Swamp azalea (*Rhododendron viscosum*)
Sweetbrier rose (*Rosa eglanteria*)
Swamp rose (*R. palustris*)
Shrub willows (*Salix*)
Elderberries (*Sambucus*)
Withe rods
    (*Viburnum cassinoides, V. nudum*)
Yellowroot (*Xanthorhiza simplicissima*)
Most bamboos (*Arundinaria, Bambusa,*
    Phyllostachys, Sasa, etc.)

PERENNIALS

Sweet flag (*Acorus*)
Swamp milkweed (*Asclepias incarnata*)
Cast-iron plant (*Aspidistra elatior*)
New England aster (*Aster novae-angliae*)
Hybrid astilbe (*Astilbe × arendsii*)
False indigo (*Baptisia australis*)
Boltonia (*Boltonia asteroides*)
Most sedges (*Carex*)
Turtleheads (*Chelone*)
Hardy ageratum (*Eupatorium coelestinum*)
Joe-Pye weed (*E. purpureum*)
Queen-of-the-prairie (*Filipendula rubra*)
Queen-of-the-meadow (*F. ulmaria*)
Manna grass (*Glyceria maxima*)
Sneezeweed (*Helenium autumnale*)
Swamp sunflower
    (*Helianthus angustifolius*)
Wild red mallow (*Hibiscus coccineus*)
Rose mallow (*H. moscheutos*)
Some kinds of iris (*Iris ensata, I. laevigata,*
    I. pseudacorus, I. versicolor, I. virgini-
    ana, Louisiana hybrids)
Cardinal flower (*Lobelia cardinalis*)
Moneywort (*Lysimachia nummularia*)
Flame grass (*Miscanthus sinensis* var. *pur-*
    purascens)
Bee balm (*Monarda didyma*)
Cinnamon fern (*Osmunda cinnamomea*)
Royal fern (*O. regalis*)
Some species of phlox (*Phlox carolina, P.*
    maculata, P. paniculata)
Obedient plant (*Physostegia virginiana*)
Prairie cord grass (*Spartina pectinata*)
Many violets (*Viola*)

(ABOVE): *Japanese primroses thrive in poorly drained sites with heavy clay soil and can even tolerate periodic immersion, conditions that would cause most perennials to rot. However, they can't survive drying out.*

(BELOW): *Cardinal flower is more adaptable than primroses. Like many plants that tolerate poor drainage, it grows just as well or better in average garden soil.*

street. On a smaller scale, you can raise the soil level in a garden bed, either by raking or hoeing the soil into low mounds or by building low walls or edges and filling the area with soil. Raising the soil level even a few inches improves the drainage enough that you can grow plants that would otherwise have drowned.

BREAKING THROUGH THE COMPACTION. When poor drainage is due to surface compaction, you may be able to relieve the problem by breaking apart the dense layer. For example, if you're trying to reclaim an area previously used as a walkway, a playground, or a parking spot, the ground will be very hard on top but might be okay underneath. Breaking through compacted soil is a tiring job with hand tools such as a pickax, mattock, or crowbar, but it's not impossible, although you may be able to loosen only a few square feet in an hour's hard work.

It's more difficult to get at and break apart a subsurface impermeable layer, such as the hardpan found when farmland with clay soil has been plowed repeatedly, or the caliche deposits typical of the Southwest. If the layer isn't too deep or too thick, landscape contractors can sometimes break it apart with a tractor-drawn implement that slices deep into the ground. That's feasible only on large, open sites. To prepare smaller areas by hand, such as a planting bed or the hole for planting a tree, shovel aside the surface soil, break apart the subsurface layer, and then refill the hole. Obviously, this is a big job, but you have to do it only once to gain long-term benefits.

CHOOSING TOLERANT PLANTS. The easy way to develop a poorly drained site is to acknowledge the problem and look for plants that tolerate it. You can't have a nice lawn or grow vegetables or annual flowers in poorly drained soil, but there are plenty of perennials and shrubs and a few trees that will survive there. Avoid plants that are described as needing "moist" soil, since that almost always implies "moist but well-drained" soil. Instead, stick with plants that are specifically listed as tolerant of poor drainage.

❧AVERT PEST AND DISEASE PROBLEMS

The world is full of large and small creatures that eat plants and diseases that infect them. This is how things always have been and always will be. It's unrealistic to strive for a perfect landscape with no blemishes or losses. You just can't achieve that level of control, and you'll get frustrated trying.

Choose your battles

Consider applying some sort of triage policy in regard to plant pest and disease problems. For example, many pests and diseases cause only minor,

Japanese beetles gang up like this as they feast on your roses, hollyhocks, and other flowers and plants. The various methods recommended for controlling them are frustrating, disgusting, and ultimately ineffective. Regretfully, you may decide to give up on roses rather than fighting the beetles.

superficial, or occasional damage that you can easily overlook. Affected plants will recover even if you don't do anything about the problem. Much landscape plant damage falls into this category, and most of the time you can pick plants without worrying about their susceptibility to pests and diseases.

Other problems cause damage that's so ugly or distressing that you can't ignore it, even though the plant might actually look worse off than it is. This leads to some hard decisions that only you can make. How much damage are you willing to accept before you get so frustrated and discouraged that you feel compelled to take action? What action will you take? How much effort and heartache is any plant worth? Should you fight a problem or replace the plant? Your answers will depend on the nature and scope of the problem, how much you value the plant(s), and how you feel about using insecticides and fungicides. These are often the most emotional and difficult choices in landscaping.

Get local advice and avoid known risks

Some pests and diseases can seriously disfigure or even kill certain plants, especially if those plants are stressed by unfavorable growing conditions, and there's little if anything you can do to stop the problem once a plant is attacked. For example, if a borer penetrates a birch tree or a cotoneaster gets infected with fire blight, those plants will almost certainly die.

Some regionally serious pests affect just a few kinds of plants. Others, such as pine voles, gophers,

---

DIAGNOSING PLANT PROBLEMS

Identifying what's wrong with a plant that doesn't look right or isn't growing well requires a certain aptitude and years of experience. The symptoms are usually confusing and unspecific. Yellow leaves, for instance, could indicate that a plant needs shade from the sun, needs more nitrogen or iron, is growing in soil that's too wet or too dry, has been exposed to cold, or is infested with spider mites. A plant whose stems or leaves have been chewed off could have been visited by deer, rabbits, woodchucks, voles, slugs, or caterpillars.

It's very difficult to diagnose plant problems simply by consulting reference books, because interpreting the symptoms depends on context. You have to think about where the plant is growing, how old it is, how vigorous it is, what the weather has been, what season it is, and what pests and diseases occur in your area at that season. Even if the problem is caused by a specific pest or disease, it's often hard to identify that organism by looking at pictures.

The best way to get answers is by asking a local expert. There may be a landscape-plant specialist at the Cooperative Extension Service, the state department of agriculture, a university department of agriculture or horticulture, or a public garden. Perhaps you'll find knowledgeable staff at a local nursery or garden center or working for a local landscape service.

- **DESCRIBE THE SYMPTOMS AND SITUATION**. The more you can say about your plant, the better the chance that an expert can identify its problem and make a recommendation. Be prepared to say what kind of plant it is and what symptoms you've noticed — yellow leaves, distorted or damaged leaves and buds, spots or blemishes on the leaves, failure to bloom, slow growth, dead shoots, sudden wilting, and so forth. Did the symptom(s) appear slowly or suddenly? How long has the plant been growing there? Have you done anything in that vicinity recently that might have affected it — applied fertilizer or herbicide, torn up the ground, cut down a tree, done construction? Has there been any unusual or extreme weather?

- **TAKE A SAMPLE FOR IDENTIFICATION**. Cut off a damaged part of the plant, wrap it in a damp paper towel and put it in a plastic bag (so it won't wilt en route), and take that along when you go to ask for help.

  If you see specific signs of insect damage, such as chewed leaves, distorted tips and buds, cut-off stems, tiny scrapes or punctures on leaves and stems, odd specks, fine webbing, stickiness, or frass (insect droppings), determine how widespread it is. Is it just on one plant, on other plants of the same kind, or on different kinds of plants, too? Try to find the insect that's causing the damage. If you don't see it at first, look again at a different time of day. If you spot the pest, try to catch it in a jar to take it to an expert for identification.

- **FOLLOW THE RECOMMENDED TREATMENT PROGRAM**. Depending on what's affecting the plant, an expert may advise you to disregard the symptoms and expect the plant to recover on its own, or recommend something you can do. This might involve moving the plant; changing how you water, fertilize, prune, or otherwise care for it; treating it with some kind of pesticide or fungicide; or using a fence, traps, or repellent to protect it from critters.

  If chemicals are recommended, ask for the "least toxic" alternative. Few occasions call for strong poisons with scary labels. Most insect pests that attack landscape plants can be controlled with insecticidal soap, oil sprays, or botanical compounds such as pyrethrum, neem, chili pepper, and rotenone. There are effective fungicides based on copper, sulfur, and hydrogen peroxide. These relatively safe-to-handle products are available at most garden centers and chain discount stores.

  If any recommended treatment program sounds like too much trouble, you can always give up. Sometimes the best thing to do with a beleaguered plant is dig it out and start anew.

Look at all the flowers on this 'Royal Standard' hosta, and think about how wonderfully sweet-scented they are. Then look at the leaves. All those holes and shredded edges are slug damage. Where slugs and snails are abundant, it's hardly worth trying to grow hostas.

slugs, root-knot nematodes, grasshoppers, gypsy moths, lace bugs, and Japanese beetles, feed on many different kinds of plants. Depending on the pest populations, which vary from year to year, they can do major or minor damage across a region. You can try to eradicate these pests from your own yard, but it's a never-ending battle because they outnumber and surround you. Trying to protect susceptible plants with repellent sprays or strategies is also a struggle.

It's easier to just give up on plants that are vulnerable to these pests and grow something else instead. Of course, this limits the selection of plants you can use, just as living in a cold climate or having a shady lot limits your landscaping choices, but it's an honest and direct response to a situation that's really beyond your control.

To learn which pests and diseases are most troublesome in your area and which plants are most susceptible to these problems, follow the gardening column in your local newspaper, any garden talk-shows

on local radio stations, and newsletters from local nurseries or public gardens. A good local nursery should steer you away from buying trouble-prone plants and toward suitable substitutes. In some plant groups there are individual species or cultivars, often newly released, that are resistant to the problems that affected older or more common varieties.

Deer

In many parts of the United States, high deer populations (sometimes reaching 50 deer per square mile, or even more than that!) pose the most serious problem that gardeners face. Insects, diseases, drought, poor soil, and difficult climates are modest challenges compared with a neighborhood herd of hungry deer.

Deer—including white-tailed deer and mule deer, and also elk—are troublesome for many reasons: (1) They're not specialists. Unlike pests or problems that affect just one or a few target species, deer eat many kinds of plants. (2) They're big eaters.

One deer can do more damage than a dozen rodents or a plague of insects. (3) They never stop. Most other garden problems are seasonal, but deer eat 365 days a year. (4) In addition to browsing, bucks disfigure trees by rubbing on them.

FENCING. Where deer pressure is intense, the best way (many gardeners would say it's the only way) to protect your plants is by installing a suitable fence. An effective deer fence has to be tall, wide, or electrified, or all of the above. Several different designs have been developed and tested by researchers around the country. Two that are relatively inexpensive and easy to install are baited electric fences and plastic mesh fences.

A baited electric fence is a single strand of wire attached to stakes and carrying current provided by a solar, battery, or AC charger. When the current is on, anything—deer, you, your children or pets—that stands on the ground and touches the wire will get a mild shock. Attaching bait (usually peanut butter smeared on pieces of aluminum foil) to the fence attracts deer so they will locate and learn to avoid the wire. However, they can easily jump the fence and will do so if they haven't learned to fear it, if they're very hungry, if the current is turned off, or if any green plants have come in contact with the wire and grounded the current.

Plastic mesh fencing is a grid of black plastic that comes in lighter and heavier weights, typically in rolls 8 feet wide by 100 or more feet long. It's installed by clipping it to tall stakes (or to trees) spaced about 15 to 20 feet apart, then adding shorter stakes to secure the bottom edge to the ground so deer can't push underneath. It's almost invisible and quite effective, although deer can jump over it or break through it if they're panicked or desperate. You can install it yourself or hire a contractor. Handling the rolls is clumsy work, especially if you're installing the fence through brushy areas or on rough ground. It's also hard to drive the stakes, and you need to work off a ladder to reach the top edge and fasten it in place. Once installed, this kind of fencing requires minimal maintenance; just check after windstorms to make sure no tree limbs have dropped onto it.

OTHER BARRIERS AND DETERRENTS. Fencing your entire yard or garden is impractical or not allowed in many neighborhoods and situations. Instead, you might try caging individual plants, laying chicken wire or similar mesh on the ground around a planting (deer hesitate to step onto a wire mesh), covering plants with large sheets of lightweight plastic bird nettings, using an ultrasonic noisemaker, or connecting a motion-detector switch to an outdoor light or a water sprinkler. An active dog that's free to run around your property, perhaps confined by one of those buried invisible fences, may be able to keep deer away. These various deterrents and gizmos have worked for some gardeners and are worth a try, but they're not always successful.

REPELLENTS. Gardeners report mixed results with commercial and homemade repellents whose smell or taste is offensive to deer. Sometimes these concoctions provide good protection, but repellents fail if deer learn to disregard them or are extremely hungry.

The main drawback with most repellents is that you have to spray or spread them repeatedly to protect new growth and to replace what's lost when previous applications wash off in a rain or decompose and become ineffective. Some of the newer commercial repellent products, such as Tree Guard, do last longer than homemade remedies, but even so, fast-growing plants need to be sprayed at least two or three times a summer.

Here's a recipe for a popular homemade deer repellent: Mix three rotten eggs or a quart of sour milk in a gallon of water. Add a teaspoon of garlic powder and a teaspoon of finely ground chili pepper. Spray or sprinkle (with a watering can) this mixture on deer-prone plants, renewing it after any heavy rain or at least once a month. Although it's unpleasant to prepare and apply this mixture, you won't notice the smell in your garden after it has dried.

Other products that are sometimes effective as deer repellents are blood meal or Milorganite fertilizer, sprinkled on the ground around target plants; bars of strongly perfumed soap hung among the plants; or a scattering of human hair trimmings or dog hair.

PLANTING DEFENSIVELY. If you have a deer problem, you probably know which plants in your yard or region suffer the most damage. The challenge is determining which plants deer are likely to ignore or avoid. Those listed in the box on pages 258–259 typically go unharmed in most gardens. Deer may nibble at them, but they're unlikely to devour them. Expand or revise the list with your own observations of how different plants fare in your area, and compare notes with other gardeners and local experts.

Rely on deer-resistant plants for unfenced areas, especially if you don't want to bother using repellents. Deer will bypass an undesirable planting if other food is available in the neighborhood.

Some gardeners have experimented with putting deer-resistant plants around the perimeter of their yard or around individual garden beds as a deterrent, hoping deer will thus be averted from favored plants that are encircled within these natural barriers. Sometimes this works, but often it doesn't. Deer easily detect their favorite foods even when those preferred plants are surrounded by other species.

DEER-RESISTANT PLANTS

Deer taste preferences vary from one region to another and from season to season. Typically deer browse heavily on apple and other fruit trees, most vegetables, most roses, most euonymus, arborvitae, yews, daylilies, hostas, and tulips. They may also ravage many other conifers, broad-leaved trees and shrubs, and perennials. In general, the plants listed below are fairly resistant to deer damage, but even these plants will sometimes be eaten if the deer are curious or extremely hungry. Where only a genus name is given, most species and cultivars within that genus are relatively resistant.

TREES

Japanese maple *(Acer palmatum)*
Serviceberries *(Amelanchier)*
Birches *(Betula)*
Hawthorns *(Crataegus)*
Ashes *(Fraxinus)*
Ginkgo *(Ginkgo)*
Kentucky coffee tree *(Gymnocladus dioica)*
American holly *(Ilex opaca)*
Magnolias *(Magnolia)*
Spruces *(Picea)*
Pines *(Pinus)*

SHRUBS

Abelias *(Abelia)*
Bearberries *(Arctostaphylos)*
Barberries *(Berberis)*
Boxwoods *(Buxus)*
Butterfly bushes *(Buddleia)*
Bluebeards *(Caryopteris)*
Shrub dogwoods *(Cornus)*
Daphnes *(Daphne)*
Forsythias *(Forsythia)*
Rose-of-Sharon *(Hibiscus syriacus)*
Lantanas *(Lantana)*
Drooping leucothoe *(Leucothoe fontanesiana)*
Mahonias *(Mahonia)*
Bayberry and wax myrtle *(Myrica)*
Myrtle *(Myrtus)*
Nandinas *(Nandina)*
Oleanders *(Nerium oleander)*
Andromedas *(Pieris)*
Potentillas *(Potentilla)*
Spireas *(Spiraea)*
Lilacs *(Syringa)*

Deer will eat almost anything when they are desperate, but they generally avoid these plants: Japanese maple, variegated liriope, and pachysandra (RIGHT); *ornamental grasses and violets* (OPPOSITE TOP); *lavender, santolina, and other pungent herbs* (OPPOSITE BOTTOM).

GROUND COVERS AND PERENNIALS

Plants marked # may be used as ground covers.

#Yarrows (*Achillea*)
Flossflowers (*Ageratum*)
Hollyhock (*Alcea rosea*)
Butterfly weed (*Asclepias tuberosa*)
#Astilbes (*Astilbe*)
#Heathers (*Calluna*)
Coreopsis (*Coreopsis*)
Cosmos (*Cosmos*)
Crocuses (*Crocus*)
Daffodils and narcissus (*Narcissus*)
Bleeding hearts (*Dicentra*)
Foxgloves (*Digitalis*)
#Heaths (*Erica*)
#Spurges (*Euphorbia*)
#Sweet woodruff (*Galium odoratum*)
#Hardy geraniums (*Geranium*)
#Hellebores (*Helleborus*)
#Heucheras (*Heuchera*)
Irises (*Iris*)
Blazing stars and gayfeathers (*Liatris*)
Flaxes (*Linum*)
#Lilyturf (*Liriope*)
Bee balms (*Monarda*)
Grape hyacinths (*Muscari*)
Forget-me-nots (*Myosotis*)
#Mondo grass (*Ophiopogon*)
#Pachysandra (*Pachysandra*)
Peonies (*Paeonia*)
Poppies (*Papaver*)
Russian sages (*Perovskia*)
Salvias (*Salvia*)
Pincushion flowers (*Scabiosa*)
#Lamb's ears (*Stachys byzantina*)
Marigolds (*Tagetes*)
Nasturtiums (*Tropaeolum*)
#Verbenas (*Verbena*)
#Veronicas (*Veronica*)
#Periwinkle or myrtle (*Vinca*)
#Violets (*Viola*)

MISCELLANEOUS

Most fragrant or pungent herbs, such as artemisias, chives, germander, hyssop, lavender, mints, oregano, rosemary, sage, santolina, and thyme
Most succulents, such as agaves, aloes, cacti, and yuccas
Most ornamental grasses and bamboos
Most kinds of ferns

'Old Blush' rose is ideal for landscape use. It is easy to grow and blooms off and on throughout the season.

9 ❧ General Care of Landscape Plants

GROWING HEALTHY, shapely plants is an essential part of making a beautiful landscape. Designing lovely combinations and arrangements is important, too, but you can't do anything artistic with plants unless they're in prime condition. Even the most sophisticated design idea is a flop if the plants look scrawny, squeezed, or sloppy. By contrast, a simple display of robust, well-groomed plants can be absolutely stunning.

This chapter covers the general aspects of landscape maintenance, the techniques that apply to many situations and kinds of plants. These topics include watering, fertilizing, mulching, weed control, helping new plants get established, and providing winter protection. (For information on troubleshooting pest and disease problems, see page 255.) Special considerations related to trees, shrubs, vines, lawns, ground covers, perennials, and other particular groups of plants are covered in the following chapters.

Along with the tending of individual plants, a landscape needs enough housekeeping—the outdoor equivalent of sweeping, dusting, and putting things away—to satisfy your standards for style and tidiness. You'll do that automatically, and it's more a matter of attitude than technique, so I won't dwell on it here.

❧ WATERING

Depending on where you live, what plants you grow, and what kind of setup you have, watering may be a job you rarely do, a frequent and time-consuming task, or something that happens automatically. Your main concerns will be which plants need watering and how much and how often you should water them. Also think about what kind of watering system is best for you and your landscape. This depends on how many times a year you need to water, how many plants or how large an area needs watering, your schedule, and your budget.

Watering depends mostly on climate

Throughout most of the eastern United States, you can have a lush, green landscape without regular watering. Of course, you'll have to water plants in containers and anything you've recently planted, and you may want to sprinkle the lawn sometimes or soak a vegetable patch, but your major established plantings won't need regular irrigation. From time to time there will be a prolonged dry spell with no significant rain for weeks on end. Droughts in rainy climates are disturbing because we aren't used to seeing brown grass and wilted plants in summer, but the consequences are rarely fatal. Plants almost always recover and grow normally after it starts raining again.

In the western United States, except for some mountain regions and along the Pacific Northwest coast, the climate is typically arid with a pronounced summer dry season. The combination of low rainfall, bright sun, warm temperatures, and steady wind means it takes regular watering to keep a lawn green, sustain dense plantings of soft-leaved shrubs and shade trees, grow traditional garden flowers, or produce fruits and vegetables. Most westerners take watering for granted, and many communities are landscaped almost entirely with plants that require irrigation, although this has changed in recent decades. Now there are many examples of beautiful home landscapes designed to conserve water. There have also been great advances in watering technology, with new systems that are clever, efficient, and affordable.

DIFFERENT LANDSCAPES NEED MORE OR LESS CARE

How much time and skill is required to maintain your yard or property depends only partly on its size. Maintenance depends mostly on the style of your landscape, what kinds of plants you grow, and how many different kinds there are. The range of possibilities is really quite dramatic. Depending on how you develop it, you can spend as little or as much time as you want on caring for your landscape.

- **NATURAL VEGETATION NEEDS THE LEAST CARE.** In nature, wild plants sprout where they may and grow as they can. Nobody arranges or tends them, but they thrive anyway and create scenery we all admire. If you want a beautiful, low-maintenance landscape, build a house out in the woods, the grasslands, the mountains, or the desert. Take every precaution to preserve the existing natural vegetation; disturb it as little as possible during and after construction. Then relax and enjoy the view.

    Of course, undisturbed sites are scarce and few people get the opportunity to live in the midst of natural vegetation. But keep it in mind as a basis for comparison. A landscape that's inspired by or modeled after the native vegetation of your region will require less care (once the plants are established) than any conventional combination of shrubs, lawn, and flower beds. Depending on where you live, the natural pattern might be an evergreen or deciduous forest with an understory of shrubs and ground covers, a scattering of dryland shrubs and scrubby trees brightened with seasonal displays of annual and perennial wildflowers, or a dense sward of perennial grasses and herbaceous perennials.

- **SIMPLE VS. COMPLEX PLANTINGS.** The more kinds of plants you combine in a landscape, the more trouble it is to care for them. There's more to know about and more to keep track of, and there are more kinds of jobs to do. You need more skills and more tools. Filling the same size landscape with larger patches of fewer kinds of plants (or with fewer but larger plants; for instance, trees instead of shrubs) simplifies maintenance.

    Groves of trees underplanted with shade-tolerant shrubs, ground covers, and wildflowers; masses of sturdy, slow-growing shrubs that require minimal pruning; beds of weed-proof ground covers that need no more than an annual shearing, if that; prairie-like patches of grasses and wildflowers that can be cut down in fall or spring with a lawn mower or string trimmer; a lawn that's shaped for easy mowing—such simple plantings have a casual, contemporary look and are easy to care for.

- **YOUNG VS. OLDER PLANTS.** Young plants are more sensitive to extreme weather—drought, heavy rains, storms, severe cold, or record heat—than mature plants are. Young vines, shrubs, and trees need more pruning and training than older ones do.

Natural landscapes require very little care. At this house in the Pennsylvania woods, about all the owners have to do is have the trees pruned occasionally to remove any limbs that might drop on the roof or driveway.

Weed problems are more severe in newly planted beds. Be patient and persistent. As a landscape fills up with older, established plants, it requires less routine care.

- **CONTAINERS AND FLOWER BEDS NEED THE MOST ATTENTION.** Plants in outdoor containers, such as window boxes, hanging baskets, and pots, require daily or frequent watering throughout the growing season, regular fertilization, occasional or frequent grooming and pruning, and seasonal repotting or replacement.

    Conventional flower beds are almost as demanding. Most annual and perennial flowers need attention at least once a week and extra care at the beginning and end of every growing season. Along with routine maintenance, these plants typically need deadheading, staking, and periodic division, renewal, or replacement.

- **HOW DO LAWNS COMPARE?** Although lawns are accused of being high maintenance, they're a breeze compared with flower, herb, or vegetable gardens. If you have equal areas of lawn and garden, you'll spend many more hours every year taking care of the garden than the lawn. If you want to cut down on maintenance, replace the lawn with long-term plantings of ground covers and woody plants, not seasonal gardens of herbaceous perennials and annuals.

    On the other hand, if you're passionate about gardening and you want to focus on your beds and borders, you can have a big lawn, too. That's because you can easily hire competent help with lawn care. It's hard to find experienced garden helpers who are qualified to tend a mixed border, even for a week or two when you go away on summer vacation, but you can always find someone to mow your lawn.

This low-maintenance landscape fills the entire front yard of a contemporary house. The widely spaced trees and shrubs can grow for years without crowding one another. Connecting them all in a sea of evergreen foliage is pachysandra, one of the few ground covers that are virtually weed-proof. Scattered clumps of daffodils bloom in spring, but they can go decades with no attention or care. None of these plants would need watering except during severe dry spells.

This border is virtually carefree. The trees and shrubs are almost all evergreen (no leaves to rake) and need just a few hours of annual pruning to stay neat and shapely. There are clumps of perennials and mats of creeping thyme among the grasses. They'll start flowering soon and continue until fall, when you'll need to spend an afternoon cutting them back and tidying up.

Tending a border like this requires lots of knowledge, time, and enthusiasm. You must recognize every plant and know when and how to care for it. Every season will bring new challenges, and you have to continually revise the design as individual plants die out, get too big, or don't live up to your expectations.

Of course the lawn and front edge must be flawless, too, to show off the border.

The same guidelines apply when you're faced with unusually dry weather in an arid climate, but in general, western landscapers should treat decisions about watering as a basic part of garden design, not in response to a short-term crisis. In arid climates you need to set priorities on a long-term basis. Follow the principles of xeriscaping (see page 248), and you will be prepared for dry, sunny summers and can enjoy the fine weather without worrying about your plants.

HOW TO INTERPRET WILTING. Wilting occurs when the soil is dry and a plant's leaves are transpiring water faster than the roots can replace it. Wilting and drought stress are worse on windy sites, because a dry wind increases water loss through a plant's leaves.

Normally wilting means you should water generously as soon as possible. Plants with soft, broad, naked leaves wilt readily and may suffer lasting damage—their leaves may turn yellow and drop off, or get brown around the edge, or their flower buds may drop off—if they wilt even briefly. Other plants resist wilting by having leaves that are succulent, needlelike, tiny, waxy, or covered with hairs. Watch these plants closely; although their suffering is less obvious, they likewise may be in desperate need of water. Recently moved plants are likely to wilt on sunny days if their root systems are small in proportion to their leafy tops. Along with watering, what these plants need is shade. Put some kind of temporary shelter over them to relieve stress as they establish new roots.

Wilting doesn't always signal a need for water. In rainy climates plants sometimes wilt on sunny days even though the soil is moist, because they have weak root systems and soft leaves. Don't be startled if you notice this, and don't water those plants. They'll soon toughen up and grow more roots if they have to.

Wilting sometimes indicates that a plant's roots have rotted because the soil is too wet, or that a plant is infected with a fungal disease that causes wilting. In either case, watering doesn't help and can exacerbate the problem. Root rot and wilt diseases are usually fatal, but not always. If the soil dries out again, plants may recover.

Plant leaves sometimes droop in a way that looks like wilting but isn't quite the same thing. Rhododendron leaves, for example, droop into a vertical position and curl up like cigars in subfreezing weather but recover as soon as it warms up again. Many plants, especially those in the legume family, such as mimosa trees and scarlet runner beans, fold their leaves up or down at dusk in a mysterious behavior called "sleep movement" and resume their normal position at dawn. You might confuse this with wilting, but it's just something interesting that happens every night regardless of soil moisture.

Lawns suffer first during a drought, but if water is limited, overlook the brown grass and irrigate valuable trees, shrubs, and other plants instead, especially any that you've planted within the last couple of years.

SETTING PRIORITIES. When drought strikes in a rainy climate, you may not be able to water everything that wilts, because you don't have enough time or energy to keep moving a sprinkler around or because you're limited by municipal water rationing or a faltering well. Ignore the lawn and big, old, well-established trees and shrubs. Water any trees, shrubs, perennials, and ground covers that you planted earlier in the season. Five gallons of water can make a life-or-death difference to a young, new plant but is insignificant to an older one. Water anything that's rare or valuable, not your common or inexpensive plants that are easy to replace. Move containers to a shady location so they won't dry out as fast. Spread extra mulch in the vegetable garden and in flower beds. Consider using a soaker hose instead of a sprinkler, to apply water more efficiently.

Watering equipment and techniques

As far as plants are concerned, it barely matters whether you use a watering can, hose, portable sprinkler, or more sophisticated sprinkler system. What counts is how often you water and how much you apply—enough to soak deep down into the soil or merely to dampen the surface. In general, it's best to water deeply, so the water soaks to the bottom of the root zone, and then water again soon enough to prevent wilting. How soon you need to water again depends on the kinds of plants. Some wilt and even get damaged as soon as the soil surface dries out, while other plants benefit if the top few inches of soil dries out between waterings.

Different watering systems and techniques can all be effective if properly used, but they do differ greatly in how fast they deliver water, how large an area they cover, how evenly they distribute water across an area, and how much water is wasted to evaporation or runoff. They also differ in cost, although in the long run the price of any watering or irrigation equipment or system is minimal compared with the value of your plants.

HAND WATERING. Hand watering with a hose or sprinkling can works fine when you're setting out a few transplants; for watering individual plants that you set out earlier in the season; for tending window boxes, hanging baskets, and other planted containers; or for general purposes if your garden is tiny or your climate is normally rainy. Many people enjoy hand watering, because it encourages them to slow down and spend time admiring their plants. On a large scale or during dry weather, though, the task can feel overwhelming.

When watering plants in containers, apply enough water to soak through the soil and drip out at the bottom. Repeat when the top few inches dries out or when plants start to wilt. Although it's easy to overwater houseplants indoors, plants in outdoor containers dry out fast and you're not likely to drown them.

It's very unlikely that you'll overdo when hand watering plants in the ground. Few people have the attention span to hold a hose in one place for long enough to fully saturate the soil. You may think you're doing a thorough job, but take a trowel and dig down into the soil and chances are you'll find that you've barely wetted the surface. To give a good soaking to a shrub or tree, lay the hose on the ground and let the water run awhile as you do other things, then come back and move the hose to another plant.

It's hard to water evenly by hand. If you go down a row of plants, watering them one at a time, you'll almost certainly give some more water than others. But this can be a plus of hand watering in a mixed planting. You can customize the job and

deliberately strive to give each plant more or less water, according to its needs.

PORTABLE SPRINKLERS. Oscillating, whirlybird, impact, and other sprinkler heads that you attach to a hose are much more convenient than extensive hand watering, as you can set up a sprinkler and turn it on, then go away and do something else while it runs. Most inexpensive sprinkler heads have a certain distribution pattern; they cover a round, square, or rectangular area. Better models are adjustable and you can set them to cover different shapes. How large an area gets watered, and how much is delivered in an hour, will depend mostly on the water pressure. Regardless of what kind of sprinkler you use, if your water pressure is low you can

Overhead sprinklers are pretty to watch but use water inefficiently. Some evaporates, some blows away, and some falls on pavement, unplanted areas, or plants that aren't thirsty.

water only a small area at one time. It takes high pressure to cover a large area.

Sprinklers are typically wasteful. A surprising amount of the water evaporates before it hits the ground on a dry, sunny day. Depending on how well the shape of the sprinkler pattern matches the areas of your yard, some of the spray may land on a driveway, patio, or other area that doesn't need watering.

With any portable sprinkler, monitor how much water is hitting the ground by setting several empty tuna-fish cans around the area being sprinkled, at varying distances from the sprinkler. Normally you should irrigate enough to apply about 1 inch of water. See how long it takes for a minimum of 1 inch to accumulate in all the cans, and assess the distribution pattern to see if the sprinkler tends to put out more water in one area or another. The distribution should be fairly uniform. If it isn't, try to figure out what's wrong. Are some of the holes plugged? Is the spray getting deflected by nearby plants? (If so, mount the sprinkler up on a post or tripod so it sprays out over the tops of the plants.) Is wind blowing away the spray? Do you need a new, better sprinkler head?

When you know how long it takes to apply about an inch of water in an area and are sure that the sprinkler does a fairly even job, you don't have to monitor it and can water by the clock or set a timer to turn the water on and off.

Along with sprinklers that you mount on the end of a hose, there are sprinkler hoses, perforated with a row of tiny holes where water spouts out. These seem like a good idea for narrow beds, because they water a strip the length of the hose, but it's tricky getting them set up right to deliver evenly. If the hose rolls or tips to one side, the spray goes that way. You have to adjust the water pressure just right, too, or delivery will be uneven, with more water coming out near the faucet end and less at the far end of the hose.

Recently some lovely decorative sprinklers have appeared in garden centers and catalogs. These are made of copper tubing bent in simple shapes and mounted on short stakes. When you turn on the water, they whirl slowly and send out a fountainlike spray. They may not cover a large enough area or distribute water evenly enough for practical use, but they're fun to watch and they make great garden ornaments.

HOSES AND PLUMBING. It's worth investing in a good stout hose that's flexible at all temperatures and kink-resistant, with an inside diameter of ⅝ inch or ¾ inch, not just a common ½-inch hose. The fatter the hose, the more water it delivers.

Install stakes or hose guides as needed to steer the hose around corners and keep it from flattening valuable plants.

If your outdoor faucets (sometimes called hose bibs) are inconveniently located, or if you don't have enough of them, have a plumber put in some new ones. A simple extender—a portable faucet attached to a 6-foot hose—is an easy way to solve the problem of faucets that are nearly inaccessible behind foundation shrubbery. If you regularly have to water at some distance from the main tap, installing a buried 1-inch plastic pipe with a faucet at the far end will provide better water pressure and save constant hose dragging.

TIMERS. A programmable timer that turns the water on and off automatically at preset times or intervals is a great convenience. These used to be available only for permanently installed irrigation systems, but now you can get models to use with portable sprinklers. Today's timers are clever and inexpensive devices. Some can be programmed to control different multiple sprinklers or zones over a weekly time cycle. The only drawback with automatic timers is that they don't know enough to *not* water when plants don't need it (when it's raining, for example).

Permanently installed sprinkler systems

In-ground systems with buried distribution lines and permanently mounted sprinkler heads are very popular and effective for watering lawns, beds, and borders. It takes a fair amount of measuring, planning, and calculating to figure out how many sprinkler heads are required and where they should be located, and some experimenting and monitoring to program the automatic control system, but once everything's set up, these systems are relatively carefree and reliable.

One issue is that designing a sprinkler system is sort of a chicken-and-egg situation, especially if you're landscaping around a new house. It saves time and minimizes disruption if you install the irrigation system first, then add plants afterward. But to do that you have to make a master plan and decide how you're going to develop the yard; how big the lawn will be; where trees, shrubs, and other plants will go; and so on. It's hard to make all those decisions until you've lived in a house for a while. Alternatively, if you wait until the lawn and plants are established, you'll be able to tell where sprinkler heads are needed, but installing them will tear things up. Oh well. You'll have to decide what approach would work best for you.

If you want to install a sprinkler system yourself, get advice from a local irrigation-supply store. Most homeowners hire a contractor to design, install, and maintain their system. Hire carefully, and invest in a state-of-the-art system with good-quality fittings and modern controls. You'll avoid headaches that way, save money by saving water, and increase your property's value.

Drip irrigation systems

Drip systems are efficient because they're readily customized. You can design or modify them so that each plant gets just as much water as it needs and no water is wasted on bare ground, pavement, weeds, or plants that don't need watering.

Drip systems distribute water slowly and operate at low water pressure. Three basic parts that you'll probably need are a pressure regulator (this attaches to the faucet and keeps the water pressure below about 30 psi, or pounds per square inch), a backflow device (this keeps hose water from getting drawn backward into the house water system), and a filter (this removes fine particles and sediment that would otherwise clog the emitters). A timer, although optional, is very helpful also, so you can set the system to turn on and off automatically while you're busy or away from home.

You'll need header or supply lines (usually ½-inch or larger plastic tubing) to distribute the water out to different parts of your yard or garden, ¼-inch feeder tubing to carry water from the main lines to individual plants, and emitters, from which the water drips out. These parts are usually all made of plastic and you can just screw, pop, or plug them together.

Both mail-order suppliers and local garden centers sell drip-system components, although the parts aren't necessarily compatible or interchangeable, so if you find a supplier you like, order everything you want from them.

Drip systems can be installed into existing plantings, or you can lay out the principal parts of the system first and then plant around them. The main supply lines can be buried or aboveground. The biggest challenge is figuring out where to put the emitters, how many of them you need, and how often and how long you should run the water. To take advantage of drip's potential efficiency, you need to monitor your system, continually tinker with it and refine it, and alter it whenever you change the plantings. This isn't difficult, but it's an ongoing chore that ordinarily requires a little attention every few weeks or months.

Keep an eye out for unexpected wet spots, which generally indicate that a connection has come undone (or a rodent has chewed through a tube) and water is leaking out. Also watch for wilted plants or

Drip irrigation systems put water where it's needed. You can install a drip system yourself using inexpensive plastic pipes and fittings.

dry spots, which may indicate clogged emitters that need to be unplugged. If you have hard water and lime builds up inside the emitters, remove them all from time to time and soak them in vinegar overnight, then rinse and reinstall them.

SOAKER HOSES. These are special hoses with tiny holes or pores through which water leaks out and soaks into the soil. Like drip emitters, soaker hoses release water slowly and efficiently; little is wasted. Also like drip systems, soaker systems require low water pressure and a filter to remove particles that would clog the pores in the hose. Drip and soaker systems are easily combined, to provide different patterns of water distribution in different parts of a garden. A drip emitter wets a circle of soil. A soaker hose wets a stripe or band of soil, usually about 1 to 3 feet wide.

Soaker hoses are typically 50 or 100 feet long and are meant to emit a maximum 60 to 100 or more gallons of water per hour per 100 feet, although they're often set to emit much more slowly, at rates of 5 to 10 gallons per hour per 100 feet. At this slow rate, all the water soaks into the soil with virtually no waste or runoff. You can snake a soaker hose through a bed, coil it around a tree or large shrub, or run it lengthwise between rows. You can leave it on the surface, cover it with mulch, or bury it a few inches deep in the soil.

If you need to water repeatedly, buy several soaker hoses so you can leave them in place throughout the season, rather than trying to move a single hose around. It's hard to insert or remove a hose where plants are growing without breaking some stems. You can join the different hoses to a main supply line with tee fittings and connect a total of up to 600 feet of soaker hose (in separate runs of no more than 100 feet each) to a single faucet.

How wide and deep an area gets watered by the soaker hose depends on soil type and how long you let the water run. To monitor the output, dig down into the soil at intervals along the length of the hose and see what you find. You'll have to do some observing and experimenting with a newly installed soaker system to figure out how often and how long to run the water, but once you've decided what's appropriate, you can put the system on a timer.

FERTILIZING

There's much truth in the old saying that "water is a poor man's fertilizer." Think of how exuberantly plants respond to a rainy season or wet climate. Lush growth can't happen without enough water.

Nutrients are important, too. Just as humans require vitamins and minerals, plants require tiny but indispensable amounts of nitrogen, phosphorus, potassium, calcium, magnesium, sulfur, iron, and other elements. These nutrients can come from

Plants in containers demand more attention than those in the ground. Watering, the primary concern, is often a daily chore. Potted plants need fertilizing, and they perform best if you apply soluble fertilizer, mixed at half the recommended dosage, every week or two during the growing season.

many sources—mineral particles in the native soil, mineral supplements that you add, compost and composted manure, processed organic fertilizers, or synthetic fertilizers. But in all cases, the nutrients have to be dissolved in water before they can be absorbed by a plant, usually through its roots but sometimes through its leaves.

Why fertilize?

Good garden soil supplies enough nutrients to sustain mature perennial and woody plants. If you have established plants that are growing normally, have good leaf color, and bloom well, they probably don't need to be fertilized. But whenever you take away plant parts, such as lawn clippings, hedge trimmings, perennial stalks and leaves, brush, tree leaves, nuts and seedpods, or vegetables and fruits that you harvest, you're removing nutrients from the site. Over time, this gradually depletes the soil and the plants go into decline unless you compensate by fertilizing somehow.

Fertilizing is also important when you're starting a new landscape on a site that was graded, filled, or disturbed, because the soil on these sites is typical-ly poor. (Even if you improve the texture of such soil by tilling it and adding organic matter, it's still low in nutrients.) In this situation, adding a moderate dose of fertilizer once or twice a year will help young plants grow faster and produce more vigorous and impressive specimens.

Getting a sample of your soil tested (a service that's available through your Cooperative Extension Service or from mail-order testing labs) is the most accurate way to determine whether you should fertilize your soil and how much of which nutrients is needed. Less precise, but often adequate, is asking the advice of an experienced gardener or landscaper in your area.

Choosing a fertilizer

Fertilizers take many forms, which vary greatly in cost, bulk, smell, ease of handling and application, purity, concentration, rate of release, and drawbacks and side effects. They also vary in nutrient content.

Federal law requires that all packaged fertilizers clearly state the analysis, or concentration of active ingredients. Look for a three-number rating, such as 5-10-5. These numbers indicate the percentage, by

A garden like this needs a balanced fertilizer in one form or another, applied at the full recommended strength on a regular basis. That's because the area is crowded with so many plants, including masses of annuals and a dozen hybrid tea roses. These plants are heavy feeders and they're competing with each other here. They won't grow and flower like this unless you give them what they need.

weight, of nitrogen, phosphorus, and potassium compounds that are included in that product. There are many "designer" fertilizers with varying amounts of nutrients, intended to stimulate maximum growth and performance of particular plants such as lawn grasses, roses, broad-leaved evergreens, or bulbs. It's interesting to experiment with these products, but don't feel you have to invest in them. Normally a balanced fertilizer—one with equal percentages of these three nutrients, such as 10-10-10—is suitable for most situations.

Sometimes a soil provides or stores adequate supplies of some nutrients but insufficient amounts of others. In this case, adding fertilizer that supplies a missing element can greatly enhance plant growth and appearance. For example, iron compounds dissolve more readily—and thus are more easily absorbed by plants—in acid soil. Hollies, rhododendrons, gardenias, and other broad-leaved evergreens often develop a yellow tinge if planted in neutral or alkaline soil because they aren't getting enough iron. A special fertilizer product called chelated iron was developed for this very situation. You mix it with water and spray it on the leaves, and they soon turn green again.

This planting of prairie wildflowers and perennial grasses needs little if any fertilizer because the plants have deep, extensive roots that penetrate far into the soil. Besides, they grow up to 6 feet tall naturally; if fertilized, they get even taller and are liable to tip over.

NATURAL VS. SYNTHETIC. Natural fertilizers include compost, composted manure, slaughter by-products such as blood meal, agricultural wastes such as cottonseed meal, sewage sludge, worm castings, seaweed extracts, wood ashes, and pulverized minerals such as limestone, rock phosphate, and greensand. Some of these products are sold primarily by the truckload from local suppliers. Others are available in 50-pound bags or in much smaller packages such as 1- or 5-pound bags. The cost per pound is always much higher when you buy small packages, so unless you're experimenting or the product is available only in small packages, buy big bags. You can store the extra in a dry place and use it in the future.

Most natural and mineral fertilizers work best if you work them several inches deep into the soil before planting, but fish emulsion and seaweed products can be mixed with water and sprinkled onto plant leaves. (This is called foliar feeding, and it works very well.)

Synthetic fertilizers include granular forms that you sprinkle or mix into the soil, pellets and spikes that you stick into the soil, and soluble products that you mix with water and sprinkle onto the soil or

Composting is a way to deal with yard, garden, and kitchen wastes. Rather than sending these materials off to a landfill, recycle the plant nutrients and organic matter by making compost and using it as a soil amendment or mulch.

The best results come from a process called hot composting, in which the materials heat up to a temperature of 140° to 160°F. That's hot enough to kill weed seeds, disease organisms, and insect pests, and the process happens so quickly that few nutrients are lost via leaching or evaporation. Making hot compost, however, is not a casual or carefree activity. It takes lots of raw material—enough to make a pile at least 4 feet wide and tall—that includes a suitable mix of ingredients, and you need to assemble the pile all at once, monitor it daily, maintain just the right moisture level, and "turn" the pile two or three times over the span of a month or so. Few gardeners make compost this way.

Most people use the alternative system called cold composting, in which materials decompose at air temperature over a time span of several months or longer. Basically, cold composting is what happens if you just toss plant debris onto a pile and ignore it, but you'll get better results if you follow these guidelines.

- **WHAT CAN YOU COMPOST?** Vegetable and fruit trimmings from the kitchen, coffee grounds, grass clippings, tree leaves, garden plant stems and stalks, chopped brush, unwanted sod, immature weeds (but not weeds with seeds or persistent roots), farm animal bedding and manures (but not dog or cat droppings), seaweed, dredgings from a fish or water-lily pond, discarded houseplants or holiday plants (roots, potting soil, and all).

- **DON'T ASK FOR TROUBLE.** Instead of composting them, discard any diseased plant parts and the rhizomes or seed heads of weedy or invasive plants.

- **CHOP COARSE OR BULKY MATERIAL.** A gas- or electric-powered chipper/shredder is the best tool for this job, and a worthwhile investment if you have to dispose of many shrub and tree trimmings, perennial stalks and stems, annual bedding plants, vegetable plants, and/or tree leaves. Chipping greatly reduces the volume of a pile and makes compost that is easier to handle and spread. In addition, tough old plant material breaks down a lot faster if you cut it into shorter or smaller pieces.

- **INCLUDE SOME SOIL.** A sprinkling of good garden soil, or the soil attached to uprooted plants, contains enough microorganisms to begin the composting process. You don't need to buy special inoculants.

- **CONFINE THE PILE.** Putting the plant material into a wooden bin, wire cage, or drum keeps it from getting scattered and helps you tend and retrieve the compost.

- **TURN OR STIR THE PILE.** This helps blend the ingredients and exposes them to oxygen, which stimulates the good bacteria, speeds the decay process, and improves the results. The more you turn the pile, the better—that's why those rotating compost drums work so well.

- **USING THE COMPOST.** When it looks fairly dark and homogeneous and the ingredients are no longer recognizable, the compost is ready to use. If most of the material has decomposed but some fresh, tough, or woody parts remain, pick them out or set them aside while you use what's ready, then put them back in the bin afterward. Spread a layer of compost 2 to 3 inches thick and mix it into the soil when you're preparing a new bed, incorporate one or more shovelfuls of compost into individual planting holes for shrubs and perennials, or apply the compost as a mulch around established plantings.

(BELOW): *Cutting down annuals and perennials after they finish blooming or when they freeze in fall yields cartloads of debris. Sort as you go, then dispose of any plant parts that are diseased or laden with potentially weedy seeds. You can compost everything else to recycle the nutrients and organic matter.* **(RIGHT)**: *Composting bulky stalks doesn't work well, though. It's much better to run everything through a chipper, which reduces a heap of coarse, scratchy, tangled stalks to a manageable pile or bagful of homogeneous chips.*

spray onto the leaves. Compared with natural fertilizers, synthetic fertilizers typically are more concentrated and the nutrients are released more quickly, although timed-release or slow-acting synthetic fertilizers are designed so that nutrients dissolve slowly and become available to plants over a period of weeks or months, not all at once.

In terms of cost per pound of nitrogen or other nutrients supplied, a large bag of an all-purpose, balanced, granular, synthetic fertilizer is usually by far the best buy. Smaller packages, specialty formulas, soluble or liquid fertilizers, processed organic fertilizers, and even bulky organic fertilizers can cost several times as much without providing any additional nutrient to your plants.

I think there's a role for both organic and synthetic fertilizers and I use them both in my gardens. Bulky organic fertilizers such as compost and manure add organic matter to the soil and provide a wide variety of nutrients over a long period of time. But a balanced synthetic fertilizer is much more economical and convenient to apply when you're maintaining a large landscape, and synthetic fertilizers generally work better than natural ones for plants in containers.

Applying fertilizer

Normally the best times to fertilize are early spring, when most plants start putting out new growth, and/or mid- to late fall. If possible, fertilize before a rain; at any rate, don't fertilize during a dry spell unless you're able to water well afterward. It's convenient to apply a year's worth of fertilizer in a single dose, but better for the plants if you make two or more smaller applications spaced a few weeks or more apart. Also, you're less likely to accidentally apply too much fertilizer in one location if you're working with smaller amounts.

Whatever fertilizer you use, be careful to apply an appropriate amount. Usually this is determined by area. Measure the plot you intend to fertilize and figure its area in square feet, then follow the label directions and weigh out a suitable amount of the product, using a kitchen or bathroom scale. Apply granular fertilizers or processed natural fertilizers evenly across the plot with a spreader or by hand. Use a watering can or hose-end device for soluble fertilizers.

Finally, remember that it's always better to err on the side of caution. Fertilizing soil is like salting food. Never use too much at once. You can always add more later, but you can't take it away.

THE CONSEQUENCES OF OVERFERTILIZATION. Using too much fertilizer of any kind, including farm manure, is wasteful at best. At worst, it can damage or even kill plants, accumulate in the soil, contaminate wells and watersheds, and pollute rivers and lakes. Those severe problems are commonly associated with farming, not gardening, although they can occur on a backyard scale. More typically in home landscapes, the result of overfertilization is exaggerated growth. That means the lawn needs to be mowed more frequently, shrubs need extra pruning, trees develop weak wood that's vulnerable to storm damage, and annual and perennial flowers get top-heavy and flop over. If you have any of these problems, stop fertilizing and wait a year or two for plants to absorb nutrients that have accumulated in the soil before you resume. When you do start again, apply smaller amounts.

WEEDING AND MULCHING

Although hundreds of kinds of plants can be weedy, you'll never encounter most of them. Usually just one or two dozen species are truly troublesome at any particular site. Chance and circumstance determine which weeds you'll focus on. Each property has its own weed problems. You may curse a plant that's totally absent from a friend's garden a few blocks away, while she laments a different weed that never shows up at your place.

Weeds are like dental problems. It's better to spend five or ten minutes every day on prevention than to deal with the consequences of neglect. Fortunately, many weed problems subside as landscape plantings mature. By tackling the current and potential weed problems soon after you move onto a piece of property or whenever you develop a new part of it, you can relax some in subsequent years.

Suppressing weed seedlings

Most weedy plants produce thousands of seeds that germinate readily and grow quickly. Weed seeds can arrive at your property in many ways. Seeds of annual and perennial weeds, such as crabgrass, plantain, and ragweed, are often present in purchased soil or mulch. Oxalis and chickweed frequently grow in nursery containers and come home with the plants you buy. Several weedy trees, such as certain ashes, maples, and cottonwoods, have wind-borne seeds. Birds distribute the seeds of berrying trees, shrubs, and vines, such as honeysuckles and wild cherries. Many annual and perennial garden flowers and herbs tend to self-sow or "volunteer," and these seedlings can be so numerous that you consider them weedy.

Most weed seeds need light to germinate and grow. They're quick to invade an open patch of bare soil, such as a newly worked bed, a hole where you removed some other plant, or ground disturbed by grading or construction. This is especially true in rainy climates or rainy weather, where weeds can fill an untended patch of bare ground in a matter of weeks. Don't give them the opportunity. When soil is disturbed in any way, proceed as quickly as possible to replant there and apply mulch to shade the surface and to inhibit weed growth.

Weed seeds may fail to sprout and grow if they land in a lawn of vigorous turf, a dense patch of ground cover, or a bed filled with perennials, shrubs, or other plants spaced close enough to totally shade the soil around and between them. This suppression of seedlings is why healthy mature plantings tend to have fewer weeds than young or weak plantings. But weeds are very competitive and sometimes pop up where you wouldn't expect to find them.

PULLING WEED SEEDLINGS. Whether or not you can name them, you'll soon learn to recognize the weeds that sprout from seed on your land. Be vigilant about pulling weed seedlings as soon as they appear. Don't let them get established. It takes only a month or two for fast-growing annual weeds to flower and produce a new crop of seeds, or for perennial and woody weeds to form such a strong root system that if you break off the top, it will sprout up again.

Some gardeners prefer to cut weed seedlings with a sharp hoe or cultivating tool, rather than pulling them up. Suit yourself. Cutting works as well as pulling and is faster for larger areas, but you have to be careful when cutting weeds that have sprouted up close to "good" plants, lest you accidentally cut the wrong stem.

USING HERBICIDES. Preemergent herbicides are chemicals designed to keep weed seeds from sprouting. Like other strategies that sound too good to be true, preemergents are effective only under specific conditions. You have to apply exactly the right amount—not too little or too much—before the targeted weed seeds begin to sprout but after the soil has reached a certain temperature, and you can't disturb the treated soil afterward without reducing the product's effectiveness. Any garden center stocks various kinds of preemergents intended for use in different situations, such as controlling crabgrass in lawns or annual weeds in flower beds. Read the labels carefully. Although they can be helpful, these herbicides work only if used exactly as directed.

Removing established weeds

You're likely to encounter well-entrenched weeds when you buy a property that's been neglected for several years. You may find an invasive ground cover that has spread into the lawn, a hedge that's infested with vines, or a flower bed that's been overtaken by bindweed or Bermuda grass.

It takes uncommon persistence to eliminate established perennial or woody weeds by hand pulling. You might have to pull hundreds of sprouts every week or two for a few growing seasons before the weed finally gives up.

(TOP): *Annual weeds, such as crabgrass and carpetweed, sprout from seed and are easy to pull out if you get them while they're still small. They usually don't sprout up through a layer of mulch, but any seeds that land on top of the mulch can grow. That ubiquitous black landscaping fabric, which you see heaving up here, offers no protection against annual weeds.*

(BOTTOM): *Perennial weeds such as oxalis are more difficult to control. All these shoots are connected by underground runners; this is all one plant. If you pull up all the shoots, the runners send up new ones right away. Eradicating a perennial weed is a very frustrating chore. As you see, mulch doesn't inhibit oxalis at all.*

Systemic herbicides, such as Roundup, work miracles in these situations. The herbicide is absorbed through the leaves of the weed and affects the entire plant, killing roots and all. Applying the herbicide is tedious and painstaking work, because you need to be careful not to spill any on the landscape plants you're trying to rescue. Obviously you can't just spray the whole area. Instead, use a swipe-type applicator or a disposable sponge paintbrush to

If an area of your yard is seriously infested with perennial or woody weeds and you want to reclaim it for desirable plants, it's generally easier and better to clear the whole area down to the ground than to do selective clearing, trying to eliminate some plants while preserving others. Although you can work around a few trees or large shrubs, if you want to save any small plants that are growing in the area, move them out of the way by digging them up and replanting them elsewhere before you tackle the weeds.

The following weed-killing techniques work best during the growing season. It takes at least a few weeks, and sometimes up to a year, to eliminate a major weed problem. Be patient, and wait until you're sure that the weeds are totally eradicated before you replant.

- **CUTTING.** Cutting it down once usually isn't enough to kill an established weed, but it does weaken the plant. And if you continue cutting new shoots whenever they appear, you can conquer tree saplings, most shrubs, and perennials with erect stems, such as milkweed and goldenrod. This may take more than one growing season, but don't give up. Use hand pruners, a lawn mower, or a string trimmer, and keep cutting those stems as close to the ground as possible.

- **SMOTHERING.** You can eliminate many perennial weeds and weedy grasses by smothering, or covering them with a dense, lightproof barrier that blocks out the sun and air. In most cases, if you cover the weeds soon after they start growing in spring, they'll be dead by fall. You can replant the area then or wait until the following spring.

  To smother weeds, first cut or mow the stems close to the ground. Then cover the weedy area with flattened cardboard boxes or sections of newspaper, overlapped like shingles, with no gaps. Top that with a layer of shredded leaves, hay, com-

posted wood or bark chips, or other organic matter, spread several inches thick. All these materials (even the cardboard) gradually decompose and can later be worked into the soil.

- **"SOLARIZING."** This works well only on sunny sites in hot climates. Cut the weeds to the ground, water well, cover the area with a sheet of clear plastic, and leave it in place for six to eight weeks in the heat of summer. Enough heat builds up under the plastic to kill shallow-rooted weeds and weed seeds.

- **SPRAYING.** A systemic herbicide, such as Roundup, will destroy persistent, mature, deep-rooted weeds that aren't intimidated by cutting or smothering. Follow the label directions exactly when mixing and applying the product, and note how soon you should expect to see results and how long you should wait before cutting down the sprayed plants and replanting in that area. Vigorous, well-established, deep-rooted perennial or woody weeds may not be eradicated by a single application. Check the label to see how long you should wait before spraying them again.

- **GRAZING.** If you live in the country and have an overgrown area that's too big to clear by hand, consider using livestock. Goats in particular, but also sheep, cattle, horses, and even pigs, will devour or trample many kinds of herbaceous weeds and woody brush. Of course, you'll need fencing, a water supply, a shed or barn for shelter from severe weather, and some basic animal-management skills to raise livestock, but you can learn what you need to know from books and by asking advice from local farmers. Caution: Some weeds are poisonous to livestock, so have a local farmer or adviser explore the area with you to identify any plants that should be cut down and removed before you put animals there.

Clearing ground is a daunting task. This property had been neglected, its large front yard overrun with forsythia. Cutting down the forsythia took many weekends and yielded a mountain of brush that had to be chipped. Then the stumps and roots had to be removed, to keep it from growing back.

apply the herbicide (diluted to the concentration recommended for spraying perennial weeds) to every sprout of the weed. Do this when the weed is in active growth, temperatures are above 60°F, and no rain is expected for at least six hours. A single application is often sufficient, but keep close watch and if any weed sprouts reappear a month or two later, treat them immediately.

Controlling invasive plants

Some of the worst "weeds" in home landscapes are garden plants that spread via roots or runners and pop up where you don't want them. Some shrubs act this way, but usually perennials, ground covers, and grasses are the culprits. Bamboo is a notorious example.

As always, prevention is better than cure. Invasive plants shouldn't be put beside a lawn or included in a flower bed or border. Instead, use them to fill large areas where it's okay if they spread, or grow them in beds that are confined by deep or wide permanent barriers, such as a strip of ground between two areas of pavement or between a paved driveway or walkway and a building foundation.

If you're troubled by invasive plants that came with the house or that you planted unknowingly, you may be able to regain control by cutting, pulling, or digging up wayward shoots. When sprouts appear in a lawn, mowing will keep them short, although the stubs may be conspicuous and annoying; if so, cut them off at or below ground level with pruning shears. Define the edge between a lawn and adjacent invasive plants by cutting a trench with an edging tool, and pull out any runners you find there. Pull sprouts that come up through neighboring plants in a flower bed.

Some invasive plants send out new runners just once a year. By removing them promptly you can easily keep the situation under control. Others continue to send out runners throughout the growing season, so you have to respond repeatedly. If you get frustrated, consider removing the invasive plant altogether and replacing it with something that doesn't spread.

Using herbicide to treat peripheral shoots of invasive plants is a little risky. A systemic herbicide, such as Roundup, would effectively kill the shoots but might weaken the mother plant. If you want to try using herbicide, experiment by treating a few shoots (paint Roundup on the leaves, as described above in the section on removing established weeds) and see what happens. Better yet, try one of the new soap-based herbicides. These products work very quickly—you see results in an hour or so—but they're too weak to actually control vigorous perennial or woody plants. You can use them to kill individual shoots without hurting the rest of the plant.

Mulching

In nature, leaves and other plant parts drop onto the soil and accumulate on the surface. This surface layer of organic material helps protect plant roots from temperature extremes, retains soil moisture, and releases nutrients as it decomposes. Mulching landscape plants provides the same benefits, and it can also inhibit weed growth. Because I live in a rainy climate, I think of weed suppression as the main advantage of mulch. In arid regions, water retention is the most important benefit. Either way, a uniform mulch also makes your landscape look neat.

Organic materials such as compost, tree leaves that you've raked and shredded, pine needles, ground or shredded bark, chipped brush trimmings, wood chips, nut hulls, grass clippings, composted agricultural wastes, and other materials can all be used as mulches. Consider appearance, availability, cost, convenience, and rate of decomposition when you're comparing different products and deciding

Faced with a stand like this of golden bamboo, most people would give up and let it be. It's hard to cut down and it keeps growing back. You need a backhoe to dig out the roots. Think twice before buying land that is infested with such a powerful, invasive plant, and don't underestimate how much trouble it would be to eradicate it.

what to use. Most garden centers have a few kinds of bagged mulch materials; for mulching large areas, it's much cheaper to have a landscape contractor or other supplier deliver a truckload of bulk mulch. A landscape looks best if you see the same mulch throughout the entire planted area, rather than a patchwork of different materials. You can achieve a uniform look by spreading a base layer of homemade compost, shredded leaves, grass clippings, or other free materials and topping it off with neater, purchased mulch such as shredded bark or hulls.

Mulch a new bed as soon as you've finished planting it. Spread the material evenly to cover the soil between plants, but don't push it up against their stems—leave some space for air to circulate there. A layer 2 to 3 inches thick is deep enough. Using too much mulch can keep the soil too wet and cause plant stems and roots to rot.

Most organic mulches decompose so fast, especially in warm climates, that you need to add a new layer every year. You can do this in any season, but it's easiest to do it when herbaceous plants are dormant and you've trimmed off their stalks so they're out of the way—that can be anytime from fall to spring. Again, a layer 2 to 3 inches deep is enough mulch to add at one time.

MINERAL MULCHES. Gravel, marble chips, crushed rock, and coarse grit can also be used as mulch. Plants respond well to these mulches because these materials dry quickly at the surface yet the soil below stays moist; this reduces humidity and associated leaf-disease problems. In addition, they reflect heat and light up onto nearby plants, and many plants like that.

But mineral mulches have drawbacks. Compared with organic mulches, they're more work to apply in the first place and much more tedious to remove if you change your mind later. If you dig up or pull out a plant, soil gets mixed with the gravel or grit, and it's hard to clean leaves and other plant debris off the surface of a gravel or rock mulch. Seeds find a bed of gravel an ideal germination site, so weeds can be a real problem in a mineral mulch. In general, rock or gravel mulches work best in arid climates for casual-style, long-term plantings of shrubs, succulents, ornamental grasses, and perennial and annual wildflowers. Using a rock or gravel mulch simply to cover bare ground as a lawn substitute in dry climates isn't a very good idea—it gets too hot, glares in the sun, and looks boring.

PLASTIC, PAPER, AND FABRIC MULCHES. Various kinds of plastic and paper mulches can be helpful in a vegetable garden, but these rarely belong in the landscape. Likewise, porous landscape fabrics are fine to use for a few special jobs, but in general they don't work well as mulches. All of these sheetlike materials are conspicuous, hard to hide, tricky to install, and messy to remove from any kind of permanent planting.

❦ CARING FOR NEW PLANTS

Most plants need some extra care for the first year or so after they are put in the ground. During this critical period, what's most important is that they develop a deep, broad root system. Once that's established, the plants will be better equipped to endure unfavorable weather conditions, to absorb water and nutrients from the soil, and to put forth vigorous top growth. There are a few important steps you can take to protect new plants from unnecessary stresses and to encourage them to send out roots. These basic steps apply to most kinds of plants and are discussed below. Special treatments for particular plants are covered in the following chapters.

Because plants are so vulnerable to poor growing conditions, accidents, or lack of care, nurseries never used to offer guarantees. That policy is now changing for various reasons, and some chain stores, mail-order nurseries, and garden centers do offer a limited one-year guarantee or partial refund on trees, shrubs, and perennials. If you're concerned, ask about this when you're shopping. You may need to present the receipt, the original container, and the dead plant to make a claim, and you'll have to convince the supplier that the loss was unavoidable and not due to negligence.

If a plant dies young, don't automatically assume that it was a bad plant or an unsuitable kind of plant. Failure simply means that something went wrong this time. If you think that kind of plant was a good choice, buy another one and try it again. Seasoned gardeners often say that you shouldn't give up on a particular type of plant until you've lost it three times.

When to plant

You see landscape crews out planting almost year-round, but they're just trying to satisfy impatient customers. They know, even as they're doing the job, that some plantings will probably need to be

The success of a border like this depends on patient, thorough soil preparation. Note how the soil here was built up a few inches higher than the adjoining lawn, by adding amendments or topsoil. That improves the drainage and increases the depth of the rooting zone. Also note the neatly cut edge between the bed and the lawn; that's a detail worth tending, as the condition of the edges affects your judgment of an entire yard.

GENERAL CARE OF LANDSCAPE PLANTS

replaced because they went in the ground at the wrong time of year. Not all seasons are suitable for planting.

Where winters are cold, the best time for planting is spring, starting as soon as daffodils bloom and continuing until deciduous trees are fully leafed out. This gives a plant a full growing season to establish a deep, wide root system. The second-best season is early fall, after the weather has started to cool but at least four to six weeks before hard frost. If you wait too late, plants are more susceptible to winter damage, such as freezing back, root rot, desiccation, and frost heaving. (For tips on combating such damage, see page 283.)

Where both winters and summers are mild, you can plant year-round.

Where winters are mild and summers are hot, planting in fall works best. If you wait until spring, plant at least four to six weeks before the onset of hot weather.

Although you can buy plants all summer, in most areas it's risky to do much planting then. A sudden spell of hot, windy weather is very stressful to a newly set plant. Even if you keep the soil moist, the root system isn't ready to absorb water as fast as it evaporates from the leaves.

Plan to put new plants in the ground as soon as possible after you bring them home or have them delivered. If you're not ready to plant yet, set them in a protected area and water them every day or as needed to keep them from drying out and wilting. If you are a regular customer or are purchasing several plants, most nurseries will tag an order for you and hold it for a week or two while you prepare the site for planting.

Soil preparation

That old saying "Dig a $10 hole for a $5 plant" is good advice for most home-landscape situations. Unless you're planting in an area that's been previously developed for use as a vegetable garden or flower bed, or you live in a region with unusually deep topsoil, plan to invest some time and money preparing the site before you stick a plant in the ground. This makes it easier for the plant's roots to extend throughout the area and absorb water and nutrients, ensuring its subsequent vigor and growth. Nothing you can do afterward compares with the benefits won by preparing the soil before you plant.

GENERAL GUIDELINES FOR SOIL IMPROVEMENT. Almost any plot of ground can be improved. Working with the soil to make it more favorable for the plants you want to grow involves these basic steps.

First, outline the area you want to improve. Remove all the existing vegetation, roots and all. Recycle good plants by transplanting them elsewhere or potting them in containers until you can replant them. Put unwanted turf and soft-stemmed plants on the compost pile. Chip, burn, or discard woody brush and woody roots.

Next, pause to consider whether there might be any underground utility lines, pipes, or wires in the area. If so, proceed cautiously with a digging fork or spade. If not, you can use a rototiller. Either way, loosen the soil throughout the area, digging as deep as the tool will reach — preferably at least 8 inches — and remove any buried debris or rocks that you discover as you dig. A single pass may leave the soil in large, rough clods. Break these apart by hitting them with a fork, or wait a few days and dig or till the area again. If the soil was quite compacted, it may take more than two passes to loosen it, and you should tackle this job when the soil is moist, not soaking wet or dust-dry.

Finally, spread a 2- to 3-inch layer of peat moss or composted organic matter — leaves, manure, agricultural or food-processing wastes, ground bark, municipal compost, or whatever is readily available and commonly used in your area — across the surface of the bed. On top of that, evenly sprinkle any mineral amendments and fertilizers that are recommended by a soil test or local authorities. These recommendations typically include small amounts of ground limestone, dolomite, gypsum, greensand, and/or superphosphate. Dig or till the entire area again, trying to distribute the organic matter and mineral amendments as uniformly and deeply as possible. Then use a rake to level and smooth the surface of the bed. You can plant into the bed now or wait until later.

In situations where the soil is particularly shallow or compacted, your initial efforts to improve it will make a big difference but won't achieve all that's possible. In such cases, it's a good idea to do your best at preparing a bed, then plant annual flowers or vegetables there. They'll grow well enough to give you a sense of progress. At the end of the growing season, remove the annuals and rework the soil, following the same steps of digging deep, adding organic matter and amendments, and mixing them in. You'll be surprised how much easier it is to dig the second time around, how much deeper you can go, and how much better the results appear. After this second go-round, the bed should be ready for perennials, shrubs, ground covers, or other permanent plantings.

SOIL SETTLES DOWN AGAIN. Loosening, tilling, and amending soil will raise the surface of a bed higher than it was before. This raised or swollen appearance is usually quite appealing. However, the soil will subside owing to gravity and the effects of rain and snow, and as any organic amendments decompose. After a while the bed will seem deflated or even sunken. You'll probably notice the difference, since it can add up to several inches—definitely enough to change the level of the bed with reference to nearby hardscape.

Post-tillage settling is inevitable, and the only way you can mitigate it is by deliberately compacting the soil after you prepare a bed. Landscape contractors often do that, but home gardeners rarely do, as it seems counterproductive to loosen soil and then pack it down again. And even if you do compact a bed, there will be further settling as the organic matter breaks down. The only way to prevent that kind of settling is by planting into unamended soil.

Plants that are established in the bed adjust to the soil as it settles, and I don't think there's anything you can or should do to bring the level back up. If you're aware that the soil has settled, just try to accept it that way and look at the plants instead.

Raised beds are often made with flimsy edging that becomes a nuisance as it warps or falls apart. By contrast, these concrete edgings are permanently sturdy and square. If you think you need or want raised beds, do the job right and make the best edgings you can build. You'll never regret it.

RAISED BEDS. Plant selection is limited by situations where the existing soil is uncommonly compacted, infertile, or poorly drained. Although you can always find some candidates for any site, the list may not include your favorite flowers or vegetables. Making raised beds is a way to get around these soil problems and grow a wider variety of plants on an otherwise difficult site. Raised beds have the further advantage of bringing the plants up closer to you, which is handy if you need or want to spend a lot of time tending them, or if you want to display them more prominently. A raised bed is also ideal for a little nursery area where you can grow plants to evaluate them or to let them get bigger before putting them out into your landscape.

One way to make raised beds is simply to shovel, hoe, or rake the existing soil into low, broad mounds separated by depressed pathways. This doesn't work very well, partly because rain or irrigation water runs off the sloping sides of the mounds and collects in the paths. You can't easily grow plants on those sloping sides either; they tip over. Finally, the amount of soil you can add to the beds by removing it from the paths is quite limited and raises the beds only a few inches or less.

If you're sure you want a raised bed and you know where you want it, the best long-term approach is to build a sturdy timber or masonry edging, equivalent to a low retaining wall (see page 214) or a permanent path edging (page 154). Don't bother with flimsy edgings made from 1x4s or other lightweight boards; they'll warp and tip and need replacement after just a few seasons.

Unless you're convinced that no plant would ever want to root down into it, prepare the existing soil inside the area framed by the new edging. Then add additional soil (usually you'll have to purchase this; see the box on page 279) on top of what you've prepared, to bring the bed surface up above the edging (knowing that it will settle down level with the edging after a while).

PLANTING INTO THE EXISTING SOIL. Although countless displays of beautiful, thriving plants support the theory that soil preparation produces outstanding results, there is another school of thought on this topic. Some people think that making the soil too soft and rich pampers, spoils, and misleads plants. Also, they say, soil amendments are an expensive, short-term fix. This "hard-knocks" school advocates accepting the soil as it is; choosing plants that will adapt to its texture, drainage, and chemistry; and encouraging them to root directly into the existing, unimproved soil.

This approach works best on sites where the soil hasn't been severely compacted, eroded, or otherwise disturbed, and it's particularly appropriate for three situations: planting trees, large-scale efforts to restore native plants, and planting on sloping or rocky sites. It's impractical to try to improve soil on a scale commensurate with the eventual spread and life span of a tree, so the tree may as well start off by rooting into the existing soil. A suitable tree can adapt to the site. It may grow more slowly at first than it would if you gave it a $10 hole, but it will catch up later and do at least as well in the long run. On large-scale naturalization or revegetation projects, such as creating a few acres of prairie, reforesting a cut-over hillside, or stabilizing a streambank, it's often an unaffordable and sometimes undesirable undertaking to work the soil. (Potential drawbacks of tilling a large or vulnerable site are that it exposes

PURCHASING SOIL AND AMENDMENTS

Buying and spreading truckloads of sand, gravel, topsoil, soil amendments, or mulch is a preliminary of many landscaping projects. Whenever you need to order materials, keep these points in mind.

- **CAVEAT EMPTOR.** Be aware that any material you buy could be a Trojan horse loaded with weed seeds or rhizomes that can turn into a persistent and discouraging problem. Weeds are most likely to be found in farmyard or stable manure, hay, and topsoil. To avoid trouble, visit the site where these materials are collected or stored; if the area is overrun with weeds, shop elsewhere. (On the other hand, sometimes purchased soil includes pleasant surprises; I've had toads arrive that way.)

- **DIRT VS. SOIL.** What's called topsoil is usually just sifted dirt. This may be okay for tolerant, adaptable trees, shrubs, and perennials, but to succeed with most garden plants you'll need to add peat moss, compost, or other organic matter, plus mineral amendments and fertilizer. To save time and trouble, many suppliers sell amended mixtures of soil and compost. These premixed products cost a little more but are ready for planting and give very good results.

- **FIND A TRUSTWORTHY SUPPLIER.** Word of mouth or recommendations from local nursery staff may help you locate a good supplier. You can order directly from a supplier or through a landscape contractor or nursery. Check the classified ads in a local newspaper and the Yellow Pages. If you're not sure what to buy, explain what kind of job you're doing or what you want to achieve and ask for advice. Many suppliers sell a variety of materials and can suggest what would be best for your situation.

- **ARRANGE FOR DELIVERY.** Bulk materials are usually sold by the cubic yard. When spread evenly, 1 cubic yard (which equals 27 cubic feet) covers an area of about 100 square feet to a thickness of just under 4 inches. Unless you have a truck and want to go get it yourself, have the supplier deliver the material. When it arrives, ask the driver to back as close as possible to the site where you'll be using it. Lay out a big tarp and have him dump the pile on it for easier cleanup afterward.

- **WORK FAST.** Spread the material as soon as possible, before the pile settles. If rain is forecast, fasten a second tarp over the pile to keep water from soaking and compressing the material. Spreading a freshly dumped pile is like playing in a sandbox compared to working with material that's gotten wet and packed down.

Shop carefully when you buy topsoil and be sure you're getting something worthwhile, not just dirt. The driver will be reluctant to go off-road and will want to dump it on your driveway. Be prepared for that. Plan to spread it immediately, while it's still soft and loose. The longer it sits, the heavier and denser it becomes, especially if it gets rained on.

the soil to erosion and can generate an unmanageable crop of annual weeds.) On steep banks or hillsides, it can be awkward or outright dangerous to try to dig or till the soil.

If you choose to plant without amending the soil, dig individual planting holes no deeper than the root ball or container but three to five times as wide. Jab your digging fork or tool here and there across the bottom and around the sides of the hole, to loosen the underlying and adjacent soil and make it easier for roots to penetrate. Set the plant in place and spread its roots out. Break apart any lumps and

Sometimes you can't, don't want to, or don't need to improve the soil. This moss phlox, for example, is growing right on the rock.

clods as you backfill the hole with the soil you removed.

If you plant into untilled soil, you must kill off any weeds, turf, or other existing vegetation that would compete with whatever plants you're trying to establish. Competition always favors the established plant over the newcomer. For a project like this, you need to be sure that the new plants you're setting out will get a full share of water and nutrients and not be starved. Spraying a systemic herbicide such as Roundup is the easiest and fastest way to kill existing vegetation. Follow label directions. As the sprayed plants die down, they'll form a sort of mulch, which you can poke through or push aside in order to dig planting holes. After planting, add more mulch to help suppress any subsequent weed growth and give your chosen plants some additional protection. Smothering (see the box on page 274) works also if the existing plants aren't very vigorous.

Root treatments and planting tips

Growers treat landscape plants in different ways to prepare them for transport and transplanting. Each method has its pros and cons, but container-grown plants are the most popular nowadays because they're easy for growers and garden centers to handle, they look good, they can be sold and transported in any season, and they get established quickly when planted in a garden.

BARE-ROOT PLANTS. "Bare-rooting" means the plant was grown in a field and dug when dormant, and its roots were washed free of soil and then wrapped in damp sphagnum moss and plastic. Such treatment destroys almost all of a plant's fine roots and frequently damages the larger ones, yet amazingly many plants recover and grow well. This method is often used for peonies, daylilies, and some other kinds of herbaceous perennials; roses and certain other shrubs; and many kinds of deciduous trees.

One big advantage is that bare-rooting reduces weight and volume and saves on transportation costs, so this method is sometimes used by mail-order nurseries. Bare-root plants have a short shelf life, though, so garden centers stock them infrequently.

If you bring home a bare-root plant or receive one from a mail-order nursery, unwrap it right away, soak the roots overnight in a container of water, and trim off any broken roots before planting. Set the plant in its hole and adjust the roots so they point outward; don't leave any roots in a bent or folded position.

BALLED-AND-BURLAPPED, OR B&B, PLANTS. This method is used mostly for evergreen trees and shrubs as well as for deciduous ones. The plants are grown in nursery rows and dug in a way that preserves a ball of intact soil around the central roots. This ball is wrapped in burlap, then secured with rope ties or a sturdy wire basket. The B&B process causes considerable root loss and damage, but not nearly as much as bare-rooting does. Fairly large plants can be safely moved this way, but you should arrange for delivery and planting of any B&B tree or shrub with a root ball bigger than 2 to 3 feet in diameter, since that much soil is more than you can lift.

If you're moving a B&B plant yourself, always support its root ball. Don't lift the plant by its trunk, as the weight of the soil can break fragile roots. When planting, remove all tie ropes, and if there's a wire basket around the root ball, take it away. Real burlap is biodegradable, so it's okay to bury it, but if you suspect that the burlap is made from synthetic fiber, remove it.

CONTAINER-GROWN PLANTS. This method is currently the most popular, because the plants suffer less root damage and shock than bare-root or B&B stock and because they're easier to transport and care for during the transition from wholesale grower to garden center to your backyard. There are a few problems with it, however. Plants in containers need frequent watering and are often stressed by getting dried out on hot days when nursery staff can't keep up with the weather. Tall or top-heavy plants in containers blow over easily and are liable to get damaged. If the plants weren't repotted often or carefully enough, the roots can get crowded, coiled, or damaged. Still, container growing is here to stay and will probably always dominate the landscape-plant market.

Before planting a container-grown plant, water it thoroughly. It's important to saturate the soil before you bury it in the ground, as water you apply afterward often runs around the root ball and does not soak down through it. If water seems to run through extremely quickly and the pot feels lightweight, the soil may have gotten dried out too many times and shrunken. In that case, the best and fastest way to wet it is to immerse the pot in a bucket of water and hold it there until it stops sending up air bubbles. (This may take a minute or two.) Then lift it out, let it drain, and proceed.

It's sometimes difficult to remove the container at planting time. First try to slide it off the root ball, but if it's stuck, give up. Don't jerk on the plant's trunk or stems, as that can be harmful. Use a utility knife or tinsnips to cut from top to bottom on opposite sides of the pot, and pull the two halves apart and away from the root ball.

Although one of the advantages touted for container growing is that it minimizes root disturbance, in most cases you actually *should* disturb the roots at

Plant bare-root shrubs in spring, when they are still dormant. Dig a hole (or trench, in this case, since he's planting a hedge) that's wide enough so you can spread the roots in all directions. Step back to check how you've positioned the plant, then refill the hole with soil and water well.

If a container-grown plant has densely matted roots, do something to separate them. Make a few vertical cuts with a pruning saw or knife, tease the roots apart by hand, or loosen them with a jet from the hose. It seems drastic, but doing something like this stimulates new root growth and the plant roots out into the ground much faster than it would if you left it undisturbed.

Sometimes you have a plant that's been growing in one place for a year or more, long enough to have established roots there, and you decide you want to move it. Perhaps you've decided it's not sited right, or it's too close to adjacent plants, or you just think it would look better someplace else. Can you move it?

Gardeners often have a cavalier attitude about moving, or transplanting, established plants, but there are reasons to be cautious about undertaking this task. It's hard work, and it's risky; digging and moving a plant disturbs its roots, which usually causes at least a minor setback. If you do decide to move a plant, follow these guidelines.

- **LOOK IT UP FIRST.** Consult plant encyclopedias or reference books to see if the plant is described as easy or hard to transplant and if any particular season is recommended.

- **TIMING.** Where winters are cold, most plants recover best if moved just when they are beginning to grow in early spring; second choice is when they start to go dormant in early fall, at least four to six weeks before hard frost. Where winters are mild, you can move most plants throughout the fall or in early spring. Wherever you live, don't move leafy plants in midsummer. Watch the five-day weather forecast, and try to move plants before a spell of mild, rainy weather. If there are dry, sunny days ahead, leave the plant where it is now. Don't risk desiccating it.

- **DIGGING THE ROOT BALL.** The size of the root ball must be in proportion to the top of the plant. As a rule of thumb, if a plant has a rounded or spherical shape, dig a circle the same width as the plant's crown. If the plant is narrower and more upright, divide the height by two and make the root ball

about that wide. For example, to move a slender shrub about 4 feet tall, dig a circle about 2 feet in diameter to outline its root ball. Work around the perimeter first, using a sharp spade to cut straight down.

Next dig a trench or pull back the soil around the outside of the circle, to give yourself some working space. Now use the spade to cut underneath the root ball, making it at least half as deep as it is wide. (It's hard to make sideways cuts when you're working underground; that's why you need the trench. If you can't cut deep enough, don't make a shallow root ball; stop and enlarge your working space.) Walk around the circle and insert the spade from all sides toward the center.

- **LIFTING AND MOVING THE PLANT.** For any but the smallest plants, this is a two-person job. Soil is very heavy. Pry underneath with a spade and rock the root ball back and forth to make sure it's loose. If it's stuck and it doesn't rock, there's still a place on the bottom that needs to be cut free. Once this is done, lift the root ball out of the ground by holding it directly, or slide a tarp underneath it as you rock it back and forth, then drag the root ball out of the hole by pulling on the tarp. *Don't* lift the plant by pulling on its stems or trunk.

- **DIVIDE PERENNIALS NOW.** If you've dug a big clump of aster, astilbe, daisy, daylily, hosta, phlox, or other perennials in order to move it, you may also want to divide it now (see page 344).

- **REPLANT PROMPTLY.** The sooner you get a plant back in the ground, the better. Planting and follow-up care are the same for plants you move as for plants you buy, so follow the general guidelines.

planting time. This stimulates new roots to grow outward into the surrounding soil and helps the plant get established.

Here are some techniques to use. If you spot any big roots that were coiled around the inside of the pot, peel them loose and cut them off a few inches from the root ball. Likewise, cut any roots that emerged from the bottom of the pot back to stubs; don't fold or coil them to make them fit in the planting hole. If the root ball is a mass of smaller roots, use a sharp knife to cut three or four vertical slits along the sides of the root ball, or use your fingers to tease some roots loose from the surface of the root ball. Another technique, which I find quite effective, is using a strong spray from a hose to wash some of the potting soil off the top, sides, and bottom of the root ball, thus loosening and exposing the roots. Don't worry about hurting a plant when you uncoil, cut, tease, or wash the roots like this; in each case, disturbing the roots improves their future growth.

SETTING PLANTS INTO THE GROUND. Here are a few tips for successful planting. First, set the plant where you want it, or arrange a group of plants by setting them on the surface of a bed, then step back and assess the placement and appearance. Most trees and shrubs are asymmetric and have one side that looks better or fuller than the others; rotate the plant if needed to put its best face forward. Go inside the house or across the street to check the positioning. Tweak the spacing and arrangement until everything looks just right before you actually start planting.

Work quickly once you've removed the root balls from their containers, as exposing the roots to air dries and damages them. If possible, plant on a cloudy or overcast day or in the evening.

Make sure that the top of the plant's root ball is at or above—never below!—grade level. If the hole is too deep, set the plant aside and add enough soil to raise it up before continuing.

Various brands of organic products called transplant boosters or growth stimulants contain plant hormones, vitamins, and micronutrients. Although scientists can't explain just how they work (they aren't comparable to conventional fertilizers) these products seem to speed root establishment and subsequent top growth.

Watering, shading, mulching, and weeding

Unless you expect rain within a few hours, water as soon as you've finished planting. Apply plenty, as it helps settle the soil into place around the plants' roots. Afterward, water as often as needed to keep the soil in the planting hole and adjacent area moist, continuing for at least a year after planting. Some experts recommend less frequent, deep watering; they say that letting the soil near the surface dry out encourages plants to send their roots downward. That's good advice after a plant has been in place for at least a month or two, but for the first few days and weeks after planting I recommend light sprinklings as often as needed to prevent wilting. At this initial stage, it's important not to stress a plant. There's plenty of time for it to grow deep roots later, after it has recovered from being transplanted.

Another unnecessary stress to be avoided if possible is severe wilting due to hot sun or dry wind. This is most likely to affect plants with large soft leaves that are set out in late spring or early summer. In this situation, protect the plant with a temporary shelter, such as an A-frame made of two sheets of lattice, a tepee of leafy twigs, or an inverted basket. Remove the shelter after a week or so, once the plant appears to have adapted and isn't wilting anymore.

Mulching provides the same benefits to new plants as to established ones, and it's especially helpful in hot weather, because it shades the soil and keeps the surface cooler. Because new plants still have only shallow roots, they get fried if the soil is hot as a griddle. (Later, after they've sunk some roots down into the cooler subsurface soil, they'll be less vulnerable to the heat.)

Annual weeds are likely to pop up around new plants because the process of soil preparation stimulates buried seeds to germinate and subsequent watering makes weed seedlings grow fast. Pull weeds promptly to keep them from competing with your plants. At the base of young trees and shrubs, maintain a clear area about 3 to 4 feet wide; don't let any weeds, grass, or ground cover grow there.

Winter protection

Plants that will be hardy in subsequent years are subject to various kinds of cold damage during their first winter in the ground and may need some extra attention or protection. Plan ahead, and where winters are cold, plant early in the growing season if possible. A well-established root system is critical for winter survival. In addition, take the following precautions.

PREVENT DESICCATION. Newly planted broad-leaved evergreen shrubs and trees and perennials and vines with evergreen foliage are particularly vulnerable to drying out in the winter. Give the ground around their roots a good soaking during any spells of dry weather. Spraying the foliage of these plants with an antidesiccant, such as Wilt-Pruf, reduces water loss through the leaves and is especially helpful on windy sites.

Another effective way to protect young evergreen shrubs is by screening them with burlap. Drive four 5- to 6-foot stakes into the ground around the shrub and staple 4-foot-wide burlap to the stakes. Leave the top open. The burlap shields the shrub foliage from winds and from the low winter sun.

PREVENT ICE AND SNOW DAMAGE. Young broad-leaved evergreen shrubs are liable to get broken, knocked down, or at least bent over by heavy wet snow or ice accumulations. If such storms are typical in your climate, it's worth protecting new shrubs for the first few winters by covering them with an A-frame made of two sheets of plywood hinged together at the top, an inverted wooden crate, or a similar sturdy structure. This prevents breakage and setbacks. As the shrubs mature, their stems and limbs grow strong enough that they can stand up to or spring back from normal winter storms.

USE A WINTER MULCH. A winter mulch is an extra layer of protection that you put out in late fall or early winter and remove in mid- to late spring. Unlike standard mulches, which are typically fine-textured and break down into a fairly dense layer, good materials for winter mulch are coarse and bulky. Hay made from salt-marsh grasses is a traditional winter mulch, along with conifer boughs, recycled Christmas trees, oat or rye straw, pine needles, or tree leaves that don't pack down, such as red oak leaves. Whatever you use, spread it several inches thick over the roots and around the base of an upright plant, or right over the crown of a dormant perennial or small or low-growing shrub, ground cover, or vine.

The purposes of winter mulch are to offer some insulation against cold, particularly cold winds, and to keep the ground frozen and prevent alternate freezing and thawing. This freeze/thaw cycle can lift or heave a root ball out of the ground. (It can also displace flagstones, hard edgings, and other inanimate objects.) Frost heaving exposes plant roots to cold and desiccation and is often fatal, so it's important to prevent it if possible.

Trees and shrubs are the backbone of a landscape. They're the biggest, oldest, most valuable plants on your property.

10 ❧ Caring for Trees, Shrubs, and Vines

WOODY PLANTS, including conifers, broad-leaved trees and shrubs, and many kinds of vines, along with palms, yuccas, cacti, and bamboos, are generally long-lived specimens that get taller and/or wider year after year. Once established on a suitable site, most woody plants require little routine care. They just grow and grow as you stand by and watch.

But eventually many woody plants outgrow the site where they were planted. Trees tower above houses, shrubs crowd against paths and windows, vines smother everything within reach, and you know about bamboo. So after years of low-input enjoyment, you're finally faced with the challenge of removing or cutting back a plant that's undeniably gotten too big. For that reason, I've included advice on evaluating and dealing with overgrown or otherwise problematic trees, shrubs, and vines in the following sections, plus guidelines for avoiding potential problems when you initially choose and site these plants as well as directions for planting and tending them.

Although there are particular tips for enhancing the appearance or performance of certain plants (different kinds of roses, for instance), those are optional refinements for advanced gardeners. This may seem surprising, but you don't necessarily have to identify all the plants in your yard before you can care for them. For example, you don't have to be able to name a tree to know that its limbs droop too low and hit you in the face when you're trying to mow the lawn. Few species need customized care. You'll usually do fine by following the general guidelines I've given here.

❧ TREES

Trees are the most valuable plants in your landscape. A healthy, well-placed specimen tree is an asset to your property and a beloved landmark. Because they grow so large, there isn't room for many trees on a typical lot. You may have just a few. That makes it all the more important for each one to be as outstanding and attractive as possible. Because they live so long, you'll mostly be caring for the trees you already have, but sometimes you get the opportunity to plant a new tree.

The category "tree" includes plants of many sizes and shapes—towering spruces, shrubby dwarf fruit trees, stout oaks with widespread limbs, graceful weeping willows, picturesque Japanese maples. And trees may occur as single specimens, in groves, or as part of a woods. Despite this range, the basic issues in tree care, as discussed below, apply to nearly all situations and cover conifers, deciduous trees, and broad-leaved evergreen trees, but not palms. (For more on the latter, see page 316.)

Preserving and protecting existing trees

Any tree that's old enough to have grown taller than your house is probably well adapted to its site. Over the years, it's experienced all kinds of weather, and its roots have found their way into the native soil. An established tree that appears to be healthy, sound, and in good shape doesn't need any routine care from you, but it does need your respect and protection.

WHEN BUILDING, RESPECT THE TREE'S ROOTS. Tree roots are closer to the surface and extend farther away from the trunk than most people realize. The *drip line* is an imaginary line on the ground directly under the perimeter of the crown. Tree roots always spread at least as wide as the drip line, and they often grow many feet beyond it. There may also be some big support roots that

Sooner or later most woody plants get too large for their site and your yard gets so crowded that you have to cut a peephole to see out of the house. At this point, it's time to consider a landscape renovation.

To expand the parking area in front of this red maple tree, the homeowner added truckloads of fill last year. That smothered the tree's roots, and now it's dying. It will have to be removed.

reach down and out, but for most trees, the network of fine, fibrous roots that absorb water and nutrients is shallow enough to be vulnerable.

Tree roots are easily damaged or destroyed by heavy equipment when a wooded site is developed for new construction or when an older house is expanded or remodeled. If you're planning to have any work done, consult with both an architect and a landscape architect to decide which trees should and can be saved and how the house, driveway, and utilities can be positioned to minimize tree damage. Before the actual work starts, have the contractor install temporary fencing along the drip line around each tree you want to preserve, so that no one can accidentally or unknowingly drive a truck, bulldozer, or backhoe there. Where root damage is unavoidable because the design calls for excavation, trenching, or grading near a tree, you may decide to take a chance and see if the tree survives, but the results can be deceptive. Root damage kills trees slowly; a damaged tree may look fine right after construction but die a few years later. Removing it at that point is more difficult and expensive than it would have been to take the tree down before construction began. The risk varies from case to case and tree to tree, so get advice on your particular situation.

KEEP THE BARK INTACT. Protect the limbs and upper part of a tree's trunk by avoiding unnecessary or careless pruning. Protect the base of the trunk by keeping lawn mowers and string trimmers away. These tools can gauge out a slice of bark in a flash, opening an ugly and vulnerable wound. Hand-clip the grass around the base of trees growing in a lawn, replace it with a ground cover that doesn't need mowing, or install a protective border around the tree. If you have a tree growing where children at play, pedestrians, vehicles, or animals might damage its trunk, build a fence or barrier (sometimes a psychological barrier is enough) to protect it.

In cold climates, young trees with thin, tender trunk bark are vulnerable to a wound called sunscald that usually strikes the south or southwest side of the trunk. This happens on clear cold days when the bark gets warmed by the sun and then cools abruptly after sunset or when clouds drift by. The damage is intensified if snow reflects sunlight and heat up onto the bark. You can protect trees from this kind of damage by painting their trunks white or enclosing them with tree wrap, a narrow strip of coated paper sold by the roll at garden centers. If you use tree wrap, remove it in early summer, as it can harbor insect pests during the growing season. As trees mature, their outer bark normally gets thick enough to provide some insulation and protect the trunk from this kind of stress.

In hot, sunny climates, trees with thin bark are vulnerable to sunscald at any time of year, and it's conventional to paint their trunks white, shade them with vines, or wrap bamboo or cane matting around them. A local nursery can advise you which, if any, of your trees would benefit from this treatment.

DON'T BURY THE BASE OF THE TRUNK. It's normal for a tree trunk to flare out at the base.

That broad, flaring area should be visible above-ground. If you bury it under a layer of soil or mulch the bark will stay too moist and is liable to rot. That harms a tree and can even kill it. People sometimes get carried away with the idea of mulching and heap shredded bark or wood chips several inches deep right around the trunk of a tree. That's too much mulch in the wrong place. It's fine to spread such mulch a few inches deep out by the drip line, but taper the layer to nothing as you get close to the tree, and don't put any mulch directly against the flaring part of the trunk. A mulch of gravel or crushed stones is less troublesome because these materials don't retain much moisture, but even so there's no reason to pile mulch against the trunk of a tree and it's better not to.

WATERING. In average or wet climates, an established tree that's adapted to its site needs watering infrequently, if at all. Normal precipitation is usually sufficient, except during severe or prolonged dry spells. A dry spell rarely kills a tree, but it can make the tree more susceptible to insect damage, diseases, or temperature extremes. When (or better yet, before) conditions get so dry that a tree's leaves wilt, give it a good deep soaking if you possibly can. Of course, the water supply is often limited during droughts. In that case, allocate the water to smaller, younger plants and let big old trees fend for themselves.

In arid climates, some popular landscape trees cannot survive on rainfall alone; they need more water. Sometimes this requirement can be met by

The landscaping crew went overboard here and piled heaps of wood chips around the base of each littleleaf linden tree. What a mistake. This can rot the bark and weaken the tree. They should pull that mulch away from the trunk and spread it in a thin layer that reaches out to the drip line.

directing roof runoff toward the tree via drainpipes or careful grading, so that when rain does come, the tree gets an extra share. More commonly, these trees are sustained by irrigation. There's no shortcut to figuring out how often and how much to water a tree. Local experts, your home's previous owner, or neighbors can offer some guidelines and advice, but even so, you have to monitor your sprinkler system's output, observe how fast and how deep a given amount of water soaks into your soil, monitor the weather, and watch the tree.

FERTILIZING. An established landscape tree that has healthy-looking leaves and seems to be growing normally does not need fertilizing, especially if it's surrounded by lawn or flower beds that you do fertilize. A tree's feeder roots are usually close enough to the soil surface to absorb nutrients that you apply on top of the ground in the form of composts, manures, or granular fertilizers. (But be careful never to apply fertilizer/weed-killer mixtures to the lawn under a tree, as the herbicides can damage shallow tree roots.) If a tree doesn't look right, seek advice from an experienced horticulturist or arborist. The problem may not be related to nutrients at all, and if it isn't, feeding the tree won't help it.

RAKING LEAVES. Mother Nature doesn't rake leaves, and you don't have to, either, when they land among shrubs, in casual mixed plantings, or on deciduous ground covers. In fact, it's good to *put* leaves in those places, as mulch. People sometimes say that leaves are harmful and that you have to get rid of them, but that isn't so. Tidiness is the main reason for raking leaves, to clean them off paved areas, paths, and lawns.

Dealing with large quantities of leaves is daunting, but the task becomes quite manageable if you run over the leaves with a lawn mower or put them through a shredder. Shredding can reduce eight or ten bags of leaves to one bag of mulch.

Leaves are an excellent ingredient for the compost pile, but you don't have to compost them before using them as mulch. It's okay to spread a layer of freshly shredded leaves 2 to 6 inches deep under and around shrubs and perennials. This saves trekking back and forth to the compost bin. Shredded leaves decompose quickly, so the layer will have flattened by spring, and you can keep adding fresh leaf mulch to the same bed year after year.

Removing a tree

Felling a large tree is trickier than it looks. There's a knack to controlling (or at least anticipating) which direction it will fall. Sometimes things go wrong and it behaves unexpectedly. Trees are very heavy, and once they've started to drop you can't do anything but run out of the way. The more trees you cut, the more you respect the hazards involved. This explains why arborists charge so much to remove a big tree,

When autumn leaves fall, rake them off the lawn and use them to mulch beds and borders, or compost them over the winter and distribute the composted mulch in spring.

especially in close quarters, and why the alternative — cutting it down yourself — is rarely a good idea.

Part of the danger comes from misusing chain saws. They cut through wood so quickly and easily that you get a sense of power and confidence that can be very misleading. Using a chain saw safely requires constant vigilance and great awareness. In the hands of an inexperienced, nervous, or fatigued user, a chain saw is an extremely dangerous tool. I know more otherwise competent people who have hurt themselves with chain saws than with any other power tool.

WHEN TO HIRE AN ARBORIST. Don't ask for trouble. If you have any doubt about whether or not you can cut a tree yourself, don't do it. In particular, stay clear of trees close to a house or other building, trees that are leaning, trees with huge limbs, trees near overhead utility lines, and trees close to the street (they may be on public property, and at any rate you don't want to be responsible if they fall onto the roadway).

The best way to find a good arborist is by word-of-mouth recommendations. Ask your friends and neighbors for advice. The best tree men are often booked up months in advance, so unless it's an emergency you'll probably have to wait awhile, but that's worth it to get someone who does careful, considerate work.

FELLING SMALL TREES WITH A HAND-SAW. It's perfectly feasible to cut down and clear away a skinny little tree (up to about 20 to 25 feet tall, or the height of a two-story house) with one of those inexpensive, replaceable-blade bow saws sold at most hardware stores. I've cut scores of trees this way. The standard-size bow saw, with a blade 21 inches long, will cut through tree trunks up to about 6 inches thick.

The performance of these saws depends on the blade. Not only must it be sharp, but seemingly minor differences in the size and angle of the teeth have a big effect on how well the saw works. If the saw seems to bind or doesn't cut quickly and easily, replace the blade with a new one or one from a different supplier. With a good fresh blade, it's surprising how fast you can cut a tree by hand.

It's usually easier to saw through green wood (that is, living trees) than dead wood, so if a tree dies, cut it as soon as possible, before the wood dries and hardens. Likewise, when you fell a living tree, do all the subsequent cutting and cleanup right away.

DISPOSING OF THE BRUSH AND WOOD. Cleaning up afterward is a bigger job than felling a tree. Of course, you can have everything hauled away, but if you have a place to stack and dry it, the wood from most hardwoods (broad-leaved trees) makes good firewood for a fireplace or woodstove.

Softwood (from conifers) tends to spark and doesn't give off as much heat, but many people burn it anyway.

What about the smaller limbs and twigs? Again, you can have the brush hauled away. In some settings, it's permissible to burn a brush pile outdoors. Dry brush (hardwood or softwood) makes excellent kindling for indoor fires; just prune some broomstick- to pencil-thick twigs into fireplace lengths, pile them in cardboard boxes, and let them dry in the basement or garage for several months. If you have a lot of brush and want to chip it for use as mulch or path surfacing, rent, borrow, or buy a gas-powered chipper.

GETTING RID OF SPROUTS AND STUMPS. Cutting a tree close to the ground may not kill it; some trees sprout back. If so, keep cutting off those sprouts until the tree gives up, or paint brush killer on the cut ends once or twice, following label directions.

Better yet, remove the stump. To do that, dig

Have the stump removed, too, when you get a tree cut down, or it will remain as an obstacle or may regenerate from brushy sprouts. This maple tree, cut a year ago, is sprouting profusely.

away the soil to expose the big roots and chop through them with an ax, or hire someone with a stump grinder. These are portable, gas-powered tools that saw down through the stump and the big roots, leaving a hole you can easily refill and a pile of wood chips. Grinding goes fast, and it's an inexpensive and very satisfactory alternative to the annoying problem of having to work around or disguise a stump. Most tree services do stump grinding and private contractors do also; check the Yellow Pages and classified ads to find someone in your area.

Tree complaints, worries, and problems

Common concerns about trees fall into two main groups. You might see something about the tree itself as a problem — perhaps it's messy, intimidating, or badly placed. Such problems should have been prevented, as they can rarely be solved. Sooner or later, you'll probably decide to get rid of a tree like this. By contrast, if you have a desirable tree growing in just the right place and something bad happens to it, you'll want to restore and preserve it if possible. This kind of problem often can be solved, but you may need professional help to do so.

The following guidelines will help you think about tree problems and solutions. When it comes to actually making final decisions and getting tree work done, you'll probably want to hire an experienced local arborist or tree service. Don't risk hurting yourself in an accident with a saw or ladder, and don't risk hurting a valuable tree by ignoring or mistreating its symptoms.

THORNS. Unless you're deliberately using it as a barrier, don't plant a tree with spiny leaves, prickly needles, or sharp thorns near a walkway or building, and never put one beside a play area or parking spot. Some cities forbid the planting of certain thorny trees in public areas. On the other hand, thorny or prickly trees and shrubs make excellent habitat for nesting songbirds, so don't hesitate to plant these trees in appropriate contexts — casual settings away from human activity.

Trees that are typically thorny include citrus, hawthorns, black locust, honey locust, palo verde, devil's club, prickly ash, and Osage orange. In a few cases, thornless varieties are available.

ROOTS. Tree roots can cause several problems. They can penetrate and clog leaky water mains and septic or sewer pipes. They can lift sections of a paved driveway or sidewalk and crack a concrete or masonry house foundation. They can snake along the surface of the ground and trip you or jam the lawn mower. They can soak up all the water and nutrients from the soil beneath and around them, out-competing any grass or other plants that you're trying to grow there.

Where roots have caused structural damage, the only solution is to remove the tree, dig up its roots, and make repairs. This is usually a messy and expensive job. Work around surface tree roots in a lawn by replacing the grass with a tough, carefree ground cover that doesn't need mowing or with mulch, stones, gravel, or decking.

Problems with tree roots and foundations are almost always due to close spacing; if you plant trees a minimum of 8 feet away you're unlikely to encounter foundation problems. As for roots clogging water, drain, or septic lines, almost any tree's roots can find and enter a leaky or perforated pipe, but willows, cottonwoods, poplars, and tamarisk are notoriously thirsty. Don't plant them anyplace near a buried water line.

SUCKERS AND WATER SPROUTS. Suckers are shoots that typically grow faster than ordi-

nary branches or twigs and commonly point straight up. They may pop up around the base of a tree, close to the trunk, or they can sprout up from the roots, appearing at distances up to several feet from the main trunk. Apples, crab apples, aspens, cottonwoods, black locust, pin cherry, and sassafras are all prone to forming suckers around the base or farther away. This is troublesome, because once suckers appear, cutting them off or pulling them up irritates the tree's roots and stimulates the production of more suckers. Once this cycle starts, it may never stop, and you have to keep removing more suckers year after year.

Suckers may also appear around wounds where major limbs or large branches were removed, especially if the tree was pruned severely. These suckers, often called water sprouts, may form in profusion during the first growing season after the tree was pruned, but they don't continue to form in subsequent years unless you do severe pruning repeatedly. If you've pruned a tree and water sprouts form, thin them by cutting or pulling off most of them. It's okay to let a few water sprouts grow into new limbs, but a crowded mass of water sprouts tends to be weak, brittle, and prone to diseases.

TREE IS TOO TALL. Have it cut down. Don't let someone just take the top off, or "top" it. Not only is topping extremely ugly, it's usually ineffective, too, as most trees quickly grow back.

(**ABOVE**): *It's normal for big old trees such as these Norway spruces to flare out at the base and have shallow roots that snake along the surface of the ground. This is a nuisance if you're trying to maintain a lawn there. But don't complain that you can't grow anything under trees like this. It's hard to grow turfgrass, true, but look at how well the hydrangeas are doing, and there are lush ferns and wildflowers immediately behind the fence.*

(**BELOW**): *Under utility lines plant only dwarf trees or species that respond well to repeated hard pruning, such as these tree-of-heavens on a streetside in Albuquerque. When they're leafless in winter, you see the massive gnarled trunks on these old trees.*

That big old red maple and the smaller red pine in front of it are beautiful specimens, but it was a mistake to plant them so close to the house. See how the maple is rubbing on the roof? Plan ahead. Trees grow faster and get bigger than you expect. Plant them well away from any building.

do your best to learn how wide the crown is likely to spread, and plant the tree at least half that distance away from the house. You might think it would be okay to set it closer and let the crown develop in a semicircle that's flattened on the side next to the house. Don't. Limbs would soon rub against the house, and you'd get all scratched up and cranky trying to squeeze in there and prune them back. Besides, a half-shaped tree doesn't look nearly as nice as a fully round specimen set farther away.

LIMBS ARE TOO LOW, SO YOU CAN'T WALK UNDER THE TREE. In the right setting—out in the open on a roomy site, surrounded by lawn or ground cover—a tree whose lower limbs sweep the ground like a long skirt is one of the most graceful and elegant sights in the landscape. A beautiful tree such as this adds to your quality of life and also to your property's value, so cherish and preserve it. It's okay to crawl underneath and reach up to remove dead branches, but don't take off leafy limbs—just lift them up when you want to mow or trim underneath.

A tree whose low-hanging limbs make you duck needs pruning. You can do this in winter or summer. Reach up with a pole saw or work from a stepladder with a bow saw or pruning saw, and remove whatever limbs get in your way by cutting them off at the branch collar (the thickened area at the limb's base).

On many trees, if you remove the lowest limbs one year, the next-higher layer of limbs will droop and you'll need to remove them the following year. This may continue for several years before you've finally pruned high enough to maintain some headroom underneath the tree.

LITTER. It's normal for any tree to drop leaves and other parts from time to time, but some trees make an extra mess—they coat everything with yellow pollen, drop bushels of sticky fruits that rot on the ground and attract wasps, shed a steady trickle of brittle twigs or flaking bark, or bear innumerable seeds that sprout up like weeds in your lawn and flower beds. Complain all you want to, advise other people not to plant that kind of tree, and then carry on with the cleanup. There's not much you can do about a messy tree except cut it down, and that would be an overreaction if the tree looks nice, casts welcome shade, provides privacy, or has other redeeming features. Getting reconciled to a messy but otherwise worthwhile tree is like having a pet that's naughty or that sheds a lot; try to accept its faults and love it anyway.

CONFLICTS BETWEEN TREE LIMBS AND STRUCTURES. In general, letting big trees grow too close to a house is asking for trouble. Limbs that overhang the roof can fall during a storm. Whole trees can tip over. Falling limbs or trees can pull down utility lines. Limbs that rub against the roof, gutters, or siding scar the surface and may break through and cause leaks. The actual risk depends on the particular tree; some trees are benign, while others are real hazards. If you're surrounded by existing large trees and have any suspicion of them, have an arborist come do an evaluation followed by any required pruning or removal. Almost always, an intrusive or overhanging tree should be cut down (not simply cut back—it will just grow out again), and the sooner the better.

When you're choosing and planting a new tree,

TREE IS COVERED WITH VINES. Whether or not vines are a problem depends mostly on the kind of vine, its vigor and ultimate size, and how it climbs (for a discussion of the latter, see the box on page 314). Small or short vines that cling tight

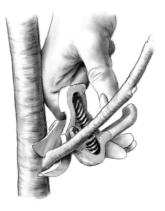

REMOVING A SMALL LIMB

Use pruning shears or loppers to cut the limb just outside the branch collar (the place where it swells out as it meets the trunk). Cutting at the right place is important because this affects how the wound heals. Don't slice into the trunk, but don't leave a stub either.

REMOVING A LARGE LIMB

If you simply saw off a limb in a single cut, the weight of the falling limb may tear a strip of bark down the trunk. Prevent that by making a three-part cut.

1. *About 1 foot away from the trunk, saw halfway up into the limb.*
2. *Just beyond that cut, saw down through the limb until it falls off. This removes the heavy part of the limb.*
3. *Saw off the stub, just outside the branch collar. Use one hand to catch it as it breaks free.*

against the trunk do little damage, but a robust vine with a heavy mass of foliage that sprawls out over the tree's canopy shades the tree's leaves, which weakens it, and makes the tree more susceptible to wind and storm damage.

In any case, the problem is that once a vine has climbed up into a tree, it's hard to pull it back down. Severing the vine's stems close to the ground kills all the top growth, but then you have a tree full of dreary-looking dead vines. Remove everything you can reach with a telescoping pole saw or trimmer. After a few years, the upper parts will break apart and fall down in bits and pieces. Meanwhile, keep an eye on the base of the vine and keep cutting off any new shoots that appear. Even if you paint the cut stubs with brush killer, a vigorous vine may resprout several times before it finally dies.

TREE HAS DEAD OR BROKEN LIMBS.

It's natural for limbs at the bottom or interior of a tree's crown to die because their leaves don't get enough light. It's also natural, although disappointing, for tree limbs to get broken during heavy storms. It doesn't necessarily hurt a tree to be loaded with dead or damaged limbs—you see plenty of trees like this surviving out in the woods, providing welcome perches and nest holes for birds and squirrels.

Closer to home, you'll probably want to remove these limbs for appearance' sake. This kind of

Never let honeysuckle, bittersweet, or any other twining vine get started up a tree. It will choke the tree and make a tangled mess, too.

(RIGHT): *Like most of the woods in the eastern United States, this grove of spindly second-growth pines has sprouted up on land once used for farming. These trees are only about 30 years old. They're weak and unhealthy because they're too close together, and most of them will probably die within the next 10 years. You could intervene and save a few of the biggest ones by cutting down all the others.*

(ABOVE): *Use a pole saw to remove dead, weak, crowded, crossing, or low-lying limbs from your trees. A telescoping pole lets you reach way up into the tree while standing safely on the ground.*

cleanup pruning can be done at any time of year. Remove whatever limbs you can reach yourself with a pruning saw and a pole saw. Hire help removing limbs too big for your saw or too tall for you to reach.

Safety is another reason for removing dead and damaged limbs, especially big ones, from trees in your yard. These limbs can break and drop — usually during windstorms but sometimes spontaneously — with no warning. It's unlikely that anyone will be standing underneath at the moment a limb falls, but it could land on your car, blow against the house, or crush some shrubs.

TREE IS UNHEALTHY. Dead limbs don't necessarily imply that anything is wrong with a tree, but discolored, disfigured, or damaged leaves are warning signs that you shouldn't neglect. Keep watch over your trees, and if you notice anything irregular, seek help. Interpreting a tree's distress symptoms is difficult, and you probably can't diagnose the problem yourself.

When a tree — or any other plant — doesn't look right, most homeowners assume that there's a pest or disease problem, but often the symptoms are caused by a sudden change in the tree's environment or growing conditions. An established tree is affected by the removal of nearby trees, increased foot traffic that compacts the soil around its roots, construction or paving in the vicinity, ground work that changes the drainage and soil moisture, increased or

decreased irrigation, or the use of broad-leaf weed killers such as those contained in weed-and-feed lawn fertilizers. If you have a distressed tree, try to think of anything you might have done to disturb it, and describe these possibilities when you seek an expert's diagnosis of the tree's problem.

Whoever identifies the problem for you can give you a prognosis. If it sounds serious, get a second opinion from another expert before beginning any treatment program. Arborists will go to great lengths to try to save a tree for you by spraying it or injecting it with chemicals, but these costly treatments may only postpone the inevitable. Sometimes you just have to admit that a tree is going to die. In other cases, the tree can take care of itself and really doesn't need your attention.

For example, it looks devastating when insect pests such as gypsy moths, Japanese beetles, or lace bugs eat a tree's leaves. Severe leaf loss can weaken a tree, but it's rarely fatal. By contrast, many trees are killed by borers and bark beetles, which drill holes into the trunk and disappear inside to do their damage. You may not realize they're present until it's too late and the tree is dead and has to be removed. Even if you detect these pests, there's little you can do about them once they're inside a tree. If attacked by borers or bark beetles, a tree usually dies within a year or two.

Trees are susceptible to a host of fungal and bacterial diseases. The many symptoms include wilting,

dead twigs, spots or smudges on the leaves, and leaves dropping in summer instead of fall. Sometimes the damage is superficial and the tree will recover by itself and grow normally the next season. It's uncommon for a single tree to die from a plant disease. The most serious diseases that afflict trees tend to spread throughout a region and cause extensive, not scattered, losses. That's what happened with the chestnuts, elms, and dogwoods in eastern North America; in each case, a disease killed millions of specimens over a period of years. Typically local experts are aware of these problems and can identify them for you, but they rarely can offer any solution. If a tree is infected with a fatal disease, you may delay its death, but you probably can't prevent it.

NOTHING GROWS UNDER THE TREE. A big bare spot under a tree ordinarily indicates that the tree's roots are so pervasive and dominant that other plants can't get enough water to survive and/or that the tree's canopy casts too much shade, but sometimes the area under a tree is barren because the soil is so meager. Tree seeds sprout and grow on rocky hilltops, gullied slopes, and cracked pavement — conditions that would vanquish plants with weaker roots. In many cases, the best response is to spread mulch or porous pavement under the tree and accept its priority. Don't try growing anything else there. Use the space for a sitting or storage area, or put a birdbath, sculpture, or big rock under the tree.

If you're determined to grow plants under the tree, it's probably possible. You'll most likely have to thin the canopy and remove the tree's lower limbs to let in more light, and to give plants underneath a chance to get rooted by adding thin layers of topsoil and mulch, building raised beds, or planting in containers.

Bare ground beneath a tree is sometimes attributed to a phenomenon called allelopathy, in which a plant releases chemicals that harm or stunt other species. Black walnut trees, in particular, are accused of allelopathy and blamed for "poisoning" the soil around them, but that story has been blown way out of proportion. A few plants, notably tomatoes, are harmed by black walnuts, but most shrubs, perennials, ground covers, and grasses grow happily beneath these and other allegedly villainous trees, oblivious to all the rumors and warnings.

TOO MUCH SHADE. If the area beneath an individual tree is so shady that plants lean and stretch, you can improve their situation by removing the tree's lower limbs and thinning its canopy. Do this pruning in summer for deciduous trees or anytime with evergreens. Crouch underneath the tree, as if you were a plant trying to grow there, and look up to see how much sky is visible. Identify particular tree limbs that block large areas of sky, and cut them off to create openings. This allows dappled light to reach the ground. You can remove about one-fifth to

To develop this site, which was once second-growth woods, someone selected the straightest, strongest tulip trees and pines and removed their lower limbs, then cleared out dozens of smaller, weaker trees and brush. This lets in enough light and air to allow an underplanting of flowering dogwood trees, which tolerate part shade, along with flower beds and lawn.

On this site, existing black locust trees were "limbed up" and the brush between them cleared away. Now gravel paths wind between slightly raised beds filled with hostas, rhododendrons, and other shade-tolerant perennials and shrubs.

one-quarter of a tree's foliage without doing serious harm.

Do the thinning yourself if you're comfortable tackling such a job. Using a pole saw, you can remove limbs up to 3 to 4 inches thick and reach up to about 15 feet high. Take your time, and don't feel you have to finish in a single session. Hire an arborist if you have any hesitation about what you're doing or if the job is too big for you.

Some trees have such dense foliage or so many branches, or they grow back so quickly, that pruning isn't an effective or practical way to reduce the shade they cast. Then you have to decide: Would you rather keep the tree or cut it down so you can grow other plants there?

Buying and caring for a new tree

Trees are sold in a wider range of sizes than any other landscape plants. You can buy year-old seedlings the size of a pencil, or massive, decades-old specimens with trunks as thick and tall as a utility pole, at prices ranging from a few dollars to many thousands of dollars. Most homeowners choose a middle course, buy trees about 5 to 10 feet tall, and are satisfied with the results. A medium-size tree, somewhat taller than you are but still small enough that two workers can handle it, has some treelike presence immediately after planting, is moderately priced, and usually

recovers fairly quickly from the shock of being transplanted.

Why would anyone go to the extremes of buying tiny or huge trees? It's mostly a matter of attitude, style, and time frame. Creating immediate impact is the main reason for transplanting specimen trees (although sometimes mature trees are moved to rescue them from sites slated for clearing and development). There's an element of bravado in moving big trees. Success requires expert skills, the right equipment, diligent aftercare, and luck. If all goes well, the tree survives, but it will probably remain static for years afterward, with little gain in height or spread, before it resumes active top growth, if it ever does.

By contrast, a child with a trowel can transplant a seedling. It won't look like anything at first, but in the years from kindergarten to college that tree will grow 20 to 30 feet or taller, radiating youthful vigor and beauty, and it will continue developing afterward. Planting baby trees may seem naively optimistic, but it's actually quite wise, and watching them grow brings priceless satisfaction. People like me who enjoy this process usually have a nursery area where we grow new trees in rows or pots for a few years before moving them to their permanent location. If you plant a tiny tree directly where you want it to grow, be sure to mark its place and protect it from encroaching weeds, the lawn mower, and the like.

PLANTING UNDER A TREE

Since most tree roots are close to the surface, digging holes to plant shrubs, ground covers, or other plants beneath a tree is likely to damage some of its roots. Minimize this damage by preparing individual planting holes—don't try to till or cultivate the entire area. Watch for tree roots as you're digging holes, and if you encounter a large root or a mass of little ones, move the hole rather than severing the roots.

If you want to end up with a mass planting, choose plants that spread sideways as they grow. That way you can start with fewer plants, spaced farther apart, than you would need if you used upright or clump-forming plants.

Another approach, helpful when you're planting large num-bers of small ground-cover or perennial plants, is to raise the bed under the tree by adding a layer of topsoil. This can be up to 6 inch-es thick at the drip line but should taper to nothing beside the trunk. If the tree has a mass of shallow, surface roots, spread over-lapping layers of newspaper on the ground first before adding the soil. Otherwise, the tree will immediately send roots up into the new soil, and such tree roots are so aggressive that it's hard for a new planting to compete with them for water and nutrients. The newspaper will decompose after a few months, but that's enough time to give new little plants a chance to get started. Adding a layer of soil won't hurt the tree if you don't overdo it.

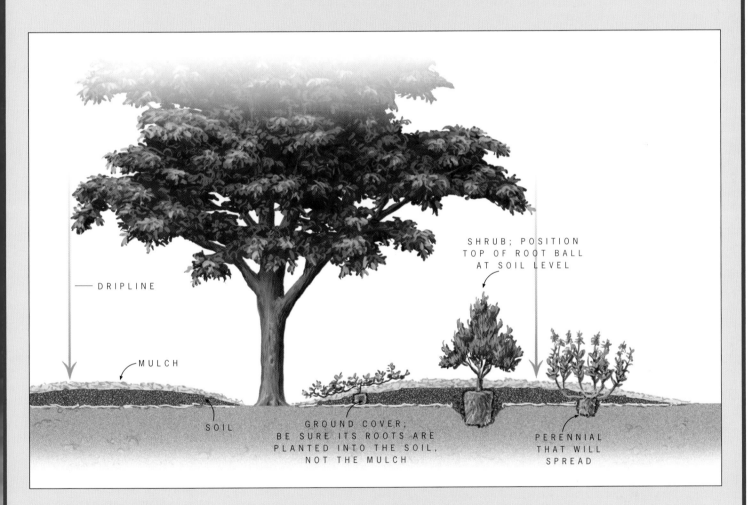

SHRUB; POSITION TOP OF ROOT BALL AT SOIL LEVEL

DRIPLINE

MULCH

SOIL

GROUND COVER; BE SURE ITS ROOTS ARE PLANTED INTO THE SOIL, NOT THE MULCH

PERENNIAL THAT WILL SPREAD

PLANTING UNDER A TREE

(LEFT) *Spread newspapers several sheets thick, overlapping the edges, to form a temporary barrier between the tree roots and the added soil. Add topsoil, piling it up to 6 inches deep at the drip line but tapering to nothing at the trunk. Top with 2 to 3 inches of mulch, tapering to nothing at the trunk.*

(RIGHT) *Choose ground covers that spread. Be sure to plant their roots down into the soil, not just in the mulch. Dig individual planting holes for shrubs, digging into the old soil below the newspaper if nec-essary to make a deep enough hole. Choose perennials that spread to form a patch, to minimize the number of holes you have to dig.*

WHAT TO LOOK FOR. If you're at a local garden center trying to select a tree to buy, set it apart from the group (ask for help if you can't move it yourself) and examine it from all sides. In general, a tree should have a single trunk that's fairly straight and strong enough to stand up without a stake. If you want a multitrunked specimen, the trunks should diverge at or near the ground. Either way, the tree's limbs should spread in all directions, forming a fairly uniform crown. No tree is perfectly symmetric, but it shouldn't be too crooked or lopsided. Typically there's one shoot in the center of the tree—called the leader—that points up and is taller than the side shoots. If the leader is missing or broken, the trunk will fork or bend; that might be okay, but it's something to consider. The leader and other limbs should be stiff and shapely, with leaves or buds all along their length, not straggly, floppy, bare shoots with tufts at the tips.

Examine the trunk and limbs for wounds or scars, and don't buy a tree with obvious damage. Look for dead or broken twigs; a few are okay, but there shouldn't be many. If leaves are present, they should have a healthy color.

PLANTING AND STAKING A TREE. Plant a small, young tree like other plants (see page 276).

Make sure you don't set it too deep. The top of the root ball should be at or slightly above ground level. If you're planting a bare-root tree, look for a color change on the bark near the base of the trunk. That indicates how deep it was planted before. Align the color change at ground level. Before refilling the planting hole with soil, make sure the tree's trunk is vertical and that its "good" side is facing the way you want it.

Mound the soil into a low berm around the perimeter of the planting hole to make a watering basin, and test it to make sure that the berm holds water until it soaks in and doesn't let any leak out and get away. A good way to water young trees is by putting the end of a hose inside the berm, adjusting the tap to a slow flow, and letting the water run for an hour or so.

Most trees don't need staking, and you should not stake a tree if you don't have to—it can do more harm than good. The best reason for staking is to hold a leafy tree upright on a windy site just long enough for it to establish strong roots. In that situation, drive two sturdy stakes on opposite sides of the tree, about 3 feet away from the trunk, at right angles to the prevailing wind. Loosely loop rope or wire ties between the stakes and the trunk, just below the lowest branches; thread the ties through cut-off sections

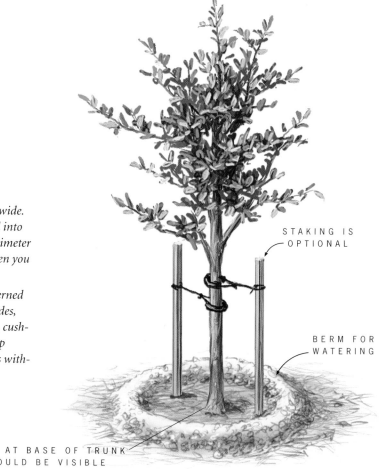

STAKING IS OPTIONAL

BERM FOR WATERING

FLARE AT BASE OF TRUNK SHOULD BE VISIBLE ABOVE THE SOIL

PLANTING A TREE

Dig a hole no deeper than the root ball and three to five times as wide. Position the tree and refill the hole, watering well to settle the soil into place around the tree's roots. Shape a berm of soil around the perimeter of the hole, so that water soaks down rather than running off when you irrigate the tree over the coming year.

Staking is optional and generally not required, but if you're concerned that the tree may blow over, drive two stakes firmly at opposite sides, perpendicular to the direction of the prevailing wind. Attach ties, cushioning them with lengths of old hose or strips of inner tube to keep them from cutting into the tree's bark. Remove the ties and stakes within one year after planting the tree.

This 'Zumi' crab apple has been well trained and pruned. The limbs diverge at wide angles, and all the weak twigs and interior clutter have been removed. Thoughtful pruning makes the tree stronger and healthier.

This maple tree was neglected when young. Extra limbs should have been thinned out, and the narrow crotches should have been eliminated. Now the crown is badly formed, with too many limbs crowded much too close together. Such contorted growth is more than unsightly. It means the tree is vulnerable to decay and breakage, and the leafy crown casts extra-dense shade on the ground below.

of an old rubber hose to keep them from cutting into the trunk. Remove the stakes and ties within one year.

If a young tree's trunk is so floppy that it doesn't stand up straight, that probably means it has been overfertilized and is growing too fast. It's better not to buy a tree like this, but if you do, use a stake to support it for no more than one year, and don't fertilize it during that time. Tie it to the stake loosely, so it can blow in the wind—that helps strengthen and stiffen the trunk. If it doesn't stand up after a year, the tree may never straighten up right, and you should replace it with a stronger specimen.

If you buy a tree that's too tall and heavy for you to handle, ask the nursery to deliver and plant it for you. (This service is often included in the price of a large tree.) With their trucks, hoists, and crews, a nursery or a landscape contractor can move large trees safely. Large trees may need staking. Let the planting crew decide and do it for you. Stakes and ties should be removed as soon as the tree is firmly rooted, usually within one year of planting.

PRUNING AND TRAINING A YOUNG TREE. Old-timers used to say that you should prune back the top of a tree when you plant it to compensate for roots lost when it was dug. Disregard that old advice. It never did apply to container-grown trees, and research has shown that there's no need to reduce the tops of bare-root or B&B trees either. According to today's tree experts, you should prune only to remove any broken branches at the time you plant a tree. Wait until the tree has been growing for a full season before you begin to direct and shape its growth.

When pruning a tree, always use sharp tools and make clean cuts. To remove a limb, cut just outside the little ridge, or "collar," where it joins a larger limb or the main trunk, and leave that collar intact, as it helps heal the wound. Cutting too close to the trunk makes a larger, more vulnerable wound. Cutting too far away leaves an unsightly, decay-prone stub.

Identify the central stem, or leader, that forms the main trunk of the tree; it's the tallest shoot and it should head straight up. Leave it alone. If there seem to be two or more parallel leaders, choose the strongest one and cut off the other(s) to produce a single-trunked specimen. If you want a multi-trunked tree, buy one that's already started that way, with trunks diverging at ground level.

Leaving lower limbs in place helps the trunk grow thicker and stronger, so remove them gradually. Each year, remove a few of the lowest limbs and cut the ones above them back partway. Continue this until the trunk is clear for roughly 8 feet — high enough so you can walk under the branches, or higher than that if you want to let more light reach under the tree to benefit plants beneath it.

The lowest limbs that you permanently leave in place should form a strong, attractive framework for the leafy crown. For these main limbs, choose three to five side branches that head off in different directions and diverge from the trunk at a wide angle (preferably at least 60°).

Start with shrubs when you're creating a garden and you may not need any other kinds of plants. Shrubs come in a full range of sizes, shapes, textures, and colors.

It's particularly important to eliminate narrow crotches or shallow forks — places where two main branches or a branch and the main trunk form a skinny vee. These intersections are very likely to split apart during storms. One way to prevent this problem is by removing the weaker branch. Other solutions are to widen the angle by inserting a block of wood between the branches while they are still young and pliable, by attaching weights to a limb to lower it away from the trunk, or by tying the limb to a stake to pull it down into a better position.

Also watch for limbs that cross and rub against each other. Rubbing damages the bark and can eventually kill one or both of the limbs, so prevent this by removing whichever limb is thinner or weaker any time you spot a pair of crossing limbs.

Otherwise, young trees need little further pruning. Simply remove any limbs that are damaged by storms or accidents and any dead twigs.

SHRUBS

Evergreen and deciduous shrubs of all shapes and sizes are the building blocks of a home landscape, useful as single specimens, in mixed borders, as an understory beneath tall trees, in foundation plantings, as ground covers, and for hedges and edgings. Their versatility reflects the variety of shrub shapes and sizes. The category of shrubs includes lilacs and ligustrums with upright, treelike trunks; fountain-like forsythias that form huge mounds of arching stems; dwarf boxwoods that make compact bush-balls; and creeping bearberry that hugs the ground. Some shrubs grow just a few inches a year, while others can grow 6 feet in a season. Some shrubs can be ignored for decades, while others are fussy and need frequent attention. It's a wide and wonderful group of plants.

Because they're so diverse in terms of mature size and shape, rate of growth, and adaptation to different growing conditions, it's very important to choose shrubs carefully before you plant. Many, perhaps most, problems result from planting a shrub in a site that's too sunny or shady, too wet or dry, or — nine times out of ten — too small for its ideal growth. If planted in favorable conditions and given plenty of space, shrubs provide years of pleasure and require only routine care. But if they're stressed or squeezed, you'll do more work for less reward.

If you're disappointed, annoyed, or bored by any of the shrubs you have now, you might be able to solve the problem, but often the best solution is to get rid of the problematic old shrub and plant a fresh new one. The typical life span for a landscape shrub is one to three decades. Old shrubs may be too vigorous and outgrow their space, or they may go into decline and gradually get straggly and weak. Sometimes they lose their charm, go out of fashion, or

NATURAL

EXTENSIVE THINNING

SHEARING

PRUNING STYLE

A shrub such as this yew can be shaped in different ways, depending on how you prune it. To simply enhance its natural shape (ABOVE LEFT), do routine thinning and only head back shoots that stick out too far. Shearing (LEFT) imposes a geometric shape on the shrub. Extensive thinning (ABOVE) opens the shrub into an irregular, artistic shape and exposes its trunks.

look dated. Meanwhile nurseries keep introducing new kinds of shrubs that are prettier, healthier, and better than ever, so choosing replacements is lots of fun. Replacing some shrubs is a great way to change the looks of your yard. It has a big impact but is fast, easy, and inexpensive to do.

Another encouraging point is that compared with trees, shrubs cause few worries. Although shrubs can make fine specimens, they're rarely considered as valuable or as irreplaceable as trees are. You may feel sad about losing or removing a big old shrub, but it takes only years, not a lifetime, to grow a replacement. Because they're smaller than trees, shrubs are generally easier to care for. You can plant, prune, or remove them yourself, without special equipment or professional help. And shrubs never endanger people or property as trees sometimes do; if a limb breaks off a lilac bush, it won't break your arm or dent your car.

Pruning shrubs

Aside from watering, fertilizing, and mulching, pruning is by far the major activity in caring for shrubs. Pruning keeps shrubs healthy and attractive and promotes vigorous growth and generous flower-

ing. Only a few kinds of shrubs never need pruning. Most require at least one or two sessions a year; these may take a few minutes or an hour or more.

The most common reason for pruning a shrub —to control its size—is not the best reason. Don't compare pruning to mowing a lawn; shrubs shouldn't need constant cutting back. Instead, think of pruning as a way to enhance a shrub's natural beauty, to groom it, refine its shape, keep it dense, and stimulate strong shoots, healthy foliage, and abundant bloom.

I don't think it's necessary to itemize different guidelines for pruning every different kind of shrub. Basically there are three principles to remember. (1) Any stem or branch that's dead or damaged can and should be removed. (2) Cutting into live wood has an immediate effect on the shrub's appearance, but more important, it influences how future growth will develop. (3) Take your time, don't cut off too much at once, and step back frequently to judge the results and decide where to cut next. Don't worry if you botch a cut. Try to learn a lesson so you'll do better next time. Most shrubs recover from amateurish pruning just as quickly as you recover from a bad haircut.

Many shrubs have a characteristic shape, or habit. **(RIGHT)**: *Double-file viburnum has over-lapping layers of arching limbs.* **(BELOW)**: *Garden hydrangea forms a hemisphere, while trailing cotoneasters spread horizontally across the ground.*

shearing, you work over the surface of the plant. To thin, you reach way down inside. Shearing cuts the ends off the most vigorous shoots. Thinning removes the weak or dead shoots. Shearing prematurely ages a shrub, but thinning keeps a shrub healthy and prolongs its life.

You can thin a shrub at any time of year. Use sharp pruning shears for most limbs, and a small pruning saw for thicker trunks. Pull aside the outer branches and peer inside a leafy or evergreen shrub. Crouch down at the base and look up into a shrub that grows upright. Lift the upper layers of limbs and examine the "underskirts" of a shrub that spreads horizontally. In every case, look for shoots or limbs that are dead and bare, weak and nearly leafless, or skinny and straggly. Remove them all by pruning them off where they join a larger stem or close to the ground. Also look for limbs that cross or rub against each other and remove whichever one is thinner. Look for limbs that are heading toward the center of the shrub and remove them; growth should face outward, not inward.

Getting rid of weak, dead, crossing, and wayward limbs lets more air and light into a shrub, reduces sites that host diseases and pests, and makes the shrub look neat and cared for.

Shrubs that get an annual checkup may need only a few shoots removed, but a shrub that hasn't been thinned for years or that has never been thinned may need a major cleaning. This can take an hour or more and yield quite a pile of dead brush.

If you try to thin a shrub that's been sheared, proceed cautiously. Look inside, and you'll see that most of the stems are basically bare. But you can't remove them all, or there won't be anything left. Remove just a few at a time, working here and there,

RESPECT THE SHRUB'S NATURAL HABIT.
If allowed to develop naturally, most shrubs take on a characteristic shape, or habit. This may be a narrow upright column, a grove or thicket of erect stems, a vase-shaped or fountainlike clump, a ball, a dome-shaped mound or cushion, a stack of layered limbs, a creeping mat, or a vinelike sprawl. Whatever it is, if you accept and work with a shrub's natural habit, rather than trying to force it into a different shape, your life will be easier and your landscape will be more interesting, varied, and distinctive.

MAKE A HABIT OF THINNING. Thinning, the best technique for routine pruning of most shrubs, differs from shearing in many ways. When

Shearing means cutting a few inches off the top and sides of a shrub in order to create a clear, simple shape with a dense, uniform, close-textured surface. Shearing is not an all-purpose technique. It's popular because the job goes fast, especially if you use an electric hedge trimmer, and because it requires little skill. Most shrubs tolerate annual shearings year after year, and some seem to thrive on this treatment, but that impression is almost always superficial. Although a sheared shrub may look healthy and green on the surface, if you pull the branches apart and peer inside you'll see a mass of dead twigs. When a plant has more dead than live wood, it's inevitably weaker than normal and more subject to various problems such as pests, diseases, and weather damage. There are sheared hedges in England that have been going for centuries, but in a typical American home landscape, sheared plantings usually look worn out or shabby (or simply dated) after ten or twenty years and need to be replaced then.

- **WHEN TO SHEAR.** The occasion for shearing is when the overall shape or size of a planting is more important than the particular kind of plant or its characteristics. For example, a landscape architect or designer might specify certain dimensions for a hedge, to make it suit the scale of the house and property. By shearing, you can maintain a hedge at approximately the desired height, width, and profile for many years. Shearing is also the technique for maintaining closely clipped edgings, topiary, and formal espaliers.

- **HOW TO SHEAR.** Clip off some or almost all of the new growth at least once a year or as often as several times dur-

ing the growing season, depending on how fast the shrub grows and how precisely shaped you want it to look. Use an electric hedge trimmer or hand hedge shears. Sharpen the blades as often as needed to make clean cuts that slice, not tear, through stems and leaves.

Generally, you can shear year-round where winters are mild. Where winters get cold, shear anytime from midfall through the winter and spring and into midsummer, but avoid shearing in late summer or early fall, as it can stimulate new growth that is extra susceptible to frost damage.

If the shrub has been continually sheared in the past, follow its established contours. The trickiest thing about shearing is establishing and maintaining level tops, straight edges, flat planes, uniform curves, and other conspicuous geometric features. Proceed slowly and stop often to step aside and scrutinize your work, or have a helper stand back and give you directions and feedback.

Try not to cut back into older wood; just remove new growth. Normally there's an incremental size increase in sheared plants; you might let them get an inch or so taller and wider every year. At that rate, it can take a decade (or a lifetime) for a sheared planting to outgrow its space, and by then it will probably need replacing anyway.

- **SHEARING A NEW PLANT.** If you plant a new shrub or hedge that you intend to maintain by shearing, prune it hard the first season you plant it to encourage it to branch out near the base, then continue shearing on a regular basis, leaving it a few inches taller and wider each time until it reaches the desired size.

Shearing can be used to create a deliberate, architectural effect. Here the shapes are very precise, and the plants are carefully positioned and aligned with relation to the house and hardscape.

Shearing hedges takes a good eye. Step back often to check yourself and make sure you're getting the shape right.

THINNING A SHRUB

Look inside the shrub to identify old, dead, weak, damaged, or crossing limbs, and remove them by cutting them off at a main stem or close to the ground. If the shrub has been neglected for years, there will be a lot of stems that need to be removed. If you thin regularly, you may find only a few to take out. You can thin a shrub at any time of year.

HEADING BACK

Heading back a shrub makes it shorter or smaller and also affects subsequent growth.

(ABOVE): *Cutting off the end of a stem makes a bushier plant, because it encourages buds below the cut to develop into side shoots.*

(RIGHT): *A new shoot grows out in the same direction as the bud closest to the cut was pointing. If there are two opposite buds there, you can remove one of them if you choose.*

taking out only the weakest, deadest-looking stems. Thinning is good for a sheared shrub, since it eliminates old wood and opens up the interior. It does leave gaps in an otherwise flush surface, but these soon fill in with new growth.

DO HEADING BACK TO SHAPE NEW GROWTH. "Heading back" means cutting the end off a long, unbranched stem to encourage lower side shoots to develop. This is the way to make young shrubs grow fuller and bushier, and it's useful for trimming older shrubs, too.

To head back, use pruning shears and do one stem at a time. Cut right next to a healthy bud or leaf (or pair of opposite buds or leaves). How much should you cut off? It depends. If you buy a young shrub that has only a few tall straggly stems, you might cut them back severely, leaving stubs only 6 to 12 inches tall. More typically you just cut a shoot back by about one-third to one-half its length, or enough to bring it in line with the rest of the shrub.

In general, do heading back of most young shrubs once a year in early spring, just before new growth starts. The exception is shrubs that flower in spring; with them, wait until right after the flowers fade, and prune then. With older shrubs, which usually need less heading back, simply cut back wayward or too-tall shoots right after they elongate in spring or summer. Lower side shoots may develop right away, or they may form the following year.

HOW PRUNING RELATES TO FLOWERING AND FRUITING. Most shrubs that bloom in late winter, spring, or early summer flower on *old growth*, or shoots that formed the previous growing season. Shear, thin, or head back these shrubs right after they bloom. If you wait until mid- or late summer, you risk cutting off the next year's flowers. Most shrubs that bloom in summer or fall flower on *new growth*, formed during the current growing season. You can prune these anytime between late fall and late spring without sacrificing any blooms.

(LEFT): *Use a combination of thinning and heading back to enhance the natural grace of an arching shrub like this bridal-wreath spirea. Once a year, thin out some of the oldest stems by cutting them off at ground level. Then cut the remaining stems back partway to encourage branching. Buds form on old growth, so do this pruning in late spring, right after the flowers fade.*

(BELOW): *Don't deadhead shrubs whose flowers ripen into showy fruits, as on this Siebold viburnum.*

DEADHEADING. The blossoms on some shrubs look messy or faded as they age and you may choose to remove them for appearance' sake. This is called deadheading. Snap the flowers off by hand if that makes a clean break, use sharp pruning shears to head back individual stems, or shear the surface of a bush that's covered with small flowers.

Deadheading isn't always necessary or feasible. It's commonly recommended because producing seeds or fruits requires energy that a shrub could otherwise direct to new leaf growth, repeated bloom during the current growing season, or more abundant bloom next year. However, the impact of dead-

(BELOW): *With rhododendrons, it's important to deadhead, or snap off the flower heads, right after the petals drop. This prevents seed formation and directs the plant's energy toward forming the next year's buds.*

heading varies from shrub to shrub, especially in terms of stimulating rebloom. Sometimes it really matters, other times it's a waste of energy. For any particular shrub, try it and see if you notice any results.

Some shrubs are so stressed by fruit production that if their seeds are allowed to ripen one year, the plants bloom sparsely or not at all the next. This sets up an alternation of "on" and "off" years and is typical of untended lilacs, mountain laurels, and rhododendrons. The same shrubs bloom annually if you prune off their seeds as soon as they form, soon after the flowers fade. Many other shrubs, though, including hollies, pyracanthas, and viburnums, can bloom reliably year after year even though they also produce tremendous crops of colorful fruits.

PRUNING A DAMAGED SHRUB. When a shrub gets damaged by accident, wind, ice or snow, foraging deer, or other causes, tend it as soon as possible, partly for its sake and partly for your own—you'll feel better when the damaged parts are out of sight. Remove all the broken limbs and jagged stubs, making neat cuts next to a main trunk or close to the ground. If this leaves just a few undamaged stems sticking up at random, shorten them by one-third or more. Then watch what happens the next growing season. Many shrubs have the ability to send up new shoots from the roots or stubs and recover from storm damage and subsequent hard pruning in just a few years to look better than ever.

In winter, if a sudden or severe cold spell freezes the tops of a marginally hardy shrub and turns its leaves and stems tan, brown, or black overnight, don't cut off the discolored parts right away, because you can't tell yet how severe the damage is. Wait until spring, then look closely to distinguish live stems with supple "green" wood and swelling buds from brittle, dead, budless stems. Prune away all the dead parts. In the worst-case scenario, cut the shrub to the ground in early spring and wait until summer to see if any new growth comes up from the roots; if not, uproot and discard it then.

WHEN, WHY, AND HOW TO DO SEVERE PRUNING. In a few situations, the best thing to do is cut all a shrub's stems off close to the ground, or no more than about 1 foot tall. Early spring is the best time for this job. Severe pruning has an all-or-nothing effect. It can kill some shrubs, especially old broad-leaved evergreens and conifers, but most deciduous shrubs and some evergreens respond to this drastic treatment by sending up a flush of vigorous new shoots.

Severe pruning can rejuvenate an old shrub that's gotten sparse and leggy after many years of neglect. If you try this, be brave enough to go all the way. Cut the old stems off close to the ground; don't be timid and leave waist-high stubs. A shrub looks best if new growth sprouts up from the base.

More often, a severe pruning in early spring is used as an annual treatment for shrubs that freeze

Certain deciduous shrubs grow best if you shear them hard every year in late winter. This cutleaf elderberry will bloom on new wood in summer and get 6 feet tall by fall. In the meantime, daffodils add color around its base.

(ABOVE): *Red-twig dogwood has the reddest bark on young twigs, so it's a good idea to cut it to the ground every spring. If that's unnerving to you, cut only half of them. Either way, it will grow back 6 to 8 feet tall by late summer and form a wider clump every year. This plant, grown from a rooted cutting and pruned every spring, is only 6 years old.*

(ABOVE): *'Shibori' and other summer-flowering spireas bloom on new growth. If you cut all the old stems close to the ground in spring, this shrub will form a flower-covered dome like this in July.*
(RIGHT): *Crape myrtles also flower on new growth, but cut them back only partway, not to the ground, because old crape myrtles develop handsome sinuous trunks with colorful mottled bark.*

back more or less every winter and flower on new growth, such as blue-mist shrub, butterfly bush, chaste tree, crape myrtle, summer-flowering spireas, and many kinds of roses (if they're grown on their own roots, not grafted).

An annual hard pruning in early spring is also a good way to maintain certain fast-growing shrubs that are valued for fancy or colorful foliage or colorful twigs. This produces a fresh, lush display of new growth every year and keeps the plants neat and compact. Shrubby willows, red-twig dogwoods, smoke tree, purple-leaf sand cherry, and fancy-leaved elderberries are some deciduous shrubs that respond well to this treatment.

Addressing common shrub problems

Unlike trees, which can pose dangerous or expensive problems, a problematic shrub is usually just an annoyance or a disappointment, and you rarely need expert help or advice. Here are some typical situations and what you can do about them.

SHRUB IS IN THE WRONG PLACE. Sometimes you can save an otherwise desirable but poorly sited shrub by moving, or transplanting, it. (For more on moving established plants, see the box on page 282.) This works best with small or medium-size shrubs. Moving anything that's more than 4 to 5 feet tall or wide is risky, but if you have a place to put it, you might as well try transplanting the shrub instead of just throwing it away.

SHRUB IN A LAWN HAS GROWN VERY LARGE. How do you feel about the shrub? Is it beautiful? Does it attract praise? If it's lovely or special, you could simply leave it alone as a specimen framed by the lawn. Better yet, feature it by creating a bed beside or around it and adding plants that complement or contrast with its flowers and foliage.

If the shrub is upright, is taller than you are, and has some trunks that are at least a few inches in diameter (not just skinny stems), you could prune it into a treelike shape. This would give it more character, especially if the trunks bend in an interesting way or have conspicuous bark. It also lets you see through to what's beyond the shrub, and it opens some space around the base for growing other plants.

Do this pruning by thinning, not by heading back. Choose the trunks you want to expose, follow them upward to make sure they support a healthy growth of foliage, and then mark them with tape or string so you won't accidentally cut them as you proceed. Remove all the weaker trunks by cutting them as close to the ground as possible, and trim all the lower side shoots and branches back to the main trunks. After you've removed the obvious limbs, keep stepping back and forth to check the overall shape; this will help you decide what to cut next and when to stop.

If you don't like the shrub in your lawn, if you think it's too big, or if it's misshapen, unattractive, or boring, get rid of it. Cut it down, dig out the roots, and plant something else there.

This collection of evergreens and conifers is overcrowded and has reached a critical point. It's time to remove some of the plants so that others can continue to grow. Otherwise they'll all get misshapen and distorted.

SHRUB CROWDS BUILDING OR BLOCKS WALKWAY. This is likely to be an evergreen that blocks your front door, rubs against the house, or covers half the sidewalk. As a rule, there's no attractive solution to this situation short of removing and replacing the shrub. Once a shrub has grown too wide, you can't make it narrow again. Cutting the sides off exposes a mass of dead wood inside. If you go that far, you might better prune it severely, cutting everything to the ground in hopes of rejuvenating the shrub. But evergreens may die or respond very slowly to that treatment.

Chances are the shrub was one of those inexpensive, common, fast-growing varieties known as "builders' specials." Dig it out and plant something more desirable.

GROUPED SHRUBS ARE TOO CLOSE TOGETHER. A mixed planting of shrubs may look attractive for several years, but sooner or later the taller or more vigorous plants will start to crowd and shade the shorter or slower-growing ones. If you act soon enough, you may be able to rescue the overall planting by removing some shrubs altogether, by

cutting them to the ground and treating the stumps with brush killer. In this case, you usually can't dig a shrub to move it without damaging the roots of the adjacent shrubs.

Which shrubs should you remove? There are no general guidelines. It's a case-by-case decision. Sometimes it's best to take out the bullies—the bigger, fast-growing shrubs—and give the smaller plants a chance. Other times it's better to take out the shorter and weaker shrubs and favor the big specimens. Try to imagine both ways, and compare what the results would be. Consider the value, appearance, and possible life span of the shrubs you would be saving.

After removing some of the shrubs, carefully prune the remaining ones. Do a good thinning and head back any extra-long shoots. Give the plants a boost by applying a moderate dose of fertilizer and adding a fresh layer of mulch. With luck, they'll soon respond to the extra space, light, and air by developing a full, natural shape.

SHRUB HAS TOO MANY BARE STEMS, NOT ENOUGH LEAVES. This may indicate that pruning has been neglected, but it can also mean that the shrub needs more sun. Decide which is the more likely explanation and take appropriate action.

CHOOSING TROUBLE-FREE SHRUBS

Along with matching the shrub to the site and situation and responding to its appearance, here are a few more practical points to consider when choosing shrubs for your landscape.

- **THORNS AND SPINES**. Don't underestimate how exasperating it is to prune or shear a thorny shrub and dispose of the trimmings. Roses, barberries, pyracanthas, hollies, and mahonias can jab you through a leather glove or denim jacket. Do you appreciate their looks enough to put up with their barbs?

- **SUCKERS**. These are sprouts that pop up from a shrub's roots, close to the main trunks or some distance away. If you let them grow, the shrub spreads to form a patch. If you cut or mow them off, the shrub sends up more. This can become a battle of wills. Bayberry, summersweet, sumac, red-twig dogwood, winterberry holly, and many other native shrubs, along with common lilac, deutzia, spirea, and other garden favorites, all tend to form suckers. Use suckering shrubs in informal settings or in transition zones between cultivated and wild landscapes, but not in tidy, formal, or crowded yards where you'll be annoyed if they start to spread.

- **WEEDY SEEDLINGS**. Shrubs that produce berries, such as chokeberry, burning bush euonymus, Tartarian honeysuckle, privets, common lantana, buckthorn, Scotch broom, Russian olive, and buffaloberry, are liable to pop up here and there as unwanted volunteer seedlings. This isn't inevitable; shrubs that go wild in one region may be scarce in another, because seed germination depends on climate. But just in case, if you're considering a berry-producing shrub, ask local gardeners whether or not it's likely to turn weedy in your yard.

Roses are a beautiful nuisance. They need pruning and deadheading, but they're so thorny. Some kinds sucker, others produce unwanted seedlings. It would take a few weekends every spring and hours a week all summer to keep up with a rose garden like this.

Some shrubs tend to be leggy, or bare at the base; this is their normal habit. If you think that's the case with your shrub, just plant something short in front of it.

SHRUB DOESN'T BLOOM. There are several reasons why a shrub that's growing well may fail to flower. It may be too young or small. Many shrubs must reach a certain age and/or size before they bloom. Perhaps you pruned it at the wrong season and cut its buds off. It may need more sun; try pruning nearby trees or moving it away from a shady site. It may need fertilizing. Most shrubs bloom better if you feed them once or twice a year, in spring and/or fall, with a fertilizer that's high in phosphorus. That's the middle number in a fertilizer formula, so look for something such as 3-6-3 or 5-10-5.

Buying, planting, and caring for new shrubs

The key issues in starting shrubs are planning ahead and choosing suitable and desirable kinds, shopping discriminately for the best specimens you can buy, spreading the roots when you set the shrub in the ground, and pruning deliberately for the first few seasons.

SHOPPING FOR SHRUBS. There's a time in spring when it seems as if every garden shop, discount center, chain store, and convenience mart has a truckload of shrubs for sale, and if you're at all susceptible to the puppylike charms of baby bushes, you'll get one and happily carry it home. That's the fun way to get shrubs, but it's not the smart way. Landscapes across America are dotted with shrubs that people bought on impulse, then planted in their yards without thinking about why, where, or how they would fit.

The better way, when you're tempted by a shrub, is to make a note of it but go home empty-handed. Look up the shrub in a garden reference book to learn more about its needs and features and to see how big it gets. Walk around your yard, decide where you'd plant the shrub, and measure to determine if there's enough space for it to grow there. Then go back and buy it, if you still want it.

Better yet is to plan ahead, think about your site over a period of time, do some research and consider what shrubs are good candidates for your growing conditions (see page 232) and which ones would complement your landscape design (page 48), and then go shopping to see if you can find what you want, or ask a friendly nursery or garden center to order the plant(s) for you.

SELECTING THE BEST PLANTS. Finding neat, well-shaped, nicely proportioned specimens is a big challenge when you're shopping for shrubs. This is because most shrubs are produced as an agricultural commodity, on a huge scale at very low margin. At the giant wholesale nurseries where most plants are grown, the containers are packed so close together that shrubs don't have room to grow round and full. They're "pruned," if at all, as quickly as possible, often with hedge trimmers. Land and labor are expensive, the market is competitive, and no one makes enough money growing shrubs to give individual plants optimal space and care.

So don't be surprised if many of the shrubs you find for sale look pinched, lopsided, or hacked. Pick out the best specimens you can find, those with vigorous shoots and healthy-looking foliage. Given enough space, thoughtful pruning, and a little TLC, a skinny but viable shrub can recover from its deprived youth and mature into a bushy adult.

If you want two or more of the same kind of shrub to use for a hedge, ground cover, or other grouped planting, buy them all at once from the same supplier. Take time selecting the individual plants to make sure they match. Line them up side by side, and choose the ones that are most similar in height, bushiness, foliage color, and flower and/or fruit color. For plantings where uniformity is very important, it's a good idea to buy a few extra shrubs as potential replacements in case of damage or loss; plant them in a spare corner and you can transplant them if needed.

PLANTING SHRUBS. Some mail-order and local nurseries still sell certain shrubs in bare-root or balled-and-burlapped form, but nowadays the majority of shrubs are grown and sold in plastic containers. This simplifies storage, shipping, and sales for the nursery business, and it means you can buy a shrub in any season and plant it at your convenience. Don't push your luck, though. In theory, container-grown shrubs can be planted anytime during the growing season. In practice, it's best to plant in spring or fall at least six weeks before the onset of either hot or cold weather.

When planting shrubs, follow the general guidelines for planting (see page 281) and pay special attention to the roots. It's so easy to just pop a container-grown shrub in the ground as if you were planting a bulb, but that's not the right approach. Look for large roots coiled around the edge or the base of the pot; peel them loose and trim their ends off, leaving stubs that point outward like the spokes of a wheel; and spread these stubs as you position the shrub's root ball in its hole. If the shrub has a dense, tangled mat of thin, wiry, or hairlike roots, use a sharp knife to make three or four vertical slits around the edge of the root ball and tease the cut ends of the roots free so they stick out like short

fringe. Work quickly and do one shrub at a time, so the roots don't have time to dry out before you get the shrub planted, then water it promptly.

Because they're typically misshapen when you buy them, shrubs usually need remedial pruning at planting time. Thin out any weak or dead stems, and head back any extra-long shoots. Then wait a full growing season while the shrub gets its roots established. The following spring, do another thorough round of thinning and heading back, or give the shrub a severe pruning. Make a gentler pass the year afterward. Treating a shrub like this while it's young makes it branch near the base and become dense and full rather than skinny and straggly.

CARING FOR SHRUBS. In addition to pruning, newly planted shrubs need routine care, as described in chapter 9. Be sure to water as needed for at least the first year after planting. Use mulch to retain moisture and to stabilize the soil temperature. Keep weeds under control, and don't let any neighboring garden plants flop over onto new shrubs or shade them. Apply winter protection if needed in your climate (see page 283).

VINES

Vines can be herbaceous or woody, with deciduous or evergreen foliage. In almost every case, they're eager or even rambunctious growers that grow faster, get bigger, and live longer than you'd expect. Even vines that start out slowly can be vigorous and tenacious once established. Don't underestimate them.

Your attitude about a vine is likely to proceed through three stages. For a while after planting it, you'll impatiently wonder why it's taking so long to make a show. Then there will be a happy period for a few to several years when the vine looks gorgeous and requires little if any care. Eventually the vine will outgrow its space, look decrepit, or annoy you somehow, and you'll want to do something about it.

Dealing with established vines can pose some serious practical problems. Keep these in mind whenever you're lured by romantic photos of vine-covered cottages or vine-draped trees. What looks lovely in a picture of someone else's garden might prove to be a real headache in your own backyard. To live happily with most vines, you need to either deliberately maintain control or disregard impending chaos. I favor order myself and think the best place for vines is on a freestanding fence or trellis, away from buildings, trees, and shrubs, and I keep my pruners sharp and use them commandingly.

Complaints and concerns about established vines

These issues often arise when you buy property where one or more vines are well established, especially if the vines were neglected by previous owners. They can also develop with vines you planted unknowingly.

VINE HAS GONE UP INTO A TREE.

Whether or not a vine hurts a tree depends on the kind of vine and how it climbs, and on which is more vigorous: the vine or the tree. Sometimes the tree clearly dominates and the vine is just harmless decoration. Other times a bullying vine smothers a weak tree. Sometimes it's a fair but ongoing contest. Whether or not to pull down or kill a vine is usually a judgment call based on your feelings about how it looks and your tolerance for uncontrollability and for risk.

Vines that climb by means of adhesive roots and cling tight against a tree's bark, such as climbing hydrangea and Boston ivy, do little damage. English ivy and wintercreeper euonymus also belong to this group, and it's generally okay to let them run up into your trees, although both eventually (after several

Vines can get huge. The weight of this big old trumpet creeper is pulling down the porch.

decades) can become quite massive, and as big old plants high above the ground they change habits and turn into upright shrubs, not clinging vines.

Vines that climb by twining around a tree's trunk and limbs, such as bittersweet, wisteria, and honeysuckle, cause swollen contortions and may even squeeze to death a young or weak tree. Vines that clamber loosely over a tree and catch hold here and there by means of thorns or twining tendrils, such as grapes, clematis, and climbing roses, weaken a tree by shading its foliage and kill individual limbs by rubbing through their bark. I think twining, tendrilled, and scrambling vines should be removed from any delicate, slow-growing, or valuable lawn or patio tree. You may choose to let these vines remain in big old forest trees around the edge of your property, but realize that they are potentially harmful. If nothing else, the sheer weight and bulk of the vine makes the tree more likely to break apart in wind- or ice storms.

Since many vines can climb 40 feet or higher

and send out new runners that reach 10 feet or longer in a single season, the total volume and weight of an established vine equals that of a small tree. If you have a vine that's threatening to overwhelm a tree, cut through its main stem(s) close to the ground and paint brush killer on the stump right away, according to the directions on the product label. This should kill the vine without hurting the tree. Repeat applications may be needed to kill some vines.

VINE IS THREATENING YOUR HOUSE. Vines that cling to a house or twine around parts such as porch railings can cause problems with dampness and mildew and will interfere with cleaning, painting, repointing mortar joints, and other maintenance. Vines can also lift shingles or cause trouble by growing over gutters or onto a roof and trapping leaves and debris. Big old vines get so heavy that they can sag a porch roof. Removing an entrenched vine is a big job, but the sooner you do it, the better.

Cut the main stem(s) at the ground. You probably won't be able to pull down the vine's runners. You'll have to climb a ladder and cut them loose, unwind them, or scrape them away.

VINE IS BARE AT THE BASE AND BUSHY ON TOP. It's common for woody vines to have one or a few main trunks that are leafless for several or many feet off the ground and a mass of smaller shoots above that produce all the foliage and flowers. If a vine has been growing this way for several or many years, cutting the main trunk(s) close to the ground is a little risky. It might make the vine bush out profusely, but there's also some chance that the vine won't recover. Try to think of those mature bare trunks as a sign of "character," or if for some reason you don't like how they look, plant something in front of them.

VINE IS CLUTTERED WITH DEAD STEMS. Deciduous and herbaceous or tender vines whose leaves and stems freeze back usually look quite messy in winter. Cut off the ugly, dead, and discolored parts at any time before new growth starts in spring.

Evergreen vines may also accumulate a conspicuous tangle of dead twigs inside a veneer of live growth. Every few years, get rid of that old growth by cutting the whole vine down in late winter or early spring.

When used as ground covers, both deciduous and evergreen vines sometimes form a mat of stems that can gradually thicken from ankle-deep to knee-deep. Don't let the tangle build up too deep. Mow or shear it down every few years.

VINE INTENDED AS A GROUND COVER KEEPS TRYING TO CLIMB. Most vines will shoot up vertically if they can, by climbing a wall,

fence, tree trunk, or other structure. You can't prevent this. Just watch for runaway shoots and pull them down whenever you spot them.

VINE IS INFESTED WITH VERMIN. For some reason, house sparrows, rats, wasps, and other unwelcome visitors often take up residence in vines planted against or near a house. An exterminator may be able to solve your problem, or you may end up removing the vine.

Vines don't know when to stop. It's okay to let clinging vines such as Boston ivy or English ivy climb on brick or masonry siding, but trouble begins when they attach to any wooden trim or windows.

VINE DOESN'T FLOWER. Most vines need plenty of sun to bloom well, and too much shade is the most common cause of poor flowering. Other reasons vary from plant to plant. In some cases the flower buds are formed in fall and may freeze during cold winters, or you may inadvertently remove buds by pruning them off. Although some vines bloom as young plants, even while still growing in 1-gallon nursery pots, others don't start to flower until they reach a greater age or size. Most vines bloom better if you feed them once or twice a year, in spring and/or fall, with a fertilizer that's high in phosphorus. That's the middle number in a fertilizer formula, so look for something such as 3-6-3 or 5-10-5.

Planting and tending a new vine

Vines are usually grown and sold like shrubs, in 1- or 5-gallon containers. In general you can buy, plant, and care for a new vine as you would handle a shrub (see page 310), if you take these additional steps.

First, have the support ready. One special consideration for vines is that if you're planning to build or install a trellis, arbor, fence (page 208), or other support, you should finish the construction first and plant the vine afterward. Don't plant the vine now, thinking you'll build something later, because that way the vine would get in your way and you'd probably damage its top or roots as you worked.

HOW VINES CLIMB

Vines climb in different ways, and this affects how far they reach, how tightly they hold on, what kind of support they need, and how hard it is to remove them. You can tell how any particular kind of vine climbs before you buy it by observing it, by asking the nursery staff, or by consulting a reference book.

- **TWINING.** Twining vines, such as akebia, bittersweet, honeysuckle, kiwi, and wisteria, wrap their stems around a support as they climb. They can grip something as thin as a toothpick or as thick as your leg, and they can climb a wire, rope, pipe, metal rod, round or square piece of wood, tree trunk or limb, or any other support, and the support can be smooth- or rough-surfaced.

  The good thing about twining vines is that they don't need to be guided; once started, they climb on their own. However, they're hard to remove. You can't pull twiners down from a tree or off a fence; you have to unwrap them. (It's particularly tedious to extract twiners from a chain-link fence.) And you may have seen what happens when a twining vine coils around a tree; over the years, it distorts the tree's growth into a characteristic pattern of bulges. As you can imagine, getting squeezed into such a weird shape eventually kills the tree.

- **TENDRILS.** Vines such as grapes and passionflowers bear curly tendrils that wrap around and hang onto a wire, string, rope, or other slender support. Clematis, whose leaf petioles act like tendrils, climbs in a similar manner.

  Tendrils can't wrap around anything thicker than your fingers, so vines like this can't climb a smooth post, bare wall or fence, or large tree trunk. To help this type of vine cover a smooth surface, you first have to install netting, a wire grid, or some other support made from elements that are skinny enough for the tendrils to grip. If given something they can hang onto, these vines will climb on their own. Otherwise you have to keep tying them up.

  When these vines freeze, the tendrils often get brittle and break, so it's usually not too difficult to pull down last year's growth in late winter if you want to prune or remove the vine. If these vines grow up into trees and go untended for a few years, though, they get tangled among the twigs and then it's quite hard to pull them down.

- **ADHESIVE ROOTLETS OR TENDRILS.** English ivy, Boston ivy, Virginia creeper, and euonymus are popular vines that form special adhesive rootlets or tendrils. These *holdfasts* can attach the vine to almost any surface, rough or smooth, and they cling so tight that it's quite difficult to peel them away. If you do manage to pull clinging vines off a fence, house wall, or chimney, the rootlets or tendrils leave scablike marks that are almost impossible to remove.

  These vines normally don't adhere to horizontal surfaces and are often used as ground covers, but once they discover a vertical surface and start climbing, they start producing those holdfasts and hang on tight. They're carefree if you want them to climb, but watch out if you don't.

  Although it's generally safe to let a clinging vine climb onto a sound brickwork, masonry, or stucco wall or chimney, keep your pruners handy and trim runners before they attach to window frames, molding, soffits, or shingles. Don't let clinging vines grip the walls of a wooden building.

- **SCRAMBLING.** Climbing roses, Cape plumbago, bougainvillea, smilax, potato vine, and other vinelike shrubs can't climb vertically by themselves. They angle upward by clambering over any nearby plants or structures. Usually their stems have thorns that catch against a surface to help hold them in place.

  If you want a scrambling vine to cover a lattice or an arch, you'll probably have to steer its shoots and tie them in place. If you don't keep fastening them up, the stems are likely to flop forward or sideways. Because they'll need attention, perhaps from a ladder or stepladder, don't use scrambling vines in an awkward or inaccessible location, and don't plant valuable or fragile plants around the base of a scrambler or you'll have to watch your step every time you go to tuck in stray ends.

  For pruning or removal, it's fairly easy to pull down scrambling vines. Wear sturdy clothing and leather gloves, because the thorns are sharp and scratchy.

Be sure the support is appropriate for the kind of vine — strong enough to bear its weight. You may have to lead the vine to the support and tack or tie it in place to get it started. Whether it needs continued guidance will depend on the kind of vine.

After you've planted, be patient. Vines are sometimes slow to get started. They may not shoot up for the first few years, and they may flower sparsely if at all during that time. Once their roots are established, though, they'll take off, and you'll be surprised at how fast they grow then.

PRUNING NEW VINES. When you buy them, most vines have just one or a few thin stems, often attached to a thin bamboo stake. When planting a new vine, remove the stake and head back the stem(s) to about 6 inches tall, cutting just above a healthy leaf or bud. This should stimulate the vine to send out new shoots near the base. After those shoots have each grown several inches long, cut each of them back to a healthy leaf or bud. Doing this kind of severe pruning when a vine is young makes it grow much fuller and bushier. Not only does it look better than a vine with a single stem, it also spreads wider and does a better job of covering a surface.

This Carolina jasmine twines around a heavy guy wire. It is separated slightly from the wall and can be let down if needed. The old bare stems, on the left, have "character."

A ladderlike trellis provides a simple, sturdy support for Confederate jasmine and holds the vine away from the house.

❦OTHER WOODY PLANTS

Palms, yuccas, cacti, bamboos, and various other specialty plants don't quite fit the standard categories of "tree" and "shrub," but they serve similar landscape roles. Most of these plants are heat lovers that do best where summer temperatures regularly climb into the 90s or higher. They are more or less sensitive to frost. Some species are killed outright when temperatures drop much below freezing. Others suffer leaf damage but recover and send out new growth from the stem, trunk, or ground. A few members of these groups are actually quite hardy and easily survive subzero conditions, but that's uncommon.

In general, these specialty woody plants should be planted in summer, when the soil is warm. Buy plants grown in 1- or 5-gallon nursery cans, and plant them like container-grown shrubs (see page 310). Don't be deceived by a plant's small initial size. Research how big it will get and allow plenty of space for it to develop. On suitable sites, most of these plants will live for decades and may eventually grow quite tall and/or spread to form wide patches. Once the plants are established, they're usually difficult to move or transplant because of their extensive root systems and heavy, often spiny or thorny, top growth.

Special care guidelines and tips

Most of these plants prefer full sun and well-drained soil, but you'll have to research particular species to learn their individual preferences. Among palms, for example, some species are drought-tolerant but others need regular deep watering. Among bamboos, some kinds need full sun, while others take part shade. You may have to read between the lines in plant reference books to distinguish between what a plant prefers and what it will tolerate, or just take a chance and hope for the best if you're trying to grow one of these plants in a region where it's uncommon or untested.

These plants typically have fewer pest and disease problems than many common trees and shrubs do, so if you can provide the right growing conditions, they're likely to be trouble-free and nearly carefree. I'll just highlight the special issues you're likely to face when caring for any of these plants.

PALMS. Tall tree palms are normally started from seed and have a single growing point. If that gets damaged somehow, because the top of the plant gets broken off or frozen, the plant usually dies. Shrubby palms often form clumps with several trunks close together, so if one trunk gets damaged or dies, a replacement will probably grow up beside it. As with any other tree or shrub, try to avoid damaging the bark, trunk, or roots of any kind of palm.

Palm fronds can stay green for years unless damaged by frost, wind, or stress, but eventually the older, lower fronds die and turn tan or brown. Sometimes dead fronds fall off spontaneously, but they often persist and build up as thatch around the base of a clump or up the trunk of a palm tree. Thatch generally looks messy, it can get infested with insects and rodents, and it's also a fire hazard. Removing dead fronds is a rough job that calls for protective clothing and thick leather gloves. Watch out for sharp spines, which occur on many palms. If you can't pull off the old fronds, cut them with a pruning saw or machete, leaving stubs a few inches long. Call a landscaper to dethatch a tall old palm tree that's been neglected for years; that's a job you don't want to tackle yourself.

YUCCAS, AGAVES, ALOES, NEW ZEALAND FLAX, AND SIMILAR PLANTS. These plants form large rosettes of tough, often spine-tipped, leaves. New leaves emerge from the center of the rosettes, while the old leaves around the bottom edge gradually die away. You don't have to do anything about those old dead leaves, especially if you can't see them down there, but if the plant is placed so that you can't overlook them, use a pruning saw, pole saw, long-handled loppers, or machete to reach in and cut them off. This is usually an awkward, scratchy, and dusty job, but the plant does look neater afterward. Use similar tools to cut off old flower stalks.

The sap from certain kinds of agaves, in particular, and sometimes from other plants can cause rashes and irritation, so wear protective clothing and wash the sap off right away if any gets on your skin.

Most of these plants eventually form clumps or patches with multiple rosettes or offsets crowded close together. If you decide you don't want it anymore, you have to dig up the whole patch, roots and all—a daunting task that really calls for a bulldozer, although you can do it with hand tools. New shoots may sprout up from any chunks of root that get left behind; if so, squelch them with weed killer.

CACTI AND OTHER SPINY SUCCULENTS. Spiny plants pose two aggravating maintenance problems: they host hard-to-get-at weeds, and they catch windblown litter. Controlling the weeds calls for long-handled weed pullers and herbicide applicators. If you can't find these tools at a local garden center, you can order them from specialty tool catalogs. Use barbecue tongs or a sharp stick to remove paper, litter, and dead leaves that get skewered on the thorns, and a leaf blower or vacuum cleaner to get at debris around the base of the plant.

Cacti are not just spiny, they're also surprisingly heavy. The combination makes them hard to handle if you want to move them. However, their roots are fairly tolerant of disturbance, so it's often possible to transplant or sell a desirable or valuable cactus that you don't want anymore.

If you just want to get rid of an established cactus that's turned ugly or become an annoyance, cut it off at the ground and throw the top away. Dig out the stump, but don't worry about the rest of the root system, as it won't sprout back.

BAMBOOS. Bamboos are very diverse. They range from dwarf, turflike species to tree-sized plants 40 feet tall and have grassy leaves attached to hollow woody stems, or culms, that can be as thin as a knitting needle or as thick as a telephone pole. Learn about its mature size, rate of growth, and hardiness before you buy or plant any kind of bamboo, but even more important, learn about its growth habit.

Basically, there are two groups of bamboos. Clumping bamboos stay where you put them; their culms all emerge from a concentrated central area. Over the decades, a clump gradually widens and typically forms a broad leafy dome, but it never gets out of bounds. It's easy to live with clumping bamboos.

By contrast, running bamboos spread to form a patch or grove. They have underground stems that run horizontally, spreading anywhere from a few inches to many feet each year before emerging as upright culms. These are the bamboos that are notorious for taking over backyards, running under walks or driveways and emerging on the other side, and popping up in neighbors' lawns. In theory, running bamboos can be controlled by breaking off the new

culms as soon as they appear around the edge of the grove, by mowing them off, or by surrounding the patch with a concrete, sheet-metal, or fiberglass barrier that extends 18 inches underground. But in practice, bamboo owners are sometimes naive, busy, tired, lazy, or forgetful. Then the neglected patch of running bamboo turns into a bully.

Getting rid of unwanted bamboo is hard work. First cut all the culms as close to the ground as possible. You'll need to keep changing or sharpening the saw blade, as bamboo quickly dulls a cutting edge. Then keep trimming off new culms as soon as they appear, with a lawn mower or string trimmer, continuing for a year or so until the rhizomes are finally so weakened that no more shoots appear. Alternatively, cut down the culms and then use a mattock to dig up all the underground plant parts. Certain herbicides will kill bamboo if used as directed, but other products are ineffective, so read the fine print on the label.

It usually takes a few years for newly planted bamboo to get established. Afterward, it's nearly carefree. Thin out individual dead or broken stems by sawing them off anytime, or renew an entire patch by cutting it to the ground in early spring. Dead leaves and bud sheaths will drop off and accumulate under any bamboo plant, but they make a good mulch, so it's okay to leave them there.

Bamboos have three stages of hardiness. When exposed to increasing cold, first the leaves turn brown and drop off, then the culms die, and finally the underground rhizomes freeze. This happens in stages—say, at 20°F, 10°F, and 0°F. If the rhizomes survive (the natural leaf mulch helps protect them), established plants can recover from frost damage to aboveground parts by sending out new growth in spring.

(ABOVE LEFT): *Removing the old fronds from palm trunks leaves a spiral pattern of stubs. This Mediterranean fan palm is one of the hardiest palms. It is slow-growing and forms a shrubby clump.*

(ABOVE RIGHT): *Cacti and succulents are associated mostly with frost-free climates, although some kinds are hardy. These plants are sized like regular trees and shrubs but have much more dramatic shapes and silhouettes.*

Don't be a slave to your lawn. If there's more than you want to mow and maintain, replace some areas with other plantings.

11 ❧ Caring for Lawns, Ground Covers, and Perennials

ALTHOUGH THESE three groups require quite different care, I've grouped them here because they're often posed as alternatives. For any given area—a strip of land along the edge of your driveway, for example—it's fairly easy to substitute one option for another. You can dig up an area of lawn and develop it into a flower bed. You can abandon a perennial border and reestablish lawn there. Or you can replace either lawn or perennials with a stand of ground cover. So these are interchangeable, but certainly not equal, ways to fill space in your yard. Which treatment you choose makes a big impact on the design and maintenance of your landscape.

In terms of appearance, lawn is the simplest. It's smooth, homogeneous, and plain green or brown year-round. A big patch of ground cover can look almost as uniform as a lawn, especially if viewed from a distance, but may be more colorful. Ground covers can have gray, blue-green, gold, purple, or variegated foliage and flowers in all colors. Also, ground covers usually have a coarser, more distinct texture than lawn grasses do. Perennials offer the most variety in size, shape, and color and are frequently planted in complex combinations rather than simple masses.

As for maintenance, lawns need frequent mowing, but they don't need skilled care. You can easily hire someone to tend your lawn. By comparison, a well-chosen ground cover needs only periodic grooming, weeding, and trimming (and watering, perhaps) once it's established on a suitable site. Perennials vary. Some are totally carefree and persist for decades even if you ignore them. Others need an annual once-over plus occasional trimming or treatment during the growing season. A few demand lots of special attention and die if they don't get it. (They may die anyway; many perennials live for only a few years.)

True annuals, along with tender perennials and tropicals that are treated like annuals (that is, planted for one season's enjoyment, then discarded), are too ephemeral to count as landscape plants, although they are helpful as prototypes in planning a design and as temporary fillers while permanent plants are still young, small, and far apart. Annuals are also ideal for large and small outdoor planters, window boxes, and other containers. But they're so easy to grow and so thoroughly discussed in other books that I won't include them here.

❦ LAWNS

Lawns are the most common and familiar way to cover ground, and despite the jokes and laments of critics, lawns have real virtues. Turf is soft and resilient and makes a great play surface for children. It's unequaled in its resistance to foot traffic; you can walk all over a lawn, day after day, without hurting it. No other plant tolerates such wear. Turf's fine texture and uniform color make it a useful design element for balancing the richness of varied plantings.

Regarding lawn care, there are two big questions. What are your expectations: do you want golf-course-quality grass, or can you overlook some flaws? And what are your circumstances: does grass grow readily in your yard, or is it a continuous struggle to keep it vigorous and green?

If your standards are reasonable and your site, soil, and climate are favorable for growing grass, maintaining a lawn is not a big deal, and even half-hearted attempts to boost its appearance via fertilizing or weed control bring good results. Since that's my situation, I'm a lawn enthusiast. Ours is far from perfect—a turf purist would scoff that it's laced with clover, but I love to look at it, walk on it, and smell it.

I truly enjoy mowing, with its simple back-and-forth rhythm and the very tangible sense of progress, and I get a lot of satisfaction from hand pulling plantains, dandelions, and other coarse weeds. In this climate, the grass (and clover) stays green most years from April through December with no watering; during the cool, moist weather of spring and fall the color is so vivid that it makes you stare. I spend about an hour a week on lawn care, and at least that much time admiring the results.

The majority of complaints about lawns and lawn care stem from a mismatch of exaggerated expectations and difficult growing conditions. If your standards are too high and your situation is too challenging, you're bound to be frustrated. Take time out and think it over. It's possible to have perfect grass, but is that a worthwhile goal for an average homeowner? Wouldn't very good grass be enough? Or maybe just so-so grass?

And why grow grass at all in places where it doesn't thrive naturally? Most turfgrasses prefer plenty of sun and deep, fertile, well-drained soil with regular rainfall or watering. If you're basically mowing weeds, not grass, rethink your situation. On shady lots, in arid climates, and on poor soils or dry slopes, it's often better to forget about lawns and think about pavement or ground covers instead.

Use mowing to make decisions

Since the size and shape of your lawn determine, to a large extent, how much time and trouble it takes to mow, it makes sense to plan a lawn with mowing in mind.

Try this. Decide how much time you want to spend each time you mow, check your watch, start mowing, and stop when that time is up. How far did you get, what's left over, and what could you do about it? Well, you could sigh and resign yourself to spending more time on mowing. You could get a bigger mower that covers more ground faster. You could compare how much an hour of spare time is worth to you with the hourly wage of local lawn-care crews. You could decide to let some of your grass go unmowed and hope nobody complains. Or you could replace the unmowed area with different plantings.

Here's another exercise. Some day when you're

The "lawn" in the foreground here is a creeping thyme with fragrant evergreen leaves and rosy flowers. Back by the house, the lawn is blue grama grass, a native grass for sunny, dry sites. It needs little if any irrigation.

GROUND COVERS TO REPLACE A LAWN

KEY:

S = needs full sun

PS = tolerates or prefers part shade

Sh = can tolerate full shade

Many plants that make good ground covers for other situations grow too tall to substitute for a lawn, or their surface is too bumpy and irregular. The plants suggested here tend to stay close to the ground (under 4 to 6 inches tall) most of the year, although they may send up taller flower stalks. Most can be cut back with a lawn mower or string trimmer after they flower or if they get too tall or look unkempt. They all tolerate occasional light foot traffic. All stay green throughout the growing season in suitable climates, and most are evergreen or nearly so.

Follow the guidelines (see page 330) on establishing and caring for ground covers, and remember: Don't gamble by planting a ground cover on a large scale until you've already proven its suitability by growing it in a small patch for a year or more, or you've seen it thriving in a nearby garden. This is especially important when choosing a plant for your front yard, where you don't want to risk public disappointment.

- **Yarrow** (*Achillea millefolium*). **S or PS.** Ferny, finely cut, fragrant leaves. Rose-pink or white flowers all summer. **ZONE 3.**

- **Bugleweed, or ajuga** (*Ajuga reptans*). **PS or S.** Low mats of green, bronze, or variegated leaves. Blue (rarely pink or white) flowers in late spring. **ZONE 3.**

- **Catlin sedge, or Texas sedge** (*Carex texensis*). **S or PS.** Looks almost like grass, but a little disheveled. **ZONE 7.**

- **Chamomile** (*Chamaemelum nobile*). **S or PS.** Finly cut, fragrant, bright green leaves; tiny daisylike flowers. **ZONE 4.**

- **Green-and-gold** (*Chrysogonum virginianum*). **S or Sh.** Bears cheery little yellow flowers almost nonstop. **ZONE 5.**

- **Wild strawberries** (*Fragaria chiloensis, F. virginiana*). **S or PS.** Glossy three-part leaves turn maroon in cold weather. Small white flowers; edible berries. **ZONE 5.**

- **Sweet woodruff** (*Galium odoratum*). **PS or Sh.** Leaves in neat whorls. Masses of tiny white flowers in spring. Turns brown in winter and goes dormant in hot summers. **ZONE 4.**

- **Creeping lilyturf** (*Liriope spicata*). **PS or Sh.** Looks like grass with a slight curl. **ZONE 5.** Regular lilyturf (*L. muscari*) has longer, wider leaves and white or violet flowers in late summer. **ZONE 6.**

- **Moneywort** (*Lysimachia nummularia*). **S or Sh.** Trailing stems lined with pairs of round leaves. Bright yellow flowers in summer. 'Aurea' has golden yellow leaves. **ZONE 3.**

- **Mazus** (*Mazus reptans*). **S or Sh.** Almost flat, with fresh-looking foliage and tiny violet or white flowers. **ZONE 5.**

- **Moss** (various kinds). **PS or Sh.** Good under trees or in acid soil. Mosses are evergreen but go dormant and turn brown in dry weather. Most are very hardy to cold but can't take extreme heat.

- **Moss phlox, or thrift** (*Phlox subulata*). **S.** Forms mats of pinlike leaves. Forms a carpet of bloom in spring, usually bright rose or pink, but also comes in white and blue-purple. Mow it right after it blooms. **ZONE 2.**

- **Gold moss sedum** (*Sedum acre*). **S or PS.** Can be weedy and you'll never get rid of it, but tolerates poor soil and neglect. Plump little leaves turn purplish in winter. Bright yellow flowers in early summer. Other evergreen creeping sedums don't spread as fast; some have pink or white flowers. **MOST ARE HARDY TO ZONE 5.**

- **Creeping thymes. S.** Caraway thyme (*Thymus herba-barona*), mother-of-thyme (*T. pulegioides*, often listed as *T. serpyllum*), and 'Reiter' thyme all make good dense lawns. Tiny leaves are green in summer, purple in winter. Tiny rose, pink, or purple flowers are very showy in summer but attract many bees. **ZONE 4.**

- **Creeping verbenas** (*Verbena* 'Homestead Purple', 'Sissinghurst', and other cvs.). **S.** Bright pink, purple, or red flowers are borne from spring to fall. Forms broad mats of lacy foliage. **ZONE 7 OR 6.**

- **Creeping veronicas** (*Veronica liwanensis, V. rupestris* 'Heavenly Blue', and others). **PS.** Tight low mats of glossy leaves topped with stunning blue flowers in early summer. **ZONE 5.**

- **Periwinkle, or myrtle** (*Vinca minor*). **PS or Sh.** Justly popular, because it's so attractive and adaptable. Glossy evergreen leaves; violet-blue flowers in late spring. There are white-flowered and variegated forms, all lovely. **ZONE 4.**

- **Sweet violet** (*Viola odorata*). **S or Sh.** Stays low and spreads by runners to form dense mats. Bears masses of very fragrant blue-violet (sometimes pink or white) flowers in early spring, sometimes again in fall. **ZONE 5.**

(TOP): *Where moss wants to grow, welcome it. It makes an excellent substitute for grass on shady sites with acid soil.*

(MIDDLE): *Creeping juniper is an alternative to grass on a steep bank that would be hazardous to mow. A planting like this needs trimming once or twice a year and a spot check for emergent weeds every month or so.*

(BOTTOM): *Lawn is the default ground cover around older houses like this, but it's fussy to mow narrow strips on split levels. To simplify care and to update the appearance, you could expand that brick walk to make it as wide as the porch and replace the turf with a tough, low, evergreen ground cover.*

feeling hurried or impatient, mow only the parts of your lawn that are easy and enjoyable to mow. Call it quits when you get bothered, and skip the portions that annoy or worry you for any reason, such as steep slopes, tight corners, bumpy ground, detached areas, or places next to buildings or under trees where there isn't enough clearance and you have to swerve or duck. Why put up with mowing in places where it's too much trouble? Convert the unmowed areas to something other than lawn.

Wherever lawn abuts other plantings, or when you undertake to convert an area of lawn into some kind of bed or border, use the lawn mower to outline shapes, particularly curves. Then follow the path of the mower to determine where the edges should lie. If a shape is easy to mow, so you can swing around the edge in a continuous path and never have to back up, turn the mower, and go again, chances are it will look graceful and natural. Curves and corners that are too sharp for easy mowing are likely to look artificial and fussy (and messy, too, because you'll neglect them when you're hot and tired).

Routine lawn care

Mowing—the first thing you think of in terms of lawn care—is actually secondary. First, you have to keep the grass healthy and vigorous, so it grows fast and full enough to need regular cutting. Weed control—the other big issue with lawns—is also related to the health of the grass. A dense stand of vigorous grass is a strong competitor and can inhibit or outgrow most weeds, but a lawn that's sparse or stressed in any way is open to invasion.

The specifics of watering, fertilizing, pest and disease control, weed prevention and control, and other aspects of lawn care vary with the kind of grass you have and your climate, soil, and growing conditions. Rather than trying to give general guidelines here, I recommend that you seek advice from local experts. They can outline a program for you to follow, which may be simple or demanding, depending on how much of a challenge it is to grow good grass where you are.

SHOULD YOU HIRE A LAWN SERVICE?

If you want a nice lawn but don't want to bother caring for it yourself, hire help. More than any other aspect of landscaping, you can easily get competent but inexpensive help with lawn care. Talk to friends and neighbors for feedback on local lawn specialists, interview the owners who manage those businesses, and see what range of services is available. Sign up on a short-term or trial basis first, then if you're satisfied with the workers and the appearance of your lawn, extend the contract.

There are advantages to getting help. A competent, experienced lawn-care service should be familiar with grasses and conditions in your area and know what needs to be done and when to do it. They should be able to recognize and treat common problems that you might not be able to diagnose or wouldn't know how to solve. Whereas you might postpone lawn care because of schedule conflicts, distraction, or bad weather, they just drive up, do the job, and continue on to the next site. Hiring help saves you time, and it means you don't have to invest in lawn-care equipment and supplies. I'm not saying you can't or shouldn't do your own lawn work, but if you feel pressed for time or have other priorities, making someone else responsible for your lawn will give you some relief.

CAN YOU FORGO CHEMICALS?

Since the 1950s, our vision of the ideal American lawn has been shaped by the development and widespread use of specialized chemical products. The flawless lawns that you see in some neighborhoods, in many commercial landscapes, and at golf courses are achieved only through carefully scheduled and measured applications of fertilizers, herbicides, pesticides, and fungicides.

It isn't possible to produce lawns of that quality without using at least some of these products. Even in good growing conditions, an "organic" or "natural" lawn won't be as lush, green, and uniform as a "chemical" lawn. This may change, as researchers and suppliers keep trying to develop alternatives such as disease-resistant strains of grass, natural fertilizers, and nontoxic (to mammals, birds, and fish) or biodegradable herbicides and pesticides. But so far the gains have been incremental; the new products work, but not remarkably well, and they're usually much more expensive than conventional methods.

Meanwhile, there are other easy ways to reduce your use of lawn chemicals. First, adjust your expectations and settle for a less-than-perfect lawn. Cut back to the minimum dosage and frequency of application. Reduce the size of your lawn, or divide it

This lawn isn't perfect; it's got thin spots and clover. But who cares? It's good enough for most neighborhoods, and the edges are neat.

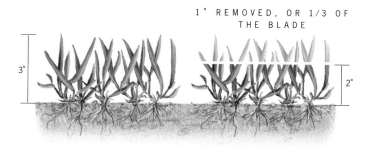

1" REMOVED, OR 1/3 OF THE BLADE

3"

2"

MOWING THE GRASS

Ideally, you should mow often enough that you never cut the grass back by more than one-third its height. So, for example, if you want to keep your grass at 2 inches, cut it as soon as it reaches 3 inches. This minimizes stress on the grass and produces sparse, short clippings that soon decompose.

2" REMOVED, OR 1/2 OF THE BLADE

4"

2"

If you wait until the grass is 4 inches or taller and then cut it back to 2 inches, the grass plants will be weakened and a much greater volume of clippings will be produced.

into zones that are treated differently depending on how prominent they are. Keep up with the mowing and maintain neat edges so your neighbors can't complain about shagginess, and they may be willing to overlook other flaws. Expand, diversify, and take good care of your other plantings so the lawn won't dominate so much of your landscape.

MOWING. The primary rule of lawn care is to mow the grass so often that you never remove more than one-third of its length. So, for example, if you want to maintain a lawn at 2 inches tall, you should mow as soon as it reaches 3 inches. Hardly anyone follows this rule, because to do so would require mowing every few days, and most people don't have the time, energy, or budget to mow more than once a week. Mowing more frequently is probably the best single change you could make in how you care for your lawn. (Don't be afraid that mowing often makes the grass grow faster; that's an old wives' tale.)

A second change is to mow higher than usual. Taller grass doesn't look as trim and neat, but it stays healthier. That's partly because you remove a smaller fraction with each mowing. (For instance, mowing from 2 inches to 1½ inches cuts off one-quarter of the grass, while mowing from 2½ inches to 2 inches removes only one-fifth.) Also, taller grass is more weed-resistant. Try raising the mower blade up a notch, maintain the lawn at that cutting height for a few weeks or longer, and see what you think.

Cut even higher, and less frequently than usual, during hot, dry weather, so the grass blades can shade the soil and keep it from getting quite as hot as

it would otherwise. Cut lower than usual at the last mowing in fall, to reduce disease problems caused when grass mats down during the winter, especially in snowy climates.

It's a good idea to change the path you follow and not always mow in the same direction. Make different patterns of stripes from week to week. Go back and forth from north to south, then from east to west. Go diagonally in one direction, then another. Start at the outside and make a continuous spiral to the center. Varying your path like this reduces the wear and tear on the grass and minimizes soil compaction from repeatedly running the mower wheels in the same tracks.

Sharpen the mower blade more often. The sharper it is, the cleaner it cuts; it should slice through the grass, not tear at it. Sharpening is a bothersome job, so everybody postpones it, but it really makes a big difference in the ease of mowing and the appearance of the grass.

CLIPPINGS. The problem of clippings relates mostly to mowing frequency. Consider that a lawn produces a certain volume of new growth every week. For example, if your lawn grows 2 inches a week, the total quantity of clippings is the same whether you mow once and cut off 2 inches or mow twice and take 1 inch each time. The consequences, though, are different.

Frequent mowing produces clippings so short that they dry up and disappear after a few hours in the sun; you don't have to collect them. And you don't need a special "mulching" mower either. Any mower produces short clippings that decompose quickly and recycle nitrogen and other nutrients back to the soil, if you mow often enough.

If you can't or don't mow often enough and always end up with conspicuous windrows or clumps of clippings, what should you do? First, mow only when the grass is dry, since clippings clump up worse when they're wet. A few hours later, use a lawn rake to disperse the biggest clumps and scatter the clippings more evenly. It rarely hurts to leave conspicuous clippings on the lawn; they soon decompose. Removing them is more for appearance' sake than for the health of the grass, unless you've skipped mowing for weeks and the lawn looks like a hayfield; then the crop of clippings might be thick enough to smother the grass below.

If you prefer to catch clippings as you mow or rake them up afterward, don't send them to the landfill. Recycle the nutrients and organic matter they contain. Pure grass clippings don't compost well alone, especially if you just dump them in a pile and let it sit, but clippings compost fine if you mix them with equal quantities of coarser, drier materials, such as perennial flower stalks or hedge trimmings, and

aerate the pile by turning it often. You can also spread grass clippings as a mulch in vegetable gardens or flower beds. Apply a layer less than 2 inches thick, and renew it as often as the clippings decompose and disappear.

WEED CONTROL. Modern herbicides that are designed to kill weeds without hurting desirable turfgrasses are responsible for many problems. Along with environmental consequences—groundwater contamination and accidental injuries to shade trees—the ease and efficiency of using herbicides has set an artificially high standard for how weedless lawns should be and has distorted our thinking.

It's misleading to focus on weeds in a lawn as if the weeds are the problem. Almost always, excessive weeds are a symptom of other, more basic problems or mismanagement, such as too much shade, extremely compacted or poorly drained soil, infertile soil, dryness, patches where the grass has been killed by insects or diseases, starting with inferior grass seed or sod, choosing grass that's inappropriate for the site, or mowing too low. If your grass is thin, weak, or stressed for any of these reasons, weeds will

Making striped patterns is one of the pleasures of mowing. Vary your route from week to week so the stripes go in different directions.

germinate and grow in any bare spots. Sure, you can spray and kill the weeds, but they'll try again. You'll never get ahead unless you identify and solve the basic problem and do whatever's required to grow a dense turf of vigorous, healthy grass. Sometimes, chronic weed problems are a sign that you should give up on lawn altogether and design a different solution for that site.

There's a role for lawn herbicides, but it's a limited one. Using a preemergent can prevent crabgrass and other annual and perennial weed seedlings from sprouting up in a newly seeded lawn that hasn't got-

RENOVATING A LAWN

There are a few likely explanations and solutions when a lawn gets overrun with weeds or the turf is weak and sparse on a site that seemingly *should* support a good lawn.

- **DETHATCHING**. Thatch looks like a buildup of uncollected clippings, but it isn't that. Instead, it's a dense layer of tough dead stems and runners that may accumulate at the base of some kinds of grasses. Thatch forms when these materials don't decompose normally, usually because the soil is deficient in earthworms and microorganisms. You may never see thatch in your yard, or it may be a recurrent problem.

  Where it occurs, thatch weakens a lawn because it keeps rain or irrigation water from soaking into the soil. Look for thatch by getting down and peering between the blades of grass. If you find a continuous, crusty, dried-out layer of dead debris, poke through it to see how thick it is. If the layer of thatch is thicker than about ½ inch, it should be removed. You can dethatch a lawn by hand with a sharp rakelike tool, but it's much easier and more effective to rent a gas-powered dethatcher or to hire a lawn service to come do the job. If you dethatch before the grass has deteriorated too far and then water and fertilize regularly afterward, the lawn should recover within one growing season and shouldn't need dethatching again for at least a few years.

- **AERATION**. Over time, walking or playing on a lawn can pack the ground hard as a rock, especially if the soil has much clay in it. Compacted soil is problematic because water doesn't soak in readily and air can't penetrate either. Grass doesn't grow well in these conditions, but some weeds do, and they're liable to take over.

  If you suspect that soil compaction is weakening your lawn, test it by trying to insert a spade or digging fork here and there. If the soil's too hard to dig, yes, you have a problem. You can rent a gas-powered machine to solve the problem, or hire a lawn service to do the job. The machine digs lots of little holes about 3 inches deep all over the surface of the lawn and pops out lipstick-sized plugs or "cores" of soil. You can break up the cores by raking over them, or disintegrate them the next time you mow the lawn (if you try that, be sure to sharpen the mower blade afterward).

  Catalogs and magazines sometimes advertise simple lightweight coring or aerating tools, such as a set of long spikes that you strap onto the soles of your shoes. These are rarely worth the money. If your soil is compacted enough to need aeration, it's exhausting to poke holes without using a power tool.

For compacted areas too small to justify renting a coring machine (or confined areas that would be inaccessible with a machine), you can use a power drill to make holes ¼ to ½ inch wide and 3 to 4 inches deep. Drilling lots of holes in your lawn may sound absurd, but it does help the grass grow better, and it's no more far-fetched than walking around in spike-soled shoes.

- **TOP-DRESSING**. Spreading a thin (½ inch or less), even layer of screened topsoil, aged manure, or fine-textured compost over the surface of a lawn often serves to reinvigorate it, probably by supplying a gentle, balanced dose of nutrients. The material must be fairly dry and lump-free, so it's easy to rake and it sinks right down around the blades of grass. The time to top-dress is just before or as the grass starts to grow, in either spring or fall. Spread it, water well, and watch the results. Professional groundskeepers sometimes top-dress once a year, and you can, too, unless you find it's too much trouble to bother with that often. One cubic yard (about a pickup-truck load) of soil or compost is enough to top-dress 650 square feet of lawn with a layer ½ inch deep.

- **TOPSEEDING**. It's sometimes recommended that you can thicken a sparse stand of grass by topseeding, or sowing seeds on top of the existing lawn. This rarely works. Although weed seeds readily germinate and grow up through grass, most turf seeds fail unless they're planted on bare soil. You might as well throw them in the trash as sprinkle good grass seeds on top of a lawn.

  If you want to replace shabby old grass or a mixture of grass and weeds with a healthy stand of new grass, the best thing to do is clear the area and start from scratch. First spray the weak or weedy lawn you want to renovate with a contact herbicide, such as Roundup. Do this a few weeks before optimal seeding season (get local advice on the best time to plant in your area). A couple of weeks after spraying, when you're sure the grass and weeds are dead, rake up all the litter. (If weed seeds are present, discard it. Otherwise, you can put it on the compost pile.) Very vigorously rake the soil in order to loosen the surface; better yet, till the soil and then rake it smooth. Or rake and loosen the surface, then top-dress with a layer of rich topsoil. Finally, sow seeds and follow up as you would for starting a new lawn.

Most turf grasses turn brown for part of the year. This perennial rye grass goes dormant in hot, dry weather, but the ragweed and plantain keep growing. Pull them out now while they're easy to spot.

ten established and filled in yet. But annual weeds shouldn't be a problem in established lawns; if they are, you probably need to fertilize and/or irrigate more and mow higher. Annual weed seeds need bare soil and light to germinate. Where grass is dense and tall enough to shade the soil, very few weed seeds manage to sprout and grow.

A prompt and targeted application of broad-leaf weed killer is good for killing perennial weeds that spread by underground runners, such as ground ivy and oxalis. It's very difficult to control these invasive weeds by hand pulling. Be vigilant and treat these weeds immediately as soon as you spot them, before they get a chance to spread. Otherwise, a single seedling of ground ivy, for example, can run through an area the size of your living room in just a year or two.

But there's no reason to use an herbicide to kill coarse, rosette-forming weeds such as dandelion and plantain. Simply pull or dig them out as you would weed a flower bed. Again, if there are so many of these weeds that hand pulling them all is unimaginable, it's time to figure out what's wrong with your lawn and tackle the problem, not the symptom.

PESTS AND DISEASES. Seek advice from local experts right away if dead or discolored patches in the lawn make you suspect a problem. Take a sample of the damaged grass and/or a photo for identification. It's hard to diagnose a problem yourself, but a local lawn specialist or horticulturist will recognize any problem at a glance because they've no doubt seen it a hundred times already. (If a problem strikes in your backyard, it's probably all around town.) When you know exactly what the problem is, you may seek second opinions on how to treat it. Often there's a choice of "chemical" and "organic" responses. In some cases, you'll be told to simply wait as the problem goes away on its own.

Hand weeding is an efficient way to remove dandelions, plantain, and other lawn weeds that form rosettes. Work when the soil is moist, and try to get out as much of the roots as possible.

EDGING. The condition of edges where lawn abuts a mulch-covered bed, a ground-cover planting, or a paved area makes a big impact on your overall impression of a lawn. If the edges are shaggy, you tend to think the whole lawn is messy. If the edges are crisp and neat, you overlook some weeds or thin spots in the lawn itself. This isn't rational or fair, but it's how most people see things. Use hand shears, a string trimmer, a power edger, or whatever tool(s) you prefer and trim lawn edges whenever—or before—they get out of line.

Be careful around trees, though. It's better not to let grass grow right up to the trunk of a tree, so you don't risk damaging the tree's bark when you trim the grass. A lawn mower or string trimmer can wound a tree in a heartbeat, leaving an ugly scar that will never disappear. Use mulch to suppress grass around a tree, or grow a ground cover there instead of grass.

Starting a new lawn

The keys to success in starting a new lawn are choosing suitable grass, preparing the soil, working at the right time of year, and watering the new grass diligently. Of course, you can hire a lawn service to make a lawn for you. If you want to do it yourself, here is some advice.

First, prepare the site and soil. Most people recognize the importance of soil preparation in starting a vegetable garden or flower bed but don't realize that it's just as important when you're making a lawn. Lawn grasses struggle in poor (that is, shallow, compacted, and infertile) soil. Nothing you can do afterward gives results as good as you get from planning ahead and investing in soil preparation before you start the lawn. Eradicate all existing vegetation (see page 274), then follow the general guidelines for soil improvement given on page 277.

SELECTING A TURFGRASS. To many people, grass is grass, but if you're in the situation of starting or renovating a lawn, you'll have to decide which grass to use. For any climate, soil, and region, there are just a few widely used turfgrasses, so those are your main options. You can soon learn to recognize and distinguish between the grasses that are most common in your neighborhood.

Although special new strains of common turfgrasses and various uncommon alternative grasses are often mentioned in magazines, few suppliers sell anything out of the ordinary. You'll have to go out of your way to locate something you've read about. If you're interested in a new or uncommon grass, start by seeking more information about it; don't assume that it's marvelous just because one article praised it highly. Get a second opinion, preferably from a local expert.

As with any other plants, selecting a turfgrass starts with the basics of matching the grass to the site. Does the grass need full sun or tolerate part shade? Does it prefer acid or alkaline soil? Does it survive on normal rainfall or require irrigation? Is it notably resistant or susceptible to diseases and insect pests that are common in your area?

Other questions have to do with appearance and care. Are the blades coarse- or fine-textured? How fast does it grow, how short should it be mowed, and how often does it require mowing?

What months of the year is it green, and when does it turn brown? Most turfgrasses fall into either of two groups. Cool-season grasses, including Kentucky bluegrass, perennial ryegrass, and most fescues, grow best in cool, moist weather. They tend to stay green until temperatures reach the high 80s or so, then go dormant and turn brown. In general, cool-season grasses don't do well where summers are hot or dry.

Warm-season turfgrasses, including Bermuda, St. Augustine, zoysia, and buffalo grass, thrive in hot weather. They turn green in late spring or early summer, then go dormant and turn brown when the weather cools off in fall. Their drought- and humidity-tolerances vary, so inquire about recommended varieties for your area.

Most homeowners prefer the looks of a uniform, homogeneous lawn planted with just one kind of grass, but sometimes it's better to plant a mixture, or to choose different grasses for different parts of your yard. For example, many people have experimented with mixing cool- and warm-season grasses, hoping to achieve year-round green color. That's worth a try, although usually one grass does better than the other and gradually takes over the lawn.

SEED VS. SOD. Check the Yellow Pages and classified ads, then call a few different sod dealers, garden centers, and lawn services to see what's available in your area. Some grasses are normally started from seed, while others are produced as sod; some come both ways. Some grasses can be installed by plugging, or setting little starts of sod about 12 to 18 inches apart; the plugs spread to fill in completely after a year or so. Others can be planted by sprigging, or scattering bits of rooted stems over the surface of the prepared area and then covering with a thin layer of topsoil.

Seed and sod are the most common options, and the tradeoff between them is price versus time. Laying sod costs a lot more—often more than 10 times the price of sowing seed—but gives almost instant results. It looks impressive, makes you feel good, and also minimizes or prevents possible problems with weed growth and soil erosion. Seeding can produce an excellent lawn, but it takes more skill and patience than laying sod. Right after seeding, a new lawn is vulnerable to getting dried out, washed away, torn up by accidents or animals, or invaded by weeds. Seeded grass starts to look good after about six to eight weeks but doesn't fill in completely until several months later.

HOW TO SUCCEED WITH SOD. It's usually best to lay sod for cool-season grasses in early fall, several weeks before hard frost, and sod for warm-season grasses in late spring, just as the weather warms up. You can buy and lay sod in other seasons, but it may not do as well.

Sod's a little heavy to handle, but even a novice can do a good job of installing it and be proud of the results. Get the site all ready before you have the sod delivered, and water the soil if it's dry. Go examine the very sod you're buying to be sure it's green and fresh-looking, not at all faded, wilted, or yellowed. Line up help, and plan to lay the sod as quickly as possible.

Start beside a straight-edged driveway, walk, or wall, or stretch a string between stakes and use that as a starting line. If your site slopes, lay the strips lengthwise across the slope, not running up and down. Lay one strip after another, butting them as close together as possible along all edges. Stagger the joints from one row to the next so they don't line up. When you encounter obstacles or reach the edge of the yard, use an old butcher knife to cut the sod to fit.

Right after you've laid it, use a roller to press the sod down against the soil, then water the entire area. Sprinkle again every day or two (unless it rains) for a couple of weeks. You'll be able to tell when the sod is taking root because it will appear to perk up and start growing. That means you can start caring for it according to the normal recommended program for that kind of grass.

HOW TO SUCCEED WITH SEEDS. You might get lucky and have good results sowing grass seeds at inappropriate seasons, but generally it's best to pay close attention to temperature and timing. Sow warm-season grasses in late spring. Wait until the soil feels comfortably warm against your skin and night temperatures stay above 60°F. Don't sow too soon, or the seeds are likely to rot in the soil and fail to grow. Sow cool-season grasses in late summer or early fall, as soon as daytime highs stop climbing above 80°F. Don't wait too late, or the seedlings will grow too slowly and still be small and weak when winter comes.

Keep the cost of sod in mind as a basis for comparison when shopping for grass seeds, and don't hesitate to pay the price for top quality. Good seed is already a bargain compared with sod, so there's no reason to save an extra nickel by sowing cheap seeds of inferior grasses.

Read the fine print on the label to ascertain that the seed germination rate is at least 80 percent, and

Hair-fine grass seedlings sprout right up through a protective layer of straw mulch.

check the date. Seed should be sold and planted within one year of the test date; if it's much older than one year, it may not germinate well or at all.

Prepare the seedbed, measure its area, and weigh out the appropriate amount of seeds to sow (this varies from one grass to another, so check the label). Sowing evenly is very important. You're unlikely to get good results if you simply toss the seeds by hand. Use a drop or rotary spreader. Divide the seeds in half, and sow them in two bouts. First go back and forth across the area in one direction, then work crosswise as you sow the second half of the seeds.

Use a roller to gently press them against the surface, walk back and forth making very close steps, or lightly scratch the area with a leaf rake. One way or another, you want to make sure that the seeds are in direct contact with the soil, not just perched on top of it. Now cover the area with a layer of wheat or oat straw, spread one stem thick. You should be able to see between the straws to the soil. The straw helps keep the soil moist and provides the seed with a little protection from the weather and from birds. It will serve as a mulch to the new seedlings and decompose soon afterward—you don't have to, and shouldn't try to, remove it.

Use a sprinkler to gently water the entire area once a day or whenever the soil surface gets dry, con-

tinuing until the grass is about 2 inches tall. Then provide a deeper soaking every two to three days, and gradually taper off to the normal recommended watering schedule as the grass gets established.

Watch for and hand pull weeds as soon as you spot them. It's risky using any kind of weed killer on a newly seeded lawn.

Start mowing the new grass as soon as it gets a little taller than the desired height. Be sure to cut it with a sharp blade, as a dull mower can actually uproot fragile-rooted seedlings.

GROUND COVERS

Ground covers are frequently used on dry or shady sites where lawns wouldn't thrive, on slopes or rough ground, around rocks or trees, in narrow or confined places where mowing would be awkward, and in any areas where you don't need or want to walk. Dozens of plants, including many perennials and shrubs and some vines, can be used in these situations to make dense, attractive, often colorful patches or beds. Ideally, an established planting needs minimal maintenance, resists weeds, looks good year-round or at least from spring to fall, and lasts for many years or even decades without requiring renovation or replacement.

Patches of snow-in-summer and scarlet flax brighten this rocky hillside, but look more closely and you'll be disappointed. This area is infested with dandelions, thistles, sow thistles, and weedy grasses. A few hours of diligent weeding would take care of things for now, but not forever.

But problems often arise. The most common troubles are a pair of opposites. If a plant used as a ground cover is too weak and sparse (perhaps because it's not a good match for the site), weeds will grow up through it. But if a ground cover is too vigorous and dense, it will compete with and inhibit other plants growing in its midst, including desirable but weaker perennials, shrubs, and trees. So it's a balancing act. You want to choose a ground cover that's strong enough to hold its own but not too aggressive.

Another concern is that any ground cover, like any other massed grouping of a single kind of plant, is vulnerable to plague-like diebacks. An uncommonly severe winter, a prolonged drought, an insect invasion, or a new disease can wipe out an entire bed. The larger an area you fill with one kind of plant, the more you'll lose if something happens to it. But that's a chance worth taking, I think, and you can minimize the risk by test-growing (see page 334) a plant before you invest in it on a large scale.

I'll discuss general guidelines for ground-cover maintenance here. For more information on tending shrubs, vines, or perennials used as ground covers, see the sections on those groups of plants. For questions or problems that are related to one particular kind of plant, such as leaf spots on English ivy or winterkill on creeping rosemary, get advice from local plant experts.

Routine care of established ground covers

Some ground covers require no annual care at all, but most need some care and attention in order to look their best. When ground covers are planted as a solution for difficult sites, they're subject to more stress than plants in favorable situations. So, for example, watch for wilting during dry spells and give ground covers on dry sites a good soaking if possible. Where ground covers are competing with tree roots for nutrients, watch for slow growth, yellowing, or other hunger signs and fertilize if needed. Stressed plants are typically more susceptible to insect and disease problems, so watch for signs of trouble and seek advice if you need to diagnose and treat them.

WEEDING. Several times a year, spaced throughout the growing season, scrutinize your ground covers, looking for weeds. There's a knack to this; it's like scanning a page in a book to look for a certain word. In scanning for weeds, you look for anomalies, leaves that have a different size, shape, or color than the ground cover does. With practice, you learn to do this automatically. Your eye spots a weed and your hand reaches to pull it out. Hand-pulling weeds on a regular schedule is often enough to keep a bed of ground cover from getting infested. You may pull only a few weeds each time, but it's important to remove them promptly, before they spread by underground runners or set seed.

Prevention is crucial because trying to eradicate a perennial weed once it's gotten established and

Weeds are less of a problem on shady sites. These crescents of Christmas fern, variegated hosta, and pachysandra are usually weed-free, but it's a good idea to check them every month or so just in case.

spread through a patch of ground cover is a difficult job. For instance, imagine a sloping bank covered with creeping junipers but infested with weedy grasses. If you ignore the situation, the grasses will take over within a year or two, covering and shading the junipers. To remove the grass by hand, you need to pull out every shoot you can see at least once a week, continuing indefinitely. A contact herbicide such as Roundup can be very helpful in this situation, but you have to apply it by carefully painting it onto the weed's leaves with a disposable-sponge-type applicator, since spraying an herbicide would damage or kill the ground cover.

In extreme cases where a neglected ground-cover bed has gotten totally infested with weeds, the only solution is to dig it up, eradicate the weeds, and start over again. You may be able to salvage starts of the ground cover to propagate and replant, but don't bother unless you're sure you can totally extract and destroy any weed rhizomes or runners that are intertwined with the ground cover's roots.

DEFINING THE EDGE. Most plants used as ground covers spread sideways, reaching a few to several inches farther each year. That's how they fill in an area, but it also enlarges the patch. Spreading may not pose a problem. In casual or natural landscapes or little-used areas, you may actually welcome a ground cover's takeover tendencies; the farther it grows, the better.

Next to a lawn, though, you'll probably want to define an edge and keep the ground cover separate from the turfgrass. Various kinds of built or buried edgings, such as brick or paver-stone mowing strips, steel or black-plastic edging strips, or landscape timbers, promise more than they deliver. They serve as a visual reminder of where the edge is supposed to be, but they rarely prevent a vigorous ground cover from crossing over or under into the lawn. If you've installed some kind of edging, monitor it and prune back or pull up every runaway shoot that crosses the line. Some ground cover plants have one annual growth spurt, and if you trim the edge soon after the current season's shoots or runners have formed, you won't have to worry about it again until the following year. Other plants grow continually throughout the season, and you have to check them repeatedly.

Keeping a narrow strip of soil bare is another

A low timber edging and mowing strip marks the line between English ivy and turf. Ivy runners that cross the line must be trimmed off a few times every year.

Two weeks after a mid-summer trim to remove shabby, faded foliage (BELOW), *variegated bishop's weed has begun a flush of new growth* (BOTTOM) *that will stay fresh-looking until winter.*

good way to maintain a definite edge between ground cover and lawn. Use a hand or power edging tool to cut straight down along the edge of the turf and lift away all the roots and runners (of both grass and ground cover) that have crossed the line in either direction. Then peel or trim the ground cover back a few inches away from the line. It will grow out into or onto the bare soil again. Depending on the kinds of ground cover and turfgrass you're dealing with, you may have to recut the edge as often as several times a year, but the job goes fairly quickly and looking at the neat edge makes you feel good afterward.

Where a ground cover is confined by pavement or architecture, its underground spread is usually controlled (although an aggressive ground cover can run under a sidewalk and pop up on the other side, or force its way up through a blacktop driveway). But shrubs and vines used as ground covers, and running perennials, too, can stick out or flop over onto an adjacent walkway, patio, or driveway and get in the way. Simply shearing them even with the paved edge typically doesn't look very nice—it makes a raw, woundlike cut and often exposes dead inner stems. In cases like this, a better way to maintain the edge is to lift up the ground cover where it's flopped over onto the pavement, reach way back underneath it, cut off the longest stems and runners with pruning shears, and pull them out and away. Then let the top layer of stems flop down again and trim their ends, like cutting bangs. This makes a leafy, tapered, sloping edge rather than a vertical face of bare, blunt-cut twigs.

GROOMING. Grooming involves removing dead leaves, stems or stalks, and flowers or fruits. It's done to neaten the appearance of the patch, stimulate new growth and keep the plants vigorous, and remove material that might host disease spores or insect pests.

Depending on the kind of plants and the size and nature of the site, you can groom ground covers in different ways. Many plants — such as lilyturf, dianthus, creeping phlox, moss phlox, lamium, lamiastrum, and geraniums — should be sheared once or twice a year to remove fading flowers, to prune off weathered leaves and stimulate fresh new growth, or to keep them from getting too tall or building up an interior tangle of dead leaves and twigs. The easy way — and this is appropriate for most plants that need shearing — is to sharpen the lawn-mower blade, set the cutting height as high as possible, and mow over the patch. But mowing is awkward, dangerous, or impractical on steep or rough sites, small or narrow sites, or around trees or rocks. In those cases, you may be able to shear the ground cover with a string trimmer. For small patches with woody stems, you may have to use a hedge trimmer or hedge shears. Old-fashioned grass shears work well for shearing small patches of soft-stemmed ground covers.

Ground covers that don't grow too fast and appear fairly neat and healthy year after year probably don't need shearing, but you can freshen their appearance and remove dead twigs and leaves by gently raking the patch with a lawn rake that has pliable rubber, plastic, or bamboo tines. A rake like this is also good for pulling out autumn leaves that have blown into a patch of ground covers and lodged among the stems.

Some ground covers rarely need grooming. For example, bearberry, creeping rosemary, and cranberry have extremely weatherproof and long-lasting evergreen leaves and small flowers that drop off naturally. Hostas, dwarf plumbago, and sundrops die down totally in winter and their leaves and stems decompose quickly and are hidden by the next season's growth. And, of course, in casual or natural settings you may not want to bother grooming ground covers at all.

Choosing a ground cover

Fairly few plants form short, dense, evergreen, long-lasting stands and are also easy to propagate and hence available and affordable in large quantities, so the same ground covers are used repeatedly in American landscapes. Although common and conservative, these familiar plants, including English ivy, pachysandra, vinca or myrtle, Asian jasmine, creeping junipers, lilyturf, and mondo grass, are often the best choices for filling large areas.

Many other plants can also be used as ground covers, especially if you're willing to consider plants that grow taller than 8 to 12 inches, that have deciduous leaves or die down in winter, that cost more or take longer to get established, or that need additional care, such as grooming in spring, deadheading in summer, and trimming and raking in fall. Uncommon ground covers can be practical and attractive alternatives to the familiar mainstays, and doing something creative with ground covers is a good way to make your landscape unique. For examples of ground covers for shade, see page 245; for dry sites, see page 249; to replace a lawn, page 321; resistant to deer, page 258; with colored foliage, page 56; to use around steppingstones, page 180; to trail over the edge of pavement, page 150.

TEST-GROW POTENTIAL CANDIDATES. If you're interested in experimenting with an unconventional ground cover, try it on a small scale with just one or a few plants. See if it is adapted to the site and grows vigorously there. Note how tall it gets. Assess how dense a stand it forms and whether it resists weeds. Watch how fast it spreads and whether or not it's invasive, and see how much trouble it is to

A ground-cover installation can be a big, expensive disappointment if the plant doesn't thrive. Lily-of-the-valley, shown here, survives in the shallow dry soil under this tree, but it turns brown and shabby by mid-July, then dies to the ground until spring. In cooler, moister soil it would stay green all summer. For this site, a sedum would be a better choice.

PROPAGATING YOUR OWN GROUND COVERS

It's practical to produce large quantities of many ground covers by starting with a few plants and dividing them repeatedly. Many perennials can be divided every year or two into 3 or more pieces each time. So, for example, you might buy one pot of a fast-spreading perennial, divide it into 4 pieces after one year, 16 pieces the second year, 64 pieces the third year, and so on. Like compound interest, the numbers soon increase at an impressive rate.

If you set aside a small area and use it as a nursery bed, you can easily produce enough of your plants to make impressive patches of uncommon ground covers. Also, by growing the plants yourself, you'll learn about how they perform and be sure that they're adapted to your conditions, so you can plant them on a large scale with confidence.

To learn more about the technique of division, see page 343. Some ground covers that are easily propagated this way include:

Variegated bishop's weed (*Aegopodium podagraria* 'Variegatum')
Bugleweed, or ajuga (*Ajuga reptans*)
Dwarf Chinese astilbe (*Astilbe chinensis* 'Pumila')
Dwarf plumbago (*Ceratostigma plumbaginoides*)
Green-and-gold (*Chrysogonum virginianum*)
Lily-of-the-valley (*Convallaria majalis*)
Hay-scented fern (*Dennstaedtia punctilobula*)
Pinks (*Dianthus*)
Epimediums (*Epimedium*)
Sweet woodruff (*Galium odoratum*)
Hostas (*Hosta*)
Spotted dead nettle (*Lamium maculatum*)
Blue star creeper (*Laurentia fluviatilis*)
Lilyturfs (*Liriope*)
Moneywort (*Lysimachia nummularia*)
Mazus (*Mazus reptans*)
Sword fern (*Nephrolepis cordifolia*)
Monkey, or mondo, grass (*Ophiopogon japonicus*)
Common pachysandra (*Pachysandra terminalis*)
Creeping phlox (*Phlox*)
Lungworts (*Pulmonaria*)
Sedums, or stonecrops (*Sedum*)
Wood fern (*Thelypteris kunthii*)
Foamflower (*Tiarella cordifolia*)
Periwinkle, or myrtle (*Vinca minor*)
Sweet violet (*Viola odorata*)
Japanese sweet flag (*Acorus gramineus*)
Lady's mantle (*Alchemilla mollis*)
Beach wormwood (*Artemisia stelleriana*)
Bergenias (*Bergenia*)
Bolax (*Bolax glebaria*)
Serbian bellflower (*Campanula poscharskyana*)
Hardy ice plants (*Delosperma*)
Wild strawberries (*Fragaria*)
Hardy geraniums (*Geranium*)
Dwarf crested iris (*Iris cristata*)
Sundrops and evening primroses (*Oenothera*)
Christmas fern (*Polystichum acrostichoides*)
Irish moss, Scotch moss (*Sagina subulata*)
Thymes (*Thymus*)
Speedwells (*Veronica*)

Sweet woodruff is an adaptable, shade-tolerant ground cover that's easy to divide. Dig up a patch, cut it into fist-sized chunks, space them about 15 inches apart, and the new planting will form a solid mat within a year or two.

confine it and maintain an edge. Does it need grooming or trimming? Does it have a dormant season? Watch the plant for at least a year, then if you're convinced that it's a good ground-cover candidate, you can propagate it or buy more to use on a larger scale.

Some problems related to particular groups of plants don't show up for more than one year, so let me warn you about them. Most low, spreading shrubs used as ground covers, such as creeping junipers, can spread at least 1 foot in all directions every year and eventually form patches 10 feet or wider. This means they're ideal for big sites but not for next to a walkway. Deciduous vines, such as Virginia creeper, are often disappointing as ground covers because they offer little defense against weeds and look particularly bleak and dead in winter. Vines in general are suitable only for large sites away from valuable or delicate trees or shrubs. Some perennials multiply so fast and get so crowded after a few years that they go into decline unless you dig, divide, and replant them—a daunting task if you're facing a large bed packed full of plants.

Along with testing a would-be ground-cover plant in your own yard to make sure it's adapted to the growing conditions there, do some additional research before you plant anything on a major scale. Ask local experts if they have any experiences or observations to share regarding that plant's long-term performance. Consult different reference books to see what they have to say, and crosscheck their descriptions of the plant. When you think you've found a winning candidate, you can confidently plant masses of it.

These divisions of lamb's ears, spaced 12 inches apart in spring, filled in to make a continuous cover by the end of the growing season.

COST CONSIDERATIONS. Since cost is a factor in filling a large area with plants, some homeowners hesitate to replace lawn or fill bare spots with ground covers. The price can range from around $1 to over $5 per square foot, depending on what kind of plants you choose and how many you need to buy in order to fill the area.

The most expensive approach is buying compact, clump-forming perennials, normally sold in 4- or 6-inch pots, and spacing them about 1 foot apart. By comparison, it's a bargain to cover a large area with low-growing or creeping shrubs or woody vines, since these plants are relatively inexpensive and you don't need to buy many of them. Usually you can buy them in 1-gallon cans and space them roughly 4 feet apart. Some ground covers are sometimes sold as flats or bundles of rooted cuttings, which you can separate and plant about 4 to 6 inches apart. These are inexpensive because nurseries can produce them so quickly, but they require extra TLC after planting and are available only for a few of the most common varieties.

It's generally okay to cut costs by spacing plants a little farther apart than the distances you see recommended in a nursery catalog or reference book, but wider spacing means it will take longer for the planting to get dense and full and you'll have to be extra vigilant about mulching and weeding between the plants in the meantime.

Starting a new bed of ground covers

New ground covers don't necessarily need special care. Basically you should treat them as you would any other plants and do your best to give them a good start. I mention this in order to contradict an idea that people sometimes have, that ground covers are miracle workers that can transform a rough weedy site into a lovely smooth patch of green, with no help from you. That's simply unrealistic. Ground covers can only perform well if you give them the opportunity.

ELIMINATE WEEDS FIRST. Be sure to destroy any existing perennial weeds, such as poison ivy, bindweed, ground ivy, quack grass, or Bermuda grass, before you do any planting. Use one of the methods described on page 274. Eradicating these weeds takes patience and persistence, and the site will look ugly until the job is done, but if you don't destroy them before you plant a ground cover, you'll be sorry later.

SOIL PREPARATION. How to prepare the soil depends on the nature of the site and how far apart the plants will be spaced. On fairly level sites and for plants spaced closer than 3 feet apart, work the whole bed, loosening the soil to a depth of at least 6 inches with a spading fork or rototiller. Remove any rocks, roots, or debris. On steep slopes or rocky sites or for plants spaced 3 feet or farther apart, you can dig individual holes rather than working the whole bed. Measure a typical root ball, and dig the holes as deep as it is high and three to five times as wide. Some ground covers don't need it, but in general it's a good idea to amend the soil with a small dose of balanced, slow-release fertilizer and a generous portion of organic matter. Work these amendments into the soil; don't just scatter them on top.

PLANTING. Consult plant encyclopedias and ask nursery staff for advice about how close to space any plant you're using for a ground cover. As a rule, the recommended spacings are intended to make a bed fill in quickly, within two years. If you're patient, you can set the plants farther apart and expect closure by the third or fourth year. I usually set small plugs or starts of low-growing perennials about 8 to 12 inches apart and taller perennials 18 to 30 inches apart. Shrubs and vines should ordinarily go 3 to 4 feet apart, at least. It looks empty at first, but they really will fill in and in the long run it's better for plants not to be too crowded.

As you're planting, use a yardstick and check the spacing as you set each plant in place. Arrange the plants in straight or curving rows, usually parallel to the long edge of the bed. Offset the plants from one row to the next so the spacing is equal in all directions (that is, arrange the plants like the cells in a honeycomb, not like the squares of a checkerboard).

Almost all ground covers benefit from a 2-inch layer of organic mulch. Some gardeners like to spread the mulch first and rake it out into an even layer, then dig down through it to set in the plants. That's okay *only if* you make sure that the plant roots are placed firmly in the soil, not just tucked into the mulch. I think mulch gets in the way of careful planting, and would rather plant first and mulch later.

BE READY TO WATER. Water the area as soon as you finish planting and mulching unless rain is imminent. Water again as often as needed throughout the first growing season, because new ground covers have shallow roots.

❧ PERENNIALS

Perennials are sometimes described as "flowers that come back every year." Don't believe that. A perennial is more than a flower. A perennial is a plant. For most landscape purposes, flowers are a bonus. In landscaping, leaves are what really matter, along with a plant's overall size, shape, and performance. And the truth is, many perennials don't come back every year. They die young, or they disappoint you and you throw them away.

Many perennials that are popular for flower beds have no other role in landscaping. Tulips, Ori-

A perennial is a plant, not just a flower. Consider their leaves, too, when you're deciding what perennials to grow. Do you recognize this lovely foliage? It's a peony, in October.

'Autumn Joy' sedum epitomizes the ideal perennial for landscaping. Massed here beside a stream, it's unfussy and trouble-free, with neat foliage that stays healthy all summer. Colorful fall flowers are a welcome bonus.

ental poppies, and delphiniums, for example, flower briefly, have insignificant foliage, or require special conditions and care to do well. But other perennials are adaptable, long-lived, and versatile, and some kinds bloom profusely for weeks at a time, year after year. These stalwarts deserve prominent positions as specimens and accents, or they can serve as ground covers, mass plantings, edgings, or hedges. Throughout this book I've included many perennials in the lists of plants for particular landscape roles. Perennials can be very effective in the landscape if you regard them as whole plants, not simply flowers, when you're choosing and siting them.

Practical considerations in choosing perennials

As with other plants, when you're choosing a perennial for landscape use, think about the basics of matching the plant to the site. Then investigate how it behaves over time and what kind of care it requires on a routine or periodic basis. Here are some questions to ask.

HOW LONG DOES IT LIVE? On suitable sites, some perennials endure for decades, even with minimal or no attention or care. Others simply

don't. They grow and bloom for a few years, then peter out and die. For example, daylilies are typically long-lived, while asters and daisies are short-lived. Often plant failure is related to summer temperatures. Some perennials prefer cool summers, while others require heat. A season or two at the wrong temperature weakens, then kills, an unadapted plant. For instance, lily-of-the-valley persists for decades in the North but falters and dies after a year or two in the South, while lavatera thrives where summers are hot but doesn't amount to much in cool regions.

It's no problem to replace a single short-lived plant, but doing early replacement on a large scale is expensive and disappointing. Catalogs rarely distinguish between perennials that are short-term or long-lived, but reference books often do tell you this. Seek advice from local gardeners, too, on which perennials fare best in your climate.

WHAT ABOUT DORMANCY? Some perennials are evergreen, especially where winters are mild, but many die down to the ground in fall — or even in summer — and don't resume growth until months later. Their dead stalks may look interesting for a while, if they're stiff enough to stand up, but sooner or later you'll probably want to clear them away. That

(ABOVE): *Delphiniums bear gorgeous flowers in unrivaled shades of blue, but the plants themselves are prima donnas.*

(LEFT): *Perennials can grow quite large; this single three-year-old plant of 'Venus' chrysanthemum is 8 feet wide. Sometime in winter or spring you'll have to cut down all its stems. The flame grass behind it, a similar-size clump, will get cut down, too. Perennials are impressive for part of the year, but they leave big gaps when they're dormant.*

(RIGHT): *When perennial flowers or seed heads start to look messy, cut them off. Sometimes this simply involves snapping or trimming off the tops of the stems. Usually, as with these hostas, it's better to reach down and cut the stalks off close to the ground.*

(BELOW): *Within a few weeks after the finished flower stalks were cut off and the tattered foliage was removed, this foxglove has sent out fresh new growth at the base. This is midsummer. By fall it will have formed a lush, broad rosette.*

leaves a blank spot in your yard. Perhaps your own memory of a plant in its glory is vivid enough that you don't notice when it's dormant, but anyone else looking at the void might wonder, why isn't anything growing there?

If a perennial is truly outstanding at some point during the year and you love it so much that you simply have to have it, you'll find a place for it, but perhaps you can put it in a rarely visited corner, or in the back of a bed where other plants will grow up in front of it. Or maybe you can grow it in a large container and set it aside when it's dormant, or grow something else in a pot and use that to fill the gap in a bed when the perennial is dormant.

WILL IT NEED CUTTING BACK? Many perennial wildflowers are virtually carefree when established on a suitable site; you really don't have to do anything to keep them healthy and attractive. Most garden-variety perennials, though, need to be trimmed at least once or twice a year or perhaps more often, especially on a small property where you see everything up close. You'll probably want to clip or shear off the spent flowers as they fade, remove weathered or yellowed foliage, and cut down old stalks when they get discolored or droopy. These trimming sessions take time, and if you've got any large-scale perennial plantings, cutting back the stems and stalks generates a mountain of debris that you have to haul away and compost or dispose of somehow.

DOES IT CLUMP OR RUN? Most perennials do one or the other—either their stems crowd close together in a compact clump, or they run sideways in all directions, spreading inches or feet every year. Clump formers tend to stay where you put them, so they make well-behaved specimens and are easy to combine with other perennials or other plants. The clump thickens gradually but doesn't surprise you or threaten to take over.

Running, or invasive, perennials are good for filling large open areas and can make an outstanding display. Short ones can be useful as ground covers in situations where you don't care how far they spread or where their spread is limited by permanent barriers such as pavement, buildings, or water. Used alone in suitable situations, running perennials are useful choices. The problems come when you unknowingly combine them with other plants. They can crowd out or suppress any smaller or weaker plants that are growing nearby, and once their roots or runners have intermingled with those of neighboring plants, it's very hard to extract and separate them. Many gardeners have been dismayed because they failed to anticipate how fast and how far a running perennial would spread.

DOES IT SELF-SEED? Whether or not a perennial self-seeds depends on what kind it is, whether or not you let the seeds develop, and particulars of temperature and soil moisture. Perennials that grow as wildflowers in your area are quite likely to self-seed in a garden, along with some garden-variety plants. Self-seeding can be charming or annoying. Get feedback from local gardeners if you're curious about how a perennial is likely to behave for you.

(**ABOVE**): *Clump-forming perennials, such as Siberian iris, stay where you put them.*

(**LEFT**): *Running perennials, such as 'Croftway Pink' monarda, spread fast in all directions and interweave with anything else that's growing nearby.*

(ABOVE): *Lady's mantle makes a frothy edging as it cascades over this stone retaining wall, but those innocent-looking flowers drop countless seeds that sprout all over the yard.*

(RIGHT): *What now? This coreopsis fell over during a rainstorm. It won't stand up again by itself, and it's too late to install stakes or supports. The best thing to do now is to cut off the flopped flower stalks. (Leave the basal foliage, which is in good condition.) A plant in this situation may or may not produce a second flush of flowers later in the season.*

DOES IT STAND ON ITS OWN? Some popular garden perennials have such large, heavy flowers that their stalks won't support them, especially if the plants are growing in overly rich or moist soil or in part shade. Other perennials, including some ornamental grasses, don't necessarily have large flowers but flop anyway, particularly after a rain- or windstorm. Staking plants to discreetly but securely support their stems is painstaking and time-consuming work. Unless you really love the plant, you probably won't want to bother with this. For any large-scale or low-maintenance plantings, look for the magic words "never needs staking."

Dividing perennials

Dividing means digging up a perennial that has gotten too crowded, spread too far, died out in the center, or declined in vigor, and then cutting or pulling it apart and replanting the separate portions (or just one piece of the original, if that's all you want). Avid gardeners view dividing perennials as a fun way to make lots of free starts that they can use to expand their plantings. Typically you can make at least three or four new starts each time you divide a plant, and many perennials can be divided every few years, so the numbers add up fast. For example, I bought a 'Stella d'Oro' daylily in a 4-inch pot in 1990. Ten years later, divisions from that one original plant fill a bed

6 feet deep and 60 feet long along the road in front of my house. On the other hand, if you don't want to bother with division (it's often heavy, messy work), some perennials can go almost indefinitely without it. If I had left it alone, my daylily would still be a single clump, perhaps 5 feet wide by now.

Check any standard plant encyclopedia or reference book to learn if a particular perennial routinely needs division and, if so, how often and at what season you should do it. For instance, asters should be divided every year or two, in spring, whereas bearded irises need division about every three years, in late summer, and hostas can go indefinitely without division, but if you do want to divide them (usually to make more plants), you can do it in spring or fall.

Some perennials, such as perennial flax and lupines, aren't made to be divided, either because their shoots are squeezed so close together that you can hardly split them apart, or because they have big or deep roots that don't recover well from damage or disturbance. It's also hard to divide perennials that form a spreading mat and are woody at the base, such as basket-of-gold (*Aurinia saxatilis*) and evergreen candytuft (*Iberis sempervirens*). Hard-to-divide perennials are normally propagated from seeds or cuttings.

THE BASICS OF DIVISION. A calm, cloudy day is the best time to divide a plant. The roots will

Perennials with good stiff stalks stand up straight all season. This queen-of-the-prairie, with flowers like pink cotton candy, is 6 feet tall. The other perennials in this bed range from 4 to 8 feet tall. They create a hedgelike effect in summer (although they all have to be cut down in winter) and never need staking.

This is just part of a roadside bed of 'Stella d'Oro' daylilies, all divided from one starter plant over a span of ten years. The violets beside the daylilies also came from one mother plant, but there are seedlings as well as divisions there.

be exposed while you're working on them, and too much wind or sun can desiccate them. If you want to replant a division in the same place where the mother plant was growing, rework the soil first. Fill the hole with compost, loosen the surrounding soil with a fork, and then mix it all together and level it out. If you're putting the divisions in a new bed, just prepare the soil as you usually would.

If you have some divisions that are too small or too valuable to put out in the open, plant them in containers, or in a nursery bed where you can watch them closely, watering as needed and sheltering them from extreme heat and cold.

If you don't have the time or place to plant them right away, wrap the divisions in damp newspaper, then with plastic, and put them in a cool dark place. You can store them for a week or more in spring, and at least a few days in summer or fall.

Normally you should replant a division at the same depth as it was growing before. Sometimes it's okay to plant divisions a little deeper, to keep them from tipping over or to bury a section of rhizome so it will bear roots. When planting a division, don't cram its roots into a tight hole. Make the hole big enough that you can spread them out and put soil between and around them. Be sure to cover all the roots as you fill the hole and pat the soil into place. Thoroughly water each plant, or the whole bed, as soon as possible.

Plants divided when their new leaves are just

starting to grow settle in quickly with no special care. Later in the season, leafy divisions are liable to wilt on sunny or windy days. It's a good precaution to protect them for a week or so after planting with an inverted basket or box, a tepee of leafy twigs, or some other temporary shelter.

In mild climates, you can safely divide perennials throughout the fall or even in the winter. Where the ground freezes, though, try to finish about six weeks before hard frost, so the divisions will have time to anchor themselves with strong new roots. Otherwise frost heaving may pop them out of the ground, where they'll get dried out or frozen before spring. For added insurance, apply a winter mulch such as evergreen boughs after the ground freezes.

DIVIDING CLUMP-FORMING PERENNIALS. Astilbes, bergenias, catmints, daylilies, hardy geraniums, hostas, lady's mantle, lamb's ears, lilyturf, lobelias, lungworts, primroses, violets, and many ferns and grasses form clumps that gradually widen and also get denser over time. Eventually they may get so crowded that they don't flower well anymore, or they may even die out in the middle.

How to divide a clump depends on how big it is and how dense it is. Unless it's huge, dig all the way around the clump, a few inches beyond the spread of its leaves, and lift it out of the ground. Then shake or wash away some of the soil to make it easier to see

(Text continued on page 348)

(LEFT): *Dividing perennials by pulling apart a clump is a free and easy way to produce more plants. This one clump of lungwort yielded a dozen starts.* (BELOW): *Spaced about 18 inches apart, they're well established a few months later.*

True meadows and prairies are mixtures of many kinds of perennial wildflowers and grasses, sometimes with a small number of annuals and biennials present as well. Once established, these are long-term plantings that can persist for decades or indefinitely. The plants are all herbaceous, so the tops die every fall, but fresh new shoots appear in spring.

Back in the 1970s and '80s, making wildflower meadows by scattering seeds on a patch of bare dirt was widely promoted as a carefree, natural approach to gardening. That was naive nonsense, as anyone who tried it soon discovered. Nearly all the seed mixes that were (and still are) being sold as wildflowers included only a tiny percentage of perennial species native to any particular region. Instead, they were loaded with a hodgepodge of adaptable annuals. If they performed at all, these seeded meadows were colorful for a year or two as the annuals bloomed and then more and more disappointing as weeds took over. Finally the owner would give up and convert the area back to lawn or a conventional garden planting.

And yet, wildflower meadows aren't just some marketing man's dream. Meadows and prairies are real, and they're glorious. The problem came from pretending that you could re-create a complex, dynamic ecosystem via some miraculously simple product and technique. Now that the hype has subsided, it's worth reconsidering the idea of creating a meadow or prairie in a home landscape. What are the pros and cons of attempting such a project? Would it work on your land? Do you want to give it a try? Here's some advice.

- **WHAT PLANTS WOULD BE APPROPRIATE FOR YOUR CLIMATE AND SITE?** There are mountain meadows and woodland meadows, tallgrass prairies and shortgrass prairies. What grows naturally in any area, if indeed a meadow or prairie would occur there at all, depends on annual precipitation, elevation, and soil. If you're interested in a project like this, why not do it right? Use only native plants, plants that would have occurred naturally on the site before the area got settled and developed. You can find out what these plants would be by joining statewide wildflower or native-plant societies, local land trusts or nature sanctuaries, or similar organizations. Obtaining seeds or starts of the plants you want will take some research, and some of the desired plants will elude you, but you can always make a start with some species and add others later.

- **SOIL PREPARATION, WEED CONTROL, AND STARTING PLANTS.** What's the history of the site you want to use? What's there now—crops, pasture, hayfield, lawn, vacant lot, weed patch? Making a meadow or prairie is a long-term project. It will take several growing seasons to transform what you have now into the planting of your dreams.

  For most people, dealing with weeds is one major problem in trying to establish a meadow or prairie. The other problem is helping the chosen plants get established. Direct-seeding into newly bared soil is the technique least likely to succeed. Weeds will rush in to take advantage of the opportunity and overwhelm the tiny grass or perennial seedlings.

Most people who try this method give up in despair.

You're much more likely to succeed if you face the two challenges separately. Spend a year or two growing seedlings of your chosen perennial wildflowers and grasses in a nursery bed while you make every effort to eliminate perennial and annual weeds from the intended planting site.

Prepare a nursery bed in a place where you can monitor it closely, water as needed, destroy all weeds, fertilize, and protect the seedlings from grasshoppers, rabbits, woodchucks, starlings, and other rascals. Sow the seeds in rows and make sure the soil never dries out. As the seedlings appear, thin or transplant them to about 6 inches apart. Tend the seedlings—and you'll need hundreds or thousands of them, depending on the area you're planting—for one or two growing seasons. By the end of that time they'll be big enough to survive when you transplant them, but still small enough that they won't be too big or heavy to handle, and that transplanting won't shock them.

Meanwhile, kill or remove the existing vegetation. Then till, rake, and seed the entire area with a fast-growing annual cover crop or green manure such as buckwheat, oats, winter rye, or crimson clover. As soon as the cover crop flowers and before it goes to seed, mow it off short and till the stubble into the ground. Immediately replant with another cover crop, let it grow, and till it in. Each time you till, annual weed seeds are brought to the surface and can germinate, but the weed seedlings get crowded out by the fast-growing cover crops, so doing this repeatedly reduces the weed population. It also improves the soil by adding organic matter.

- **PLANTING.** Plan to plant the meadow or prairie in early spring. Mow the current cover crop as short as possible. Dig the seedlings and transplant them to their permanent sites, arranging them as you choose. You can make some clumps here and there where you group a few plants of one kind, or mix all kinds evenly throughout the area. You'll probably want to space the seedlings about 2 to 4 feet apart, depending on the kind of plant. Water well immediately after planting, and pray for a rainy spring and summer so the plants can get off to a good start and won't have to suffer dryness.

  Do you want a network of paths that wind through your planting? If so, lay them out before you start planting and surface them with a thick layer of wood chips (see page 175).

- **SUBSEQUENT CARE.** It takes a few more years for the perennials and grasses to form full-size clumps and fill the area. By that time they'll be flowering and ripening seeds every year, and they may start to self-seed, which will thicken the planting. Meanwhile, keep watching for weeds (including tree seedlings) and destroying them as soon as you spot any.

  Other than weeding, an established meadow or prairie needs little if any maintenance. You could simply observe it. But if you want to play a more active role, go out and mow the area once a year. You'll need a bush hog or its equivalent for large areas, or a heavy-duty string trimmer for smaller plots. When you mow, let the clippings lie where they fall;

they'll soon rot away. Mowing speeds the decomposition of old dead stalks and leaves, returning their nutrients to the soil.

You could mow after hard frost in fall, but there's no reason to. The tan and russet stalks and seedpods still look pretty then, and if you leave them standing they provide valuable seeds and shelter for birds and small wildlife in winter. A better time to mow is early spring. By that time the old stalks have toppled or gotten knocked over and the area looks pretty shabby, so mowing then gives you a feeling of accomplishment, and it sets the stage for the fresh new growth that will soon appear.

This "backyard prairie" features a dozen or so perennial wildflowers and grasses native to the northern Great Plains. Even though the area is small, the effect is exhilarating because the plants are so robust.

Tulips add welcome spring color to this border, then disappear as the other plants expand. To make a successful combination like this, position the shrubs, long-lived perennials, and other permanent plants first, then add bulbs afterward.

(*Text continued from page 344*)

how to proceed. Try to identify the separate growing points, which will show up as buds in spring or as tufts of leaves or stems in summer. The goal is to pull, pry, or cut apart the clump, separating it between the growing points. Focus on those buds or shoots as you pull the clump apart and the roots will split along the same lines, so each piece will have its own roots. Usually you can divide a clump into at least three or four pieces. An old or broad clump may yield as many as a dozen or more new starts.

Sometimes you can poke your thumbs or fingers into a clump to pull it apart by hand, but often you need a sturdy tool. Lightweight trowels, kitchen knives, and the like are useless, as they'll immediately bend or break. Use a great big screwdriver, a sharp spade, a machete, an old pruning saw, or even a hatchet. Be decisive, and try to make a clean snap or cut as you pull the clump apart—don't tear at it if possible. Or try stabbing the clump with two garden forks arranged back to back, then split it by pushing apart the fork handles.

If a clump is so large that you don't think you could dig it all out of the ground, leave it in place,

slice it into wedges with a sharp spade, and lift out one division at a time.

When dividing a dense clump, you can hardly avoid breaking a few of the individual rosettes. Don't worry—there are usually more good divisions than you have space for. Sort out the best ones for replanting, and discard any small or broken pieces.

DIVIDING RUNNING OR MAT-FORMING PERENNIALS.

Yarrows, several types of anemones and artemisias, asters, phloxes, bee balms, loosestrifes, sundrops and evening primroses, sweet woodruff, and various ferns and grasses spread by means of slender horizontal stems called rhizomes that are located right under the surface of the soil. The rhizomes reach out in all directions, often branching as they go and overlapping each other to form tangled mats. New shoots sprout up from all parts of the mat, forming a dense patch.

To divide a perennial that's formed a patch, first cut any flower stalks or shabby old foliage down close to the ground, so you can see what you're doing. Then there are various ways to proceed.

To renew a plant that you're going to replant in

the same place, study the patch, choose the best part, dig around it, lift it out, and set it aside. Tear out the rest of the patch, amend the soil, and replant the division you saved.

To start a few new plants without disturbing the mother patch, use a sharp spade to cut blocks or wedges about 3 to 6 inches square from around the edge of the patch. Lift them out and refill the holes with fresh soil.

To divide an entire patch into several new plants, cut it all into squares, like cutting a pan of brownies, and lift them out one at a time. Or lift the patch as a whole, set it on the ground or on a tarp, and then cut it and take the squares apart.

To replant the divisions, dig a shallow hole, set the division in place, firm the soil around it, and water. Big divisions rarely need further care. Small divisions are liable to dry out and wilt, so watch them and water as needed.

Caring for special groups of perennials

The term *herbaceous perennial* describes any plant that lives from year to year but doesn't develop woody stems and branches. So this plant category includes favorite hardy garden flowers such as peonies and chrysanthemums along with all kinds of bulbs, ferns, ornamental grasses, and many tender or tropical plants. Aside from basic routine maintenance, there are just a few special considerations for each of these different groups.

BULBS. Many perennials form bulbs, corms, tubers, or other underground storage organs. You notice these organs only when you're planting, transplanting, or dividing these plants; otherwise such plants are just like any other perennials, so I don't think there's much basis for the common practice of treating "bulbs" as a distinct category of plants.

Bulbs serve only a limited role as landscape plants since they're grown almost exclusively for their flowers, which last only for days or weeks. The rest of the year, the plants' foliage is insignificant or absent. Certainly you shouldn't think of designing a planting around bulbs. Instead, think of them as something to insert after you've framed a design with woody plants and more substantial perennials. Frankly, bulbs get in the way while you're trying to

Spanish bluebells naturalize easily in a woodland and spread to form a sea of blue flowers in spring. Bulbs that naturalize are good landscape plants.

Ferns are surprisingly tough and trouble-free. Hay-scented fern, shown here, makes a lush ground cover on sites too rough, rocky, or shady for grass. It's deciduous, but the dead fronds release a pleasant aroma.

cuses, tulips, and lilies are especially popular as rodent fare. Gardeners troubled by these pests have various strategies for protecting their bulbs with homemade repellents or by planting them in buried plastic-mesh bags or wire-mesh cages. I'm not sure any of these ploys is ultimately effective, and they all sound like a lot of trouble.

If bulbs survive and don't get eaten, they're likely to multiply and form clumps. After several years, the clumps may become so dense that flowering is reduced. If so, you can rejuvenate the plant by division. More frequent division is appropriate if you want to make more plants. The best time to divide most bulb-forming perennials is when their leaves start turning from green to yellow but before the leaves die down altogether. Carefully dig up the entire clump. Be careful—the bulbs are probably deeper than you'd expect them to be, and you don't want to stab them. Once you've gotten it out, grab the clump by its leaves and shake it. Extra soil will fall off and the bulbs will come loose. Simply pick, pluck, or snap them apart. Leave the roots and leaves attached to the bulbs—it's okay if they break off accidentally, but don't pull them off.

Sort through the bulbs you've divided, discard any damaged or puny ones, and replant the biggest, best ones right away. Unlike the dormant bulbs you buy, in the fall, these plants are still growing, so they belong in the soil. Plant them individually, burying them as deep as they were before. The leaves will continue turning yellow and then disappear after a month or so.

FERNS. Like other perennials, different kinds of ferns tend to have either a running or a clumping growth habit. Either type can be divided just before new growth begins in spring if you want to thin a crowded planting or to multiply your stock. Otherwise, ferns established on a suitable site need virtually no care. You can cut off old fronds when they turn brown if you want to, or just let them flop over and die down naturally.

Although most ferns prefer moist, well-drained soil, a few tolerate soggy or waterlogged conditions, and many can survive through seasonal dry spells by going dormant. Ferns are also fairly adaptable to different light conditions. They are among the best ground covers for densely shaded sites and actually grow well even in dark places where other perennials would weaken and die. But many ferns grow quite well in part or even full sun if they get enough water.

prepare a bed and lay out a permanent planting. Wait until the major plants are in place, then add bulbs between and around them.

Most bulb-forming perennials are fairly adaptable, but they do vary in how much cold or heat they can endure and also in how much cold or heat they require. Bulbs that are suited to your climate are likely to be fairly long-lived and trouble-free. If they aren't suited, they'll die within the first year or two.

With the notable exception of daffodils and narcissus, most bulbs are quite attractive to squirrels, chipmunks, gophers, voles, and other critters. Cro-

ORNAMENTAL GRASSES. The most widely grown ornamental grasses are all perennials. Most are clump-forming types. A few spreading kinds are sometimes grown as ground covers, but these are too invasive and hard to control for most sites.

Grasses are sorted into two groups, warm-season and cool-season, according to their growing habits. Most ornamental grasses are warm-season types. They don't start sending out new growth until soil and air temperatures climb into the 60s or higher in spring or early summer, and they go dormant when the weather cools off in fall. A few kinds are cool-season grasses, which send out new foliage in fall and spring (or all winter in mild zones) and they go dormant in the heat of summer. Grasses turn tan when they're dormant. You might think they're dead, but wait until the season changes and chances are they'll start growing again.

Most grasses grow back year after year even if you neglect them, but they gradually build up a thick mound or layer of dead thatch. Burning is a dramatically fast and effective way to get rid of grass thatch, but it's not safe or legal in most neighborhoods. The alternative, cutting the grass close to the ground, is a dusty, itchy, scratchy job. You can do this in late fall or winter after the grass turns tan and starts to shatter or break apart, or wait until just before new growth begins in spring. Tackle a patch of grass that's not too big and tough with a lawn mower set high. Use hand shears, a power brush trimmer, a pruning saw, or a machete to cut through a densely crowded clump of any tall or coarse grass. Whatever tool you use, you'll have to sharpen it afterward because dead grass quickly dulls a cutting edge.

Over time, clump-forming grasses sometimes die out in the center and splay apart, or they may stay intact but spread too wide. To correct (or better yet, prevent) either problem, you can divide a clump every few years in midspring, just before new growth starts. Cut off the old leaves, then dig around the perimeter of the clump, following a circle at least 2 to 3 feet in diameter. Push, pull, or heave the root ball up out of the ground and shake it back and forth to dislodge soil, mulch, and debris that's lodged around the crown (the place where the stems and roots come together). To divide the crown, you may have to split it with an ax, like chopping wood, or cut through it with an old pruning saw. Divide it into three or more sections. Replant each division so its crown is level with or slightly above the surface of the soil.

TENDER AND TROPICAL PERENNIALS.

There are countless perennials that thrive in warm

Fountain grass bears rustling foliage and fluffy plumes from midsummer until fall. When killed by hard frost, it turns pale tan and stands up partway through the winter.

climates but are more or less sensitive to cold. Some die back partway if frozen but recover in spring, while others are killed outright.

This huge group includes gingers, philodendrons, bird-of-paradise, cast-iron plant, agapanthus, cannas, various ferns, and many succulents. Most can be grown in containers or treated like annuals in cold climates. Where they survive outdoors, they can be used in many ways, according to their size and growth habit. Shrub-sized, clump-forming tropicals make outstanding specimens or accent plants, while shorter, spreading tender perennials are often used as ground covers.

These plants need little more than routine maintenance. Remove old leaves when they turn yellow or brown. If plants get frosted, remove damaged parts and then wait to see if new growth appears in spring.

Most tender perennials can be divided if they get too crowded or if you want to increase your stock, although digging and dividing big specimens is a challenging job. If the plant goes dormant each year (during winter or during dry weather), do the division at the end of the dormant season, just before active growth begins. If leaves are present, you'll almost certainly break or bruise some of them, but new growth will compensate for the damage. Don't be surprised if the root systems are massive and quite tough. Use a sharp tool to cut through the roots and divide the clumps into a few smaller pieces that you can replant or give away.

Taylor's Master Guide to Landscaping

PHOTO CREDITS

INDEX

Photo Credits

RITA BUCHANAN: viii-1, 10, 13 top, 13 bottom, 15, 24 left, 24 right, 25, 27, 30-31, 33, 35, 38 right, 47 left, 50 left, 52 top, 54, 55, 57 left, 57 right, 58 top right, 58 bottom, 64 left, 64 right, 65 top, 65 middle, 65 bottom, 66 top, 66 bottom, 68 top, 68 bottom, 78 top, 91, 98 left, 98 right, 109 left, 123, 134 bottom left, 146, 152, 153, 157 top, 157 bottom, 164, 181, 190, 195 left, 195 right, 198 bottom, 199, 203, 206, 210 left, 210 right, 216 top, 216 bottom, 217, 228, 229, 232, 239, 243 bottom, 244 bottom, 250 bottom, 251, 253 top, 253 bottom, 254, 256, 259 top, 264, 265, 271 left, 271 right, 273 top, 273 bottom, 274, 275, 279, 281 left, 281 right, 286 top, 286 bottom, 287, 288, 289, 291 top, 291 bottom, 292, 293, 294 left, 294 right, 299 bottom, 302 top, 305 left, 306, 307 top left, 307 top right, 312, 315 top, 317 left, 318 insert, 323, 327 left, 327 right, 331 bottom, 333 top, 333 middle, 333 bottom, 334, 335, 336, 337, 339 bottom, 340 top, 340 bottom, 341 bottom, 342 top, 343, 344, 345 top, 345 bottom, 350

TODD BUCHANAN: 76 insert, 99

C. COLSTON BURRELL: 347

KAREN BUSSOLINI: 13 middle, 80 left, 103, 142 left

CRANDALL & CRANDALL: 47 right

R. TODD DAVIS PHOTOGRAPHY: 5 top, 20, 36 top, 71, 79 top right, 82, 116 middle, 116 top, 117 bottom, 131 bottom, 163 top, 165 top, 171, 173 left, 230 insert, 241, 247 bottom, 260-261, 270, 296, 318-319, 328, 332

THOMAS ELTZROTH: viii (insert), 9 left, 51, 83, 97, 112, 158 insert, 163 bottom, 170, 247 top, 284 insert

DEREK FELL: ii-iii, iv-v, 5 bottom, 7 bottom, 8 top, 9 right, 11, 34, 43, 45, 46 left, 52 bottom, 74, 76-77, 78 bottom, 79 bottom left, 79 bottom right, 80 right, 95 bottom, 101, 104, 109 right, 115, 116 bottom, 117 top, 118, 120, 121, 125 top left, 125 top right, 127 right, 134 bottom right, 142 right, 147, 151 right, 155 top left, 155 bottom, 161, 162 top, 168 top, 183, 188, 200, 202 top, 204 bottom, 205, 220, 223 top, 223 bottom, 224, 230-231, 244 top, 246, 259 bottom, 262, 267, 269, 278, 284-285, 300, 303 right, 307 bottom, 309, 317 right, 322 top, 322 middle, 325, 330, 331 top, 351

DEREK FELL/BRICKMAN GROUP, LANGHORNE, PA: 110 bottom

CHARLES MARDEN FITCH: 32, 233, 235, 238

MARGE GARFIELD: 8 bottom, 18 bottom, 53 top, 94, 119, 127 left, 148 top, 160 left, 305 top, 322 bottom

GORDON HAYWARD/POSITIVE IMAGES: 166 bottom, 180

JERRY HOWARD/POSITIVE IMAGES: 44, 92

CHARLES MANN: vi-vii, 3, 6, 16 bottom, 18 top, 19 top, 30 insert, 36 bottom, 38 left, 40, 48, 53 bottom, 61, 88, 90 top,

90 bottom, 129, 132-133, 134 top left, 141 bottom, 149 top, 155 top right, 156 middle, 156 bottom, 162 bottom, 166 top, 176, 194, 202 bottom, 204 top, 207, 211, 212, 219, 222, 243 top, 248, 260 insert, 263 bottom, 320, 339 top, 353-354

IVAN MASSAR/POSITIVE IMAGES: 174 bottom left

RICK MASTELLI: 16 middle, 17 top, 17 bottom, 19 bottom, 36 middle, 42, 79 top left, 81 top, 89, 96 top, 100, 108, 113 top, 125 bottom, 128 top, 128 bottom, 130 top, 138 top, 138 bottom, 141 middle, 143, 151 left, 160 right, 167, 168 bottom, 169, 175, 177, 184 bottom, 198 top, 201, 208, 213, 215 right, 226, 276, 280, 303 left, 305 right, 310, 338, 341 top, 342 bottom, 348

JERRY PAVIA PHOTOGRAPHY, INC.: 7 top, 12, 16 top, 21, 28, 29, 41, 46 right, 49, 50 right, 58 top left, 59, 60, 81 bottom, 84, 93 left, 93 right, 95 top, 96 bottom, 102, 106 insert, 106-107, 110 top, 111, 113 bottom, 130 bottom, 131 top, 132 insert, 135, 136, 141 top, 148 bottom, 149 bottom, 156 top, 158-159, 165 bottom, 173 right, 174 top, 174 bottom right, 178, 184 top, 189, 192 insert, 192-193, 196, 215 left, 218, 231-232, 237, 240, 245, 250 top, 252, 258, 263 top, 263 middle, 268, 295, 299 top, 302 bottom, 308, 313, 315 bottom, 349, 352

POSITIVE IMAGES: 44, 92, 166 bottom, 174 bottom left, 180

STEVEN STILL: 234

Index